Driving Innovation and Business Success in the Digital Economy

Ionica Oncioiu
Titu Maiorescu University, Romania

A volume in the Advances in E–Business Research
(AEBR) Book Series

www.igi-global.com

Published in the United States of America by
    IGI Global
    Business Science Reference (an imprint of IGI Global)
    701 E. Chocolate Avenue
    Hershey PA, USA 17033
    Tel: 717-533-8845
    Fax: 717-533-8661
    E-mail: cust@igi-global.com
    Web site: http://www.igi-global.com

Library of Congress Cataloging-in-Publication Data

Names: Oncioiu, Ionica, 1972- editor.
Title: Driving innovation and business success in the digital economy /
   Ionica Oncioiu, editor.
Description: Hershey : Business Science Reference, [2016]
Identifiers: LCCN 2016045415| ISBN 9781522517795 (hardcover) | ISBN
   9781522517801 (ebook)
Subjects: LCSH: Technological innovations--Management. | Information
   technology--Management.
Classification: LCC HD45 .D75 2016 | DDC 658.5/14--dc23 LC record available at https://lccn.loc.gov/2016045415

This book is published in the IGI Global book series Advances in E-Business Research (AEBR) (ISSN: 1935-2700; eISSN: 1935-2719)

British Cataloguing in Publication Data
A Cataloguing in Publication record for this book is available from the British Library.

All work contributed to this book is new, previously-unpublished material. The views expressed in this book are those of the authors, but not necessarily of the publisher.

For electronic access to this publication, please contact: eresources@igi-global.com.

Advances in E-Business Research (AEBR) Book Series

In Lee
Western Illinois University, USA

ISSN:1935-2700
EISSN:1935-2719

MISSION

Technology has played a vital role in the emergence of e-business and its applications incorporate strategies. These processes have aided in the use of electronic transactions via telecommunications networks for collaborating with business partners, buying and selling of goods and services, and customer service. Research in this field continues to develop into a wide range of topics, including marketing, psychology, information systems, accounting, economics, and computer science.

The **Advances in E-Business Research (AEBR) Book Series** provides multidisciplinary references for researchers and practitioners in this area. Instructors, researchers, and professionals interested in the most up-to-date research on the concepts, issues, applications, and trends in the e-business field will find this collection, or individual books, extremely useful. This collection contains the highest quality academic books that advance understanding of e-business and addresses the challenges faced by researchers and practitioners.

COVERAGE

- Web advertising
- E-business technology investment strategies
- E-business models and architectures
- Trends in e-business models and technologies
- Online consumer behavior
- E-Business Management
- Mobile Business Models
- E-business strategies
- Interorganizational information systems
- Web 2.0

IGI Global is currently accepting manuscripts for publication within this series. To submit a proposal for a volume in this series, please contact our Acquisition Editors at Acquisitions@igi-global.com or visit: http://www.igi-global.com/publish/.

Titles in this Series

For a list of additional titles in this series, please visit: www.igi-global.com

Social Media Listening and Monitoring for Business Applications
N. Raghavendra Rao (FINAIT Consultancy Services, India)
Business Science Reference • copyright 2017 • 470pp • H/C (ISBN: 9781522508465) • US $205.00 (our price)

Analyzing the Strategic Role of Social Networking in Firm Growth and Productivity
Vladlena Benson (Kingston University, UK) Ronald Tuninga (Kingston Business School, UK) and George Saridakis (Kingston University, UK)
Business Science Reference • copyright 2017 • 525pp • H/C (ISBN: 9781522505594) • US $220.00 (our price)

Securing Transactions and Payment Systems for M-Commerce
Sushila Madan (University of Delhi, India) and Jyoti Batra Arora (Banasthali Vidyapeeth University, India)
Business Science Reference • copyright 2016 • 349pp • H/C (ISBN: 9781522502364) • US $205.00 (our price)

E-Retailing Challenges and Opportunities in the Global Marketplace
Shailja Dixit (Amity University, India) and Amit Kumar Sinha (Amity University, India)
Business Science Reference • copyright 2016 • 358pp • H/C (ISBN: 9781466699212) • US $215.00 (our price)

Successful Technological Integration for Competitive Advantage in Retail Settings
Eleonora Pantano (Middlesex University London, UK)
Business Science Reference • copyright 2015 • 405pp • H/C (ISBN: 9781466682979) • US $200.00 (our price)

Strategic E-Commerce Systems and Tools for Competing in the Digital Marketplace
Mehdi Khosrow-Pour (Information Resources Management Association, USA)
Business Science Reference • copyright 2015 • 315pp • H/C (ISBN: 9781466681330) • US $185.00 (our price)

The Evolution of the Internet in the Business Sector Web 1.0 to Web 3.0
Pedro Isaías (Universidade Aberta (Portuguese Open University), Portugal) Piet Kommers (University of Twente, The Netherlands) and Tomayess Issa (Curtin University, Australia)
Business Science Reference • copyright 2015 • 407pp • H/C (ISBN: 9781466672628) • US $235.00 (our price)

RFID Technology Integration for Business Performance Improvement
In Lee (Western Illinois University, USA)
Business Science Reference • copyright 2015 • 317pp • H/C (ISBN: 9781466663084) • US $225.00 (our price)

DISSEMINATOR of KNOWLEDGE

www.igi-global.com

701 E. Chocolate Ave., Hershey, PA 17033
Order online at www.igi-global.com or call 717-533-8845 x100
To place a standing order for titles released in this series, contact: cust@igi-global.com
Mon-Fri 8:00 am - 5:00 pm (est) or fax 24 hours a day 717-533-8661

Editorial Advisory Board

Table of Contents

Detailed Table of Contents

Section 1

This chapter is studying strategic turning points in ICT business using Nokia as an example. Though several transformational phases of Nokia, the business is going on and being profitable. The main branch in the business has changed several times, also during the last decades. The activities of Nokia are still in the ICT, however. The previous main branch of Nokia, mobile and smart phones, has changed into networks technology and business. The case of Nokia proved to be the good example about the business development, transformation and evolution possibilities in the ICT business. This chapter also introduces a long-term perspective strategic turning points and path dependency in the case of Nokia and considers the potential (unintentional) co-evolution development between Nokia and Ericsson.

This study examined the impact of innovation on the entrepreneurial success in selected business enterprises in South-Western Nigeria. The paper dwelt on the extent to which the selected enterprises innovation effort affects the quality of their product as well as the company image. Data were analysed using descriptive and inferential statistics. Hypotheses were tested at 0.05 significant levels with the aid of parametric student t-test. The results revealed that there is a positive relationship between innovation and product quality as well as a positive relationship between innovation and good corporate image and that both of them significantly affect entrepreneurial success. The study recommends that business enterprises should engage more on innovation of their production process to improve their product quality and even enhances good corporate image. This will help them to sustain their position in the face of stiff competition.

In large-scale Open Source Software (OSS) innovation ecosystems that incorporate firms, a variety of measures are taken to tame the potentially chaotic activities and align the contributions of various participants with the strategic priorities of major stakeholders. Such taming rests on the dual desires of this emergent community of firms to unleash the innovation potential of OSS and to drive it to a certain direction, and it emerges in the form of various organizational activities. By drawing on a sample of large-scale OSS ecosystems, we discuss that methods employed for taming are isomorphic, and overview the emerging strategic pattern for establishing systems of innovation. This pattern involves a related set of practices to balance virtues of OSS community while introducing corporate discipline. In contrast to approaches such as open innovation, which favor isolated reasoning, we present a systemic and historical perspective to explain the continuum in emergence and establishment of strategic patterns.

Chapter 4

Due to rapid evolution of technology, innovations are vital to most organizations. Nevertheless, the results of innovations are in many cases not satisfying. Several studies have shown that an organization's failure to benefit from an adopted innovation can often be attributed to a deficient implementation process rather than to the innovation itself. Thus, the implementation process is a critical interface between the decision to adopt and the routine usage of an innovation. Ways and methods to implement innovation effectively have been under scholarship for some time now. Despite the number of studies which identify multiple causes of unsuccessful implementation processes, literature is lacking regarding the strategic facets of innovation implementation. Building on the derived knowledge of the underlying dynamics of innovation processes, through grounded theory and in-depth literature review, the present study aims to contribute to existing implementation literature by examining the strategic facets of innovation implementation.

Section 2

India is a country with a population of 1.2 billion and around 400 million poor people remain excluded from the formal economy. India does not offer a social security number for its residents. Rather, there exist variant forms of identification documents. In 2009, the Government of Indian initiated the Aadhaar project to create biometric technology-enabled unique identities for Indian residents. In a short timespan span, the project has made remarkable progress by enrolling more than 600 million people. The objective of this paper is twofold: (1) to review the emerging literature on inclusive innovation and (2) to examine the case of Aadhaar Project in India, which aims to address the issue of poverty and inclusive development. Findings of the study reveal that the Aadhaar project has the potential to create an ecosystem of inclusive innovation and entrepreneurship, which can be beneficial for developing economies like India.

Chapter 6

This paper is aimed at making the diffusion of the technological innovation and their role in affecting the agricultural sector in the three-sided (social, economic and environmental), a hand, it can participate to resolve problems of the agricultural sector: the effects of the climatic changes, the farming exodus and the migration and the problems of poverty. The theoretically and empirically studies analyze the mechanical innovation role in improving agricultural sustainability through the impact of mechanization on agricultural productivity, CO_2 emission and demographic growth for a panel of three Maghreb countries (Algeria, Morocco and Tunisia) during the period 1999-2012. By using simultaneous equations, the authors' finding that mechanical innovation cannot achieve the purpose of sustainable development in the agriculture sector in the Maghreb countries through the negative impact of mechanization and research and development on agricultural productivity.

Section 3

Chapter 7

This chapter deals with the copyright issues faced by authors once their books enter the digital sphere, as well as the difficulties associated with overseas publications of their books, from a territorial perspective. It examines whether territorial copyright borders still afford book authors effective copyright protection in the digital economy, and further, whether the culture of the book is being eroded through the prevalence of extra-territorial publications. Relevantly, this article examines the landmark US Supreme Court decision of Kirtsaeng v Wiley and Sons, Inc. and considers its likely future impact on the enforcement of territorial copyright by authors and publishers. Finally, the article concludes that territorial copyright borders have become blurred, difficult to enforce in view of recent precedent, and are ineffective in preserving authors' copyright and the cultural dimensions of their books.

Chapter 8

The purpose of this book chapter is to test the importance of trust to increase the loyalty of e-news brand readers in Indonesia and to test its antecedents. Trust becomes a central factor in the electronics news brand to increase the loyalty of its readers. Within this chapter, trust in news electronics brand influenced by the reader's experience and customer confusion. Exciting experience and unforgettable experiences influenced by the attributes of the news brand electronics. The readers' experiences will be able to reduce customer confusion and will increase confidence in the electronics news brand significantly. Basically, consumers are not confused in the electronics news brand. Other results showed that the attached attributes to electronics news brand will be able to significantly increase readers' loyalty.

The purpose of this chapter is to provide some insights into advertisements on the Iranian websites. Firstly, in publisher side, is the ethic a matter of fact in accepting Internet advertisements to publish? Second, to provide a preliminary insight into the advertising of pleasant and objectionable products, which one is more? Third, what kind of the involvement (rational or emotional) used more to publish Internet advertisements? Content analysis was used to verify the data. In order to avoid the miscoding of contents, two researchers conducted the analysis and Intercoder reliability used to this goal. we found that (1) all 649 analyzed ads in Iranian websites are belonged to ethical ads and no unethical advertisement found at websites, (2) the majority of published advertisements are belonged to "high involvement product with rational appeal", (3) the "objectionable product ads" at Iranian weblogs was more "pleasant product ads". This study by analyzing 1400 advertisements gives managers some insights and solutions regarding to advertising on the Iranian Internet domains.

Chapter 10

Digitalization can be regarded as a megatrend which results that both brand building and brand management must adapt to new challenges. The growing role of digitizing points to both challenges and risks, as well as to opportunities. This chapter conceptualizes digitizing as a resource for brand development with the help of two tourism destinations. It focuses on the role Web-based platforms play in destination brand development, using the examples of two seemingly nearly similar Christmas tourism destinations as case studies: Santa Claus, Indiana, and Santa Claus Village, Rovaniemi. The chapter highlights the contribution of a customer-oriented digitalization to creating a competitive advantage, even a sustainable one, for tourism destinations with theoretical connections to a resource-based view (RBV) and discusses its potential for incremental and radical innovative brand development processes.

Section 4

Chapter 11

Advancements in organizational information systems and developments in business environments have brought important changes to the contemporary management practices and business models. Organizations have evolved beyond their specific and general environments towards business ecosystems. This study investigates the evolutions of organizational information systems and business environments in the contexts of business ecosystem. Based on an evolutionary study of organizational information systems and business ecosystem an ontological model is proposed for the adoption of new technologies in the real world designs with particular attention to the application of technology. We call for further empirical and conceptual research in understanding and exploring the role of business ecosystems in organizational operations and industrial ecosystems.

The aim of this chapter is to answer calls for more studies on the role of materialities in enabling or restricting the participation of larger numbers of people beyond managerial ranks in strategy-making. Drawing on sociomateriality as a practice philosophical perspective, the chapter studies strategy-making in a community-based organization and explores how human actions and materialities interweave to enhance the participation of rank-and-file members in strategy-making. The results show how different sociomaterial configurations gain strategic agency in different phases of a strategy-making process and the implications of these for participation in strategy-making. The authors argue that it is not sufficient to focus on technologies or other materialities as such, but it is also necessary to acknowledge the whole sociomateriality of practices. Furthermore, they also argue that participation in strategy could be seen as a dialectic process of exclusion and inclusion.

The old idea of segmented macroeconomics of the financial sector competing with the real economy is replaced by a new model. This model formalizes the new architecture for the macro economy, and its relationship to the stock market. In this model relating to a reconstructed state of the economy and the emergent structure of the financial architecture, money and spending are treated as complementary elements of growth and development. The overarching structure in the end is the Money, Finance, Spending and Real Economy (MFSRE) with its extensively complementary inter-variables relationship in a general system and cybernetic form of interrelationships. The stock market, exemplified by the empirical case study of Bangladesh's state of the economy and the Dhaka Stock Exchange, bring out the true example of the macroeconomic analysis. The new financial architecture with its stabilization, sustainability and growth and wellbeing as basic-needs regime of development is contrasted with old macroeconomic belief and policies based on outmoded macroeconomic beliefs and futures.

Section 5

The objective of this study is to investigate the influence of life creativity contests held by museums for elementary school children and their parents on the participants' conceptual cognition of water conservation technologies. A survey is designed to evaluate the change in the participants' conceptual cognition of the technologies, and includes questionnaires on water consumption habits in daily lives, understanding of the water resources in the Taiwan region, and uses of and opinions on water-saving devices. A method on which the assessment of the conceptual knowledge of the participants was based was a content analysis of the interviews. The findings of this study suggested: (a) the creativity contest provided diverse opportunities to improve the participants' cognitive concepts of water conservation; (b) this activity also has positively influenced the learning of knowledge, attitudes, and behaviors of water conservation technologies.

Chapter 15

This paper presents a critical review and synthesis of research literature in higher education exploring teachers' conceptions of blended learning and their approaches to both design and teaching. Definitions of blended learning and conceptual frameworks are considered first. Attention is given to Picciano's Blending with Purpose Multimodal framework. This paper builds upon previous research on blended learning and conceptual framework by Picciano by exploring how objectives from Picciano's framework affect teachers' approaches to both design and teaching in face-to-face and online settings. Research results suggest that teachers use multiple approaches including face-to-face methods and online technologies that address the learning needs of a variety of students from different generations, personality types and learning styles.

Chapter 16

Among billions of Internet enabled devices that are expected to surround us in the near future, many will be resource constrained, i.e., will have limited power supply, processing power and memory. To cope with these limitations, the Constrained Application Protocol (CoAP) has been recently introduced as a lightweight alternative to HTTP for connecting the resource limited devices to the Web. Although the new protocol offers solid technical advantages, it remains uncertain whether a successful uptake will follow, as it depends also on its economic feasibility for the involved stakeholders. Therefore, this paper studies the techno-economic feasibility of CoAP using a systematic methodological framework. Based on eleven expert interviews complemented with a literature survey, the paper identifies potential deployment challenges for CoAP, both technical and business-related, and suggests approaches to overcome them. The findings should facilitate the uptake of CoAP by supporting the potential adopters of the protocol in their decision-making.

Preface

In today's digital world, rapid changes in organizations and their management are one of the basic conditions that are necessary for an organization's success. The development and mastery of digital computing are the most important areas for the new digital economy, while its impact will also include new emerging uses of innovation technology. Innovation is a broad concept; the term "innovation system" has often been used to describe the interaction between an individual firm, on one hand, and firms and institutions that can provide such resources on the other hand. Innovation systems have received attention from researchers, as well as policy-makers, as possible instruments for improving the innovation capacity of enterprises.

Furthermore, innovation is the most important part of the modern world. The best approach to this world would be to seek solutions when problems occur, for it is clear they do. A possible idea of modern e-business would be the development of a knowledge-based society that can be shared by everyone on the planet: Knowledge Society for All. This concept involves total mobility for anyone - anywhere - anytime. Therefore, eBusiness has emerged as a solution to the problem of carrying the weight of the international trade.

The innovation capacity of an enterprise thus rests on the foundation of its resources, which have been accumulated as a result of their previous activities. These resources have been shaped by the needs of the past and are subsequently applied in the current innovation process to respond to the needs of the future. The ability to come up with new solutions will therefore depend on the ability to adapt the resources in response to the new requirements of the innovation process (see Eisenhardt & Martin, 2000; Pek-Hooi, Mahmood, & Mitchell, 2004; Teece, Pisano, & Shuen, 1997).

As suggested by its title, the Driving Innovation and Business Success in the Digital Economy volume displays various cross- and multi-disciplinary approaches. Against the background of the complex landscape of issues in the field of digital economy, the volume explores several known or less known research directions, while approaching topics on which there has been said a lot, but never enough.

The target audience of this book can be composed of researchers, professionals and university students working in the field of information systems with an interest in innovation and business success in the digital economy. The people about whom I am going to write in the following pages, as well as their contributions to the International Journal of Innovation in the Digital Economy, are part of a world in which not only the scientific result is important, but also its impact on the society. The authors of the papers in this volume propose practical solutions to the need to implement new innovative technologies that help enterprises to adapt to changes in the markets as well as to exploit digital market opportunities. For this reason, I believe that the content of this volume represents a starting point for finding answers to demands posed by today's world.

Therefore, the 18 papers published in *Driving Innovation and Business Success in the Digital Economy* invite any reader to explore the main factors that contributed to the configuration of the digital economy, such as the use of IT and telecommunication technology within educational environments, using new technology effectively in the organizations, the digital divide and the effects of the digitalization.

The first part of the book includes some papers that address subjects related to the business innovation. Innovation is inevitable in today's dynamic business environment; thus, companies are increasingly forced to become more innovative and faster in their product development, in order to bring new products into markets and in this way, remain competitive in order to survive. The call for innovations and creativity within the efficiency frames is not restricted to profit-oriented companies, but also includes public sector government organizations. The advantages of the information and communication technology, as a direct result of innovatively approaching the old management tools regarded in the context of the new economy, are emphasized by Rauno Rusko, the author of the first chapter "Strategic Turning Points in ICT Business: The Business Development, Transformation, and Evolution in the Case of Nokia". Starting with an in-depth literature review, the author discusses further of the business development, transformation and evolution possibilities in the ICT business. This study introduces a long-term perspective turning points and path dependency in the case of Nokia and considers the potential (unintentional) co-evolution development between Nokia and Ericsson. Therefore, his article argues that it is important to provide a framework comprising of research agenda explaining the relationships between IT Capability and Firm Innovation.

The key message of the article "Impact of Innovation on the Entrepreneurial Success in Selected Business Enterprises in South-West Nigeria" is that the business enterprises should engage more in the innovation of their production process to improve their product quality and even enhance a good corporate image. Olu Ojo presents the impact of innovation on the entrepreneurial success in selected business enterprises in South-West Nigeria. The results revealed that there is a positive relationship between innovation and product quality, as well as between innovation and a good corporate image and that both of them significantly affect entrepreneurial success.

The focus of the chapter "Taming of Openness in Software Innovation Systems" is on the fact that the innovation-related practices of two different open source software communities differentiates them into corporate- and community-led. Such taming rests on the dual desires of this emergent community of firms to unleash the innovation potential of open source software and to drive it to a certain direction, so as to emerge in the form of various organizational activities. By drawing on a sample of large-scale open source software ecosystems, Mehmet Gençer and Beyza Oba discuss that the methods employed for taming are isomorphic and overview the emerging strategic pattern for establishing systems of innovation. After reviewing the fragmented literature on project success in software research, the authors argued that while these two different worlds collaborated, they adopted and transformed some of the practices and structures from each other and retained some others.

The fourth chapter of this book, entitled "Innovation Implementation: The Critical Facets", presents the implementation of innovations in successful organizations. After a critical analysis of innovation-implementation literature, Neeta Baporikar pursues questions such as: How does the implementation of technological innovations like new computer systems differ from the implementation of non-technological innovations such as new managerial, educational, training, or patient-treatment interventions? How does success or failure at implementing an innovation in one team or location spread through an organization or community? More exactly, the author concludes that in the absence of effective implementation, the benefits of innovation adoption are likely to be null.

The second part of the book addresses issues related to sustainable development and the growth of the green economy. The objective of Vanita Yadav in "Sustainable Development Challenges in Developing Countries: Can Technology Provide Inclusive Solutions?" is twofold: to review the emerging literature on inclusive innovation and to examine the case of the Aadhaar Project in India, which aims to address the issue of poverty and inclusive development. Moreover, Yadav explains that in a sustainable development process, there is basically a need for a harmonious, balanced use of three types of capital - economic, social and natural. The paper also explores the inclusive innovation ecosystem around the Aadhaar project and discusses its potential to address institutional voids in India. As a result, new innovative business models can be built through exploiting the benefits offered by the Aadhaar platform.

The next chapter "The Challenge of Mechanical Innovation and Their Impact on Agricultural Sustainability of Maghreb Countries: An Empirical Analysis by 3SLS" makes an interesting contribution regarding the concept of sustainable development. This concept has spread during the '90s in scientific research, both locally and worldwide. All the researches agrees that the achievement of sustainable development depends on the respect of three essential principles: equity between nations and generations, the equilibrium of the economic situation and the protection of the environment. Rachida Khaled tests the effects of mechanical innovation on the agricultural sector in the three Maghreb countries (Tunisia, Morocco and Algeria) by a model of simultaneous equations. The estimation results show that mechanization used by Maghreb farmers is unsustainable. For this purpose, it is unable to achieve the sustainable development objectives in the agricultural sector of Maghreb countries.

The third part of the book refers to the Internet Advertising. For decades, marketers and advertisers have amassed an array of strategies, tactics and principles that, it is claimed, can be applied to any particular advertising campaign. In today's technological world, the challenge is to apply that knowledge to the discipline of Internet Advertising. At the same time, companies whose target users have mostly interest-driven e-lifestyles must be aware that the click rate on internet ads by these users is very low. They must work on developing strategies for attracting such users to internet advertisements, or try to communicate their advertising messages in another way.

Francina Cantatore in "The Migration of the Book across Territorial Borders Copyright Implications for Authors in the Digital Economy" examines whether territorial copyright borders still afford book authors effective copyright protection in the digital economy, and furthermore, whether the culture of the book is being eroded through the prevalence of extra-territorial publications. She discusses how this changing publishing sphere has impacted on authors' copyright protection. The article concludes that territorial copyright borders have become blurred, difficult to enforce in view of recent precedent, and are ineffective in preserving authors' copyright and the cultural dimensions of their books.

"The Importance of Electronics News Brand Trust: The Case of Online Newspapers in Indonesia" is an article which tests the importance of trust to increase the loyalty of e-news brand readers in Indonesia and to test its antecedents. Throughout this study, Elia Ardyan and Vincent Didiek Wiet Aryanto state that it is difficult to predict the readers' loyalty. Based on these considerations, authors launch the idea that there are three things that must be built in order to increase the trust of readers. Firstly, make it an interesting attribute of electronic new brands. Secondly, create positive experiences to the reader, and last but not least, reduce consumer confusion.

According to Mehdi Behboudi and Hamideh Mokhtari, the authors of the chapter "Online Advertising: Experimental Facts on Ethics, Involvement and Product Type", answers to the following concerns; from the publisher's point of view, is the ethic a matter of fact in accepting Internet advertisements to publish? Secondly, provided a preliminary insight into the advertising of pleasant and objectionable products, which one is more important? Thirdly, what kind of involvement (rational or emotional) used to publish more Internet advertisements? In pursuing these goals, the content of 649 ads through 205 websites and 751 ads through 138 weblogs was analyzed by authors. They used content analysis to verify the data and observed that there are different behavior on weblogs and websites.

Merenheimo and Rusko in the chapter "Cocreating the Christmas Story: Digitalizing as a Shared Resource for Shared Brand" want to widen the perspective from planned development projects to approaches within the large internet society. The authors study tourism destination branding as a co-creative process of the destination and consumers. It is a process that cannot be fully controlled by any single participant. They consider how branding approaches within a wide internet society can create opportunities for co-created value, and scrutinize their contribution to sustainable competitive advantage. Following this resource-based view, they argue that the internet society can contribute to changes in societal meanings related to the digitalization itself and in its relation to a particular destination. Such a change can improve a destination's position compared to its competitors.

The fourth part of the book includes three articles which are intended to present some aspects related to a practical perspective of using the Digital Economy tools in business environment.

The study "Applications Driven Information Systems: Beyond Networks toward Business Ecosystems" by Kayvan Lavassani and Bahar Movahedi investigates the evolutions of organizational information systems and business environments in the contexts of business ecosystem. Based on an evolutionary study of organizational information systems and the business ecosystem, an ontological model is proposed for the adoption of new technologies in real-world designs, with particular attention to the application of technology. The authors interpret the results of the two sides of the paper (theoretical and practical) and propose concrete solutions, founded by the used instrumentation.

Apart from the single organization perspective, industry and society level questions arise as well. Laine and Parkkari focus their attention on a project within entrepreneurship society in Finland and describe how practices within this project create strategic agency for both a large number of people, and for the IT technology. They consider how the co-constitution of the social and material produce strategic agency. They draw from "sociomateriality as a practice" the dynamic construction of strategic agency in and through the continuous (re)configuring of human actions, information technology and other materialities. The authors describe how strategy making within the entrepreneurship society follows a top-down mode and constructs project members with the identity of an IT entrepreneur. The article shows how agency gets both enabled and constrained through the entanglement of human action and IT, leading to the effects of inclusion and exclusion.

Masudul Alam Choudhury discusses in "Cybernetic Approach for the Stock Market: An Empirical Study of Bangladesh" the implementation of a model which formalizes the new architecture for the macroeconomy and its relationship to the stock market. The author argues that this model is related to a reconstructed state of the economy and the emergent structure of the financial architecture. Also, money and its spending are treated as complementary elements of growth and development. Data used are topical, refer to issues addressed in the article and have representativeness and utility value for analytical approach.

The fifth part of the book addresses issues related to education and the educational system. The economic, social and political landscape in which future development will take place has therefore also changed. It is widely accepted that the use of IT and telecommunication technology within educational environments has increased dramatically over the last years and that it will keep increasing in the future. In the three dimensions of technology implications (i.e., technology development, application, and innovation) categorized in "Comprehension of Technology in Parent-Child Activities Using Bloom's Taxonomy of the Cognitive Domain", the participants exhibited improved performance after the activity, indicating that the creativity competition activity helped the students understand water-saving technologies during the activity, trained them to proactively engage in exploratory learning and improved their creative thinking and problem-solving skills. The authors - Tzu-Hsiang Ger, Yao-Ming Chu and Mei-Chen Chang - investigate the influence of water conservation technology contests on the cognition of school children and their family members. The results suggest that the creativity contest provided diverse opportunities to improve the participants' cognitive concepts of water conservation and that this activity also has positively influenced the learning of knowledge, attitudes and behaviors of water conservation technologies.

The article "Teachers Conceptions and Approaches to Blended Learning: A Literature Review" builds upon previous research on blended learning and conceptual framework by Picciano, by exploring how objectives from Picciano's framework affect teachers' approaches to both design and teaching in face-to-face and online settings. Vicki Caravias presents a critical review and synthesis of research literature in higher education exploring teachers' conceptions of blended learning and their approaches to both design and teaching. She also suggests that teachers use multiple approaches including face-to-face methods and online technologies that address the learning needs of a variety of students from different generations, personality types and learning styles.

As indicated in the title of the chapter "A Techno-Economic Perspective of Constrained Application Protocol", Tapio Levä et al. investigate a subject which continues to generate intense debates among academia society. The article examines how to be economically feasible for the potential adopters and other stakeholders participating in protocol deployment. Based on eleven expert interviews complemented with a literature survey, the authors identify potential deployment challenges for the Constrained Application Protocol, both technical and business-related, and suggest approaches to overcome them. The dense content, the accuracy of formulated ideas and the creative use of statistical and econometric tools make the presented research work authentic and valuable. Therefore this study takes interest in understanding the importance of the organizations to adopt technological innovations for competitiveness in the knowledge-based economy and it also discusses the role of the Constrained Application Protocol in the evolving the Internet of Things ecosystem.

Ionica Oncioiu
Titu Maiorescu University, Romania

REFERENCES

Eisenhardt, K. M., & Martin, J. A. (2000). Dynamic capabilities: What are they? *Strategic Management Journal*, *21*(10-11), 1105–1121. doi:10.1002/1097-0266(200010/11)21:10/11<1105::AID-SMJ133>3.0.CO;2-E

Pek-Hooi, S., Mahmood, I. P., & Mitchell, W. (2004). Dynamic inducements in R&D investment: Market signals and network locations. *Academy of Management Journal*, *47*(6), 907–917. doi:10.2307/20159630

Teece, D. J., Pisano, G., & Shuen, A. (1997). Dynamic capabilities and strategic management. *Strategic Management Journal*, *18*(7), 509–533. doi:10.1002/(SICI)1097-0266(199708)18:7<509::AID-SMJ882>3.0.CO;2-Z

Acknowledgment

I think that in life nothing is accidental, and sometimes when you least expect, there are people coming into one's life who are able to see in one's person more than she can see. Looking back, I realize that I am tremendously indebt to Ms. Elena Druică. I want to thank her for trusting me, for our extremely positive collaboration and for opening thus a door to a new challenge for me: the editorial activity. I wish to thank Ms. Druică for each virtual encouraging smile, for each piece of advice and especially for her on-going generous and kind support.

I wish to express further my thankful thoughts to Sean Eckman for his confidence, high-professional guidance and continuous support all through the activity of editing the *International Journal of Innovation in the Digital Economy*.

Last, but by no means least, I wish to thank all the persons who made the publishing of the present volume possible: Jan Travers, Eleana Wehr, Melissa Wagner, Erin Wesser, Christina Henning, Nicole Elliott, Kristina Byrne, Lindsay Johnston, Joshua Witman, Nick Newcomer and many other IGI-Global team members, reviewers, collaborators, and all the contributing authors. without your efforts and dedication this editorial project would have never been possible.

Section 1

Chapter 1
Strategic Turning Points in ICT Business:
The Business Development, Transformation, and Evolution in the Case of Nokia

Rauno Rusko
University of Lapland, Finland

ABSTRACT

This chapter is studying strategic turning points in ICT business using Nokia as an example. Though several transformational phases of Nokia, the business is going on and being profitable. The main branch in the business has changed several times, also during the last decades. The activities of Nokia are still in the ICT, however. The previous main branch of Nokia, mobile and smart phones, has changed into networks technology and business. The case of Nokia proved to be the good example about the business development, transformation and evolution possibilities in the ICT business. This chapter also introduces a long-term perspective strategic turning points and path dependency in the case of Nokia and considers the potential (unintentional) co-evolution development between Nokia and Ericsson.

INTRODUCTION

Information communication technology (ICT) business has been and still is a significant part of the global economy. The telecommunication revenue as a percentage of GDP in OECD countries was 2.8% in 2009. For example, in 1985 this revenue as a percentage of GDP was already 2.1% and after that it has been varied between 2.23-3.23 percentage of GDP (OECD communication outlook, 2011). In 2013, the share of ICT sector and its sub-sectors was 5.5 percentage of GDP. In Finland, for example, the share was 5.6 per cent and in Sweden 6.82 per cent of GDP (OECD 2015). The importance of the technical progress of ICT over the globalization and business and consumption practices in global economy is even higher. Therefore, because ICT sector is a significant part of Global economy, changes in this business

DOI: 10.4018/978-1-5225-1779-5.ch001

cuts a dash. This research is focused on the ICT business and especially in one significant company in this business: Nokia.

The strategic analysis of study is based on path-dependency analysis, in which the history of the research object is important. According to Koch (2008, p. 52), path dependency "can be understood as a conceptual framework that explains emerging phenomena in a processual perspective. It does so by focusing on self-reinforcing mechanisms and shaping specific strategic practices (routines and resources), that finally lead to a strategic lock-in situation and thus to a lack of strategic responsiveness" (See, also Sydow et al., 2005)

Besides the strategic moves of Nokia, this study emphasizes other turning points of the technology in ICT and mobile phone business. The long-term strategic process of Nokia is not unique: there are several dramatic strategic turns among the other companies in the ICT business. One good example is Swedish company Ericsson. However, Nokia provides a good example about the turbulent business and business environment of ICT branch. This chapter is focused on the strategic paths of Nokia compared with some other paths of companies in the ICT branch, such as Ericsson. The development of Ericsson, especially, resembles the development of Nokia. Thus, the perspectives of study also lean on the perspectives of institutional theory and isomorphism, where the firms follow the same paths and strategies with each other. (Haveman, 1993)

This study is organized as follows: after introduction part is a short description about the methodology of this research. Sub-chapter 3 is focused on the meanings of strategy and strategic perspectives in this research. After that, is described the history of Nokia and more generally the development the whole mobile phone branch. In Sub-chapter 5 we have the strategic analysis over the turning points of Nokia. Finally, there are conclusions which include also some analyses of the contemporary markets of mobile phones and need for further research.

RESEARCH DESIGN

This study is based on case study research strategy in which the case is the strategic processes of Nokia. Social sciences have various definitions for case study research. Typically, case study research is not tied to any particular method. It enables several alternative methods to use - both qualitative and quantitative (see e.g. Eriksson and Kovalainen, 2008; Yin, 2002). Therefore, case study research could be considered more like a research strategy (Laine et al., 2007; Yin, 2002) without any exclusionary tight definitions about the methods suitable or unsuitable for the category of "case study research".

Most of the case studies have some of these following features (Laine et al., 2007, 10; see also e.g. Yin 2002):

1. Holistic and meaningful characteristics of real life events or cases.
2. Organizational and managerial processes.
3. The use of several materials and methods.
4. The exploitation of previous researches.
5. The dimness of the case and context.

This research has most of these features: it considers the strategic processes of Nokia, which are "real life events". It is focused on processes by using several materials, such as annual reports, articles and other scientific or practical materials. In addition to case study strategy, this study is based on the explanatory content analysis, which is a typical method in analysing the annual reports of the companies (see, e.g. Carduff, 2010). Furthermore, because of the relatively long research period for 40 years, this study also has the features of path dependency analysis (Lamberg et al., 2007) in which the history of the research object is important. Underlying assumption in path dependency analysis is some kinds of self-reinforcing mechanisms and shaping specific strategic practices (routines and resources), resembling strategic lock-in situation. (Sydow et al., 2005; Koch, 2008, 52). According to Vergne and Durand (2010, 736) path dependence is used to describe a mechanism that connects the past and the future with an abstract way, which sometimes leads successful outcomes and sometimes not.

THE LONG-TERM STRATEGIC PERSPECTIVES OF MANAGEMENT STUDIES

This research is focused on the development and long-term strategic paths of one firm, Nokia. In this sub-chapter, Nokia is a case study example about the long term strategic changes of ICT company. For this reason, it is important to define the concepts and meanings of the strategy and perspectives of "history matters" (Vergne & Durand, 2010).

Because of the importance of long term perspective and history, the analysis emphasizes strategic turning points. For example, Sylvander and colleagues (2004, 21) make, in the context of strategic turning points, a distinction between internal cohesion (internal stakeholders i.e. the producers and employees) and external cohesion (external stakeholders). In this case study, the focus is on meso or macro perspectives (external cohesion), that is to say, on the information and knowledge available for external stakeholders: statistics, annual reports and other written materials. Vergne and Durand (2010,737) find in path dependence three levels of analysis, where two out of three (macro and meso levels) resemble the category of external stakeholders and one out of three resembles internal stakeholders: "at macro level institutionalists use path dependence to account for (harmful) institutional persistence", ..."at the meso level economists rely on path dependence to explain suboptimal governance or technology outcomes" and "... at the micro level the dynamic capability view refers to path dependence as surrogate for organizational rigidity while paradoxically insisting on its positive impact on competitive advantage".

Vergne and Durand (2010) notice that path dependence is only one of several alternative "history matters" notions, such as absorptive capacity, institutional persistence, resource accumulation, structural ineartia, imprinting, first mover advantage and chaos theory (cf. Perello-Marin, Marin-Garcia, & Marcos-Cuevas, 2013). In addition, Vergne and Durand (2010) see that instead of a theory, path dependence is rather a process, where history is unfolding in a self-reinforcing manner and an outcome of "lock-in" effect.

Because path dependence is closely related to strategies of the firm, this study also considers strategic perspectives (see Dunning, 2000). This study understands the concept of strategy in a multifaceted way by following e.g. the perspectives of Mintzberg and his colleagues (1998). They found 10 strategic schools: design school, planning school, positioning school, entrepreneurial school, cognitive school, learning school, power school, cultured school, environmental school and configuration school. They defined term "strategy" by following five Ps for strategy: Plan (intended strategy), Pattern (realized strategy), Position and Ploy (specific maneuver against competitor) (Mintzberg et al., 1998, 9-15). This study mainly follows the mainstream perspective of strategy research emphasizing, instead of micropraxis of the management and organization which are typical for strategy as practice perspective (see, e.g. Laine, 2010), meso- and macro-activities (c.f. Jarzabkowski & Spee, 2009), and technological changes.

Among the categories of Mintzberg and colleagues (1998) the most important perspectives for strategy in this paper are intended strategy, emergent strategy, deliberate strategy and realized strategy. Furthermore, configuration school, which is combining the elements of all other nine strategic schools, contains two interesting phases: configuration (steady state) periods and transformation periods. During configuration periods it is possible to carefully plan the strategies of the organization and during transformation periods the organization is following some kinds of re-engineering processes.

In addition to frameworks introduced by Mintzberg and his colleagues (1998), this study touches other two discussions: strategy as practice and different forms of collaborative strategies. Actually, strategy as practice perspective is near the ideas of emergent strategy by Mintzberg and his colleagues (1998). Namely, strategy as practice framework is based on the idea that operational actions of organization are important part of the strategy-making. Therefore, the everyday practices and doings in the organization generate the whole strategy of organization (See, e.g. Laine, 2010). Indeed, strategy as practice -principle and emergent strategy defined by Mintzberg and his colleagues (1998) resemble each other.

Other interesting discussion considers the dimension between cooperation and competition. Whether organization is following cooperative strategy or competitive strategy? Actually this not the "right" question, because e.g. Kylänen & Rusko (2011) noticed, by using development work in Pyhä-Luosto destination as an example, that simultaneously there can be cooperative (deliberative) actions on the organization on the strategic level and competitive actions on the operational level. Actually in this case there is unintentional coopetition strategy in this kind of development work, which is also some kind of emergent strategy (cf. Mariani et al., 2007).

This part of the chapter contains several different concepts or frameworks in order to understand and define "strategy". We will meet many of these perspectives once again in Sub-chapter 6 in the context of Nokia and its strategic processes. resent your perspective on the issues, controversies, problems, etc., as they relate to theme and arguments supporting your position. Compare and contrast with what has been, or is currently being done as it relates to the chapter's specific topic and the main theme of the book.

THE HISTORY OF NOKIA AND MOBILE PHONE BRANCH

The history of mobile phone industry and business has strong connections with innovations and technological inventions and systems. Therefore, this section includes, in addition to the managerial or strategic turning points of business, also several technical turning points in the wireless networks and solutions.It is noteworthy that often the same technical systems have been used and even invented nearly simultaneously in different parts of the world.

General Landmarks of Mobile Phone Business

As already mentioned, technological improvements have marked out the turning points of the mobile phone business. For this reason, we consider at first the technological framework of the business (Table 1). There have been dozens of systems in the history of mobile phones. Perhaps it is the easiest is to categorize these systems with 5 classes: 1 G, 2G, 3G, 4G and 5G systems or networks. In Table 1 mobile phone systems are classified into these five categories.

It is difficult to define when and who invented and provided the first one mobile phone for the use of the market. The role of Scandinavia has been very important in the field of pioneering work in this

Table 1. Five generations of wireless phones and communicators

	1 G	2 G	3 G	4 G	5 G
Systems or standards (examples)	Nippon Telephone and Telegraph (NTT) Tokyo 1979 . Nordic Mobile Telephone (NTM) 1981, Advanced Mobile Phone Service (AMPS) 1983 in USA	GSM (Europe) IS-95 (USA) iDEN D-AMPS PDC CSD PHS GPRS HSCSD WiDEN CDMA2000 EDGE (2,5G) EGPRS (2,5G)	W-CDMA (UMTS, FOMA) TD-CDMA IS-856 TD-SCDMA GAN/UMA HSPA	UMB UMTS (Revision 8 (LTE)) WiMAX CDMA Unified IP and seamless combination of broadband, LAN/WAN/ PAN/WLAN	CDMA LAN//WAN/ PAN/WLAN and wwww Unified IP and seamless combination of broadband, LAN/WAN/ PAN/WLAN, ?
General features	Analog service No data service	Digital voice service 9.6K to 14.4 K bit/sec One-way data transmissions only Enhanced calling features like called ID	Superior voice quality Up to 2M bit/sec always-on data Broadband data services like video and multimedia Enhanced roaming	Up to 100 Mbit/s or even 1Gbit/s (loading) and 20 Mbit/s (sending). Combination of several services and networks which increase the usability.	1 Gbts and higher
Period (in which system is in general use).	1979-2002	1991-2011	2001-	2011-	2015?

(see, e.g. Nurvitadhi, 2003; Halonen et al., 2003; Dahlman ct al, 2008; Akhtar, 2013)

branch. However, perhaps the earliest commercial mobile phone service provided in US as a result of cooperation with Motorola and Bell System in 1946. Service based on MTS system (Mobile Telephone System). Also in Scandinavian one of the first mobile phone solutions have been invented 60 years ago. Those days Swedish enterprise Ericsson provided the first commercial automatic mobile phone system. They had a couple of hundreds customers and equipment of mobile phone needed a lot of space. Equipment weighed 40 kilograms and filled the whole boot of the car. The first technology based on MTA system (Mobile Telephony A) and the users were professional from different branches such as advocates, physicians and mass media. The system was based on a framework provided by Swedish national phone company (current Telia-Sonera). Those days network used 160 MHz frequency domain. (Tietokone, 2006). MTS, MTA and later version MTB are so called zero generation products (0G) within the history of mobile phones. However, these earlier technologies were not any commercial successes.

Next step was to launch NMT system (Nordisk Mobiltelefon) in Scandinavian 1981. Nearly at the same time or actually a bit earlier established the earliest commercial 1G mobile phone system by Nippon Telephone and Telegraph (NTT) in Tokyo on December 1979 (Balston, 1993; Nurvitadhi, 2003). In Finland NMT system started in 1982. This system used 450 MHz frequency domain. Actually both Swedish Ericsson and Finnish Nokia introduced the same system nearly at the same time. In US, the Advanced Mobile Phone Service (AMPS) was not started until 1983 (Nurvitadhi, 2003). The first NMT car phone Nokia Talkman launched in 1984. In 1987 publicized the first mobile (hand)phone. In 1987, they changed the system by NMT-900 network in order to attach wider capacity.

The first production-ready digital GSM-phone in the world was introduced by Nokia in 1991. This was actually the first second generation mobile phone. Later on Nokia launched the first pocket size mobile phone Nokia 1011. Fast GSP -system developed as a world-wide system during 1990's. (Tietokone, 2006). There were several different standards for 2G phones, such as IS-95 which was used especially in US, GPRS and more advanced (actually 2,5 G) cellular phones EDGE and EGPRS. In the case of 2G cellular phones, Nokia was initially technical and finally also commercial market leader in the world (see also Table 1).

3G phase started in 2001 when first 3G networks established in Japan. Technology based on FOMA standard. Perhaps, the most popular UMTS 3G standards have taken place generally in 2005 all over the world. Contemporary mobile phone standards are based on 3G, 4G and gradually also 5G solutions. The main differences between these three generations are, according to Janevsk (2009, 1), that 5G "is seen as user-centric concept instead of operator-centric as in 3G or service-centric concept as seen for 4G. In the proposed concept, the mobile user is on the top of all". However, it is difficult to define the actual (technological) content of the 5G solutions.

This sub-chapter showed that the role of Scandinavia, and especially the role of two Scandinavian companies, Ericsson and Nokia, seems to be important in the development process of mobile phones. Furthermore, this paper shows that in spite of the enormous strategic changes of these two companies, they development still resemble each other.

The Development of Nokia

Above in Sub-chapter 4.1, we have come to know a technology of mobile phones better. The description was focused only on some technical turning points of the mobile phone business. For example, the turning points in the management and in the markets shares of the branch were ignored. In this section also some of these details have been introduced, especially in the case of Nokia. However, the real strategie analysis for Nokia is in Sub-chapter 5.

Nokia has had a long history, for about 150 years. Thus it is clear that during the history of Nokia, there have been many products and technologies. Most of these products have been passed. Nokia divided its history into four phases in 2011 and in 2013 Nokia divides its history with 15 different phases, (including the nameless early state). The updated historical steps of Nokia basing mostly on these phases are on Table 2.

During the first phase Nokia produced paper, rubber and cables." Between 1865 and 1967, the company would become a major industrial force; but it took a merger with a cable company and a rubber firm to set the new Nokia Corporation on the path to electronics". (Nokia, 2011). One important turning point was based on merger 1967 in which Nokia Ab, Finnish Rubber Works and Finnish Cable works formally merge to create Nokia Corporation.

After the merger, according to Nokia (2011), they were "ideally positioned for a pioneering role in the early evolution of mobile communication". During second phase (1968-1991) they have some pioneering products, such as radio telephone equipment provided by Mobira Oy. Mobira established via a joint venture (1979) between Nokia and leading Finnish television maker Salora. Furthermore, 1981 was built NMT, "the first international mobile phone network", 1982 Nokia makes its first digital telephone switch, Nokia DX200, 1984 Mobira Talkman (portable phone) launched, 1987 Mobira Cityman, which was the first handheld NMT phone, 1991 they make world's first GSM call.

Table 2. The divisions for the history of Nokia

Division of Phases According to Web- Pages 2011	Division of Phases According to Web-Pages 2013
1) Nokia's First century: 1865-1967	1898 The galoshes revolution
	1912 Electronics go boom
2) The move to mobile: 1968-1991	1967 Three become one
	1979 The mobile era begins
	1984 Good enough for Gorbachev
3) Mobile revolution 1992-1999	1991 A new direction
	1994 Name that tune
	1997 Snake bites
	1998 On top of the world
4) Era before Microsoft 1999-2010	1999 Multi-tasking mobiles
	2005 One billion and counting
	2006 Nokia Siemens networks
	2009 Treading lightly
	September 2010 A fresh face at the helm (Elop as CEO)
5) Era of Nokia with Microsoft 2/2011-9/2013	February 2011 A meeting of minds
	October 2011 Let battle commence, Nokia &Microsoft phones
	Microsoft buys Nokia Mobile phones by 5.44 billion euro. New CEO: Rajcev Suri, (temporarily before Suri: Risto Siilasmaa)
6) Era of Networks 9/2013-	Nokia buys Alcatel-Lucent
	Five business areas: Mobile Networks, Fixed Networks, IP/Optical Networks, Applications & Analytics ja Nokia Technologies.

(Modified from Nokia, 2011; Nokia, 2013)

In 1992, was important turning point in the history of Nokia. Jorma Ollila becomes a president and CEO of Nokia. Earlier Jorma Ollila has been a manager in one of the divisions of Nokia, namely in Nokia Mobile Phones. He focused the company on the branch of telecommunications. The other turning points during the third phases of Nokia were for instance 1992 (Nokia's first GSM handset), 1998 (Nokia became world leader in mobile phones) and 1999 when Nokia launches the world's first WAP handset, the Nokia 7110. (Nokia, 2011).

According to the web-pages of Nokia (2011) the fourth phase consists especially of 3G, mobile multiplayer gaming and multimedia devices. The turning points are following years: 2002 (first 3G phone), 2003 (Nokia launches the N-game, 2005 (Nokia N-series is born), 2006, when Olli-Pekka Kallasvuo became as a CEO and president of Nokia. At the same time, Jorma Ollila stays as part-time chairman of Nokia. In 2007 "Nokia recognized as 5th the most valued brand in the world. Nokia Siemens Networks commences operations. Nokia launches Ovi, its new internet services brand" (Nokia, 2011). In 2008 Nokia's three mobile device business groups and the supporting horizontal groups are replaced by an integrated business segment, Devices & Services.

Actually, it is also easy to find 5th era for Nokia, which begins in 2010 and consists of a change in the executive management and in the systems of mobile phones. Namely, Stephen Elop started as a

CEO and president of Nokia in the autumn of 2010. Previously, Elop worked as the head of the Business Division Microsoft. Another turning point was spring 2011 when Elop announced the cooperation between Nokia and Microsoft. With the same, Elop announced that Nokia mobile phones will be used in the future Microsoft platform instead of Nokia's own Symbia platform. According to Nokia (2013), "The goal is to establish a third ecosystem to rival iOS and Android. The industry has shifted from a battle of devices to a war of ecosystems… ". Already during 2011 Nokia launched its first Nokia with Windows phones, the Nokia Lumia 800 and the Nokia Lumia 710 (in October 2011).

Nokia has 130 050 employees in the end of 2011. Over half of them (73 686) were in Nokia Siemens Network, 38% in Devices & Services (49 406) and the rest of them in Location & communication (6 659) and in Corporate Common Functions (219). (Nokia, 2012) Most of the employees were outside of Finland and Europe. Especially amount of Chinese and other Asian employees had increased recent years at the cost of Europe and North America. According to Gartner (2013, via Talouselämä, 2013), the market share of Nokia had decreased to 18 per cent in the last quarter of 2012. As late as 2011, Nokia estimated that their mobile device volume market share was 32% in 2010. (Nokia, 2011b). The total volume of mobile phones in the world for year 2012 was about 1.750 million units, which is a bit lower level than previous year. Furthermore, total profit of Nokia in 2011 was negative (-1073 million euro) (Nokia, 2012).

Because of the declining market development of Nokia-Microsoft mobile and smart phones, Microsoft decided to buy Nokia Mobile department using 5.44 billion euro. Nokia is still independent company focusing on mobile networks and innovations. Nokia had January 2016 about 104 000 workers (Nokia, 2016).

The marketing strategy of Nokia has been multidimensional: it is both general and diversified. Nokia has used a lot of money to build up one of the most famous brands in the world. It had succeeded rather well: Nokia –brand was ranked as the world's sixth most valuable brand in 2005. Today the situation is different, the value of the brand has decreased remarkably. Part of the general marketing of Nokia is to build up some kind of cultural approach to support the demand for the products of Nokia (compare Moisander and Valtonen 2006).

The Nokia is an international multi-product enterprise, which have many subsidiaries. In 2011, the most important locations for them were the USA, Germany, Great Britain, South-Korea, China, the Netherlands, Hungary, Brazil, and India. (Nokia 2011b). Now the role of French workers has increased because of the Alcatel-Lucent acquisition of Nokia. Nokia focuses on networks and technologies. Their four networks businesses are associated with virtual networks, mobile broadband, IP routing and optical technologies, and the Cloud applications and services to manage network performance. Nokia Technologies focuses on advanced R&D for licensing and new product businesses. (Nokia, 2016b)

All in all, Nokia as a whole company, experienced a remarkable recovery in 1990's. From the multi-branch company, it changed into a one-branch company covering both mobiles and mobile networks. This branch is focused on enabling electric mobile communication, which has many sub-industries or sub-branches, however. Still Nokia, as a firm, is relatively complicated entirety although nearly all of its products are focused in one way or another on information, telecommunication and networks. Because of the relative complicated entirety of Nokia, this section told only part of the features and story of Nokia. More specific strategic analysis is presented in the previous section.

THE STRATEGIC ANALYSIS OVER THE TURNING POINTS OF NOKIA: REFLECTIONS OF ERICSSON

Nokia

We have familiarized some technical details and development about mobile phone industry and Nokia. This section deepens the perspectives of Nokia and mobile phone business in the context of strategic discussions and processes. However, this section shows that technical turning points also have connections with strategic ones.

Therefore, this Sub-chapter is following the same periodic structure as four (or actually five) technical turning points introduced above in the Sub-chapter 4.2.

Afterwards the first century of Nokia appears to follow emergent strategy: the main branches changed and developed during the century gradually and peacefully. Even the world war didn't have significant effects on the performance of Nokia. There were at the same time 2-3 main branches: at first mechanical pulp mill, which changed towards a paper mill. Gradually, the main products of Nokia turned to be rubber, paper and cables.

After merger 1966 Suomen Gummitehdas Oy and Suomen Kaapelitehdas Oy combined as the parts of Nokia Ab. (Nokia, 2011c). This event was important because it started new strategic doctrine in Nokia. Previously, Nokia followed emergent or entrepreneurial strategic school. There were not remarkable eras of transformation. Therefore Nokia followed in its early phases more like configuration strategies. Collaboration (and mergers) strategies are part of the power school in the typology of Mintzberg and his colleagues (1998). Merger 1966 started a chain of numerous another mergers and cooperation which leaded Nokia as an international multi-trade company. Some of these mergers were profitless. Especially CEO and president of Nokia Kari Kairamo (during period 1977-1988) followed deliberative strategy for internationalizing Nokia with multi-trade mergers. Kairamo was strong and visionary leader in Nokia, which means also that there were nuances of entrepreneurial leadership in Nokia those days. After his death, Nokia drifts into crisis of economy and leadership. Two managers of Nokia compete to get power in Nokia: Kalle Isokallio and Simo Vuorilehto. Temporally Vuorilehto was a couple of years as a CEO and president of Nokia. In 1991 Jorma Ollila was chosen as a new CEO and president of Nokia. Earlier Ollila has specialized in the mobile phone sector. Therefore he noticed the possibilities of this branch and soon the entire Nokia specialized in mobile phones. This was a remarkable strategic turning point in Nokia which enables the enormous success of Nokia during 1990's. Nokia became as a leading producer of mobile phones in the world. This strategic turning point was based on more like emergent than deliberative strategy (cf. Mitzberg, 1998). However, after 1991 strategy of Nokia followed deliberative intentional strategy without any significant strategic transformation. Of course there were technical changes in the frameworks and platforms of mobile phones, but operational mechanisms of Nokia took care of these changes successfully. It is also possible to claim that Ollila followed visionary strategy in the same way as Kairamo, but the main contents of the visions were totally different.

There have been in the era of Ollila also some minor strategic changes in Nokia: at first production units were in Finland but later on the importance of China and India increased in production and marketing. There were also some interesting new strategies in the context of these kinds of internationalising: Nokia and Motorola cooperated with each other with the local government in order to establish new production units in China. Luo (2004) noticed this cooperation and called these actions to be as coopetition activities in which the competing firms cooperate with each other.

Olli-Pekka Kallasvuo followed the same strategic doctrines and configuration strategy as Ollila. It is possible that this decision was a mistake because it seems that turbulent markets needs more transformation in the mobile phone business for example in the forms of platform decisions. Actually, Kallasvuo based his actions on the typical cultural school attitude. Perhaps therefore Stephen Elop becomes as new CEO and president of Nokia. At the same time there was once again a remarkable turning point in the strategy of Nokia: cooperation with Microsoft started collaborative strategy which possibly threats the existence of Nokia as an independent company. Again there was also emergent strategy on the background: Nokia drifts to the transformation phase.

The style of the company changed during the phase of Elop: several Finnish units abolished and the focus of the manufacturing, and research and development moved more abroad. However, a head office is still in Finland after Elop. Furthermore, Nokia has still maintained its independency. However, the prevailing period of Elop has already shown that there is a strategic turning point in the development of Nokia in 2010/2011. This provides further evidence that there was really a transformation phase in progress of Nokia, at least during 2010-2013. The success of this turning point was missing. Therefore, during 2013 started a new turning point, where the CEO changed (Raeev Suri via Siilasmaa) and Microsoft bought the mobile phone department of Nokia by 5.44 billion euro. Nokia focused on mobile networks and innovation. In 2016, the acquisition of Alcatel Lucent will strengthen the new strategic choice.

Some Eras in the Development of Ericsson

In 1876, Lars Magnus Ericsson started a telegraph repair shop with help from his friend Carl Johan Andersson. In 1878, Ericsson began making and selling his own telephone equipment. Thus, the history of Ericsson started directly among the branch of telephone. The business was successful in Swedish market and they expanded their business into foreign markets. Only markets in America were problematic for Ericsson (The History of Ericsson, 2016).

Ericsson introduced the world's first fully automatic mobile telephone system, MTA (Mobile Telephony A), in 1956. MTA is one of the zero generation products (0G) within the history of mobile phones. It released one of the world's first hands-free speaker telephones in the 1960s. These first innovations in the branch of mobile phone were not any commercial success (The History of Ericsson, 2016; Tietokone, 2006).

Ericsson was one of the leading mobile phone companies in the 1990's. However, in 2001 Ericsson's cell phone division merged with the major Japanese home electronics firm Sony and formed SonyEricsson Communications. Sony acquired Ericsson's share in the venture on February 16, 2012. Practically this means that recently lately Ericsson has focused on mobile networks (e.g. mobile broadbands, network design), cloud systems, consulting and management of immaterial property rights and technology licenses. (The History of Ericsson, 2016)

Comparison of the Development Between Nokia and Ericsson

Though the history of Nokia is as old as of Ericsson, early phases are very different. Nokia established in 1865 and Ericsson in 1876. The first products of Nokia were pulp for paper, gradually also rubber and cables whereas the first products of Ericsson were telephones. Both of these companies were interested in mobile communication and e.g. radio telephone equipment. Both of the companies had a pioneering role in the development of mobile phones. Ericsson met remarkable cooperation with Sony in 2001 and Nokia with Microsoft in 2011. In both cases, this cooperation activity has abated.

In spite of some differences in the selection of products and services, both Nokia and Ericsson contemporarily focus on networks, patents and technology licensing. The main branches of the business have been nearly the same since 1980's: mobile phones, smart phones and finally especially broadbands, mobile networking and patents. From the management perspectives, this joint development might be based on isomorphism and mimetic (Haveman, 1993). Already in 1993 Haveman (1993) noticed that the organizations imitated large and profitable companies, not similar sized organizations. However, she found also that especially large firms imitated other large firms.

Yet, there any not any marks of deliberative strategic copying or mimetic between Nokia and Ericsson. In both cases the market development and market shares in mobile phones declined and this caused that firms had business arrangements with collaboration (in the case of Nokia with Microsoft and in the case of Ericsson with Sony). Finally, in both of the cases, the companies leaved off their former core business: mobile phones and concentrated in other existing business areas, such as mobile phone networks, patents and technology licensing. It seems that the core mobile phone and smart phone business drifted from blue ocean strategy to red ocean strategy (cf. Kim & Mauborgne, 2005) and Ericsson and Nokia are seeking either new blue ocean strategies or at least more profitable market niches. In this sense, Ericsson moved first from the core business of mobile phones and Nokia later on. Ericsson does not have any first mover advantage due to fact that Nokia was already acting in the same "new" markets as Ericsson. However, Ericsson started this new allocation of resources and Nokia made nearly similar moves later on. Thus, if there is mimetic isomorphism in the ICT business, it might be asymmetric: possibly Nokia followed the strategic changes of Ericsson, but not vice versa.

In addition, this kind of similar strategic development is possible to call "co-evolution". Co-evolution means according to Kemp, Loorbach and Rotmans (2007) a situation, where different subsystems are shaping but not determining each other (relative autonomy). Because Nokia and Ericsson do not have any tight connection or collaboration now and nor in their history, this kind of loose relationship between them, which is based on co-evolution, might be possible.

CONCLUSION

The evolution of Nokia includes several turning points. Technical innovations and development was one important feature in these junctions. Furthermore, strategic changes and processes have appeared hand in hand with these technical changes of mobile phone systems and platforms. One of the main aims of this article is to clarify the content of these strategic changes. In Sub-chapter 5, the analysis based, for example, on the typology of Mintzberg and his colleagues (1998) in their seminal of book of strategic discussions: Strategy Safari. Table 3 concludes and compresses the strategic analysis of Nokia and ICT business.

It is possible to notice that many strategic turning points really associated with the technical platforms. However, the first strategic turning point in 1967 was not based on the general technological evolution. The merger in 1967 by chance enabled the excellent future of Nokia: it focused on the technology industries. In this sense, there was also emergent strategic doctrine in Nokia. However, the era of 1968-1991 was mainly based on multi-trade mergers and internationalisation and therefore it was an era of deliberative strategy. In spite of this, these multi-trade mergers did not have any clear direction. This period meant

Table 3. Strategic and technical turning points of Nokia

Period	1865-1967	1968-1991	1992-1999	2000-2010	2011-2013	2013-
Technical system/ platform	0 G	0 G and 1 G	2 G	3 G	4 G	5 G
Strategic schools and doctrines of Nokia	Emergent/ entrepreneurial strategy. Configuration Competition	Deliberative strategy with aim of international multi-trade company via numerous international mergers. Learning. Transformation Cooperation	Initially emergent strategy, finally deliberative visionary (entrepreneurial) strategy, which focused on mobile phones. Configuration Competition (Cooperation with subcontractors)	Deliberative strategy. Configuration Competition	Emergent strategy, deliberate strategy (in OS) Transformation Cooperation (Coopetition)	Deliberate strategy (mobile networks the main branch) Transformation Learning (New focuses)
Reasons and events associated with the strategic turning points	National multi-trade company via merger 1966. New goals of CEOs in order to internationalise the multi-trade business.	Problems to choose continuer for CEO position after Kari Kairamo. Jorma Ollila was selected as a new CEO. New system: GSM (2G) for mobile phones	The change in system of mobile phones (3 G)	New CEO (Kallasvuo 2006) continued the prevailing strategies. Market shares decreased both in mobile phones and smart-phones. Nokia's Symbian platform has many problems. 2011 new CEO (Elop) whom started to cooperate with Microsoft and takes Microsoft as a new platform (OS) of mobile phones.	New CEO Rajeev Suri (via Siilasmaa). Small market shares of mobile phones caused the strategic turn, where Nokia focuses on mobile networks and innovation

the significant strategic and technical learning period for Nokia: it learnt the rules of the international business and possibilities of new technology. (Table 3)

The second turning point means enormous change for Nokia: it met remarkable success in mobile phones after it had specialized in mobile phones. Technologically Nokia was pioneering company in 2 G technology during 1990's. Ollila's and Kallasvuo's strategies based on the maintaining situation with deliberative strategy and superior technological competence. However, especially in the branch of smartphones Nokia has lost its hegemony in the market and in technology: Symbian platform was not competitive with some other competing platforms, such as Android (Google). This change was really fast (Table 5). Thus, in the period of Elop, Nokia chosen Microsoft's operating systems as a platform for its most advanced smartphones. For Nokia, this was one important turning point. Also, the value of the brand for Nokia has decreased fast recently, this OS changing will also mean the changing brand for Nokia: the brand of Nokia was partly connected with the OS and brand/ecosystem of Microsoft family (cf. Kenney & Pon, 2011). In the era of 5G Nokia leaved off its core business: mobile phones and it concentrated in other existing business areas, such as mobile phone networks, patents and technology licensing. At the same time the CEO of Nokia changed and the collaboration with Microsoft practically ended.

Generally, the fact that each time, when changing the management of Nokia in the cases of Kairamo, Ollila, Elop and Suri, has meant remarkable changes in the strategy of Nokia partly confirms the existence of some kinds of (top-level) internal cohesion in Nokia. Furthermore, in ICT, and especially in mobile phone industry, have been technical external turning points (external cohesion) simultaneously with these changes in top management: Kairamo (1G), Ollila (2G), Kallasvuo (smartphones (Symbian) and 3,5G), Elop (smartphones (Windows) and 4G) and Suri (5G). It seems that new technology might need a new management and new directions in Nokia in order to survive in business. In the period of Ollila, there were several steps from the end of 1G via 2G towards 3G, however. This simultaneous (top-level) internal cohesion and simultaneous external cohesion (changes in technology and operating systems) provides evidence about Nokia for path dependence and lock-in phenomena in the forms of simultaneous internal and external cohesion and strategic turning points (cf. Sydow et al., 2005; Koch, 2008, 52; Vergne and Durand, (2010, 736). One form of external cohesion or mimetic isomorphism might be based on the similarities of the strategic development of Ericsson and Nokia. Possible mimetic isomorphism is asymmetric, however. Though the missing linkages and practical cooperation between Nokia and Ericsson their strategic choices resemble each other during the latest decades. It is even possible to notice some kind of weak co-evolution with relative autonomy between them. This potential co-evolution might be unintentional, however.

The collaboration with Microsoft threatened the independency of Nokia, a company which have seen as a part of the Finnish patriotism. This long-term analysis shows that Nokia had good conditions for growth in the 1990's but it is possible that company has met the Penrose effect: the concept of managerial limits of growth (see, e.g. Pitelis, 2002). Until now the change in the management has mostly meant in Nokia the new ways to survive in business.

This research also provides some hints for further studies. In the case of Nokia strategic and technical turning points mostly hand in hand followed each other. It will be important to study whether this finding has more general extensions in the other branches and industries, thus confirming these kinds of general internal and external cohesion and path dependence. Furthermore, what kinds of differences this phenomenon contains between industries.

REFERENCES

Akhtar, S. (2010). 2G-4G Networks: Evolution of technologies, standards, and deployment. In *Encyclopedia of Multimedia Technology and Networking*. Ideas Group Publisher. Retrieved from http://faculty.uaeu.ac.ae/s.akhtar/EncyPaper04.pdf

Balston, D. M. (1993). *Cellular Radio Systems*. Artech House.

Carduff, K. (2010). *Corporate Reporting: From Stewardship to Contract*. The Annual Reports of the United States Steel Corporation (1902-2006).

Dahlman, E., Skold, J., & Beming, P. (2008). *3G Evolution: HSPA and LTE for Mobile Broadband*. Academic Press.

Dunning, J. H. (2000). The eclectic paradigm as an envelope for economic and business theories of MNE activity. *International Business Review, 9*(2), 163–190.

Eriksson, P., & Kovalainen, A. (2008). *Qualitative Methods in Business Research*. Sage Publications Ltd.

Halonen, T., Romero, J., & Melero, J. (2003). *GSM, GPRS and edge performance: evolution towards 3G/UMTS*. John Wiley & sons Ltd. doi:10.1002/0470866969

Haveman, H. A. (1993). Follow the leader: Mimetic isomorphism and entry into new markets. *Administrative Science Quarterly*, 593–627.

Janevski, T. (2009). 5G mobile phone concept. In *Consumer Communications and Networking Conference*, (pp. 1-2). IEEE.

Jarzabkowski, P., & Spee, P. (2009). Strategy-as-practice: A review and future directions for the field. *International Journal of Management Reviews*, *11*(1), 69–95.

Kemp, R., Loorbach, D., & Rotmans, J. (2007). Transition management as a model for managing processes of co-evolution towards sustainable development. *International Journal of Sustainable Development and World Ecology*, *14*(1), 78–91.

Kenney, M., & Pon, B. (2011). Structuring the Smartphone Industry: Is the Mobile Internet OS Platform the Key? *Journal of Industry, Competition and Trade*, *11*(3), 239–261. doi:10.1007/s10842-011-0105-6

Kim, W. C., & Mauborgne, R. (2005). Blue ocean strategy: From theory to practice. *California Management Review*, *47*(3), 105–121. doi:10.2307/41166308

Koch, J. (2008). *Strategic Paths and Media Management-A Path Dependency Analysis of the German Newspaper Branch of High Quality Journalism*. Available at SSRN 1101643

Kylänen, M., & Rusko, R. (2011). Unintentional coopetition in the service industries: The case of Pyhä-Luosto tourism destination in the Finnish Lapland. *European Management Journal*, *29*(3), 193–205. doi:10.1016/j.emj.2010.10.006

Laine, M., Bamberg, J., & Jokinen, P. (2007). Tapaustutkimuksen käytäntö ja teoria. In Tapaustutkimuksen taito, (pp. 9-38). Gaudeamus.

Laine, P.-M. (2010). *Toimijuus strategiakäytännöissä: Diskurssi- ja käytäntöteoreettisia avauksia*. Turku School of Economics.

Lamberg, J.-A., Näsi, J., Ojala, J., & Sajasalo, P. (Eds.). (n.d.). *The Evolution of Competitive Strategies in Global Forestry Industries*. Dordrecht, The Netherlands: Springer.

Luo, Y. (2004a). *Coopetition in International Business*. Copenhagen Business School Press.

Mariani, M. M. (2007). Coopetition as an emergent Strategy. *International Studies of Management & Organization*, *37*(2), 97–126. doi:10.2753/IMO0020-8825370205

Mintzberg, H., Ahlstrand, B., & Lampel, J. (1998). *The Complete Guide through the Wilds of Strategic Management*. FT Prentice Hall.

Moisander, J., & Valtonen, A. (2006). *Qualitative Marketing Research: A Cultural Approach*. London: Sage Publications. doi:10.4135/9781849209632

Nokia. (2011a). *Story of Nokia (Nokia's first century to Nokia Now)*. Retrieved from http://blog.a4add.com/story-of-nokianokias-first-century-to-nokia-now/special-news/create-free-Website-a4add.com

Nokia. (2011b). *Form 20-F 2010 (Annual Report of Nokia 2010)*. Nokia.

Nokia. (2011c). *Historia lyhyesti*. Retrieved from http://www.nokia.fi/nokia/tietoa-yhtiosta/historia/historia-lyhyesti

Nokia. (2012). *Annual report 2011*. Nokia.

Nokia. (2013). *The Nokia Story*. Retrieved from http://www.nokia.com/global/about-nokia/about-us/the-nokia-story/

Nokia. (2016a). *Nokia ja Alcatel-Lucent juhlistavat tänään toimintansa aloittamista yhdistyneenä yhtiönä.* Retrieved from http://company.nokia.com/fi/uutiset/lehdistotiedotteet/2016/01/14/nokia-ja-alcatel-lucent-juhlistavat-tanaan-toimintansa-aloittamista-yhdistyneena-yhtiona

Nokia. (2016b). *Our businesses*. http://company.nokia.com/en/our-businesses

Nurvitadhi, E. (2003). *Trends in Mobile Computing: A Study of Mobile Phone Usage in the United States and Japan*. Oregon State University.

OECD. (2015). Retrieved from: http://www.oecd.org/internet/broadband/oecdkeyictindicators.htm

OECD Communication Outlook. (2011). OECD.

Ong, J. (2011). *Google overtakes Nokia as top smartphone platform maker*. Retrieved from: http://www.appleinsider.com/articles/11/01/31/google_overtakes_nokia_as_maker_of_top_smartphone_platform.html

Pitelis, C. (2002). *The Growth of the Firm. The Legacy of Edith Penrose*. Oxford University Press.

Rosario Perello-Marin, M., Marin-Garcia, J. A., & Marcos-Cuevas, J. (2013). Towards a path dependence approach to study management innovation. *Management Decision, 51*(5), 1037–1046. doi:10.1108/MD-08-2012-0605

Rusko, R. (2012). Strategic Processes and Turning Points in ICT Business: Case Nokia. *International Journal of Innovation in the Digital Economy, 3*(3), 25–34.

Sydow, J., Schreyögg, G., & Koch, J. (2005). *Organizational paths: Path dependency and beyond*. Free University of Berlin.

Sylvander, B., Schieb-Bienfait, N., Le Floch-Wadel, A., & Couallier, C. (2004). The strategic turn of Organic Farming in Europe: a resource based approach of Organic Marketing Initiatives.*XI World Congress of Rural Sociology Special session II: Peasant between Social Movements and the markets*.

Talouselämä. (2013). *Gartner: The market share of Nokia declined extremely low*. Author. (in Finnish)

The History of Ericsson. (2016). Retrieved From: http://www.ericssonhistory.com/

Tietokone. (2006). *Matkapuhelintekniikka täyttää 50 vuotta*. Tero Lehto.

Vergne, J.-P., & Durand, R. (2010). The missing link between the theory and empirics of path dependence: Conceptual clarification, testability issue, and methodological implications. *Journal of Management Studies, 47*(4), 736–759.

Yin, R. K. (2002). *Case study research: Design and methods*. Newbury Park, CA: Sage.

Chapter 2

Impact of Innovation on the Entrepreneurial Success in Selected Business Enterprises in South–West Nigeria

Olu Oju
Osun State University, Nigeria

ABSTRACT

This study examined the impact of innovation on the entrepreneurial success in selected business enterprises in South-Western Nigeria. The paper dwelt on the extent to which the selected enterprises innovation effort affects the quality of their product as well as the company image. Data were analysed using descriptive and inferential statistics. Hypotheses were tested at 0.05 significant levels with the aid of parametric student t-test. The results revealed that there is a positive relationship between innovation and product quality as well as a positive relationship between innovation and good corporate image and that both of them significantly affect entrepreneurial success. The study recommends that business enterprises should engage more on innovation of their production process to improve their product quality and even enhances good corporate image. This will help them to sustain their position in the face of stiff competition.

INTRODUCTION

A number of business enterprises are craving for survival within the stiffened economy as it is presently being witnessed in Nigeria and many other countries of the world. The enterprises' actions to survive and be relevant in the agenda of things need to be studied to identify whether such action as innovation can lead to success of such enterprises. Enterprises are constantly seeking ways to grow, advance and survive in a dynamic environment characterised by complexity and uncertainty. Thus, business enterprises engage in one form of innovative activities or the other in order to cope with the market challenges and gain competitive advantage and wide acceptance of its product in different markets.

DOI: 10.4018/978-1-5225-1779-5.ch002

The role of entrepreneur in inter-industry relationship cannot be over emphasised, particularly, as they affect a number of activities in a number of industries. The nature of innovative process that affects enterprises survival and economic growth revolves around the active and inactive functions of the entrepreneur. In fact, scholars view entrepreneur variously but more importantly as innovator who is responsible for the creation of new products and new methods of production, new processes and capable of identifying new markets (Schumpeter, 1949).

From this background, it follows that if entrepreneurs are viewed as innovators, creators, and sometimes as developers, it will not be out of place to see them as vital function in national and institutional development. It is important therefore to study the impact attached to innovation on entrepreneurial success.

Despite the plethora of studies on innovation in the last few decades, there is no widely accepted causal relationship between innovation and entrepreneurial success. Besides, the impact of innovation on entrepreneurial success of manufacturing firms in Nigerian has not received adequate research attention. This study becomes imperative because many empirical studies that have been carried out and many articles that were written on the subject of innovation placed more emphasis on the developed economies. For example, Heunk (1998) conducted a study on the role of innovation in small and medium sized firms in relation to the firm's success. In their study, Brazeal and Herbert (1999) examined innovation process as an important attribute that eventually triggers the entrepreneurial event or performance. Litz and Kleysen, (2001) observed that innovation is a significant issue, while Hanif and Marnavi (2009) opined that knowledge based economy required the use of innovation measures in addition to quality initiatives for achieving competitiveness.

Thus, a review of academic literature on the subject of innovation reveals that there is a dearth of literature on it in the developing countries including Nigeria and that this creates a major gap in knowledge that has to be filled. This research attempts to fill this gap by studying innovation as it relates to product quality and good corporate image and their effects on entrepreneurial performance in selected manufacturing firms in Nigeria.

LITERATURE REVIEW

Concept of Innovation

The Oxford Advanced Learner's Dictionary of Current English (2015) defines innovation as the introduction of new things, ideas, or ways of doing things or something, which is yet to be carried out by anyone or that is unique. According to Trott (2005), innovation is any good service or idea that is perceived by someone as new while Henrik (2007) sees innovation as the successful implementation of a creation and this innovation seems to foster growth, profits and success. In the words of Trott (2005), innovation is the management of all the activities involved in the process of idea generation, technology development, manufacturing and marketing of new (or improved) product or manufacturing process or equipment. He explained further with simple equation that shows the relationship between the two terms: Innovation = theoretical conception + technical invention + commercial exploitation. Combining the various views, Zaltman, Duncan and Holbek (1973) defined innovation as any idea, practice, or material artifact perceived to be new by the relevant unit of adoption. In other words, organisational innovation has been consistently defined as the adoption of an idea or behavior that is new to the organization (Zaltman *et al.*, 1973). The innovation can either be a new product, new technology, new service or new administrative practice (Hage, 1999). Many companies today are innovative bringing about new ideas and modifying existing ones into their offerings because of the competitive nature of the market. Innovation is different from invention. While innovations are concerned with the launch or introduction of new products, services and processes, inventions are not necessarily introduced into the market (Riederer, Baier & Graefe, 2005).

Types of Innovation

According to Litz and Kleysen (2001), innovation can be classified into product innovation and process innovation. Product innovation refers to the new or improved product, equipment or service that is successful on the market. Process innovation involves the adoption of a new or improved manufacturing or distribution process, or a new method of social service. Riederer *et al.* (2005), identify four different types of product innovation. These are:

1. Incremental innovation is a kind of sustaining innovation by which present technology is used to improve products and services that have gained prominence in the market place.
2. Technological substitution innovation involves the use of new technology developments to make entirely new products that fill existing market opportunities.
3. Market innovation involves combining and using existing technologies in such a way that is new to the market, therefore bring about the existence of a new market segment.
4. Radical innovation is a form of disruptive innovation. It creates a new product or service with new technology that will in turn create a new market segment.

Another classification of innovation also has two main categories; the sustaining innovation and the disruptive innovation (Riederer et al., 2005). By its name, sustaining innovation improves upon already existing products or processes. On the other hand, disruptive innovations are those that are practically different from existing process or product or service already in the market.

Besides, according to Oman (2008), the newness that innovation portrays in the improvement of products, services or process can be described in two ways, technical innovations and administrative innovation. The technical innovation has to do with technology, products and services. The administrative innovations on the other hand, deal with improved procedures, policies and organisational form.

Innovation and Entrepreneurship

There is a close association between innovation and entrepreneurship (Hung & Mondejar, 2005). The boundaries of entrepreneurship embrace an important attribute of the innovation process which eventually triggers an entrepreneurial event or performance (Brazeal & Herbert, 1999; Bygrave & Hofer, 1991). There are some features that are peculiar to innovation. These features are relative advantage which is the degree to which innovation appears superior to existing product, compatibility which is the degree to which the innovation can go with existing product of the organisation, complexity which defines the degree to which the innovation is relatively difficult to understand, divisibility which defines the degree to which the innovation can be tried on a limited basis, and communicability which is the degree to which the beneficial results of usage are observable or describable to others.

Schumpeter (1934) sees the entrepreneur as an agent of change and describes the carrying out of the change or innovations as enterprise. In considering Schumpeter's theory of innovation and entrepreneurship, it would not be overstatement to say that innovation is linked with entrepreneurship. Therefore, the success of an entrepreneurial business or entrepreneur depends on to an extent on innovation, the changes initiated by the entrepreneur.

Entrepreneurship results in the creation of new firms and it is important that entrepreneurs create and adapt the resource base of the new firm (Stam, Gibcus, Telussa, & Garnsey, 2008). New firms are often faced with resource base weakness which makes it impossible for them to compete favorably in the market or business environment with the well-established firms. Therefore, these new firms must demonstrate dynamic capabilities to recognise the resource base as needed (Eisenhardt & Martin, 2000). The dynamic capabilities indicate innovation. They include specific and identifiable processes such as Research and Development (R&D), inter-firm alliancing, new product development and exporting. Innovation comes from the combination of competence, technology and vision in bringing improved products, services and processes to the market more quickly and profitably than the competition (Chandler, Keller, & Lyon, 2000).

Entrepreneurial Success

According to Bosma, Van Praag, and Gerrit de Wit (2000), entrepreneurial success is measured by success of the firm as well as the success of individual entrepreneur's that results from the ownership and conduct of the new firm. Entrepreneurial success can also be measured by other non-financial indicators. Thus, a business organization or an entrepreneur can measure its performance or success rate using the financial and non-financial measures (Chong, 2008). Profit making is a major measure of entrepreneurial success. Other measures of entrepreneurial success are generated employment and the organization's survival.

The association between the successful entrepreneur and profit making is almost undisputed in literature (Bosma *et al.*, 2000). A number of theoretical frameworks exist on how the successful performance of business as well as the owner can be measured. The commonly used success measurement is the goal approach. In this approach, information is easily accessible by the owner-managers for evaluation process (Pfeffer & Salancik, 1978). The goal approach measures the extent to which an organization or an entrepreneur achieves its goals, making use of its available resources.

Other approaches to the measurement of entrepreneurial success include the system resource approach, stakeholder approach, and competitive value approach. The system resources approach assesses the ability of an organization or entrepreneur to obtain its resources (Yutchman & Seashore, 1967). The stakeholders approach and the competitive value approach evaluate performance of an organization or entrepreneur based on its ability to meet the needs and expectations of the external stakeholders like shareholders, creditors, employees, customers, suppliers, competitors, government and local communities among others (Daft, 1995).

The goal approach focuses on making use of the financial measures of entrepreneurial or organizational success which include profits, revenues, return on investment, return on assets, return on equity and cash to total assets among others. The non-financial measures that are used by organization or entrepreneur include the number of employees (Kuo & Wu, 2008), revenue per employee (Johannisson, 1993). Walker, Loughton and Brown (1999) give some other non-financial measures of success and their relevance to success measurement. Such measures include

1. **Lifestyle:** This encompasses such issues as having the capability to use the business and its assets to do things for personal gratification, and
2. **Autonomy:** Entrepreneurs are into business to achieve independence.

Other popular measures of entrepreneurial success or performance include growth, income, wages, survival, innovation and productivity, profitability and satisfaction. The most typical performance measure at the individual level of observation is individual earnings (Audretsch, 2002).

Finally, in the words of Oman (2008), a well-planned organizational innovation should achieve the following within an enterprise among others.

- Improve quality of goods and services and flexibility of production or service provision.
- Reduce unit labor costs, consumption of materials and energy, product design costs.
- Increase range of goods and services, and replace of products being phased out as well as developing environment-friendly products.
- Improve communication and interaction amongst various business activities within the enterprise, and develop stronger relationships with the customers.
- Increase ability to adapt to different clients demands.
- Reduce adverse environmental impact or improve health and safety.
- Increase efficiency or speed of supplying and/or delivering goods or services and reduce operating costs for service provision.
- Increase visibility or exposure for products and enhance entering into new market.

Management of Innovation

Entrepreneurial innovation need to be taken with all seriousness because it determines the growth and future of an organization. Innovation is extremely complex and involves the effective management of a variety of different activities. Thus, innovation management is the economic implementation and exploration of new ideas and discoveries (Riederer et al, 2005). Innovation management also involves the promotion of organizational culture that would encourage and boost the development of new ideas and opportunities. The organizational integration of innovation in the corporate structure takes place through innovation management (Brem & Voigt, 2007). Therefore, innovation management should be treated as a part of business strategy. Innovation management is the development, introduction and as the case may be, implementation and enforcement of technical and social-technical initiatives of the management of the business. Thus, innovation management comprises the decisions about innovation and the innovation processes (Hauschildt, 2004)

METHODOLOGY

This study used survey research design. Survey research design was used because it is perceived as a good method in identifying changes in corporate performance due to strategic planning. The study population is limited employees of five manufacturing firms in South-Western geo-political zone of Nigeria. The companies' selection was done through purposive sampling method and these companies are in the Food and Beverages line. They were chosen because of their contributions to economic development of Nigeria. They are Cadbury Nigeria PLC, Flour Mills of Nigeria PLC, Nestle Nigeria PLC, United African Company Nigeria PLC, and Unilever Nigeria PLC. Both primary and secondary data were used in the study. Primary data were collected through the administration of questionnaire while secondary data were garnered from annual report and accounts of the selected companies. Simple random sampling technique was used to select the respondents through which primary data were collected. Eighteen employees were selected from each company. This gives a total of 90 employees as the respondents. However, only 72 of the respondents filled their questionnaire properly and were for the analysis. This gives 80% response rate. To ensure the validity and reliability of the instrument used for the study and to minimize the element of bias that could emerge from the research, the questionnaire was carefully constructed (Ojo, 2003). Before the final version of the questionnaire was sent out, it was pilot-tested. A pilot test which took the form of test-retest method was conducted using ten employees to determine the appropriateness and relevance of the questions in the instrument and to see whether the respondents actually understand the questionnaire. The first draft of the questionnaire was circulated to selected experts who are experienced researchers on innovation and business performance management. Based on the feedback from these experts, modifications were made. Data were analyzed with the use of descriptive and inferential statistics through Statistical Package for Social Sciences (SPSS), version 19.0.

Testing of Hypotheses and Discussion of Results

The hypotheses for this study were tested with the aid of parametric student t- test.

Hypothesis One

Ho: There is no significant relationship between innovation and product quality.

From one-sample statistics Table 1, the number of variables is 72, the mean is equal to 2.01, the standard deviation is .986 while the standard error mean is .116. Therefore, the mean value of 2.01 which shows the average response indicates that the respondents agree that innovation is positively related to product quality.

Similarly, from Table 2, the t-test value is 17.336, the degree of freedom is 71, and the mean difference is 2.014. Since p-value of .000 is less than 0.05, then the t test value is significant. Hence there is a significant relationship between innovation and product quality in selected manufacturing firms. The null hypothesis is therefore rejected. The alternative hypothesis which says that there is a significant positive relationship between innovation and product quality is therefore formulated and upheld.

Table 1. One-sample statistics

	N	Mean	Std. Deviation	Std. Error Mean
Organizational innovation has impact on quality product.	72	2.01	.986	.116

SPSS Output from Field Survey, 2016.

Table 2. One-sample test

.	Test Value = 0					
	t	df	Sig. (2-tailed)	Mean Difference	95% Confidence Interval of the Difference	
					Lower	Upper
Organizational innovation has impact on quality product.	17.336	71	.000	2.014	1.78	2.25

SPSS Output from Field Survey, 2016.

Hypothesis Two

Ho: There is no significant relationship between innovation and company image.

In addition, from one-sample statistics Table 3, the number of variables is 71, the mean is equal to 1.99, the standard deviation is 1.049 while the standard error mean is .124. Therefore, the mean value of 1.99 which shows the average response indicates that the respondents agree that innovation is related to company image.

In the same vein, from Table 4, the t-test value is 15.956, the degree of freedom is 70, and the mean difference is 1.986. Since p-value of .000 is less than 0.05, then the t test value is significant. Hence there is a significant relationship between innovation and company image of selected manufacturing firms. Thus, the second null hypothesis is also rejected. The researcher therefore formulated and upheld alternative hypothesis which says that there is positive relationship between innovation and company image.

Table 3. One-sample statistics

	N	Mean	Std. Deviation	Std. Error Mean
Organizational innovation has impact on company image.	71	1.99	1.049	.124

SPSS Output from Field Survey, 2016.

Table 4. One-sample test

.	Test Value = 0					
	t	df	Sig. (2-tailed)	Mean Difference	95% Confidence Interval of the Difference	
					Lower	Upper
Organisational innovation has impact on company image.	15.956	70	.000	1.986	1.74	2.23

SPSS Output from Field Survey, 2016.

SUMMARY OF FINDINGS

The findings revealed that change is inevitable in any organization. Business enterprise that has the objectives of existing till time indefinite and wants to maximize profits for its investors, shareholders and creditors must continuously engage in diverse forms of innovation and be able to quickly adapt to changes that occur within its industry as well as its operating environment. Ability to innovate and manage the existing products and services will improve product quality, boost corporate image, and enhance healthy competition among its rivals as well as improving enterprise success and performance.

In the first hypothesis tested, the research finding revealed that the existing relationship between innovation and product quality is positive. The mean value of 2.01 shows that the average response of the respondents. In the same vein, the t-test value is 17.336, the degree of freedom is 71, and the mean difference is 2.014. Since p-value of .000 is less than 0.05, then the t test value is significant. This means that innovation is positively related to product quality. The reason is that the average customer will appreciate innovative and quality product.

In the second hypothesis, the mean value of 1.99 shows the average response which indicates that the respondents agree that innovation is related to company image. Similarly, the t-test value is 15.956, the degree of freedom is 70, and the mean difference is 1.986. Since p-value of .000 is less than 0.05, then the t test value is significant. Hence there is a significant relationship between innovation and company image of selected manufacturing firms. Thus, the null hypothesis two was rejected. This means that entrepreneur that involve in innovation will enjoy positive public corporate image for his business.

CONCLUSION

This research work examined the impact of innovation on the entreprencurial success in selected business enterprises in South Western Nigeria. The study has proven that innovation has a significant and positive relationship with product quality and corporate image. The different variables under the study have shown valuable relationship which is a pointer for enhanced performance in selected business enterprises. Innovation was found to improve product quality and corporate image and these have subsequently enhanced entrepreneurial success and performance Therefore, based on the above, it can be concluded that engage in innovative activities will achieve bumper success in his entrepreneurial ventures.

RECOMMENDATIONS

In view of the fact that innovation has become an important business strategy for improving product quality and for boosting corporate image in the eyes of the public, the following recommendations are offered to business enterprises' operating in South Western Nigeria to improve their entrepreneurial success and performance.

1.   Since there is a relationship between innovation and business performance, it is recommended that entrepreneurs should be more innovative in their orientations. They should try to generate and test many different business ideas and bring a different perspective to business and trading opportunities.

2. Given the importance of entrepreneurship to the economy of a country, it is essential that entrepreneurs adopt innovation in their daily operations to enhance their productivity as well as corporate image because innovation has a significant positive impact on the success of enterprises.
3. Organization should strictly adherence to innovation management policy to achieve their vision. Since it has been revealed that a company's success is a measure of its innovativeness.
4. They should maintain a continuous and effective research and development, and allow all its staff to act as agents of change by giving them free hands to operate. This will increase the level of innovativeness and will enhance business success in the society.

REFERENCES

Audretsch, O. B. (2002). *Entrepreneurship: A survey of literature.* London: CEPR.

Bosma, N., & Van Praag, M., & de Wit, G. (2000). Determinants of successful entrepreneurship. Scientific analysis of Entrepreneurship and SMEs (SCALES) Research Report 0002/E The Concept of an Integrated Idea Management. *Int. J. Technology, Policy, and Management, 7*(3).

Brazeal, D. V., & Herbert, T. T. (1999). The genesis of entrepreneurship. *Entrepreneurship Theory and Practice, 23,* 29–25.

Brem, A., & Voigt, K. (2007). Innovation management in emerging technology ventures –The concept of an integrated idea management. *Int. J. Technology, Policy, and Management, 7*(3).

Bygrave, W. D., & Hofer, C. W. (1991). Theorizing about entrepreneurship. *Entrepreneurship Theory and Practice, 16,* 13–22.

Chandler, G., Keller, C., & Lyon, D. (2000). Unravelling the determinants and consequences of an innovation-supportive organizational culture. *Entrepreneurship Theory and Practice, 25,* 59–76.

Chong, H. G. (2008). Measuring performance of small and medium sized enterprises: The grounded theory approach. *Journal of Business and Public Affairs, 2,* 1.

Daft, R. L. (1995). *Organization theory and design.* New York: West Publishing.

Eisenhardt, K. M., & Martin, J. A. (2000). Dynamic capabilities: What are they? *Strategic Management Journal, 21*(10-11), 1105–1121. doi:10.1002/1097-0266(200010/11)21:10/11<1105::AID-SMJ133>3.0.CO;2-E

Hage, J. T. (1999). Organizational innovation and organizational change. *Annual Review of Sociology, 25*(1), 597–622. doi:10.1146/annurev.soc.25.1.597

Hanif, A., & Marnavi, I. A. (2009). Influence of quality, innovation and new product/services design on small and medium enterprises.*Proceedings of the World Congress on Engineering.*

Hauschildt, J. (2004). *Innovation management.* Munchen: Vahlen.

Henrik, B. (2007). Risk conception and risk management in corporate innovation: Lessons from two Swedish cases. *International Journal of Innovation Management*, *11*(4), 497–513. doi:10.1142/S1363919607001849

Heunks, F. J. (1998). Innovation, creativity and success. *Small Business Economics*, *10*(3), 263–272. doi:10.1023/A:1007968217565

Hornby, A. S. (2015). *The Oxford advanced learner's dictionary of current English*. Oxford, UK: Oxford University Press.

Hung, H., & Mondejar, R. (2005). Corporate directors and entrepreneurial innovation: An empirical study. *Journal of Entrepreneurship*, *14*(2), 117–129. doi:10.1177/097135570501400203

Johannisson, B. (1993). Designing supportive contexts for emerging enterprises. In C. Karlsson, B. Johannisson, & D. Storey (Eds.), *Small business dynamics: International, national and regional perspectives*. London: Routledge.

Kuo, T., & Wu, A. (2008). *The determinants of organizational innovation and performance: An examination of Taiwanese electronics industry*. Unpublished Paper. National Chengchi University, Taiwan.

Litz, R. A., & Kleysen, R. F. (2001). Your old men shall dream dreams, your young men shall see visions: Toward a theory of family firm innovation with help from the Brubeck family. *Family Business Review*, *14*(4), 335–352. doi:10.1111/j.1741-6248.2001.00335.x

Ojo, O. (2003). *Fundamentals of research methods*. Lagos: Standard Publications.

Oman, M. (2008). *Measuring innovation in developing countries*. Regional Workshop on Science and Technology Statistics by Institute of Statistics. Retrieved from: www.uis.unesco.org

Pfeffer, J., & Salancik, G. R. (1978). *The external control of organization: A resource dependence perspective*. New York: Harper and Row.

Riederer, J. P., Baier, M., & Graefe, G. (2005). Innovation management – An overview and some best practices. *C-LAB Report*, *4*, 3.

Schumpeter, J. A. (1934). *The theory of economic development*. Cambridge, MA: Harvard University Press.

Stam, E., Gibcus, P., Telussa, J., & Garnsey, E. (2008). *Employment growth of new firms*. JENA Economic Research Papers, 08-005.

Trott, P. (2005). Innovation management and new product development (3rd ed.). Essex, UK: Pearson Education Limited.

Walker, E., Loughton, K., & Brown, A. (1999). The relevance of non-financial measures of success for micro business owners.*International Council for Small Business*, *NaplesConference Proceedings*.

Yuchtman, E., & Seashore, S. (1967). A system approach to organizational effectiveness. *American Sociological Review*, *32*(6), 891–903. doi:10.2307/2092843

Zaltman, G., Duncan, R., & Holbek, J. (1973). *Innovations and organizations*. New York: Wiley.

Chapter 3
Taming of "Openness" in Software Innovation Systems

Mehmet Gençer
İstanbul Bilgi University, Turkey

Beyza Oba
İstanbul Bilgi University, Turkey

ABSTRACT

In large-scale Open Source Software (OSS) innovation ecosystems that incorporate firms, a variety of measures are taken to tame the potentially chaotic activities and align the contributions of various participants with the strategic priorities of major stakeholders. Such taming rests on the dual desires of this emergent community of firms to unleash the innovation potential of OSS and to drive it to a certain direction, and it emerges in the form of various organizational activities. By drawing on a sample of large-scale OSS ecosystems, we discuss that methods employed for taming are isomorphic, and overview the emerging strategic pattern for establishing systems of innovation. This pattern involves a related set of practices to balance virtues of OSS community while introducing corporate discipline. In contrast to approaches such as open innovation, which favor isolated reasoning, we present a systemic and historical perspective to explain the continuum in emergence and establishment of strategic patterns.

INTRODUCTION

Collaborative innovation is becoming increasingly commonplace in many industries, ranging from biotechnology to computer hardware/software. Many organizations are struggling with volatility in consumer demands, stiff competition, and try to respond in a creative and agile manner to these market pressures. The consequences, as it appears, frequently involve seeking innovation beyond traditional locus of internal R&D departments. Accordingly, various organizations pursue bilateral or multilateral arrangements to actively cultivate inter-organizational networks of collaborative innovation.

For firms in volatile markets, acknowledging the need to reach out to networks is a first move that open up new challenges. Most of these firms have established practices and strategies based on closed forms of innovation. Some others have experience with 'open innovation', which involves exchanges with

DOI: 10.4018/978-1-5225-1779-5.ch003

other organizations (firms and research institutions), often using established forms of legally binding bilateral arrangements such as licensing. However, network types of organizing defy existing bilateral forms to enable their participants to get organized with one another easily. Firms intending to benefit from networked, collaborative, and open innovation face various challenges regarding how to reason about, interact with, and profit from the networks they are embedded within. Organization of these open innovation practices is a chaotic forefront of innovation, which demands organizational forms of its own, developed through ongoing trials and errors of its current adopters.

Among several other industries, software industry has been one in which attitudes towards collaborative innovation strategies are changing rapidly. It seems that 'adaptation' is replacing 'planning' as the fundamental principle of innovation in software technology development. Within this changing mindset, Open Source Software (OSS), once a marginal movement, is finding its way into mainstream inter-organizational innovation practice in the industry. OSS provides proven methodologies, which stimulate rapid software product evolution at the expense of process predictability (as opposed to the established practices of software engineering), and promote product interoperability which facilitate a more efficient coordination medium (Behlendorf, 1999; Benkler, 2005; Ritala, 2001). Leading players in the computing industry, such as IBM, Apple, and Google, actively cultivate open source innovation networks and/or use software technologies coming out of these networks as components in their key products or operations (West 2003).

However, despite the rhetoric of `openness' surrounding these practices, considerable effort is vested in to tame the `mess'. Within the multitude of often conflicting business agendas in a collaborative innovation system, each participant faces the dilemma of converting collaborative outcomes into competitive advantage. Accessing knowledge resources through networks overcomes rigidities of innovating in isolation (Jorde & Teece 1989; Ring & van de Ven 1994; Leonard-Barton 1992; von Hippel 2006). Yet, an organization expects some predictability, and would like to drive this distributed and emergent, rather than centralized and planned innovation process in a direction that makes sense for its own priorities. While `openness' in OSS is associated with unleashing the bottom-up innovation, blending and aligning it with a business strategy unavoidably faces the dilemma of re-leashing this innovative power so that it is manageable in a `top-down' way and becomes useful `business-wise'.

In this exploratory study we examine how practices in OSS, which is a non-commercial community organized as "collaborative innovation model" (von Hippel and von Krogh 2003), blends into a hybrid innovation model of the emergent community of commercial firms who adopt these practices. The major theoretical concern of the paper is to explore how the collaboration of two distinct worlds (OSS/bazaar and firms/hierarchies) incrementally changes the established activities and lead to the transformation of a community. In this vein, we investigate six cases (Apache, Linux, Eclipse, Mozilla, GCC, Android) of 'community-led' and 'corporate-led' collaborative innovation projects based on OSS, and attempt to identify common patterns in structures and processes which address the above mentioned dilemma while empowering collaborative, open innovation. In explaining the transformation of the OSS practices, we utilize an activity-based model developed by Jarzabowski (2005). This approach incorporates actors, activities of actors, and the collective structures developed by the shared activities of involved actors. We define the two communities as activity systems comprising distributed actors, shared activities of these actors (recruiting, strategic decision making, licensing, leadership, and quality assurance) and collective structures (governance) developed during the pursuit of these shared activities.

These activities are sites where interactions among actors are promoted and arise from their interactions with the collective structures. Through time these iterated interactions around shared practical activities legitimizes them and provides domains of signification, domination, and legitimization. Furthermore, in this study, practices like governance and appropriation regimes are taken as instruments of mediation between divergent goals and interests of distributed actors. Through the mediation of these practices various constituents reach an agreement about the actions to be taken, and whether these actions are legitimate and acceptable.

Such an approach has been instrumental in understanding the transformation process and especially its duality because it address both the strategic concerns of firms participating in open source software innovation systems, and why certain strategic practices are available for mutual, multilateral acceptance, while others are not. The analysis of data reveals that recent corporate-led open source innovation systems legitimize themselves by drawing from practices developed in community-led systems. Once a set of practices is worked out - by incremental improvements - for the new strategic challenges, they are mimicked within the emerging community. For example, governance mechanisms developed in one innovation ecosystem are reproduced in others without the need for exogenous policies and policy-makers imposing them. In this sense, OSS innovation model today appears to be an avant-garde category of inter-organizational collaborative innovation system which, by the virtue of owing its advantages to aggregation of resources (human and financial) is a valuable case of collaborative, open innovation but does not fit in the related literature which portrays such systems as entities which are shaped by exogenous forces, regulations and policies.

The paper is organized as such; in the following section we present our theoretical framework, which is based on activity-based approach. Then we discuss extant research on the transformation of OSS. The next section covers our research design and data, followed by our findings. Building on six well-known, large-scale OSS-based collaborative innovation projects, we identify common activities and practices that prevail for taming 'openness'. Finally, we discuss how the new practices emerged and transformed the OSS community, with its theoretical and practical implications, followed by conclusions.

THEORETICAL FRAMEWORK

OSS community brings together geographically dispersed actors (i.e. firms and developers) with diverse interests around a common issue: innovation in software. As a situated activity, innovation practice both shapes and is shaped by various activities of the OSS community and its situated actors cannot be decoupled from the context in which they act. In this vein, the study of how innovation practice is constructed within the community must take into consideration the social situation that provides embedded norms of conduct and the micro interpretations of the same social situation by the agents (Jarzabowski, 2005).

This interplay between context (macro) and actors (micro) in the construction of innovation practice reflects the activity, which is the basis of such a reconstruction process and endorses a deeper understanding of the community transformation processes. In such collective action domains like OSS, transformation is a complex social process, which requires collective action of numerous actors. In the process of such a change, besides the purposive actions of multiple actors, structures and processes embedded within the collaboration network play a role in initiating new and disrupting existing practices (Wijen & Ansari, 2007). Thus, we will be utilizing activity-based approach in order to explore how certain innovation related activities like recruitment of developers, development of new projects, and decision making can trigger and lead the transformation of the existing innovation. Accordingly, we study innovation as a situated activity, which is always constructed and reconstructed by the "practical-evaluative agency" (Emirbayer & Mische, 1998).

This process of transformation can follow various courses: change, recursiveness and stabilization (Jarzabowski, 2005). This paper focuses on the change course of innovation practice and its construction among multiple, distributed actors (mainly developers and firms). Distributed actors while pursuing their own divergent interests reason, question, discuss and challenge the existing innovation practice; as active agents they exploit social contradictions, tensions, conflicts between the system they are part of and the society. This very process of contestation makes the practice itself prone to fragmentation. Thus, various "structural" and "interpretive" actions must be generated to align the interests of distributed actors so that a collective action can be generated.

Such an approach to change deems the study of prevailing community (its structure and philosophy), goal-directed behavior of agents, and the interaction between these two levels. In this framework agents are taken as practical-evaluative, future oriented, and iterative. In the specific case under study, their actions are mediated through governance regimes and licensing arrangements, which enable interaction between them and the community they are part of. These mediating activities also enable coordination of distributed actions and contributions so that collective action is achieved. In this vein OSS is conceptualized as an activity system comprised of actors, their community, and the goal directed innovation practice in which they are involved.

Practices provide continuity in activities by enabling interaction between the actors and collective structures (Jarzabowski, 2005). However, as the constituents of a community (the two communities of community-led and corporate-led projects in our case) interact with another tensions arise due to emergent interpretations of the new activities that are introduced. The same practices, which promote continuity within a software project ecosystem during the interaction with other ecosystems serve as mediators between contradictory views to leverage new patters of activity, change the context and the meaning attributed to the activities.

The focus of this paper is this transformation process in OSS after collaboration among the two communities in software industry. More specifically we study the change in OSS activities and practices after collaboration in various projects with other activity systems that are characterized as firm-centered hierarchies.

Studying Change and Transformation in OSS

Existing research on OSS mostly views the phenomenon from its community roots (see, for example, the summary in von Krogh et al, 2012). Some of the recent studies on OSS focus on the transformation of the various constituents of the ecosystem. By studying processes like development life cycle, product support, licensing and business strategies adopted Fitzgerald (2006) claims that OSS "has metamorphosed into a more mainstream and commercially viable form" (p. 587). O'Mahony and Ferraro (2007) in a multi-method research studied the emergence of a governance system and the introduction of bureaucratic mechanisms in one OSS project ecosystem. Results of their study indicate how through time bureaucratic values were incorporated to the governance of the project community. Further, they claim that by combining elements of both bureaucratic and democratic mechanisms the community was able to develop a governance mechanism where both regimes coexisted. Similarly, West and O'Mahony (2008) in their comparative study of sponsored and autonomous open source projects found out that governance mechanism utilized by each were different; autonomous projects had a pluralistic governance mechanism and in the sponsored projects major decisions were controlled by the sponsor.

One explanation of this transformation process is the inevitable interaction between open source communities and software companies and the experimentation of new business models. Strategic alliances between corporations and open source communities like Eclipse have been domains for the development of hybrid governance mechanisms (Gençer & Oba, 2011). Corporate involvement in OSS projects has promoted change in the perceptions, development processes, and business models employed by the OSS community (Lundell, Lings, & Lindqvist, 2010). The relationships between firms and OSS communities naturally influence the way of doing business (Dahlender & Magnusson, 2005, 2008; Frey et al., 2011). Another explanation for the transformation is related to work related activities of the developers; employees of corporations during work are allowed to participate in OSS projects with OSS developers (Hauge, Sorensen, & Conradi, 2008). This daily mundane activity of work related exchange creates a milieu where different worlds experience each other and carry their experiences to their own realms. Bergquist et al. (2011) claim that free and open source software (FOSS) has transformed from an ideological movement to a commercially viable form of software development and this process of transformation has been characterized by various justifications of utilizing open source at different time periods. Rajala, Westerlund and Möller (2012), discuss market oriented OSS business model transformation of MySQL open innovation activity; firms operating in the field of OSS require adaptation to community values and respond to the needs of customers so that community resources are mobilized to enhance innovation capabilities.

This paper, analyzes the transformation of OSS community practices that resulted from the interaction with other software ecosystems within the industry that have a divergent rationale for recruitment, quality assurance, strategic decision making, intellectual property, and governance regimes. In terms of exploration, OSS communities are not controlled hierarchically by the companies with which they establish various forms of cooperation, and there are no binding contracts between the companies and community members. Similarly, exploitation of economic value from the jointly created products by various legal mechanisms is against the basic assumptions of the OSS community. Thus, as we argue, the transformation is not induced by business models or legal adjustments but rather is an inherent outcome of the interaction of two different ecosystems.

RESEARCH METHODS

In order to qualitatively explore the transformation of open source software communities and their practices we have selected a sample of six software projects that are still in operation. Selection of cases was guided by theoretical sampling process on the basis of difference in business models, size, production capacity, and founding date. In so doing, we have included "transparently observable" (Pettigrew, 1990) cases from two major categories of business models: community-led and corporate-led OSS projects. Some of these projects started as small non-commercial projects led by a small group of developers, but later meet corporate interest while some others are initiated by one or a group of firms, and later enjoyed support of individuals from OSS community. These six cases, Apache, Linux, Eclipse, Mozilla, GNU Compiler Collection (GCC), and Android were regarded as appropriate to study the transformation process.

Data for the cases were collected from documents archives. We have analyzed documents published by projects on their websites including statements, announcements, software release logs, developer guidelines, and committer policies. For each case we collected longitudinal data about each issue included in our model. To complement and provide an outsider view, besides publicly available company statements, we have collected news in journals, blogs, and scholarly articles. Collecting data from different sources and opposing opinions counteracted possible bias that can result from relying on a single and coherent source.

The qualitative data set we developed is utilized for a thematic analysis, which started with broad categories and then reduced to key issues under investigation. In order to explore how governance regime has transformed we focused on decision-making process. Our central question was designed to analyze how and by whom decisions are made in software project communities and how this decision making process differed in time. The first part of our main question, how decisions are made reflected the collective structures (units, foundation, lieutenants and committers) and the styles (top-down or grass-roots) developed over time in relation to governance. Major decisions in OSS projects are related to:

1. Setting design goals of software products by selecting among proposed features,
2. Creating sub-projects as needed (i.e. re-bundling the existing features), and
3. Promoting some contributors to 'committer' status who has the right to change or accept changes to the master copy of a software source code.

These decision categories are related to human resources (staffing), quality assurance, and structuring of activities. Thus, as goal-directed practical activities we have studied staffing, recruitment, structuring, and quality assurance because these activities are related to:

1. Coordination of responsibilities/outcomes,
2. Making common sense and appealing to the participants for collective decision making, and
3. Influencing the goals or outcomes of participants (firms and developers) that promote the reconstruction of existing arrangements.

The data analysis of this cross-case study is comprised of three phases. Firstly, we analyzed each case to identify the related activities and came up with a chronological list of such elements, which involved type of decision, actors involved and the type of structure. With this within-case analysis we were able to develop an in-depth understanding of the transformation process that is revealed in each case and expand the extant arguments. Later this list was redesigned to include only those that are common in all the cases comprising the sample. In the second phase, we examined each element across all the cases, to identify how and why it has emerged, who were involved and what were the subsequent outcomes. During this phase we also checked how activities and actors interact with each other and how these patterns differ between cases. And finally, at the third phase we analyzed how these activities and actors contributed to the transformation of OSS, especially in the governance regime.

FINDINGS

In this section, we present the results of our cross-case analysis of the data. The documentation of decision paths revealed six generic outcomes that are commonly observed in all cases: licensing, governance structure, acceptance of new (sub) projects, human resources (promotion), organizational leadership, and quality assurance. The comparison of community-led and corporate-led projects in these activities is given in Table 1.

Table 1. Identification of activities

Project	Overview
Apache (community-led)	• Web server software which has a *liberal license* allowing use in commercial products. • A community project since its start in 1999 but enjoyed a lot of corporate support early on from firms like IBM who use the technology in some of their products. • Governed by the Apache Group which later became a foundation. • New activities are put through an *incubation* process for taming "providing guidance and support to help each new product engender their own collaborative community, educating new developers in the philosophy and guidelines for collaborative development as defined by the members of the Foundation"
Linux (community-led)	• An operating system whose development is led by a vast global community, with a public license (General Public License, GPL) limiting commercialization. But it is used as infrastructure element by many firms. • Some key developers were later hired by leading companies in the industry. It lacks any formal governance body, and led by its originating leader Linus Torvalds since 1991, and has a closed and small leadership team. • Accelerating corporate contributions have prompted creation of a foundation in 2007 dedicated to fostering the technology, and hosts several events where influential community members are brought together.
Eclipse (corporate-led)	• A software development platform initiated by IBM in 2001. • The alliance has later become a foundation which oversees the development ecosystem in a more transparent way. Foundation members are leading firms of the computing industry who pay dues and dedicate developers to the project. • Contributing individuals are promoted to the committer status by existing committers, provided that they demonstrate 'discipline and good judgment'. • New projects are put through an incubation process, similar to Apache case. • The liberal license of Eclipse software was later refined by the foundation and made compatible with GPL to facilitate reuse in appropriation, along with changes in code acceptance policies.
Mozilla (corporate-led)	• A project with web browser and e-mail software. • Initiated by the firm Netscape upon its failure to compete with Microsoft's Internet Explorer. • Its license has gone through several changes from one that explicitly favored Netscape, to a more standard liberal license compatible with the broader open source ecosystem (de Laat, 2005). • Mozilla considers itself as a "hybrid organization, combining non-profit and market strategies to ensure the Internet remains a shared public resource". • Uses an incubation process similar to Apache for taming new projects.
GCC (community-led)	• The GNU Compiler Collection is a piece of software which is used for compiling much other software for a variety of platforms. • Is licensed with GPL. • Its development, started in 1987, was confined within the GNU team led by Richard Stallman, a prominent figure of the open source movement. • As it became a fundamental technology for many firms targeting the UNIX platform, a steering committee was formed in 1999 with representatives from leading firms and universities, but the project leadership emphasizes that the committee members represent communities, not their employers.
Android (corporate-led)	• An open software platform for mobile devices had an impact in the market in only three years following its announcement in November 2007. • The software is licensed using the liberal OSS license used in the Apache project. • Although promotion policies are transparent, these are less meritocratic compared to more mature projects like Eclipse; for example it is only the project leaders (who happen to be Google employees) who promote others, etc. • It is unclear how new projects are approved.

Similar Practices Across the Cases

One common element among the community and corporate-led projects is the human resource activity based on meritocratic promotion of developers. Meritocratic promotion is seen as an important basis of OSS model and seems to be fully adopted in corporate-led OSS projects as well. Besides somewhat exceptional case of Android, both community-led and corporate-led projects adopt voting-based schemes for developer promotion. Contributors who demonstrate skills and adapt to community norms are voted into ranks by existing committers. Norms are (re)articulated by existing meritocracy implementation and thus become an important element of taming within corporate-led collaborative projects.

Quality assurance methods such as software testing and peer review are very important to reduce the adverse effects of defects in software engineering. In terms of quality assurance, OSS is commonly praised as hosting processes in which software quickly evolves into high quality products despite the lack of central control which empowers it. The general quality assurance strategy in OSS has been to transfer testing and bug reporting activities to software user base. Many OSS projects make frequent releases of 'testing' versions of software, which in turn put into use by a large group of enthusiasts and those who are in need of new features not yet offered in 'stable' releases of software. Existing evidence (Zhao & Elbaum, 2003) indicate that frequent releases is often the case for OSS projects for promoting high quality products. In large OSS projects such as Gnome, Mozilla, and Debian, quality assurance has become a part of the community awareness. These projects explicitly stated

1. Their quality goals such as to improve the product where it is needed, and to keep the quality of the distribution as high as it should be,
2. Who the quality participants are, and
3. What are typical quality assurance actions and to which part of software they should be applied.

The development guidelines of the projects studied indicate that the OSS style of quality assurance is applied in all types of projects. However there are differences related to their usage and organization. All the cases followed OSS pattern of releasing frequently. Community projects such as Linux and GCC, and to some degree corporate-led projects like Eclipse and Mozilla, follow the pattern of releases marked as 'testing' or 'release candidate'. These releases are targeted to the user community who are willing to take the risk of using buggy software (in many cases for the sake of accessing new functionality) and provide feedback/bug-reports which in turn assist the developers to carry the software quality to a more mature level. Additionally, both types of projects have clear -even formal- test plans and procedures. In the case of Apache, which is a collection of numerous sub-projects, the quality assurance activities reveal some variation which depends on the nature of the developer community (e.g. size of the development team, type of project sponsorship, project complexity, and release policies). At the other extreme, in Android, the development of the core system is pretty much closed within Google and the quality assurance activities appear to be similar to the ones in closed innovation systems, i.e. they are shaped by the fact that the product goes live on millions of mobile devices of non-tester users. Although they make frequent releases much like OSS style, they work hard (behind closed doors) to ensure that software developed is stable. On the other hand the Android ecosystem consists of thousands of other, higher level pieces of software (Android applications), which are developed by strategic partners and are not subject to such centrally administered quality assurance policies and procedures.

One noteworthy fact in quality assurance activities is that as the some projects become more commercially oriented, they incorporate additional steps to quality assurance process to ensure that contributions meet the license framework and legal requirements related to the commercialization of the software developed. This is the case with Apache and Eclipse. These projects ensure the code contributions go through several steps related to software quality assurance (automated tests, dependency checks, etc.) and also license sanitation. Overall the case of quality assurance in both corporate-led and community-led projects seem to retain proven OSS methods (much like the case for promoting developers) and extend it with context specific requirements.

Differences Between the Cases

Strategic decisions related to the creation of new sub-projects is handled in a more 'transparent' and 'planned' way in corporate-led projects where the process is given names as 'incubation period/process'. In Apache and Eclipse examples, this period involves tempering of the new project and its leadership so that the software development process meets certain quality standards. In community-led projects, on the other hand, all is decided by meritocratic leadership. There may even be cases where leadership makes decisions despite strong opposition (Gençer et al., 2006) which is hard to imagine in case of corporate-led projects.

The difference in property regimes and corresponding licensing schemes reflect the difference of concerns with wider adoption (in community-led type) and suitability for use in commercial products (in corporate-led type). The experience seems to have shown that replacement of intellectual property hostile regime of free software movement with more liberal licenses is generally welcomed. Despite minor variations liberal licenses (with archetypes such as Apache and Mozilla licenses) seem to be the established norm for new corporate-led OSS projects, whereas more restrictive and viral licenses such as GPL is the norm for community-led projects.

In comparing the two types of projects, it is interesting to note that community-led projects are less transparent in terms of governance regime employed. This situation may look somewhat counter-intuitive at first, but there are strategic advantages of transparent governance in an inter-organizational setting. Such transparency serves well for directing community attention and goal setting. Fitzgerald (2006), notes how such transparency has been utilitarian for avoiding the strategic planning vacuum, in which software development followed any 'itch worth scratching'. Corporate-led projects aim to be inclusive and flexible in their planning process, but nevertheless such planning vacuum is avoided by careful outlining of targeted software features and development road-maps, and making them widely available. Hence, using transparency as an instrument has been valuable for directing community attention and setting goals effectively.

Similar to governance mechanisms, organizational leadership is more transparent and works through formal bureaucracy in corporate-led projects community, as in the example of Eclipse where each major participant dedicate certain amount of resources (human and financial) to the project and have seats in decision-making bodies. On the other hand, corporate influence in community-led projects, when it exists, is evidenced by having seats in governance committees. Generally, as Watson et al. (2008) notes it's rather the amount of contribution rather than formal ownership that is the basis of control and influence in community-led projects.

DISCUSSION

A summary of similarities and differences of cross-case analysis is given in Table 2. The findings of our study provide a picture of what is being 'tamed' in business adoption of OSS, and in what direction the process heads. Most noticeable OSS element that is left intact in this taming process is the meritocratic promotion of developers. Watson et al. (2008) note how OSS enables companies to access high quality talent base while reducing risks associated with recruitment. Appreciation of a large group of software developers is a reliable criteria for screening new talent. Thus, retaining the meritocratic promotion does not only ensure software quality, but also provide access to relevant talent pool. In similar vein, adjustments to OSS licensing (see de Laat 2005 for a review) are designed in such a way that while it attracts high quality and increasing volume of contributions, at the same time it allows these contributions to be used in commercial products. Use of more liberal licenses in the corporate-led OSS community is a key instrument in capturing collaboratively created value out of new software.

On the other hand, formal governance practices and goal setting activities are specific to corporate-led realm of OSS and it appears to be still experimental. Some popular success stories like Eclipse are likely to set emerging norms in this respect. Furthermore, comparison of the Android case with Eclipse and Apache suggest that developing a supportive base for collaborative innovation deems increasing transparency in governance structures and practices. Such transparency not only improves trust among partners, but also makes the process more predictable. Additionally, it allows participants to cast a direction in terms of goals and outcomes of the collective process, thus contributing to the taming of OSS. In a business environment where there are established bilateral forms such as joint ventures, such multilateral forms of governance are rather new.

Theoretical Implications

This phenomenon further highlights the need for ontological commitment to network in inter-organizational collaboration research, since the networks start to become concrete entities with some sort of controlling bodies and norms of their own. Despite the awareness about advantages of innovation networking, the business environment is at an infancy phase in terms of institutionalization of collaborative innovation

Table 2. A comparison of corporate-led and community-led OSS projects

	Community Led Projects	**Corporate Led Projects**
Licensing schemes	GPL, targets largest adoption	Liberal, balances adoption and appropriation
Governances regimes	Not formal, meritocratic	Foundation/bureaucratic, transparent
Strategic decision making process	Not transparent, left to leadership	Well defined incubation processes
Developer promotion	Meritocratic promotion of developers	Meritocratic promotion of developers
Organizational leadership	Imposed by hiring lead developers, or through committees	Imposed through formal bureaucracy
Quality assurance	Community powered	Community powered, with additional measures for legal issues

networks (Whittington et al., 2011). Collaborative innovation is prone to a variety of problems; the initiation of inter-firm relations relies on a variety of antecedent factors (Oba & Semerciöz, 2005), and development of relations and mutual trust that sustain them is hard to predict or control (Ring & van de Ven, 1994). Developing collaborative relations entail sharing critical knowledge (Gächter et al., 2010) and taking risks as committing to relation specific investments.

Our study focused on the emergence and role of practices and structures that are associated with taming of collaborative innovation networks based on OSS model. We have used six cases of community-led and corporate-led projects, and attempted to identify common elements in both types of projects as well as differences, after collaborating with each other. We contend that community-led and corporate-led OSS communities differ: (1) practices and formal arrangements for taming are more explicit and transparent in corporate-led community, (2) meritocratic basis of developer promotion is retained in both, and, (3) the means of asserting influence by corporations is different in both, but considered legitimate as far as the meritocratic basis is retained.

Studies on collaborative innovation mainly focus on the ability of a firm to attract ideas and resources from external actors and appropriate benefits of innovation. As indicated by Langlois (1990) firms are pursuing ways to improve innovation performance beyond the hierarchical structures and thus, mix of new organizational forms are emerging. Studies such as van der Linden et al. (2009) present economic frameworks within which the OSS innovation model is being employed by companies. During the last decade, research reports such as van der Linden et al. (2009) and Fitzgerald (2006) appealed to mainstream practice, unlike the preceding decade where OSS-related literature was rather marginal. Such literature offers a retrospective account of the open source experience in economic terms such as value chain and differentiation. While we lack any extensive evidence at the global level, there are regional studies whose results support that adoption of OSS model is on the rise (Hauge et al., 2008; Nikula & Jantunen, 2005).

Accordingly, OSS is an appropriate case to study how due to certain endogenous and exogenous pressures, innovation regimes can incorporate some elements of other innovation regimes. In the background of these developments is the increasing speed of innovation, driven by variety and volume of demand, high connectivity of devices, and high degree of transferability of information. This makes it hard for even the biggest players to control or supply complex products on their own. When a complex system such as the software industry is on the verge of a fundamental transformation, various marginal practices can become common as they fit well into the new environment. Furthermore, these market pressures trigger creation of software ecosystems where different types of innovation and governance regimes had to cooperate in order to cope with the emergent changes. Innovation regimes build on in-house software production and revenue generation by patented products gradually has adopted elements of the OSS community. Traditionally, the major concern of firms operating in this innovation regime was whether to buy or make the software, and recently this problem has been transformed to collaborate or not; and if the decision is to collaborate then how the relations with the partners should be governed so that efficiency and appropriation would be achieved. The consequences of such a transformation unavoidably lead to transformation of the OSS innovation regime as well. Some authors have already pointed to fundamental shifts in OSS processes, and noted that these indicate alteration of ground rules in both the OSS movement and the software industry (Fitzgerald, 2006). Fitzgerald also explains how 'OSS 2.0' balances "a commercial profit value-for-money proposition while still adhering to acceptable open source community values" (2006 p: 588).

Our findings extend this argument and present the organizational elements that are associated with the shifts in the open source process towards more corporate involvement. There appears to be an emergent, stable pattern of proven mechanisms, strategies, and processes. Thus, the transformation indicated by Fitzgerald's OSS2.0 is institutionalized into common workable governance mechanisms that emerged from the daily activities, and enabled participant market actors to set-up collaborative software ecosystems. Furthermore, emergence of such innovation and governance practices seems to be isomorphic; since they make common sense in most situations and they are practical, actors do not seek other ways of doing things, and avoid introducing disturbance of their respective systems.

Managerial Implications

We call for due attention to the state of the change and transformation in the software industry. We suggest that emergence of the transformation mentioned by Fitzgerald (2006) has already been institutionalized and legitimated, hence will soon lead to faster adoption of OSS strategies by a wider community. The new hybrid innovation regime incorporates activities and mediating practices of previously existing innovation regimes. Such a new design has developed from existing patterns and practices, in incremental steps such that each modification is recognizable and makes sense to stakeholders. Yet, the emergent attractor is radically different from its dual origins (of OSS and proprietary models). Its elements are different from those common in corporate hierarchies; rather than targeting a top-down control or planning in the strict sense, they are instruments of taming. It is through these elements that an corporate-led OSS continues to be an emergent system which retain advantages of bottom-up innovation, while at the same time its major stake-holders can "invite it to emerge" (Jelinek, 2004) in certain ways rather than others, hence avoiding the planning vacuum.

Greater acknowledgment of the need for collaborative innovation is one side of the transformation in the software industry, and OSS seems to be the organizational model of choice in many sub-contexts of the industry. Its emergence triggered by the success of popular community products such as Linux and Apache, but its true admittance to business strategies went through a series of experiments, which in turn transformed OSS practices as well. As far as this emergent combination of solutions work, they can be the first choice of future collaborative software innovation ecosystems in software industry. Nokia's Symbian project might as well continue to be as innovative as Android, but the players of the industry seem to be connected much more easily to OSS model at the moment. Phrasing the current situation rather dramatically, OSS makes a lot of sense, and makes all others look like nonsense.

Software industry innovation practices indicate that free software and open source software are settling in which focus shifts to co-endowment rather than stressing their differences. The community now enjoys more interest in terms of resources provided by corporate ventures, while the corporate circles keep finding ways to turn community experience to viable business practices. Benefits of firms are not much different (e.g. sharing costs of innovation by the help of aggregation), but more than that they have a fundamental interest in capturing value that is created during their collaboration with OSS ecosystems; ensuring legal conditions (software licensing) for capturing value they have helped to create, or assuring quality of software partially built by others, but they will be liable for once it is sold. Therefore a fundamental shift in the requirements and expectations of the practitioners calls for a change in OSS innovation model as well.

CONCLUSION

This study focused on the innovation related practices of two different OSS communities: corporate-led and community-led. We have used a sample of six cases to identify similarities and differences in practices. In so doing we were able to identify various structural properties and practices that emerged in both communities while they collaborated in innovation. Thus, we argued that while these two different worlds collaborated they adopted and transformed some of the practices and structures from each other and retained some others. Our findings indicate how innovation based cooperation changed the dominant logic prevailing both communities and lead to convergence.

REFERENCES

Behlendorf, B. (1999). Open Source as a Business Strategy. In C. DiBona, S. Ockman, & M. Stone (Eds.), *Open Sources: Voices from the Open Source Revolution* (pp. 149–170). O'Reilly.

Benkler, Y. (2005). Coase's penguin, or, linux and the nature of the firm. In R. A. Ghosh (Ed.), *CODE: Collaborative Ownership and the Digital Economy* (pp. 169–206). Cambridge, MA: The MIT Press.

Bergquist, M., & Ljungberg, J. Bertil Rolandsson. "A Historical Account of the Value of Free and Open Source Software: From Software Commune to Commercial Commons. In S. Hissam, B. Russo, M. de Mendonça Neto, & F. Kon (Eds.), *Open Source Systems: Grounding Research* (pp. 196–207). Boston: Springer.

Dahlander, L., & Magnusson, M. (2008). How do firms make use of open source communities? *Long Range Planning*, *41*(6), 629–649. doi:10.1016/j.lrp.2008.09.003

Dahlander, L., & Magnusson, M. G. (2005). Relationships between open source software companies and communities: Observations from Nordic firms. *Research Policy*, *34*(4), 481–493. doi:10.1016/j.respol.2005.02.003

de Laat, P. B. (2005). Copyright or copyleft?: An analysis of property regimes for software development. *Research Policy*, *34*(10), 1511–1532. doi:10.1016/j.respol.2005.07.003

Emirbayer, M., & Mische, A. (1998). What is agency? *American Journal of Sociology*, *103*(4), 962–1023. doi:10.1086/231294

Fitzgerald, B. (2006). The transformation of open source software. *Management Information Systems Quarterly*, *30*(3), 587–598.

Frey, K., Lüthje, C., & Haag, S. (2011). Whom should firms attract to open innovation platforms? The role of knowledge diversity and motivation. *Long Range Planning*, *44*(5), 397–420. doi:10.1016/j.lrp.2011.09.006

Gächter, S., von Krogh, G., & Haefliger, S. (2010). Initiating private-collective innovation: The fragility of knowledge sharing. *Research Policy*, *39*(7), 893–906. doi:10.1016/j.respol.2010.04.010

Gençer, M., & Oba, B. (2011). Organising the digital commons: A case study on engagement strategies in open source. *Technology Analysis and Strategic Management, 23*(9), 969–982. doi:10.1080/095373 25.2011.616698

Gençer, M., Oba, B., Özel, B., & Tunalıoğlu, V. S. (2006). Forking: The GPL coherent technology for flexible organizing in foss development. European Group of Organizational Studies 2006 Colloqium, Bergen, Norway.

Hauge, O., Sorensen, C. F., & Conradi, R. (2008). Adoption of open source in the software industry. In B. Russo, E. Damiani, S. Hissam, B. Lundell, & G. Succi (Eds.), Open Source Development, Communities and Quality. Springer.

Jarzabkowski, P. (2005). Strategy as practice: An activity-based approach. *Sage.*

Jelinek, M. (2004). Managing Design, Designing Management. In R. Boland & F. Callopy (Eds.), *Managing as Designing.* Stanford.

Jorde, T. M., & Teece, D. J. (1989). Competition and cooperation: Striking the right balance. *California Management Review, 31*(3), 25–37. doi:10.2307/41166568

Langlois, R. N. (1990). Creating external capabilities: Innovation and vertical disintegration in the microcomputer industry. *Business and Economic History, 19,* 93–102.

Leonard-Barton, D. (1992). Core capabilities and core rigidities: A paradox in managing new product development. *Strategic Management Journal, 13*(S1), 111–125. doi:10.1002/smj.4250131009

Lundell, B., Lings, B., & Lindqvist, E. (2010). Open source in Swedish companies: Where are we? *Information Systems Journal, 20*(6), 519–535. doi:10.1111/j.1365-2575.2010.00348.x

Nikula, U. (2005, July). Quantifying the Interest in Open Source Systems: Case South-East Finland Sami Jantunen. *Source,* 192-195.

O'Mahony, S., & Ferraro, F. (2007). The emergence of governance in an open source community. *Academy of Management Journal, 50*(5), 1079–1106. doi:10.5465/AMJ.2007.27169153

Oba, B., & Semercioz, F. (2005). Antecedents of trust in industrial districts: An empirical analysis of inter-firm relations in a turkish industrial district. *Entrepreneurship and Regional Development, 17*(3), 163–182. doi:10.1080/08985620500102964

Pettigrew, A. (1990). Longitudinal field research on change: Theory and practice. *Organization Science, 1*(3), 267–292. doi:10.1287/orsc.1.3.267

Rajala, R., Westerlund, M., & Möller, K. (2012). Strategic flexibility in open innovation–designing business models for open source software. *European Journal of Marketing, 46*(10), 1368–1388. doi:10.1108/03090561211248071

Ring, P. S., & van de Ven, A. H. (1994). Developmental processes of cooperative interorganizational relationships. *Academy of Management Review, 19*(1), 90–118.

Ritala, P. (2001). Coopetition Strategy - When is it Successful? Empirical Evidence on Innovation and market performance. *British Journal of Management.*

van der Linden, F., Lundell, B., & Marttiin, P. (2009). Commodification of industrial software: A case for open source. *Software, IEEE.*, *26*(4), 77–83. doi:10.1109/MS.2009.88

von Hippel, E. (2006). *Democratizing Innovation*. MIT Press.

von Hippel, E., & von Krogh, G. (2003). Open source software and the "private-collective" innovation model: Issues for organization science. *Organization Science*, *14*(2), 209–223. doi:10.1287/orsc.14.2.209.14992

von Krogh, G., Rossi-Lamastra, C., & Haefliger, S. (2012). Phenomenon-based research in management and organisation science: When is it rigorous and does it matter? *Long Range Planning*, *45*(4), 277–298. doi:10.1016/j.lrp.2012.05.001

Watson, R. T., Boudreau, M. C., York, P. T., Greiner, M. E., & Wynn, D. Jr. (2008). The business of open source. *Communications of the ACM*, *51*(4), 41–46. doi:10.1145/1330311.1330321

West, J. (2003). How open is open enough?melding proprietary and open source platform strategies. *Research Policy*, *32*(7), 1259–1285. doi:10.1016/S0048-7333(03)00052-0

West, J., & O'Mahony, S. (2008). The role of participation architecture in growing sponsored open source communities. *Industry and Innovation*, *15*(2), 145–168. doi:10.1080/13662710801970142

Whittington, R., Cailluet, L., & Yakis-Douglas, B. (2011). Opening Strategy: Evolution of a Precarious Profession. *British Journal of Management*, *22*(3), 531–544. doi:10.1111/j.1467-8551.2011.00762.x

Wijen, F., & Ansari, S. (2007). Overcoming inaction through collective institutional entrepreneurship: Insights from regime theory. *Organization Studies*, *28*(7), 1079–1100. doi:10.1177/0170840607078115

Zhao, L., & Elbaum, S. (2003). Quality assurance under the open source development model. *Journal of Systems and Software*, *66*(1), 65–75. doi:10.1016/S0164-1212(02)00064-X

Chapter 4
Innovation Implementation:
The Critical Facets

Neeta Baporikar
Namibia University of Science and Technology, Namibia

ABSTRACT

Due to rapid evolution of technology, innovations are vital to most organizations (Choi & Chan, 2009, p. 245). Nevertheless, the results of innovations are in many cases not satisfying. Several studies have shown that an organization's failure to benefit from an adopted innovation can often be attributed to a deficient implementation process rather than to the innovation itself. Thus, the implementation process is a critical interface between the decision to adopt and the routine usage of an innovation. Ways and methods to implement innovation effectively have been under scholarship for some time now. Despite the number of studies which identify multiple causes of unsuccessful implementation processes, literature is lacking regarding the strategic facets of innovation implementation. Building on the derived knowledge of the underlying dynamics of innovation processes, through grounded theory and in-depth literature review, the present study aims to contribute to existing implementation literature by examining the strategic facets of innovation implementation.

INTRODUCTION

Due to rapid evolution of technology, innovations are vital to most organizations (Choi and Chan, 2009, p. 245). In addition, a growing number of customers are expecting organizations to act ecologically and socially responsible. Those circumstances force enterprises to adopt and implement innovations even beyond their core businesses. Nevertheless, the results of innovations such as improvements in efficiency due to total quality management, statistical process control, and manufacturing resource planning are in many cases not satisfying (Klein, Conn, and Sorra, 2001, p. 811). Several studies have shown that an organization's failure to benefit from an adopted innovation can often be attributed to a deficient implementation process rather than to the innovation itself (Klein & Sorra, 1996, p. 1055; Aiman-Smith & Green 2002, p. 421; Gary, 2005, p. 644; Karimi, Somers, & Bhattacherjee, 2007, p. 123). The implementation process, as the critical interface between the decision to adopt and the routine usage of an innovation

DOI: 10.4018/978-1-5225-1779-5.ch004

(Klein & Sorra, 1996, p. 1057), has received increasing attention by scholars. The degree of implementation success is considered a better indicator for innovation quality than the degree of adoption success due to the fact that not all adopted innovations get ultimately implemented (Karimi et al., 2007, p. 103). Despite the growing number of studies which identify multiple causes of unsuccessful implementation processes, literature is lacking multidimensional models that explain the difference between successful and unsuccessful implementation efforts. Such models should take into account multiple and to some extent interrelated drivers of implementation success (Dean Jr. & Bowen, 1994, p. 393; Klein & Sorra, 1996, p. 1056; Klein et al., 2001, p. 811; Repenning, 2002, p. 110). In addition, Choi and Chan (2009, p. 245) point out that existing implementation studies tend to focus either on employee-related aspects, mostly on an individual level, or on organizational aspects such as management support, structure, and resources of the implementing organization. By combining these two approaches, Choi and Chan (2009, p. 251) show that management support significantly improves the implementation effectiveness as well as the innovation effectiveness by strengthening the collective innovation confidence and the collective innovation acceptance of employees.

The present study aims to contribute to existing implementation literature by examining the strategic facets of innovation implementation. In contrast to Choi and Chan (2009), this study does not focus on the strength of causal relationships between factors of influence and implementation success. Instead, the strategic facets within the organizations, which affect implementation success over time, are of particular interest.

LITERATURE REVIEW

In defining innovation, there is a need to distinguish the subtle difference between an "invention" and "innovation." According to Merriam-Webster On-Line Dictionary, invention is "a device, contrivance, or process originated after study and experiment".[1] However, the same source defines innovation as "the *introduction* (emphasis is ours) of something new, a new idea, method, or device." Schumpeter (1996, p. 81-86) describes innovation as a process of creative destruction which is continuously revolutionizing macro level markets and structures. The widespread sub-categorization of the innovation process into the consecutive phases of invention, innovation, as well as diffusion and imitation can also be attributed to Schumpeter (1939, p. 84-102; Milling and Maier, 1996, p. 17). The invention phase is characterized by the discovery of a previously unknown solution to a problem. In form of an innovation, the invention is economically used for the first time during the innovation phase. In the subsequent diffusion and imitation phase, the innovation spreads through the market, thereby increasingly realizing the potential technological progress (Milling & Maier, 1996, p. 17-18).

On a micro level, innovations diffuse between actors of a social system or an organization through an existing or emerging set of relationships (Allen, 1977, p. 234-265; Roger, 2003, p. 5). Rogers (2003, p. 5-6) defines *diffusion* in the standard work *Diffusion of Innovations* as a process by which information is exchanged over certain communication channels between members of a social system. He differentiates between the five stages *knowledge, persuasion, decision, implementation*, and *confirmation*. The *knowledge stage* is initiated by the first encounter with the innovation and ends after a general understanding of the innovation has been acquired. In the following *persuasion stage*, an affirmative or negative attitude towards the innovation emerges. Next, *decision stage*, the innovation is at least partially tested before it is decided whether the innovation will be adopted or disregarded. In case of a positive adoption decision, the innovation will be used for the first time during the *implementation stage.* Within the final *confirmation stage,* the adoption decision is continuously challenged and where appropriate revoked based on newly acquired information about the innovation (Roger, 2003, p. 168-169).

Within an organizational context, the innovation process is subdivided into two main processes: the *initiation process* and the *implementation process* (Zaltman, Duncan, & Holbeck, 1973, S. 58; Roger, 2003, p. 420), which is similar to the stages mentioned. Figure 1, gives the generic innovation process.

The *initiation process* comprises the collection of information, the creation of concepts, the planning of the adoption process, and the final decision to adopt or disregard the innovation (Roger, 2003, p. 420-430). It consists of the two sub-processes *agenda-setting* and *matching*.

In contrast to the initiation process, the implementation process comprises all events, activities, and decisions which ideally lead to a routine usage of the innovation. It consists of the sub-processes *Reorganizing/Restructuring, Exposing/Clarifying, and Routinizing.* Within the first sub-process of the *implementation process,* the innovation is adjusted to organizational needs as well as to the organizational structure. During the second sub-process, the innovation is increasingly understood and used by the members of the respective organization. Finally, the innovation loses its autonomous character and becomes fully integrated into the organization in the course of the last sub-process (Roger, 2003, p. 435).

Within the initiation process, Rogers (2003, p. 403) also differentiates between three kinds of innovation decision approaches at organizational level as:

- **Optional:** An individual independent from the members of the respective social system decides over the adoption or disregard of the innovation.
- **Authority:** A minority of the social system, which is characterized by high social esteem, expert knowledge or power, decides in favour or against the innovation. This decision must then be accepted by all other members of the organization.
- **Collective:** A decision is based on the consensus of the members of the social system.

Even though both, the initiation as well as the implementation process, have a substantial influence on the success of an innovation and its use, this chapter focuses on the internal implementation process

Figure 1. Generic innovation process

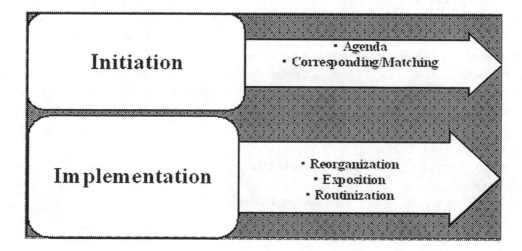

of an organization as highlighted in Figure 1. It is assumed that this process is initiated by an authority innovation-decision, which is by the call made by senior management. Ettlie (2006) described three stages of innovation in developing a successful industry. The first is: product design and innovation, second is when resulting innovation begins to become dominant and firms with ability to manufacture [with] quality [will] more efficiently dominate [the market] and the last is, when those firms can compete based on the economies of scale and capital intensity dominate industry. On the other hand, Luecke and Katz (2003) identified three different types of innovation: incremental, radical, and disruptive. "Incremental innovation is generally understood to exploit existing forms or technologies", Luecke and Katz (2003). This type of innovation is appropriate for improving the organization's current processes and products to capture more of the market share. On the other hand, radical innovation is "something new to the world, and a departure from existing technology or methods" Luecke and Katz (2003). The terms *breakthrough innovation* and *discontinuous innovation* are often used as synonyms for radical innovation. Lastly, disruptive technology is used "to describe a technical innovation that has the potential to upset the organization's or the industry's existing business model" Luecke and Katz (2003).

Thus, innovation is the process and outcome of creating something new, which is also of value (Baporikar, 2017a). Schumpeter argued that innovation comes about through new combinations made by an entrepreneur, resulting in:

- A new product.
- A new process.
- Opening of new market.
- New way of organizing the business.
- New sources of supply.

Accordingly, innovation involves the whole process from opportunity identification, ideation or invention to development, prototyping, production marketing and sales, while entrepreneurship only needs to involve commercialization. Today it is said to involve the capacity to quickly adapt by adopting new innovations (products, processes, strategies, organization, etc.) Also, traditionally the focus has been on new products or processes, but recently new business models have come into focus, i.e. the way a firm delivers value and secures profits. Innovation is the first appearance or use of a particular practice. It is the commercially successful exploitation of ideas. This definition associates innovation with a tangible outcome. Successful innovation is about creating value (Baporikar, 2015). It does so either by improving existing goods, processes or services (incremental innovation), or by developing goods, processes or services of value that have not existed previously (radical innovation).

However, both kinds of innovation require doing the following: have an understanding of and insights into consumer needs and developing imaginative and novel solutions. In addition, innovation is generally associated with the following:

- The willingness to take risk.
- Accepting high levels of ambiguity and uncertainty.
- Original thinking.
- A passion to drive the idea through to conclusions.
- The ability to inspire passion in others.

Research on the implementation of organizational innovations is both labours intensive and rare (Baporikar, 2017b). The ideal study of team or organizational innovation implementation, we believe, is one that examines the implementation of a single innovation, or a common set of innovations, across a sample of adopting organizations or teams over time. For example, Edmondson, Bohmer, and Pisano (2001) combined qualitative and quantitative data collection in a longitudinal study of 16 surgical teams' efforts to implement a new technique—minimally invasive cardiac surgery—in the operating room. Klein, Conn, and Sorra (2001) conducted a multilevel, longitudinal study of the implementation of a single type of computerized manufacturing technology (manufacturing resource planning or MRP II) across 39 manufacturing plants. And Holahan, Aronson, Jurkat, and Schoorman (2004) examined the implementation of computer technology inscience education in 69 schools. The findings of these studies and of in-depth qualitative case studies of organizational innovation implementation (e.g., Nutt, 1986; Nord & Tucker, 1987; Repenning & Sterman, 2002), illuminate stumbling blocks and best practices in innovation implementation.

Obstacles to Innovation Implementation

The implementation of team and organizational innovations is difficult for numerous reasons. Six inter-related reasons figure prominently in the implementation literature. First, many innovations—particularly technological innovations—are unreliable and imperfectly designed. The newer the technologies, the more likely it is to have bugs, break down, and are awkward to use. This "hassle factor" can render even the most enthusiastic technophile frustrated and annoyed (Baporikar, 2015c). In their review of the literature on computerized-technology implementation, Klein and Ralls (1995) reported that 61% of the qualitative studies they reviewed documented the negative consequences of low technology quality and availability on employee satisfaction and innovation use. Second, many innovations require would-be users to acquire new technical knowledge and skills. For many people, this may be tedious or stressful (Baporikar, 2017a). In an individual-level study of project engineers' implementation of information-technology innovations, Aiman-Smith and Green (2002) found that innovation complexity—the extent to which the new technology was more complicated than the technology it replaced—was significantly negatively related to user satisfaction and the speed required to become competent in using the innovation.

Third, the decision to adopt and implement an innovation is typically made by those higher in the hierarchy than the innovation's targeted users. Targeted users, however, often have great comfort in the status quo and great scepticism regarding the merits of the innovation. Nevertheless, they may be instructed by upper management to use the innovation against their wishes. Indeed, based on interviews in 91 organizations, Nutt (1986) concluded that managers' most common strategies in guiding innovation implementation are "persuasion" and "edict"—both of which involve little or no user input in decisions regarding adoption and implementation.

Fourth, many team and organizational innovations require individuals to change their roles, routines, and norms. Innovation implementation may require individuals who have previously worked quite independently to coordinate their activities and share information (Klein & Sorra, 1996). It may also disrupt the status hierarchy, requiring individuals who have previously worked as boss and subordinates to now work as peers (Baporikar, 2016a). In a qualitative study of the implementation of an empowerment education intervention for diabetes patients, Adolfsson, Smide, Gregeby, Fernstro''m, and Wikblad (2004) found that doctors and nurses struggled with the role changes that the intervention required. Although the doctors and nurses believed that the empowerment approach was beneficial for their patients, they found it difficult to step out of their expert roles to interact with their patients as facilitators.

Fifth, implementation is time consuming, expensive, and, at least initially, a drag on performance. Effective innovation implementation often requires hefty investments of time and money in technology start-up, training, user support, monitoring, meetings, and evaluation. Thus, even the most beneficial innovation is likely to result in poorer team and/or organizational performance in the short run, as Repenning and Sterman (2002) documented in their study of the implementation of two process improvement innovations—one designed to reduce expensive stores of work-in-progress inventory and one designed to speed new product development—in a division of a major U.S. automaker. Good things—implementation benefits—may come to those who wait, but targeted users and their managers may feel greater pressure to maintain pre-existing levels of performance than to invest in the uncertain and long-term potential of innovation implementation.

Last but not the least, the sixth one is that, organizations are a stabilizing force. Organizational norms and routines foster maintenance of the status quo (Baporikar, 2014a). Even when organizational members recognize that a specific change would be beneficial, they often fall prey to the "knowing– doing gap" (Pfeffer & Sutton, 2000). That is, they often fail, for a variety of reasons, to actually do the things that they know would enhance performance or morale (Baporikar, 2014b). Organizational members may adhere rigidly to the past, fear reprisal for suggesting bold changes, or substitute talk for action, for example (Pfeffer & Sutton, 2000). The result, unfortunately, is a failure to adopt, and certainly to implement, potentially beneficial innovations.

Given these challenges to implementation success, it is perhaps no wonder that observers estimate that nearly 50% or more of attempts to implement major technological and administrative changes end in failure (e.g., Aiman-Smith & Green, 2002; Baer & Frese, 2003; Repenning & Sterman, 2002). Indeed, a 2002 report by financial giant Morgan Stanley estimated that, of the $2.7 trillion that companies pour into technology each year, more than $500 billion is wasted—in large part due to implementation failure. Moreover, there are different innovations like: several types of innovation process, product/service, strategy, which can vary in degree of newness: incremental to radical, and impact: continuous to discontinuous, which further may have their own and unique implementations hassles. If innovation is today's hot commodity, how can business leaders harvest it? They must create conditions in which innovation can thrive in their companies (Baporikar, 2015a).

Drivers for Innovation

- Financial pressures to reduce costs, increase efficiency, do more with less, etc.
- Increased competition.
- Shorter product life cycles.
- Value migration.
- Stricter regulation.
- Industry and community needs for sustainable development.
- Increased demand for accountability.
- Demographic, social and market changes.
- Rising customer expectations regarding service and quality.
- Changing economy.
- Greater availability of potentially useful technologies coupled with a need to exceed the competition in these technologies.

Barriers to Innovation in Organization

- The organization tends to pursue line extensions rather than developing totally new business models.
- The organization has prioritized short-term financial results over investing for the long term.
- Opportunities to exploit underdeveloped areas/markets often die because they can never find a home to nurture them.
- The organization is looking for the next silver bullet rather than pursuing a portfolio of opportunities.
- The organization fails to learn from past mistakes and has become more risk averse when it comes to new ideas (Baporikar, 2015b).

Greatest Innovation-Related Challenges Facing Organization

- Changing the organizational culture.
- Reducing time to market for an innovation.
- Transforming ideas into marketable goods/services.
- Creating the proper execution strategy.
- Getting teams to work together better.
- Identifying changes in customer behaviour or emergent and unmet needs.
- Containing development costs.
- Creating the proper incentives to maximize creativity among employees and external partners.
- Difficulty in predicting future trends.
- Leadership's openness to and enthusiasm for innovation as a major lever for growth.
- Leveraging new technology.
- Eliciting and using customer feedback.
- Identifying and collaborating with suppliers, subcontractors, or other external partners.

Source of Organization's Most Successful Innovation

- New product/service—developed in-house.
- Improvement of an existing product/service that was developed in-house.
- New product/service—developed in collaboration with a partner.
- New product/service—acquired from the outside.
- Improvement of existing product/service that was acquired from the outside.

STRATEGIC FACETS OF INNOVATION IMPLEMENTATION

Innovation is more than an idea -- it takes place when great ideas actually happen and make their mark on the world (Baporikar, 2015a). So implementation is crucial. Our review of the literature on innovation implementation suggests that there are six strategic facets that can be considered as critical factors which shape the process and outcomes of innovation implementation. They are:

- **Implementation Policy and Practice:** One key factor is the package of implementation policies and practices that an organization establishes (Klein & Ralls, 1995). Implementation policies and practices include, for example, the quality and quantity of training available to teach employees to use the innovation; the provision of technical assistance to innovation users on an as-needed basis; the availability of rewards (e.g., praise, promotions) for innovation use; and the quality, accessibility, and user-friendliness of the technology itself. The influence of such policies and practices is cumulative and compensatory. No single implementation policy or practice seems to be absolutely critical for an organization's innovation implementation effectiveness. But, the overall quality of an organization's implementation policies and practices is predictive. Klein et al. (2001) found that manufacturing plants that established numerous high-quality implementation policies and practices were more successful in implementing manufacturing-resource planning, a major technological innovation, than were manufacturing plants whose implementation policies and practices were meagre and of lesser quality.

- **Climate for Innovation Implementation:** Organization's or team climate for innovation implementation—that is, employees' shared perceptions of the importance of innovation implementation within the team or organization is important. When a unit's climate for innovation implementation is strong and positive, employees regard innovation use as a top priority, not as a distraction from or obstacle to the performance of their "real work." Both Klein et al. (2001) and Holahan et al. (2004) found that implementation climate was a significant predictor of innovation use.

- **Role of Managers:** Managers play a critical role in the implementation process, so their support of the innovation is the third critical factor. In the absence of strong, convincing, informed, and demonstrable management support for implementation, employees are likely to conclude that the innovation is a passing managerial fancy: Ignore it and it will go away (Baporikar, 2016b). As Repenning (2002) warned, "Managers may be understandably suspicious of the recommendation that, once they choose to adopt an innovation, they support it wholeheartedly irrespective of any reservations concerning lack of appropriateness. To do otherwise, however, insures that the implementation effort will fail" (pp. 124–125). Sharma and Yetton (2003) found that the more an innovation requires employees to work together—as the innovations on which we focus in this article do—the stronger the positive relationship between management support and implementation success.

- **Financial Resources:** Availability of financial resources is crucial as generally implementation is, of course, not cheap. It takes money to offer extensive training, to provide ongoing user support, to launch a communications campaign explaining the merits of the innovation, and to relax performance standards while employees learn to use the innovation. Like Nord and Tucker (1987), Klein et al. (2001) found that financial-resource availability was a significant predictor of the overall quality of an organization's implementation policies and practices and thus, indirectly, a predictor of the organization's implementation effectiveness.

- **Learnability:** Existence of learning orientation, that is a set of interrelated practices and beliefs that support and enable employee and organizational skill development, learning, and growth is a prerequisite for implementation of innovation to be fruitful. In organizations and teams that have a strong learning orientation, employees eagerly engage in experimentation and risk taking; they are not constrained by a fear of failure (Baporikar, 2016c). A learning orientation is critical during innovation implementation because implementation is rarely an easy, smooth process or an instant success. Bugs, errors, and missteps are likely. A strong learning orientation allows organizational members to overcome such obstacles, experimenting, adapting, and persevering in innovation use (Baporikar, 2016d). The research of Edmondson et al. (2001) suggests that leaders create a shared team learning orientation by (a) articulating a compelling and inspiring reason for innovation use; (b) expressing their own fallibility and need for team members' assistance and input; and (c) communicating to team members that they are essential, valued, and knowledgeable partners in the change process. As a result, team members— targeted innovation users—come to see innovation implementation as an exciting learning opportunity, not as a burden to be endured. Further, team members must feel sufficient psychological safety (Edmondson, 1999; Baer & Frese, 2003) to express their ideas and opinions, as well as to admit their errors. A psychologically safe social environment is one in which group members collectively feel secure taking interpersonal risks (Edmondson, 1999). Indeed, Baer and Frese (2003) found that psychological safety moderates the effects of process innovation on organizational performance: The greater an organization's climate for psychological safety, the stronger the positive relationship between the organization's adoption and implementation of process innovations and its financial performance.

- **Perseverance and Patience:** Managerial patience—that is, a long-term time orientation (Baporikar, 2014d). Managers who are committed to achieving the long-term benefits of innovation implementation understand that the implementation process may diminish unit productivity and efficiency in the short term (Baporikar, 2014d; 2014e). The more managers push employees to maintain or improve immediate task performance, the less time and energy employees can devote to the implementation of innovations that offer long-term, and potentially more enduring, performance gains (Repenning & Sterman, 2002).

Strategic Implications

- The role of the CEO with respect to innovation needs to evolve from vision setting to enabling and driving innovation execution.
- To drive execution of innovation, organizations need to appoint a c-level executive to take on that role and drive the required change while addressing the organizational and execution challenge. For innovation to become part of the organizational fabric, it has to be managed as every other business discipline, such as marketing, finance, operations or HR.
- Organizations need to focus on finding ways to accelerate innovation frequency and speed. This is a major weakness, which has been identified by the survey, and which can serve as a major source of competitive advantage, particularly in industries faced with intense global competition.
- Ideas may increasingly come from new markets. Companies can benefit by being open to lessons drawn from the experiences of companies in Asia and putting them into practice in other parts of the organization (Baporikar, 2014c).

The innovation organization must be legitimized and professionalized — the accountability must connect with line management to ensure transparency of the CEO's vision for innovation along with the commitment for execution. A robust innovation process must be established to support the organization to facilitate the frequency, speed and consistency of innovation results. The innovation organization will need to keep an open mind as new ideas will increasingly come from overseas operations in emerging markets as the multi-polar world continues to mature (Baporikar, 2016b). Ownership and accountability for innovation is diffused. The difficulty with innovation also appears to have roots in organizational design.

Companies with a chief innovation executive believe they are more competitive and have managed to achieve better innovation performance. Nurturing innovation and shepherding new ideas to market requires a concerted effort—the lack of organizational clarity may be keeping some companies from achieving the results they expect from innovation Baporikar, 2015b). In fact, companies that are successful with innovation are more likely to have a chief innovation executive. Having a senior executive in charge can help solve one common difficulty with innovation: that new ideas languish because they can't find an internal champion. Despite the importance of innovation, many companies are still too cautious. Part of the problem is the 'disconnect' between what companies hope to achieve from innovation and the steps they are taking. Although most companies say that their strategy is business transformation or major improvement, they are often taking incremental steps to implement these strategies (Baporikar, 2014f).

Organizations that indicate a higher importance of innovation to their success are more likely to designate a single executive-level point of accountability for innovation. Those organizations with a single point of accountability for innovation will have higher innovation performance and capabilities as compared with their peers. Innovation will remain a top priority on the corporate agenda across most industries and today, more and more organization's strategy is either totally or largely dependent on innovation (Baporikar, 2016b). Especially in retailing, IT/technology, media, publishing & entertainment, these industries being consumer based or service place significantly higher emphasis on innovation while logistics and aerospace & defence industries rank innovation lower in importance. Strategic imperatives that must be addressed in order for companies to shift from a vision of innovation to a high performance innovation organization: it is not sufficient for organizations to create a vision for an innovation culture —CEOs must create ownership and accountability for execution, but also to deliver results companies must treat innovation as any other business discipline by aligning resources, tools and processes with a clear set of performance goals and metrics.

Without an innovation structure established and legitimized, putting new ideas into practice is proving difficult. Stakeholders – especially employees, customers are concerned not only about their ability to generate new ideas, but also with their ability to transform innovation into action (Baporikar, 2016e). In the language of innovation researchers, an innovation is a product or practice that is new to its developers and/or to its potential users. Innovation adoption is the decision to use an innovation. Innovation implementation, in contrast, is "the transition period during which [individuals] ideally become increasingly skilful, consistent, and committed in their use of an innovation. Implementation is the critical gateway between the decision to adopt the innovation and the routine use of the innovation" (Klein & Sorra, 1996, p. 1057). The difference between adoption and implementation is fundamental: Individuals, teams, organizations, and communities often adopt innovations but fail to implement them successfully.

Consider an example that is as mundane as it is close to home. Do you own a new high end camera with advanced features? If so, that's innovation adoption. When you bought the camera, you adopted it. If you own that camera, did you in fact use its advanced features in the past week? That's innovation implementation. If you use the camera advanced features regularly, in a skilled, consistent, and committed manner, you've excelled at implementation.

As a general rule, adoption is much easier—although sometimes more expensive—than implementation. Many innovations, like high end camera, are implemented ineffectively. Thus, innovation failure—the failure of an innovation to achieve the gains expected by the adopting individual or individuals—often reflects not the ineffectiveness of the innovation per se but the ineffectiveness of the implementation process (Klein & Sorra, 1996). In short, the innovation fails because it is not used with the consistency, skill, and care required achieving its expected benefits.

CONCLUSION

This paper has analysed implementation processes assuming that an organization is well structured with proper hierarchy and top-down management approach and based on formal communication network. In contrast to most studies, the present study does not only focus on the diffusion of rational innovations, which show the typical bandwagon-like behavior, but also on ambiguous innovations. Following Choi and Chan (2009) structural aspects, predominant in diffusion literature, and employee-oriented aspects, mainly discussed in implementation literature, have been combined in order to understand better why so many implementation efforts fail. Hence, the structural aspects of a network have been combined with other crucial aspects like drivers of innovations. Assuming that senior management of an organization pushes the adoption of an innovation button; managers still need to use their limited resources more effectively by considering the dynamics of organizational theory as applicable to their organizations. Future research in this area can focus on the limitations of this study, which is the secondary data based approach. Therefore, the implementation of innovations in successful organizations could be undertaken on case based approach to bring out the best practices in innovation implementation.

Researchers have begun to identify the practices and characteristics that allow organizations to overcome the challenges of innovation implementation. Clearly, top management cannot close the book on an innovation after they have decided to adopt it. To ensure targeted users' sustained and skilful use of innovative technologies and practices, managers must devote great attention, conviction, and resources to the implementation process. While important strides have been made in understanding the process of innovation implementation, more research is needed and important questions remain. How does the implementation of technological innovations like new computer systems differ from the implementation of non-technological innovations such as new managerial, educational, training, or patient-treatment interventions? How does success or failure at implementing an innovation in one team or location spread through an organization or community? Do units that succeed in implementing one innovation succeed in implementing others as well? Though questions remain, the growing innovation-implementation literature draws needed attention to the challenge and the importance of effective innovation implementation. In the absence of effective implementation, the benefits of innovation adoption are likely to be nil. After all, how many wonderful memories' you can capture if you buy a top-of-the-line camera but never use it?

REFERENCES

Adolfsson, E. T., Smide, B., Gregeby, E., Fernstro¨m, L., & Wikblad, K. (2004). Implementing empowerment group education in diabetes. *Patient Education and Counseling*, *53*(3), 319–324. doi:10.1016/j.pec.2003.07.009 PMID:15186870

Aiman-Smith, L., & Green, S. G. (2002). Implementing New Manufacturing Technology: "The Related Effects of Technology Characteristics and User Learning Activities. *Academy of Management Journal*, *45*(2), 421–430. doi:10.2307/3069356

Allen, T. J. (1977). Managing the Flow of Technology: Technology Transfer and the Dissemination of Technological Information Within the R&D Organization. Cambridge, MA: Academic Press.

Baer, M., & Frese, M. (2003). Innovation is not enough: Climates for initiative and psychological safety, process innovations, and firm performance. *Journal of Organizational Behavior*, *24*(1), 45–68. doi:10.1002/job.179

Baporikar, N. (2015). Drivers of Innovation. In P. Ordoñez de Pablos, L. Turró, R. Tennyson, & J. Zhao (Eds.), *Knowledge Management for Competitive Advantage During Economic Crisis* (pp. 250–270). Hershey, PA: Business Science Reference; doi:10.4018/978-1-4666-6457-9.ch014

Baporikar, N. (2015a). *Innovation Knowledge Management Nexus. In Innovation Management* (pp. 85–110). Berlin: De Gruyter.

Baporikar, N. (2016a). Organizational Barriers and Facilitators in Embedding Knowledge Strategy. In *Business Intelligence: Concepts, Methodologies, Tools, and Applications* (pp. 1585–1610). Hershey, PA: Business Science Reference.

Baporikar, N. (2016b). Strategies for Enhancing the Competitiveness of MNEs. In M. Khan (Ed.), *Multinational Enterprise Management Strategies in Developing Countries* (pp. 50–71). Hershey, PA: Business Science Reference.

Baporikar, N. (2016c). Lifelong Learning in Knowledge Society. In P. Ordóñez de Pablos & R. Tennyson (Eds.), *Impact of Economic Crisis on Education and the Next-Generation Workforce* (pp. 263–284). Hershey, PA: Information Science Reference.

Baporikar, N. (2016d). Talent Management Integrated Approach for Organizational Development. In A. Casademunt (Ed.), *Strategic Labor Relations Management in Modern Organizations* (pp. 22–48). Hershey, PA: Business Science Reference.

Baporikar, N. (2016e). Stakeholder Approach for Quality Higher Education. In W. Nuninger & J. Châtelet (Eds.), *Handbook of Research on Quality Assurance and Value Management in Higher Education* (pp. 1–26). Hershey, PA: Information Science Reference.

Baporikar, N. (2017a). Knowledge Transfer Issues in Teaching: Learning Management. In N. Baporikar (Ed.), *Innovation and Shifting Perspectives in Management Education* (pp. 58–78). Hershey, PA: Business Science Reference.

Baporikar, N. (2017b). *Innovation and Shifting Perspectives in Management Education* (pp. 1–352). Hershey, PA: IGI Global.

Choi, J. N., & Chan, J. Y. (2009). Innovation Implementation in the Public Sector: An Integration of Institutional Collective Dynamics. *The Journal of Applied Psychology*, *94*(1), 245–253. doi:10.1037/a0012994 PMID:19186909

Dean, J. W. Jr, & Bowen, D. E. (1994). Management Theory and Total Quality: Improving Research and Practice Through Theory Development. *Academy of Management Review*, *19*(3), 392–418.

Edmondson, A. C. (1999). Psychological safety and learning behaviour in work teams. *Administrative Science Quarterly*, *44*(2), 350–383. doi:10.2307/2666999

Edmondson, A. C., Bohmer, R., & Pisano, G. P. (2001). Disrupted routines: Team learning and new technology adaptation. *Administrative Science Quarterly*, *46*, 685–716. doi:10.2307/3094828

Ettlie, J. E. (2006). *Managing Innovation, New Technology, New Products, and New Services in a Global Economy*. Burlington, MA: Elsevier Butterworth-Heinemann Publications.

Gary, M. S. (2005). Implementation Strategy and Performance Outcomes in Related Diversification. *Strategic Management Journal*, *26*(7), 643–664. doi:10.1002/smj.468

Holahan, P. J., Aronson, Z. H., Jurkat, M. P., & Schoorman, F. D. (2004). Implementing computer technology: A multiorganizational test of Klein and Sorra's model. *Journal of Engineering and Technology Management*, *21*(1-2), 31–50. doi:10.1016/j.jengtecman.2003.12.003

Karimi, J., Somers, T. M., & Bhattacherjee, A. (2007). The Impact of ERP Implementation on Business Process Outcomes: A Factor-Based Study. *Journal of Management Information Systems*, *24*(1), 101–134. doi:10.2753/MIS0742-1222240103

Klein, K. J., Conn, A. B., & Sorra, J. S. (2001). Implementing Computerized Technology: An Organizational Analysis. *The Journal of Applied Psychology*, *86*(5), 811–824. doi:10.1037/0021-9010.86.5.811 PMID:11596799

Klein, K. J., Conn, A. B., & Sorra, J. S. (2001). Implementing computerized technology: An organizational analysis. *The Journal of Applied Psychology*, *86*(5), 811–824. doi:10.1037/0021-9010.86.5.811 PMID:11596799

Klein, K. J., & Ralls, R. S. (1995). The organizational dynamics of computerized technology implementation: A review of the empirical literature. In L. R. Gomez-Mejia & M. W. Lawless (Eds.), *Implementation management of high technology* (pp. 31–79). Greenwich, CT: JAI Press.

Klein, K. J., & Sorra, J. S. (1996). The Challenge of Innovation Implementation. *Academy of Management Review*, *21*(4), 1055–1080.

Klein, K. J., & Sorra, J. S. (1996). The challenge of innovation implementation. *Academy of Management Review*, *21*, 1055–1080.

Luecke, R & Katz, R. (2003). *Managing Creativity and Innovation*. Boston, MA: Harvard Quarterly.

Milling, P. M., & Maier, F. H. (1996). Invention, Innovation and Diffusion: A Simulation Analysis of the management of new products. Berlin: Academic Press.

Nord, W. R., & Tucker, S. (1987). *Implementing routine and radical innovations*. San Francisco: New Lexington Press.

Nutt, P. C. (1986). Tactics of implementation. *Academy of Management Journal*, *29*(2), 230–261. doi:10.2307/256187

Pfeffer, J., & Sutton, R. I. (2000). *The knowing–doing gap: How smart companies turn knowledge into action*. Boston: Harvard Business School Press.

Repenning, N. P. (2002). A Simulation-Based Approach to Understanding the Dynamics of Innovation Implementation. *Organization Science*, *13*(2), 109–127. doi:10.1287/orsc.13.2.109.535

Repenning, N. P., & Sterman, J. D. (2002). Capability traps and self-confirming attribution errors in the dynamics of process improvement. *Administrative Science Quarterly*, *47*(2), 265–295. doi:10.2307/3094806

Roger, E. M. (2003). Diffusion of Innovations. New York: Academic Press.

Schumpeter, J. A. (1939). *Business Cycles: A Theoretical*. New York: Historical, and Statistical Analysis of the Capitalist Process.

Schumpeter, J. A. (1996). *Capitalism*. London: Socialism and Democracy.

Sharma, R., & Yetton, P. (2003). The contingent effects of management support and task interdependence on successful information systems implementation. *Management Information Systems Quarterly*, *27*, 533–555.

Zaltman, G., Duncan, R., & Holbeck, J. (1973). *Innovations and Organizations*. New York.

ENDNOTE

[1]   Merriam-Webster On-Line Dictionary. http://www.merriam-webster.com/dictionary.

Section 2

Chapter 5
Sustainable Development Challenges in Developing Countries:
Can Technology Provide Inclusive Solutions?

Vanita Yadav
Institute of Rural Management Anand, India

ABSTRACT

India is a country with a population of 1.2 billion and around 400 million poor people remain excluded from the formal economy. India does not offer a social security number for its residents. Rather, there exist variant forms of identification documents. In 2009, the Government of Indian initiated the Aadhaar project to create biometric technology-enabled unique identities for Indian residents. In a short timespan span, the project has made remarkable progress by enrolling more than 600 million people. The objective of this paper is twofold: (1) to review the emerging literature on inclusive innovation and (2) to examine the case of Aadhaar Project in India, which aims to address the issue of poverty and inclusive development. Findings of the study reveal that the Aadhaar project has the potential to create an ecosystem of inclusive innovation and entrepreneurship, which can be beneficial for developing economies like India.

INTRODUCTION

India does not have something like the American Social Security Number and multiple forms of identity documents exist in India. India is a country of 1.2 billion where only 33 million pay taxes and 60 million possess a passport (Parker, 2011). There are millions of Indians who do not possess any form of identity proof and remain excluded from the formal economy. There is a growing stream of researchers who view inclusive innovation as a solution to this inclusion problem.

In literature, inclusive innovation is being proposed as an important and socially relevant concept. However, it is still in its nascent stage of conceptualization (George, McGahan & Prabhu, 2014; Foster & Heeks, 2013) and this paper is an attempt to add to the growing body of knowledge in this area.

DOI: 10.4018/978-1-5225-1779-5.ch005

The objective of this paper is to first present a review of literature on inclusive innovation. The second objective is to study the case of Government of India's Aadhaar project using the lens of inclusive innovation. The paper presents a discussion of the Aadhaar project and its operations. The paper also explores the inclusive innovation ecosystem around the Aadhaar project and discusses is potential to address institutional voids in India.

BACKGROUND

'Inclusive' Innovation

Innovation literature has come a long way from Joseph Schumpeter's definition of innovation. Schumpeter defined innovation as producing new goods, production methods, sources of supply, and new organization of any industry (Fagerberg, Mowery & Nelson, 2006). Innovation is a widely used term having multiple definitions in literature. In general, it entails producing something new of commercial value. This definition is now being extended in the social realm and here it implies providing novel solutions to complex social problems.

Traditionally, innovation recognizes development as generalized economic growth. In contrast, inclusive innovation views development as active inclusion of people excluded from the mainstream development. The difference refers to the inclusion involving some aspect of innovation for/by the marginalized groups (Foster & Heeks, 2013).

The first objective of this study was to review the emerging literature on inclusive innovation and summarize key conceptualizations. A search using keywords "inclusive" and "innovation" in major e-Databases like Proquest and Ebsco resulted in only six relevant peer reviewed journal papers. Few of these papers attempted to put forward definitions of inclusive innovation. Further, I expanded the search on definitions to include published reports and conference papers. A list of definitions on inclusive innovation is presented in Table 1.

Table 1. Definitions of inclusive innovation in literature

George, McGahan & Prabhu (2012)	"Inclusive innovation as the development and implementation of new ideas which aspire to create opportunities that enhance social and economic wellbeing for disenfranchised members of society."
Foster & Heeks (2013)	"Inclusive innovation is the means by which new goods and services are developed for and/or by the billions living on lowest incomes."
Mashelkar (2012), Global Research Alliance	"Inclusive innovation is any innovation that leads to affordable access of quality goods and services creating livelihood opportunities for the excluded population, primarily at the base of the pyramid, and on a long term sustainable basis with a significant outreach."
Paunov (2013), OECD Report	"Inclusive innovation… harnessing science, technology and innovation know-how to address the needs of lower-income Groups."
Heeks, Amalia, Kintu, & Shah (2013)	"Inclusive innovation… is the means by which new goods and services are developed for and/ or by those who have been excluded from the development mainstream; particularly the billions living on lowest incomes. "

Paunov (2013) reports heterogeneous terminology used in practice and literature for inclusive innovation. For example, terms like "frugal innovation" "pro-poor innovation" and "innovation for the bottom of the pyramid" have been used to depict inclusive innovation. Such innovations are considered inclusive and can possibly provide solutions for reducing gaps between the rich and the poor.

Frugal innovations in simple terms are typically cheaper and simplified product versions, which are within the purchase limits of lower-income groups. These low cost products and services can in turn help improve welfare of the poor and are likely to provide business opportunities. Paunov (2013) suggests business process innovations as the other dimension of inclusive innovation, which can potentially provide access to goods and services for the lower-income groups/poor.

Inclusive Innovation for Sustainable Development

Developing nations face complex challenges and need innovative solutions to alleviate poverty. As a result, there was an emergence of literature on base of the pyramid (Prahalad, 2004). OECD and non-OECD economies have actively been engaged in policy discussions on generating inclusive growth (Paunov, 2013). Even in Latin America, top down policy interventions failed to deliver the proposed economic development.

Government in developing nations like India acknowledge that growth needs to be inclusive such that significant resources are provided towards strengthening government programs targeting poverty reduction, employment generation, and provision of essential amenities like water, electricity, roads, sanitation and housing especially for the poor (Planning Commission, 2011). Inclusive innovation is proposed as an extension of this inclusive growth (George et al., 2012).

Inclusive Development Challenges in India

India is a diverse country, which is home to some of the world's richest billionaires and at the same time is home to the world's poorest poor. According to the Millennium Development Goals report (2014) by the United Nations, one third of the world's poorest people live in India. The number of people who are poor in India has increased from 421 million in 1981 to 456 million in 2005 as per the $1.25 a day standard of poverty measurement (Narayan, 2009).

Researchers like Narayan (2009) suggest that the poor in India are not lazy. In fact, he states that like the rich, the poor take initiatives but still remain poor. The reasons for this situation are described constraints they face, for example inadequate access to capital, lack of business skills and inability to formally participate in markets.

A question of significance then is- who should be responsible to build and maintain institutions for proper market functioning? To build markets is not a straightforward task. Further, institutional assembly efficiency is likely to vary across different contexts (Mair et al, 2012). Based on prior literature (Fligstein & Mara- Drita, 1996; North, 1990; McDermott, 2002), a study by Yadav (2014) suggests that the state, implying the government, should ideally take responsibility for building such formal institutions. However, many developing economies like India have weak and corrupt government structures, which raises concerns on governments' role in creating institutions for market building.

CASE OF INCLUSIVE INNOVATION IN INDIA- THE AADHAAR PROJECT

Need for the Project

Establishing a proof of a person's identity using some form of documentation has been the practice in India. In this regard, the Government of India has undertaken various efforts in the past. Some examples being-the photo identity cards issued by the Election Commission in 1993 and the Multipurpose National Identity Card (MNIC) in 2003. In addition, cards like the driving license or passports are also used for identification purposes.

However, these efforts resulted in multiple forms of identity proofs. Further, many cases of duplicate and fake identity creation were uncovered by the media. For instance, a press release reported nearly 4,000 fake identity cases in the state of Maharashtra in India (TNN, 2012a). There were speculations in the press that there would be thousands of similar cases across others states in India.

Project Initiation and Implementation

To deal with the problems of multiple forms of identity proofs, the Government of India initiated the Aadhaar project. This began in January 2009 by setting up an attached office to the Planning Commission of India (http://planningcommission.nic.in). This attached office was called the Unique Identification Authority of India (UIDAI, http://uidai.gov.in). The major aim was to create a robust and cost-effective biometric-based identity solution for all the residents of India (Yadav, 2014). The Aadhaar project primarily involved issue of unique identification numbers to residents of India. This was built around two primary criterions- the identification number or the Aadhaar number should be "(a) robust enough to eliminate duplicate and fake identities, and (b) can be verified and authenticated in an easy, cost-effective way" (UIDAI, 2010, pp. 1).

It was projected that the Aadhaar project will replace all forms of identity verifications existing in India (Yadav, 2014). Total of 1004533560 residents in India had enrolled for the Aadhaar number by April 17, 2016. The growing trend of Aadhaar enrollments is illustrated in Figure 1. The gender and age related enrollment data are illustrated in Figure 2. The data shows that there are 36.75 percent enrollments in the female age group of 18 years and above and 10.35 percent enrollments in the female child age group of 5 to less than 18 years. For males, there were 38.85 percent enrollments in the age group of 18 years and above and 11.65 percent enrollments in the male child age group of 5 to less than 18 years.

Project Operations

Aadhaar project is one of the largest technology-oriented initiatives launched by the Government of India. The project technology was envisaged to offer three key functions- enrollment, de-duplication and online authentication (Khanna & Raina, 2012). Aadhaar is 12-digit unique number linked with biometric information like the iris scan and/or fingerprints scan. Numerous agencies such as the state government, central government, enrollment agencies like the technology firms, hospitals issuing birth certificates, and groups like the civil society and community networks, have been involved in the operations of the Aadhaar project. All these organizations have partnered with the UIDAI to enable implementation of the project in India.

Figure 1. Aadhaar enrollments trend

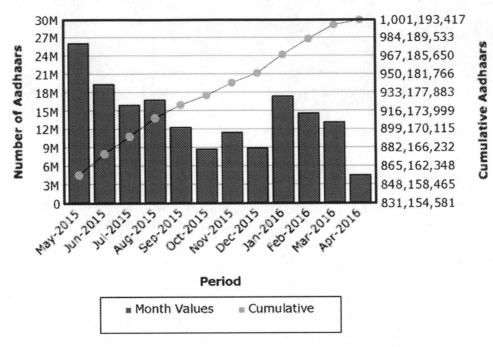

Figure 2. Aadhaar enrollments by age and gender

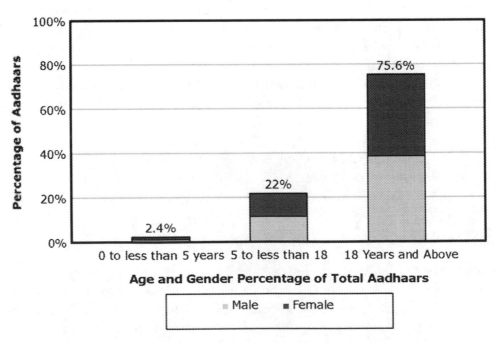

Figure 3. Partnerships with Different Agencies to Implement Aadhaar

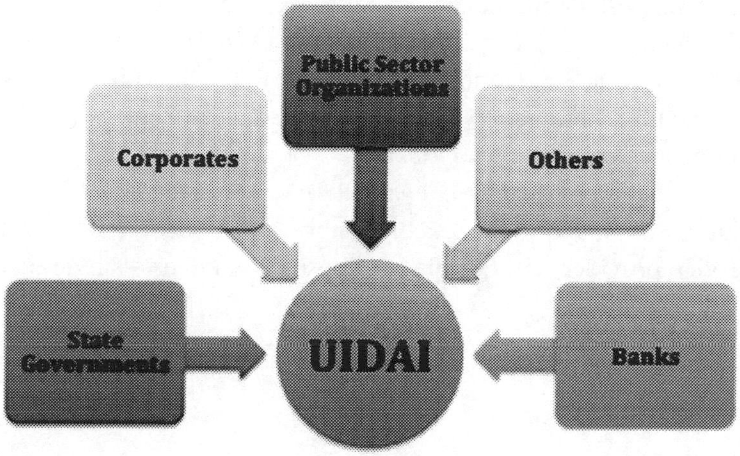

UIDAI partnered with numerous registrars for the enrollment process (see Figure 3). The enrollment equipment comprises of a laptop loaded with the enrollment software, a fingerprint reader, an iris scanner, a webcam, and a laser printer. All this equipment come packed together in a briefcase, which made it portable and easy to carry around. The enrollment was allowed in English as well as regional Indian languages. Registrars were mainly the organizations interfacing with a large numbers of people. These included organizations that had managed the Public Distribution System (PDS) or the government sponsored rural employment schemes, or distributed cooking fuel etc. In September 2011, UIDAI had partnered with 69 of such registrar organizations (Khanna & Raina, 2012). These included state governments, public sector units, National Stock Depository Limited, India Post, the Life Insurance Corporation of India, public sector banks, and telecom companies. The role of the registrars was to set up enrollment camps and they were also allowed to partner with other agencies to enroll residents.

Next, the Identification process is done to perform an identity authentication check. In other words, it checks whether the person is who she/he claims to be. The Identification process involves the following steps (UIDAI, 2012):

1.   The person holding the Aadhaar number / card approaches a service provider to seek services like banking, credit cards, getting a mobile connection or availing other government sponsored services.
2.   The service provider in order to authenticate the identity of the person connects with the Authentication User Agency that establishes a secure leased line to the Central Information Data Repository at UIDAI.
3.   The Central Information Data Repository verifies the submitted Aadhaar data with the data stored on the Central Information Data Repository and responds with a simple "yes/no" to indicate a "match/no match" response.

By using this method, a person's identity, address and demographic data can be verified for provision of various services like getting a telephone connection or using banking services or government services etc.

However, the Aadhaar number alone cannot be used in the authentication process. The Aadhaar number is to be used along with demographic attributes like the name, address, or date of birth of the resident; or with a one-time generated pin password delivered to a mobile number or email address of the resident; or with biometrics data like the finger print and/or iris scan. This way it is possible to provide a single factor or multi-factor (combination of attributes) identity authentication service based upon the authentication requirement of the service provider.

The government of India's report on UID enabled service delivery (UIDAI, 2012) highlights that Aadhaar will potentially provide multiple ways of identity authentication for any kind of service delivery. As a result, a service provider will be able to choose from either a single-factor or a multi-factor authentication.

DISSCUSSION

Many developing countries like India have weak formal institutions, which impede participation of poor in markets or the formal economy. These are often referred to as institutional voids in literature. These institutional voids highlight that absent or weak institutions can prevent access to and entry into markets. They are also viewed as sources of business opportunity for entrepreneurs. However, informal market intermediaries do exist in developing country markets but they are usually not open for all market participants (Khanna & Palepu, 2010). For instance, a moneylender residing in rural India is unlikely to view a business idea merit as the right approach of lending money to rural entrepreneurs.

The Aadhaar project is attempting to address the institutional void issue in India by creating a technology enabled formal mechanism for inclusion of the poor. UIDAI had entered into formal partnerships with various organizations illustrated in Figure 3. Yadav (2014) examined Aadhaar's potential to fill institutional voids in India by adopting Khanna and Palepu's (2010, 2005) methodology for identifying and responding to institutional voids. This paper extends Yadav's (2014) study and exemplifies that Aadhaar is able to address three institutional voids.

1. **Non-Participation of Poor in Markets and Formal Economy:** The first institutional void that Aadhaar attempts to fill is the non-participation of poor in markets and formal economy. The information on consumer base at the bottom of the pyramid and in far flung rural areas is either absent or poorly available. As a result, this segment is quite inaccessible to entrepreneurs and corporations. Aadhaar had enabled creation of biometric based unique identity proofs for the residents of India. Current status of Aadhaar enrollments indicates 643,866,779 Aadhaar numbers issued for Indian residents by July 2014 (see Figure 1). As a result, it is creating a formal mechanism for market based transactions by/for the poor.

2. **Unreliable Methods/Processes for Identity Authentication:** The second institutional void that Aadhaar attempts to fill is of unreliable methods and processes for identity authentication in India. Aadhaar enabled authentication can possibly provide secure and reliable identity authentication services for firms and entrepreneurs to facilitate market transactions in future. It is enabling the process of identity authentication for organizations and entrepreneurs by offering a single or multi-factor consumer authentication solution, which the service providers can embed in their service delivery process. Though most of the firms and entrepreneurs have not yet started using Aadhaar for customer authentication in India, there are some major organizations that are coming forward

to try this technology-enabled authentication. For example, Visa announced a partnership with five Indian banks in December 2013 allowing Aadhaar holders access to a Visa account. This new account was called "Saral Money", which will use Aadhaar enabled biometric authentication for verifying and authorizing payments to customers (Krowne, 2012).

3. **Absence of Mechanisms to Facilitate Banking in Far-Flung Rural Areas in India:** Finally, the third void it attempts to fill is of unavailability of mechanisms to carry out banking transactions in all the rural areas across India. As a result, monetary transactions are unlikely to be carried out in a formal, reliable and secure manner with the residents of India especially with those living in far-flung rural areas. Aadhaar is likely to enable secure monetary transactions through MicroATMs and mobile phones in all rural areas across India. Banking correspondents are being proposed to facilitate these transactions in rural areas.

CONCLUSION

At present, the Aadhaar project is a work-in-progress. However, if it is successful, even partly, it is likely to bring India to the forefront of citizen-identification technology. Parker (2011) reports that Aadhaar is likely to outperform the social security number and other biometric based systems across the globe. This paper presented the case study of the Aadhaar project using the research lens of inclusive innovation. This concept of inclusive innovation is evolving and this paper attempts to bring forward emerging definitions in this area. This area offers immense potential for future research.

The case study of Aadhaar project reveals its potential to unlock numerous innovative opportunities. The project creates an ecosystem of inclusive innovation and as a result the excluded poor and other actors like public and private organizations and entrepreneurs stand to gain. Aadhar is based on an open API platform and the cloud-based authentication that Aadhaar uses can enable organizations like banks, insurance companies, telecom companies, hospitals, educational institutions, government organizations and nongovernment organizations to offer numerous kinds of services to the billion people in India. New entrepreneurial opportunities exist for startups and entrepreneurs who can create different mobile apps using Aadhaar authentication for provision of numerous kinds of services that require identity proofs.

Consequently, new innovative business models can be built exploiting the benefits offered by the Aadhaar platform. It is being projected that by embedding the Aadhaar number in different public and private services an ecosystem like the Google search ecosystem can be evolved (Polgreen, 2011). As a result, it can potentially be used to create an underlying infrastructure for offering commercial services in India (Economist, 2012).

The Aadhaar project enables creation of a formal mechanism to fill three institutional voids existing in the Indian markets. If the Aadhaar project becomes successful then banking institutions will lend money to the poor, telecom firms will provide mobile connections to the poor, healthcare and educational institutions will be able to keep portable records and offer services to the poor. In other words, buying and selling process will be easier for Indian residents including the poor.

REFERENCES

Fagerberg, J., Mowery, D. C., & Nelson, R. R. (Eds.). (2006). *The Oxford handbook of innovation*. Oxford, UK: Oxford University Press. doi:10.1093/oxfordhb/9780199286805.001.0001

Fligstein, N., & Mara-Drita, I. (1996). How to make a market: Reflections on the European Union's Single Market Program. *American Journal of Sociology*, *102*, 1–33. doi:10.1086/230907

Foster, C., & Heeks, R. (2013). Conceptualising Inclusive Innovation: Modifying systems of innovation frameworks to understand diffusion of new technology to low-income consumers. *European Journal of Development Research*, *25*(3), 333–355. doi:10.1057/ejdr.2013.7

George, G., McGahan, A. M., & Prabhu, J. (2012). Innovation for inclusive growth: Towards a theoretical framework and a research agenda. *Journal of Management Studies*, *49*(4), 661–683. doi:10.1111/j.1467-6486.2012.01048.x

Heeks, R., Amalia, M., Kintu, R., & Shah, N. (2013). Inclusive Innovation: Definition, Conceptualisation and Future Research Priorities.*Annual Conference of the Academy of Innovation and Entrepreneurship*.

Jaipuriar, V. (2012, Jan 6). *Aadhaar ATMs on doorstep*. Retrieved June 15, 2013, from The Telegraph: http://www.telegraphindia.com/1120106/jsp/jharkhand/story_14969269.jsp#.Ucd_fhYtslI

Khanna, T., & Palepu, K. G. (2005). *Spotting Institutional Voids in Emerging Markets*. Harvard Business School Publishing Note 106-014.

Khanna, T., & Palepu, K. G. (2010). *Winning in emerging markets: A road map for strategy and execution*. Harvard Business School Press.

Khanna, T., & Raina, A. (2012). *Aadhaar: India's' Unique Identification' System*. Harvard Business School Strategy Unit Case, 712-412.

Krowne. (2012, Dec 13). *Visa launches new payment service in India – links Indian UID with Visa accounts*. Retrieved June 18, 2013, from C-ITV: http://security-news-tv.com/2012/12/13/visa-launches-new-payment-service-in-india-links-indian-uid-with-visa-accounts/

Mair, J., Marti, I., & Ventresca, M. J. (2012). Building inclusive markets in rural Bangladesh: How intermediaries work institutional voids. *Academy of Management Journal*, *55*(4), 819–850. doi:10.5465/amj.2010.0627

Mashelkar, R. A. (2012). *Global Research Alliance Working Paper*. Retrieved on 16 July 2014 from http://www.theglobalresearchalliance.org/en/What-we-do/~/media/Files/Resources/What%20is%20Inclusive%20Innovation_Global%20Research%20Alliance.ashx

McDermott, G. A. (2002). *Embedded politics: Industrial networks and institutional change in Postcommunism*. Ann Arbor, MI: University of Michigan Press. doi:10.3998/mpub.12137

Narayan, D. (2009). *Moving Out of Poverty: The Promise of Empowerment and Democracy in India* (Vol. 3). Washington, DC: World Bank. doi:10.1596/978-0-8213-7215-9

North, D. C. (1990). *Institutions, institutional change and economic performance.* New York: Cambridge University Press. doi:10.1017/CBO9780511808678

Parker, I. (2011, Oct 3). *The ID Man: Can a software mogul's epic project help India's poor?* Retrieved Oct 5, 2012, from The New Yorker: http://www.newyorker.com/reporting/2011/10/03/111003fa_fact_parker

Paunov, C. (2013). *Innovation and Inclusive Development: A Discussion of the Main Policy Issues (No. 2013/1).* OECD Publishing. doi:10.1787/18151965

Planning Commission (2011). *Faster, Sustainable and More Inclusive Growth: An Approach to the Twelfth Five-Year Plan (2012-17).* Government of India, Planning Commission Document.

Polgreen, L. (2011, Sept 2). *Scanning 2.4 Billion Eyes, India Tries to Connect Poor to Growth.* Retrieved Oct 10, 2012, from New York Times: http://www.nytimes.com/2011/09/02/world/asia/02india.html?pagewanted=all

Prahalad, C. K. (2004). *The fortune at the bottom of the pyramid: Eradicating poverty through profits.* Philadelphia: Wharton School Publishing.

PTI. (2012, Oct 18). *Micro-ATM using Aadhaar data delivers cash to villagers.* Retrieved June 20, 2013 from The Hindu: http://www.thehindubusinessline.com/news/microatm-using-aadhaar-data-delivers-cash-to-villagers/article4009641.ece

The Economist . (2012a, Jan 14). *India's identity scheme- The magic number: A huge identity scheme promises to help India's poor—and to serve as a model for other countries.* Retrieved April 5, 2012, from The Economist: http://www.economist.com/node/21542763/print

TNN. (2012, Oct 22). *UID helps detect 4k fake beneficiaries.* Retrieved 29 Oct, 2012, from The Times of India: http://timesofindia.indiatimes.com/city/mumbai/UID-helps-detect-4k-fake-beneficiaries/articleshow/16907738.cms

UIDAI. (2010). *UIDAI Strategy Overview: Creating a Unique Identity Number for every resident in India.* Planning Commission, Government of India Document.

UIDAI. (2012). *Aadhaar Enabled Service Delivery.* Planning Commission, Government of India Document.

United Nations (2014). *Millennium Development Goals report.* Author.

Yadav, V. (2014). Unique Identification Project for 1.2 billion People in India:Can it fill Institutional Voids and enable 'Inclusive' Innovation? *Contemporary Readings in Law and Social Justice, 6*(1), 38–48.

Chapter 6

Impact on Agricultural Sustainability of Maghreb Countries:
An Empirical Analysis by 3SLS

Rachida Khaled
University of Sousse, Tunisia

ABSTRACT

This paper is aimed at making the diffusion of the technological innovation and their role in affecting the agricultural sector in the three-sided (social, economic and environmental), a hand, it can participate to resolve problems of the agricultural sector: the effects of the climatic changes, the farming exodus and the migration and the problems of poverty. The theoretically and empirically studies analyze the mechanical innovation role in improving agricultural sustainability through the impact of mechanization on agricultural productivity, CO2 emission and demographic growth for a panel of three Maghreb countries (Algeria, Morocco and Tunisia) during the period 1999-2012. By using simultaneous equations, the authors' finding that mechanical innovation cannot achieve the purpose of sustainable development in the agriculture sector in the Maghreb countries through the negative impact of mechanization and research and development on agricultural productivity.

INTRODUCTION

The agriculture is a sector which plays a crucial role in the enhancement of territories, since this sector contributes to the increased growth of the country, nourishes all living things, but meeting a sustainability problem especially in developing countries. Agriculture is introduced into the sustainable development plan to improve and modernize this sector for agriculture called 'environmentally responsible' (Ambroise et al, 1998).

At the beginning of the seventy years, agriculture has found its place in political debate through the exposure of these issues such as: the mode of production productivist, environmental degradation, political and institutional structures etc.

DOI: 10.4018/978-1-5225-1779-5.ch006

This is a great debate that is open to the world in all commissions and United Nations organizations that is related to sustainable agriculture to set new targets for renewable and sustainable development.

This debate based on the work of UN member states, seeks to combine a consensus around vital of a new human world politics, fair and concerned with protecting the environment.

The birth of this new concept "political ecology" began to spread in the world where some developed countries were changing their mode of production by the substitution of industrial processes of physical or chemical to biological processes. For example, with the use of nitrates substituting nitrogen fixation by bacteria as herbicides and pesticides will have been replaced with natural antagonists of weeds and insect pests (Estevez et al, 1999).

The Sustainable increase in agricultural yields each time was not achieved without the destructive effects of the environment. The transition from conventional mode to sustainable ways of agriculture has formed a long journey that has supported both socioeconomic and environmental terms.

On this basis, in the early ninety, the concept of sustainable agriculture began to appear officially. This new agriculture aims to protect resources in agriculture (soil, water, energy ...) and stimulating the biological process that is the basis of stability by the mastery of pests and weeds (Estevez et al, 1999) and find a quick way to balance the three aspects already mentioned in the economic, social and environmental occurrence and in the agricultural sector.

Although the word sustainability was popularized by the spread of the concept of sustainable development (Delchet, 2004), the term sustainable agriculture and sustainable society have been discussed in the North American continent (The limits to growth, Meadows and al, 1972). On this basis, the author has initiated a debate on the production-growth and its environmental and social consequences in a period characterized by an energy crisis. Since then, the concept of sustainable agriculture has been distributed increasingly in all environmental debates.

While the question of whether technological innovation, particularly the mechanization improves or prevents the agricultural sustainability opens the door to the birth of several economic and political debates, there are little theoretical and empirical studies on the factors of development and economic durability of irrigation system in Maghreb countries.

The objective of this paper is to make up the void in the literature and make an in-depth analysis the sustainability agriculture sector of the Maghreb countries in order to identify their socioeconomic and environmental factors.

To better understand what leads the mechanization effect on the Maghreb agriculture sustainability, we browse in these paper three types of factors, social, economic and environmental. The scope of our study covered 3 Maghreb countries during the 1999-2012 periods. We utilized an econometric methodology based on the 3SLS.

Our results show that the mechanical innovation, research and development cannot achieve the sustainable development purpose in the agricultural sector of the Maghreb country in particular economic efficiency.

The rest of the paper is organized as follows. Section 2 furnishes a brief literature review of the impact of technological innovation in the agricultural sustainability. Section 3 presents the trend of agriculture and mechanization in the Maghreb countries. Section 4 shows the data and the adopted econometric methodology. The empirical results are obtained and interpreted in section 5. The rest of the paper is devoted to the presentation of some solutions, policy implications, suggestions and conclusion.

Technological Innovation and Sustainable Development: A Brief Literature Review

Major prior studies related to the present paper include Alani (2012), Blazy and al (2011), Esposti (2002), Van Rijn and al (2012), Feder and al (1993), Ruttan (1974), Khaled and al (2014, 2016). These studies focus on the effects of technological innovation such as mechanization, on the development of agricultural sustainability in developed and developing countries.

The concept of "innovation" is developed by the neoclassical approach as Adam Smith, David Ricardo, Marx etc. and improved by the Austrian school as Joseph Schumpeter. Technological innovation is defined as the set of innovations that induce transformation or a disruption of resources and methods of production, organization of work, products and markets, economic structures.

Schumpeter distinguished five types of innovation such as product innovation (production of a new product, process innovation (new method of production), discovered a new source of raw materials or energy, commercial innovation and new types of organizations (Dubouloz, 2006).

The neoclassical school indicates that the technological innovation and technological progress are factor that enhances the production quantities of capital and labor unchanged. This is an unexplained residue like manna falling from heaven. While Schumpeter explains that technological innovation is the engine of economic development.

Several authors analyze the impact of mechanical innovation and their role in the development of agricultural sustainability. For example, Alani (2012) shows that the improving agricultural productivity is linked with technical progress, he argues their work by a theoretical model derived from a production function type Cobb–Douglas to measure the impact of technological innovation and the productivity on economic growth in Uganda. He found that as technological innovation enhances economic growth. While the labor and capital productivity has reduced economic growth. He explains this result by the low productivity of the workforce who prefers leisure than work.

Fadavi et al (2010) analyzed the impact of mechanization on production through a survey of a diverse swatch contains 80 apple growers in Iran. They have obtained results as mechanization could not vary significantly because of the increased labor and energy cost during the harvesting operation. According to these authors, the agricultural mechanization is a destruction source of the land and natural resources.

Blazy et al (2011) indicate that, the improvement in agricultural production based on the reduction of pesticide use and renovation of soil fertility in the fight against weed, provide the nitrogen to the soil without insecticides increases in numbers, each of this way has led to technological innovation. According to the authors the innovations also have different effects on the net operating income and the productivity. The implementation of some innovating method in the agricultural sectors based on environmental, social and economic conditions.

Blazy et al (2011) conducted a survey on conventional farmers and organic banana farmers to have the most efficient technology adopted in the French Antilles (Guadeloupe and Martinique). They are found as a result that mechanization will be a source of sustainability in the production of organic banana due to its negative impacts on the environment.

Recent research shows that agricultural development is improving by the technological innovation, but whereas the durability can affect positively or negatively by the mechanization as it explains Khaled and al (2016) in his empirical analysis that is founded on the OLS modeling.

The innovation in agriculture and rural enterprise comes from whatever source (formal or informal) of new modes in the production and organization of agricultural activity.

The rural populations have a human capital integrating essential sources of knowledge and new procedures through their knowledge and modes of organization.

Good solutions found by small farmers themselves are a necessary source for enhancing agricultural productivity of developing countries.

Poole (2006) explains that, the mechanism and the level of research and innovation in the formal agricultural system have increased in the eighteenth and nineteenth century later has the use of scientific methods in relatively advanced economies (quoted by Khaled et al, 2016).

The R&D preferences in agriculture were encouraged during the last century by the government, which led to the birth of the formal national research systems in advanced and developing countries and the creation of organism's international research.

The green revolution is represented as a result of public research or as a classic example of a method giving land ownership to the farmer.

At this point, we can say that innovation is constituted by various researches and it can be spread through different distribution procedures by economic historical, political, institutional and climate contexts. In recent years, the increasing advances in technology led to the creation of technology platforms such as information and communication technology (ICT) and biotechnology (Khaled et al, 2016).

EVALUATION OF SOCIOECONOMIC AND ENVIRONMENTAL FACTORS

Energy

The farming surroundings and the agricultural sectors endure mediocrity of the infrastructure and the lack of information. These two difficulties cause the reduction of the outputs of the agricultural production and the decrease of the level of employment in this sector, what conducted to the apparition of poverty in these surroundings (Khaled et al, 2016).

For solving these problems, it is necessary to encourage the investment in the energy since he/it is considered like means of enhancing the life quality for rural populations, while being based on the technologies, in particular of information and the communication.

The lack of infrastructure and high costs are often explained by the lack of rural energy associated with various social, economic and political difficulties.

The energy is necessary to reinforce the nonagricultural farming economy directly and the agricultural farming economy indirectly.

The current price of oil and its derivatives can release hazardous effects that affect various areas such as air pollution, sea pollution that led to the decline the marine resources and soil pollution and thus to reduce the fertility of agricultural land and subsequently to lower yields and lower employment in this sector, Which encourages migration from rural to industrial or other services.

Energy supply associated with conventional technologies in rural areas can be more expensive. The social and environmental benefits of the development of services based on energy sources other than oil are viable.

We must invest in the energy sectors other than oil for environmental and economic reasons, such as wind and solar energy, which are technically feasible for local markets in rural areas.

Poverty Reduction

The project " objectives of the millennium for the development " (OMD) defined real strategies to avoid poverty while improving the investments in the infrastructure and the human capital in the farming surroundings, what permits to improve the agricultural sector by a qualified manpower, as well as the increase of production following the increase of the transportation means and thereafter a growth of the outputs and a reduction of poverty in the background farming, while motivating the equality between the sexes and the protection of the environment (Khaled et al, 2016).

The project of the OMD includes the science, the technology and the innovation and permits to apply the knowledge to the development.

The difficulties faced by developing countries in innovation are not related to the creation of new knowledge, but the effective use of existing techniques.

The System of Supermarkets

The impact of the international proliferation of large series on food retail sectors was generally analyzed for developing countries and also in several other regions such as Latin America, Central and Eastern Europe, sub-Saharan Africa and Asia (Khaled et al, 2016).

In developing countries, to reason at a time of demand bound to the tendency of the local life forms and to the big international business entry, the food systems are quickly going to be complex. In Tunisia the international supermarket entry is increasing with the time the sample Carrefour Market that has developed in most regions of Tunisia.

However, the international supermarket is a novelty that ensures the sale of food products, such as fresh produce, namely fruits, vegetables, meat and fish, which promotes the growth of production in the two sectors agriculture and fisheries.

So the international supermarket is an innovation that improves several areas such as fisheries and agriculture, and for industry.

Khaled et al (2016) indicates that, the international supermarket system offers the advantages that are the development of the employment in these stores and in their specific supply chains, an overall increase in the quality of food coming from the technology transfer and commercial uses of farmers.

National supermarkets are represented as major suppliers and demanders of local products, in the less advanced countries. These companies run into relationship marketing and ensure the root of supply series. This new business model is distinguished by low margins and high quality, creating new opportunities and new challenges for providers, such as self-service sales, healthy environments, indicating prices, the aggressive marketing and the promotions are henceforth the strategic norm (Cadilhom et al, 2006).

The development of monopsony system and economies of scale associated with the production, the basis of the standards and the organization rule and multiplication of knowledge to make, transmission of the markets that explains the situation of the small agriculturists of the difficult zones that is outside of these markets.

Agricultural Evolution in the Maghreb Country

The Maghreb region includes richest country in oil and gas (Libya, Algeria) and countries whose resources are very limited compared to their populations (Tunisia, Morocco and especially Mauritania) throughout the region of Africa north (Khaled et al, 2016).

To solve this problem of limited natural resources, many economic and political leaders put agriculture in question. For all the Maghreb countries, the agricultural sector remains of major importance in the economic, social and political level.

The sector must continue to achieve two strategic objectives: the protection of the development of basic agricultural products so-called strategic (cereals, milk, potatoes and sugar) and compensation for producers in the event of agricultural disasters.

Globally, on the basis of the green revolution goal, the success of these R&D should result increased the production volume of basic agricultural products, by increasing yields and agricultural productivity and lower the level of agricultural imports expensive and rarely by the degree of respect and apply the principles of sustainable development (Khaled et al, 2016).

So the use of new technologies such as cultural diversity or animal genetic material shows very contradictory results, with rising environmental costs (protection of forest areas and backgrounds, the use of mechanization on fragile soils with increased erosion, ...) and the social costs (loss of a genetic heritage applied to the arid conditions, deterioration of the collective actions with the individual production motivations).

In some difficult areas, these new technologies do not find their place because of the lack of infrastructure for production and transport, and low participation in services such credits to finance the costly inputs.

Also applied research, partly in experimental research institutions overlooked the local expertise of the actors and the spread of this research was done at the expense of local knowledge which ensured a balance between the medium and the community.

In the arid media, the options distribution difficulties are in intensive systems, which have been frequently reduced for social reasons, such as non-rationality of producers or low level of education in marginal and disadvantaged areas, etc.

The basic consequence is the reduction of the actions to the destructive technical applications of the nature to restrict the environmental risks, in particular the risks of drought.

However, facing the demographic increase of the Maghreb countries, and in light of the urbanization and unemployment increases rates attached to the emigration from the marginal surroundings, of the pastoral zones deterioration, the increasing desertification problem, and the weak technological transfer of research in the difficult zones that correspond to more of 85% of the territory, the agricultural research was interested again controlled in the small and medium agricultural farmers of the arid and semi-arid zones, but this new orientation made itself it in a setting of liberalization, from the years 80, named pre – adjustment period.

The above table measures the evolution of socioeconomic factors (agricultural productivity, number of mechanization and net revenue per capita) and the environmental factor (energy production) in the two years 2005 and 2010.

The table showed that, in Algeria, the all socioeconomic factors increase by against the environmental factor such as energy production is dropped. In Morocco, the number of mechanization remains constant during the years 2005-2010. While the net income per capita increases despite declining agricultural

Table 1. Summarize the tendency of socioeconomic and environmental factors such as the agriculture productivity, energy production, number of mechanization and the net income per capita in the three Maghreb countries in 2005 and 2010

Country	Agriculture Productivity		Energy Production		Number of Mechanization For 100 Square km		Net Income Per Capita	
	2005	2010	2005	2010	2005	2010	2005	2010
Algeria	8.221	9.0	166662.44	150524.713	128	141	10270	12630
Morocco	14.677	14.4	610.282	879.445	490	490	4710	6200
Tunisia	10.127	8.2	6681.4	8120.509	127	120	7360	9800

(WDI, 2014).

productivity and increases of energy production. In Tunisia, the number of mechanization has decreased, as well the agricultural productivity. While net revenues per capita and energy production have increased.

This table indicates that mechanization has evolved with the same sense of agricultural productivity and inversely to the energy production. This trend explains that mechanization is the motor of productivity (Feder et al, 1993) and production in Maghreb countries.

The Maghreb countries are characterized, in recent years, by the introduction of green and not productivist technologies, for this reason the number of mechanization is reduced as the case of Tunisia (Boughanmi 1995).

However, the adoption and dissemination of this model seem to be moving very slowly because mainly of its uniformity and lack of adaptation to regional diversity and heterogeneity of production systems in Maghreb countries. The biological and chemical technologies (improved seeds, chemical fertilizers) are basically neutral about the size of the operation and can be adopted by both large and small farmers, provided that an effective extension system, closely related research and near the farmer (Ruttan, 1985; Boughanmi 1995). The Tunisian experience related to extension remains too rigid administrative and involving little agricultural profession, despite some reforms in the direction of decentralization and coordination of extension programs.

Econometric Methodology and Data

The approach selected in this paper was to model the mechanical innovation impact on the agriculture sustainability in the Maghreb countries. Our initial intention was to cover all countries in the Maghreb, but given that some countries have not yet data of agricultural productivity (for example, Libya, Mauritania), the samples are included only 3 Maghreb countries: over the period of 1999-2012.

Data

Data were extracted from two sources, the data will be used for the measurement of variables are taken from the database of the World Development Indicators (WDI 2014) and food agriculture organization (FAO 2014).

Information related the expenses in research and development "R&D" (ERD), the expenses in information and communication technology "ICT" (EICT), the CO2 emission (CO2_E) and the demographic growth (DG) are collected from Worlds Development Indicators (World Bank, 2014). Other information related to agricultural productivity (AP), the mechanization, the Labor (L), the farming population (FP) is collected from food agriculture organization (FAO, 2014).

The dependent variables of interest are agriculture productivity, energy production and net income per capita.

The Variables

Our analysis founded on macroeconomic factors:

- **Agricultural Productivity (AP):** Agriculture in value added by the worker (% of GDP) (WDI, 2014). V. Ruttan (1974) indicates that the agricultural growth, improvement begins with the apparition of one sustained increase period in the total productivity via the use of new factors and new technologies; our technology is the system of irrigation (Khaled and al, 2014).
- **The Expenses in Research and Development (ERD):** Clark and Youngblood (1992) showed that the variable " technology ", as the expenses of the R&D changes the supple utilitarian shape with time is included in the specification of the function of profit, this variable permits to solve the problem of tendency of time (Thirtle and al, 1995). The R&D is the key of development and modernization of the agricultural sector (quoted by Khaled and al, 2016).

Even in the developed country, the agricultural systems of research meaningful are dedicated to testing and refined the innovations of the agriculturists and to test the adaptation of exotic exploitation varieties and the species of the animal (Ruttan, 1974).

- **The Expenses in Information and Communication Technology (EICT):** Permits to improve the sector by the diffusion of innovation to the world level and the diffusion of the R&D toward the producers and the consumers.

The ICT decreases the uncertainty of the producers concerning the bought input and of the consumers concerning the consumed product (Feder et al, 1993).

- **The Mechanization (M):** It is a very important technology to improve the outputs of producers. (Clay, 1982).
- **The labor (L):** Alani (2012) proved that the labor is considered as a technology that permits of replaced the machinery in some cases to keep the durability of the sector.
- **The Farming Population (FP):** Himself the producers, the consumers and the manpower. The farming sociologist research has contributed to the diffusion efficiency of technology (Ruttan, 1974).
- **The CO2 Emission (CO2_E):** Carbon dioxide emissions are those stemming from the burning of fossil fuels and the manufacture of cement. They include carbon dioxide produced during consumption of solid, liquid and gaseous fuels and flaring (WDI, 2014). This variable is defined by Soni and al (2013) as environmental determinant.
- **Demographic Growth (DG):** The population growth (annual %) corresponds to the exponential growth rate of the population in the middle of the year n-1 to n, expressed as a percentage. (WDI, 2014). SemihAkc-omak et al (2009) and Van Rijn and al (2012) indicates that, the demographic growth is a factor of social aspect.

Econometric Methodology

From a methodological viewpoint, we chose to value the involvement of the innovations technological to the durability and the growth of the agricultural sector based on the standard production function of Cobb - Douglas type (1928) improves by Dowricks and Rogers (2002) respecting the properties traditional neoclassical (Khaled and al, 2016).

$$Y = AK^{\alpha k}H^{\alpha h}L^{\beta} \text{ or } \beta = 1 - (\alpha_k + \alpha_h) \tag{1}$$

Where, Y is a dependent variable which is defined by agricultural productivity, CO2 emission and demographic growth. K, H, L and A are, respectively, the physical capital, the human capital, the labor that grows to the rate exogenous and constant " n ", the technical progress is neutral in the sense of Hicks (1932) and αk, α_h, β are the production elasticity's (Khaled et al, 2016).

However to evaluate the participation of mechanical innovation, we decomposed the stock of physical capital in two parts: the material, physical capital is the mechanization (M) and the immaterial physical capital is the expenses in the information and communication technology ICT (EICT).

The ERD is the investment in human capital, according to the theory of human capital (Nafiou, 2009).

The expenses in R&D (ERD) and the expenses in the technology of information and communication, ICT (EICT) are considered like an investment in the innovation (OECD, 1999).

The stock of the labor is decomposed into two parts: the labor in the agricultural sector (L) and the farming population (FP).

The goal of this paper is to examine the relationship between mechanical innovation and agricultural sustainability through the impact of mechanization on agricultural productivity, CO2 emission and demographic growth.

This relationship is measured by a simultaneous equations model (3SLS) extended as follows:

$$AP_{it} = \alpha + \beta_1(EICT)_{i,t} + \beta_2(M)_{i,t} + \beta_3(ERD)_{i,t} + \beta_4(L)_{i,t} + \beta_5(FP)_{i,t} + \beta_6(CO2\_E)_{i,t} + \beta_7(DG)_{i,t} + \xi_{i,t} \tag{2}$$

$$CO2\_E_{it} = \alpha + \beta_1(EICT)_{i,t} + \beta_2(M)_{i,t} + \beta_3(ERD)_{i,t} + \beta_4(L)_{i,t} + \beta_5(FP)_{i,t} + \beta_6(AP)_{i,t} + \beta_7(DG)_{i,t} + \xi_{i,t} \tag{3}$$

$$DG_{it} = \alpha + \beta_1(EICT)_{i,t} + \beta_2(M)_{i,t} + \beta_3(ERD)_{i,t} + \beta_4(L)_{i,t} + \beta_5(FP)_{i,t} + \beta_6(AP)_{i,t} + \beta_7(CO2\_E)_{i,t} + \xi_{i,t} \tag{4}$$

i = 1, 2,…N, t = 1,2,…Ti

Where AP, CO2_E and DG are the dependent variables, are defined respectively as agricultural productivity, CO2 emission and demographic growth. The Independent variables are the expenses in research and development (ERD), the expenses in information and communication technology (EICT), the mechanization (M), the labor (L), and the farming population (FP).

Equation (2), allows measure the impact of mechanical innovation on economic sustainability through the effect of the mechanization (M) on the agriculture productivity (AP), as well as the spending of research and development (ERD) and spending of information and communication technology (EICT) impact.

Equation (3), allows examine the impact of mechanical innovation on environmental sustainability through the effect of the mechanization (M) on CO2 emission (CO2_E), as well as the spending of research and development (ERD) and spending of information and communication technology (EICT) impact.

Equation (4), examines the impact of mechanical innovation on social sustainability through the effect of the mechanization (M) on the demographic growth (DG), as well as the spending of research and development (ERD) and spending of information and communication technology (EICT) impact.

Our methodology is based on an estimate of the simultaneous equations model (3SLS), a sample of 3 Maghreb countries (Algeria, Morocco, Tunisia) and a measurement of the variables from the data for the countries will of 1999 until to 2012.

This simultaneous equations model is estimated by the generalized method of moments (GMM). Since generally, the results of GMM are robust.

RESULTS AND INTERPRETATION

Table 2 provides summary statistics on the variables.

The above table shows that the average agricultural productivity, the entire sample is 2.437398%. The inter-individual variance (between) 0.0908%, while the intra individual variance (time) is equal to 0.0172%, in our case the inter-individual dimension (3 countries) is very important that the intra-individual dimension (17 years country) (0.0908%> 0.0172%). The same for the regression (3) and (4).

Table 3. summarized the results of three least squares (3SLS) models for the sample of the 3 Maghreb countries from 1999 to 2012.

The first column presents the effect of mechanization on economic sustainability through their impact on agricultural productivity. The second column indicates the effect of the mechanization on environmental sustainability through her effect in CO2 emission. The third column shows the impact of mechanization on social sustainability through her effect on demographic growth.

Table 2. Descriptive statistics

Variable	Mean	Std. Dev	Min	Max
AP	12.04083	3.502358	6.68	20.223
ERD	.5452381	.331392	.07	1.5
EICT	4.497619	3.163703	1.5	14.5
L	6.506214	2.970074	2.3	10.9
FP	39.64065	4.713145	33.902	47.6508
M	5.632143	2.200882	2.45	8.1
CO2_E	2.215405	.717636	1.132	3.529
DG	1.201214	.2298503	.928	1.776

N 42

n 14

T 3

Note. — N, total number of observation; n, number of observation for only one country; T, number of country.

Table 3. The model estimation by the 3SLS method

Models	(2)	(3)	(4)
Variables	AP	CO2_E	DG
AP	---	.0213774 (0.386)	.0679745 (0.000)***
CO2_E	.8139869 (0.386)	---	.3073321 (0.010)***
DG	3.887044 (0.000)***	.4615501 (0.01)***	---
M	**-1.747371 (0.000)***	.0752307 (0.000)***	-.0032265 (0.962)**
ERD	2.011479 (0.023)**	-.3136046 (0.021)**	-.2275172 (0.043)**
EICT	.0069395 (0.936)	.0263234 (0.049)**	-.0141828 (0.206)
L	-.4338862 (0.000)***	.076319 (0.000)***	.0193965 (0.202)
FP	.1810303 (0.107)	.0436239 (0.013)**	-.028774 (0.057)*
Constant	9.928643 (0.106)	-3.26619 (0.000)	.9223143 (0.264)
Observations	42	42	42
R²	0.9220	0.9524	0.6737

Note. — Panel estimations of the 3 Maghreb countries. The dependant variable is the agriculture productivity (AP), CO2 emission (CO2_E) and the demographic growth (DG). Variables in parentheses are at the significance level of 1% *, 5%** and 10%***.

According to the regression (2), we show that, the variables: population growth (DE) and expenditure of R&D (ERD) are positive and significant at the 5% and 10% level. The variables: labor (L) and mechanization (M) are negative and significant at the 1% level. While the variables: expenditure of ICT (ECIT), farming population (FP) and a CO2 emission (CO2_E) are positive and not significant.

The above table (regression 2) shows that, where agricultural productivity (AP) increases by 1 percentage points, mechanization (M) decreases by 1.747371 percentage points and labor (L) decreases by 0.4338862 percentage points. By against, demographic growth (DG) rise by 3.887044 percentage points and R&D expenditure (ERD) increase by 2.011479 percentage. This result is similar to the study of Fadavi and al (2010) and Khaled et al (2016).

This negative impact of mechanization on the economic sustainability explains that the mechanization cannot achieve economic efficiency in the Maghreb countries due to the intensive use of mechanization in the sector, allowing deteriorate soil fertility over time and eventually lowers productivity and performance in the agricultural sector (Fadavi and al, 20101).

The variables: expenditure of ICT (ECIT), farming population (FP) and a CO2 emission (CO2_E) are not significant because the relationship is indirect with agricultural productivity. This relation is created through other factors such as labor, energy production, etc.

In the regression (3), we mark that, the variable expenditure on R&D (ERD) is negative and significant at the 5% level and the: expenditure on ICT (EICT), labor (L), farming population (FP), mechanization

(M) and population growth (DG) are negative and significant at the 1% and 5% level. While the variable: agricultural productivity is positive, but not significant.

The above table indicates that, when CO2 emission (CO2_E) rises by 1 percentage points, mechanization (M) increases by 0.0752307 percentage points, labor (L) increases by 0.0752307 percentage points, demographic growth (DG) rise by .4615501 percentage points, communication and information technology expenditure (EICT) increase by 0.0263234 percentage points and farming population (FP) raises by 0.0436239 percentage points. However, R&D expenditure (ERD) drops by 0.3136046 percentage points.

According to the study of Kallivroussis et al (2002); Soni et al (2013), the use of mechanization in the agricultural exploitation causes diffusion of pollution in the soil and in the air as CO2 which leads eventually to the reduction of soil fertility, development of diseases in rural areas, etc.

The variable agricultural productivity is not significant because of its indirect relation with the issuance of CO2.

Regression (4), indicates that, Variables: expenditure of R&D (ERD) and rural population (FP) are negative and significant at the 5% and 10% and the variables: agricultural productivity (AP) and a CO2 emission (CO2_E) are positive and significant at 1%. While the variables: mechanization (M) and expenditure on ICT (EICT) are negative and not significant and variable labor (L) is positive but not insignificant.

The above table suggests that, demographic growth (DG) increases by 1 percentage points, the CO2 emission (CO2_E) rises by 0.3073321 percentage points and the agriculture productivity (AP) increases by 0.0679745 percentage points. Whereas, R&D expenditure (ERD) and farming population (FP) decreases respectively by 0.2275172 percentage points and 0.028774 percentage points.

The variables mechanization (M), expenditure of ICT (EICT) and labor (L) are not significant. These results explain the indirect relation between this factor and demographic growth.

According to the regression 2 and 3 analysis, mechanization (M) can affect negatively the demographic growth by diffusion of CO2 in the soil and air (regression 3) which subsequently leads to disease development and subsequently the reduction of population growth. The CO2 diffusion induces to soil degradation and subsequently the decline in productivity and production (regression 2) agricultural which causes the increasing undernourishment and decreased demographic growth.

Mechanization improves the purchasing power of Employers in the industrial sector such as an equipment manufacturing society, for against the rural population suffers from very high level of poverty. As he explains Timmer (1992), the agricultural sector is like a black box, it provides power to all the other sectors against it is not growing.

In the Maghreb countries, the mechanization affects negatively the environmental, economic and social sustainability's.

According to the results of the simultaneous equations model (3SLS) estimation, we noticed that the workforce has a negative role in the functioning of agricultural machines (Ruttan, 1974). The regressions (2) show that the relationship between agricultural productivity and labor is negative (0.4338862).

Labor recruited in the agricultural sector of the Maghreb countries is unqualified. It is malfunctioning agricultural machinery and deteriorates the production by ecological footprint (Fersino et al, 2002).

The impact of mechanization on economic, social and environmental aspects is explained by the effect of labor on the three durability's. The workforce in agriculture of the Maghreb countries is unqualified. The lack of learning by doing in the agricultural sector prevents increasing performance and productivity through ecological footprint, poor use of fertilizers, spreading pollution and over-exploitation of water resources (Feder et al, 1993).

The result of the estimated regression 2 and 3 shows that the level of research and development have a negative impact on the environmental and social aspects through their impact on CO_2 emission and demographic growth, this result can be interpreted by the novelty of the sustainable agriculture in the Maghreb countries, such as organic farming. These results are similar to studies of Esposti (2002), and Khaled et al (2016).

Biological research and development remains until today in the laboratories and has not yet applied to a field.

The information and communication technology (ICT) has a positive effect on environmental aspect, this result is explained by the introduction of new technology (mobile, internet, etc.) in rural areas and their participation in the agricultural sector through improved marketing of an agricultural product line, development and definition of sustainable agriculture concept and organic products in the Maghreb countries (Khaled et al, 2016).

The result of the estimated regression 3 indicates the farming population affects negatively the environmental aspect through their impact on CO_2 emission.

The population increase in rural areas increases the pollution in the zone and increases the use of water resources, leading to over-exploitation of natural resources.

Mechanization used by Maghreb countries is not sustainable since it cannot achieve the sustainable development aims in the agricultural sector of the Maghreb countries.

RECOMMENDATION POLICY

The results of the model estimation 3SLS include policies of very important implications for producers and consumers of sustainable agriculture in the Maghreb countries are listed as follows:

1. The government support for funding and Development: The Maghreb Farmers need for state subsidies to buy sustainable agricultural machines with good quality. They also need the development of their rural areas by building infrastructure to attract investors to invest in the agriculture sector.
2. Improve training in the rural middle, especially how to operate farm machinery: the workforce in the agricultural sector of the Maghreb countries is not qualified because of their limited education level. The majority of labor worked in agriculture is the farming population.
3. The development of environmental protection strategy and implementation in the rural middle, for example, the payment of fees for people that generate negative externalities in the rural areas.

SUGGESTION

In order to enhance the estimation model, this section suggests some recommendations for future studies. There are a few studies that examine the mechanical innovation and their role in determining the agricultural sustainability. Research on the innovation of sustainable agriculture, in recent years, begins to develop, but many questions remain unanswered or their answers are ambiguous. This section provides suggestions for future study. The empirical studies that are performed on innovation for sustainable agriculture focus on the Maghreb countries. Future studies on the mechanization factors and their impact on the agriculture sustainability could focus on a large sample of developing countries that exceeds 3 countries. This is to analyze the trend of impact method of sustainable and innovative culture on socioeconomic (the cost of production and transportation, the qualification of manpower, funding for agricultural sector), institutional, policies (agricultural sustainability policy) and biophysical (protection of natural resources) factors in these countries. The future studies should compare the level of development of sustainable agriculture in developed countries and developing countries.

CONCLUSION

The concept of sustainable development has spread during the 90s in scientific research both locally and planetary. All this research agrees that the achievement of sustainable development depends on the respect of three essential principles: equity between nations and generations, the equilibrium of the economic situation and the protection of the environment (Khaled et al, 2016).

On this basis, several economists and scientists believe that the diffusion of technological innovation is a basic means to ensure sustainable development in the agricultural sector.

To verify this effectiveness, we tested the effects of mechanical innovation on the agricultural sector in the three Maghreb countries (Tunisia, Morocco and Algeria) for a period from 1999 to 2012 by a model of simultaneous equations, as well as their ability or non to achieving the objectives of sustainable development in agriculture sector.

The estimation results show that mechanization used by Maghreb farmers is unsustainable. For this it's unable to achieve the sustainable development objectives in the agricultural sector of Maghreb countries. The mechanized agricultural land use may lead to reduced fertility and increased pollution. This result is similar to the study of Khaled and al (2016).

A recent study done by CEMA (2014) indicates that there are 12 types of agricultural mechanization in the world. The weak type is used by developing countries, particularly Africa. It can be concluded that the poor quality of mechanization used by Maghreb countries negatively affects the agricultural sector sustainability.

REFERENCES

Akçomak, İ. S., & ter Weel, B. (2009). Social capital, innovation and growth: Evidence from Europe. *European Economic Review*, *53*(5), 544–567. doi:10.1016/j.euroecorev.2008.10.001

Alani. J. (2012). Effects of Technological Progress and Productivity on Economic Growth In Uganda. *Revue Procedia Economics and Finance*, (1), 14 – 23.

Ambroise, A., Barnaud, M., Manchon, O., & Vedel, G. (1998). Bilan de l'expérience des plans de développement durable du point de vue de la relation agriculture-environnement. *Courrier de l'environnement de l'INRA, 34.*

Blazy, J.-M., Carpentier, A., & Thomas, A. (2011). The willingness to adopt agro-ecological innovations: Application of choice modelling to Caribbean banana planters. *Revue Ecological Economics*, *72*, 140–150. doi:10.1016/j.ecolecon.2011.09.021

Boughanmi. H. (1995). *Les principaux volets des politiques agricoles en Tunisie: évolution, analyse et performances agricoles.* CIHEAM-options méditerranéennes, ser.B/n 14, les agricultures maghrébines à l'aube de l'an 2000.

Cadilhon, J.-J., Fearne, A. P., Giac Tam, P. T., Moustier, P., & Poole, N. D. (2006). Quality incentives and dependence in vegetable supply chains to Ho Chi Minh City. *Acta Horticulturae,* (699), 111–117. doi:10.17660/ActaHortic.2006.699.11

CEMA. (2014). *Promouvoir le développement rural et agricole en Afrique grâce à la mécanisation agricole (MA) avancée.* Comité Européen des groupements de constructeurs du machinisme agrico.

Clark, J. S., & Youngblood, C. E. (1992). Estimating Duality Models with Biased Technical Change: A Time Series Approach. *American Journal of Agricultural Economics, 74*(2), 353–360. doi:10.2307/1242489

Clay, E.J. (1982). Technical innovation and public polic: agricultural development in the Kosi Region, Bihar, India. *Agricultural Administration, 9,* 189-210.

Delchet, K. (2004). *Qu'est-ce que le développement durable?.* Academic Press.

Dubouloz, J. (2006). Acception et défense des loca publica dans les Variae de Cassiodore, Un point de vue juridique sur la cité. dans M. Ghilardi, Ch. J. Goddard et P. Porena dir., Les cités de l'Italie tardo-antique (IVe –VIe siècle), Institutions, économie, société, culture et religion. *Actes du colloque de l'Ecole française de Rome, 369,* 53-74.

Esposti, R. (2002). Public agricultural R&D design and technological spill-ins a dynamic model. *Revue Research Policy, 31,* 693–717.

Estevez, B., & Domon, G. (1999). Les enjeux sociaux de l'agriculture durable un débat de société nécessaire? Une perspective nord-américaine. *Courrière de l'environnement, 36.*

Fadavi, R., Keyhani, A., & Mohtasebi, S. S. (2010, December). Estimation of a Mechanization Index in Apple Orchard in Iran. *The Journal of Agricultural Science, 2*(4).

Feder. G & Umali. D. L. (1993). The Adoption of Agricultural Innovations. *Technological Forecasting and Social Change, 43,* 215-239.

Fersino, V., & Petruzzella, D. (2002). Organic agriculture in the Mediterranean area: state of the art. Options Méditerranéennes: Série B. Etudes et Recherches, 40, 9- 51.

Kallivroussis. L, A. Natsis. N & Papadakis. G. (2002). The Energy Balance of Sunflower Production for Biodiesel in Greece. *Biosystems Engineering Revue, 81*(3), 347–354.

Khaled, R., & Hammas, L. (2014). Macroeconomic and institutional determinants of the irrigation system and their impact on development and economic sustainability of the agricultural sector in MSEC: A new result by using panel data. *International Journal of Sustainable Economies Management, 3*(3), 54–66. doi:10.4018/ijsem.2014070104

Khaled, R., & Hammas, L. (2016). Technological innovation and the agricultural sustainability: What compatibility for the mechanization? *International Journal of Innovation in the Digital Economy, 7*(4).

Meadows. D, Randers. J & William. W. (1972). *The limits to growth. A report for the club of Rome's project on the predicament of mankind.* Academic Press.

Nafiou. M.M. (2009). Impact de l'aide publique au développement sur la croissance économique du Niger. *Revue africaine de l'Intégration, 3*(2).

OCDE. (1999). *Développement durable les grands questions?.* Author.

Poole. N. (2006). *L'innovation: enjeux, contraintes et opportunités pour les ruraux pauvres.* Document de synthèse, Janvier.

Ruttan, V.-W. (1974). Induced innovation and agricultural development. *RE:view, 64*(May), I-14.

Ruttan, V.-W. (1989). Institutional-Innovation and Agricultural Development. *Review World Development, 17*(9), 1375–138. doi:10.1016/0305-750X(89)90079-X

Soni, P., Taewichit, C., & Salokhe, V. M. (2013). Energy consumption and CO2 emissions in rainfed agricultural production systems of Northeast Thailand. *Agricultural Systems, 116*, 25–36. doi:10.1016/j.agsy.2012.12.006

Thirtle, C., Townsend, R., & Van Zyl, J. (1998). Testing the Induced Innovation Hypothesis in South African Agriculture (An Error Correction Approach). *Agricultural Economics,* (19), 145–157. doi:10.1016/S0169-5150(98)00030-9

Timmer, C.P. (1992). agricultural and economic development revisited. *Agricultural Systems, 40*, 21-58.

Van Rijn, F., Bulte, E., & Adekunle, A. (2012). Social capital and agricultural innovation in Sub-Saharan Africa. *Revue Agricultural Systems, 108*, 112–122.

Section 3

Chapter 7

The Migration of the Book across Territorial Borders:
Copyright Implications for Authors in the Digital Economy

Francina Cantatore
Bond University, Australia

ABSTRACT

This chapter deals with the copyright issues faced by authors once their books enter the digital sphere, as well as the difficulties associated with overseas publications of their books, from a territorial perspective. It examines whether territorial copyright borders still afford book authors effective copyright protection in the digital economy, and further, whether the culture of the book is being eroded through the prevalence of extra-territorial publications. Relevantly, this article examines the landmark US Supreme Court decision of Kirtsaeng v Wiley and Sons, Inc. and considers its likely future impact on the enforcement of territorial copyright by authors and publishers. Finally, the article concludes that territorial copyright borders have become blurred, difficult to enforce in view of recent precedent, and are ineffective in preserving authors' copyright and the cultural dimensions of their books.

INTRODUCTION

It should be stated at the outset that there is no concept of 'international copyright', which will automatically protect authors' copyright globally. Instead, copyright protection is territorial in nature and relies on the laws of individual countries for protection in that country. For example, in the USA the 1976 *Copyright Act* (together with a number of other statutes) regulates copyright use; in Australia the *Copyright Act* of 1968 (as amended) applies.

Most countries, however, (including the USA and Australia) are members of international copyright treaties, namely the *Berne Convention for the Protection of Literary and Artistic Works* (1971) where

DOI: 10.4018/978-1-5225-1779-5.ch007

copyright works are defined as 'literary and artistic works' (Article 2(1), 102). Under this treaty authors receive recognition for their foreign rights under the 'national treatment' requirement, which provides that a qualifying 'foreign work' must receive the same protection as a 'local work' [Article 7(8)]. Thus member States' copyright laws should have certain 'minimum standards' of copyright protection to comply.

In practice, however, it has become apparent that digital publishing and global book sales have eroded these principles and have impacted on authors' ability to protect and monetise their copyright internationally. In dealing with the migration of the book across territorial borders this article considers two aspects of the migration process:

First, it discusses the impact of electronic publishing or the digitalisation of the book across bordersand what this means to authors in relation to their copyright. Whilst these advances have positively impacted on the availability and accessibility of books, and the creation of increased publishing opportunities for authors, there have also been corresponding negative consequences. Problem areas for authors have included pirating of their work on the internet though unauthorised copying, as well as a lack of knowledge on digital publishing and copyright protections on the internet.

Secondly, the issue of extra-territorial print publications – another area of book migration – is examined in relation to authors' copyright, as traditional publishing also faces cross-border issues which cannot always be readily resolved. This global trend in publishing may lead to territorial copyright infringements. One increasing problem faced by Australian authors and publishers is the issue of unlawful parallel importing, which is difficult to police, especially in relation to digital copies. Parallel importing restrictions apply in the USA, Australia, Canada and the UK, but in reality these provisions are often breached by:

- Wholesalers or discounters who import illegally printed copies of books from the Far East into Australia and sell books at discounted prices: In these instances, authors don't benefit from royalties as printing typically takes place in third world countries without regard to copyright. These books are often text books with poor quality printing and binding.
- Where books are lawfully published for an overseas market, and are then imported back into the country in breach of parallel import restrictions, or sold online across territorial borders at cut-rate prices: Again authors don't benefit from royalties and these books are sold in competition with local publishers, who suffer losses as a result.

In Australia the issue of the sale of books on the internet has not been addressed in Court but the landmark US case of *Kirtsaeng v John Wiley & Sons* (2013) could have a far-reaching impact on authors and local publishers in the US, and potentially worldwide. In this case Kirtsaeng purchased text books from Thailand and then resold them on eBay to students in the US. The Court held that US copyright owners may not prevent importation and reselling of copyrighted content lawfully sold abroad, due to the application of the 'first sale doctrine'. This case, discussed in more depth below, is a clear illustration that the availability of books online and cross-border selling may affect the application of territorial copyright, essentially rendering it inoperative in practice.

This article aims to provide insights on these issues by including references to research conducted with a purposive sample of published Australian authors, which examines authors' views on these concerns from a 'grassroots' perspective. A brief synopsis of the methodology applied in this research follows below.

The Research Component and Methodology

A national online survey of published Australian authors (Cantatore, 2011) investigated the perceptions of authors on the dissemination of written work on the internet and the effects of digitalization on authors' copyright, amongst other issues. Responses were obtained from 156 authors, including fiction, non-fiction and academic authors. Additionally, 17 in-depth interviews with a range of authors, as well as additional interviews with small and large publishers, provided further qualitative insights into these issues. The methodology incorporated qualitative interviews, as well as qualitative and quantitative information obtained through the online survey. Approximately one third of the surveyed authors were full-time authors and the balance part-time

A Multi-Method Approach

A multi-method approach, characterized by a combination of qualitative and quantitative research methods, was employed. In this process the use of multiple methods or triangulation (Denzin and Lincoln, 2005) assisted with an in-depth investigation of the research issues. In-depth face-to-face interviews with a number of authors, underpinned by qualitative data obtained through online survey questionnaires, distributed through the *Australian Society of Authors* (ASA) and Writers' Centers throughout Australia, formed the nucleus of the research. This information was supplemented by primary documents such as legislation and publishing contracts, a comprehensive literature review and background research on legislative and publishing issues.

The Denzin and Lincoln (2005) view of the qualitative researcher being described as 'bricoleur and quilt maker', a person who assembles images into montages (a method of editing cinematic images), using a variety of methods, strategies and empirical materials (p. 4) was a relevant consideration in structuring the research. The assembling of authors' viewpoints through in-depth interviews and online surveys, together with legal research, literature review and economic considerations, resembled such a 'quilt' as envisaged by these authors. This viewpoint also supported the idea of 'purposive sampling', as described by Patton (2002).

Three important factors in particular merited consideration, described by Gray, Williamson, Karp and Dalphin (2007) as: 'the type of information to be gathered, the resources available for research and the access to individuals, groups and institutions' (p. 43). These factors were taken into account in both stages of the research model, and more particularly, in the construct of purposeful sampling, as proposed by Patton (2002) and discussed below.

Purposeful Sampling

The strategy described by Patton (2002) as 'purposeful sampling' (p. 45) has also been referred to as 'purposive sampling' (Stake, 2004, p. 451). Stake explains 'purposive sampling' as follows: 'For qualitative fieldwork, we draw a purposive sample, building in variety and acknowledging opportunities for intensive study' (p. 451). Patton regards such sampling as 'information rich and illuminative', offering insight about the phenomenon studied rather than empirical generalisation from a sample to a population (p. 40). In comparing the differences between 'qualitative purposeful sampling' and 'statistical probability sampling', he describes purposeful sampling as follows: 'Qualitative enquiry typically focuses on a relatively small sample… selected purposefully to permit enquiry into and understanding of a phenomenon *in depth'* (pp. 234-235).

The type of purposeful sampling used in this research can best be described as 'maximum variation sampling' as envisaged by Patton (2002). This type of sampling aims to capture and describe central themes that cut across a great deal of variation. It relies on the identification of common patterns in the diversity of responses. In the case of authors and copyright, it would aim to recognise common themes emerging from the results of a diverse group of authors from different age groups, backgrounds and geographical areas.

Purposive sampling was implemented in two stages, namely: the first sample of face to face interviews with 17 published authors, including 'elite' interviews - as perceived by Marshall and Rossman (2010, p. 155) - who comprised more than half of the sample. A second sample of online surveys was completed by a larger group of 156 participants from the ranks of published Australian authors. The researcher considered elite authors as those who have been published over an extended period of time and have made continued contributions to the development of the book industry. Because of this naturalistic approach, it was envisaged that such a sample would provide an authentic and relevant result.

Purposive sampling through the combination of surveys and interviews allowed for a more goal-oriented investigation and for more introspection and reflection on the part of the researcher. The emphasis was not purely on data collection, but on the assimilation and critical analysis of research results, bearing in mind Brannen's cautionary remarks against the risks inherent in qualitative research:

For example, the current turn to reflexivity in qualitative research in respect of the focus upon the researcher risks neglecting research participants. By contrast …there is the opposite risk whereby researchers attribute to their research participants a monopoly over meaning. There is a danger of downplaying the interpretive role of the researcher (Brannen, 2004, p. 313).

With these caveats in mind, care was taken to identify and acknowledge the viewpoints of participants in the in-depth interviews where they were specific on certain issues. Furthermore, the online survey provided a means of utilising a larger sample group to obtain qualitative data against which the subjective interviewee comments and observations could be examined.

Scope of the Research

Two main groups of participants were identified in the research - full time authors and part time authors, with only data obtained from published authors utilised. In addition, three publishers (two small and one large/mainstream) and a publishing contract consultant were interviewed to provide background information and a further perspective on the research issues.

Certain sources, especially those regarded as 'elite interviews', could provide valuable information on the research issues, such as author Frank Moorhouse, who had played an instrumental part in copyright protection for Australian authors. Marshall & Rossman (2010) note some of the advantages of elite interviews as their possible familiarity with legal and organisational structures and their broad views on the development of policy fields (pp. 155-156). It was thus envisaged that the findings of the research would be strengthened by the inclusion of a purposive sample of such high-profile or 'elite' participants with a high level of knowledge on the subject matter, as proposed by Patton (2002).

In respect of the online survey all responses were anonymous, with no identifying features other than broad demographic information, such as the respondent's state of residence, age, type of writing engaged in and income. The non-identifying approach was selected as the underlying basis for this strategy as it was aimed at encouraging prospective respondents to participate in the survey due to the assurance of anonymity (Buchanan, 2004, p. 146). The scope of the research therefore sought to include a number of different 'types' of authors, who could be classified as full time or part time writers, and also according to profession (for example fiction writer, non-fiction writer, academic writer, etc.).

The Two Stages of Data Collection

As explained above, the research process was executed in two stages, a first stage which consisted of limited open-ended face to face interviews with 17 authors, three publishers and a publishing contract consultant, followed by a second stage, which comprised an online survey which was distributed through the Australian Society of Authors (ASA), the professional association for Australia's literary creators, and various writers' centres nationally. This approach allowed for the collection of rich qualitative data through the in-depth interviews (Denzin & Lincoln, 2005, p. 12), together with a wider scope of data collection through the online survey.

An interview guide was used to facilitate the in-depth interviews, in line with Patton's suggestion that the use of an interview guide leaves the interviewer 'free to explore, probe and ask questions that will elucidate and illuminate the particular subject.' According to Patton (2002) 'it provides for better use of the limited time available for an interview; interviewing is more systemic and comprehensive and the issues to be explored are delineated in advance' (p. 343).

The open-ended structure of the interviews with this sample group provided the first valuable source of qualitative data and informed the second stage of the research by providing more insight into the research issues. Furthermore, the scope of the research questions evolved through the process of interviewing as key trends and changes in the industry became more evident and synthesized as the research progressed.

The second research stage allowed for a more focused approach by utilizing an online web-based survey questionnaire, consisting of limited open-ended and multiple choice questions. Significantly, the online survey provided a purposive sample of data on the research issues, larger in scope than the face to face interviews. It was envisaged that the use of this additional instrument would increase the validity of the findings, as proposed by Marshall & Rossman (2010, pp. 104-105) and as favoured by Patton (2002, p. 306). Web-based surveys have become more widely used in the last ten years and are regarded as inexpensive, with a short response time and able to achieve satisfying response rates compared to questionnaires delivered by 'classical' mail (Ganassali, 2008, p. 21). Web-based surveys are also regarded as having lower respondent errors and increasing the completeness of response (McDonald & Stewart Adam, 2003, p. 85).

Fontana and Frey (2005) recognized the fact that computer surveys were becoming more widely used as part of the data gathering process and stated that developments in computer-assisted interviewing had called into question the division between traditional modes of interviewing such as the survey interview and the mail survey (p. 703) They observed that:

...today we are really looking at a continuum of data-collecting methods rather than clearly divided methods; in fact... many surveys today incorporate a variety of data-gathering methods driven by concerns such as time constraints, financial demands, and other practical elements (p. 703).

Consequently, it was envisaged that an online survey promoted by the ASA (a national organization with approximately 3,000 members from all Australian States and Territories) would obtain pertinent responses from a wide geographic spectrum of authors, implemented by using a web-based survey mechanism such as 'Survey Monkey', a user-friendly research tool commonly used by academics.

The substantive content of the survey, entitled '*Authors, Copyright and the Digital Evolution*' consisted of seven pages, which included '*Demographic information*', '*Your views on copyright*', *The existing copyright framework*', '*The publishing industry*' and '*Publishing on the internet.*' The questions were presented in three formats, which included limited open-ended questions, allowing for a paragraph of comment per subject. The second format used was that of multiple questions, where the subject matter lent itself to such a format. The third type of questions used was 'likert' scale choices, employed to scale participants' responses in relation to the questionnaire topics. The survey instrument allowed for 'filtering', which enabled the elimination of unpublished author responses to focus on results related to published authors. It further provided a function for cross tabulating results. This facility also enabled comparison of the results of part time and full time authors.

Limitations

There were certain inherent limitations in the techniques employed during the two stages, due to practical considerations associated with in-depth interviews and the procurement of online survey respondents. The limited number of author interviews conducted (17 out of 40 requests) was reflective of the limitations of this method, such as unavailability, a reluctance to be interviewed, expense considerations and time factors. However, the purposive sample nevertheless allowed for in-depth discussion and provided insight into authors' subjective viewpoints on the research issues as proposed by Patton (2002, p. 45).

Whilst the online survey had the advantage of being cost effective and accessible to a large group of authors, there were limitations to a web-based approach. The total number of 177 responses obtained in the online survey represented a relatively small group in view of the number of possible respondents. Possible respondents included members of the ASA (3,000) and an unknown number of members of the various Writers' Centres that provided links to the survey. These response figures were reflective of the limitations imposed by the online survey method. One significant limitation was the fact that responses were limited to users of the internet. This created a risk of non-response bias, which presented a threat to making inferences from the data obtained (Bech & Kristensen, 2009, p. 3). As a result, the data was utilized as targeted qualitative, rather than quantitative data, providing the researcher with insight into the research questions rather than the ability to draw generalisations.

Limitations on the part of respondents may include: a lack of online facilities (although it would be presumed that most authors would have access to the internet), a lack of interest in the subject matter, apathy on the issue of copyright, a lack of understanding of the issues involved resulting in a reluctance to participate, a lack of motivation, a lack of time and a general reluctance to complete surveys. However, in the context of similar surveys, such as the national *Queensland University of Technology Survey on Academic Authorship, Publishing Agreements and Open access* (Austin, Heffernan & David, 2008) - where emails with survey links were sent directly to 27,385 academics, and only 509 responses were received - it appears that the level of interest displayed by authors in the present survey was not unusual.

However, whilst these limitations are acknowledged, based on the purposeful sampling strategy with the inherent purpose of 'in-depth understanding' as identified by Patton (2002, p. 230), the results of the survey provided sufficient data for meaningful analysis and discussion within the framework of this paper. The findings are thus incorporated into this discussion to provide some meaningful insights from authors' viewpoints on the effect of books being sold across territorial borders, whether in digital or print form (Cantatore, 2012). In the discussion below, authors' and publishers' comments were made within the context of this research, unless otherwise indicated.

A Global Milieu: Digital Copyright Challenges

The concept of a 'heavenly library' where books resided in digital form was discussed in some depth by Sherman Young (2007) in his book *The book is dead, long live the book*. This was by no means a new thought – the idea was previously framed as a 'heavenly jukebox' by Goldstein (2003) in his book where he predicted 'a digital repository of books, movies and music available on demand' (p. 184).

Young (2007) subsequently extended this idea of a 'heavenly jukebox' by relating music to books and imagined the 'heavenly library' 'as the world's collection of books available in an instant.' (p. 15). This concept, according to Young, had a number of advantages over printed books, including more flexibility and ease of publishing for publishers, greater accessibility for readers, environmental advantages, lower costs and portability. As early as 1993, Rawlins had enumerated the advantages of e-books as being 'cheap, long lasting, easily copied, quickly acquired, easily searched and portable in bulk' (1993, p. 475).

The research findings showed that these advantages were recognized by many authors who saw the digital market as a new way to connect with readers and transform the book supply chain. Full time authors in particular appreciate the growing significance of the internet market place and the advantages of making their books available in digital form. During the course of this research, over a period of 3-4 years, e-reading technology has also advanced rapidly and most of the interviewees and survey participants were conscious of the inroads made into traditional publishing by devices such as iPhones, iPads, Kindle, etc. New devices are constantly being introduced into the marketplace, and the concept of a digital environment where all books, music and films are available at the click of a button has become a reasonable expectation rather than a potential promise.

So what are the perceived disadvantages of a 'heavenly library'? Apart from considerations that book lovers may no longer have a library filled with printed books due to the smart economics of buying e-books online, and that we may see a demise of the traditional book culture as a result, authors raised concerns about digital copyright protection.

Although authors have obtained new publishing and distribution opportunities in the decentralised publishing sphere of the internet, copyright enforcement has become more onerous as a result of electronic publishing. In a recent paper delivered by Richard Hooper CBE (2012) in Sydney he recognised that there was a global 'battlefield' between supporters of the notion that the internet should be free on the one hand, and the creative industries wanting to protect their intellectual property and copyright on the other. The Hooper Report included a feasibility study for the *Digital Copyright Exchange*, a key recommendation of the *Hargreaves Report* (2011).

The complexity of copyright law and licencing has been a stumbling block for many authors in asserting their copyright online. The Australian survey findings showed that nearly 80 per cent of all respondents were concerned about their digital copyright. Most of the author comments related to theft of work on electronic media or 'online piracy'. Some authors cited instances of copyright breaches on their internet publications without any apparent solutions.

It is significant that, although they acknowledged that illegal online copying was a real concern for them as the current copyright structure did not seem to address the problem adequately, more than half of the survey respondents admitted to doing nothing to protect their copyright online. Several respondents specifically cited a lack of knowledge on e-book copyright as a problem and voiced concerns about a lack of time and funds to pursue copyright breaches on the internet. Whilst these concerns were common amongst authors, equally prevalent was the lack of any action taken with regard to copyright breaches. In addition, publishers did not provide a shield for authors against online copyright infringement, with most authors and publishers apparently accepting the inevitability of copyright infringements on the internet.

Those authors who took protective steps employed different measures to protect and regulate the use of their online copyright material. Significantly, less than one-fifth of survey respondents used digital rights management (DRM) to prevent the copying of their work. Some expressed reservations about the use of DRM and described it as 'a barrier' to readers buying their books. Whilst most respondents stated that it was 'impossible' to protect their copyright online, just under a tenth favoured flexible licensing models - such as the Creative Commons - which recognise authors' moral rights and provide licensing options in the Australian *Copyright Act* 1968 (section 89).

Although the Creative Commons had been in operation for over 10 years, slightly less than half of survey respondents admitted that they were not familiar with the concept, while approximately 36 per cent expressed support for the Creative Commons. Considering the nature of the respondents (published authors) one may have expected a greater awareness of this licensing option. It is noted however, that interviewees who supported the Creative Commons were generally also bloggers, who had more internet knowledge than others who had not previously published work online. It appears that this provides an opportunity for the Creative Commons concept to be better marketed to this group of professionals who would be a logical stakeholder group. However, a significant perceived drawback of the Creative Commons licensing scheme is that it does not prescribe licensing fees or financial remuneration for participants due to its voluntary character.

As an alternative protective measure, nearly 36 per cent of the survey respondents stated that they posted warnings on their websites or on the creative work itself, and 13 per cent used 'other means' of copyright protection such as relying on their publishers and taking note of daily Google alerts advising of illegal file sharing sites.

Significantly, as some authors pointed out, the problem with protecting online copyright was that it was usually not commercially viable to pursue offenders in the case of a breach. It was noted that international copyright was a grey area and that legal advice would not necessarily help to resolve practical issues. The findings showed that the prohibitive costs of protecting their copyright and litigating overseas was a stumbling block for most Australian authors, which was evidenced by the absence of Australian copyright litigation on books.

An issue of specific concern to authors was how the digital economy impacted on their existing territorial copyright, the dilution of which seemed inevitable. It was suggested by some authors that it would be short-sighted for countries to attempt territorial changes - such as the suggested lifting of parallel import restrictions - when publishing agreements were already being impacted by digital technologies. Others saw no reason for dividing territories up geographically where digital rights were concerned, arguing that consumers would expect to have access to digital contents worldwide, irrespective of where they lived. The findings also showed that the possibility of self-publication had effectively removed traditional territorial barriers for authors.

It is evident that most publishers have already come to the realisation that they need to acquire worldwide digital rights when they purchase a book and that authors and organisations such as the ASA are becoming acutely aware of the importance of world digital rights (Loukakis 2010, p.4). Although the Productivity Commission study on parallel importing (2009) raised authors' awareness of the dilemma of territorial copyright - which relies on the enforcement of copyright law as a national prerogative - the digital sphere has made it increasingly difficult to cling to existing copyright models. In Australia, the Harper Panel (Competition Policy Review, 2015) reviewing competition law and policy recommended abolition of the remaining restrictions on parallel importation. The Government subsequently announced support for removing parallel import restrictions on books.

Territorial copyright protection is in a state of flux, as is evidenced by the inevitable encroachment of online booksellers, such as Amazon, on these rights by selling books across international borders. Significantly, the Australian *Copyright Act* 1968 (section 44F) of provides that there are no restrictions on importation of an electronic literary work, except that it must be a 'non-infringing copy' (i.e. made lawfully in the country of origin), thus significantly affording no parallel import protection on digital books.

Sally Collings, Australian author and publisher, expressed the view that the territorialism that had existed in publishing for decades, would become a non-issue as digital books became more prevalent (Cantatore 2012). This viewpoint was supported by author and self-publisher John Kelly, who said that the possibility of self-publication has effectively removed traditional territorial barriers. In an online article '*Publish and be damned* (2009)' he stated that self-publishers 'have access to a world-wide market by submitting their book to Google Books and Amazon and Lulu's websites, all available for a start-up cost of less than $100.00.' On the issue of the deregulation of publishing and parallel importing, he said:

The very nature of competition has been turned on its head and the once revered retail bookstore is staring its use-by date down the barrel just like the neighbourhood hardware store. But it isn't the threat of de-regulation that places it in this invidious position. The internet already has! One can debate the positive and negative impacts of this development, but it has nothing to do with government regulation.

Kelly's observations were pertinent as he raised two issues, not only that of self-publication and the greater freedom it allowed, but also the fact that many books were bought online today across territorial copyright borders, rendering government regulation secondary to practical realities.

These authors' and publishers' comments support the argument that the internet has expanded the boundaries of copyright protection and that current legislative structures may not offer authors the necessary protection in the digital economy. Several authors mentioned the need for new copyright solutions, although the findings showed divergent views on the subject. While some suggested that authors should be more proactive in their approach to copyright, others were of the view that the existing copyright structure was insufficiently suited to copyright use in the digital domain. Most authors showed an awareness of the challenges facing their profession in the expanding literary sphere in the digital domain but - perhaps not surprisingly - not many solutions were being offered. Authors who were most optimistic about the future of online publishing acknowledged the limitations of DRM technology, yet there appeared to be few other viable income producing copyright options available.

In a fairly recent report, the Australian Book Industry Strategy Group (BISG) (2011) recognised the problems associated with protection of digital copyright and the necessity for reform. They recommended that the Australian Law Reform Commission (ALRC) should 'consult directly with the book industry through its author and publishers associations when it next reviews copyright issues' (p. 68), Furthermore, they suggested that the Government should work with internet industries, to adopt a binding industry code on copyright infringement by internet service providers, to protect online copyright. These recommendations are commendable, but would require not only a focused intention by the ALRC and Government to alleviate current digital copyright concerns, but also practical and enforceable measures, such as the punitive sanctions and anti-piracy copyright education campaign proposed by the ASA (Loukakis, 2011, p. 6).

In more recent copyright developments in Australia, the ALRC has released a Discussion Paper on *Copyright in the Digital Economy* (2013), calling for submissions from stakeholders. It considers several options for reform, set out in the Terms of Reference, one of which is the possible recognition of 'fair use' of copyright material in the *Copyright Act* 1968 (as opposed to the current closed list of permitted purposes for 'fair dealing'), which will allow for expanded transformative use (2012, p. 24). Such an inclusion will align the Australian copyright approach with US provisions for 'fair use', and will create a wider range of copyright exceptions, especially relevant on the internet.

The collection of royalties internationally continues to be a problem. A number of authors voiced the concern that copyright measures and royalty schemes based in Australia did not sufficiently address the issue of loss of revenue from overseas sources, such as sales on the internet and copyright infringements which occurred overseas. This concern is being fuelled by the blurring of territorial copyright zones as a result of new media structures and the expanding use of electronic devices. It is evident that these problems can only exacerbate as online publishing becomes more prevalent and territorial borders become less defined.

Surprisingly, the findings revealed that many authors did not favour a hard line enforcement of electronic copyright, which may account for their lack of preventative action. There were those who saw the internet as a marketing opportunity and employed 'soft' licensing practices such as the Creative Commons, and others who were happy to provide their creative work not only DRM free, but also free of charge. The findings also showed an increased awareness of the necessity for changing business models and a need to embrace the digital market, as proprietary branded electronic readers become more widespread.

It has also become apparent that licensing terms and conditions are becoming paramount in the digital milieu, especially in relation to e-books, such as Kindle sales. This trend reflects the observations of John and Reid (2011), that owners' and users' copying rights are now being determined more by individual licenses and less by provisions in copyright law than in the past. It also supports Young's contention that copyright requires a re-assessment in the digital environment (2007, pp. 158-159). At the very least, publishers and authors must now apply close scrutiny to the terms and conditions of international electronic licensing agreements such as Google and Kindle agreements, to avoid the power of the individual –both author and localised publisher—sliding backward as global publishing giants advance forward.

The Demise of Territorial Copyright

It has been noted above that the *Berne Convention* provides guidelines on the treatment of copyright in extra-territorial works, requiring that foreign works should enjoy the same protection as local works. These guidelines are implemented by various national copyright protections such as the USA *Copyright Act* 1976, the UK Copyright, Designs and Patents Act 1988 and the Australian *Copyright Act* 1968. Restrictions on the parallel importation of books have regulated the importation and sale of printed books, and are enforced in these countries. However, internet publications and sales of printed books in the digital economy have limited the usefulness of these measures, as seen in the recent US *Kirtsaeng* (2013) case, discussed below.

The Parallel Import Debate in Australia

In Australia, current parallel importation provisions allow a restriction on importation of printed copyright material into Australia, which provide Australian publishers with a 30-day window to distribute a local version of a book (and 90 days to resupply) before competing overseas publishers may distribute the same product in Australia (*Copyright Act 1968* (Cth) ss 102 and 112A). The US *Copyright Act* 1976 (s 104) provides a similar protection for copyright works of national origin.

The Australian parallel import provisions were under review between 2006-2009, with lobbyists advocating the removal of these restrictive provisions in the legislation. The Australian Productivity Commission conducted an investigation into the nature, role and importance of intangibles, including intellectual property, to Australia's economic performance, as well as the effect of copyright restrictions on the parallel importation of books. Two hundred and sixty-eight (268) submissions were put forward to the Productivity Commission during 2008 by authors on the issue of parallel importing (Productivity Commission Report, 2009).

In their submissions to the Productivity Commission, many authors provided examples of how they felt the current parallel import restrictions (PIRs) had benefited them, or how the potential removal of the restrictions might affect them. Nick Earls argued that, allowing parallel imports would 'undermine authors' incomes', 'destroy the local market', and present 'a serious disincentive towards Australian publishers publishing new Australian books' (Submission, 2008, pp. 8-9). Garth Nix pointed out that territorial copyright provided publishers with certainty, which encouraged them to invest in Australian authors and Australian books (Submission, 2008, p. 7). Without that certainty there would be less incentive to invest in Australian books, and consequently the opportunities for Australian authors would be fewer. In addition, Thomas Keneally foresaw the gradual demise of the Australian publishing industry, cautioning: 'Both authors and literary agents, particularly those whose interest is explicitly Australian, would be facing shrinking resources and contracts'(Submission, 2008, pp. 4-5.) Many authors also stated that, in the absence of parallel import restrictions, they would lose control over the sales of their books. Once the rights to books were sold overseas, authors would no longer be able to control which edition of the book was sold in Australia, potentially impacting on their returns. Furthermore, some new or undiscovered authors could find it more difficult to gain attention in an open market (Productivity Commission Submissions 2008). Despite the 268 author submissions (in addition to those of publishers and booksellers), against the proposed abolition of the parallel import restrictions, the Productivity Commission recommended that the Government repeal Australia's parallel import restrictions for books (Productivity Commission Report, 2009).

However, the final result of the investigation was that the Government, under pressure from authors and publishers, rejected the recommendations of the Productivity Commission to phase out parallel import control, and instead retained the status quo. Whilst the brief euphoria in the midst of Australian publishers and authors was well founded, it has since become evident that these protective provisions in s 102 of the Australian *Copyright Act* would not protect authors and publishers from infringements occurring in the digital sphere. As noted above, the Australian *Copyright Act* does not place any restrictions on importation of electronic literary works - except that they must be 'non-infringing copies'. It also remains to be seen what the effect of the current review (ALRC, 2013) of the Act will be. To be adequately informed in making recommendations, significant research by the ALRC and broad consultation with the Australian community and copyright creators will be required (Loukakis, 2012). The final report of the ALRC is due on 30 November 2013.

During their interviews, authors and publishers participating in the research stated specific instances in which they had encountered copyright problems. A mainstream publisher explained the difficulties in enforcing copyright internationally as follows: 'The thing that is probably the most confusing here is the way that book rights are transacted internationally. You can have an originating publisher in one country with rights to sell in another country.' She saw this as a major problem in the Google book scanning case [*The Authors Guild et al v Google, Inc*, (2009)], where the American edition of an Australian publication may have been scanned by Google, but the Australian metadata applied. This caused confusion about who the actual rights holder of such a book was and, consequently, made it difficult to enforce copyright. The Google settlement falls outside the scope of this article; however, the issues raised by Google's unauthorised book scanning initiative are inextricably linked to the operation and inadequacy of existing copyright structures.

Another publisher observed that, even though Australia applied parallel import restrictions, authors routinely experienced problems with illegal parallel importation of their books from countries such as China or India. Where illegal copies were being sold by reputable booksellers, whether online or in the retail market, the problem could be addressed by sending a letter requesting them to cease and desist from selling the book, but it was difficult to control offshore operators and internet marketers. She explained that authors did not benefit financially from remainder deals that are sold at cost or below cost, as contracts generally provide that the author does not benefit once the book is sold by the publisher for less than the printing costs. This means that if a book by an Australian author is remaindered in the USA and sold into Australia at remainder cost, the author does not receive anything, even if the book is sold at full price in Australia.

Frank Moorhouse recognised further problems with regard to the collection of royalties internationally. 'It is difficult to police copyright zones in English speaking countries', he said, referring to the problems of international collecting agencies. He ascribed this difficulty to the difference in the law and ethos of different English speaking countries, which was evidenced in the 'tricks, fraud and danger' inherent in protecting copyright internationally. These problems were less evident in compact cultural groups, such as the Danish, for example, who were confined to one country. For this reason, collecting agencies in Scandinavian countries were more successful than English speaking, European countries.

Nick Earls also experienced a problem with his copyright when he discovered that copies of his novel *ZigZag Street* were being sold on remainder tables outside newsagents in Australia, in breach of copyright provisions. In this instance, his UK publisher had overstocked and copies of the novel found their way to a remainder house in the UK, where they were bundled up and sent to Australia with other books, in breach of his territorial rights. He recognised, however, that it was difficult to prevent this from happening or to stop the newsagents from selling the books, as they had bought the books in good faith, thinking that they were legally entitled to sell them.

These comments accord with the concern voiced by a number of authors: that copyright measures and royalty schemes based in Australia do not sufficiently address the issue of loss of revenue from overseas sources, such as sales on the internet and copyright infringements which occur overseas. This concern is being fuelled by a number of issues: the blurring of territorial copyright zones as a result of new media structures (and the expanding use of electronic devices) and actions by organisations such as Google, who actively defy traditional copyright expectations.

In Australia - as in the case of the UK and US - territorial rights remain in existence. Although the ASA has cautioned authors to ensure that these rights remain protected in the digital domain (Loukakis, 2010) it is clear that authors will find this advice more and more difficult to implement, considering the global reach of the online book market, which has made it unlikely for any publisher to accept a book without securing the world rights. This trend points to a dilution of the value of territorial rights in the digital economy, which supports Young's (2007) contention that the industry requires a new copyright infrastructure (pp. 158-159).

Additionally, the realities of applying the 'first sale doctrine' to books imported from another country and then sold in the country of origin, as was the case in *Kirtsaeng,* puts paid to the idea that territorial rights will necessarily protect US rights holders from the impact of cross-border sales.

The Kirtsaeng Case

In the recent US case of *Kirtsaeng v John Wiley & Sons* (2013), Kirtsaeng, a Cornell University student, purchased mathematics text books from his home country Thailand (with the assistance of friends) and then resold them on eBay to students in the US. The texts were English foreign editions and only authorised for sale in Europe, Asia, Africa and the Middle East. The issue to be decided was how s 602 (which prohibits the importation of works into the US without the copyright owner's permission) and s 109 (dealing with the first sale doctrine) of the *Copyright Act* applied to copies of books made and legally acquired abroad, and then imported into the US. The Supreme Court held by a 6-3 majority that US copyright owners may not prevent importation and reselling of copyrighted content lawfully sold abroad, due to the application of the 'first sale doctrine' (2013, p. 2). The effect of the first sale doctrine (also referred to as an 'exhaustion of rights'), is that the publisher's copyright is exhausted once a book is lawfully purchased. The majority opinion in this case stated from the outset that the first sale doctrine applied to lawfully made copyright works, even when made in a foreign country (2013, p. 2).

It is significant that the Court read the Act as imposing no geographical limitation. This approach was in contrast to the Lower Court decision in the case *John Wiley & Sons, Inc. v Kirtsaeng* (2011). In the earlier decision the Court had found in favour of Wiley, who relied on s 602 of the Act and argued that Kirtsaeng could not rely on the first sale doctrine (s 109) as it only applied to works manufactured in the US.

The 6-3 division in the Supreme Court decision is reflective of the controversy surrounding the interpretation and application of these two provisions in the Act. Previously, in the *Costco Wholesale* case (2010) the Court was divided 4-4 on this issue, and in the earlier decision *Quality King* (1998) the Court held that s 109 limited the scope of s 602, leaving open the question whether US copyright owners could retain control over the importation of copies manufactured and sold abroad (p. 135).

In her dissenting judgment in *Kirtsaeng* Justice Ginsburg criticised the reasoning of the majority, stating that the majority's interpretation of the *Copyright Act* was 'at odds with Congress' aim to protect copyright owners against the unauthorized importation of low-priced, foreign made copies of their copyrighted works (2013, p.10).' She also expressed the viewpoint that 'the Court embrace(d) an international-exhaustion rule that could benefit US consumers but would likely disadvantage foreign holders of US copyrights (2013, p. 28).'

The Supreme Court in *Kirtsaeng* thus resolved the case in favour of permitting parallel importation by relying on the first sale doctrine. Despite the argument that this interpretation favours consumers by providing them with cheaper options, the flipside is that rights holders in written work could be disadvantaged by the erosion of their territorial rights. Principally, this decision illustrates how easily territorial copyright provisions may be circumvented, and the potential far-reaching impact on authors and publishers globally in the future.

CONCLUSION: FUTURE SOLUTIONS

In conclusion, it has become evident that the traditional application of territorial copyright and parallel import restrictions no longer serve to protect copyright holders, due to the impact of digital sales and also due the application of the 'first sale doctrine' in the US. For now, parallel import restrictions apply to printed books, but will they become obsolete in the digital age? It is apparent that new copyright solutions are required, which require authors and publishers to embrace digital technology, improve their knowledge of online publishing and apply alternative creative publishing models. As internet publishing and cross-border sales increase, new business models are needed. We have seen that DRM has been criticised as being too restrictive, yet for many authors and publishers its use has been instrumental in protecting their copyright. On the internet a variety of licencing solutions have been proposed, including models such as the Creative Commons and various 'pay-per-view' schemes, the most widely used of which is possibly the licensing of *Kindle* books by Amazon.

More recently, the implementation of a 'Digital Copyright Exchange' has been investigated and recommended by the Hooper Report in the UK (2012). This system takes the form of an automated licensing machine on a web portal, which allows the user to agree on a price and use of the content, in order to obtain a licence and download the content. It is proposed that this exchange will be part of a 'Copyright Hub' which will serve an educational function, introduce a voluntary Rights Registry and provide access to the digital copyright exchange. Whilst the system will predominantly accommodate low transaction amounts associated with music downloads, it will also serve the book industry by providing licensing options for digital publications (Hooper, 2012, p. 30).

Savikas (2013), CEO of *Safari Books Online*, has described the benefits of running subscription-based e-book service models similar to the cloud entertainment subscription services. Services such as *Spotify, Rdio* and *Netflix* are widely used by consumers, and whether or not this will be feasible for digital books remains to be seen. Clearly future solutions for authors and publishers in the book industry will need to be flexible and internationally focussed. In order to effectively monetise their creative efforts, authors will need to be pro-active, embrace the realities of the marketplace and revise their views of what constitutes a 'book sale' in the digital economy.

REFERENCES

Austin, A. C., Heffernan, M., & David, N. (2008). *Academic Authorship, Publishing Agreements and Open Access (Research Report)*. Brisbane, Australia: Queensland University of Technology.

Australian Law Reform Commission. (2012). *Copyright and the Digital Economy (IP 42)* (Government Report, Canberra). Retrieved June 18, 2013, from http://www.alrc.gov.au/publications/copyright-ip42

Australian Law Reform Commission. (2013). *Copyright and the Digital Economy (DP 79)* (Government Report, Canberra). Retrieved on June 18, 2013, from http://www.alrc.gov.au/publications/copyright-ip42

Bech, M., & Kristensen, B. (2009). Differential Response Rates in Postal and Web-based Surveys among Older Respondents. *Survey Research Methods, 3*(1), 1–6.

Berne Convention for the Protection of Literary and Artistic Works, July 24, 1971.

Brannen, J. (2004). Working Qualitatively and Quantitatively. In C. Seale, D. Silverman, J. F. Gubrium, & G. Gobo (Eds.), *Qualitative Research Practice* (pp. 312–315). London: Sage Publications. doi:10.4135/9781848608191.d25

Buchanan, E. A. (2004). *Readings in Virtual Research Ethics: Issues and Controversies*. Hershey, PA: Idea Group Publishing. doi:10.4018/978-1-59140-152-0

Cantatore, F. (2011). *Authors, Copyright and the Digital Evolution*. Retrieved on November 20, 2011, from http://www.surveymonkey.com

Cantatore, F. (2012). *Negotiating a changing landscape: Authors, Copyright and the Digital Evolution* (Unpublished doctoral dissertation). Bond University, Queensland, Australia.

Copyright Act 1968 (Cth) (Australia).

Copyright Act 1976 (USA).

Copyright, Designs and Patents Act 1988 (UK).

Costco Wholesale Corp. v Omega, SA 131 S.C. 565 US (2010).

Denzin, N. K., & Lincoln, Y. S. (Eds.). (2005). *Handbook of Qualitative Research* (2nd ed.). London: Sage Publications.

Earls, N. (2008). *Submission to Productivity Commission, Canberra*. Retrieved on November 20, 2011, from http://www.pc.gov.au/projects/study/books/submissions#initial

Fontana, A., & Frey, J. H. (2005). The Interview: From Neutral Stance to Political Involvement. In N. K. Denzin & Y. S. Lincoln (Eds.), *Handbook of Qualitative Research* (3rd ed.; pp. 695–728). London: Sage Publications.

Ganalassi, S. (2008). The Influence of the Design of Web Survey Questionnaires on the Quality of Responses. *Survey Research Methods*, 2(1), 21–32.

Goldstein, P. (2003). *Copyright's highway: From Gutenberg to the Celestial Jukebox*. Stanford, CA: Stanford University Press.

Hargreaves, I. (2011). Digital opportunity: A review of intellectual property and growth. London: Government Research Report.

Harper, I. (2015). *Competition Policy Review*. Australian Government. Retrieved on 13 April at http://competitionpolicyreview.gov.au/

Hooper, R. (2012). *The Hooper Report*. London: Government Research Report. Retrieved on June 6, 2013 at http://www.ipo.gov.uk/types/hargreaves.htm

John Wiley & Sons, Inc. v Kirtsaeng 54F. 3d 210 (2d Cir. 2011).

Jones, B. (2011). Book Industry Strategy Group Report. Canberra, Australia: Government Research Report.

Kelly, J. (2009). *Publish and be damned*. Retrieved on May 19, 2011 from http://www.abc.net.au

Keneally, T. (2008). *Submission to Productivity Commission, Canberra*. Retrieved on November 20, 2011, from http://www.pc.gov.au/projects/study/books/submissions#initial

Kirtsaeng v John Wiley & Sons 568 U.S. WL 1104736 (U.S. Mar. 19, 2013).

Loukakis, A. (2010) *Warning: More ebook loopholes*. Retrieved on December 10, 2010, http://www.asauthors.org

Marshall, C., & Rossman, G. B. (2010). *Designing Qualitative Research* (5th ed.). London: Sage Publications.

McDonald, H., & Adam, S. (2003). A Comparison of Online and Postal Data Collection Methods in Marketing Research. *Marketing Intelligence & Planning, 21*(2), 85–95. doi:10.1108/02634500310465399

Nix, G. (2008). *Submission to Productivity Commission, Canberra*. Retrieved on November 20, 2011, from http://www.pc.gov.au/projects/study/books/submissions#initial

Oakes, L. (2001). *Language and national identity: Comparing France and Sweden*. Philadelphia: John Benjamins Publishing Company. doi:10.1075/impact.13

Patton, M. Q. (2002). *Qualitative Research and Evaluation Methods* (3rd ed.). London: Sage Publications.

Productivity Commission. (2009). *Restrictions on the Parallel Importation of Books*. Retrieved on November 20, 2011, from http://www.pc.gov.au/projects/study/books/report

Quality King Distributors, Inc. v. L'anza Research Int'l, Inc. - 523 U.S. 135 (1998).

Rawlins, G. J. E. (1993). Publishing over the next decade. *Journal of the American Society for Information Science, 44*(8), 474–479. doi:10.1002/(SICI)1097-4571(199309)44:8<474::AID-ASI6>3.0.CO;2-3

Savikas, A. (2013). *The future of publishing*. Podcast, January 15, 2013. Retrieved on June 18, 2013 from http://nextmarket.co/blogs/conversations/7178184-andrew-savikas-ceo-of-safari-books-on-book-publishing-models-social-reading-and-more

Stake, R. E. (2005). Qualitative Case Studies. In N. K. Denzin & Y. S. Lincoln (Eds.), *Handbook of Qualitative Research* (3rd ed.; pp. 443–466). London: Sage Publications.

Survey Monkey. (2013). Retrieved on June 17, 2013 from http://www.surveymonkey.com

The Authors Guild et al v Google, Inc , (2009) US District Court, Southern District of New York, No. 05-08136 1.

Young, S. (2007). *The book is dead, long live the book*. Sydney: The University of New South Wales Press Ltd.

Chapter 8

The Importance of Electronics News Brand Trust:
The Case of Online Newspapers in Indonesia

Elia Ardyan
STIE Surakarta, Indonesia

Vincent Didiek Wiet Aryanto
Universitas Dian Nuswantoro, Indonesia

ABSTRACT

The purpose of this book chapter is to test the importance of trust to increase the loyalty of e-news brand readers in Indonesia and to test its antecedents. Trust becomes a central factor in the electronics news brand to increase the loyalty of its readers. Within this chapter, trust in news electronics brand influenced by the reader's experience and customer confusion. Exciting experience and unforgettable experiences influenced by the attributes of the news brand electronics. The readers' experiences will be able to reduce customer confusion and will increase confidence in the electronics news brand significantly. Basically, consumers are not confused in the electronics news brand. Other results showed that the attached attributes to electronics news brand will be able to significantly increase readers' loyalty.

INTRODUCTION

Newspaper is considered as the world's information resources (Strebler, Robinson, & Heron, 1997) that has developed over the years. Originally, newspaper is produced in a print version, but the Internet is revolutionizing it (Nilssen, Bertheussen, & Dreyer, 2015) and the development of online newspapers increases so rapidly (Arikunto, 2010). The development of the Internet forced many companies to redefine how to reach and remain relevant to its target audience (Harden & Heyman, 2009). Some well-known brands such as Tribune Co. newspaper, New York Times, the Tucson Citizen, Boston and many popular newspaper brands in USA should close his business. Ranaweera and Prabhu (2003)found out that a

DOI: 10.4018/978-1-5225-1779-5.ch008

decrease in audience is caused by several things, such as the change towards free news, failed model of alternative income, advertisers for online media is reinforced by the current economic crisis, changes in the production process of news and changes in the usage patterns of news. Besides, the Internet also plays a role in the decline of the traditional newspaper circulation. The Internet has changed the access, production and circulation of information (Shen, Wu, Chen, & Fang, 2016). Internet provides access speed that is not owned by traditional media. Internet makes everything easier. The development of the Internet is also supported by the development of a variety of media that can access the Internet directly, such as mobile phone, smartphone, and a variety of other media. The emergence of "net native" or "digital net" generation (Carrol, 1991) or the generation that grew and comfortable with the Internet environment makes an online newspaper preferred over the traditional one. Developments that trigger various online brands began to appear, either because of the development of communication, technology, or information (Morgan-Thomas & Veloutsou, 2013).

Online newspaper provides a variety of important benefits to readers. Some of the benefits of online newspaper is helping the increase in frequencies and create a platform for sharing information quickly across countries (Nilssen et al., 2015), supporting environmental perspective (Attaran, Divandari, & Adinov, 2012), and it is more interactive than the print media (Capaldo, Iandoli, & Ponsiglione, 2004; Cheng & Dainty, 2003). Chaston, Badger, and Sadler-Smith (1999), Explain that online use in the newspaper industry gives a speed for news to reach readers. A low cost of distributing information, a possibility for news updates constantly, and an opportunity to build a more direct contact and interaction with the users. Development of the Internet, like Web 2.0, allows people to instantly produce and disseminate news items online (Atakan-Duman & Ozdora-Aksak, 2014). Although online newspaper has many benefits, but the emergence of online newspaper will be cannibals for the print newspaper (Shen et al., 2016; Shnayder, van Rijnsoeve, & Hekkert, 2016).

Trust becomes an important part in the online environment. Trust is one of the success factors that can enhance the competitive advantage in electronic commerce environment. The increase of confidence by 75% occurs in the use of social media (Eldeman Trust, 2012). Managers should be able to increase customer confidence in the brand. Some literature explain that consumers' trust in the brand is caused by several things, such as satisfaction, experience, perceived value, perceived risk, service quality and reputation (Benedicktus, 2011; Delgado-Ballester & Munuera-Aleman, 2001; Eastlick, Lotz, & Warrington, 2006; Ha & Perks, 2005; Harris & Goode, 2004; McKnight, Choundhury, & Kacmar, 2002b; Sahin, Zehir, & Kitapci, 2011; Singh & Sirdeshmukh, 2000; Tanrikulu & Celilbatur, 2013). The increase of trust will be able to influence the behavior of customer loyalty (Gommans, Krishnan, & Scheffold, 2001; Harris & Goode, 2004; Sahin et al., 2011).

The increase in electronic news brand (e-news brand) does not only give positive effect on journalistic industry, the easiness in making news-themed website also give effect to the increase in the interest to make e-news brand. The phenomenon in Indonesia is that there are various e-news brands emerge but the news provided is not the real fact. For instance, e-news brand is used for black campaign in political world. There is a lot of hoax news given to assassin someone's character. There are many e-news brands copying news from other e-news brand. Those are some causes of the decrease in the trust of newspaper readers.

The aim of this research is to test the importance of trust to increase the loyalty of e-news brand readers in Indonesia and to test its antecendent.

BACKGROUND

Electronic News Brand

Brand is an important thing in a company. It is the heart of marketing and business strategy (Mascarenhas, Kesavan, & Bernacchi, 2006).The managers should use a systematic approach to build a strong brand. The reason of doing this is that brand can influence business performance(Newton, 2001). A negative brand reputation will ruin the company and decrease the business performance.

In general, brand is a name that is attached to the product. Kotler and Keller (2012) Defines brand as the name, shape, signal, symbol, or design or a combination of these that identify and distinguish our products with competitors. Technically, this definition makes the manager would have to create a new name, logo, symbols, and others (Schindehutte, Morris, & Kocak, 2008). The name was created to be unique and different from its competitors, because the brand is used as a differentiator with competitors. Brand is a name that has the power to influence the market (Kapferer, 2008). In its development, the brand is no longer just the name that is attached to the product. Peteraf and Barney (2003) explain that the brand is not just a name but a firm promise, a promise to give something to the consumer

The focus of this study is online brand in the newspaper company. The concept developed is electronic news brand (e-brand news). We define e-brand news as a name in the form of an online newspaper that provides a variety of information and news openly.

E-News Brand Attribute

Attributes defined as a description of characteristics attached to a product or service (Keller, 1993)or what customers thought about a product or service. Attribute is divided into 2 types: intrinsic and extrinsic attribute. Intrinsic attributes are attributes that are associated with the product / brand. Extrinsic attributes are external aspects of the products or services associated with purchase. Keller (1993) explains 4 types of extrinsic attribute:

1. Price information.
2. Packaging or product appearance information.
3. User imagery.
4. Usage imagery.

Some experts say that there are some attributes that have a significant effect on online branding (de Chernatony & Christodoulides, 2004; Phillips, 2001).
The attributes include:

1. Fulfillment / reliability.
2. Customer service / responsiveness / care.
3. Website design / ease of use / site design.
4. Financial security / privacy / security / trust.
5. Interactivity / customization / personalization.

Sheng and Teo (2012) uses a utilitarian dimension attribute (ease of use and perceived usefulness) and hedonic (entertainment and aesthetics) to see the effects on brand equity. Sheng and Teo (2012) developed the concept of e-airline brand attributes into six indicators, the efficiency of the site, system availability, privacy, site's attractiveness, and price. In the context of an online newspaper, Chaston et al. (1999) explained that there are five essential attributes, namely usability, reputation, trust, privacy and familiarity.

We define e-news brand attribute as the inherent characteristics of online news brands. Online news brands must have four attributes, the information provided should be intact, ease of using e-news brand, e-news brand must be organized properly, and the news must be up to date. First, the information provided should be intact. Information obtained by the editor should all be given to the public. News Media will be able to sharpen the reader's perception of the world (Alan, 2004; Jia, Lansdall-Welfare, Sudhahar, Carter, & Cristianini, 2016). If not all the information is given full and transparent, then the reader would be wrong to receive information. The reader's perception on what is happening in the world to be one because of lack of information or the information given is not the actual information. At this time, many emerging e-news brands are prone providing misinformation. They give wrong information for wanting so many e-news readers to visit their brand. Secondly, the ease in using e-news brand, in the online context, we recognize the Technology Acceptance Model (TAM). TAM has identified two measures that profoundly affect the adoption of new technology, the perceived usefulness and perceived ease of use (Davis, 1989). In the context of e-news brand, ease of use of e-news brand becomes important. Ease of use defined the degree to believe that roommates a person using a particular system would be free from effort (Davis, 1989). The ease of use will be able to influence a person's attitude (Pinho & Soares, 2011; Sanchez, Hueros, & Ordaz, 2013). The attitude in question is the attitude to continue using e-news brand. In addition to affecting the attitude of the reader, the reader easily opens any content in the e-news brand makes the readers easy to use (Linsey, Jackson, & Cooke, 2011) and will be motivated to continue to read e-news specific brand. Thirdly, e-news brand is well organized. Structuring content is important for the reader. News content in the layout based on certain topics, such as football content, national news, international news, and more. Fourth, the news should be up to date. Readers will be delighted if the news that there is always the latest news. News must be continuously up to date, so that the reader is motivated to keep reading.

E-News Brand Experience

Experience occurs when consumers consume the product or service that interact with brands (Brakus, Schmitt, & Zarantonello, 2009), starting from the search and terminated the purchase and after-purchase services (David Aviciene, Gatautis, Paliulis, & Petrauskas, 2009), It is vital to ensure the brand experience can improve a positive attitude in the context of brand. Online consumers will interact with the brand online.

Online brand experience covers all points of interaction between customers and brands in the virtual space (Christodoulides & de Chernatony, 2004). Morgan-Thomas and Veloutsou (2013) defines online brand experience as a person's subjective response when in contact with online brand. Web experience can be defined as customers total impression on online company resulting from exposure to a combination of virtual marketing tool (Asim & Hashmi, 2005; Constantinides, 2004). In this regard, there is searching, browsing, finding, selecting, comparing and evaluating information, interacting and doing transaction with online companies (Constantinides, 2004). Ha and Perks (2005) define online brand experiences as a consumer's positive navigations (i.e., using web-based communities and participating in events) and perceptions (i.e., the attractiveness of cookies, variety and uniqueness of visual displays and value for money) with a specific website'.

In this study, we define e-news brand experience as the interaction between the customer and the stimulus related to online news brands in which occurs a search, browse, find, select, compare and evaluate the required information or news. The experience of online news brands can change thinking experience, feelings experience, visual experience, and action experience.

Customer Confusion

Edward and Sahadev (2012) defined customer confusion as customer uncomfortable psychological experience when exposed to an overload of marketing information which are often very similar, misleading, ambiguous and unnatural. Mitchell, Walsh, and Yamin (2005) defines customer confusion as a lack of understanding caused by consumer being confronted with the overly rich information environment that can't be processed in the time available to fully understand and be confident in the purchase environment. Walsh and Mitchel (2010) Give the example of customer confusion as the condition of anxiety, frustration, lack of understanding and uncertainty that influence decision making. Sometimes, confusion is also called "decision difficulty" (Walsh & Mitchel, 2010).

Consumer confusion will decrease the preference in making decision, choosing qualified and best product, and enjoying shopping experience(C. Huffman & Kahn, 1998; V. W. Mitchell & Papavassiliou, 1999). Consumer confusion is associated to some things, they are, negative word of mouth (Turnbull, Leek, & Ying, 2000), cognitive dissonance (V. W. Mitchell & Papavassiliou, 1999), decision postponement (Walsh, Hennig-Thurau, & Mitchel, 2007), dissatisfaction (Foxman, Muehling, & Berger, 1990), and decreased trust (Walsh et al., 2007).

There are three dimensions of customer confusion, they are, similarity confusion proneness, overload confusion proneness, and ambiguity confusion proneness (Walsh et al., 2007). Similarity confusion proneness's is the tendency of customer to think that different products have similarities visually and functionally. Customers have such kind of confusion tend to have negative experience causing dissatisfaction. Overload confusion proneness is defined as "consumers' difficulty when confronted with more product information and alternatives than they can process in order to know, to compare and to comprehend alternatives". Ambiguity confusion proneness is defined as "consumers' tolerance for processing unclear, misleading, or ambiguous products, product-related information or advertisements."

E-News Brand Trust

There are some definitions of brand trust.Chaudhuri and Holbrook (2001) defines brand trust as someone's willingness to rely on brand ability to run its function. Other expert defines brand trust as secure feelings of customers in their interaction with brands which is based on the perception that the brand is reliable and responsible for customers' interest and prosperity (Delgado-Ballester, 2001). Brand Trust is viewed as the bond between customers and the brands (Delgado-Ballester et al., 2003).

The literature consistently explain that trust is a key element in the web-based business success (Baum & Locke, 2004). Brand trust is the most essential factor for a success and a competitive advantage against competitors in e-commerce (Tanrikulu & Celilbatur, 2013). Brand Trust has a very important role both for creating commitment (Morgan & Hunt, 1994) and building loyalty (Singh & Sirdeshmukh, 2000), and brand equity (Chaudhuri & Holbrook, 2001).In the online environment, trust explains the relationship between businesses and consumers (Yusuf, 1995). Trust is able to accept the risks and uncertainties of the transaction or relationship (McCole, Ramsey, & Williams, 2010). In online world, trust does not only lead to the role of trusted and trustee. Salo and Karjaluoto (2007) concluded that trust also leads to a third party, such as information systems, third-party users, in privacy protection, and engine and online systems. In his research, Tanrikulu and Celilbatur (2013) concluded that there are some of the most important factors that must be considered when building consumer trust, among others are: transactions security, timeliness, accuracy and policy on privacy (Eastlick et al., 2006; McCole et al., 2010). Another factor is the past experience of consumers, their support to customers, the size and popularity of vendor (Gaskill, Van Auken, & A., 1993).

In this study, we define e-news brand trust as the willingness of news readers to believe that news, information systems, or other third party have the reliability, credibility, responsibility and competence. The dimensions of e-news brand trust used this research is reliability, credibility, responsibility, and competency (Delgado-Ballester et al., 2003; Morgan & Hunt, 1994).

E- News Brand Loyalty

Consumer characteristics are quite heterogenic, leading to company's difficulties in maintaining their customers particularly in the online context. Consumers have various options of news websites in the internet. They tend to switch from one website to another website. The daunting task of the company is to maintain its website to retain its customer's loyalty.

Some experts proposed their definition on brand loyalty. Brand loyalty is a deeply held commitment to re-buy or re-patronize a preferred product/service consistently in the future, thereby causing repetitive same brand or same brand-set purchasing, despite situation influences and marketing efforts having to potential to cause switching behaviors *(Oliver, 1997)*. (2) Attitudinal Loyalty. Mascarenhas et al. (2006) Divides brand loyalty into some sections, among others are (1) Behavioral Loyalty. The general form of behavioral loyalty is re-purchasing behavior. From behavioral perspective, loyalty is defined as a re-purchase or recommendation (Abdillah & Husin, 2016). (2) Attitudinal Loyalty. It is often expressed with a positive preference towards the brand and its effect on others is very significant; (3) Situational Loyalty. It is usually measured by purchasing in certain situations. Kotler and Lee (2005) add another kind of loyalty that is oppositional brand loyalty (the rate at which customers excrete a negative vote on a competing brand).

The concept of e-loyalty is a continuation of the concept of brand loyalty in the context of online customer behavior (Al-Hawari, 2014; Gommans et al., 2001). E-loyalty is customer attitudes to e-business that results in repeat purchases (Anderson & Srinivasan, 2003). In this study, e-news brand loyalty is defined as a person's commitment in using online news brands (or often called a website) where a person consistently chooses the electronic brands compared to other electronics brand to achieve its stated objectives.

Hypothesis

Consumer experience is positioned as a moderator between utilitarian and hedonic attributes on brand equity (Sheng & Teo, 2012). Brand equity refers to the brand loyalty. The brand synonymous with the incorporation of various attributes. Attributes are exactly what will be able to build a brand to become a strong brand in the minds of consumers. Consumers are already feeling the various attributes of the brand or product will have interesting experiences about the product. In his research, Mahadeoa, Oogarah-Hanumana, and Soobaroyen (2011) uses the attributes TAM to measure the effect on the consumer experience on the website. Other researchers have found that there is a relationship between attributes utilitarian / hedonic and consumer experiences (Moon & Kim, 2001). In these paper hypotheses are proposed that:

E-News Brand Attributes Positively Affect to the E-News Brand Experience

Vigneron and Johnson (1999) explains that the function of the brand is based on five characteristics or attributes, among others: the symbol of the individual's power and social status, reflection of social approval, exclusivity or limitation of the offer to small number of people, the contribution of emotion la experience, technical superiority. Various characteristics or attributes have an influence on consumers' willingness to pay a price premium for the brand and recommend it to other. The two influenced variables are the dimensions of loyalty. Research conducted by (Anisimova, 2007) concluded that the multi-dimensional attributes of corporate brands is a very important predictor of customer loyalty. In this paper hypotheses is proposed that:

E-News Brand Attributes Positively Affect to the E-News Brand Loyalty

Various marketing efforts often make consumers will be confused. The more information you enter to the consumers' mind create confusion increased. The experience is more personal (Pullman & Gross, 2004; Schmitt, 1999a, 1999b) and created during the learning process when in need of use, maintain and sometimes arrange the goods or services (Carbon & Haeckel, 1994). This experience is making consumers understand about the product characteristics more clearly. The experience can be used to counter customer confusion (Mitchell et al., 2005). The higher one's own experience, the more people are not confused about something. In a study conducted by Simonin (1999) found that experience and significant negative effect on knowledge ambiguity (for smaller scale companies). Ambiguity is one dimension of customer confusion (Walsh & Mitchell, 2010). Dimensions of customer confusion are likely to have a negative experience (Walsh & Mitchell, 2010). In these paper hypotheses is proposed that:

E-News Brand Experience Negatively Affect to the Customer Confusion

Information received by consumers is often confusing. This is because the information is not given in full elaboration. There are things added to attract readers. The confusion experienced by consumers can reduce consumer confidence to the brand. Walsh and Mitchell (2010) also found that consumer confusion will tend to reduce market confidence. The market started to be unbelievable because the information received tend to ambiguous and sometimes contradictory. In the study conducted by Tjiptono, Arli, and Bucic (2014), the dimensions of customer confusion (Similarity confusion proneness) a significant negative effect on confidence. In these paper hypotheses is proposed that:

Customer Confusion Negatively Affect to the E-News Brand Trust

Tanrikulu and Celilbatur (2013) said that one of the factors that build consumer confidence is past experience. In offline purchasing contexts, some researchers concluded that the brand experience positively and significantly influence in the brand trust effect (Ha & Perks, 2005; Sahin et al., 2011). Ha and Perks (2005), conducted research on online consumer behavior in Korea, they described that online consumer experience influence significantly on trust, based on the said previous studies, it is proposed that:

E-News Brand Experience Positively Affect to the E-News Brand Trust

In the context of offline purchasing, brand trust is the antecedent of consumer loyalty (Chaudhuri & Holbrook, 2001; Sahin et al., 2011; Singh & Sirdeshmukh, 2000). Consumers who believe in a brand will strive to recommend the brand re-purchase or take action. In the concept of loyalty in internet media, trust is a variable that affects consumer loyalty (Gommans et al., 2001; Harris & Goode, 2004). In these paper hypotheses is proposed that:

E-News Brand Trust Positively Affect to the E-News Brand Loyalty

Data Collection and Sample

We test our model on two e-news brand. Those e-news brand are Kompas.com and Detik.com. This study population are people who had read Kompas.com and Detik.com. Questionnaire was distributed to 535 respondents where only 418 questionnaires were returned and worthy for further analysis. The response rate of this study was 78%. Samples took 418 respondents, of which 239 respondents are Kompas.com's reader and Detik.com's reader 179 respondents.

Table 1. describes about the characteristics of respondents. There are 4 respondents characteristics: gender, age, education, and employment affiliation.

First characteristic is about gender. Detik.com's respondents are 56.42% are male and 43.58% are female. The most respondent of Detik.com are 20-30 years old. 49.93% respondents of Detik.com have an undergraduate education and 42.46% are postgraduate. Students are the most dominant job as a reader of detik.com. The gender of Kompas.com's respondents are 55.65% male and 44.35% are female. The most Kompas.com's respondents are 20-30 years old. 46.44% of Detik.com's respondents have a undergraduate education and 42.26% are postgraduate. Students are the most dominant job as a reader of Kompas.com

Measurement

The measurement scale used in the questions is using a scale of 1 to 10, from strongly disagree to strongly agree. E-news brand attribute is measured from: full information(X1), easy to use(X2), well organized(X3), Up-to-date(X4). E-news brand experience is measured from: Thinks experience(X6), feel experience(X7), visual experience(X8), behavioral experience(X9). Customer Confusion is measured from the indicators such as similarity confusion proneness(X10), confusion proneness overload (X11), ambiguity confusion proneness(X12). E-Brand Trust is measured from reliability (X13), (2) credibility, responsibility (X14), and competent (X15). And E-Loyalty is measured from re-reading (X16), positive word of mouth (X17) commitment to make comment (X18).

Table 1. Respondent Characteristics

DESCRIPTION	DETIK.COM	Frequency %	KOMPAS.COM	Frequency %
Sex				
Male	101	56.42	133	55.65
Female	78	43,58	106	44.35
Age				
<20 years	9	5.03	11	4.06
20 – 30 years	131	73.18	177	74.06
30 – 40 years	33	18.44	45	18.83
41 – 50 years	3	1.68	4	1.67
>50th	3	1.68	2	0.84
Education				
Undergraduate	84	49.93	111	46.44
Postgraduate	76	42.46	101	42.26
Doctoral	19	10.61	27	11.30
Occupation				
Lecturer	11	6.15	20	8.37
Civil servants	24	13.41	24	10.04
Private Employee	51	28.49	60	25.10
Entrepreneur	31	17.32	53	22.18
Student	52	29.05	71	29.71
Another Job	10	5.59	11	4.60

ISSUES, CONTROVERSIES, PROBLEMS

The first study is to analyze the Detik.com. When seen in Table 2, we can conclude that this study has been valid and reliable for further analysis. The validity of this study using convergent validity and reliability using AVE whereas the construct validity.

If we look at Table 2 in the column convergent validity, each item / indicator variable has a value greater than 0.5 so that no items / indicators are released from the analysis. All values AVE of each variable was also above the required value of 0.5. Here are the values AVE each variable: E-Brand Experience (0.672), E-News Brand attribute (0.828), Customer Confusion (0.8), E-News Brand Trust (.788), E-News Brand Loyalty (0,625).

In Table 2 column construct reliability, it can be concluded that this study data has been reliable since the value of each variable construct reliability is greater than the cut-off (> 0.60). Here is the values construct reliability: E-Brand Experience (0.735), E-News Brand attribute (0.800), Customer Confusion (0.800), E-News Brand Trust (.798), E-News Brand Loyalty (0,703).

Table 4 describes the results of hypothesis testing both for study 1 and study 2. In Table 2 column detik.com, we can see the model fit investigator on the study 1. GFI value of 0.905 is greater than the required value (> 0.90) so this model is good. NFI value amounted to 0.954 greater than the required

Table 2. Validity and reliability study 1

DETIK.COM	ITEMS	CONVERGENT VALIDITY	CONSTRUCT RELIABILITY	AVERAGE
E-News Brand Experience	X1	0.949	0.735	0.672
	X2	0.701		
	X3	0.717		
	X4	0.885		
E-News Brand Attribute	X5	0.999	0.800	0.828
	X6	0.626		
	X7	0.994		
	X8	0.967		
Consumer confusion	X9	0.980	0.800	0.800
	X10	0.665		
	X11	0.999		
E-News Brand Trust	X12	0.998	0.798	0.788
	X13	0.795		
	X14	0.933		
	X15	0.808		
E-News Brand Loyalty	X16	0.833	0.703	0.625
	X17	0.724		
	X18	0.810		

conditions (> 0.90) so that this model is good. TLI value amounted to 0.986 greater than the required conditions (> 0.90) so that this model is good. RMSEA value of 0,042 is smaller than the required condition (<0.08) so that this model is good. We conclude that the data were fit with a model developed

Hypothesis testing in one study, it can be seen in Table 4 column detik.com. Each of the H1, H2, H5, H6 accepted. While the H3 and H4 was rejected because of the influence of independent to dependent variable is not significant.

Study 2 was a study to analyze the Kompas.com. If we see in Table 2, we can conclude that this study has been valid and reliable for further analysis. The validity of this study using convergent validity and reliability using AVE whereas the construct validity. If we look at Table 2 in the column convergent validity, each item / indicator variable has a value greater than 0.5 so that no items / indicators are released from the analysis. All values AVE of each variable was also above the required value of 0.5. Here are the values AVE each variable: E-Brand Experience (0.880), E-News Brand attribute (0.798), Customer Confusion (0.714), E-News Brand Trust (0.727), E-News Brand Loyalty (0.560).

In the Table 2 column construct reliability, it can be concluded that this study data has been reliable since the value of each construct reliability variable is greater than the cut-off (> 0.60). Here is the values construct reliability: E-Brand Experience (0.891), E-News Brand attribute (0.815), Customer Confusion (0,747), E-News Brand Trust (0.763), E-News Brand Loyalty (0.610).

Table 4 describes the results of hypothesis testing both for study 1 and study 2. In Table 2 column Kompas.com, we can see the model fit investigator on the study 2. GFI value of 0.871 is slightly smaller

Table 3. Validity dan reliability study 2

DETIK.COM	ITEMS	CONVERGENT VALIDITY	CONSTRUCT RELIABILITY	AVERAGE
E-News Brand Experience	X1	0.826	0.891	0.880
	X2	0.966		
	X3	0.974		
	X4	0.806		
E-News Brand Attribute	X5	0.946	0.815	0.798
	X6	0.951		
	X7	0.763		
	X8	0.900		
Consumer confusion	X9	0.884	0.747	0.714
	X10	0.825		
	X11	0.825		
E-News Brand Trust	X12	0.624	0.763	0.727
	X13	0.821		
	X14	0.966		
	X15	0.821		
E-Loyalty	X16	0.973	0.610	0.556
	X17	0.675		
	X18	0.906		

Table 4. Model fit and hypotheses study 1 and study 2

HYPOTHESIS	KOMPAS.COM	DETIK.COM
E-News Brand Attribute → E-News Brand Experience (H1)	0.154**	0.274*
E-News Brand Attribute → E-Loyalty (H2)	0.276*	0.297*
E-News Brand Experience → Customer Confusion (H3)	-0.049 (ns)	-0.055 (ns)
E-News Brand Experience → E-News Brand Trust (H5)	0.340*	0.206*
Customer Confusion → E-News Brand Trust (H4)	-0.009 (ns)	-0.010 (ns)
E-News Brand Trust → E-Loyalty (H6)	0.310*	0.285*
Model FIT		
GFI	0.871 (marginal)	0.905 (good)
NFI	0.917 (good)	0.954 (good)
TLI	0.939 (good)	0.986 (good)
RMSEA	0.079 (good)	0.042 (good)

*significant 0.01

** significant 0.05

than the cut-offnya, but as it approaches the value cut-off of 0.9 so that the model is still considered good. NFI value amounted to 0.917 greater than the required conditions (> 0.90) so that this model is good. TLI value of 0,939larger compared with the terms of the required (> 0.90) so that this model is good. RMSEA value of 0.079 is smaller than the required condition (<0.08) so that this model is good. We conclude that the data was fit with a model developed.

Hypothesis testing in one study, it can be seen in Table 4 column detik.com. Each of the H1, H2, H5, H6 accepted. While the H3 and H4 was rejected because of the influence of independent to dependent variable is not significant.

The trust is a very important factor in the online environment, particularly in the electronics news brand. There are several reasons why the vital trust in the online environment, among others: (1) on-line environment is fraught with uncertainty. Uncertainty often makes consumers become hesitant to make a decision. Trust enables consumers to deal with uncertainty (Koufaris & Hampton-Sosa, 2004; McKnight, choundhury, & Kacmar, 2002a). These conditions will enable the company to reduce costs, improve efficiency, more flexible and supports long-term planning (Chen and Dhillon, 2003). The ability to deal with uncertainty will also enable consumers to capture and perform a variety of decisions, one of which was the decision to be loyal to a brand. (2) increased competition in the online environment. Many e-news emerging brand that always delivers good news or interesting content. Therefore, the trust must be built by detik.com and kompas.com. (3) The trust will motivate customers to be active in the online environment.

The news can not be trusted to make the reader will not be back to read both detik.com or kompas.com. In this chapter, shows that trust is an important factor to create loyalty for the the readers. The result same as previous studies, in which the trust is able to increase loyalty (Gommans et al., 2001; Harris & Goode, 2004). One dimension of trust is able to build brand loyalty is kredibilitas. Chung, Kim, and Kim (2010) found an online news paper must establish credibility. Credibility is meant is the source, the message and the medium credibility (Metzger, Flanagin, Eyal, Lemus, & McCann, 2003). Sources of information must be people who really trusted, expert, or people expert in a particular field. Sources must have credibility so the news awake accuracy (Gaziano & McGrath, 1986). Sources of information must be objective and impartial to one particular party. Beebrapa skilled experts explain that the credibility of the website (electronics news brand) credibility of interpersonal source credibility (Berlo, Lemert, & Mertz, 1969; Infante, Parker, Clarke, Wilson, & Nathu, 1983; Posner & Kouzes, 1988; Sundar & Nass, 2001). Source will give an important message or information to the public. Messages must have credibility. Messages credible means information provided from sources not contrived or what it is. Often to increase traffic to electronics brand news, the news that there are exaggerated. The news is not true. Media also must be trustworthy (Kim & Tohnson, 2005). Website as a medium must be credible, with confidence, skill, charm and dynamism (Flanagin & Metzger, 2007).

In this study, electronics news brand experience is able to increase the confidence of the reader. Building a positive experience readers an important part in the online environment. In the literature, the experience tends to exist in research in the field entertiment and hospitality. In the online environment, the experience tends to occur the use of technology in the interaction between human being and a computer or a machine (Ding, Huang, & Verma, 2011). Previous research has examined expressed cognitive construct flow in human-computer interaction and shows the flow of which can be determined by the focus of attention, interactivity, sense of control, the level of challenge and skill (DL Huffman, Kalsbeek, & Novak, 1996; Novak, Huffman, & Yung, 2000). Commitment and trust in a website depends on the perception of the website and how to meet expectations on the integrity and reliability and how well give promises (Bart, Shankar, Sultan, & Urban, 2005). Readers should receive appointments through their experiences when reading the news brand electronics. This is a pleasant experience will make people committed and believe in electronics news brand.

The research found the smaller the degree of consumer confusion, the higher the higher consumer confidence in the electronics news brand. Customer confusion will create some problems, one of which too much information accepted by the reader. Too much information becomes a problem because a lot of information very similar, ambiguous, unnatural and misleading (Edward & Sahadev, 2012). It will make the decision making consumption or purchase would be very confusing (Leek & Kun, 2006) .Informasi ambiguous, unnatural and misleading readers will be no trust in electronics brand news tersebut.Tjiptono et al. (2014) found that the dimensions of customer confusion (overload confusion and ambiguity confusion proneness proneness) but not signigikan negative effect on trust. Overload confusion is a condition in which the consumer will be very difficult to explain back various information and alternative (Walsh et al., 2007). The cause is too much information about the product or brand specific. Overload confusion will make the trust readers will go down, because the reader is not able to clearly identify the uniqueness and otherness electronics news brand with its competitors. All look the same.

In this chapter, antesenden of electronics news reader experience is the brand attribute. The results show that the electronics news brand attribute can influence the reader's experience. Readers who interact with the various attributes of the news brand electronics, where the reader a feel for how the information provided should be intact, ease of using e-news brand, e-news brand must be organized properly, and the news must be up to datewill provide a positive experience to the reader. Attributes can be semaca clue. In the literature, the clue will be able to stimulate a person to experience not easily forgotten (Berry, Wall, & Carbon, 2006; Brakus et al., 2009; Schmitt, 2009). Readers can experience perceived cognitively experience, feelings, sensory, and behavioral (Brakus et al., 2009)

Positive Experience experienced news reader electronics brand will be able to reduce customer confusion. The higher one's readers have the experience, the more people are not confused to use electronics news brand. In his research conducted by Simonin (1999) found that experience and significant negative effect on knowledge ambiguity. The experience would eliminate the things that associated with ambiguity, uncertainty, and lack of comprehension on electronics news brand.

SOLUTIONS AND RECOMMENDATIONS

In the literature, trust is an important part of the business based websites (Ba, Whinston, & Zhang, 2003; Hoffman, Novak, & Peralta, 1999; Keat & Mahon, 2004; Kim & Benbasat, 2003). Within this research, the trust becomes an important part in the development of electronics news brand. The trust is able to increase the loyalty of readers in re-reading, recommending, and is active in providing comments. There are three things that must be built in order to increase the trust of readers. First, make it interesting attribute of electronics news brand. Second, to create positive experiences to the reader. One way is to make the reader to participate. Participation can be done by making the reader will comment the news that appeared in detik.com and kompas.com. In addition, readers can also provide material detik.com news on the editorial board and kompas.com. Third, reduce consumer confusion. One way is to give the correct and reliable news.

CONCLUSION

The aim of this chapter is to test the importance of trust to Increase the loyalty of readers e-news brand in Indonesia and to test its antecedents. Trust becomes a central factor in the electronics news brand to increase the loyalty of its readers. Within this research, the belief in electronics news brand is influenced by the reader's experience and customer confusion. Exciting experiences and unforgettable experiences influenced by the attributes of the electronic news brand. The reader experiences will be able to reduce customer confusion and will increase of confidence in the electronics news brand significantly. Consumers are not confused about influential confidence in the electronics news brand. Other results showed that the attached attributes to the electronics news brand will be able to significantly increase reader's loyalty trust. It is a very important factor in the online environment, particularly in the electronics news brand.

REFERENCES

Abdillah, A., & Husin, N. M. (2016). A longitudinal examination corporate social responsibility reporting practice among top bank in Malaysia. *Procedia Economics and Finance*, *35*, 10–16. doi:10.1016/S2212-5671(16)00004-6

Al-Hawari, M. A. A. (2014). Does customer sociability matter? Differences in e-quality, e-satisfaction, and e-loyalty between introvert and extravert online banking users. *Journal of Services Marketing*, *28*(7), 538–546. doi:10.1108/JSM-02-2013-0036

Alan, S. (2004). *News Culture* (3rd ed.). Maidenhead, UK: Open University Press.

Anderson, R. E., & Srinivasan, S. (2003). E-satisfaction and E-Loyalty: A Contingency Framework. *Psychology and Marketing*, *20*(2), 123–138. doi:10.1002/mar.10063

Anisimova, T. A. (2007). The Effect of Corporate Brand attributes on Attitudinal And Behavioral Consumer Loyalty. *Journal of Consumer Marketing*, *24*(7), 395–405. doi:10.1108/07363760710834816

Arikunto, S. (2010). *Prosedur penelitian: Suatu Pendekatan Praktik*. Jakarta: Rineja Cipta.

Asim, M., & Hashmi, Y. (2005). *E-Loyalty: Companies Secret Weapon On the Web*. Lulea University of Technology.

Atakan-Duman, S., & Ozdora-Aksak, E. (2014). The role of corporate social responsibility in online identity construction: An analysis of Turkey's banking sector. *Public Relations Review*, *40*(5), 862–864. doi:10.1016/j.pubrev.2014.07.004

Attaran, H. J., Divandari, A., & Adinov, H. (2012). Identifying effective factors in market integration (realization of sustainable co mpetitive advantage) the banking services in Mellat Bank based on source -centered approach. *Journal of Public Administration*, *12*(4), 91–112.

Ba, S., Whinston, A. B., & Zhang, H. (2003). Building trust in online auction markets through an economic incentive mechanism. *Decision Support Systems*, *35*(3), 273–286. doi:10.1016/S0167-9236(02)00074-X

Bart, Y., Shankar, V., Sultan, F., & Urban, G. L. (2005). Are the drivers and role of online trust the same for all web sites and consumers? A large scale e xploratory empirical study. *Journal of Marketing*, *69*(4), 133–152. doi:10.1509/jmkg.2005.69.4.133

Baum, J. R., & Locke, E. A. (2004). The relationship of entrepreneurial traits, skill, and motivation to subsequent venture growth. *Journal of Applied Phycology*, *89*(4), 589–598.

Benedicktus, R. L. (2011). The Effects of 3rd Party Consensus Information on Service Expectations and Online Trust. *Journal of Business Research*, *64*(8), 846–853. doi:10.1016/j.jbusres.2010.09.014

Berlo, D. K., Lemert, J. B., & Mertz, R. J. (1969). Dimensions for evaluating the acceptability of message sources. *Public Opinion Quarterly*, *33*(4), 563–576. doi:10.1086/267745

Berry, L. L., Wall, A. E., & Carbon, L. P. (2006). Service clues and customer assessment of the service experience: Lesson from marketing. *The Academy of Management Perspectives*, *20*(2), 43–57. doi:10.5465/AMP.2006.20591004

Brakus, J. J., Schmitt, B. H., & Zarantonello, L. (2009). Brand Experience: What is It? How Is It Measured? Does It Affect Loyalty? *Journal of Marketing*, *73*(3), 52–68. doi:10.1509/jmkg.73.3.52

Capaldo, G., Iandoli, L., & Ponsiglione, C. (2004). *Entrepreneurial competencies and training needs of small firms*. Paper presented at the 14th Annual International Entrepreneurial Conference, Napoli.

Carbon, L. P., & Haeckel, S. H. (1994). Engineering Customer Experiences. *Marketing Management*, *3*(3), 9–19.

Carrol, A. B. (1991). The pyramid of corporate social responsibility: Toward the moral management of organisasional stakeholders. *Business Horizons*, *34*(4), 39–48. doi:10.1016/0007-6813(91)90005-G

Chaston, I., Badger, B., & Sadler-Smith, E. (1999). Organisational learning: Research issues and application in SME sector firms. *International Journal of Entrepreneurial Behavior & Research*, *5*(4), 191–203. doi:10.1108/13552559910293146

Chaudhuri, A., & Holbrook, M. B. (2001). The Chain of Effects From Brand Trust and Brand Affect to Brand Performance: The Role of Brand Loyalty. *Journal of Marketing*, *65*(2), 81–94. doi:10.1509/jmkg.65.2.81.18255

Chen, S. C., & Dhillon, G. S. (2003). Interpreting dimensions of consumer trust in e-commerce. *Information Technology Management*, *4*(2-3), 303–318. doi:10.1023/A:1022962631249

Cheng, M. I., Dainty, A. R. J., & Moore, D. R. (2003). The differing faces of managerial competency in Britain and America. *Journal of Management Development*, *22*(6), 526–537. doi:10.1108/02621710310478495

Christodoulides, G., & de Chernatony, L. (2004). Dimensionalising on- and offline brands' composite equity. *Journal of Product and Brand Management*, *13*(3), 168–179. doi:10.1108/10610420410538069

Chung, C. J., Kim, H., & Kim, J. H. (2010). An anatomy of the credibility of online newspapers. *Online Information Review*, *34*(5), 669–685. doi:10.1108/14684521011084564

Constantinides, E. (2004). Influencing The Online Consumer's Behavior: The Web Experience. *Internet Research*, *14*(2), 111–126. doi:10.1108/10662240410530835

Davidaviciene, V., Gatautis, R., Paliulis, N., & Petrauskas, R. (2009). Electronic Business. Vilnius: VGTU.

Davis, F. D. (1989). Perceived usefulness, perceived ease of use and user acceptance of information technology. *Management Information Systems Quarterly, 13*(3), 319–340. doi:10.2307/249008

de Chernatony, L., & Christodoulides, G. (2004). Taking the brand promise online: Challenges and opportunities. *Interactive Marketing, 5*(3), 238–251. doi:10.1057/palgrave.im.4340241

Delgado-Ballester, E. (2001). *Development and validation of a brand trust scale.* Twin Cities, MN: University of Minnesota.

Delgado-Ballester, E., & Munuera-Aleman, J. L. (2001). Brand trust in the context of consumer loyalty. *European Journal of Marketing, 11*(12), 1238–1258. doi:10.1108/EUM0000000006475

Ding, X. D., Huang, Y., & Verma, R. (2011). Customer experience in online financial services: A study of behavioral intentions for techno-ready market segments. *Journal of Service Management, 22*(3), 344–366. doi:10.1108/09564231111136863

Eastlick, M. A., Lotz, S. L., & Warrington, P. (2006). Understanding Online B-toC Relationships: An Integrated Model of Privacy Concern, Trust and Commitment. *Journal of Business Research, 59*(8), 2006. doi:10.1016/j.jbusres.2006.02.006

Edward, M., & Sahadev, S. (2012). Modeling The Consequences of Customer Confusion in A Service Marketing Context: An Empirical Study. *Journal of Service Research, 12*(2), 127–146.

Flanagin, A. J., & Metzger, M. J. (2007). The role of site features, user attributes, and information verification behaviors on the perceived credibility of web-based information. *New Media and Society, 9.*

Foxman, E. R., Muehling, D. D., & Berger, P. W. (1990). An investigation of factors contributing to consumer brand confusion. *The Journal of Consumer Affairs, 24*(1), 170–189. doi:10.1111/j.1745-6606.1990.tb00264.x

Gaskill, L. A. R., & Van Auken, H. E. (1993). A factor analytic study of the perceived causes of small business failure. *Journal of Small Business Management, 31*(4), 18–31.

Gaziano, C., & McGrath, K. (1986). Measuring the concept of credibility. *The Journalism Quarterly, 63*(3), 451–462. doi:10.1177/107769908606300301

Gommans, M., Krishnan, K. S., & Scheffold, K. B. (2001). From Brand Loyalty to e-Loyalty: A Conceptual Framework. *Journal of Economic and Social Research, 3*(1), 43-58.

Ha, H.-Y., & Perks, H. (2005). Effect of Consumer Perceptions of Brand Experience on The Web: Brand Familiarity, Satisfaction, and Brand Trust. *Journal of Consumer Behaviour, 4*(6), 438–452. doi:10.1002/cb.29

Harden, L., & Heyman, B. (2009). *Digital engagement: internet marketing that captures customers and builds intense brand loyalty.* New York: AMAKOM.

Harris, L. C., & Goode, M. M. H. (2004). The Four of Loyalty and The Pivitol Role of Trust: A Study of Online Service Dynamics. *Journal of Retailing, 80*(2), 139–158. doi:10.1016/j.jretai.2004.04.002

Hoffman, D. L., Novak, T. P., & Peralta, M. (1999). Building consumer trust online. *Communications of the ACM, 42*(4), 80–85. doi:10.1145/299157.299175

Huffman, C., & Kahn, B. E. (1998). Variety for sale: Mass customization or mass confusion? *Journal of Retailing, 74*(4), 491–513. doi:10.1016/S0022-4359(99)80105-5

Huffman, D. L., Kalsbeek, W. D., & Novak, T. P. (1996). Internet and web use in the United States: Baselines for commercial development. *Communications of the ACM, 39*, 36–46.

Infante, D. A., Parker, K. R., Clarke, C. H., Wilson, L., & Nathu, I. A. (1983). A comparison of factor and functional approaches to source credibility. *Communication Quarterly, 31*(1), 43–48. doi:10.1080/01463378309369484

Jia, S., Lansdall-Welfare, T., Sudhahar, S., Carter, C., & Cristianini, N. (2016). Women are seen more than heard in online newspapers. *PLoS ONE, 11*(2), 1–11. doi:10.1371/journal.pone.0148434

Kapferer, J.-N. (2008). *The New Strategic Brand Management: Creating and Sustaining Brand Equity Long Term*. London: Kogan Page.

Keat, T. K., & Mahon, A. (2004). Integration of TAM based electronic commerce models for trust. *Journal of American Academy of Business, 5*(1/2), 404–410.

Keller, K. L. (1993). Conceptualizing, Measuring, and Managing Customer Based Brand Equity. *Journal of Marketing, 57*(1), 1–22. doi:10.2307/1252054

Kim, D., & Benbasat, I. (2003). Trust-related arguments in internet stores: A framework for evaluation. *Journal of Electronic Commerce Research, 4*(2), 49–64.

Kim, D., & Tohnson, T. J. (2005). *Media credibility: comparing internet and traditional news sources in South Korea*. Paper presented at the International Communication Association Conference, New York, NY.

Kotler, P., & Keller, K. L. (2012). *Marketing Management*. Pearson Education, Inc.

Kotler, P., & Lee, N. (2005). *Corporate Social Responsibility Doing the Must Good for Your Company and Your Couse*. John Wiley and Son Inc.

Koufaris, M., & Hampton-Sosa, W. (2004). The development of initial trust in an online company by new customers. *Information & Management, 41*(3), 377–397. doi:10.1016/j.im.2003.08.004

Leek, S., & Kun, D. (2006). Consumer Confusion in the Chinese Personal Computer Market. *Journal of Product and Brand Management, 15*(3), 184–193. doi:10.1108/10610420610668621

Linsey, R., Jackson, T. W., & Cooke, L. (2011). Adapted technology acceptance model for mobile policing. *Journal of Systems and Information Technology, 13*(4), 389–407. doi:10.1108/13287261111183988

Mahadeoa, J. D., Oogarah-Hanumana, V., & Soobaroyen, T. (2011). Changes in social and environemntal reporting practices in an emerginh economy (2004-2007): Exploring the relevance of staeholder and legitimacy theory. *Accounting Forum, 35*(3), 158–175. doi:10.1016/j.accfor.2011.06.005

Mascarenhas, O. A., Kesavan, R., & Bernacchi, M. (2006). Lasting Customer Loyalty: A Total Customer Experience Approach. *Journal of Consumer Marketing, 23*(7), 397–405. doi:10.1108/07363760610712939

McCole, P., Ramsey, E., & Williams, J. (2010). Trust Considerations on Attitudes Toward Online Purchasing: The Moderating Effect on Privacy and Security Concerns. *Journal of Business Research, 63*(9-10), 1018–1024. doi:10.1016/j.jbusres.2009.02.025

McKnight, D. H., Choudhury, V., & Kacmar, C. (2002a). Developing and validating trust measures for e-commerce: An integrative typology. *Information Systems Research, 13*(3), 334–359. doi:10.1287/isre.13.3.334.81

McKnight, D. H., Choundhury, V., & Kacmar, C. (2002b). The Impact of Initial Consumer Trust on Intentions to Transact With a Website: A Trust Building Model. *The Journal of Strategic Information Systems, 11*(3-4), 297–323. doi:10.1016/S0963-8687(02)00020-3

Metzger, M. J., Flanagin, A. J., Eyal, K., Lemus, D. R., & McCann, R. M. (2003). Credibility for the 21st century: integrating perspectives on source, message, and media credibility in the contemporary media environment. In P. J. Kalbfleisch (Ed.), *Communications Yearbook* (Vol. 27, pp. 293–335). Mahwah, NJ: Lawrence Erlbaum Associates. doi:10.1080/23808985.2003.11679029

Mitchell, V. W., & Papavassiliou, V. (1999). Marketing causes and implications of consumer confusion. *Journal of Product and Brand Management, 8*(4), 319–339. doi:10.1108/10610429910284300

Mitchell, V.-W., Walsh, G., & Yamin, M. (2005). Towards a Conceptual Model of Consumer Confusion. *Advances in Consumer Research. Association for Consumer Research (U. S.), 32*, 143–150.

Moon, J., & Kim, Y. (2001). Extending the TAM for a World-Wide-Wen Context. *Information & Management, 38*(4), 217–230. doi:10.1016/S0378-7206(00)00061-6

Morgan, R. M., & Hunt, S. D. (1994). The Commitment-Trust Theory of Relationship Marketing. *Journal of Marketing, 58*(3), 20–38. doi:10.2307/1252308

Morgan-Thomas, A., & Veloutsou, C. (2013). Beyond technology acceptance: Brand relationships and online brand experience. *Journal of Business Research, 66*(21-27), 21-27.

Newton, K. (2001). *Management Skills for Small Business*. Small Business Policy Brand.

Nilssen, J., Bertheussen, B. A., & Dreyer, B. (2015). Sustained competitive advantage based on high quality input. *Marine Policy, 52*, 145–154. doi:10.1016/j.marpol.2014.10.011

Novak, T. P., Huffman, D. L., & Yung, Y. (2000). Measuring the customer experience in online environments: A structural modeling approach. *Marketing Science, 19*(1), 22–42. doi:10.1287/mksc.19.1.22.15184

Oliver, C. (1997). Sustainable Competitive Advantage: Combining Institutional and Resource-based View. *Strategic Management Journal, 18*(9), 697–713. doi:10.1002/(SICI)1097-0266(199710)18:9<697::AID-SMJ909>3.0.CO;2-C

Peteraf, M., & Barney, J. (2003). Unraveling The Resource-Based Tangle. *Managerial and Decision Economics, 24*(4), 309–323. doi:10.1002/mde.1126

Phillips, D. (2001). Managing reputation in cyberspace. *Journal of Communication Management, 5*(3), 300–304.

Pinho, J. C. M. R., & Soares, A. M. (2011). Examining the technology acceptance model in the adoption of social networks. *Journal of Research in Interactive Marketing, 5*(2/3), 116–129. doi:10.1108/17505931111187767

Posner, B. Z., & Kouzes, J. M. (1988). Relating leadership and credibility. *Psychological Reports, 63*(2), 527–530. doi:10.2466/pr0.1988.63.2.527

Pullman, M. E., & Gross, M. A. (2004). Ability of Experience Design Element to Elicit Emotin and Loyalty Behaviors. *Decision Sciences, 35*(3), 551–578. doi:10.1111/j.0011-7315.2004.02611.x

Ranaweera, C., & Prabhu, J. (2003). The influence of satisfaction, trust and switching barriers on customer retention in a continuous purchasing setting. *International Journal of Service Industry Management, 14*(4), 374–395. doi:10.1108/09564230310489231

Sahin, A., Zehir, C., & Kitapci, H. (2011). The Effects of Brand Experiences, Trust and Satisfaction on Building Brand Loyalty; An Empirical Research On Global Brands. *Procedia: Social and Behavioral Sciences, 24*, 1288–1301. doi:10.1016/j.sbspro.2011.09.143

Salo, J., & Karjaluoto, H. (2007). A Conceptual Model of Trust in the Online Environment. *Online Information Review, 31*(5), 604–621. doi:10.1108/14684520710832324

Sanchez, R. A., Hueros, A. D., & Ordaz, M. G. (2013). E-learning and the University of Huelva: A study of WebCT and the technological acceptance model. *Campus-Wide Information Systems, 30*(2), 135–160. doi:10.1108/10650741311306318

Schindehutte, M., Morris, M. H., & Kocak, A. (2008). Understanding Market-Driving Behavior: The Role of Entrepreneurship. *Journal of Small Business Management, 46*(1), 4–26. doi:10.1111/j.1540-627X.2007.00228.x

Schmitt, B. H. (1999a). Experiential Marketing. *Journal of Marketing Management, 15*(1-3), 53–67. doi:10.1362/026725799784870496

Schmitt, B. H. (1999b). *Experiential Marketing: How to Get Customers to Sense, Feel, Think, Act, and Relate to Your Company and Brand*. New York: The Free Press.

Schmitt, B. H. (2009). The Concept of Brand Experience. *Journal of Brand Management, 16*(7), 417–419. doi:10.1057/bm.2009.5

Shen, C.-H., Wu, M.-W., Chen, T.-H., & Fang, H. (2016). To engage or not to engage in corporate social responsibility: Empirical evidence from global banking sector. *Economic Modelling, 55*(June), 207–225. doi:10.1016/j.econmod.2016.02.007

Sheng, M. L., & Teo, T. S. H. (2012). Product attributes and brand equity in the mobile domain: The mediating role of customer experience. *International Journal of Information Management, 32*(2), 139–146. doi:10.1016/j.ijinfomgt.2011.11.017

Shnayder, L., van Rijnsoeve, F. J., & Hekkert, M. P. (2016). Motivations for Corporate Social Responsibility in the packaged food industry: An institutional and stakeholder management perspective. *Journal of Cleaner Production, 122*(May), 212–227. doi:10.1016/j.jclepro.2016.02.030

Simonin, B. L. (1999). Transfer of Marketing Know-How in International Strategic Alliances: An Empirical Investigation of the Role and Antecedents of Knowledge Ambiguity. *Journal of International Business Studies*, *30*(3), 463–491. doi:10.1057/palgrave.jibs.8490079

Singh, J., & Sirdeshmukh, D. (2000). Agency and trust mechanisms in consumer satisfaction and loyalty judgments. *Journal of the Academy of Marketing Science*, *28*(1), 150–167. doi:10.1177/0092070300281014

Strebler, M., Robinson, D., & Heron, P. (1997). *Getting the Best Out of Your Competencies*. Brighton, UK: Institute of Employment Studies, University of Sussex.

Sundar, S. S., & Nass, C. (2001). Conceptualizing sources in online news. *Journal of Communication*, *51*(1), 52–72. doi:10.1111/j.1460-2466.2001.tb02872.x

Tanrikulu, Z., & Celilbatur, N. (2013). Trust Factor Affectng E-Ticket Purchasing. *Procedia: Social and Behavioral Sciences*, *73*, 115–119. doi:10.1016/j.sbspro.2013.02.030

Tjiptono, F., Arli, D., & Bucic, T. (2014). Consumer confusion proneness: Insights from a developing economy. *Marketing Intelligence & Planning*, *32*(6), 722–734. doi:10.1108/MIP-05-2013-0082

Turnbull, P. W., Leek, S., & Ying, G. (2000). Customer confusion: The mobile phone market. *Journal of Marketing Management*, *16*(January-April), 143–163. doi:10.1362/026725700785100523

Vigneron, F., & Johnson, L. W. (1999). A Review and a Conceptual Framework of Prestige-Seeking Consumer Behavior. *Academy of Marketing Science Review*, *99*(1), 1–15.

Walsh, G., Hennig-Thurau, T., & Mitchel, V.-W. (2007). Consumer confusion proneness: Scale development, validation, and application. *Journal of Marketing Management*, *23*(7/8), 697–721. doi:10.1362/026725707X230009

Walsh, G., & Mitchel, V.-W. (2010). The Effect of Consumer Confusion Proneness on Word of Mouth, Trust, and Customer Satisfaction. *European Journal of Marketing*, *44*(6), 838–859. doi:10.1108/03090561011032739

Yusuf, A. (1995). Critical success factors for small business: Perceptions of South Pacific entrepreneurs. *Journal of Small Business Management*, *33*(2), 68–73.

Chapter 9
Online Advertising:
Experimental Facts on Ethics, Involvement, and Product Type

Mehdi Behboudi
Islamic Azad University, Iran

Hamideh Mokhtari
Islamic Azad University, Iran

ABSTRACT

The purpose of this chapter is to provide some insights into advertisements on the Iranian websites. Firstly, in publisher side, is the ethic a matter of fact in accepting Internet advertisements to publish? Second, to provide a preliminary insight into the advertising of pleasant and objectionable products, which one is more? Third, what kind of the involvement (rational or emotional) used more to publish Internet advertisements? Content analysis was used to verify the data. In order to avoid the miscoding of contents, two researchers conducted the analysis and Intercoder reliability used to this goal. we found that (1) all 649 analyzed ads in Iranian websites are belonged to ethical ads and no unethical advertisement found at websites, (2) the majority of published advertisements are belonged to "high involvement product with rational appeal", (3) the "objectionable product ads" at Iranian weblogs was more "pleasant product ads". This study by analyzing 1400 advertisements gives managers some insights and solutions regarding to advertising on the Iranian Internet domains.

BACKGROUND ON ADVERTISING

Before starting the study and how we can find the responses of those questions, it is necessary to speak about advertising and how it communicates with people. For this reason, in following sections we provided some ideas and quotations regarding to advertising in order to give you preliminary background on advertising. So, Advertising is an entity of concepts which marketers are be able to use to introduce products to the market, mostly based on formerly created communication. Advertising is based on two

DOI: 10.4018/978-1-5225-1779-5.ch009

premises: the first is marketing, which attempts to communicate and establish a relationship with customers by transferring value (Darroch, 2004); the second is communication, which serves as a process to create a unified idea between a sender and a receiver (Schramm, 1995). In other words, advertising is the process of sharing concepts among people (Dibb & Simken, 1991). However, some scholars like Richards and Curran (2002) are not agreed with this argument and stated, those processes must be termed as "advertising" that embrace "persuasion". They believe that promotional activities without persuasive cues cannot be named as advertising. Marketing and communication theories have the same origins and thus reinforce each other. The combination of marketing and communication created the emergence of the new subject of marketing communication.

Advertising has been defined in many different ways. Since the definitions are based on researchers' observational approaches, finding the best one is impossible. In order to find a definition upon which many researchers agree, a content analysis was undertaken, and the following definitions seem to be compatible with Internet advertising. Based on study which conducted by Richards & Curran (2002), "advertising is a paid non-personal communication from an identified sponsor, using mass media to persuade or influence an audience" (p. 63). It is believed that the purpose of advertising is to create an image of the product and persuade the customer to buy it. Therefore, advertising is a part of an organization's communications policy in its marketing mix. Decisions on types of advertising formats should be made with respect to introducing a product. According to recent studies, Online advertising is an Internet-based process by which advertisers communicate, interact with, and persuade online users in order to position a brand, which allows a company to promote both consumer awareness and preference in a customized and personalized way, and decrease the time needed to make a buying decision (Hanafizadeh & Behboudi, 2012). However, the question raised here is; do the people show the same manner in facing the online ads? Of course, not, but how they do behave differently? Following parts give us some idea on this matter.

Gender Differences in Behavior, Attitude, and Belief

One of the effective variables in forming a behavior is human nature. Any behavior of a human being is affected by rational and emotional factors like gender. Depending on their gender, human beings have different reactions toward most natural or unnatural phenomena. The Internet is not exempt from this rule. Consumers use the Internet differently depending on whether they are male or female, and these differences are observed in Internet ads as well. The users' perception based on gender has three dimensions in advertising:

- Use patterns.
- Online privacy concerns.
- Behaviors (Wolin & Korgaonkar, 2003).

If users are different in their attitude, communication and behavior pattern due to their gender, it is important to consider the processes that should be utilized to assess the effectiveness of the advertising. Since appropriate evaluation of advertising effectiveness regarding gender allows the advertiser to achieve the target group with a lower cost, many studies have been published on the effectiveness of advertising with gender consideration; these show that gender differences are effective when paying attention to an advertisement. Gender is a key variable in classifying the market, and. there are some factors which should be taken into account when advertising as these factors are different for males and females:

- Identifiability.
- Accessibility.
- Measurability.
- Responding to marketing mix factors.
- Profitability (Darly & Smith, 1995).

Advertisers must recognize the beliefs, attitudes and behavioral patterns based on gender and apply them in advertising design. To understand users' beliefs, attitudes and behaviors, advertisers should focus on message content, because forming the primary framework of these behavioral characteristics depends on the effectiveness of the advertisement on user perception. In analyzing the different factors, which can result in an effective ad, some characteristics should be considered as advertising topics:

- The current stereotyping about differences between the perceptions of men and women.
- The way in which information is analyzed by men and women (For example, consider the clues and cucs that persuade female users to follow ads and apply them in designing an objective and effective advertisement.).
- Positioning gender-based brands (This is critical in order for the organization to be aware that its brand is popular among men or women.).

According to gender, in what dimensions are customers' perceptions different? Studies show that men in general have a more positive attitude toward online ads than women. Men usually search the Internet for entertainment, searching for information and shopping in particular, while women usually use it for communication purposes. Wolin and Korgankar (2003) showed that men perceived online advertisements as either profitable, enjoyable or informative.

- Men find Internet ads more enjoyable than magazine and newspaper ads.
- Men find Internet ads more useful than magazine, newspaper and radio ads.
- Men find Internet ads more informative than magazine, newspaper and radio ads.

The study also focused on aggressiveness, deceptiveness and usefulness, and concluded that women believe that online ads arc:

- More annoying than magazine and newspaper ads.
- More annoying than radio and TV ads.
- More deceptive than TV ads.
- More useful than TV ads.

Due to this report, we can conclude that men have more positive impressions of online advertisements than women and prefer them to traditional advertising.

Behavioral Differences in Terms of Internet Usage

Internet usage has influenced customer motivation to peruse online advertising and to purchase. A customer's reaction to an online advertisement stems from his own beliefs and attitudes toward the Internet. One factor that helps form customers' beliefs and attitudes is the amount of time a customer spends on the Internet. According to Wolin and Korgankar (2001), customers are classified as either heavy or light users. Users from the heavy group have some or all of the following characteristics:

- Higher education.
- Higher revenue.
- Young age group.
- Professional business owners.

Heavy users usually have more positive attitudes toward Internet ads. Compared to light users, heavy users believe that Internet ads are more enjoyable, entertaining, useful and less boring or annoying than traditional ads. Consequently, creating a common ad for all users may not result in reaching the target audience. When advertisers design ads for heavy Internet users, one point should be considered; since these visitors have used the Internet for a long time, they may find that some Internet advertisements promote objectionable products. When advertisers broadcast objectionable or unpleasant products, they usually use unethical cues and materials to appeal to customers. Therefore, in designing ads for heavy Internet users, advertisers must take ethical issues into consideration. When designing advertisements for light users, it should be noted that whereas users assess product features on the basis of their own beliefs and use the Internet to satisfy their needs, they do not think that the Internet is as much of a powerful device for business as do heavy users. Thus, the security aspect of Internet advertising and buying should be emphasized for light users. Also, to persuade light users to follow an advertisement, marketers must stress the informative and enjoyable nature of online advertising (Wolin & Korgankar, 2001). Heavy users believe that Internet advertising and buying will decrease customer costs and that Internet advertising is necessary. In order for advertisers to have more influence on heavy users, they must focus their designs on comparative prices and show comparisons with their competitors. For light users who are less familiar with online advertising and buying advantages, marketers should highlight the comparisons between online and traditional purchasing.

STUDY BACKGROUND

In order to enter the study we now need some statistics on ads on Iranian users' behaviors. According to *Itproportal.com* (2015), the number of currently registered domains has reached 252 million. It is a matter of fact while the number of Internet users worldwide reached 3.5 billion that shows a growth equal to 566.4 percent from 2000 until 2012. The 1.6 billions of these users are connecting from the Asia. Middle East with seventeen countries has nearly 123 million users in which, Iran with 47 billion users ranked at the second country, Bahrain with 1.2 billion ranked at the first place, and Iraq with 11 million placed at the third position (Internetworldstats.com, 2013). As a new active in adopting Internet advertising (Hanafizadeh *et al.,* 2012), Iran by developing websites with high efficiency, user-friendly contents, and appropriate e-business models could acquire high traffic and launch many relevant channels of advertising. Despite advances in online channels available to Internet advertisers, and a shift in spending towards these interactive venues, measuring the impact of Iranian online promotional efforts continues to be a challenge. On the other hand, the Internet as a personalized medium, has still some technically and theoretically difficulties to understand. Doing business through this medium, has a persuasive potential determined by the interactive possibilities of the web sites (Voorveld*et al,*. 2010), a high level of trust of consumers in Web sites (Nielsen, 2009), the opportunity they provide to consumers at all stages in the sales cycle (Voorveld*et al., 2010*), and make consumer hands free to select and go through his/her options (Hanafizadeh & Behboudi, 2012a). It pushes consumer into condition that switches to his/her another mode of behavior –"Serious vs. Playful"- (Rogers and Thorson, 2000), and does not act in accordance with his/her goal-oriented (serious) mode. In this mode, and by considering nobody is there (a private medium), he/she is expected to react to clues and hits that has never ever had a click. In comparison to offline media, this is a natural behavior, because consumer may has some hesitations or feels shame to do those works when he/she realize that other people are watching him/her.

On the other hand, the marketers who are aware of this invisible behavior, are expected to redirect their advertisements to the Internet, specifically, marketers of objectionable product. In Iran, it can be true, because of both governmental regulations in which advertisements of objectionable products is prohibited in mass media, and Islamic culture that do not permit promotion of unconventional images and texts through the society. Notwithstanding Islamic principles and rules, the Internet as a highly personalized medium is expected to turn into the main channel of advertising for these types of products. This idea can be seen true, if we consider two following reasons. First, the Internet provides private channel of advertising which occurs at the individual level not social level (Dahlen, 2004). Second, keeps Islamic society away from social concerns and hesitations regarding to objectionable product advertisements.

Therefore, it is vital to learn more about the ethics and the objectionable product advertisements in Iranian websites. Hence, the aim of this study is to investigate the current advertisements situation in Iranian websites and weblogs from an ethics standpoint, as well as to provide some insights into the nature of current Internet advertisements of Iranian websites and weblogs. Three key questions and one secondary question are designed to pursue above-mentioned goals as following:

1. Is ethics a matter of fact in accepting online advertisements to publish in Iranian website?
2. Do the number of objectionable products advertisements are more than the pleasant ones?
3. What kinds of appeals are used to publish online advertisements (rational or emotional?).

The secondary question:

*   Which types of advertising (Product/service, PSA, Issue, Political, and Corporate) can be seen more in Iranian websites?

LITERATURE REVIEW

Although there has been a significant amount of researches into Internet advertising, however, there is still no consensus about its definition and dimensions (e.g., Schlosser *et al.,* 1999; Ha, 2008). Recently, some researchers attempted to update the definition of advertising. For example, after a series of interchanges with advertising experts, Richards and Curran (2002, p.74) developed the following definition:

"Advertising is a paid, mediated form of communication from an identifiable source, designed to persuade the receiver to take some action now or in the future." Consequently, the purpose of advertising can be summarized as building an image of a product and persuading potential audience to buy that product (Hanafizadeh *et al.*, 2012). However, "Internet advertising is an Internet-based process by which advertisers communicate, interact with and persuade online users in order to position a brand, which allows a company to promote both consumer awareness and preference in a customized and personalized way, and to decrease the time needed to make a buying decision" (Hanafizadeh & Behboudi, 2012, p.22).

Numerous studies have been developed to measure consumer motives for the Internet use (e.g., Korgaonkar & Wolin, 1999; Papacharissi and Rubin, 2000) but the ethics has received less attention by Internet advertising researchers all around the world (e.g., Dahlen, 2002; Sheehan, 2002; Caiand Jun, 2003; Faber *et al.*, 2004; Francis & White, 2004; Weib, 2005; LaFerle & Kim, 2006). As an example Dahlen (2002) has investigated Internet advertising users and concluded that users show a better response to functional products which need to have "think processes". It is reported that for functional product advertising to be effective the advertisement should evoke a dynamic sequence of negative to neutral emotions (Rossiter and Percy, 1991), whereas for expressive products positive emotions should be evoked (Rossiter and Percy, 1991). In this regard, Holbrook and Hirschman (1982) believed that the psychosocial interpretation of expressive products is largely idiosyncratic and less susceptible to explicit information search. As the advertisements for functional products cater to negative purchase motivations and are mainly interesting when the consumer is 'in the market' for the product (Belch 1982; Rossiter and Percy, 1992, 1997; Dahlén & Bergendahl, 2001), repeated exposures should quickly lead to tedium (Sawyer, 1981; Tellis, 1997). Razzouk *et al.*, (2005) analyzed value-based advertising strategies for high and low involvement products, the results showed that most websites reviewed seem to comply with expected value-based advertising strategies. Some researchers have investigated ethical concerns in websites. In recent years, a lot of ethical issues have arisen among the shopping websites, such as: advertising misleading/ untruthfulness, bad product quality, cheating, privacy, property, information misuse, trust betrayal, etc. (Yang *et al*, . 2009). These all happened because the development of ethics cannot keep pace with the growth of technology in the online business, and hence bring a lot of problems whose scope is not clear yet. For example, Creyer (1997) reported that customers are willing to pay higher prices in some ethical firms and pay lower prices to punish other unethical firms. Creyer's findings imply that a firm's ethical performance will have positive impact on the shopping behavior of customers. In online circumstances, consumers will shop only if they trust the website.

In advertising context, Murphy (1998) stated that, there are three key moral principles on which advertising should be based: truthfulness, dignity of human person, and social responsibility (Murphy, 1998). Yang *et al.*, (2009), believe, apart from new problems accompanied with applications of new information technology (IT), on the whole, lack of ethical consideration and responsibility of web vendors can be regarded as one of the main factors that cause consumers to feel dissatisfied and insecure. Therefore, it is crucial to increase the ethical concern of the web vendors to make the online business successful. Radin*et al.*, (2007) listed ethical issues in EC including privacy, security concerns, websites unlabeled as advertising, cyber squatters, online marketing children, conflicts of interest, and manufacturers competing with intermediaries online. According to some studies of ethical issues facing the Internet, the most often mentioned ethical concerns regarding marketing on the Internet are security of transactions, illegal activity (e.g. fraud and hacking), privacy, honesty/trustfulness, judgment by same standard as other media, pornography, product warranty, plagiarism, targeting children, unsolicited e-mails, and false advertising (Bhattacherjee, 2002; Peslak, 2006; Ryker*et al.*, 2002).

Ethical issues related to advertising content include the use of informative versus emotional, persuasive advertising (Lppke, 1989), using messages such as fear (Rotfeld, 1989) and sexual appeals (LaTourand Hawthorn, 1994). It can be concluded that ethics concerns have different judgments among researchers, and there is a need for more research and better measures of ethics among online advertisements. Regarding to advertising, Nairnand Dew, (2007) examined the ethics of targeting children through the Internet and the evidence behind these concerns. They found that advertising tends to be for products not used by children. In particular, they reported that there is significant use of popular children's characters to incite sales. Heidarzadeh *et al.,* (2011) investigated the electronic police and its impact on the websites' sales in Iran. They found that there are two different behavioral reactions. By adding police logo to a shopping website, they found that pleasant products has a positive impact and strengthens trust-making procedure of users for more purchase. Nevertheless, this would have negative impact on those shopping websites that present objectionable products.

Although, literature shows there are many studies have conducted regarding to ethical concerns in websites, but there is still a gap need to cover in regards to published advertisements on the Internet. Specifically, no study conducted to report differences among advertisements contents appeared at websites and weblogs. There are some surmises that websites and weblogs permit advertisers to publish their non-ethical materials for getting a little more fee. Moreover, it is assumed that websites and weblogs with the purpose of getting more traffic, they feel free to use sexual and non-moral appeals. By considering Iranian religious traditions and cultures, this study is to investigate these concerns. After reviewing the literature of ethics in advertising body of tradition, we now need to consider studies, which have been conducted in web delimitation by using content analysis. The aim of reviewing these studies is to report those methods that used to analyze web-based content.

The first attempt was made by Liu (1997), analyze the content of homepages by looking for a set of features. The conclusions from his study were that the objective of Fortunc 500 companies in establishing homepages was to announce the companies' presence on the web, to promote the companies' image, to enhance public relations, to attract users to browse products and services, and to collect user responses and other related data. Two years later, Vattyam and Lubbers (1999), were also interested in homepage features and performed a content analysis of 83 of the Fortune 100 companies. Their results indicated that many activities found on these homepages are traditionally associated with public relations. Bell &Tang (1998) attempted to perform a survey of 60 companies that used the Internet, examining the effectiveness of their commercial websites, predominantly from the user's perspective. The results of an online survey found that only 30 percent of the companies had facilities for conducting transactions online and only seven percent charged users for website access. Bucy*et al.,* (1998) conducted a content analysis on 496 famous websites and reported co-features of online advertising including: animation, color, and graphic. Smith and Strahm (2000) used social network analysis to examine the links between white supremacist sites. Consistent with the expectations discussed above, they found that the movement was decentralized, but that there were no sharp divisions between the groups and that different kinds of groups frequently linked to one another. They found evidence that the Internet does assist in the creation of an international virtual extremist community: over two thirds of the links were to international sites.

Perry and Bodkin (2000) performed a content analysis of Web sites utilizing categories representing a range of marketing communications, and found considerable variability in how members of the Fortune 100 used their websites. The websites ranged from very simple ones that focused on basic company information, such as company history, to quite complex Web sites that incorporated a mix of promotional elements, such as press releases, advertisements, games, free gifts and pricing information. Weareand

Lin (2000), examined methodological issues for content analytic research of the World Wide Web. They suggest that The World Wide Web is characterized by its ubiquity, global reach, interactivity, decentralized, hyperlinked structure, and multimedia format. All of these characteristics present researchers with opportunities and challenges at each step of a content analysis: sampling, unitization, development of content categories, coding, and analysis.

Schafer (2002) rated 132 extremist sites. He concluded that these web sites provide a wide range of information, that many of the sites provide groups with the opportunity to sell products, and that the web sites are often used as tools to facilitate communication among members. Gerstenfeld *et al.,* (2003) conducted a content analysis of 157 extremist web sites using two raters per site. They found that the majority of sites contained external links to other extremist sites (including international sites), that roughly half the sites included multimedia content, and that half contained racist symbols. Moreover, they reported that a third of the sites disavowed racism or hatred, yet one third contained material from supremacist literature. According to Gerstenfeld *et al.,* (2003) these and other findings suggest that the Internet may be an especially powerful tool for extremists as a means of reaching an international audience.

Frosch*et al.,* (2007) by conducting a content analysis on television direct-to-consumer advertising reported that most ads made some factual claims and made rational arguments for product use, but few described condition causes, risk factors, or prevalence. Emotional appeals were almost universal. In order to detect the advertisements automatically, Dou *et al.,* (2010), proposed a Web-based advertising content analysis platform. Their platform consists of the following three parts: web information extraction, advertiser's named entity identification and advertiser's industry identification. To provide a fairly comprehensive background to readers, this study was developed a theoretical framework to examine its four questions in the form of study's questions.

Theoretical Framework

1. Product types

Pleasant products are those that create no shame for purchaser or seller while they are exchanged, on the other hand, objectionable products are those ones that include some kind of hesitation and shame in their buying process. In other word, objectionable products are legal products that rarely can be on the shelf of stores and need some kind of private channels of distribution. The pattern for purchase of pleasant products is different with objectionable products. It can be concluded that consumers in shopping objectionable products are willing to go to the Internet since internet is a private medium and nobody can discover their wants to buy those products. On the other hand, advertisers by being aware of this behavior of consumers are expected to publish their objectionable products advertisements through the Internet. Hence, a question is designed to check the validity of this argument as follow:

Question 1: Do the more a medium is personalized, the more objectionable products are publishing through that medium?

2. Product Involvement

Product involvement, which is related to elaboration and the amount of attention dedicated to advertising messages (Gardner *et al.,* 1985), has been reported to be a major determinant of the consumer's behavior and response to a certain ad (Laurent & Kapferer, 1985). It is a matter of fact, since product affect its advertising plan. From an appeal point of view, advertising messages with low involvement are completely different from high involvement ones (Yang, 1997). Wills *et al.,* (1991) believed that products with low involvement should be advertised through emotional appeals and products with high involvement should be advertised through rational appeals. Dahlen, (2002) stated that banner advertisement is not effective for functional products, while it works effectively for expressive products and makes positive attitude toward them. According to Vaughn, (1986), there are four types of involvement; rational involvement (high and low) and emotional involvement (high and low). High involvement customers need to be persuaded with strong arguments, whereas low involvement customers do not need strong arguments and do not need to be persuaded to the same extent as high involvement customers (Petty *et al.,* 1983; Petty & Cacciopo, 1984). By considering that the Internet is rational medium (Dahlen*et al.,* 2004), following hypotheses are designed to examine Iranian websites advertisements from an involvement point of view:

Question 2a: Do the majority of published advertisements through Iranian websites are using high involvement?

Question 2b: Do the majority of published advertisements through Iranian websites are using rational appeals?

3. Ethics in Internet Advertising

Consumer distrust of advertising (Shavitt*et al.,* 1998) and strong inclinations toward advertising avoidance (Kelly et al., 2010). One factor that is reported as affecting variable in avoiding from advertisement is irrelevant culture. Hall (1976) stated that culture is communication and communication is culture. The influence of cultures particularly important in transferring advertising strategy across the borders, because communication patterns are closely linked to cultural norms in each market (Hong *et al.,* 1987). Thus, if advertising differences across cultures can be predictable, the task of the advertiser in multiple cultures can be much simplified (Albers-Miller & Gelb, 1996). On the other hand, culture and advertising are intrinsically connected with each other. Cultural influence on consumers' beliefs and attitudes toward advertising has been well documented in the marketing literature (e.g. Durvasula & Lysonski, 2001; La Ferleet *et al.,* 2008). More specifically, Durvasula and Lysonski, (2001) systematically compared consumers' attitudes toward advertising in five countries located on four different continents and deduced that beliefs toward advertising vary across culture in general. Nevertheless, on the one hand, in religious countries like Iran, it is expected to find a opposite behaviors and on the other hand, by considering medium of Internet that has an interactive and personalized route, following hypotheses are designed to test the validity of current surmises:

Question 3a: Do ethics is a matter of fact in published advertisements in Iranian *websites*?

Question 3b: Do ethics is not a matter of fact in published advertisements in Iranian *weblogs*?

RESEARCH METHODOLOGY

The objective of this study is to analyze websites and weblogs' contents in terms of published advertisements. In order to gather data, a content analysis – a common method used in analyzing advertising and website contents (Okazaki, 2004) – is performed. Content analysis is extensively used in advertising literature in order to study cultural value appeals and it is described as an objective, systematic and quantitative way of conducting information about communication content (Tong & Robertson, 2008). Moreover, it has a wide use in cross-cultural advertisements both on the web and in TV or print media, especially in the global arena (Baack & Singh, 2007).

First, we developed an operational definition in order to identify which websites have eligibility to be at the scope of study. In this way, those websites were selected that have highest traffic rank according to *Alexa.com* statistics. *Alexa.com* is worldview website that offers websites rank and the traffic condition country by country.*Alexa.com* recently offered 500 top websites of each country based on the traffic volume. We considered 250 websites of this record as sample of study. However, in the middle of analysis, we have faced with the problem that near to 45 of these websites are filtered according to Iran's Internet Usage Regulations; consequently, we had to analyze 205 websites.

Since there was no reference website to publish statistic regarding to weblogs, we developed a heuristic methodology in order to gather weblogs. In this way, first of all, by interviewing with advertising experts, (those who had a background in teaching advertising and doing ad campaigns on the Internet); eleven keywords related to word "objectionable" (namely: Gain and Lose Weight pills, Depilatory cream, Razor, Tweezer, Devices for Men, Stimulus Drop, Infertility pills, Body whitening cream, Underwear, Breast Cream for Women, Impotence Treatment Cream) were chosen. The keywords then were searched in Google and 138 first ranked weblogs selected to perform content analysis. For selecting 138 weblogs, we have relied on saturation principal and accepted first records page of Google. This way adopted since after searching a keywords, regardless of two first pages, other pages contain unrelated links and concepts. As we know, Google search algorithms are usually designed in a way that permit a record list at the first page only because of two reasons. First one is more searches or visits, and second one is, good performance on Search Engine Optimization, SEO (Hanafizadeh & Behboudi, 2012). All search regarding eleven keywords of objectionable products were done in Google Persian and by which the homepages of 138 weblogs visited. It is necessary to mention that since some of those links have been filtered, this part of study was conducted by using anti-filters.

RESULTS AND DISCUSSION

1. Content analysis released that the number of "objectionable product ads" observed at Iranian weblogs (512 ads or 68percent) was more than "pleasant product ads" (239 ads or 32 percent). This finding verify question number one «the more a medium is personalized, the more objectionable products are publishing through that medium». But these results are not valid for websites. Because from 649 observed ads among 205 analyzed websites, we found only 33 (5 percent) objectionable product ads. It shows that Iranian websites use a formal theme and practice in regarding to accepting advertisements to publish.

2. Content analysis was restricted to websites and revealed that majority of published advertisements are belonged to "high involvement product with rational appeal". From 649 published ads in websites, 297 ads or 46 percent were "high involvement product with rational appeal" which pushes them to take the first place. After that "low involvement product with rational appeal" (165 or 26 percent), "low involvement product with emotional appeal" (122 or 19 percent), "high involvement product with emotional appeal" (65 or 1 percent) were placed respectively. Based on this statistics, we can

conclude that there are significant evidences to validate hypotheses number two (Q2a and Q2b) "the majority of published advertisements through Iranian websites are using high involvement, and the majority of published advertisements through Iranian websites are using rational appeals".

3. Content analysis showed that all 649 published ads in Iranian websites are belonged to ethical ads and no unethical advertisement found at websites. By these evidences, there is no statistic to reject question number three (Qa) "ethics is a matter of fact in published advertisements in Iranian websites". In addition, from 751 analyzed ads among weblogs, we could only find six ads that do not care ethical issues in their appeals and cues. Accordingly, we can conclude that there is no evidence to accept question number three (Qb) "ethics is not a matter of fact in published advertisements in Iranian weblogs". It is necessary to note that, although we found 512 objectionable product ads among 751 observed advertisements, but they were naturally shame product not using shame appeals to persuade consumers to react.

Regarding to secondary question: "Which types of advertisements (Product/service, PSA, Issue, Political, and Corporate) can be seen more in Iranian websites", we found that the "product/service" advertisements have highest frequency in Iranian websites. From 649 observed ads 394 were belong to "product/service" (e.g. mobile cell phone and software), 121 ads were belong to "issue ads" (e.g. job searching, symposium, contests), 99 ads were belong to "PSAs" (e.g. health care and nonprofit organizations announcements), 35 ads were belong to "corporate ads" (e.g. stock exchange), and surprisingly no political ads can be seen in this time analysis.

This study also releases some other valuable leads from Iranian websites and weblogs as follow:

1. Compared to websites, weblogs have published an addition number of advertisements. Owning the fact that from 138 weblogs we observed 751 advertisements (i.e. 5.5 ads in each weblog), while from 205 websites we only could find 649 ads (i.e. 3.2 ads in each website). It shows ads published at weblogs are almost two times in comparison to websites.
2. Most of advertisements have designed to in way that appears in cold colors (like green and blue).
3. Published advertisements in websites and weblogs ranged from all kind of products. In websites, we could see: mobile cell phone, training CDs, drugs (for losing weight and diet materials), software, watches, and internet modems. Instead in weblogs, we observed toiletries and cosmetics, products related to cohabits, and atrophy pills.

CONCLUSION

The objective of this study was to provide some insights to following questions: Is ethics a matter of fact in accepting online advertisements to publish in Iranian website. Do the number of objectionable advertisements are more than the pleasant ones? What kinds of appeals are used to publish online advertisements (rational or emotional)? Moreover, which types of advertising (Product/service, PSA, Issue, Political, and Corporate) can be seen more in Iranian websites? In pursuit of this goal, a theoretical framework was designed by reviewing the literature and body of tradition. Finally, in order to test questions, the content of 1400 advertisements that were published at 205 websites and 139 weblogs were analyzed. The possible contribution of the present study is fourfold. First, this is the foremost content analysis that has been conducted on Iranian websites and weblogs, which in turn is remarkable. Second, this paper could provide some in-depth insights into surmises regarding Iranian websites and their ethical issues. Third, the present paper identified the type of appeals which are using in Iranian websites and weblogs. Finally, it offers a categorization from all products advertisements published in Iranian websites and weblogs.

The first thing that this study learns to objectionable products marketers is that weblogs are an appropriate channel to reach right users. Since they use an informal template, which in turn permit marketers to use some beyond the scope options to publish their advertisements and follow an "open hands" practice. Moreover, the majority of weblogs are filtered. Surprisingly, we could observe that most of the high traffic weblogs are filtered, but still get their adequate users from search engines and type in. Although this is a governmental rule, however, neither advertisers nor audiences do not care it and find a route to reach their enjoyable weblogs. If we consider a pull strategy of advertisement (Hanafizadeh & Behboudi, 2012a), we can conclude those consumers that seeking objectionable products have an adequate motive to visit high traffic weblogs, even though they are filtered. It makes those weblogs an appropriate place for advertising of those products. The second thing that this study learns to international marketers is that Iranian websites are a good platform to publish those advertisements that using rational appeals. It does not matter they use low or high involvement, because the findings in this regard (high involvement with rational appeals (0.46), and 165 low involvement with rational appeal (0.26) have a significant difference in comparison to two other areas (high involvement with emotional appeals (0.1) and low involvement with emotional appeals (0.19). Hence, this study suggest to marketers that pay more attention to the type of web advertising format (Hanafizadeh & Behboudi, 2012b), type of audiences (Hanafizadeh & Behboudi, 2012a) and internet publishers (Hanafizadeh *et al.*, 2012). Since, according to those studies internet advertisements in Iran is still at the first stage of adoption and need to developing proficient publishers and ad agencies to improve this field of business. Finally, this study learns to international marketers who intent to advertise in Iran through Internet is this point that; there is no doubt that ethics are a matter of fact, specifically in websites. The more these marketers avoid using unethical cues and appeals, the more they are expected to be successful. Expect of cosmetics (although they were seldom and just 6 objectionable ones of them used to have unethical cues), weblogs show a care about ethical issues and do not publish objectionable product with unethical cues. This caused from Islamic culture of this country. Because the majority of weblogs owners are Muslims and they believed that the revenue must be *Halal* (i.e. the one revenue should not results in the other disserves). They believed that when you accept to publish unethical ads, you are implicitly put society away from its spiritual purpose.

REFERENCES

Albers-Miller, N. D., & Gelb, D. B. (1996). Business advertising appeals as a mirror of cultural dimensions: A study of *eleven* countries. *Journal of Advertising*, 25(4), 57–70. doi:10.1080/00913367.1996.10673512

Baack, D. W., & Singh, N. (2007). Culture and web communications. *Journal of Business Research*, 60(3), 181–188. doi:10.1016/j.jbusres.2006.11.002

Belanger, B., Hiller, S. B., & Smith, W. J. (2002). Trustworthiness in electronic commerce: The role of privacy, security, and site attributes. *The Journal of Strategic Information Systems*, 11(3-4), 245–270. doi:10.1016/S0963-8687(02)00018-5

Belch, G.E. (1982). The effect of television commercial repetition on cognitive response and message acceptance. *Journal of Consumer Research, 9*(1), 56–65.

Bell, H., Nelson, K., & Tang, N. K. (1998). The effective of commercial Internet websites: A user's perspective. *Electronic Networking Applications and Policy, 8*(3), 219–228. doi:10.1108/10662249810217768

Bhattacherjee, A. (2002). Individual Trust in Online Firms: Scale Development and Initial Test. *Journal of Management Information Systems, 19*(1), 211–241.

Bucy, E. P., Lang, A., Potter, R. F., & Grabe, M. E. (1998). *Structural features of cyberspace: A content analysis of the World Wide Web.* Paper presented at the 1998 Conference of the Association for Education in Journalism and Mass Communication, Theory and Methodology Division, Baltimore, MD.

Burris, V., Smith, E., & Strahm, A. (2000). White supremacist network on the Internet. *Sociological Focus, 33*(2), 215–234. doi:10.1080/00380237.2000.10571166

Cheema, A., & Papatla, P. (2010). Relative importance of online versus offline information for Internet purchases: Product category and Internet experience effects. *Journal of Business Research, 63*(9-10), 979–985. doi:10.1016/j.jbusres.2009.01.021

Chellappa, R. K., & Paol, A. P. (2002). Perceived information security, financial liability and consumer trust in electronic commerce transactions. *Logistic Information Management, 15*(5-6), 358–368. doi:10.1108/09576050210447046

Choi, M. S., & Rifon, N. J. (2010). Antecedents and consequences of Web advertising credibility: A study of consumer response to banner ads. *Journal of Interactive Advertising, 3*(1), 12–24. doi:10.108 0/15252019.2002.10722064

Creyer, E. H. (1997). The Influence of Firm Behavior on Purchase Intention: Do Consumers Really Care About Business Ethics? *Journal of Consumer Marketing, 14*(6), 421–432. doi:10.1108/07363769710185999

Culnan, M. J., & Milne, R. G. (2001). *The Culnan-Milne survey on consumers and online privacy notices: summary of responses.* Federal Trade Commission. Available at: http://www.ftc.gov/bcp/workshops/glb/supporting/culnan-milne.pdf

Dahlén, M. (2002). Thinking and feeling on the World Wide Web:the impact of product type and time on World Wide Web advertising effectiveness. *Journal of Marketing Communications, Vol, 8*(2), 115–125. doi:10.1080/13527260210142347

Dahlén, M., & Bergendahl, J. (2001). Informing and transforming on the web: An empirical study of response to banner ads for functional and expressive products. *International Journal of Advertising, 20*(2), 189–205.

Dahlén, M., Murray, M., & Nordenstam, S. (2004). An empirical study of perceptions of implicit meanings in World Wide Web advertisements versus print advertisements. *Journal of Marketing Communications, 10*(1), 35–47. doi:10.1080/1352726042000177391

Dinev, T., & Hart, P. (2006, January1). Internet privacy concerns and social awareness as determinants of intention to transact. *International Journal of Electronic Commerce, 10*(2), 7–29. doi:10.2753/JEC1086-4415100201

Dou, R., Wu, J., Zhang, S., & Liang, W. (2010). A Web-based advertising content analysis platform. *Future Information Technology and Management Engineering (FITME),International Conference.*

Durvasula, S., & Lysonski, S. (2001). Are there global dimensions of beliefs toward advertising in general: A multicultural investigation. In C. P. Rao (Ed.), Globalization and its managerial implications (pp. 184–202). Westport, CT: Quorum Books.

Ellis, S. T., & Griffith, D. (2001). The Evaluation of IT Ethical Scenarios Using a Multidimensional Scale. *The Data Base for Advances in Information Systems, 32*(1), 75–85. doi:10.1145/506740.506750

Faber, R. J., Lee, M., & Nan, X. (2004). Advertising and the consumer information environment online. *The American Behavioral Scientist, 48*(4), 447–466. doi:10.1177/0002764204270281

Frosch, D. L., Krueger, P. M., Honrik, R. C., Cronholm, P. F., & Barg, F. K. (2007). "Creating Demand for Prescription Drugs: A Content Analysis of Television Direct-to-Consumer Advertising", 1 (January). *Annals of Family Medicine*, 16–13.

Garener, M. P., Mitchell, A. A., & Russo, E. J. (1985). Low involvement strategies for processing advertisements. *Journal of Advertising, 14*(2), 4–56. doi:10.1080/00913367.1985.10672941

Gerstenfeld, P. B., Grant, D. R., & Chiang, C. (2003). Hate Online: A Content Analysis of Extremist Internet Sites. *Analyses of Social Issues and Public Policy (ASAP), 3*(1), 29–44. doi:10.1111/j.1530-2415.2003.00013.x

Ha, L. (2008). Online Advertising Research Advertising Journals: A Review. *Journal of Current Issues and Research in Advertising, 30*(1), 31–48. doi:10.1080/10641734.2008.10505236

Hall, E. T. (1976). Beyond Culture. Doubleday.

Hanafizadeh, P., & Behboudi, M. (2012). *Online advertising and Promotion, New Technologies for Marketing*. IGI-Global. doi:10.4018/978-1-4666-0885-6

Hanafizadeh, P., Behboudi, M., Ahadi, F., & Ghaderi Varkani, F. (2012). Internet Advertising Adoption; a Structural Equation Model for Iranian SMEs. *Internet Research, 22*(4), 499–526. doi:10.1108/10662241211251015

Heidarzadeh Hanzaee, K., Behboudi, M., & Sadr, F. (2011). Emerging New Concept of Electronic Police and its Impact on the Websites' Sales. *Interdisciplinary Journal of Research in Business, 1*(3), 8–14.

Hoffman, D., Novak, T. P., & Peralta, M. (1999). Building consumer trust online. *Communications of the ACM, 42*(4), 80–85. doi:10.1145/299157.299175

Hofmeister-Toth, A., & Nagy, P. (2011). The content analysis of adver-games in Hungary. *Qualitative Market Research: An International Journal, 14*(3), 289–303. doi:10.1108/13522751111137514

Holbrook, M. B., & Hirschman, E. C. (1982). The experiential aspects of consumption: Consumer fantasies, feelings, and fun. *The Journal of Consumer Research, 9*(2), 132–140. doi:10.1086/208906

IAB.net. (2011). *Internet Advertising Revenues Hit $7.3 Billion in Q1 '11 Highest First-Quarter Revenue Level on Record According to IAB and PwC*. Retrieved from www.iab.net

Internetworldstats.com. (2012). *Internet Users and Population Statistics for 35 countries and regions in Asia.* Retrieved from: http://www.internetworldstats.com/stats3.htm

Itproportal.com. (2011). *Number Of Domain Names Registered Approaching 200 Million.* Retrieved from: http://www.itproportal.com/2010/02/23/number-domain-names-registered-approaching-200-million/

Kelly, L., Gayle, K., & Drennan, J. (2010). Avoidance of Advertising in Social Networking Sites: The Teenager Perspective. *Journal of Interactive Advertising, 10*(2), 16–27. doi:10.1080/15252019.2010.10722167

Kim, W., Jeong, O., Kim, C., & So, J. (2011). The dark side of the internet: Attacks, cost and responses. *Information Systems, 36*, 675–705. doi:10.1016/j.is.2010.11.003

Korgaonkar, P. K., & Wolin, L. D. (1999). A multivariate analysis of web usage. *Journal of Advertising Research, 39*(2), 53–68.

Kotler, P. (2001). Marketing Management. Prentice Hall.

La Ferle, C., Edwards, S. M., & Lee, W. (2008). Culture, attitudes, and media patterns in China, Taiwan, and the U.S. balancing standardization and localization decisions. *Journal of Global Marketing, 21*(3), 191–205. doi:10.1080/08911760802152017

La Ferle, C., & Kim, H. (2006). Cultural influences on internet motivations and communication styles: A comparison of Korean and US consumers. *International Journal of Internet Marketing and Advertising, 3*(2), 142–157. doi:10.1504/IJIMA.2006.010296

LaTour, M. S., & Hawthorne, T. (1994). Ethical judgments of Sexual appeals in print advertising. *Journal of Advertising, 23*(3), 81–90. doi:10.1080/00913367.1994.10673453

Laurtent, G., & Kaoferer, J. (1985). Measuring consumer involvement profiles. *JMR, Journal of Marketing Research, 22*(1), 41–53. doi:10.2307/3151549

Li, D., Browne, G., & Wetherbe, J. (2006). Why do internet users stick with a specific website? a relationship perspective. *International Journal of Electronic Commerce, 10*(4), 105–141. doi:10.2753/JEC1086-4415100404

Liao, H., Proctor, R. W., & Salvendy, G. (2008). Content preparation for cross-cultural e-commerce: A review and a model. *Behaviour & Information Technology, 27*(1), 43–61. doi:10.1080/01449290601088424

Lippke, R. L. (1989). Advertising and the social conditions of autonomy. *Business & Professional Ethics Journal, 8*(4), 35–58. doi:10.5840/bpej19898417

Liu, C., Arnett, K. P., Capella, L. M., & Beatty, R. C. (1997). websites of the Fortune 500 companies: Facing customers through home pages. *Information & Management, 31*(6), 335–345. doi:10.1016/S0378-7206(97)00001-3

Murphy, P. E. (1998). Ethics in advertising, review, analysis, and suggestions. *Journal of Public Policy & Marketing, 17*(2), 316–319.

Nacar, R., & Burnaz, S. (2011). A cultural content analysis of multinational companies' web sites. *Qualitative Market Research, An International Journal, 14*(3), 274–288. doi:10.1108/13522751111137505

Nairn, A., & Dew, A. (2007). Pop-ups, pop-under, banners and buttons: The ethics of online advertising to primary school children. *Journal of Direct, Data and Digital Marketing Practice*, (May), 30–46. Available at http://www.palgrave-journals.com/dddmp/journal/v9/n1/full/4350076a.html

Nebenzahl, I. D., & Jaffe, E. D. (1998). Ethics dimensions of advertising executions. *Journal of Business Ethics*, *17*(7), 805–815. doi:10.1023/A:1005850812845

Nielsen. (2009). *Global Consumer Confidence Survey*. Nielsen Company.

Okazaki, S. (2004). Do multinationals standardize or localize? The cross-cultural dimensionality of product-based web sites. *Internet Research: Electronic Networking Applications and Policy*, *14*(1), 81–94. doi:10.1108/10662240410516336

Papacharissi, Z., & Alan, R. M. (2000). Predictors of internet use. *Journal of Broadcasting & Electronic Media*, *44*(2), 175–196. doi:10.1207/s15506878jobem4402_2

Perry, M., & Bodkin, C. (2000). Content analysis of Fortune 100 company Web sites. *Corporate Communications An International Journal*, *5*(2), 87–96. doi:10.1108/13563280010338331

Peslak, A. R. (2006). PAPA revisited: A current empirical study of the Mason framework. *Journal of Computer Information Systems*, *46*(3), 117–123.

Petty, R. E., & John, C. T. (1984). The Effects of Involvement on Responses to Argument Quantity and Quality: Central and Peripheral Routes to Persuasion. *Journal of Personality and Social Psychology*, *46*(1), 69–81. doi:10.1037/0022-3514.46.1.69

Petty, R. E., John, C. T., & Schumann, D. (1983). Central and Peripheral Routes to Advertising Effectiveness: The Moderating of Involvement. *The Journal of Consumer Research*, *10*(2), 135–146. doi:10.1086/208954

Phelps, J., Nowak, G., & Ferrell, E. (2000a). Privacy concerns and consumer willingness to provide personal information. *Journal of Public Policy & Marketing*, *19*(1), 27–41. doi:10.1509/jppm.19.1.27.16941

Phelps, J. D., D'Souza, G., & Nowak, G. J. (2000b). Antecedents and consequences of consumer Privacy concerns: An empirical investigation. *Journal of Interactive Marketing*, *15*(4), 2–17. doi:10.1002/dir.1019

Radin, T. J., Calkins, M., & Predmore, C. (2007). New Challenges to Old Problems: Building Trust In E-marketing. *Business and Society Review*, *112*(1), 73–98. doi:10.1111/j.1467-8594.2007.00287.x

Razzouk, N. Y., Setiz, V., Lamuda, K., & Kepekci, A. C. (2005). A Content Analysis of Value-Based Advertising on the Internet. *Journal of Website Promotion*, *1*(3), 61–73. doi:10.1300/J238v01n03_05

Richards, J. I., & Curran, C. M. (2002). Oracles on Advertising: Searching for a Definition. *Journal of Advertising*, *31*(2), 63–77. doi:10.1080/00913367.2002.10673667

Rodgers, S., & Thorson, E. (2000). The Interactive Advertising Model: How Users Perceive and Process Online Ads. *Journal of Interactive Advertising*, *1*(1), 42–61. doi:10.1080/15252019.2000.10722043

Rodgers, S., Wang, Y., Rettie, R., & Alpert, F. (2007). The Web Motivation Inventory Replication, extension and application to internet advertising. *International Journal of Advertising*, *26*(4), 447–476.

Rossiter, J. R., & Percy, L. (1991). Emotions and motivations in advertising. *Advances in Consumer Research. Association for Consumer Research (U. S.), 18*, 100–110.

Rossiter, J. R., & Percy, L. (1992). A model of brand awareness and brand attitude advertising strategies. *Psychology and Marketing, 9*(4), 263–274. doi:10.1002/mar.4220090402

Rossiter, J. R., & Percy, L. (1997). *Advertising Communications and Promotion Management.* McGraw-Hill.

Rotfeld, H.J. (1988). Fear appeals and persuasion: Assumption and errors in advertising research. *Current Issues and Research in Advertising, 11*(1), 221-40.

Ryker, R., LaFleur, E., McManis, B., & Cox, C. K. (2002). Online privacy policies:An assessment of the fortuneE-50. *Journal of Computer Information Systems, 42*(4), 15–20.

Sawyer, A. (1981). Repetition, cognitive responses and persuasion. In R. E. Petty, T. M. Ostrom, & T. C. Brock (Eds.), *Cognitive Responses in Persuasion* (pp. 237–262). Lawrence Erlbaum Associates.

Schafer, J. A. (2002). Spinning the web of hate: Web-based hate propagation by extremist organizations. *Journal of Criminal Justice and Popular Culture, 69–88.* Available at http://www.albany.edu/scj/jcjpc/vol9is2/schafer.pdf

Schlosser, E. A., Shavitt, S., & Kanfer, A. (1999). Survey of internet users' attitudes toward internet advertising. *Journal of Interactive Marketing*, 34–54.

Shavitt, S., Lowrey, P., & Haefner, J. (1998). Public Attitudes Toward Advertising: More Favorable Than You Might Think. *Journal of Advertising Research, 38*(4), 7–22.

Sheehan, K. B. (2002). Of surfing, searching, and newshounds: A typology of Internet users online sessions. *Journal of Advertising Research, 42*(5), 62–71. doi:10.2501/JAR-42-5-62-71

Tellis, G. J. (1997). Effective frequency: one exposure or three factors?. *Journal of Advertising Research,* 75–80. Available at http://papers.ssrn.com/sol3/papers.cfm?abstract_id=906019

Thorson, E. (1996). Advertising. In An integrated Approach to Communication Theory and Research (pp. 211-230). Mahwah, NJ: Lawrence Erlbaum.

Tong, M. C., & Robertson, K. (2008). Political and cultural representation in Malaysian websites. *International Journal of Design, 2*(2), 67–79.

Turban, E., King, D., McKay, J., Marshall, P., & Lee, L. K. (2008). *Electronic Commerce 2008: A Managerial Perspective.* Pearson Prentice Hall. Available at: www.pearsonhighered.com

U.S Census Bureau News. (2011). *Monthly and Annual Retail Trade.* Retrieved from http://www.censuse.gov/www/ecomm.htm/

Vattyam, S., & Lubbers, C. A. (1999). *A content analysis of the web pages of large U.S corporations: What is the role of public relations and marketing?.* Paper submitted to the Public Relations Division of the AEJMC for review for the 1999 Conference.

Vaughan, R. (1986). How advertising works: A planning model. *Journal of Advertising Research, 1*(1), 57–66.

Voorveld, H. A. M., Neijens, P. C., & Smit, E. G. (2011). The Relation Between Actual and Perceived Interactivity, What Makes the Web Sites of Top Global Brands Truly Interactive. *Journal of Advertising*, *40*(2), 77–92. doi:10.2753/JOA0091-3367400206

Weare, C., & Lin, W. Y. (2000). Content Analysis of the World Wide Web Opportunities and Challenges. *Social Science Computer Review, 18*(3), 272-292.

Weiss, D. (2005). Internetnutzung im studium – Erklarung and vorhersage der internetnutzung von studierenden in Deutschland und Osterreich. *Psychologie–Medienpsychologie*, *135*(1-3), 135.

Wills, J., Samli, C. A., & Jacobs, L. (1991). Developing global products and construct and a research agenda. *Journal of the Marketing Strategies: Academy of Marketing Science*, *19*(1), 1–10.

Yang, C. (1997). An exploratory study of the effectiveness of interactive advertisements on the Internet. *Journal of Marketing Communications*, *3*(2), 61–85. doi:10.1080/135272697345970

Yang, M. H., Natalyn, C., Lin, B., & Cho, H. Y. (2009). The effect of perceived ethical performance of websites on consumer trust. *Journal of Computer Information Systems*, *50*(1), 15.

Chapter 10
Co–Creating the Christmas Story:
Digitalizing as a Shared Resource for a Shared Brand

Rauno Rusko
University of Lapland, Finland

Petra Merenheimo
University of Lapland, Finland

ABSTRACT

Digitalization can be regarded as a megatrend which results that both brand building and brand management must adapt to new challenges. The growing role of digitizing points to both challenges and risks, as well as to opportunities. This chapter conceptualizes digitizing as a resource for brand development with the help of two tourism destinations. It focuses on the role Web-based platforms play in destination brand development, using the examples of two seemingly nearly similar Christmas tourism destinations as case studies: Santa Claus, Indiana, and Santa Claus Village, Rovaniemi. The chapter highlights the contribution of a customer-oriented digitalization to creating a competitive advantage, even a sustainable one, for tourism destinations with theoretical connections to a resource-based view (RBV) and discusses its potential for incremental and radical innovative brand development processes.

INTRODUCTION

Digitalization is an interesting phenomenon: despite its technological groundings it clearly points to non-technological innovation potential (Jeannerat & Crevoisier, 2011). Through digitalization, brand building is becoming a dialectic and participatory approach where managers are said losing their control over brands (Ind, 2015). Digitalization can nowadays be regarded as a megatrend which results that both brand building and brand management must adapt to new challenges (Wiedmann, 2015). One of its effects is the growing customer engagement in business, marketing and branding activities, which is

DOI: 10.4018/978-1-5225-1779-5.ch010

increasing to an extent that Boyd et al. (2014) call customer engagement a norm in today's marketplace. Indeed, brands need to become agile in order to adjust to changing situations (Lusch & Vargo, 2006), but it is not plausible to expect them to develop without brand or marketing management interference. The brand development and brand management scholars and practitioners this development situates in front of a dilemma: how to positively acknowledge societal changes without simply adjusting to the customer demands and how to integrate brand development in the management practice (Wiedmann, 2015)? Ignoring the customers is risky, as it can lead to a dissonance between what managers think customers do, and the reality how they use and build brands (Ind, 2014). These challenges implicate digitizing as a resource for innovative brand development processes with potential for value creation. Most studies on cocreational opportunities for value creation are conducted from the perspective of single companies. Research on digitalization from a multistakeholder perspective is needed (Ramaswamy & Ozcan, 2016). This chapter scrutinizes digitizing as a resource for innovative brand development processes in the tourism sector, which enables a multistakeholder perspective on the topic. The chapter discusses brand development with the help of two tourism destinations consisting of a number of companies with one shared brand: Christmas. The destination brand ownership is distributed among many interests and so differs from brands owned by individual companies. Destinations, consequently, offer a fresh perspective on the study of digitalization as a resource within co-creative brand development.

In the tourism sector, several forms of customer engagement have become more important than ever. Digitalization provides several channels over which customers can *share* their experiences of products and services with others. Digitally shared experiences have important effects on the brand of the destination (Budeanu, 2013), as well as on product design and product development (Battarbee & Koskinen, 2005; Kozinets et al., 2008). The brand is an essential part of every marketing and business model (Moore & Birtwistle, 2004) having an effect on a business's turnover and profitability. In this sense, brand development and product development become associated with each other in literature on management (e.g., See: Ambler & Styles, 1997). This chapter conceives brand development integral to product development.

Drawing from the resource-based view (RBV), this chapter examines how digitalization-based product development can contribute to a sustainable competitive advantage in form of destination brands. The study draws from two tourism destinations: Santa Claus, Indiana, USA, and Santa Claus Village Rovaniemi, Finland. The chapter starts by reviewing the presently available literature on digitalization, product development and sustainable competitive advantage, and by emphasizing the role consumers play in these processes. The subsequent section describes the methodology used, and the data section examines how the two destinations utilize digitalization to develop the Christmas brand. The proceeding section discusses how digitalization can contribute to value co-creation within the framework of RBV. The chapter concludes with a presentation of its findings.

BACKGROUND

Digitalization and Co-Creation

Digitalization has various alternative definitions. It can mean the use of Internet, social media, various digital technologies and analytics, as well as mobile applications in business activities. Especially in communications, information, media, and entertainment (CIME) industries exploit digital technologies (Gimpel & Westerman, 2012) but digitizing provides an opportunity for businesses in nearly all sectors. Digitalization has become a top-priority research topic for the tourism sector, as well (Williams, Stewart & Larsen, 2012). Digitalization has been reported as influencing the tourism business positively (Kamuzora, 2005), but as Williams et al. (2012, p. 6) point out, while social media is promoted as a vehicle for influencing traveler motivations and behavior, little is actually known about how to use the data it generates.

Digitalization has changed the everyday lives of consumers (Poster, 2004) to the extent that there is a new type of active consumer, the "creative consumer" who takes part in discussions on the features and aspects of companies' services and products (Burgess, 2006). As creative consumers, "prosumers" (Toffler, 1980), customers play an important role in digitizing products and services (Burgess, 2006). Customer-based business logic is hardly new; 'putting consumers to work' had already become a trend in the United States by the mid-1950s in, for example, self-service restaurants and filling stations and in the assembly their own furniture (Ritzer & Jurgensen, 2010; Büscher & Igoe, 2013). This phenomenon was recognized at the time but was not subject to significant theoretical discussion (Ritzer, 2013).

Although discussions of prosuming, (value) co-creation, service-dominant logic, and crowdsourcing can be considered distinct, all of them focus on customer-based perspectives and attitudes toward production. In his seminal study on presuming *The third Wave* (1980), Alan Toffler introduces the role of consumers as part of the production process. There are two alternatives for the definition of "prosumer": one combines "professionalism" with "consumer"; the other alternatively incorporates the word "producer" with "consumer." In both cases, active consumers are hobbyists who participate, one way or the other, in the production process. Toffler (1980) asserts that these two views offer alternative perspectives: "production for use" and "production for exchange." Prosuming is focused on "production for use" where "production and consumption are united in the same person" (Kotler, 1986, 510). According to Toffler (1980), prosuming was already well in use before industrialization effectively separated the roles of the consumer and producer. In the society posited by *The Third Wave*, Toffler emphasizes, the increased role of the individual consumer instigates demarketization and demassification instead

Table 1. The development of consumer-based perspectives and the most important studies of them.

Decades	1970's	1980's	1990's	2000's	2010's
Prosumer	McLuhan and Nevitt (1972)	**Toffler (1980)** Kotler (1986)	Tapscott (1995)	Toffler and Toffler (2006)	Ritzer and Jurgenson (2010) Ritzer (2013)
Co-creation	Lovelock and Young (1979)	*Toffler (1980) Kotler (1986)*	Normann and Ramirez (1993)	**Prahalad and Ramaswamy** (2000; **2004**) Bendapudi and Leone (2003); Wind and Rangaswamy 2001)	Ramaswamy and Gouillart (2010)
SDL			Day (1999) Haeckel (1999)	Grönroos (2000) Shet et al. (2000) **Vargo and Lusch (2004;** 2006)	Heinonen et al., (2010, 2013)
Crowdsourcing				**Howe (2006)** Brabham (2008) *Wind and Rangaswamy (2001)*	Doan, Ramakrishnan and Halevy (2011)

of mass production. Kotler (1986) sees the situation as challenging for marketers because it implies a demand for higher-quality, instead of mass-produced, messaging.

Co-creation or *value co-creation* are representatives of new perspective, where the borders of two counterparties, customers, and sellers, is disappearing in the traditional sense. According to Prahalad & Ramaswamy (2004), the juxtaposition between demand and supply side of markets is misleading: producers and customers are working together to create joint value. Their work stresses the importance of value co-creation in *contrast with* traditional market mechanisms. The first steps toward a concept of value co-creation were posited as early as 1979 by Lovelock & Young who note that customers can be a source of productivity gains (Bendapudi & Leone, 2003, 16). Bendapudi & Leone (2003) list twenty-three publications between 1979 and 2000 focusing on co-production and customer participation in production, including Prahalad & Ramaswamy (2000) and Wind & Rangaswamy (2000). Both papers emphasize the changing role of customers as co-creators, but notably, Wind & Rangaswamy (2001) specifically consider the digital marketplace in this context. Normann & Ramirez (1993), meanwhile, introduce value co-creation using IKEA's business logic as an example of a business whose "goal is not to create value for customers but to mobilize customers to create [their] own value from the company's various offerings" (ibid., 69). Ramaswamy & Gouillart (2010) similarly define the features of co-creative enterprises by using, among others, Nike as an example.

As for *service-dominant logic,* the seminal paper is Vargo & Lusch (2004). According to these authors, there are several preceding studies for service-dominant logic, including Day (1999) but also Haeckel (1999), and Shett et al. (2000) who both are proponents of consumer-oriented, service-centered views on marketing that influenced Vargo & Lusch (2004). In this sense, the importance of the Haeckel's study (1999) is based on the findings that many successful companies were moving from a "make-and-sell" strategy to a "sense-and-respond" strategy (Vargo & Lusch, 2000). Because the economy's focus is shifting from a focus on tangible goods toward one on intangible goods (e.g., skills, knowledge, and information), the service-dominant logic's position stronger than goods-centered philosophies and companies must integrate messages on how they benefit consumers into their mission statements; thus, focal orientation has shifted from producer to the consumer (Vargo & Lusch, 2004). In contemporary marketing and management studies, the role of service-dominant logic is strong, and there are thousands of publications focused on this perspective. Along with many others, Vargo & Lusch have continued to develop their perspective on this repositioning of marketing paradigm in their popular books and articles (e.g., See: Vargo & Lusch, 2006; Lusch & Vargo, 2006; Lusch et al., 2007; Lusch et al., 2008). One interesting correlative to service-dominant logic is "customer-dominant logic" in which the customer's perspective is at the center of any analysis (Heinonen et al., 2010, 2013). In customer-dominant logic, the focus is on "customer activities as discrete sequences of behavior aimed at creating or supporting some type of value in the customer's life or business" (Mickelsson, 2013, 534).

Finally, *crowdsourcing* emphasizes the role of customers as a part of the production process, especially as part of digital-product development (Brabham, 2008). Howe (2006, 5), introduces crowdsourcing as an alternative to outsourcing and defines it in the following way: "… [C]rowdsourcing represents the act of a company or institution taking a function once performed by employees and outsourcing it to the undefined (and generally large) network of people in the form of an open call. This can take the form of peer-production (when the job is performed collaboratively), but is also often undertaken by sole individuals. The crucial prerequisite is the use of the open-call format and the large network of potential laborers. Thus, crowdsourcing has both physical (traditional) forms and virtual, digital forms. That is, crowdsourcing is either a business practice that outsources an activity to a literal, tangible crowd or a form of outsourcing not directed to other companies but to the crowd by means of an open tender or open call via an Internet platform (See: Howe, 2006; Burger-Helmchen & Penin, 2010; Schenk & Guittard, 2009; Rusko, 2012; 2013). Literature on crowdsourcing has appeared relatively recently, but the Wind & Rangaswamy's concept (2001) of consumers as co-creators in the digital marketplace conforms well with the concept of crowdsourcing.

Customer Engagement

Customer engagement (CE) is also important perspective, which is nowadays focused mainly on virtual customer engagement (So et al., 2016). Many definitions of customer engagement are associated with brands. van Doorn et al. (2010), for instance, defines that "CE is a behavioral construct that goes beyond transactions, and may be specifically defined as a customer's behavioral manifestations that have a brand or firm focus beyond purchase, resulting from motivational drivers, a view shared by others in the field. " (see also So et al., 2016, p. 5). Especially important are new customers, which are potential repeat customers. (Bowden, 2009), especially important is feedback and its effects on the knowledge sets and knowledge structure.

Sawhney, Verona, and Prandelli (2005) divide CE into two parts: CE in physical environments and in virtual environments. CE in virtual environment is based on customer-centric co-creation perspective, where the role customer is active and dialogue is two-way and continuous. (Sawhney et al., 2005)

Often social media is part of the broader customer engagement strategy, it can be an effective and cost-efficient marketing, sales, service, insight and retention tool. According to Barry et al. (2011, p. 1) "[C]ustomers who engage with companies over social media are more loyal and they spend up to 40 percent more with those companies than other customers".

Virtual CE has been studied also in tourism (Cabiddu, De Carlo, and Piccoli, 2014). Cabiddu et al., 2014) find three forms of customer engagement leaning on social media: persistent engagement, customized engagement, and triggered engagement. Persistent engagement represents a possibility to maintain the ongoing dialogue by social media with customer even they are not physically at the destination. Customized engagement considers the possibility of interacting with customers based on prior knowledge of individual level information, that is, personalize organizational communications in a way, which threat customer as individuals. Triggered engagement enables immediately response of e.g. hotel or other service provider during the trip, when the customers are in the place and using digital platforms. (Cabiddu, et al., 2014).

Competitive Advantage through Digital Co-Creative Branding

Bogoviyev (2009, p. 25) suggests that brand co-creation should comprise not only consumer creation of a brand's image, in the form of advertisements, and identity, in the form of a logo and slogan, but also new designs for physical products. Similarly, Mladenow, Bauer & Strauss (2014) call web-based (digitalized) crowdsourcing "new-product development," based on an open-innovation paradigm. In this sense, digital brand co-creation overlaps with new-product development, and co-creative actions for improving tangible, physical products can contribute to brand development. Such a perspective overlaps with marketing research, which mainly emphasizes collective value co-creation by the *customer* and has several linkages also with customer engagement. Kosenitz et al. (2008, p. 340) call research that examines the effects of customer creativity on companies a "top-down perspective." They argue that online consumer communities can act as a counterbalance to companies' branding activities, which are seen as unethical, abusive, and irresponsible (Kosenitz et al., 2008, p. 353). Still, companies do benefit from customer involvement through the creation of superior services (Bogoviyeva, 2009), and customers' comments have been noted to flow back, feeding business with new ideas (Kozinets et al., 2008). Some critical voices have stated that active online users mainly deliver a free labor force for business (Arvidsson, 2005; Foster, 2009, Ritzer & Jurgenson, 2010). Nevertheless, researchers also emphasize the empowering role of participatory value creation (Jenkins, 2006).

According to Ramaswamy and Ozcan (2016), the concept of cocreative value creation between customers and brand is still a black box. This chapter draws from Humphrey & Grayson (2008) and suggests that value cocreation can be approached using the categories of exchange value and use value. The terms go back to Marx (1867), who defines "use value" as value that holds for a specific individual; "exchange value," in contrast, is defined as a use value that holds not strictly for given individual but for others as well. In other words, that which has exchange value is exchangeable (Humphrey & Grayson, 2008: 965). Following from this distinction, (cost) effectiveness, for example, implies direct benefits and thus offers use value for a specific company brand. Improvements, in contrast, only contain exchange value if they offer value for customers and can, therefore, be commercialized. Consequently, brand development can create both use and exchange values, even though the respective level of improvement itself can vary. Depending on its level of innovativeness, brand development can be characterized as incremental or radical (Ettlie, 1983).

METHODOLOGY AND DATA

This study utilizes a case-study strategy, which allows for several methods and materials in the analysis (Eriksson & Kovalainen, 2008; Yin, 2014). The study draws from two cases: Santa Claus, Indiana, U.S.A., and Santa Claus Village in Rovaniemi, Finland. Santa Claus Village began as the Arctic Circle Cabin built for Eleanor Roosevelt's 1950 visit to Rovaniemi. The donated land on which the welcoming ceremony was to take place was within the Polar Circle. In the core areas of Santa Claus Village, Santa .

Both destinations base their business on the legends of Christmas and Santa Claus and can be expected to contribute to the development of Christmas as a brand. As a result, Christmas represents a shared brand. The present case study's design follows an embedded case-study analysis plan, in which the embedded unit of analysis is the digital-product development of companies within these two tourism destinations (cf. Yin, 2014). The context is the tourism business environment. This study will combine the digital co-creation perspective with the resource-based view and discuss how digitilization as a resource can contribute to a sustainable competitive advantage. The present approach to digitalization as a resource for brand development complies with VRIN-criteria for a resource-based view. These criteria state a resource can contribute to a company's sustainable competitive advantage if the resource is valuable, rare, inimitable, and non-substitutable (Barney, 1991). The VRIN-criteria are explained in Table 2.

The two destinations comprise several attractions and companies. Though based on the same legend, the destinations differ in their image. Santa Claus Village, Indiana, U.S.A., "America's Christmas Hometown," consists of a wide array of Santa-themed shops and attractions: Santa's Candy Castle, the Santa Claus Museum, and Holiday World and Splashin' Safari. Santa Claus Village, Rovaniemi, Finland, is situated in the far north, in the Arctic Circle. It also has Christmas theme parks (Santa Claus Village and Santa Park in Rovaniemi), but it strongly emphasizes the Northern Lights, reindeer safaris, and

Table 2. VRIN criteria

Valuable	Rare
-Generates rents that can be captured by the firm -Resources can enable a firm to be lower cost than rival firms, or they may enable the firm to differentiate its products or services.	-A firm that possesses a rare resource can generate either superior margins or superior sales volumes from an equivalent cost base to competitors. -Resource is not commonly found across other competing firms.
Inimitable	**Non-Substitutable**
-The more difficult it is for competing firms to replicate the resource, the longer-lived will be the rent stream accruing to the resource. -Inimitability results from the presence of isolating mechanisms such as causal ambiguity, information asymmetries or social complexity.	-A resource cannot be easily replaced by another resource that delivers the same effect.

Bowman and Ambrosini (2003). See, also Barney, 1991.

Arctikum as the scientific center. Both locations are represented as destinations on Internet platforms like TripAdvisor and Facebook. Moreover, outside joint Web appearances, the destinations' attractions and companies have their own websites as well, and each is an individual member on the same Internet platforms. TripAdvisor offers a platform with customer reviews and a customer community, and Facebook is a social media platform that directly connects destination companies with each other and with customers. The companies whose websites were examined are examples of organizations that are active in digital-media creation, and they better demonstrate the potential of co-creative brand development among multiple players. The examples enable us to emphasize value creation in brand development for several companies. Within this brand development process, we analyze digitalization as a resource with the help of the VRIN-criteria and discuss its contribution to the sustainable comparative advantages. The VRIN criteria for both incremental and radical development processes are considered separately.

Data Analysis of Cases: Brand Development through Digitalization

Incremental Innovations Contributing to Brand Development

It is generally expected that digitalization, especially through social media, benefits companies. Piller et al. (2012) note, however, that a necessary requirement for benefiting from social media is that companies actively create processes to benefit from the innovations and ideas created by customers. The existence of a mass of customers is not enough. Similarly, Martin & van Bavel (2013) highlight the importance of harnessing social-media platforms for value creation, and Wiedmann (2015) and Ind (2015) point to the challenges of such task. Examples of company product development are rather easy to discern from examining individual tourism-company websites and individual Facebook pages, but how and to what extent these approaches can contribute to brand development is often not clear. Companies operating in the two locations use social platforms mainly for developing tangible products and services. The case study will begin, then, by introducing the case of the amusement park Holiday World in Santa Claus, Indiana, and discuss how digitalizing can contribute to brand development.

It is unclear whether the restaurants belong to the park or are independent companies located inside the park. Nevertheless, the examples indicate that the destination can, with the help of digitizing, easily include a large number of potential customers in the menu-development process of one or several companies located inside it. They also demonstrate building customer relations through the development of a concrete product: food offered at the destination. Because neither the voting behavior of individual customers nor the park's direct mails are visible for all, the development process itself remains veiled. It is a two-way process between a company asking and customers answering, but there is no communication among customers as there is in the case of customer community TripAdvisor.

The posting received ten publically visible suggestions and twelve "likes" in two days, and the suggestions show customers raising health-related concerns about Holiday World's food offerings. For example, they include requests for more sugar-free alternatives—which requests one might expect to benefit a large number of customers, thereby providing motivation for the overarching destination's restaurants to improve their menus. Furthermore, as previously noted, this forum-based poll is different from the website's poll format, and the comments and their writers are visible for all, including potential customers. Piller et al. (2012, p. 3) define customer co-creation as "an active, creative, and social collaboration process between producers and customers (users), facilitated by a company." They note that this can be carried out either through empowering customers to design a solution themselves or through implementing methodologies to transfer a customer-created solution into the company domain (Piller et al., 2012, p. 3). The case of Holiday World's Facebook polling fits this definition.

Still, Humphreys & Grayson (2008, p. 968) argue that, although the boundary between consumers and producers is getting porous through practices that engage customers in the production process, consumers can challenge the dichotomy only if they are asked to assist in creating *exchange value*. Consumers' posting on Holiday World's FB page is exactly the sort of situation Humphrey & Grayson (2008) are referring to: customers can create the exchange value of the food assortment, which can be co-opted by the company and resold for surplus value. The examples expose Facebook use that is close to the systematic collecting and utilization of customer ideas. Companies collect ideas and preferences, then incorporate them into their menus and dishes, rather than picking ready innovations. Lilien et al. (2002) argue that user innovations developed further by a company lead to a clear advantage for the company. The examples in their research, as well as our examples above, are based on tangible products and services produced by individual companies.

At the same time, too, these examples point to another interesting facet or digitizing: On the theme park's Facebook page, people are spoken of using their real names (e.g., "F&B director: James"), and the names are even connected with pictures of the mentioned persons (e.g., "Matt and Alan [a local contractor] making decisions this morning about Wildebeestro's roofing materials. [7 photos]" [Holiday World, 2014c]). Moreover, Facebook, as a platform, is based on the idea of communication with real names. This means that customers also take part in discussion and co-creation using their real names. Such an open-communication form (i.e., one based on real names) evinces trust, which scholars regard as crucial for the sustainable attractiveness of a destination (e.g. Macintosch, 2003). The example therefore stretches the concept of brand development toward tangible, everyday actions (e.g., Birkstedt, 2012; Bogoviyev, 2009; Närvänen, 2013). One might, therefore, argue that a brand can be improved (within a destination) through concrete, company-led action on incremental innovations in physical products (e.g., through a shift toward offering sugar- and gluten-free alternatives) and that digitalization enhances this process.

Furthermore, these examples above show the importance of customer engagement in incremental innovations. The customers are producing new content to the virtual platforms in order to develop further the services of Christmas tourism. Thus, especially virtual customer engagement is closely related with digital value co-creation activities in the examples of incremental innovations.

Towards Radical Innovations

Holiday World's company-led actions above highlight incremental innovations and their role in brand development. Different from company brands, destination brand ownership is distributed. Insch (2011) notes that tourists do not take ownership of it, and companies, or their marketers, do not directly consume it as a natural resource. This makes destination brands more difficult to study. We can next examine a joint destination brand and consider how a destination can use digitalization as a resource for value creation and, finally, for competitive advantage to a company. The character of a shared brand is more intangible than a concrete product or service and therefore offers an interesting perspective on co-creation.

For an example of shared destination brand development it is worthwhile to return to Holiday World's individual website. There Holiday World reported that the Google map showing the route to Santa Claus, Indiana, was not up-to-date. The theme park's customers complained about the issue to Google, which in turn, corrected the error, and the company responded by thanking those who complained and placing a link to the updated Google map.

This example is a case of value creation initiated by customers, then acknowledged by the company. And, importantly, it is also an instance of value creation for the destination as a whole, as its outcome helps customers find their way to the destination, not just to the theme park within it. It is an example, then, of customer-led exchange-value production, as the outcome was of value not only to several customers, but also to Holiday World and the destination as a whole.

Another example of customer-led value creation can be seen within TripAdvisor customer reviews of Rovaniemi, Finland. The website's reviews contain direct feedback from customers on destinations and are meant to help other customers select destination. The following is one TripAdvisor review specifically for Santa Claus Village:

"Kitschy but cute"

We first stopped here on a beautiful July evening after the shops and restaurants were closed. No gates, no guards, no entrance fees, no crowds. Nothing but wonderful Christmas music piped through the grounds and a painted line to indicate the boundary of the Arctic Circle. What a place! Loved it. When we revisited the following day, it was somehow less appealing with the gift shops and overpriced restaurants bustling with tourists. Overall, though, this is a delightful area. Even after a hot July day, there's a crispness to the evening, and the midnight sun is unforgettable. (TripAdvisor, 2014a)

The above review received no responses from the destination's service providers to the negative comments about prices. From the perspective of product development, such customer reviews are customer-led and one-way. Destination attractions and companies are left in the recipient, rather than the facilitator, role. However, these customer reviews *can* contribute to brand development, as individual companies place feedback in their websites for marketing purposes. Companies in both Rovaniemi and Santa Claus have placed direct links to TripAdvisor customer reviews on their own websites. Such actions indicate that destinations do follow customer reviews and enforce the articulated responses from the customers within their own domains. Still, most company websites simply link to TripAdvisor's review pages without commenting on specific reviews. The extent and means of processing the ideas customers express, therefore, remain hidden. Additionally, the example demonstrates well how companies' brand management can be affected by reviews and loss of control over them (e.g., See: Hoyer et al., 2010).

Compared with the TripAdvisor's customer reviews, TripAdvisor's "customer communities" offer a more interactive communication platform. In this community, travelers can ask anything about a destination. Other travelers and so-called "destination experts" then answer the questions. Destination experts have local knowledge. Interestingly, this service supposedly draws from volunteers:

Destination experts are the backbone of the TripAdvisor community. They are regular contributors who exemplify the best of our forums, giving helpful, friendly advice and welcoming new members. They are passionate about the destinations they represent. Whether residents, locals, or frequent visitors, they have up-to-date knowledge of what's going on in their destinations. However, destination experts are not your personal travel agents. They are also not moderators, administrators, or members of the support team, so they are not responsible for removing inappropriate content or answering site-related questions. Please note: Destination experts are volunteers, so don't be afraid to say 'thanks' when they've provided you with helpful advice! (TripAdvisor, 2014b)

The concept of destination experts is interesting. First, it mobilizes the resources of enthusiastic hobbyists who feel attached to their destination of expertise and relies on local knowledge and commitment to a destination as a whole, not merely to certain companies. Second, it shows that, due to digitizing, one expert can represent several destinations at the same time. She does not have to be physically located in the destination itself, unlike official tourist-info bureaus, which physically represent one destination alone. And, through digitizing, she is not bound to discuss certain topics but can speak to every facet of her various destinations. Through dialogues between an expert and customers, this digital form of prosuming contributes to destinations' value creation. Piller et al. (2012) point to a risk of competition growing alongside the use of customer innovations. They refer to the increasing entrepreneurship of customers: customers refusing to deliver ideas for free but, instead, selling their ideas to companies. The TripAdvisor model of destination experts demonstrates an interesting method of overcoming this "entrepreneurial danger." Emphasizing their voluntary and enthusiastic nature, the company recruits experts that contribute to destination brand development without increasing the fear of entrepreneurship and without the introduction of additional costs.

Digitalization indeed appears to be an impressive resource for such branding, which is based on real nature. Santaclausvillage.fi, for example, includes a link to Santatelevision.com, which is a collection of films about the Lapland region of Finland. The top-rated videos here include films about reindeer and ice breakers, and many of them play traditional (Sami) Lappish music. The described high degree of uniformity in the Rovaniemi destination indicates that the brand co-creation process here is controlled by the destination and its companies and processed with only selectively administered involvement from customers. Hoyer et al. (2010) note that consumer involvement at the earliest stages of branding increases the risk of focusing on incremental, rather than radical, innovations. The examples of santaclausvillage.fi and the associated companies' websites give one compelling reasons to speculate otherwise; the destination-led brand-creation process here is uniform, rather than radical.

As for this information's not appearing on any destination websites, one might claim that not only the threat is silenced, but possibly as well, so is any potential link between environmental concerns and the destination's brand development—a potential that, for example, has been demonstrated by the development of the green destination brands, which connect tourism with climate change and other environmental topics. Green destination brands are built on positive environmental values. Insch (2011) also refers to an opposite and more ironic example of destinations' reactions environmental topics: to the growing incidence of climate-change tourism, in which travelers pay to witness environmental changes. Also in these examples above customer engagement is a relevant part of customer-based branding in Christmas tourism destinations. Brand development activities seems to be one of the motivational drivers of customers (cf. So et al., 2016).

DISCUSSION

Digitizing seems to be part of the brand development process of both destinations introduced in this chapter. In this sense, digitizing, the Internet, and social media might be resources for these destinations. We will next consider in this section whether this kind of digitalization can be viewed as example of a resource-based advantage according to the previously noted VRIN criteria. We can then examine the role of active customers in this context and acknowledge digitization's contributions to the development of both gradual and radical changes. The study hence adheres to the distinction between incrementality and radicalness in regard to rates of innovation (Ettlie, 1983) and considers brand development separately, according to a distinction between incremental and radical processes. The separation between the two is largely based on differences in dealing with uncertainty, whether there is a frame within which a change will occur or the frames themselves change entirely (e.g. Norman & Verganti, 2014). The aim here is not to highlight the existence of separate categories; after all, those categories are not static or hard, as Dewar & Dutton (1986) point out. Rather the goal here is to demonstrate the potential of digitizing as a resource in as multifaceted a way as possible. It could be seen as an approach to open up the 'black box' of cocreated value between customers and brand, as Ramaswamy and Ozcan (2016) call for.

- **Valuable:** Digitizing clearly enables interplay between many diverse stakeholders. Interestingly, this interplay enhances the development of a destination brand that is not under private ownership from vast destination communities that do not own a product or service collectively, or even share motivations. On the whole, then, the examples above show incremental innovations in existing products and brands. They for example show that digitizing enables the collection of feedback and ideas digitally, which means lower costs when compared with postings. This is, first, because, through digitalization, it is possible to post a question related to product development among an unlimited number of potential customers. The costs are not related to the number of recipients, and cost savings point to the valuableness of digitalization in collecting feedback and ideas. The example of TripAdvisor volunteer experts also reveals that, due to digitizing, one expert can even represent several destinations at the same time. Her contributions consist of Web-based writings. Therefore, she does not have to be physically located in the destination's locale, unlike employees of official tourist-info bureaus, who can only be located in and, thus, physically represent one destination.

Apart from viewing value creation in terms of cost efficiency, though, digitizing enables customers to take part in the production process, which enhances *exchange* value creation. Producing exchange value is about producing use value not only for the individual, but for others, which makes it exchangeable and offers the possibility of commercialization (Humphrey & Grayson, 2008). This supports the argument that digitalization, and especially social media with its open applications' enhanced potential for exchange-value creation, enables feedback and conversation among multiple players. However, there are limitations to such value-creation practices. With platforms like TripAdvisor and Facebook, one can only target those customers already active on the platforms, and this is problematic because there are regional differences in the IT use of travelers, as Munar & Jacobsen (2014) point out. Furthermore, successfully reaching a large audience is dependent on how effectively information is spread from one user to another. Obviously, then, the architecture of the platforms might limit the value.

Concerning value creation in terms of radical innovativeness, the case of Rovaniemi must be emphasized for the discrepancies between the destination's present snowy branding and community awareness of environmental change and the destination's lack of snow. Notably, this discrepancy is neither actively processed nor utilized by the destination, whereas examples from elsewhere show that such discrepancies can contribute to brand development. This suggests the discrepancy has emerged because of the growing digital community. And, to comply with what Norman & Verganti (2014) call the process of a "meaning change," it should, therefore, be argued that digitizing can enable radical innovations in the form of new motives and meaning combinations. They can be seen reflecting the socio-cultural dynamics and offering potential for symbolic value-added (see e.g. Jeannerat & Crevoisier, 2011).

- **Rare:** Destinations use both standardized platforms, such as TripAdvisor, Google, and Facebook, as well as their own jointly functioning websites. Both platform types contribute to the creation of a rare resource, albeit such digital platforms are not rare in themselves. TripAdvisor destination experts, for example, are supposed to operate on a voluntary basis. As a result, they are not remunerated by the company. Instead, their motivation is expected to arise through connectedness to the destination in question. Through digitizing, these experts can be found and leveraged, and their detailed local knowledge and strong commitment to various destination can be mobilized; in the case of radical brand development, then, an Internet community results in a meaning change that puts a destination in a position different from its competitors', thereby contributing to rareness (see Chen at al., 2011).

- **Inimitable:** Standardized digital platforms are open and visible to all. While this might motivate heterogeneous comments and so enhance creativeness in product development, it is not protected from competitors. On social media platforms, such as Facebook and other forms of digital "multi-way communication" (Lusch & Webster, 2011), the creation process of exchange value is visible to the public. The company's own websites, on the other hand, can enjoy greater protection from the destination. Answering polls or giving feedback through the website might remain between the customer and the destination alone. Such two-way communication and its contribution to brand development is not visible to others, and therefore, harder to imitate. In contrast, neither individual companies nor their competitors can control multi-way digital communities because these communities are based on open forums. Interestingly, it is this very lack of control that can be perceived contributing to the creation of an "inimitable set of location-bound created assets" (Chen, 2011); resources with the potential for exchange value are developed through community negotiations so varied and individualized that imitating them is impossible.

- **Non-Substitutable:** Digitizing can enhance trust in customer relations: communication is fast, and customers' questions and concerns can be responded to quickly and easily. Frequent updates in websites make employees' names and faces familiar to customers. Trustful customer relations contribute to the sustainable attractiveness of a destination (Macintosh, 2003). Digital platforms where customers make suggestions with their real names can also contribute to trust-building in the product-development process.

But digitalization not only points to sustainability, it also indicates some substitutability of digitalization itself as a resource. Cheung & Lam (2009) for example point to the changing role of travel agencies as intermediaries between travelers and suppliers. TripAdvisor can be seen as such an intermediary. It provides firsthand information and advice from travelers to travelers. Of course, this alone does not contribute to the substitution of digitalization as such, since TripAdvisor is Internet-based. However, it does point to the possibility of variance in combinations of local, individual-based knowledge and e-commerce platforms. Put another way, digitalization (e.g., with pictures, webcams, or maps) is not enough, but to some extent, physical and individual experiences are also necessary so that these experiences can be delivered digitally. Again, digital community renegotiations over digitalization and/or its relation to a particular destination are led by "multi-way communications including non-customers and non-shareholder stakeholders" (Lusch & Webster, 2011). Branding within such digital negotiations can achieve a broad audience and become less substitutable.

In the cases of both Indiana and Rovaniemi, destination actors have made efforts to develop their brands and images through digitizing with their respective websites and social media pages. There are both one-way and two-way channels for customers in these digitizing activities. And, although most of these destinations' customers are relatively passive followers and readers, there is an active minority of customers that participates in these destinations' brand development. These customers are co-creating value with the destinations' companies, albeit their roles as prosumers might not be very pronounced. And, given that the sustainability of these resources might be somewhat ambiguous, these platforms and their active users are therefore real resources for the studied destinations and their service providers.

Finally, based on this analysis, it should be emphasized that digitizing might contribute to fulfilling all the VRIN criteria of a *bundle* of resources, including active and inclusive societal discussions, rather than representing an independent resource that fulfills the criteria alone.

Table 3. Digitizing as a resource of a destination

Digitizing as a resource in an incremental brand development process	Digitizing as a resource in a radical brand development process
Potential value: Digitizing enables use of simple technical applications, and so contributes to cost and time savings for firms in collecting ideas and feedback, and in improving customer relations. Improvement of the cold arctic web appearance of the Christmas destination with help of customer pictures. With customer crowdsourcing improvement of internet based map applications for better reachability and appearance of the destination.	*Potential value*: Emerging discrepancy between destination brand and community discussions. The value of such a situation of discrepancy is risky: destination brand does not fit with the community opinion, anymore. Potential change of the arctic meaning of 'Christmas destination' acknowledging the climate change. The meaning of digitizing changes: it gets connected with the (Christmas) destination.
Rareness: Even though facilitated by customers, such as improvements in the Google map, or by firms such as improvement of food products with help of digital polls, in both cases, digitizing itself is used in a standardized instead of in a unique form.	*Rareness*: Digitizing is used in an uncontrollable way. It is not facilitated by destinations, nor by single customers. Digitizing can be perceived as rare if its meaning changes and gets connected with the (Christmas) destination *other* than with other destinations. This would require more than informing about the destination.
Inimitability: Digitizing is strongly based on visibility. Customers are encouraged to participate in product development through using platforms to openly express feedback (Facebook) or make a choice between alternative products. Similarly, firms and destinations post their answers visible for all.	*Inimitability*: Through digitizing which enhances stakeholder participation, community discussions and the emerging discrepancies get hardly controllable by single firms, destinations, or by individual lead customers. They can therefore hardly be imitated.
Non-substitutability: Gradual development which rests on feedback or polls in internet can hardly be replaced by more cost effective solutions.	*Non-substitutability*: Changing the relation between digitizing and destination, or the meaning of a Christmas destination, is a slowly societal process of substitution.

CONCLUSION

The chapter demonstrated the contributions of digitizing to co-creative brand development within the tourism sector. It approached brand development as part of product development, which includes improving tangible products, and incremental innovations, as well as community discussions around totally new meanings (i.e., radical innovations). Cocreative value creation through digitalization is still considered a 'black box' (Ramaswamy & Ozcan, 2016). The present chapter aimed to open this black box focusing on the destination perspective. It examined two different conceptions of the brand development process and discussed how digitizing can enhance value co-creation

The first conception highlights customer participation through Internet applications that many customers can openly access. The destination is able to benefit from multiple perspectives and develop its products so they have use value to a greater number of customers. This means that there is a potential for creating exchange value. Research usually labels these kinds of improvements as incremental innovations. Through improvements in a product that are significant for all destination attractions and companies, such as a digital road map, digitizing can contribute to use value co-creation simultaneously, not only for several customers, but also for several companies within the same destination locale. This points to a potential for commercialization and, hence, for exchange value. Furthermore, digital applications can contribute to trust building in customer relations. Uncomplicated, cost-effective, and quick communication allows for more personal exchanges between the producer and customer. The openness of communication, evinced by use of real names on platforms like Facebook, can also contribute to trust building. Trust is necessary for the sustainable attractiveness of a destination.

This chapter also confirms the relevance of customer engagement in the co-creation and prosuming processes. Especially in the active brand development activities of the customers show the importance of virtual customer engagement also in Christmas tourism. This chapter focused on digitizing activities, which might have effects on this result. However, also the importance of physical environment is large because of the core industry of the cases, tourism.

The presented examples of incremental development emphasize the active use of standard digital platforms and social media: advising, asking, and answering. However, these also expose the very limits and conditions for digitizing as a resource contributing to sustainable competitive advantage. It is argued here that digitizing clearly can contribute to value co-creation and to a more agile brand. And, through digitizing, rare knowledge about destinations can be found and exploited independent of physical location. But digitizing, per se, is only rare if it is related to certain destinations alone or, at least, related in a different manner to specific destinations than it is for competitors. Furthermore, digitizing is only inimitable if its exchanges are not publically visible. More invisibility through direct digital communication using website polls or e-mail can contribute to stronger inimitability. But, in the case of open platforms like Facebook, visibility prevents inimitability by its very nature.

It is here argued that, theoretically, customer-oriented digitizing can become a resource according to the VRIN criteria. The chapter highlights a possible case of radical development based on a change in meanings that is related to digitalization itself. A changed relation between a destination and digitizing can put some resource bundles (destinations) in different positions than others (see Chen et al., 2011). This, in turn, can make customer-oriented digitizing a rare resource for the destination in question. Such changes in meanings point to societal processes.

The finding supports Jeannerat and Crevoisier's (2011) notion of the importance to authenticate the link between technological and non-technological values, in order the companies to be able to manage the widely dispersed digitalized communication. From the RBV perspective, however, exactly the loss of control makes societal changes hardly imitable or substitutable.

Noted too is that, in practice, a separation between incremental and radical innovation-based product development processes is very difficult. Most likely, then, the development process is a combination of the two (e.g., See: Norman & Verganti, 2014). Similarly, digitizing is often used in combination with other resources, such as local knowledge and trustful customer relations, and this underlines the incremental aspect of the process. But digitizing can also enhance a change in a destination's core meaning destination and so contribute to radical innovations and developments. Arguably, then, because of the simultaneously incremental nature of digitization, potential radical values can be processed gradually. The chapter points that the highlighted incremental and radical characteristics are useful for analyzing and developing the brand management practices, as well.

FUTURE RESEARCH DIRECTIONS

The findings of this chapter are in agreement with previous research that characterizes digitizing as inseparable from marketing and management. They also suggest that digitizing can be perceived, like immobile natural resources or capabilities, as part of a set of circumstances that contribute to a destination's sustainable competitive advantage; as with other resources, its potential for value co-creation can change over time (Line & Runyan, 2014). Consequently, identifying use value and the potential for creating exchange value within societal processes for meaning change would be an interesting area of future research within brand management.

This chapter focused on the economic value creation associated with dispersed digital innovating, but the future research should more strongly take into consideration also its non-economic dimensions and values. Similarly to the climate change highlighted in the chapter, researchers could study how digitalization based innovations reflect and construct a change in global attitudes towards for example equality or safety. Such an analysis could finally explain how global values contribute to regional economic success of certain innovations and to failure of others.

REFERENCES

Ambler, T., & Styles, C. (1997). Brand development versus new product development: Toward a process model of extension decisions. *Journal of Product and Brand Management*, 6(4), 222–234. doi:10.1108/10610429710186752

Andreu, L., Aldas, J., Bigne, E., & Mattila, A. (2010). An analysis of e-business adoption and its impact on relational quality in travel agency-supplier relationships. *Tourism Management*, 31(6), 777–787. doi:10.1016/j.tourman.2009.08.004

Arctice. (2014). *Arctice is on Facebook*. Reviewed 29 March from https://www.facebook.com/pages/Arctice/586348848092936

Arvidsson, A. (2005). Brands: A critical perspective. *Journal of Consumer Culture*, 5(2), 235–258. doi:10.1177/1469540505053093

Battarbee, K., & Koskinen, I. (2005). Co-experience: User experience as interaction. *CoDesign, 1*(1), 5–18. doi:10.1080/15710880412331289917

Bendapudi, N., & Leone, R. P. (2003). Psychological implications of customer participation in co-production. *Journal of Marketing, 67*(1), 14–28. doi:10.1509/jmkg.67.1.14.18592

Benkler, Y. (2001). Coase's Penguin, or: Linux and the Nature of the Firm. *The Yale Law Journal, 112*(3), 369–446. doi:10.2307/1562247

Birkstedt, R. (2012). *Between the deliberate and the emergent - Constructing corporate brand meaning in MNCs* (Doctoral dissertation). University of Turku.

Bogoviyeva, E. (2009). *Brand development: The effects of customer brand co-creation on self-brand connection* (Doctoral Dissertation). University of Mississippi. ProQuest LLC.

Bowden, J. L. H. (2009). The process of customer engagement: A conceptual framework. *Journal of Marketing Theory and Practice, 17*(1), 63–74. doi:10.2753/MTP1069-6679170105

Bowman, C., & Ambrosini, V. (2003). How the resource-based and the dynamic capability views of the firm inform corporate -level strategy. *British Journal of Management, 14*(1), 289–303. doi:10.1111/j.1467-8551.2003.00380.x

Boyd, D. E., Clarke, T., & Spekman, R. (2014). The emergence and impact of consumer brand empowerment in online social networks: A proposed ontology. *Journal of Brand Management, 21*(6), 516–531. doi:10.1057/bm.2014.20

Brabham, D. C. (2008). Crowdsourcing as a model for problem solving an introduction and cases. *Convergence (London), 14*(1), 75–90. doi:10.1177/1354856507084420

Brown, S. L., & Eisenhardt, K. M. (1995). Product development: Past research, present findings, and future directions. *Academy of Management Review, 20*, 343–378.

Budeanu, A. (2013). Sustainability and Tourism Social Media. *Tourism Social Science Series, 18*, 87–103.

Burger-Helmchen, T., & Pénin, J. (2010). The limits of crowdsourcing inventive activities: What do transaction cost theory and the evolutionary theories of the firm teach us. In *Workshop on Open Source Innovation*, Strasbourg, France.

Büscher, B., & Igoe, J. (2013). 'Prosuming' conservation? Web 2.0, nature and the intensification of value-producing labour in the late capitalism. *Journal of Consumer Culture, 13*(3), 283–305. doi:10.1177/1469540513482691

Cabiddu, F., De Carlo, M., & Piccoli, G. (2014). Social media affordances: Enabling customer engagement. *Annals of Tourism Research, 48*, 75–192. doi:10.1016/j.annals.2014.06.003

Cheung, R., & Lam, P. (2009). How travel agency survive in e-business world? *Communications of the IMIBA, 10*, 85–92.

Choi, . (1997). *The Economics of Electronic Commerce*. Macmillan Technical Publications.

Dalsgaard, S. (2008). Facework on Facebook: The presentation of self in virtual life and its role in the US elections. *Anthropology Today, 24*(6), 8–12. doi:10.1111/j.1467-8322.2008.00626.x

Day, G. (1999). *The market-driven organization: understanding, attracting and keeping valuable customers.* New York: The Free Press.

Dewar, R. D., & Dutton, J. E. (1986). The adoption of radical and incremental innovations: An empirical analysis. *Management Science, 32*(11), 1422–1433. doi:10.1287/mnsc.32.11.1422

Eriksson, P., & Kovalainen, A. (2008). *Qualitative methods in business research.* New York, NY: Simon & Schuster. doi:10.4135/9780857028044

Ettlie, J. E. (1983). Organizational policy and innovation among suppliers to the food processing sector. *Academy of Management Journal, 26*(1), 27–44. doi:10.2307/256133

Foster, R. J. (2009). The Work of the New Economy: Consumers, Brands, and Value Creation. *Cultural Anthropology, 22*(4), 707–731. doi:10.1525/can.2007.22.4.707

Gerschenfeld, N., & Vasseur, J. P. (2014). As objects go online. *Foreign Affairs, 93*(2), 60–67.

Gimpel, G., & Westerman, G. (2012). *Shaping the Future: Seven Enduring Principles for Fast Changing Industries.* Working Paper-MIT Center for Digital Business.

Gretzel, U., Kyung, H. Y., & Purifoy, M. (2007). *Online travel review study. Role & impact of online travel reviews.* Laboratory for intelligent systems in tourism. Retrieved from http://www.tripadvisor.com/pdfs/OnlineTravelReviewReport.pdf

Haeckel, S. (1999). *Adaptive enterprise: Creating and leading sense-and-respond organizations.* Boston: Harvard School of Business.

Hall, M. (2008). Santa Claus, place branding and competition. *Fennia, 186*(1), 59–67.

Haythornthwaite, C. (2009, January). Crowds and communities: Light and heavyweight models of peer production. In *System Sciences, 2009. HICSS'09. 42nd Hawaii International Conference* on (pp. 1-10). IEEE.

Heinonen, K., Strandvik, T., Mickelsson, K., Edvardsson, B., Sundström, E., & Andersson, P. (2010). A customer-dominant logic of service. *Journal of Service Management, 21*(4), 531–548. doi:10.1108/09564231011066088

Heinonen, K., Strandvik, T., & Voima, P. (2013). Customer-dominant value formation in service. *European Business Review, 25*(2), 104–123. doi:10.1108/09555341311302639

Holidayworld. (2014a). Retrieved from http://www.holidayworld.com/holiblog/2014/03/05/deep-fried-question-fabulous-flop/

Holidayworld. (2014b). Retrieved from http://www.holidayworld.com/holiblog/2014/03/13/sweet-question/

Holidayworld. (2014c). Retrieved from https://www.facebook.com/HolidayWorld?sid=b660a4148829021a9b66f8005420e3c1&ref=search

Holidayworld. (2014d). Retrieved from https://plus.google.com/+holidayworld/posts

Howe, J. (2006). The rise of crowdsourcing. *Wired Magazine, 14*(6), 1-4.

Hoyer, W. D., Chandry, R., Dorotic, M., Krafft, M., & Singh, S. S. (2010). Consumer co-creation in new product development. *Journal of Service Research, 13*(3), 283–296. doi:10.1177/1094670510375604

Humphreys, A., & Grayson, K. (2008). The intersecting roles of consumer and producer: A critical perspective on co-production, co-creation and prosumprion. *Social Compass, 2*(3), 963–980. doi:10.1111/j.1751-9020.2008.00112.x

Ind, N. (2015). How participation is changing the practice of managing brands. *Journal of Brand Management, 21*(S9), 734–742. doi:10.1057/bm.2014.35

Insch, A. (2011). Conceptualization and anatomy of green destination brands, *International Journal of Culture. Tourism and Hospitality Research, 5*(3), 282–290.

Jeannerat, H., & Crevoisier, O. (2011). Non-techonolgical innovation and multi-local territorial knowledge dynamics in the Swiss watch industry. *International Journal of Innovation and Regional Development, 3*(1), 26–44. doi:10.1504/IJIRD.2011.038061

Jenkins, H. (2006). *Convergence Culture: Where Old and New Media Collide*. New York University Press.

Kamuzora, F. (2005). The Internet as an Empowering Agent for Small, Medium and Micro Tourism Enterprises in Poor Countries. *e-Review of Tourism Research, 3*(4), 82-89.

Kariyawasam, R. (2010). Next Generation Networks: A New Digital Divide? *International Journal of Innovation in the Digital Economy, 1*(3), 1–21. doi:10.4018/jide.2010070101

Kotler, P. (1986). The prosumer movement: A new challenge for marketers. *Advances in Consumer Research. Association for Consumer Research (U. S.), 13*(1), 510–513.

Kozinets, R. V., Hemetsberger, A., & Jensen Schau, H. (2008). The Wisdom of Consumer Crowds: Collective Innovation in the Age of Networked Marketing. *Journal of Macromarketing, 28*(4), 339–354. doi:10.1177/0276146708325382

Law, R., Qi, S., & Buhalis, D. (2010). Progress in tourism management: A review of website evaluation in tourism research. *Tourism Management, 31*(3), 297–313. doi:10.1016/j.tourman.2009.11.007

Li, J., Merenda, M., & Venkatachalam, A. R. (2009). Business process digitalization and new product development: An empirical study of small and medium-sized manufacturers. *International Journal of E-Business Research, 5*(1), 49–64. doi:10.4018/jebr.2009010103

Lilien, G., Morrison, P. D., Searls, K., Sonnack, M., & von Hippel, E. (2002). Performance assessment of the lead user idea-generation process for the new product development. *Management Science, 48*(8), 1042–1059. doi:10.1287/mnsc.48.8.1042.171

Line, N. D., & Runyan, R. C. (2014). Destination marketing and the service-dominant logic: A resource-based operationalization of strategic marketing assets. *Tourism Management, 43*, 91–102. doi:10.1016/j.tourman.2014.01.024

Lusch, R. F., & Vargo, S. L. (2006). Service-dominant logic: Reactions, reflections and refinements. *Marketing Theory, 6*(3), 281–288. doi:10.1177/1470593106066781

Lusch, R. F., Vargo, S. L., & O'Brien, M. (2007). Competing through service: Insights from service-dominant logic. *Journal of Retailing, 83*(1), 5–18. doi:10.1016/j.jretai.2006.10.002

Lusch, R. F., Vargo, S. L., & Wessels, G. (2008). Toward a conceptual foundation for service science: Contributions from service-dominant logic. *IBM Systems Journal, 47*(1), 5–14. doi:10.1147/sj.471.0005

Lusch, R. F., & Webster, F. E. (2011). A stakeholder-Unifying, co-creation philosophy for marketing. *Journal of Macromarketing, 31*(2), 129–134. doi:10.1177/0276146710397369

McLuhan, M., & Nevitt, B. (1972). *Take today: The executive as dropout*. New York: Harcourt Brace Jovanovich.

Mickelsson, K. J. (2013). Customer activity in service. *Journal of Service Management, 24*(5), 534–552. doi:10.1108/JOSM-04-2013-0095

Miller, M. M., & Henthorne, T. L. (2007). In Search of Competitive Advantage in Caribbean Tourism Websites: Revisiting the Unique Selling Proposition. *Journal of Travel & Tourism Marketing, 21*(2), 49–62. doi:10.1300/J073v21n02_04

MITSloan Management Review. (2014, January 7). Retrieved from http://sloanreview.mit.edu/article/the-nine-elements-of-digital-transformation/

Mladenow, A., Bauer, C., & Strauss, C. (2014). Social Crowd Integration in New Product Development: Crowdsourcing Communities Nourish the Open Innovation Paradigm. *Global Journal of Flexible Systems Management*, 1-10.

Moisio, L., & Rökman, M. (2011). Musician's, fans' and record company's value creation in internet. In *Proceedings of the Naples Forum on Services: Service- Dominant-Logic, Service Science, and Network Theory*. Available at: http://www.naplesforumonservice.it/uploads//files/Moisio,%20Rokman%20Musici an.pdf

Moore, C. M., & Birtwistle, G. (2004). The Burberry business model: Creating an international luxury fashion brand. *International Journal of Retail & Distribution Management, 32*(8), 412–422. doi:10.1108/09590550410546232

Närvänen, E. (2013). *Extending the Collective Consumption of Brands* (Doctoral dissertation). University of Tampere.

Norman, D. A., & Verganti, R. (2014). Incremental and Radical Innovation: Design Research vs. Technology and Meaning Change. *Design Issues, 30*(1), 78–96. doi:10.1162/DESI_a_00250

Normann, R., & Ramirez, R. (1993). From value chain to value constellation: Designing interactive strategy. *Harvard Business Review, 71*(4), 65–77.

Palmer, A. (2004). The internet challenge for destination marketing organizations. *Destination Branding, 128*.

Pelkonen, K., & Yliniemi, A. (2005). *The history of the Arctic Circle in Rovaniemi*. Rovaniemi: Osviitta.

Piller, F., Vossen, A., & Ihl, C. (2012). From Social Media to Social Product Development: The Impact of Social Media on Co-Creation of Innovation. Die Unternehmung, *65*(1).

Poster, M. (2004). Consumption and digital commodities in the everyday. *Cultural Studies*, *18*(2-3), 409–423.

Prahalad, C. K., & Ramaswamy, V. (2000). Co-opting customer competence. *Harvard Business Review*, *78*(1), 79–90.

Prahalad, C. K., & Ramaswamy, V. (2004). Co-creation experiences: The next practice in value creation. *Journal of Interactive Marketing*, *18*(3), 5–14. doi:10.1002/dir.20015

Ramaswamy, V., & Gouillart, F. (2010). *The power of co-creation*. New York, NY: Simon & Schuster.

Ramaswamy, V. & Ozcan, K. (2016). Brand value co-creation in a digitalized world: An integrative framework and research implications. *International Journal of Research and Marketing*. 10.1016/j.ijresmar.2015.07.001

Ritzer, G. (2013). Prosumption: Evolution, revolution or eternal return of the same? *Journal of Consumer Culture*, 1–22.

Ritzer, G., & Jurgenson, N. (2010). Production, Consumption, Prosumption The nature of capitalism in the age of the digital 'prosumer'. *Journal of Consumer Culture*, *10*(1), 13–36. doi:10.1177/1469540509354673

Rusko, R. (2013). The Redefined Role of Consumer as a Prosumer: Value Co-Creation, Coopetition, and Crowdsourcing of Information Goods. In Production and Manufacturing System Management: Coordination Approaches and Multi-Site Planning (pp. 162- 174). Academic Press.

Rusko, R., Merenheimo, P., & Haanpää, M. (2013). Coopetition, Resource-Based View and Legend: Cases of Christmas Tourism and City of Rovaniemi. *International Journal of Marketing Studies*, *5*(6).

Rusko, R. T., Kylänen, M., & Saari, R. (2009). Supply chain in tourism destinations: The case of Levi Resort in Finnish Lapland. *International Journal of Tourism Research*, *11*(1), 71–87. doi:10.1002/jtr.677

Sawhney, M., Verona, G., & Prandelli, E. (2005). Collaborating to create: The Internet as a platform for customer engagement in product innovation. *Journal of Interactive Marketing*, *19*(4), 4–17. doi:10.1002/dir.20046

Schuh, G., Kuhlmann, K., Pitsch, M., & Komorek, N. (2013, July). Digitalization as a key enabler for efficient value creation networks in the tool and die making industry. In *Technology Management in the IT-Driven Services (PICMET), 2013 Proceedings of PICMET'13* (pp. 1976-1984). IEEE.

Sheth, J., Sisodia, R., & Sharma, A. (2000). The Antecedents and Consequences of Customer-Centric Marketing. *Journal of the Academy of Marketing Science*, *28*(Winter), 55–66. doi:10.1177/0092070300281006

Singh, S. (2010). Digital divide in India: Measurement, determinants and policy for addressing the challenges in bridging the digital divide. *International Journal of Innovation in the Digital Economy*, *1*(2), 1–24. doi:10.4018/jide.2010040101

So, K. K. F., King, C., Sparks, B. A., & Wang, Y. (2016). Enhancing customer relationships with retail service brands: The role of customer engagement. *Journal of Service Management*, *27*(2).

Toffler, A. (1980). *The third wave*. New York: Bantam books.

Toffler, A., & Toffler, H. (2006). *Revolutionary Wealth*. New York: Doubleday.

Tripadvisor. (2014a). Retrieved from http://www.tripadvisor.com/ShowUserReviews-g189922-d591471-r172227191-Santa_Claus_Village-Rovaniemi_Lapland.html

Tripadvisor. (2014b). *TripAdvisor.com, Community, Destination Experts*. Author.

Van Doorn, J., Lemon, K. N., Mittal, V., Nass, S. D. P., Pirner, P., & Verhoef, P. C. (2010). Customer engagement behaviour: Theoretical foundations and research directions. *Journal of Service Research*, *13*(3), 253–266. doi:10.1177/1094670510375599

Vargo, S. L., & Lusch, R. F. (2004). Evolving to a new dominant logic for marketing. *Journal of Marketing*, *68*(1), 1–17. doi:10.1509/jmkg.68.1.1.24036

Vargo, S. L., & Lusch, R. F. (2006). *Service-dominant logic. The service-dominant logic of marketing: Dialog, debate, and directions*. Armonk, NY: ME Sharpe.

Verona, G. (1999). A resource-based view of product development. *Academy of Management Review*, *24*(1), 132–142.

Westerman, G., Bonnet, D., & McAfee, A. (2014). *The Nine Elements of Digital Transformation*. Academic Press.

Wiedmann, K.-P. (2015). The future of brand and brand management – Some provocative propositions from a more methodological perspective. *Journal of Brand Management*, *21*(9), 743–757.

Williams, O. W., Stewart, K., & Larsen, D. (2011). Toward an agenda of high-priority tourism research. *Journal of Travel Research*, *51*(1), 3–11. doi:10.1177/0047287511427824

Wind, Y. J., & Rangaswamy, A. (2000). *Customerization: The Next Revolution in Mass Customization*. Marketing Science Institute Working Paper No. 00-108. Cambridge, MA: Marketing Science Institute.

Yin, R. K. (2014). *Case Study Research: Design and Methods*. New York: Sage.

Section 4

Chapter 11
Applications Driven Information Systems:
Beyond Networks toward Business Ecosystems

Kayvan Lavassani
North Carolina Central University, USA

Bahar Movahedi
North Carolina Central University, USA

ABSTRACT

Advancements in organizational information systems and developments in business environments have brought important changes to the contemporary management practices and business models. Organizations have evolved beyond their specific and general environments towards business ecosystems. This study investigates the evolutions of organizational information systems and business environments in the contexts of business ecosystem. Based on an evolutionary study of organizational information systems and business ecosystem an ontological model is proposed for the adoption of new technologies in the real world designs with particular attention to the application of technology. We call for further empirical and conceptual research in understanding and exploring the role of business ecosystems in organizational operations and industrial ecosystems.

INTRODUCTION

Organizational information platforms have advanced significantly during the past few decades. These developments have resulted in significant increase in effectiveness and efficiency of executing organizational business processes. Organizational information platforms are tightly coupled with organizational strategy and management of organizational business processes (Sauer & Willcocks, 2002; Chroneer, 2005; Zhang, Xue & Dhaliwal, 2016). Consequently, understanding developments in the patterns of organizational information platforms requires a multifaceted investigation of business processes, strategy,

DOI: 10.4018/978-1-5225-1779-5.ch011

and the environment. This study explores the development of organizational information systems from an organizational business process perspective in the context of business strategy and business ecosystem. We argue that the development of organizational structures and management of business processes has moved beyond the intra-organizational sphere of organizations and that the contemporary businesses cannot fully define their business model – i.e. customer value proposition and profit formula– within the context of their traditional business environment. The traditional view that separates organizational environment into two spheres of "specific environment" and "general environment" (Jauch & Osborn, 1981) may be useful for identifying key stakeholders and the relations among them; however for the purpose of profit formulation and strategic planning we argue that organizational environment should be viewed within the context of business ecosystems. After discussing the organizational developments in this domain, the study focuses on the evolution of adequate organizational business information systems which further supports the business ecosystem view of the organizational environment.

The Emergence of Organizational Information Ecosystem: Rational, Natural, Open System

An organization can be defined and analyzed from different perspectives. In his seminal work on organizational studies Scott (2003) explains that the early views of the organizations were mostly concerned with the management of internal elements of the organizations and were analyzing organizations as "closed systems". One example is early –and widely cited– organizational model proposed by Leavitt (1965). While this model has been widely used in studying the socio-technical aspect of organizations (Hawryszkiewycz, 2010; Nograsek & Vintar, 2014; Lyytinen & Newman, 2014; Spottke, Wulf & Brenner, 2015) it mostly focuses on the "internal elements" of organization (Scott, 2003). The elements of Leavitt's organizational model are: social structure, goals, participants and technology (Leavitt, 1965).

The intra-organizational level of analysis is evident in the early "rational" and "natural" views of the organizations where emphasize has been respectively on identifying the "distinctive features of organization" and "behavioral structure of organization" (Scott, 2003). However, in contemporary business environments, organizations are highly inter-connected. They affect their environment and are influenced by changes in their environment. Hence, Scott (2003) recommends that an open system view of organizations is more helpful for understanding and analyzing organizations. The open system view does not replace or reject previous views but rather emphasizes that a merely closed system view of the organizations is not capable of explaining the contemporary organizational functions.

Bertalanffy (1968) as one of the seminal scholars in the development of the General System Theory (GST) defined open system "as a system in exchange of matter with its environment, presenting import and export, building-up and breaking-down of its material components" (Bertalanffy, 1968, p. 141). It is important to note that this open system definition stems from the GST perspective. In the context of organizational studies in an open system, "environments shape, support, and infiltrate organizations" while inter-organizational connections are more critical to organizational survival than intra-organizational connections (Scott, 2003).

Moore (1993) describes the concept of business ecosystem to illustrate the increasing role of environment in the survival and growth of organizations. Moore's (1993) study on the changes in the organizational environments that lead to success and failure of organizations can be best explained within the open system perspective. Creation, suitability, and adaptability of the business ecosystem are viewed as some of the main contributors to the survival and growth of organizations. The rapid change in the advancements of technology and innovation during the past few decades has attracted increasing attention to the role of business ecosystems in organizational success and failure. Several stakeholders can be influenced by the actualization of open system view. Consider some of the key infrastructure projects in the U.S. during the early 2010s. The news started to circle stating that Chinese companies are going the takeover large construction projects including California Bay Bridge – which was initially considered to be funded as part of the American Recovery and Reinvestment Act (ARRA) of 2009 (also known as the U.S. stimulus package) and it was later removed from ARRA funding consideration due to the Buy American provision in the act (Public Law, 111–5, p. 303). Various stakeholders, including the government officials, businesses, and the general public were puzzled about the assignment of some key parts of this project to a Chinese construction company while the –once globally dominant – U.S. construction companies should have been in need of new projects during the recovery. The fact is, on one hand, companies compete in their business ecosystem, and on the other hand, business ecosystems are competing with each other. Business ecosystems while can have inter-connections can be differentiated based on geographic location or industry. In the above example, the ecosystem of Chinese construction companies has gained significant experience, know-how and resources during the past few decades of significant growth in China and around the world. However, the U.S. construction industry has not made similar advancements during the same period to nurture its business ecosystem. The existence of "nurturing processes" has been found to be a key success factor in the development of enriched business ecosystems in China (Rong, Wu, Shi & Guo, 2015a). In conclusion, we believe that the ecosystem view of business environment can help us to better understand the patterns of business operations; and furthermore, an open system view is the best approach in analyzing the business ecosystems. In the following, the concept of business ecosystems as open systems are further explored.

Business Ecosystem as an Open System

The business ecosystems can be viewed and analyzed at different levels. Based on our literature search in studying the business ecosystems we have identified one classification of analysis that divides analysis of business ecosystems into two categories: studying the life cycle and studying the stakeholders (Rong, Hu, Lin, Shi & Guo, 2015b). While these are important aspects of business ecosystems we realized there is a need to further clarify the concept of the business ecosystem with regards to the level of analysis. In this section, we further investigate the level of analysis of business ecosystem to provide a framework for future studies. We also acknowledge that this area of study is at its early stages of development. We call for other researchers to challenge and evaluate the proposed models in the present study as well as further studies in this domain.

Rothschild (1990) provided a macro level view of a business ecosystem in which the whole economy is viewed as an ecosystem. According to this view "no one set up the ecosystem", just like the market economy and capitalism, that "it just happened" thanks to advancements in technology and supporting/complementary industries among other known and unknown factors (Rothschild, 1990, p. 267). In contrast, Moore (1993) provided an organizational view of a business ecosystem that believes business ecosystems doesn't just happen. In Moore's (1993) view the business ecosystem is set up and shaped by entrepreneurs and businesses are further guided to expand and gain leadership in the marketplace (ecosystem). In the following, these varying levels of analysis for business ecosystems are described.

In Moore's (1993) view the level of analysis is "company", although he suggests that a company is to "be viewed not as a member of a single industry but as part of a business ecosystem that crosses a variety of industries" (Moore, 1993, p. 76). This organizational level perspective is further clarified when he gives examples of "Toyota ecosystem" or "Durant's ecosystem". Rong et al. (2015a) is another example of business ecosystem investigation at the organizational level. Similar to the Moore's (1993) view, Rong et al. (2015a) highlight the role of an organization in creating and nurturing the business ecosystem through "incubating complementary partners", "identifying leader partners", and "integrating ecosystem partners". This organizational level view of busyness ecosystem is clearly in contrast with Rothschild's (1990) view and requires clear distinction.

At the *organizational level,* all components of the organization's ecosystem (internal and external elements) come together to support the two fundamental aspects of its business model: value proposition to customers, and profit formula (Gamble, Thompson, & Peteraf, 2014). Moore's (1993) view of the business ecosystem is mostly relevant to this level of analysis. An example of this view is the competition of Toyota business ecosystem with U.S. car manufacturers' ecosystem (Moore, 1993). The discussion of "competing supply chains" can also fit into the organizational level view of business ecosystems.

Business ecosystems can also be analyzed at the *industry level.* At this level, the business ecosystem usually can be defined by its stakeholders including the industry suppliers, customers, as well as related domestic and international industries.

From industry level perspective the members of the ecosystem not only are competing with each other but also they can share resources and platforms. Following the works of Moore (1993) and Rong et al. (2015b), we recognize that the industry level analysis is not limited to one industry but includes cross-industry business processes and stakeholders. The cross-industry business ecosystems together shape Rothschild's (1990) view of the economy as an ecosystem.

Pilinkiene and Maciulis (2014) provided a classification of the ecosystem into five types: industrial, innovation, business, digital business, and entrepreneurship ecosystems. Within our –more macro - level– classification, industrial, innovation and digital ecosystems fall under the category of industry level business ecosystems; while business and entrepreneurship fall under our organizational level business ecosystem.

Two categories of business ecosystems are presented along with their prominent founders. In addition, the five categories of business ecosystems are presented from the work of Pilinkiene and Maciulis (2014). Furthermore, some examples of each of the five perspectives of business ecosystems are presented from the work of Pilinkiene and Maciulis (2014) as well as our literature search. It is important to note that due to the different views of each category the definitions of the concepts may vary. For exam the Moore's (1993) definition of "business ecosystem" is different from the classification approach of Pilinkiene and Maciulis (2014) and the authors of this study. Considering the relative novelty of the concept of the business ecosystem a unified and widely accepted classification has not formed yet; hence, this is a fruitful area of research for future studies. For the purpose of this study, the macro-level classification (Industry level ecosystem vs. Organizational level ecosystem) is utilized. However, further insight is provided to draw a clearer picture of the concept of business ecosystem.

At the organizational level, businesses are focused on designing a business model that provides a superior value proposition to customers while the profit formula is promising and sustainable. Various factors from the industry (including those related to specific-environment and cross-industry factors) shape the stakeholders' relations and industry lifecycle. At the highest level of analysis domestic as well as global micro/macro-economic factors shape or affect the industry ecosystem. The industry level ecosystems create the ecosystem view of the economy.

Developments in Organizational Information Systems: Application Awakens

We argued that organizational business ecosystems can be analyzed at two macro-levels: industry level ecosystem and organizational level ecosystem. In this section, the development of organizational information systems is explored within the framework of rational, natural and open systems. The main contribution in this section is to provide an understanding of the structure of organizational information systems within the open system (ecosystems) perspective. In this section, we present an ontological model of organizational information system development to illustrate the different levels of organizational information systems and the formation of business ecosystems. For developing the proposed model we pay particular attention to ontological development method and the relationship between technological advancement and developing a scientific view of the business ecosystem.

Ontological Development Method

Ontological models can assist us with a clear representation of a concept or a body of knowledge by highlighting its elements and their relations (Wang & Marquardt, 2009). Bunge (1977, 1979) and Wand and Weber (1990, 1993) have been credited with their seminal contributions to the area of ontological model development (c.f. Wang & Marquardt, 2009; Chan, Tan & Teo, 2014; Paschke, Athan, Sottara, Kendall & Bell, 2015). These models have been generally inspired by the GST.

Conceptual ontological models including business information systems, business processes, and business ecosystems are constructed based on the observation of real world practice and the previously proposed conceptual models. The conceptual ontological models are constructed based on the observation and interpretation of real world designs by the theorist. The conceptual model is then presented and implemented into the real world designs by empiricist (Wand & Weber, 1993; Lavassani, Movahedi, & Kumar, 2010).

While several information system models have been proposed, it should be noted that ontological models are by nature dynamic concepts. That is, the conceptual models are expected to continuously be presented/introduced by empiricists to the real world designs, be challenged and generate new real world designs that can be conceptualized into a new conceptual ontology by the theorist. This is a never ending process.

Technology Advancement and Scientific View of Business Ecosystem Development

Drucker (1976) reminded us that "young people today will have to learn organizations the way their forefathers learned farming". In Drucker's view "the application of knowledge to technology" is not "simply the application of scientific knowledge to technical devices" (Wood & Wood, 2005). Based on the study of revolution in agriculture, medicine, and mechanical arts during 1750-1857, Drucker argued that these advancements "owed little or nothing to the new knowledge of contemporary science. In fact, in every technology practice with its rules of thumb was far ahead of science. „Technology, therefore, became the spur to science" (Wood & Wood, 2005, p.355). From this perspective, technology has "an immediate impact on science" while science does not have a significant effect on technology until a useful application has been found for it (Drucker, 1993, p.287). Hence we argue that this is the application of the technology that mostly affects –and awakens– the business practices and shapes ecosystems not the technology (information technology in our study) itself.

Drucker (1961) best explained this argument by stating that "the immediate effect of the emergence of technology was not only rapid technological progress: it was the establishment of technologies as systematic disciplines to be taught and learned and finally the re-orientation of science toward feeding these new disciplines of technological application". Comparing this model to the ontology development model of Wand and Weber (1993), we identified important similarities and differences. In both models, the ontology of the business ecosystem is inspired by the real world technology adoption and design. However, the main difference is the effect of the conceptual model (in this case, business ecosystem ontology) in the real world design (in this case, practice of information technology adoption).

We name this model Wand-Weber-Drucker (WWD) ontology of information technology development. Based on the application of Wand and Weber (1993) view in organizational information system adoption, the (conceptual) business ecosystem ontology directly affects the real world design of information technology adoption in organizations. However, with support of Ducker's (1961) view we point out that the business ecosystem ontology will only affect real world adoption of information system if the empiricist is convinced that the proposed ontology will enhance the business model. Our proposed WWD model is the framework that we use in further investigating the developments of organizational information systems adoption. In the following section, we provide further evidence about the applicability of WWD model in organizational information system adoption in the context of a business ecosystem.

Information System Integration Platform: From Organizations to Ecosystems

In this section, the role of information systems as integration platforms is discussed. After a brief historical review of some technological advancement and their applications, we will focus mainly on the application of the Internet. Organizational information systems have evolved significantly over the past five decades. One of the early organizational information systems that found popular applications in the 1960s was Electronic Data Interchange (EDI) system. During the 1960s, EDI systems were widely adopted in the military, health care, and banking. Within the concept of our proposed WWD, when the application of technology was observed it rapidly affected the information technology design in many industries and businesses. Based on the interpretation of the changes very soon new information technology designs and new conceptual models were developed during the 1960s, that promised a new business environment. Decades later we observed several nonbank organizations facilitating the financial transactions (e.g. PayPal) as well as the chip embedded bank cards. Applying our proposed WWD model to this example reveals that PayPal and chip embedded bank card could have been developed years –if not decades– earlier had the scientific advancements and business ecosystem were awakened by an earlier application of technology.

The EDI systems require significant investment in the organizational infrastructure and utilization hence the technology has not been adopted significantly by "small- and medium-sized" organizations (Gunasekaran, Lai & Cheng, 2008). Advancements in computer science and production of affordable personal computers in the 1980s and 1990s increased the accessibility of technology to business and consumers. This paved the ways to the adoption of private networks across various functions of organizations. The application of computers in organizational functions coupled with the network capabilities paved the way to the emergence of multi-module Enterprise Resource Planning (ERP) systems.

Since the 1990s the e-commerce applications capable of conducting electronic transitions have expanded significantly thanks to the Internet as an "electronic medium" (Gunasekaran, Marri, McGaughey & Nebhwani, 2002). The internet has made significant changes not only in the management of organizational functions and business processes but also in the environment in which organizations operate. Here we further explore the role of Internet as a contemporary medium in organizational business models and their ecosystems.

Muzellec, Ronteau and Lambkin (2015) in their study on the role of the internet on business models and ecosystems conclude that the internet has enabled an evolution in the businesses by enabling them to have combinations of B2B and B2C value proposition to customers. Muzellec et al. (2015) argue that the internet is a driving force behind companies to adopt a "two-sided internet platform", one oriented toward business customers and another one toward individual consumers. From this perspective business ecosystem helps with the conceptualization of complex "value co-creation over time" (Muzellec et al., 2015). A successful business model, therefore, needs to be responsive to changes in the business ecosystem. Muzellec et al. (2015) argue that business models in the Internet era will be able to sustain if they can successfully help their organization to navigate in "a dynamic ecosystem which constantly changes".

Beside the changes in the business models as described here, another influential role of the internet in disrupting the business ecosystem has been the formation of Internet of Things (IoT). IoT not only affects the organizational supply chain *(i.e. at the organizational level)* but also evolves the business ecosystem *(i.e. at the industry level)* (Rong et al. 2015b). The IoT will affect both value proposition and profit formula. Looking at IoT within the context of Muzellec's et al. (2015) "two-sided" effect of the internet, it is evident that the business ecosystem will continue to experience significant evolution both at organizational and industry levels. Rong et al. (2015b) argue that industries that employ IoT will experience exposure to other industries and hence will have "cross-industry stakeholders". Therefore, in addition to changes in the business ecosystem, we should expect to see more integrated business ecosystems across different industries. From an open system view this phenomenon can be theoretically explained however for academics and practitioners who want to manage their business process in the complex business environment many complexities remain; which can be a subject of future study. For example, Rong et al. (2015b) recommends that due to complexities of studying business processes (supply chain processes) in the complex IoT domain, the concepts can be more feasibly studied only at the industry ecosystem level.

One of the main elements of our proposed WWD business ecosystem model of organizational information system development is the role of application; in which new conceptual ecosystem ontology (e.g. one infused by a new technology, new business process management practice, etc.) will only create new design in the business environment if it has useful application in terms of customer and business value creation. Interestingly, Rong's et al. (2015b) conclusion in their study is a supporting evidence for the validity of our proposed WWD business ecosystem model. Rong et al. (2015b) suggest "that new technological innovation per se has no inherent value so that a healthy ecosystem needs to be developed in order to fully realize commercial potential of the new technology". This is in line with our WWD model and Drucker's view, that scientific innovation does not have an effect on real world designs until it has found useful applications.

Information System Integration Function: From Networks to Collaboration

Earlier in the paper, we made an argument –with support from the literature– that organizational information systems not only are tightly coupled with the management of business processes, but also have become an important part of organizational strategy. Consequently, organizational information systems are influenced by and shape the business ecosystem. To determine the extent of information system deployment in an organization two aspects of technology utilization should be evaluated: depth and breadth (Zhang, Xue, & Dhaliwal, 2016). As Zhang et al. (2016) explain, *depth* of organizational information system utilization refers to the "intensity and scale of asset utilization". Organizations with more *depth* of utilization tend to have higher levels of integration across their inter-organizational business processes, and hence can take advantage of benefits resulting from higher levels of vertical integration across their internal and external supply chain. *The breadth* of information system utilization, on the other hand, refers to the "diversity and scope" of usage (Zhang et al., 2016). Organizations with higher levels of breadth tend to build more inter-organizational business process relationships. To simplify the concepts of depth and breadth in organizational information systems, it can be argued that while the depth of inter-organizational information system utilization measures the quality of the relationships, the breath demonstrate the amount (in terms of diversity and scope) of relationships. Information platforms as the backbone of organizational business process utilization enable and facilitate the depth and breadth of information system utilization. It is essential for business managers to recognize the past and current developments of organizational information systems to gain competency in leading their organizations toward the future.

We briefly discussed how organizational information platforms evolved from the EDI networks to the organizations which are part of an ecosystem in the world of IoT. The level of organizational integration defines the relationship of the organization as an actor in the network. Here we look at *integration* in terms of *depth* of information system utilization. Lavassani, Movahedi and Kumar (2010) analyzed integration at the business strategy level and identified four levels of integration based on the works of Himmelman (2001) and Romero et al. (2008). These four levels – in order – are: Networking, coordination, cooperation, and collaboration. Lavassani et al. (2010) argue that as organizations decide to employ richer integrations medium (from EDI and ERP systems to web-based exchanges and collaborations), the goal of integration evolves as well.

In the early stages of integration at 'networking' and 'coordination' levels, the goal is to merely establish a common information platform so that actors in the network can adjust their activities. Achieving just in time delivery and lean warehouse management practices would be sample expected outcomes of such integration. With the increase in the level of integration function to 'cooperation' organizations start to share resources. For example, two car manufacturers that decide to share an assembly line. At the 'collaboration' level – the highest level of integration–, the actors (organizations) start sharing responsibilities as well. An example is the collaboration of a TV brand that designs a TV to be manufactured and delivered by a manufacturer.

The fact is, in the contemporary business environment integration through collaboration in many cases is not an advantage but a requirement for organizations to survive and prosper in the business ecosystem (Panetto, Jardim-Goncalves & Molina, 2012). One of the challenges of analyzing organizational collaborative networks is that such modeling "is usually done in some organizational settings" (Krogstie, 2012, p. 138). Future studies need to be conducted to explore the modeling of organizational collaborative networks and their information systems adoption in the contexts of the business ecosystem.

CONCLUSION

Management of organizations within their business ecosystem is becoming the new art of managers and entrepreneurs. If the structure is to follow strategy (Chandler, 1962) and strategy is affected by and affects the business ecosystem, then the organizational structure and management of business processes should be conducted with the business ecosystem in mind.

We started by exploring different perspectives of analyzing organizations. From an organizational ecosystem perspective, an open system view of the organization was found to be the most appropriate view for the contemporary organizations. From an open system perspective, "organizations are viewed as a system of interdependent activities" (Scott, 2003, p. 29). Hence, the evolution of business ecosystems as it relates to organizational information systems can be best viewed and analyzed from an open system view of organizations. Our view about the importance of open system perspective in defining the organizational ecosystem, is not to overlook the importance of the natural and rational views; rather it stems from the fact that rational and natural views of organizations are more concerned with internal components of organizations, while in the open system view "external elements can be more critical" to the organizational survival (Scott, 2003, p. 29).

Following the categorization of business ecosystems to organizational and industry levels, an ontology of business ecosystem is presented. Furthermore, an ontological model for developments of information technology adoption in the context of business ecosystems has been proposed based on the seminal works of Drucker (1976) and Wand and Weber (1993). Finally, we provided a more detail discussion about the adoption of organizational information systems in the business ecosystem which entails a shift of focus from networking to collaborating. Investigating business ecosystems is an emerging field of study which requires further advancements in the development of models and concepts. We hope our proposed models can be applied to the real world designs of information technology adoption in business ecosystems, be challenged and be the inspiration for the development of new ontological models. Further research is required to enhance our understanding and application of business ecosystems.

Since "social media is already a critical part of the information ecosystem" as a "media platforms" (Zeng, Chen, Lusch & Li, 2010) we see opportunities for future research to be conducted in this domain. Future studies can also focus on the application of business ecosystems in complex industries and businesses. In particular investigating the motives, mechanism and process of building a collaborative alliance among business ecosystems can be fruitful areas for future studies; this can include proposing and evaluating the collaborative strategies along with their advantages and disadvantages in nurturing the business ecosystem.

REFERENCES

Acs, Z., Szerb, L., & Autio, E. (2015). *Global Entrepreneurship Index 2015, Global Entrepreneurship and Development Institute*. CreateSpace Independent Publishing Platform.

Barnard, C. I. (1938). *The Functions of the Executive*. Cambridge, MA: Harvard University Press.

Bendix, R. (1956). *Work and authority in industry: Managerial Ideologies in the Case of Industrialization*. New York: John Wiley.

Bertalanffy, L. (1956). General System theory. In *General Systems. In Yearbook of the Society for the Advancement of General System Theory* (10th ed.). Ann Arbor, MI: Academic Press.

Bertalanffy, L. (1968). *General System Theory: Foundations, Development, Applications*. New York: George Braziller.

Blau, P. M., & Scott, W. R. (1962). *Formal organizations: A comparative approach*. San Francisco, CA: Chandler Publishing.

Boulding, K. E. (1956). General systems theory the skeleton of science. *Management Science, 2*(3), 197–208. doi:10.1287/mnsc.2.3.197

Bunge, M. (1977). Treatise on basic philosophy: Vol. 3. *Ontology I: The furniture of the World*. Boston: Reidel.

Bunge, M. (1979). Treatise on basic philosophy: Vol. 4. *Ontology II: A World of systems*. Boston: Reidel.

Chan, H. C., Tan, C. H., & Teo, H. H. (2014). Data Modeling: An Ontological Perspective of Pointers. *Database Management, 25*(4), 17–37. doi:10.4018/JDM.2014100102

Chandler, A. (1962). *Strategy and structure*. Cambridge, MA: MIT Press.

Chroneer, D. (2005). The impact of supply chain information and networking on product development in Swedish process industry. *International Journal of Logistics Systems and Management, 1*(2), 127–148. doi:10.1504/IJLSM.2005.005968

Collins, R. (1975). *Conflict Sociology: Toward an Exploratory Science*. New York: Academic Press.

Cross, S. E., Kippelen, B., & Berthelot, Y. H. (2014). Reaching Across the Pond: Extending a Regional Innovation Ecosystem Strategy, In B. Galbraith (Ed.), *European Conference on Innovation and Entrepreneurship* (p. 128). Academic Conferences International Limited.

Drucker, P. F. (1961). The Technological Revolution--Notes on the Relationship of Technology, Science and Culture. *Technology and Culture, 2*(4), 342–351. doi:10.2307/3100889

Drucker, P. F. (1976). *The Unseen Revolution: How Pension Fund Socialism Came to America*. New York: Harper and Row.

Drucker, P. F. (1993). The Ecological Vision: Reflections on the American Condition. Transaction Publishers.

Etzioni, A. (1964). *Modern Organizations*. Upper Saddle River, NJ: Prentice Hall.

Feijoo, C., Maghiros, I., Abadie, F., & Gomer-Barroso, J. L. (2009). Exploring a Heterogeneous and Fragmented Digital Ecosystem: Mobile Content. *Telematics and Informatics, 26*(3), 173–292. doi:10.1016/j.tele.2008.11.009

Fernandez, M. T. F., Jimenez, F. J. B., & Roura, J. R. C. (2015). Business incubation: Innovative services in an entrepreneurship ecosystem. *Service Industries Journal, 35*(14),. 783–800. doi:10.1080/02642069.2015.1080243

Frosch, R. A., & Gallopoulos, N. E. (1989). Strategies for manufacturing. *Scientific American, 261*(3), 144–152. doi:10.1038/scientificamerican0989-144

Frutiger, M., Narasimhan, S., & Slaughter, S. (2014). A Business Ecosystem Perspective on Open Platforms and Outsourcing Relationships: A Software Industry Case Study. In R. Hirschheim, A. Heinzl, & J. Dibbern (Eds.), *Information Systems Outsourcing* (pp. 501–515). Mannheim, Germany: Springer. doi:10.1007/978-3-662-43820-6_20

Gamble, J., Thompson, A., & Peteraf, M. (2014). *Essentials of Strategic Management: The Quest for Competitive Advantage*. McGraw-Hill/Irwin.

Gouldner, A. W. (1959). Organizational analysis. Sociology Today, 400-428.

Gunasekaran, A., Lai, K. H., & Cheng, T. C. E. (2008). Responsive supply chain: A competitive strategy in a networked economy. *The International Journal of Management Science, Omega, 36*(4), 549-564.

Gunasekaran, A., Marri, H. B., McGaughey, R. E., & Nebhwani, M. D. (2002). E-commerce and its impact on operations management. *International Journal of Production Economics, 75*(1-2), 185–197. doi:10.1016/S0925-5273(01)00191-8

Hawryszkiewycz, I. (2010). *Knowledge Management: Organizing Knowledge Based Enterprises*. Hampshire, UK: Palgrave MacMillan.

Himmelman, A. T. (2001). On coalitions and the transformation of power relations: Collaborative betterment and collaborative empowerment. *American Journal of Community Psychology, 29*(2), 277–284. doi:10.1023/A:1010334831330

Isenberg, D. (2011). *The entrepreneurship ecosystem strategy as a new paradigm for economic policy: principles for cultivating entrepreneurship*. The Babson entrepreneurship ecosystem project. Retrieved December 20, 2015. from http://www.wheda.com/root/uploadedFiles/Website/About_Wheda/Babson%20 Entrepreneurship %20Ecosystem%20Project.pdf

Isherwood, D. & Coetzee, M. (2011). Enhancing digital business ecosystem trust and reputation with centrality measures. *Information Security South Africa (ISSA)*, 1-8.

Jauch, L. R., & Osborn, R. N. (1981). Toward an integrated theory of strategy. *Academy of Management Review, 6*(3), 491–498.

Karakas, F. (2009). Welcome to World 2.0: The new digital ecosystem. *The Journal of Business Strategy, 30*(4), 23–30. doi:10.1108/02756660910972622

Korhonen, J. (2001). Four ecosystem principles for an industrial ecosystem. *Journal of Cleaner Production, 9*(3), 253–259. doi:10.1016/S0959-6526(00)00058-5

Krogstie, J. (2012). Modeling of Digital Ecosystems: Challenges and Opportunities. In L. M. Camarinha-Matos, L. Xu, & H. Afsarmanesh (Eds.), International Federation for Information Processing, (pp. 137-145). Springer.

Lappi, T., Haapasalo, H., & Aaltonen, K. (2015). Business Ecosystem Definition in Built Environment Using a Stakeholder Assessment Process. *Management, 10*(2), 110–129.

Lavassani, K., Movahedi, B., & Kumar, V. (2010). Electronic collaboration ontology: The case of readiness analysis of electronic marketplace adoption. *Journal of Management & Organization, 16*(3), 454–466. doi:10.1017/S183336720000208X

Leavitt, H. J. (1965). Applied organizational change in industry: structural, technical and humanistic approaches. In Handbook of Organizations, (pp. 1144-1170). John Wiley & Sons.

Lu, C., Rong, K., You, J., & Shi, Y. (2014). Business ecosystem and stakeholders' role transformation: Evidence from Chinese emerging electric vehicle industry. *Expert Systems with Applications, 41*(10), 4579–4595. doi:10.1016/j.eswa.2014.01.026

Lyytinen, K., & Newman, M. (2014). A tale of two coalitions – marginalising the users while successfully implementing an enterprise resource planning system. *Information Systems Journal, 25*(2), 71–101. doi:10.1111/isj.12044

March, J. G., & Simon, H. A. (1958). *Organizations.* New York: Wiley.

Moore, J. (1993). Predators and Prey: A New Ecology of Competition. *Harvard Business Review, 71*(3), 75–86.

Moskowitz, H. R., & Saguy, I. S. (2013). Reinventing the role of consumer research in today's open innovation ecosystem. *Critical Reviews in Food Science and Nutrition, 53*(7), 682–693. doi:10.1080/1 0408398.2010.538093

Muzellec, L., Ronteau, S., & Lambkin, M. (2015). Two-sided Internet platform: A business model lifecycle perspective. *Industrial Marketing Management, 45*(2), 139–150. doi:10.1016/j.indmarman.2015.02.012

Nograsek, J., & Vintar, M. (2014). E-government and organisational transformation of government: Black box revisited? *Government Information Quarterly, 31*(1), 108–118. doi:10.1016/j.giq.2013.07.006

Panetto, H., Jardim-Goncalves, R., & Molina, A. (2012). Enterprise Integration and Networking: Theory and practice. *Annual Reviews in Control, 36*(2), 284–290. doi:10.1016/j.arcontrol.2012.09.009

Paschke, A., Athan, T., Sottara, D., Kendall, E., & Bell, R. (2015). A Representational Analysis of the API4KP Metamodel. In R. Cuel & R. Yound (Eds.), *Formal Ontologies Meet Industry,Proceedings of the 7th International Workshop 2015.* doi:10.1007/978-3-319-21545-7_1

Pilinkiene, V., & Maciulis, P. (2014). Comparison of different ecosystem analogies: The main economic determinants and levels of impact. *Procedia: Social and Behavioral Sciences, 156*, 365–370. doi:10.1016/j.sbspro.2014.11.204

Public Law, 111–5, American Recovery and Reinvestment Act of 2009. (n.d.). Retrieved December 1, 2015. from https://www.gpo.gov/fdsys/pkg/PLAW-111publ5/pdf/PLAW-111publ5.pdf

Rashidi, R., Yousefpour, S., Sani, Y., & Rezaei, S. (2013). Presenting a butterfly ecosystem for digital entrepreneurship development in knowledge age. *Proceedings of 7*[th] *conference on Application of Information and Communication Technologies (AICT).* doi:10.1109/ICAICT.2013.6722798

Romero, D., Galeano, N., & Molina, A. (2008). Innovation in manufacturing networks. In A. Azevedo (Ed.), *International Federation for Information Processing, 266* (pp. 47–56). Boston: Springer.

Rong, K., Hu, G., Lin, Y., Shi, Y., & Guo, L. (2015). Understanding business ecosystem using a 6C framework in Internet-of-Things-based sectors, *International Journal of Production Economics, 159*, 41-55.

Rong, K., Wu, J., Shi, Y., & Guo, L. (2015). Nurturing business ecosystems for growth in a foreign market: Incubating, identifying and integrating stakeholders. *Journal of International Management, 21*(4), 293–308. doi:10.1016/j.intman.2015.07.004

Rothschild, M. (1990). *Bionomics: Economy as Business Ecosystem*. New York: Beard.

Rubens, N., Still, K., Huhtamaki, J., & Russell, M.G. (2011). A network analysis of investment firms as resource routers in Chinese innovation ecosystem. *Journal of Software, 6*(9), 1737-1745.

Saur, C., & Willcocks, L. P. (2002). The evolution of organizational architect. *MIT Sloan Management Review, 43*(3), 41–49.

Scott, W. R. (2003). *Organizational: Rational, Natural, and Open Systems*. Upper Saddle River, NJ: Prentice-Hall.

Spottke, B., Wulf, J., & Brenner, W. (2015). Consumer-Centric Information Systems: A Literature Review and Avenues for Further Research. *Proceedings of Thirty Sixth InternationalConference on Information Systems*.

Wand, Y., & Weber, R. (1990). An ontological model of an information system. *IEEE Transactions on Software Engineering, 16*(11), 1281–1291. doi:10.1109/32.60316

Wand, Y., & Weber, R. (1993). On the ontological expressiveness of information systems analysis and design grammars. *Journals of Information Systems, 3*(4), 217–237. doi:10.1111/j.1365-2575.1993. tb00127.x

Wang, A., & Marquardt, W. (2009). An Ontological Conceptualization of multiscale models. *Computers & Chemical Engineering, 33*(4), 822–837. doi:10.1016/j.compchemeng.2008.11.015

Weill, P., & Woerner, S. (2015). Thriving in an Increasingly Digital Ecosystem, *MIT. Sloan Management Review, 56*(4), 27–34.

Wood, J. C., & Wood, M. C. (Eds.). (2005). *Peter F. Drucker: Critical evaluations in business and management*. New York, NY: Routledge.

Zeng, D., Chen, H., Lusch, R., & Li, S. H. (2010). Social media analytics and intelligence. *IEEE Intelligent Systems, 25*(6), 13–16. doi:10.1109/MIS.2010.151

Zhang, C., Xue, L., & Dhaliwal, J. (2016). Alignments between the depth and breadth of inter-organizational systems deployment and their impact on firm performance. *Information & Management, 53*(1), 79–90. doi:10.1016/j.im.2015.08.004

Chapter 12

Implications of the Strategic Agency of Sociomaterial Configurations for Participation in Strategy–Making

Pikka-Maaria Laine
University of Lapland, Finland

Piritta Parkkari
University of Lapland, Finland

ABSTRACT

The aim of this chapter is to answer calls for more studies on the role of materialities in enabling or restricting the participation of larger numbers of people beyond managerial ranks in strategy-making. Drawing on sociomateriality as a practice philosophical perspective, the chapter studies strategy-making in a community-based organization and explores how human actions and materialities interweave to enhance the participation of rank-and-file members in strategy-making. The results show how different sociomaterial configurations gain strategic agency in different phases of a strategy-making process and the implications of these for participation in strategy-making. The authors argue that it is not sufficient to focus on technologies or other materialities as such, but it is also necessary to acknowledge the whole sociomateriality of practices. Furthermore, they also argue that participation in strategy could be seen as a dialectic process of exclusion and inclusion.

INTRODUCTION

The digital economy enables more inclusive forms of strategy-making through new social technology, which has been seen in the area of open innovations (Afuah & Tucci, 2012; Baldwin & von Hippel, 2011; Chesbrough, 2006). More inclusive forms of strategy-making may refer to the participation of personnel or customers in strategy-making; joint strategy-making between different organizations; or the collective strategy processes of community-based or network-based organizations (Laine & Vaara,

DOI: 10.4018/978-1-5225-1779-5.ch012

2015; Whittington, 2015). However, only a few studies examine how people beyond managerial ranks participate in strategy-making (Balogun, Best, & Lê, 2015; Jarzabkowski, Burke, & Spee, 2015; Jarzabkowski, Spee, & Smets, 2013). This is because the growing interest in the role of materialities, including technology, in strategy practice research (Jarzabkowski & Pinch, 2013) has mainly been actualized by examining how top and middle managers use strategy tools, material artifacts, and technology in various ways to enhance their strategic agency (Dameron, Lê, & LeBaron, 2015; Jarzabkowski & Kaplan 2015). Hence, there is a paucity of knowledge regarding how these materialities are used to enable or restrict the participation of larger numbers of people beyond managerial ranks (Laine & Vaara, 2015; Whittington, 2015).

In our study, we draw from sociomateriality (Barad, 2003; Orlikowski & Scott, 2008; Suchman, 2007) to examine how human actions and materialities are interwoven such that they enhance the participation of rank-and-file members in strategy-making. Sociomateriality refers to a practice philosophical approach (Orlikowski, 2015) or "strong" view of materiality (Lê & Spee, 2015). It sets aside the distinctiveness of the social and material in favor of the ontological co-constitution of human activity and materialities. Thus, it allows for the full acknowledgement of the inherent immanence of the materiality of practices, which in our case are the practices of strategy-making. The social and material are in a constant process of (re) configuring, which means that they are always situationally interwoven to work together toward certain ends. These sociomaterial configurations exercise agency through their performativity, that is, through the things they do. In our study, we examine the performative effects of the sociomaterial configurations on the participation of rank-and-file members in strategy-making. In other words, we explore the strategic agency of sociomaterial configurations and the implications of this for participation in strategy-making. By strategy-making, we refer to the actions that are consequential for the strategic outcomes, directions, survival, and competitive advantage of the organization (Johnson, Melin, & Whittington, 2003). Strategic agency, in turn, refers to the capability to act and have an impact on organizational strategy-making, such as making decisions concerning the future direction and resource allocation of the organization or interpreting the strategy for employees or customers (Giddens, 2001; Mantere, 2008; Thomas, 2009).

We empirically study the strategic agency of sociomaterial configurations and their implications for participation through an ethnographic study of an "entrepreneurship society" in Finland. Entrepreneurship societies aim to promote entrepreneurship by arranging various activities around entrepreneurship (Pittaway, Rodriguez-Falcon, Ayiegbayo, & King, 2011), and they can be seen as community-based organizations (Keevers, Treleaven, Sykes, & Darcy, 2012). They make an interesting case for studying enlarged participation in strategy-making, since these societies are informal, non-accredited, volunteer-based, and mostly student-led organizations, where organizational actors have few official hierarchical relationships among each other.

Our study makes two contributions to strategy-as-practice research. First, we propose a novel practice theoretical approach to examine strategy-making: sociomateriality as a practice philosophical perspective. Drawing from this approach, we also demonstrate how material actors have strategic agency, but only when understood as ontologically entangled with and inseparable from human actions. Second, we contribute to discussions on participation in strategy-making. We show that it is not sufficient to focus on information technologies or other materialities as such, as it is necessary to acknowledge the inherent sociomateriality of strategy-making activities and practices.

STRATEGY-MAKING AND SOCIOMATERIALITY

Over the last few years, there has been a trend toward greater openness in the strategy process (Whittington, Yakis-Douglas, & Cailluet, 2011). Opening the strategy process may mean the inclusion of personnel or customers in strategy-making; joint strategy-making between different organizations; or the collective strategy processes of community-based or network-based organizations (Laine & Vaara, 2015; Whittington, 2015). The trend has been reinforced by new organizational forms and changing managerial cultures (Musson & Duberley, 2007; Whittington et al., 2011). However, in the digital economy, more inclusive forms of strategy-making have also been enabled by new social technology, which has been seen in the area of open innovations (Afuah & Tucci, 2012; Baldwin & von Hippel, 2011; Chesbrough, 2006).

Indeed, there are increasing calls within strategy-as-practice research for an emphasis on the material—including technology—in strategy-making (Jarzabkowski & Pinch, 2013; Vaara & Whittington, 2012). However, studies have been mainly focused on exploring how top and middle managers use strategy tools, material artifacts, and technology in various ways to enhance their strategic agency (Jarzabkowski & Kaplan, 2015). Jarzabkowski and Kaplan (2015) present an extensive overview of how and why actors select and apply strategy tools, what might be the various outcomes of using a tool, and how the use of a tool constrains and enables strategy-making. Some studies have examined how strategic plans gain textual agency and affect collective understanding (Spee & Jarzabkowski, 2009; Vaara, Sorsa, & Pälli, 2010). Spee & Jarzabkowski (2011), for example, elucidate how a strategic plan both shaped and was shaped by human interaction within the strategic planning process of senior managers. Werle and Seidl (2015), in turn, examine the interaction of multiple strategy tools and their impact on the development of strategic topics.

Moisander and Stenfors (2009) point out the possible inadequacy of traditional strategy tools in the context of knowledge intensive organizations, where participative dialogue and experimentation are required (see also Thomas & Ambrosini, 2015). Hence, some studies have demonstrated how three-dimensional artifacts enable more participative forms of strategy-making. Whittington, Molloy, Mayer, and Smith (2006) show how a "cube" was developed within a strategy process as a material artifact to capture and carry the message of strategy to the personnel of the organization. Heracleous and Jacobs (2011), in turn, demonstrate how participants in a strategy workshop constructed a metaphorical material structure to make sense of and discuss their organization's strategy. Jarzabkowski, Burke, and Spee (2015) explore the coordination of speech, material objects, and embodied behaviors. They show how different constellations of speech, material objects, and embodied behaviors construct different spaces for strategy work, such as "mutual space" for collaborative work, "dialogical space" for negotiating work, and "restricted space" for private work.

A few studies have also focused on the role of information technology in extending strategy-making beyond managerial ranks in the context of knowledge intensive organizations. Kaplan (2011) examines how the use of PowerPoint slides was part of the discursive practices of strategic knowledge production and enabled the participation of many people in the construction of strategy in a telecommunication company. Stieger, Matzler, Chatterjee, and Ladstaetter-Fussenegger (2012), in turn, provide a rare example of the use of information technology to involve the entire personnel in the strategy-making of a medium-sized Austrian technology company. Jarzabkowski, Spee, and Smets (2013) demonstrate how underwriting managers used photos, maps, data packs, spreadsheets, and graphs to make decisions that shaped their firm's strategy. Demir (2015), in turn, explores strategy-making as an ongoing grassroots activity in Swedish banks. He elucidates how the strategic actions of corporate advisors are affected by bundles of sociomaterial affordances, or "bundled action possibilities" provided by how social and material features are enacted together in strategy practice.

Despite the advances made, there is still room for research on the role of materialities in increasing participation in strategy-making. For this endeavor, we propose sociomateriality (Barad, 2003; Orlikowski & Scott, 2007; Suchman, 2007) as a practice philosophical perspective (Orlikowski, 2015) or "strong" view of materiality (Lê & Spee, 2015) to examine the dynamic entangling of human actions and materialities in strategy-making, and the performative effects of this. Sociomateriality is a theoretical approach that has been employed in the areas of material feminism (Barad, 2003), science and technology studies (Suchman, 2007), and research on technology and organizations (Orlikowski & Scott, 2008). To some extent, it may be seen as a counterforce to linguistic turn, which is believed to overemphasize the social by considering reality and material as constructed in and through language. Within sociomateriality, nature and material are seen as agentic—they act, and those actions have consequences for humans and non-humans. Sociomateriality intends to deconstruct the reality/language dichotomy and incorporate the material and the discursive (Alaimo & Heckman, 2008).

Hence, sociomateriality emphasizes that human subjects and material objects have no attributes as distinct entities but that they come to exist in and through mutual constitution of each other. On the other hand, "interaction suggest[s] two entities, given in advance, that come together and engage in some kind of exchange… intra-action underscores the sense in which subjects and objects emerge through their encounters with one another" (Suchman, 2007, p. 267). Intra-action focuses on materialization and meaning-making, which are the "specific material reconfigurings" that constitute the world (Barad, 2007, p. 142). Hence, sociomaterial configurations are seen as performative, which means that they act and have an impact on issues (Barad, 2003; Butler, 2006). Furthermore, practice is the space in which the social and material become constitutively entangled (Orlikowski, 2015). The social and material are embedded in practices; thus, all practices are sociomaterial. Hence, the sociomaterial philosophical perspective leads us to formulate our research question to ask how information technology, other materialities, and human actions are interwoven so as to produce strategy-making as well as participation in strategy-making.

METHODOLOGY

Our empirical research is an ongoing ethnographic study of a Finnish entrepreneurship society that we refer to as "StartingUp" (name changed). Entrepreneurship societies have become a widespread phenomenon globally (Pittaway et al., 2011). In Finland, the first entrepreneurship society was founded in Helsinki in 2009, and by 2014 there were about 15 societies throughout the country. Entrepreneurship societies are non-accredited, student-led societies that seek to educate, inspire, and encourage entrepreneurial interest (Pittaway et al., 2011). They attract students who are interested in learning about enterprise and developing enterprising skills either to start their own businesses or to become people who are more enterprising (Pittaway et al., 2011). StartingUp engages mainly in organizing startup entrepreneurship-related events at its "home base" (field notes), a small space in an industrial building. The events usually include speeches by entrepreneurs or people involved in entrepreneurial support. StartingUp's events are open to the public and there is no official membership. The people who participate in the events are usually students from two local universities, and most of them represent the fields of business, IT (programming), or design. However, the active group of people running StartingUp also includes young people who are already engaged in the working life.

As a research context, StartingUp is part of the increased interest in startups at the grassroots level (Lehdonvirta, 2013) and the rise in startup-focused activities from the bottom up (Sipola, 2015) that has come about in Finland in recent years. Startup discourse emphasizes scalability, technology, fast market entry, growth, agility, and the importance of teams (e.g., Ries, 2011; Blank, 2013). This discourse is prevalent in StartingUp as well. StartingUp is a community-based organization (Keevers et al., 2012) with little formal hierarchy. Thus, its network-like organization makes for a good case for understanding how information technology, other materialities, and human actions are interwoven such as to enhance the participation of a large number of people in strategy-making. In part, we selected StartingUp because it was founded shortly before data collection began. This allowed us to map out strategy-making in real time in the early phase of an organization's development and to see the continuous processes in which the social and the material are entangled, thereby gaining insight into how and why events play out over time (Langley, 1999).

We relied on ethnography to study the configuring of human actions, information technology, and other materialities in strategy-making. Ethnography is about understanding how a particular community (in our case, StartingUp) lives by studying events, language, rituals, institutions, behaviors, artifacts, and interactions (Cunliffe, 2010). We followed ethnography as an epistemological stance and as a way of engaging with the world around us, rather than as a clear-cut method of data collection (ibid.). As ethnographic fieldwork involves working with people for long periods in their natural setting (Fettermann, 2010, p. 33), the second author has been conducting the fieldwork since September 2013. This was when StartingUp held its first public events. We report the data generated between September 2013 and March 2014.

Data collection in ethnography is not about strict procedures or the quantity of certain kinds of data, but it is about doing what it takes to understand how we create meanings and live our lives with others (Cunliffe, 2010). Our data were mainly collected by attending the formal events and activities of StartingUp, especially the almost-weekly talks at the home base of the community. In all the activities and events, the second author took field notes, and some events were audiotaped. She also took photographs and participated in the informal discussions and activities of the community. Furthermore, she tracked StartingUp on social media platforms (Facebook and Twitter) and the community's webpage and engaged in Facebook discussions. The second author also conducted and transcribed seven semi-structured, audiotaped interviews with the project manager of StartingUp, four people actively taking part in the community, a development manager from TechCo (pseudonym for the technology and innovation center in a mid-Finnish city that established StartingUp), and a local entrepreneur involved in the community. In these semi-structured, one-on-one interviews, she followed a story-telling approach (Czarniawska, 2004). This allowed the interviewees to talk about their experiences without too much guidance on the part of the interviewer and to provide us with rich, descriptive data regarding the purpose and development of StartingUp and its network. Eventually, this fieldwork also led the second author to become an active and trusted member (Adler & Adler, 1987) of the community, which enabled her to participate in its actions and practices.

Our analysis process began with the second author constructing a thickly descriptive story (Langley, 1999) of StartingUp's development from the establishment of the project in early 2013 to March 2014, based on observations, field notes, interviews, and social media feeds. The analysis was carried out as an abductive process, which means an iterative back-and-forth process between theoretical concepts and empirical data (Klag & Langley, 2013). Based on the story, we first analytically separated and coded the actions of human and material agents (Eriksson & Kovalainen, 2015). Then, we referred back to the theorization of sociomateriality and intra-action to elicit how "subjects and objects emerge through their encounters with one another" (Suchman, 2007, p. 267). We identified various sociomaterial configurations, and analyzed their actions, i.e., what did they do. Here we used insights from textual analysis (Tischer, Meyer, Wodak, & Vetter, 2000) and focused especially on examining how these sociomaterial configurations produced strategic actions. By strategic actions, we refer to all those actions that relate to the purpose, future, survival, and competitiveness of the community (Johnson et al., 2003). We distinguished three phases of strategy-making according to discernible shifts in participation of the members of StartingUp in strategy-making: Informing the Purpose of the Entrepreneurship Society; Enacting Startup Scene Membership; and Providing IT Services. Finally, we composed our results section to elucidate the continuous co-constitutive (re)configuring of human actions, information technology, and materialities and the performative effects of these for strategy-making in general and participation in strategy-making in particular.

The claims made in the results section are based on our reading of ethnographic data, and we do not want to give the impression that no other interpretations could be (re)constructed from our material. We also recognize that the second author has played a significant role in co-constructing the story of StartingUp, both in interaction with the participants as a researcher and also as one of the actors in the story, or a member of the community. However, we see this engagement as a strength, since it allowed for the nuanced description and informed interpretation of the configurations that had agency in StartingUp's strategy-making.

RESULTS

Informing the Purpose of StartingUp

At the beginning of 2013, the entrepreneurship society StartingUp was established in and through the institutionalized project management and financing procedures of technology and innovation centers in Finland. One of the local managers of TechCo, a technology and innovation center in a mid-Finnish city, created the project by defining a project plan for two years. The procedure established StartingUp differently from most of the other entrepreneurship societies, since it provided financing for a hired project manager. In contrast, most of the other entrepreneurship societies had been student-led proposals that operated on a voluntary basis. As stated in the project plan, the purpose of StartingUp was "to establish new companies and create new jobs in the area" (Project plan of StartingUp).

TechCo set up a webpage as well as Facebook and Twitter accounts for StartingUp. They materialized the organization of StartingUp to various stakeholders such as the local community, other technology and innovation centers, and entrepreneurship societies in Finland. The webpage used English to describe StartingUp as a supporting actor who activates entrepreneurial people and aids new ventures:

We develop StartingUp in co-operation with business operators and universities from the local region. StartingUp activates people who are innovative, courageous and curious. We build networks with other Entrepreneurship Societies, Startups and Investors. We operate among the entrepreneurs of the future.

We help them to develop business concepts and to create innovative Startup Teams. We also organize inspirational events with an entrepreneurial spirit and great performers. (StartingUp webpage)

The text draws from the startup discourse. It constructs entrepreneurs as innovative, courageous, and curious forerunners with whom StartingUp wants to co-operate. By defining itself as a link to investors, StartingUp holds an important position in the field of startup businesses.

Within the startup discourse, a webpage is not seen as sufficient media; Facebook and Twitter appeal as additional communicative platforms. However, TechCo produced social media not as an interactive communication channel, but as a one-way communication channel for delivering the purpose and messages of StartingUp. The following post determines the purpose of StartingUp as a joint accomplishment between the residents in the area: "Our common goal is to create dozens of new companies in the local region within the next two years. Join us!" (StartingUp Facebook).

In May 2013, a young man, Tim (name changed), with work experience at a startup company and in municipal politics was hired as a project manager to develop the community and help it in establishing new companies. Tim started to arrange various types of events at the StartingUp facilities. He continued to use Facebook and Twitter to inform people about the events and to post photos of the events, thus enhancing the one-way communication channel through social media. The posts constructed StartingUp as a dynamic forerunner that creates great experiences for everyone who participates:

It's the beginning of a very good week! [--] The day after tomorrow [the local city] will explode because of the awesome Launch Event of StartingUp! Who is in? Show your commitment! (StartingUp Facebook)

Drawing from the startup discourse, the posts reproduced the heroic ethos for the startup entrepreneurs. They were constructed almost as saviors of the universe by commending them for "doing a grand job for humankind" (StartingUp Twitter). The character of an entrepreneur was also produced in and through the events organized by StartingUp. The ideal startup entrepreneur was embodied by Marc (name changed), a local creative industry startup entrepreneur. He applied a "cozy" presentation mode by sitting on a sofa with his two-year-old son. Moreover, he did not focus on presenting his company but spoke instead about his everyday life as an entrepreneur, which he constructed as a "life full of surprises, which I kind of love and which make me feel alive" (field notes). The sofa, the son, and Marc's presentation materialized the easy-going and autonomous lifestyle of an entrepreneur, who does what he wants with his life. For him, entrepreneurship wells up from his passion; he then enacts it. Work becomes like play and this leads to endless possibilities: "Do what you love and the rest will come. Doing the thing you love gives you power" (Marc's presentation). Marc emphasized that although he *"works 24/7"* (field notes), he does what he loves and would do it anyway, even without monetary compensation. Marc's presentation produced the startup entrepreneur as an active, independent, and restless person whose passion overrides any stress caused by work.

The startup discourse emphasizes that learning by doing and "getting things done" is appreciated more than elaborate planning. However, at StartingUp events, participants did not engage in doing "things" or working together. Rather, they sat down to listen to presentations and left the facilities after the events. This passivity was obvious on one particular occasion, when the project manager—who had planned and organized the events—had to leave early. He asked two of the participants to lead a discussion about the activities that the participants would like StartingUp to have in the future. Very few ideas were suggested and the discussion was soon terminated.

In many events organized by StartingUp, presentations were provided in a traditional type of setting, where the presenter used PowerPoint or Prezi and spoke in front of the audience, which sat in a classroom format, listening quietly. The presenters provided long presentations about their organizations. The audience consisted of students who did not seem to get too excited about the presentations. Even when Marc applied a cozy presentation style, by sitting on a sofa with his small child, the audience became quiet listeners. Thus, the space of StartingUp's facilities as well as the PowerPoint and Prezi format of the presentations oriented the other participants to sit in traditional classroom formation and listen quietly.

The configuring and reconfiguring of human actions, information technology, physical setting, and their usage constructed both the purpose of StartingUp and how the purpose and the future of the community were defined and by whom. Overall, the project plan, webpage, and posts materialized StartingUp as a community (even before public events took place). They produced StartingUp as a two-year project and as a supporting actor who activates entrepreneurial people and aids new ventures (in particular, technology- and growth-oriented startup entrepreneurship, and not just any kind of entrepreneurship). However, people other than the project manager were not invited to participate in defining the purpose of StartingUp, nor were they included in planning and organizing the events. The participants of the events were thus constructed as event attendees rather than members of StartingUp community. Hence, these sociomaterial (re)configurings restricted the participation of the members of StartingUp in the strategy-making of the organization. They also seemed to reproduce the traditional top-down type of strategy-making, with the TechCo manager and project manager as key actors. The key characteristics of the Informing the Purpose of StartingUp phase are summarized in Figure 1, as are the consequences of the strategic agency of this phase's sociomaterial configuration.

Enacting Startup Scene Membership

In January 2014, StartingUp organized a get-together event for all Finnish entrepreneurship societies in a remote location over a weekend. The purpose of the event was posted on Facebook as follows: "to 'break the ice' between the Finnish entrepreneurship societies, to get people from them to know each other, and to establish more co-operation between the societies." The post constructed StartingUp as an equal member among the community of entrepreneurship societies, who could provide suggestions for co-operation. Furthermore, the project plan guided Tim to construct the members of StartingUp as part of the representatives of entrepreneurship societies. Since the plan insisted that StartingUp would be run by voluntary forces during 2015, Tim provided the event with the purpose of allowing the active members of StartingUp to get to know each other as well as people from other entrepreneurship societies. The activity of the members was defined by their participation in previous events and engagement in discussion with Tim. Facebook was now constructed as an exclusive media by sending invitations to the event to a selected group of people.

Altogether, 30 people—young women and men—from seven different entrepreneurship societies attended the event, including nine people from StartingUp. These were the "active" (Tim, project manager, field notes) ones, who had attended previous events regularly. The event was composed of informal discussions and formal workshops. The informal occasions were set up according to Finnish traditions, such as sauna, hole in the ice for winter swimming, fireplace, and beer. The material arrangements provided the participants with a cozy atmosphere for becoming easily acquainted with each other and enhanced informal discussions about the purpose and actions of entrepreneurship societies.

Figure 1.

(Re)configuring the co-constitutive relationship of human actions, IT, and other materialities	Implications for strategy-making
Institutionalized financing and project plan procedures allow the TechCo (a local innovation and technology center) manager to construct a project plan for establishing StartingUp.　　Financing and project plan procedures　Techco manager	Establishing StartingUp as a two-year project aimed at creating new companies and jobs.　Defines the management (project manager and supervisory board) of StartingUp.
TechCo establishes a webpage and Facebook and Twitter accounts for StartingUp, which create a virtual presence before actual events take place.　TechCo　Webpage Facebook Twitter	Materializing StartingUp to various stakeholders through virtual presence.　Further defining StartingUp's purpose as being a supporting actor who activates entrepreneurial people and aids new ventures.
Project manager of StartingUp organizes events with speakers, provides posts and photos on social media.　Social Media posts and photos　Project manager	Creating a dynamic, startup-like spirit around StartingUp.　Constructs an even heroic representation of entrepreneurship.　Enhancing the role of project manager as the determiner of the purpose of StartingUp.
In StartingUp's events, local entrepreneurs tell their stories and talk about their organizations using PowerPoint and Prezi presentations, while the audience sits quietly in a classroom-like setting.　PP presentation and classroom setting　Presenter and audience	Creates the character of startup entrepreneurs as easy-going and masters of their own lives.　Produces event participants as passive listeners and event attendees, rather than StartingUp community members.
Implication for participation in strategy-making:	
These sociomaterial (re)configurations restrict the participation of the members of StartingUp in the strategy-making of the organization.	

The informal discussions in a cozy setting enabled the people from StartingUp to engage in discussions, which in turn provided them with equal membership among the representatives of entrepreneurship societies. There was lots of chitchat, but also discussion about Finnish startup entrepreneurship. The more established societies also shared their experiences. A community manager of one society—a young woman—spoke about their business acceleration program, which was targeted exclusively at new, technology-based startup companies that strive for internationalization and growth. The discussions produced the participants as part of the startup world. What is noteworthy is that identification with the startup scene was not just a consequence of the cozy setting and joint discussions, but a condition for them, since the participants embodied the coziness with their youth and comfortable presence.

There was also a formal workshop to plan the purpose and future of co-operation between the attending entrepreneurship societies. One of the ideas produced during the workshop was to establish a common website for all the Finnish entrepreneurship societies. Some of the participants started to work on this task immediately. This was possible because all the participants had laptops and smartphones with them. They reserved a domain, made a preliminary sketch of the website, and published it. The website made the co-operation of entrepreneurship societies matter, both in the sense of making it important and of materializing it. This enhanced the posting about the webpage and the event on Twitter, with tagging all of the participating entrepreneurship societies:

A couple of things have taken action, one of which is this webpage. (John, Twitter)

The webpage and Twitter posts about it enacted the action-oriented "lean startup" spirit (Ries, 2011) that is valued in the startup discourse and was emphasized in the discussions during the event. In addition to the webpage, social media provided a virtual presence for the event through photos and messages about the presentations on Twitter and Facebook and through comments on posts. Social media published this private, secluded event. The public presence enhanced postings by the participants of the event, which in turn provoked postings of other members of societies not attending the event. Hence, the virtual presence was not just a consequence of using social media, but a condition for intensified usage of social media. Virtual presence enabled more postings and hype about the event as the participants posted comments about it and as other participants and people outside the event commented on the posts.

During the event, it was noteworthy that the members of StartingUp were the ones producing the membership, not the Facebook invitation that had constructed the membership when the event was launched. The members of StartingUp were confronted with questions about their operation:

"So, what do you do in StartingUp?", "What events do you have coming up?" and "What kind of people do you have there?" (Field notes)

The questions within the ponderings about startups forced the members of StartingUp to stop and think about what they were doing and why, something that the earlier events had not done. They changed the way they spoke about StartingUp and started to talk about it as their project: "What we are doing" (field notes). They presented their ideas for future entrepreneurship-related events. Further, some of the photos posted on Twitter showed the members of StartingUp presenting their ideas (StartingUp on Twitter). All of this produced StartingUp as a joint venture and the members as "the StartingUp people" (field notes).

The configuring and reconfiguring of social actions and material objects during the Enacting Startup Scene Membership phase constructed StartingUp as a volunteer-organization-to-be, as the project plan directed the project manager to seek to establish a core group of volunteers who would run the community after the project ended. The organized get-together event, starting with the social media invitation and then the cozy setting and discussion within the event, constructed StartingUp as an equal among the Finnish entrepreneurship societies. The webpage and posts on Facebook and Twitter materialized the presence of co-operation between entrepreneurship societies, which further enhanced posting in social media. Furthermore, the cozy physical setting provided joint discussions. Participation in discussions and constructing of the webpage, posting, and presentations, as well as receiving questions about the operations of StartingUp produced the members of StartingUp as part of the larger entrepreneurship society community. Importantly, it produced StartingUp as their joint venture and them as "us." Altogether, these sociomaterial configurations enabled a large group of people to participate in the strategy-making of StartingUp. The key characteristics of the Enacting Startup Scene Membership phase are summarized in Figure 2, as are the consequences of the strategic agency of this phase's sociomaterial configuration.

Providing IT Services

After the get-together event, Tim (the project manager) invited the nine StartingUp members who had attended the event and seven other people who had actively participated in earlier events to a closed and secret Facebook group called the "StartingUp core team" (field notes). This Facebook group format meant that only the people in the group were able to see that the group exists. This core team embodied the "holy trinity, the perfect startup team [, which] consists of coders, graphic designers, and business people" (Tim, project manager, interview). The Facebook format of the group constructed certain people as the exclusive core team who were allowed to take part in planning the future of StartingUp, organizing events, and arranging co-operation. The following post provides the group with the task of formulating the future of StartingUp:

[…] We plan the communication and events/activities of StartingUp. In brief, you tell the ideas, we plan & Tim does the work! (Core team Facebook)

The post also changes Tim's role from the central planner to a member of the planning group with a specific responsibility to implement the plans.

The core team then reconstructed Facebook as their internal communication platform. It was used for holding virtual meetings, preparing upcoming events, and planning the future. The startup discourse guided an emphasis on IT in discussions. The easy-going attitude of startup entrepreneurship was reconstructed by portraying how IT people were "lured in by saying that there will be beer and pizza" (Kevin, a coder, interview). Furthermore, the IT-people were very active in the group. Hence, the discussed business ideas were related to information technology and the planned events became more IT-focused. For example, lots of time was devoted to planning a "Hackathon" (field notes), which was an event that involved software development in groups over a limited amount of time.

Constructing the core team simultaneously excluded other people from defining and developing StartingUp. However, this was produced as inevitable, as illustrated in the following extract from a Facebook chat:

Yes, the Facebook group weeds out people who come to events only occasionally from the core activities of StartingUp. [--] The good thing about this is that the core team clearly stands out and is able to act a bit more "seriously" and the bad thing is that for those who really want to take part, it is not that easy to get into the "inner circles." However, this is pretty much unavoidable. (Private Facebook chat between Peter—a coder—and the second author)

The establishment of the core team is constructed to matter because it materializes the core team in relation to the undefined others. It provides the core team with the authority to act, and it constructs the

Figure 2.

(Re)configuring the co-constitutive relationship of human actions, IT, and other materialities	Implications for strategy-making
The project plan guides the project manager to seek to establish a core group of volunteers who will take on StartingUp after the project funding runs out. Project Plan — Project manager	Constructing StartingUp as a volunteer-organization-to-be.
Invitation to co-operation for "active" members, based on event attendance and discussion with project manager. Facebook invitation — Project manager — Members' event attendance	Constructing a group of people as the "active members," who get to participate in strategy-making.
StartingUp invites Finnish entrepreneurship societies to a co-operation event. Project manager — Facebook invitation	Constructing StartingUp as an equal member among the entrepreneurship societies
Laptops and smartphones enable participants to launch a common webpage. Virtual presence enhances posting about the event on social media. Physical setting — Laptops — Event participants	Materializing their co-operation in the form of common webpage and posts, and enacting "learning-by-doing."
During event, the cozy physical setting (sauna, fireplace, beer) enhances informal discussions. Physical setting — Informal discussion	Participation in discussions provides members of StartingUp with equal membership among other representatives of entrepreneurship societies.
StartingUp members participate in discussion and workshops and receive questions about their operations. Physical setting and discussions — StartingUp members	Producing the members of StartingUp as "us" and StartingUp as their joint venture.
Implication for participation in strategy-making:	
These sociomaterial (re)configurations enable a large group of people to participate in the strategy-making of the organization.	

actions of the core team as more important than the actions of others. However, the secret Facebook group format did not expose this position to any stakeholders.

The project plan guided StartingUp to establish co-operation with local entrepreneurs. This was reformulated by the project manager: "We need to co-operate with local companies in order to start doing things, take StartingUp to the next level, and increase the resources available for organizing bigger events in the future" (Tim, project manager, field notes). Expressing the necessity of moving to the "next level" reproduces the idea that companies need to make visible the difference between the future and the present. Drawing from the startup discourse, co-operation with local entrepreneurs was defined as a "problem solving program" (field notes) in February 2014. The label of the program offers a promise for providing solutions. It was targeted at local entrepreneurs with small or medium-sized businesses who could bring a problem to the StartingUp team, which would then suggest solutions. Instead of intensive planning of the program, the team hastily met the first entrepreneur at the facilities of StartingUp. This enacted the "learning-by-doing" mode of action. The core team suggested solutions based on information technology, such as building up the business with 3D modeling for the entrepreneur, whose company was operating in a traditional field of business.

It was agreed upon that the core team would not receive any monetary compensation for their service: "Without getting paid like a real company" (field notes). This defined the operation as providing the core team members with an opportunity to gain experience and references for future business and personal CVs. However, this also defined the program differently from the common connotation of providing solutions as services. This discrepancy became apparent when there were confused expectations in the meeting with the second entrepreneur:

It feels like [the co-operating entrepreneur] is constantly asking for more and more new services: his ideas are puffing up like bread dough. He might have misunderstood a bit that it is not the purpose of StartingUp to produce or market events "like a company," but to provide him with the ideas/visions. (Private Facebook chat between Mary, a designer, and the second author)

The entrepreneur expected the team to provide services for his needs, such as organizing events for his business. The message above shows frustration, which then culminates in the team defining the services that they are willing to provide, such as IT consulting and minor software development. The team emphasized that their role was to provide ideas because they would not receive monetary compensation for their work. Furthermore, they insisted that their services would need to be available for everybody:

The point was that if we create a tool, it can be published as an open source tool so that anyone can use it if they want. (Steven, a coder, field notes)

Even though StartingUp was now enacting IT entrepreneurship by providing services for other entrepreneurs, the team emphasized that the role of StartingUp was only to provide limited services so that it would not "step on the toes of existing companies by offering free services" (Tim, project manager, field notes).

The configuring and reconfiguring of human actions, information technology, and other materialities constructed StartingUp as a community of service providers. The core team members were constructed as the active actors who took part in developing StartingUp and providing services. Thus, participation in strategy-making was limited to the exclusive people within the core team. Newcomers and other people interested in StartingUp—who were however unable to regularly attend its events—were not given an opportunity to participate in negotiations about the future of StartingUp or to co-operate with local entrepreneurs. This reproduced a traditional setting in which only a limited group of actors was able to take part in the strategy-making of the organization.

The key characteristics of the Providing IT Services phase are summarized in Figure 3, as are the consequences of the strategic agency of this phase's sociomaterial configuration.

DISCUSSION

Our study makes two contributions to strategy-as-practice research. First, we propose sociomateriality (Barad, 2003; Orlikowski & Scott, 2007; Suchman, 2007) as a practice philosophical perspective (Orlikowski, 2015) for examining materiality in strategy-making. This answers the calls for providing theoretical frameworks with which to conceptualize the use of material objects within strategy-making (Jarzabkowski et al., 2013; Lê & Spee, 2015). Sociomateriality does not consider humans and materialities as distinct entities. Instead, social and material are seen as inherently entangled and inseparable. Lê and Spee (2015) propose a "strong" view of materiality for highlighting this.

However, most of the organization studies in general and strategy studies in particular assume that humans and materialities are distinct entities, which—even though they are mutually interacting and dependent—have inherent characteristics and some a priori independence from each other (Dameron et al., 2015; Werle & Seidl, 2015). Lê and Spee (2015) acknowledge this as a "moderate" view of materiality, within which materialities are seen to afford action possibilities, which are made sense of and used by humans. We go beyond these approaches to materiality to argue that the status of current research may be due to the conceptualizations of practice that the research draws from. Wanda Orlikowski (2015) presents three approaches to practice. "Practice as phenomenon" highlights the importance of exploring of what actually happens in practice, and "practice as a perspective" draws from the insights of practice theorists to examine practices. However, the deepest ontological commitment to practices as reality—"practice as philosophy" (Orlikowski, 2015)—is rarely seen in organization studies in general and strategy studies in particular. Hence, within strategy-as-practice research, strategy practices have been (implicitly) defined as distinct entities that have some a priori existence from human actions (Chia & MacKay, 2007).

Our study provides a rare empirical example of sociomateriality (Barad, 2003; Orlikowski & Scott, 2007; Suchman, 2007) as a practice philosophical perspective (Orlikowski, 2015). We demonstrate how sociomaterial configurations have strategic agency, i.e., they have capability to act and have an impact on organizational strategy-making (Giddens, 2001; Mantere, 2008; Thomas, 2009). This adheres to views on strategic agency that acknowledge that agency is not an essence that is inherent in humans, but a capacity realized through the associations of actors (whether human or non-human), and, thus, it is relational, emergent, and shifting (Latour, 1987, 1992, 2005 in Orlikowski, 2007). It entails acknowledging that both humans and non-humans (materialities) can have strategic agency, but only as intertwined with each other. Thus, we cannot separate the social and material ontologically or understand the strategic agency of human actors without taking into account their entanglement with the material, and vice versa.

Second, we contribute to discussions on participation in strategy-making. Participation has been seen to improve the quality of strategies and commitment to them (Burgelman, 1991; Floyd & Wooldridge, 2000). In contemporary organizations and volatile environments, it has been seen as a means to increase flexibility (Thomas & Ambrosini, 2015). It has also been seen as an ethico-political issue in terms of (in) equality linked with organizational decision-making and managerial dominance (Laine & Vaara, 2015; Pullen & Rhodes, 2014). Strategy-as-practice research has explicitly focused on examining the actions and practices that enable or restrict participation (Mantere, 2005, 2008; Mantere & Vaara, 2010; Rouleau, 2005; Rouleau & Balogun, 2011). Recently, material artifacts and new technology have been acknowledged as

Figure 3.

(Re)configuring the co-constitutive relationship of human actions, IT, and other materialities	Implications for strategy-making
Establishing and using a secret Facebook-group for the core team. Format and posts of Facebook-group Project manager and Core team	Constructing certain people as the exclusive core team who are allowed to take part in planning the future of StartingUp.
Project plan guides to establish services, which was accomplished under the "Problem Solving Program." Project plan Problem Solving Program	Defining StartingUp as a service provider. Defining service production as an opportunity to gain experience and references.
Problem Solving Program guides local entrepreneurs to expect services without monetary compensation. Local entrepreneurs Services	Forcing core team to redefine the services as minor IT consulting and software development. Producing the core team as IT entrepreneurs.

Implication for participation in strategy-making:

These sociomaterial (re)configurations restrict participation in the strategy-making to the "core team" of the organization.

means to engage larger numbers of people to strategy formation and implementation (Whittington, 2015). However, there are relatively few studies that have explicitly focused on materiality and participation, although some studies have touched upon this (Heracleous & Jacobs, 2011; Jarzabkowski et al., 2015; Kaplan, 2011; Stieger et al., 2012; Werle & Seidl, 2015). Furthermore, these studies do not draw from sociomateriality as a practice philosophical perspective, and they tend to present partial demonstrations of the use of materialities in including people beyond managerial ranks in strategy-making. We, in turn, argue that, for enhancing participation, it is not sufficient to focus on information technologies or other materialities as such, but it is also necessary to acknowledge the inherent sociomateriality of strategy-making activities and practices. Participation can be either enabled or restricted by controlling the entire range of sociomaterial configurations (see also Demir, 2015) instead of relying on using individual (e.g., Kaplan, 2011) or even multiple materialities (e.g., Werle & Seidl, 2015).

Further, our study also demonstrates the dialectical dynamics of participation in strategy-making in community-based organization. We elucidate first how sociomaterial configurations perform agency by excluding members of the community and providing leadership to a project manager. Second, we then demonstrate how sociomaterial configurations include members of the community in joint strategy-making. Finally, we present how certain members are constructed as the core members and strategists by sociomaterial configurations, whereas other members are excluded from decision making.

FUTURE RESEARCH DIRECTIONS

Apart from the above mentioned contributions, we wish to highlight two limitations. First, our study is based on a single case, which raises issues regarding the generalizability of our findings. Future studies could explore the impact of sociomaterial configurations for participation in strategy-making across multiple contexts (traditional organizations, NGOs, or a larger number of community-based organizations). These studies could also be extended to highlight the role of body within sociomaterial strategy-making configurations. This is needed to gain a deeper understanding of the dynamics of inclusion and exclusion in strategy-making, since there is a paucity of knowledge regarding how different kinds of bodies and differently abled bodies are able and allowed to participate in strategy work. Second, our approach has been highlighting the extension of participation. However, future studies should also take into account the contradictory nature of diffusing strategic responsibilities, and hence, the resistance to participation by sociomaterial configurations.

CONCLUSION

We have examined the strategic agency of sociomaterial configurations and the implications of this for participation in strategy-making. We have examined the strategy-making process of a community-based organization and identified how social and material configure situationally with performative effects in strategy-making, such as defining the purpose and the objectives of the community, its competitive advantage, and the roles and responsibilities for accomplishing these. Our study also demonstrates the dialectical dynamics of enabling and restricting participation along the strategy-making process. First, in the Informing the Purpose of the Entrepreneurship Society phase the (re)configuring of human actions, IT, and other material settings produced a traditional top-down mode of strategy-making, excluding the members of the community from strategy-making. Then, in the Enacting Startup Scene Membership phase, participation was extended to a larger number of people by sociomaterial configurations. However, in the next phase, Providing IT Services, the exclusive nature of strategy work was reconstructed by appointing a restricted group of people as strategists. Hence, even though the developments in technology might have democratizing effects in regard to participation in strategy-making, we argue that the inherent inseparability of sociomateriality should be taken seriously to be able to enhance participation in strategy-making. Participation can be either enabled or restricted by controlling the entire range and whole variety of sociomaterial configurations instead of relying on using individual or even multiple materialities.

ACKNOWLEDGMENT

This work was supported by the Finnish Funding Agency for Technology and Innovation [grant number 40205/13] and the Foundation for Economic Education [grant number 3/1679].

REFERENCES

Adler, P. A., & Adler, P. (1987). *Membership roles in field research.* Newbury Park, CA: SAGE. doi:10.4135/9781412984973

Afuah, A., & Tucci, C. L. (2012). Crowdsourcing as a solution to distant search. *Academy of Management Review, 37*(3), 355–375. doi:10.5465/amr.2010.0146

Alaimo, S., & Heckman, S. (2008). Introduction: Emerging modes of materiality in feminist theory. In Material Feminisms (pp. 1–19). Bloomington, IN: Indiana University Press.

Baldwin, C., & von Hippel, E. (2011). Modeling a paradigm shift: From producer innovation to user and open collaborative innovation. *Organization Science, 22*(6), 1399–1417. doi:10.1287/orsc.1100.0618

Balogun, J., Best, K., & Lê, J. (2015). Selling the object of strategy: How frontline workers realize strategy through their daily work. *Organization Studies, 36*(10), 1285–1313. doi:10.1177/0170840615590282

Barad, K. (2003). Posthumanist performativity: Toward an understanding of how matter comes to matter. *Signs (Chicago, Ill.), 28*(3), 801–831. doi:10.1086/345321

Barad, K. (2007). *Meeting the universe halfway: Quantum physics and the entanglement of matter and meaning.* Durham, NC: Duke University Press. doi:10.1215/9780822388128

Barley, S. R. (1990). The alignment of technology and structure through roles and networks. *Administrative Science Quarterly, 31*(1), 61–103. doi:10.2307/2393551

Blank, S. (2013, May). Why the lean start-up changes everything. *Harvard Business Review, 91*(5), 63–72.

Boudreau, M. C., & Robey, D. (2005). Enacting integrated information technology: A human agency perspective. *Organization Science, 16*(1), 3–18. doi:10.1287/orsc.1040.0103

Bourdieu, P. (1990). *The Logic of Practice.* Cambridge, MA: Polity Press.

Burgelman, R. A. (1991). Intraorganizational ecology of strategy making and organizational adaptation: Theory and field research. *Organization Science, 2*(3), 239–262. doi:10.1287/orsc.2.3.239

Butler, J. (2006). *Hankala sukupuoli* [Gender trouble: Feminism, and the subversion of identity]. Helsinki: Gaudeamus.

Carlile, P. R. (2002). A pragmatic view of knowledge and boundaries: Boundary objects in new product development. *Organization Science, 13*(4), 442–455. doi:10.1287/orsc.13.4.442.2953

Carter, C., Clegg, S. R., & Kornberger, M. (2008). So!apbox: editorial essays: Strategy as practice? *Strategic Organization, 6*(1), 83–99. doi:10.1177/1476127007087154

Chesbrough, H. (2006). Open innovation: A new paradigm for understanding industrial innovation. In H. Chesbrough, W. Vanhaverbeke, & J. West (Eds.), Open innovation: Researching a new paradigm (pp. 1–14). Oxford, UK: Oxford University Press.

Chia, R., & MacKay, B. (2007). Post-processual challenges for the emerging strategy-as-practice perspective: Discovering strategy in the logic of practice. *Human Relations*, *60*(1), 217–242. doi:10.1177/0018726707075291

Cunliffe, A. L. (2010). Retelling tales of the field. In search of organizational ethnography 20 years on. *Organizational Research Methods*, *13*(2), 224–239. doi:10.1177/1094428109340041

Czarniawska, B. (2004). *Narratives in Social Science Research*. London: Sage. doi:10.4135/9781849209502

Dameron, S., Lê, J. K., & LeBaron, C. (2015). Materializing strategy and strategizing material: Why matter matters. *British Journal of Management*, *26*, 1–12. doi:10.1111/1467-8551.12084

De Certeau, M. (1984). *The practice of everyday life*. Berkeley, CA: University of California Press.

Demir, R. (2015). Strategic activity as bundled affordances. *British Journal of Management*, *26*, S125–S141. doi:10.1111/1467-8551.12083

Eriksson, P., & Kovalainen, A. (2015). *Qualitative Methods in Business Research. 2nd extended edition*. London: SAGE.

Fetterman, D. M. (2010). *Ethnography: Step-by-step*. Thousand Oaks, CA: SAGE Publications.

Floyd, S. W., & Wooldridge, B. (2000). *Building strategy from the middle: Reconceptualizing strategy process*. Thousand Oaks, CA: Sage.

Foucault, M. (1977). *Discipline and Punish: The Birth of the Prison*. New York: Random House.

Giddens, A. (1984). *The Constitution of Society. Outline of the Theory of Structuration*. Berkeley, CA: University of California Press.

Giddens, A. (2001). *Sociology* (4th ed.). Cambridge, UK: Polity Press.

Heracleous, L., & Jacobs, C. D. (2011). *Crafting strategy: Embodied metaphors in practice*. Cambridge, UK: Cambridge University Press. doi:10.1017/CBO9780511975516

Jarzabkowski, P., Balogun, J., & Seidl, D. (2007). Strategizing: The challenges of a practice perspective. *Human Relations*, *60*(1), 5–27. doi:10.1177/0018726707075703

Jarzabkowski, P., Burke, G., & Spee, P. (2015). Constructing spaces for strategic work: A multimodal perspective. *British Journal of Management*, *26*, S26–S47. doi:10.1111/1467-8551.12082

Jarzabkowski, P. & Kaplan, S. (2015). Strategy tools-in-use: A framework for understanding "technologies of rationality" in practice. *Strategic Management Journal, 36,* 537–558.

Jarzabkowski, P. & Pinch, T. (2013). Sociomateriality is 'the New Black': Accomplishing repurposing, reinscripting and repairing in context. *M@n@gement, 16*(5), 579–592.

Jarzabkowski, P., & Spee, A. P. (2009). Strategy as practice: A review and future directions for the field. *International Journal of Management Reviews, 11*(1), 69–95. doi:10.1111/j.1468-2370.2008.00250.x

Jarzabkowski, P., Spee, A. P., & Smets, M. (2013). Material artifacts: Practices for doing strategy with 'stuff'. *European Management Journal, 31*(1), 41–54. doi:10.1016/j.emj.2012.09.001

Johnson, G., Melin, L., & Whittington, R. (2003). Micro strategy and strategizing: Towards an activity-based view. *Journal of Management Studies*, *40*(1), 3–22. doi:10.1111/1467-6486.t01-2-00002

Kaplan, S. (2011). Strategy and PowerPoint: An inquiry into the epistemic culture and machinery of strategy making. *Organization Science*, *22*(2), 320–346. doi:10.1287/orsc.1100.0531

Keevers, L., Treleaven, L., Sykes, C., & Darcy, M. (2012). Made to measure: Taming practices with results-based accountability. *Organization Studies*, *33*(1), 97–120. doi:10.1177/0170840611430597

Klag, M., & Langley, A. (2013). Approaching the conceptual leap in qualitative research. *International Journal of Management Reviews*, *15*(2), 149–166. doi:10.1111/j.1468-2370.2012.00349.x

Laine, P.-M., & Vaara, E. (2015). Participation in Strategy Work. In Cambridge Handbook of Strategy as Practice. Cambridge University Press. doi:10.1017/CBO9781139681032.036

Langley, A. (1999). Strategies for theorizing from process data. *Academy of Management Journal*, *24*, 691–710.

Lê, J. K., & Spee, A. (2015). The role of materiality in the practice of strategy. In Cambridge Handbook of Strategy as Practice. Cambridge, UK: Cambridge University Press.

Lehdonvirta, V. (2013). Helsinki Spring: An essay on entrepreneurship and cultural change. *Research on Finnish Society*, *6*, 25–28.

Mantere, S. (2005). Strategic practices as enablers and disablers of championing activity. *Strategic Organization*, *3*(2), 157–284. doi:10.1177/1476127005052208

Mantere, S. (2008). Role expectations and middle manager strategic agency. *Journal of Management Studies*, *45*(2), 294–316.

Mantere, S., & Vaara, E. (2008). On the problem of participation in strategy: A critical discursive perspective. *Organization Science*, *19*(2), 341–358. doi:10.1287/orsc.1070.0296

Moisander, J., & Stenfors, S. (2009). Exploring the edges of theory-practice gap: Epistemic cultures in strategy-tool development and use. *Organization*, *16*(2), 227–247. doi:10.1177/1350508408100476

Musson, G., & Duberley, J. (2007). Change, change or be exchanged: The discourse of participation and the manufacture of identity. *Journal of Management Studies*, *44*(1), 143–164. doi:10.1111/j.1467-6486.2006.00640.x

Orlikowski, W. J. (2000). Using technology and constituting structures. *Organization Science*, *11*(4), 404–428. doi:10.1287/orsc.11.4.404.14600

Orlikowski, W. J. (2007). Sociomaterial practices: Exploring technology at work. *Organization Studies*, *28*(9), 1435–1448. doi:10.1177/0170840607081138

Orlikowski, W. J. (2015). Engaging practice in research: Phenomenon, perspective, and philosophy. In D. Golsorkhi, L. Rouleau, D. Seidl, & E. Vaara (Eds.), *Cambridge handbook of strategy as practice* (2nd ed.; pp. 33–43). Cambridge, UK: Cambridge University Press. doi:10.1017/CBO9781139681032.002

Orlikowski, W. J., & Scott, S. (2008). Sociomateriality: Challenging the separation of technology, work and organization. *The Academy of Management Annals, 2*(1), 433–474. doi:10.1080/19416520802211644

Pittaway, L., Rodriguez-Falcon, E., Aiyegbayo, O., & King, A. (2011). The Role of entrepreneurship clubs and societies in entrepreneurial learning. *International Small Business Journal, 29*(1), 37–57. doi:10.1177/0266242610369876

Pullen, A., & Rhodes, C. (2014). Corporeal ethics and the politics of resistance in organizations. *Organization, 21*(6), 782–796. doi:10.1177/1350508413484819

Reckwitz, A. (2002). Toward a Theory of Social Practices. A Development in Culturalist Theorizing. *European Journal of Social Theory, 5*(2), 243–263. doi:10.1177/13684310222225432

Ries, E. (2011). *The lean startup. How today's entrepreneurs use continuous innovation to create radically successful businesses.* New York: Crown Publishing Group.

Rouleau, L. (2005). Micro-Practices of Strategic Sensemaking and Sensegiving: How Middle Managers Interpret and Sell Change Every Day. *Journal of Management Studies, 42*(7), 1413–1441. doi:10.1111/j.1467-6486.2005.00549.x

Rouleau, L., & Balogun, J. (2011). Middle managers, strategic sensemaking, and discursive competence. *Journal of Management Studies, 48*(5), 953–983. doi:10.1111/j.1467-6486.2010.00941.x

Schatzki, T. R. (2001). Practice theory. In T. R. Schatzki, K. Knorr-Cetina, & E. von Savigny (Eds.), *The practice turn in contemporary theory* (pp. 1–14). London: Routledge.

Scott, S., & Orlikowski, W. J. (2012). Reconfiguring relations of accountability: Materialization of social media in the travel sector. *Accounting, Organizations and Society, 37*(1), 26–40. doi:10.1016/j.aos.2011.11.005

Sipola, S. (2015). *Understanding growth and non-growth in entrepreneurial economies. Analysis of startup industries and experimental winner generation in Finland, Israel and Silicon Valley* (Doctoral dissertation). Acta Universitatis Ouluensis, G Oeconomica 73.

Spee, A. P., & Jarzabkowski, P. (2011). Strategic planning as a communicative process. *Organization Studies, 32*(9), 1217–1245. doi:10.1177/0170840611411387

Stieger, D., Matzler, K., Chatterjee, S., & Ladstaetter-Fussenegger, F. (2012). Democratizing strategy: How crowdsourcing can be used for strategy dialogues. *California Management Review, 54*(4), 44–68. doi:10.1525/cmr.2012.54.4.44

Suchman, L. A. (2007). *Human–machine reconfigurations: Plans and situated actions.* Cambridge, UK: Cambridge University Press.

Taylor, C. (1985). *Philosophy and the human sciences.* Cambridge, UK: Cambridge University Press. doi:10.1017/CBO9781139173490

Thomas, L., & Ambrosini, V. (2015). Materializing strategy: The role of comprehensiveness and management controls in strategy formation in volatile environments. *British Journal of Management, 26*, S105–S124. doi:10.1111/1467-8551.12075

Thomas, R. (2009). Critical management studies on identity: Mapping the terrain. In The Oxford Handbook of Critical Management Studies (pp. 166-185). Oxford University Press.

Tischer, S., Meyer, M., Wodak, R., & Vetter, E. (2000). *Methods of Text and Discourse Analysis*. London: SAGE.

Vaara, E., Sorsa, V., & Palli, P. (2010). On the force potential of strategy texts, a critical discourse analysis of a strategic plan and its power effects in a city organization. *Organization, 17*(6), 685–702. doi:10.1177/1350508410367326

Vaara, E. & Whittington, R. (2012). Strategy-as-practice. Taking social practices seriously. *The Academy of Management Annals,* 1–52.

Werle, F., & Seidl, D. (2015). The layered materiality of strate- gizing: Epistemic objects and the interplay between material artefacts in the exploration of strategic topics. *British Journal of Management, 26*, S67–S89. doi:10.1111/1467-8551.12080

Whittington, R. (2015). The massification of strategy. *British Journal of Management, 26*, S13–S16. doi:10.1111/1467-8551.12078

Whittington, R., Molloy, E., Mayer, M., & Smith, A. (2006). Practices of strategizing/organising. Broadening strategy work and skills. *Long Range Planning, 39*, 615–629. doi:10.1016/j.lrp.2006.10.004

Whittington, R., Yakis-Douglas, B., & Cailluet, L. (2011). Opening strategy: Evolution of a precarious profession. *British Journal of Management, 22*(3), 531–544. doi:10.1111/j.1467-8551.2011.00762.x

Chapter 13

Cybernetic Approach for the Stock Market:
An Empirical Study of Bangladesh

Masudul Alam Choudhury
Sultan Qaboos University, Oman

ABSTRACT

The old idea of segmented macroeconomics of the financial sector competing with the real economy is replaced by a new model. This model formalizes the new architecture for the macro economy, and its relationship to the stock market. In this model relating to a reconstructed state of the economy and the emergent structure of the financial architecture, money and spending are treated as complementary elements of growth and development. The overarching structure in the end is the Money, Finance, Spending and Real Economy (MFSRE) with its extensively complementary inter-variables relationship in a general system and cybernetic form of interrelationships. The stock market, exemplified by the empirical case study of Bangladesh's state of the economy and the Dhaka Stock Exchange, bring out the true example of the macroeconomic analysis. The new financial architecture with its stabilization, sustainability and growth and wellbeing as basic-needs regime of development is contrasted with old macroeconomic belief and policies based on outmoded macroeconomic beliefs and futures.

INTRODUCTION

Stock market turnover rates, yields, yield rates, and stability are indicators of the health of the economy for those countries that depend upon such a financial institution. But it is not such an important support system for an economy that does not have stock market, and does not need one. Instead they depend upon real asset pricing mechanism for measuring the economic and social standards. The stock market is then not an essential institution to act as a barometer of economic change. But these two opposite views tell a much larger story about the economic processes and their social effects. Meera (2004, p. 59) puts the emptiness of the casino barometer of a stock market and its underlying financial system in value formation in the following words: "Financial institutions create money out of nothing but lend it out of interest.

DOI: 10.4018/978-1-5225-1779-5.ch013

This characteristic of fiat money called seigniorage is at the root of financial crisis, monetary instability, and unjustness. The fractional reserve requirement also makes possible the creation of additional money through multiple deposit creation. All this has brought about huge volumes of liquidity in the global monetary system, which is responsible for the huge asset price bubbles faced in many countries."

To investigate into these opposite views regarding the financial system with or without stock market we note what lies behind stock market in the organization of asset valuation to protect the wealth of savers and to contribute to and reinforce the relationship that money and finance has with the real economy. Furthermore, stock market stability also requires inflation targeting and a participatory form of development model for the protection and wellbeing of the marginal savers. The ethical principle here linked with the economic objective is derived from Rawls' Difference Principle (1971) as an example. On the point of national wellbeing Rawls wrote (op cit, p. 14-15):"... inequalities of wealth and authority are just only if they result in compensating benefit for everyone, and in particular for the least advantaged members of society." The moral theme underlying the Difference Principle is equally applicable to the purpose of financial stability and social and economic measurement of wealth. The question then stands whether stock markets can deliver such a concept of wellbeing. Likewise, we need to ask whether there is an alternative economic and socially productive activity that establishes the total wellbeing criterion for the nation.

And on this objective issue the structural changes linked with stock market and alternative financial institutions also invoke the nature of participatory role between central bank and commercial bank on the matter of money, finance and real economy complementary relationships. On this issue Mishkin (2007a, p. 55) presents his view:

First, it (central bank) should advocate a change in its mandate to put price stability as the overriding, long-run goal of monetary policy. Second, it should advocate that the price stability goal should be made explicit.... Third, the Fed should produce an 'Inflation Report' ... that clearly explains its strategy for monetary policy and how well it has been doing in achieving its announced inflation goal.

Furthermore, the issues of monetary relations involving central bank and commercial banks, and inflation targeting to stabilize prices also invoke the study of asset pricing mechanism for the common good on the wellbeing side. On this asset-pricing issue for inflation targeting Mishkin (2007b, p. 59) emphasizes the use of monetary policy for the stabilization of stock market fluctuations. He points out the importance of regulating the monetary policy effect on inflation targeting so that stock market effects on investment as a major form of spending (fiscal side) remains well maintained. Besides this there is need to maintain the transmission effect of stock market changes on household liquidity and household wealth.

Firstly, a combination of the above-mentioned socio-economic problems faced by the prevalent monetary, financial, and real economy relations is summarized in analyzing the causes of stock market turmoil. Next, the formalization of a new financial architecture with participatory linkages requires development and application of a revolutionary new form of model that is epistemologically premised on unity of knowledge. From the formalism of the new financial architecture comes out the problems of economy and society discussed above. These comprise firstly, the nature of functional relations between money, finance and real economy that leads to price stabilization, economic growth, monetary and fiscal expansion with appropriate financial instruments.

Secondly, there ought to be a dynamic basic-needs regime of development that can bring about, and that springs from the prescribed model of participative inter-relations between money, finance, and the real economy.

Thirdly, in the resulting kind of the sectorally unified model of inter-causal relations the issues of asset valuation, economic diversification, and central bank-commercial banking relations need to be designed. Fourthly, the social wellbeing implications of the emergent money, finance and real economy relations need to be evaluated in the midst of the complementary scenario of ethics and economics. In all, the emergent money, finance and real economy relationship with all the inter-variable relations between them and involving the ethical, economic and financial dimensions make up a systemic order of ethico-economic integration. We will refer to such inter-causal relations with ethics embedded in that system as the endogenous effect of ethics in the systemic context. We will infer from the analytical results of the systemic model of money, finance, and real economy how stock market stabilization by alternative design can be attained. The stabilization we will be searching for will comprise the dynamic inter-variable relations with money circulations. It will be shown how a select portfolio of financial instruments can be effective in resource mobilization of the financial and physical kinds.

Finally, we will discuss how the spending goals, productivity, technological change, and economic diversification obtained through over inter-variable participation can become effectual. The policy and structural consequences of such systemic interrelations in economic stabilization will be explained.

A REVIEW OF THE LITERATURE

Mark Blaug on Monetarism (Friedman) and Fiscalism (Keynes)

The origin of financial architecture for the stock market arises from the nature and function of money and spending and then takes the course to other critical directions relating to such inter-causal relations. This topic is cast in the incisive words of Mark Blaug (1993, p. 29):"The great debate between Keynesians and monetarists over the respective potency of fiscal and monetary policy has divided the economic profession, accumulating what is by now a simply enormous literature."

From such critical observations in the history of economic thought it is clear that financial instruments are to be appointed as ways of mobilizing financial resources into productive activity. Yet because of the relationship that arises between money and real resources by the nature of financial instruments and the institutional function of money with spending (fiscalism), the stock market acquires its specific meaning relating to such relations. If the relations implied here between money, finance and real economy along with the broader perspective of wellbeing are not proper, then instability and volatility causing loss in the wealth of shareholders and individuals disturb the stock market. The result then becomes an unwanted development in the economic system for preserving the efficiency, productivity, stability, and wellbeing that ought otherwise to be engendered by a good non-banking financial institution.

Neither Keynes nor Friedman were restful with the idea of steady-state equilibrium with learning behavior caused by interaction between choices of monetary, fiscal (spending), innovative, productive and uncertainty in a changing economic system. Such an economic system remains permanently embedded in the social order. The result is a social political economy (Holton, 1992; Parsons, 1964; Parson & Spenser, 1956).

Consequently, monetary expansion joins with fiscal (real economy spending) expansion and gets interactively causal with productivity, economic growth and prices.[1] It is unknown where exactly the conflict between monetarism and fiscalism commences near to the full-employment of (P,G). There is no precise point for this. Hence the (P,G)-points becomes a random point in the probabilistic field of many such possible points defined by the intersections of Aggregate Supply (AS) and Aggregate Demand (AD) curves. Thereby, there exists a family of aggregate supply curves (monetarism) and deflated (P,G)-points shown by E_1, E_2, ..., E_n, etc

In the end, the joint effects of monetarist and fiscal regimes cause perturbations, instability, volatility, and drawdown of productivity in random fields of (P,G)-points in the deflationary domain denoted by R (Choudhury, 2011, 2012).

The price level and growth of output are macroeconomic variables. However, if stock market is considered to be a key signal of economic change then a significant weight is attached to stock market prices and yields. Consequently, stock market (P,G)-values adversely affect all other (P,G)-values. Thereby the macroeconomic indicators of (P,G) are affected.

Mishkin on Stock Market Stability via Inter-Causality between Money, Finance and Real Economy

First we note the following mono-causal relationship explained by Mishkin in respect of monetary, fiscal, interest rate, and selected wellbeing variable (employment, E):

$$[M\uparrow\text{inclusive of f}\uparrow]\Rightarrow[\text{random variations (r,c)}]\Rightarrow [\text{Deflationary effects on}\{(P,G) \Rightarrow E] \tag{1}$$

Where, M denotes the quantity of money in circulation;

f denotes the fiscal (spending) variables;
r denotes real rate of interest;
c denotes discount rate; and
E denotes employment.

In reference we note that the bracketed term, $[M\uparrow\text{inclusive of f}\uparrow]$, causes volatility and instability in the random probabilistic field R, as shown and explained. Besides, the resulting randomness in (P,G)-probabilistic field also causes productivity to stall and employment to become unstable, as between short-term and long-term employment uncertainties. The principal cause of such randomness and unpredictable behavior of the economic and financial sectors is the variations between short-term and long-term real interest rates and discount rates (r,c). Such variations in r reflect upon the random relations between M and f. The predominance of the stock market on all such variables reigns as the determining factor of economic instability and financial market volatility.

Using the simple version of the macroeconomic IS-LM curve we note the transference of the random probabilistic field R denoted by R' that is now characterized by random equilibrium points such as e_0, e_1, e_2, ..., e_n etc. The random (r,c) effects are shown to be contained in R' as the domain of (G,r,c)-points. In the 2-dimensional diagram average values of r and c are used and denoted by 'i'.

The Contest between the Classical, Monetarist, and Fiscalist (Spending) Views of Economic Regimes

Underlying the conflicting effects on price stabilization, economic growth, productive expansion of the economy, and socioeconomic wellbeing, is the absence of complementarities between these goals, and how they can be attained in a consistent and participative way by market-polity integration. The classicists, upon who followed the new classical school, the focus of economic organization was on the market process. Consequently, monetary policy and market process formed the backbone of private sector development. An expansionary monetary policy was found to reduce the real rate of interest. A lower rate of interest ought to stimulate the economy into higher output. But our arguments given above point out that, even though real output would increase by an expansion of real monetary aggregate, this would be at the expense of increasing prices and increasing real rate of interest. Thereby, the increase in real output is adversely dampened by the joint increases in inflation and real interest rate, the very two horns of the evil economic monster. The effects of monetary regimes on the expansion of the real economy, that is the private sector, cannot be sustained under such adverse price and interest rate effects.[2]

The Austrian School of Economics was the champion of the classical school of monetary phenomenon. It promoted private monetary unit, the laissez faire concept of this monetary unit as a private regulated commodity of market exchange, and the short-term as opposed to the long-run effectiveness of monetary policy in mobilizing financial resources particularly for reducing unemployment and creating employment. On this matter Hayek (1999, p. 236) wrote: "I think it is very urgent that it becomes rapidly understood that there is no justification in history of the existing position of a government monopoly of issuing money."

Hayek's vision of private unit of currency value is echoed by leading exponents of the Austrian Economic School. On a similar note Ludwig von Mises (1981, p. 478) wrote: "Money is the commonly used medium of exchange. It is a market phenomenon. Its sphere is that of business transacted by individual or groups of individuals within a society based on private ownership of the means of production and the division of labor." The Austrian School as a great champion of the free market economic order promoted monetary regime over fiscal regime or spending regime including Government expenditure for the public good. According to the Austrian School voiced by von Mises (op cit p. 479), economic destabilization caused by inflationary pressure was due to the role of Government in trying to stimulate the economy with unwanted spending, when contrarily market correction should take care of the adjustment process to establish market equilibrium, and thereby, stable prices. Thus the role of spending regime by including government expenditure was not brought into a complementary relationship with monetary regime.

On this point von Mises (op cit, p. 481) wrote an important note on the market adjustment process of monetary aggregate on which the least role of Government interference, and thereby fiscal policy control, need to be exercised: "The main thing is that the government should no longer be in a position to increase the quantity of money in circulation and the amount of checkbook money – that is 100 percent – covered by deposits paid in by the public." This appears as an important point to note on the most efficacious and non-inflationary effect of monetary regime in a market economy.

However, the fiscal role of government expenditure to drive money into the productive directions of private sector as Keynesian would have desired, is kept outside of the equation of money and spending with productive and technological change at stable prices and increasing real output. This point has remained an unresolved approach in completing the important factors of progress. These are namely, price stability, increase in real output, decline or replacement of interest rates by inflationary targeting alternative, factor productivity and elastic full-employment point, technological change, and social wellbeing as a combination of market and non-market forces, regimes and policies. All these factors together configure the total resource mobilization under dynamic conditions of socioeconomic change.

The laissez faire monetary theory is projected in the writings of Yeager (1997, p. 412-13) whose striking words in this regard are as follows: "Government would be banished from any role in the monetary system other than that of defining a unit of account or *numeraire*. We envisage a unit defined in a bundle of goods and services comprehensive enough for the general level of prices quoted in it to be practically steady." Such a laissez faire conception of monetary exchange in concert with market exchange in real goods and services while an effective way of connecting money with the real economy, it puts ultimate independence of such monetary regime from government interference and governance that would otherwise come about by the presence of spending including government and private spending. The wellbeing objective and sustained economic stabilization by complementarities between the monetary regime and the fiscal (spending) regime as of markets and governments by their complementary roles is not targeted in the laissez faire conception of money and markets. Markets are upheld as the ultimate arbitrator of economic stabilization, growth and productivity generated by technological change.

From the above review of the literature one finds that monetarist approach is predominant in the development of the market process and the private sector. It should then be obvious that the spending regime should combine with the monetarist regime to accelerate the process of market freedom but within the reigns of regulation and controls when the market process becomes destabilizing. The monetarists did not believe in such possibility. Thus monetarism remained disjoint from the spending regimes including government spending, budgetary controls, taxation and resource redistribution. It is obvious that in the absence of fiscal regime to complement with money circulation no fresh productivity of factor inputs, innovation and technological advance can be generated.

Consequently, by leaving the two policies and regimes separate of each other the prospect of economic stabilization with price, real output growth, and lower interest rate remains at best a short-run case. The long-run stabilization is unattainable by the use of any of the two policies and regimes. Thereby, sustainability, which is a long-run target of economic stabilization, is not attained by the use of any of the two policies. This is an economic fact based on the scarcity of resources in the long-run that causes aggregate demand pressures to destabilize the (P,Y,r)-relationship. Also it is a political fact by virtue of the case that the opposite economic and policy perspectives govern the elected party in their short-term lives. These points are brought out by Farmer (2010). Farmer (2010, p. 19) writes on the political versus market adjustment of the non-inflationary stabilization problem: "I take the idea that a sound theory must explain how individuals behave and how their collective choices determine aggregate outcomes. From Keynesian economics, I take the idea that markets do not always work well and that sometimes capitalism needs some guidance. These ideas form a coherent new paradigm for macroeconomics in the twenty-first century."

We argue in this paper that Governments are subjected to participatory relationship with the private sector as two sides of the same coin. These together aim at attaining economic stabilization, productivity and growth, assimilation of technological change, and bring about social wellbeing. Consequently, the economic, social and ethical goals are mutually inter-causal and thus embedded by organic relationship in the same general system of interrelations. In this way, the political agenda of control and guidance to stem the unwanted market situation is left to the assimilation of knowledge and learning in an evolutionary and civil system of public and private sector understanding through the participatory heart and mind of the social community. Such is a maturing community, whose gaze is attaining the goal that Foucault (see Dreyfus & Rabinow, 1983) referred to as a discursive society. Its totality of mature understanding in the framework of organic unity of relations is Foucault's usage of the word Episteme.[3]

Mainstream Consequences of Monetary and Fiscal Regimes concerning Wellbeing, Money, Spending, Output, Prices, Employment and Productivity by Technological Change

We can summarize the results of our succinct review of the literature in respect of the prevailing state of relationship between monetary and fiscal regimes across the great divide for the attainment of socioeconomic wellbeing by way of economic stabilization, economic growth, and technological change with productivity. We define this comprehensive objective function as a wellbeing criterion denoted by W(.) as follows:

$$W = W(y,p,M,F,r,\rho,\theta) \tag{2}$$

Y denotes real output;
p denotes the price level;
M denotes the quantity of money;
F denotes spending;
r denotes the real rate of interest;
ρ denotes productivity of factors; and
θ denotes technological change.

$$dW/d\theta = [(\partial W/\partial y),(dy/d\theta)]^+ + [(\partial W/\partial p).(dp/d\theta)]^\pm + [(\partial W/\partial M).(dM/d\theta)]^\pm + [(\partial W/\partial F).(dF/d\theta)]^\pm + [(\partial W/\partial r).(dr/d\theta)]^\pm + [(\partial W/\partial \rho).(d\rho/d\theta)]^+ + (\partial W/\partial \theta)^+ \tag{3}$$

Our discussion in respect of the prevailing state of the given interrelations between variables point out that an overly dependence on monetary regime without complementarities with fiscal (spending) regime causes technology to be exogenous. Consequently, the simultaneous expansion of monetary and fiscal (spending) regimes is not considered in the light of what Myrdal (1957. 1958) referred to as circular causation relations between the variables signifying growth and development mentioned in this section. Likewise, there is a similar discussion by Young (1928) on the need for simultaneous interrelations between the variables. The same argument is launched against the prescription of fiscal (spending) regime. Consequently, as Blaug has pointed out, the monetary and fiscal (spending) regimes in macroeconomic stabilization and coordination have remain opposed to each other, in as much as also the private sector and public sector focus of monetary and spending regimes, respectively, remain opposed to each other.

The result of such dichotomous consequences in macroeconomic theory shows up in the indeterminate signs of the changes in the (p,M,F,θ)-variables by the exogenous effect of technological change. Since such exogenous technological change is positively related to factor productivities, therefore, the effects of M and F remain exogenous on factor productivities. The growth of output, and along with this the dynamics of employment, remain neutral to technological change and productivity growth in the long-run. That is, sustainability of economic stabilization, growth and policy coordination cannot be attained together.

In the end, since technological change denoted by θ remains exogenous to every variable in the category (y,p,M,F,u,ρ) in respect of price stabilization with increasing output, therefore, there cannot exist macroeconomic coordination between M and F regimes in the direction of non-inflationary economic growth.

The Effects of Exogeneity between Monetary and Spending Regimes on the Stock Market

It was pointed out that if the stock market was assumed to play a significant role in economic growth, the stock market will assume a high weight in the average price level. Consequently, the exogenous effect of technological change on the variables causing non-sustainability of price stabilization and economic growth will also show up in the stock prices. The inability in holding on to stable prices in the field shown now establishes a volatile relationship between stock prices and the variations in the real rate of interest. That is, the indeterminacy of nominal interest rate in the domain, will intensify the volatility of the stock price.[4]

Furthermore, as bonds and stocks represent a mirror image of the quantity of money in supply, therefore, variations in the bond and stock prices in the portfolio of financial assets cause volatility in short-term rates of interest. In the world financial markets the volatility of short-term interest-rates has been the cause of stock market volatility. Such variations in turn are the causes of intense degrees of speculation in the stock market with bonds and stocks backed mainly by financial papers. The ultimate result of such volatile movements of stock prices and short-term interest rates is a flight of capital away from the real sector to the financial sector under the force of financial speculation.

The relationship between the (y,p,M,F,i,u,ρ)-variables under the impact of exogenous technological change can be shown the exogenous effect of θ on these curves will be certain shifts that remain an empirical fact. There is no exact direction of the shifts. For example, an upward shift of the y-curve could mean an upward shift of the predominant stock price curve P_s, but a lower or higher net result on the r-curve caused by the joint effect of the monetary and spending (fiscal) curves.

Likewise, the productivity curve could shift upward along with the upward shift of r-curve due to the net effect of M and F curves on the income multiplier causing y curve to shift but at the expense of inflationary regime. The unemployment (u) effect will be similar to the y-effect at the long-run evolution of y to its full-employment level with uncertain net effect concerning M and F regimes. In the short-run the same M and F joint effect will yield an accelerated convergence towards full-employment followed by price pressure at the long-run neutrality between M and F and y along the classical version of the aggregate supply curve of output (Friedman, 1960, 1989).

On the other hand, the responses to the various variables to variations in i-variable can be shown by the following expression. The variable u will follow the same form of a random trend along with y under the net volatile effects of M and F and the y-variable and p-variable:

$$dW/di = [(\partial W/\partial y).(dy/di)]^- + [(\partial W/\partial p).(dp/di)]^\pm + \{[(\partial W/\partial M).(dM/di)]^- + [(\partial W/\partial F).(dF/di)]^+\}^\pm + [(\partial W/\partial i)]^- + [(\partial W/\partial \rho).(d\rho/di)]^- \qquad (4)$$

Expression (4) shows that the net random (volatility) effect of variations in i depends strongly on the variations in $(dp/di)^{\pm}$ and $\{.\}^{\pm}$. Here, by the predominating effect, $p = P_S$. The same kind of random effects are transmitted to the wellbeing function through the other volatility effects.

How to Stabilize the Economy from the Deleterious Effects of Stock Market Volatility with Knowledge-Induced (y,p,M,F,i,u,ρ)[θ] Variables

The principal objective and the contribution of this paper are to develop a theory of complementarities between monetary and fiscal regimes in the light of circular causal (or inter-causal) relationships between the variables mentioned here. The implications are that M-F complementarities are formed by and result in (circular causation) complementarities and endogenous interrelationships between all the variables. The exception is the replacement of interest rates and interest-bearing financial instruments by trade-related instruments. This is the meaning of the M and F complementarities that enable unified interrelationships between money (M), spending (F), finance (f), and real economy (y,p,u,ρ). We refer to the emergent model as MSFRE-model.

The emergent inter-causal relationships between all the variables in the presence of technological change and gains of productivity while replacing interest-bearing financial instruments with trade-related ones is an evolutionary learning phenomenon. Evolutionary learning is established by an epistemic view of circular causal relations in terms of systemic unity of knowledge (Maturana & Varela, 1987).

In economic terms there is an opposite movement between trade-related instruments (f) and interest rate caused by bank-savings. Bank savings cause withholding of financial resources from the real economy, while they are driven to interest-bearing opposites. Contrarily, if savings are continuously converted into productive spending by way of investment and consumption, then Savings = Spending always. An amount of savings in the bank is converted continuously into spending by way of engaging the productive process and market forces. Government integrates with the market process via specific joint ventures. This relationship yields the micro-money concept and it equates to the value of spending in the perfectly market trading venue. Government becomes an agent of market catalysis.

Consequently, the following results would hold:

$M.V = P.Y =$ Spending in nominal terms of price P and real income Y. Here $k = 1/V \to 1$ as $V \to 100$ per cent. That is, the equivalence between money and spending (fiscalism) becomes perfect when the circulation of a quantity of money is project-specific through-out the economy. This is similar to the Austrian concept of laissez faire concept of money. But in our case, the progress towards this perfect equality is through the activity of trade replacing interest rate. That is, savings are converted continuously into spending. Banks are to mobilize savings, not to hold them back -- even for future use. That is because the withdrawal of potential savings from being mobilized causes the output to remain below the potential level.[5] This is a continuous phenomenon in an economy that depends on interest rates as the basis of capital accumulation through bank savings. Keynesian idea of bank savings is based on such withdrawals from the real economy (Ventelou, 2005).

The further result is this: The necessary complementarities between the variables {y,p,M,F,f,u,ρ}[θ], mean that all these variables are positively complementary in respect of the systemic knowledge variable denoted by θ. This is an epistemological issue in unity of knowledge. In the real domain it is expressed by continuous reinforcing complementarities. Such unity of knowledge manifest by pervasive complementarities can be attained only by the action of θ on all the variables. Hence θ is of the epistemic category in unity of systemic knowledge. In fact, θ is equivalent to wellbeing, for it represents the continued cause and effect of interaction and integration forming into unity of systemic knowledge across evolutionary learning, as reconstructed interrelations proceed between the interacting and integrating variables.

The epistemic consequences are independent of time. Time is replaced by knowledge as the explanatory factor of dynamics and change. Time is treated as datum for purposes of recording the state of complementarities by endogenous forces, in which policies such as M and F and f participate.

The Generalized MSFRE Model of Unity of Knowledge

First Stage: Estimation of the circular causation relations

Let $\mathbf{x}$ denote the vector $\{y,p,M,F,f,u,\rho,\theta\}$. In this every variable is induced by θ-values. Let an element $x_i \in \{y^1,p^2,M^3,F^4,f^5,u^6,\rho^7,\theta^8\}$, $i = 1,2,\ldots,8$ as marked out against the variables.

Complementary (inter-) relations between the variables imply:

$$x_i = f_i(\mathbf{x}_i'), \text{ where } x_i' \text{ is an element of x excluding the particular } x_i. \tag{5}$$

$$\theta = F(\mathbf{x}), \tag{6}$$

θ is thus a monotonic transformation of $W(\mathbf{x})$. Hence it is itself a wellbeing criterion (Henderson and Quandt, 1971). θ-values are ranked by examining the state of .complementarities as they ought to be (note otherwise the negative relationship between i and all the other variables).

$i = 1,2,..,8.$

Second Stage: Simulation of the circular causation relations

The estimated coefficients of the system of equations (5) and (6) are next simulated by giving them improved (revised) values to normatively aim for better levels of complementarities. Such selections are set by institutional discourse and policy measures.

The simulated θ-value then results as a function in the simulated $\mathbf{x}$-values, say $\mathbf{x}^\wedge$. All other symbols abide in their simulated forms.

The simulated system corresponding to (5) and (6) is,

$$x^\wedge_i = f_i(\mathbf{x}^\wedge_i') \tag{7}$$

$$\theta^\wedge = F(\mathbf{x}^\wedge) \tag{8}$$

Such estimations and simulations will continue on over new sets of time-series or cross-sectional data. As well as, algorithmically the simulations can be continued on in reiterative processes.

Third Stage: Money, spending (fiscalism) and real economy equivalences

MV = PY, as V → 1, with θ↑ (algorithmic simulation) resulting in,

M = PY. (9)

Thus systemic unity of knowledge as episteme continuously simulates the circular causation relations with increasingly ranked θ-values in the case of a 100 per cent mobilization of micro-money circulation in real assets across the economy. A microeconomic (project-specific) outlook to macroeconomic aggregate of the strictly M1 (money supply) and liquidity type (money demand) is implied.

The principal hinge pin of the entire simulation by circular causation premised on unity of knowledge as the episteme underlying reiterative θ-values in complementary socio-economic inter-variables relations is the replacement of interest-bearing financial instruments by trade-related instruments. This in turn means the replacement of savings as financial withdrawal by banks from the real economy, by mobilization of savings into productive spending instead. Money is thereby mobilized into the real economy by using the appropriate trade-related financial instruments. The MSFRE model is now formulated by equations (5)-(8) in continuity of evolutionary learning and/or by continued sequences of estimation and simulation over time-series and cross-sectional data.

Thus an important contribution of this paper is also to note the empirical basis of estimating and simulating the MSFRE by circular causation relations in epistemic reference. This is to extend the theory of circular causation and cumulative causation beyond Myrdal (op cit), Young (op cit) and Kaldor (Kaldor, 1975; see Toner, 1999).

The Stock Market in the Circular Causation Theory of MSFRE

The stock market phenomenon appears as a question: Is the stock market a logically acceptable financial institution in the MSFRE model? The answer centers on the fact that the MSFRE mobilizes financial resources only into real economic activity. The financial instruments therefore, are simply endogenous mappings between the monetary and real economy via the circular causation relations between these sectors. The financial assets are now tied endogenously to real assets that are valued in financial terms and in which all forms of resources are mobilized. Financial assets lose their relevance to bank-savings in interest-bearing instruments.

In the presence of portfolios of real assets, real market exchange (trade) performs the sole function of valuation. Consequently, there is no speculation in such markets to generate wealth and capitalization. Price stability and responsiveness to sustainability as long-run phenomenon complementing the variables by their systemic evolutionary learning (θ-effect) establishes a dynamic basic-needs regime of development under the impact of appropriate technology (ρ) induced by θ.

Mishan's categorization of systemic interrelations for the MSFRE model can be formulated by the following chain relation:

[M↑⇔F↑⇔f↑⇔r↓⇔c↓⇔yields↑but stabilizes⇔ (P^→0) ⇔y↑⇔u↓⇔ρ↑][θ↑] (10)

⇔ implies circular causation of any one variable with the remaining variables, all being induced by evolutionary learning as systemic unity of knowledge between the variables, even as simulation is carried out with increasing θ-ranked values.

The emergence of basic-needs regime of development spells out the attained levels of wellbeing by the social choice of the 'good things of life'. In it the wellbeing function is simulated under the condition of pervasively complementary relations between the variables as shown, but with the key negative relationship with r and c. It is now logical that price stability will be maintained as output increases in the full MSFRE model.

Now in the absence of any need to have a capital market in the MSFRE form of the dynamic basic-needs regime of development, speculation and independence of the financial sector disappears. Volatility of the financial and economic sectors is annulled. The resulting regime reflects ethical integration with the socioeconomic basic-needs development regime (Streeten, 1981). We have thus established the conformable, sustainable, and complementary circular causation relations with the epistemic choice of knowledge-induced variables through simulation of wellbeing in the MSFRE model taken up in its entirety.

A Casual Reference to MSFRE Model in the Open Economy

The MSFRE model cogently maintains its consistency and completeness in the open economy case. Very briefly speaking, the foreign direct investments are now diverted away from portfolio (liquidity) investments (savings) into the real economy. The exchange rate mechanism is now determined by productivity spelled out by terms-of- trade.[6] Improving terms-of-trade depend upon effective diversification, productive transformation, and trade-orientation along the *dynamic* basic-needs regime of development. Price stability also stabilizes the terms-of-trade along with price stability. Stock markets are now segmented between the financial products and the real market exchange. Global economic integration of the real markets is causally related with the momentum of technological advance, productivity, and factor prices, prices of goods and services, fair terms-of-trade, and exchange rates.

Inter-country capital mobility occurs by way of resource mobilization into productive spending in the dynamic basic-needs regime of development through market integration in the MSFRE model applied to real markets. Money is now mobilized as financial resource by appropriate participatory financial instruments into the real economy. In these respects appropriate participatory financial instruments such as, equity participation, joint venture, trade financing, co-financing, and profit-sharing are used in a phased out situation of interest-rate and exchange rate mechanism. Inflation targeting is thereby encouraged but within the dynamics of the MSFRE model.

In the end, along with economic stabilization effective terms-of-trade and exchange rate stabilization occurs. This facilitates foreign trade and free flow of tradable goods, resources and services between countries. Along with such free flows in goods and services, capital flow liberalizes in terms of joint ventures, equity participation, co-financing, trade-financing, and profit-sharing ventures. Capital formation now becomes a productive process in the dynamic basic-needs regime of development of the MSFRE model.

The relevance of stock market is now relegated to the above kind of function of maintaining economic stabilization and wellbeing. But to maintain such sustainable future knowledge induction on the continuity of such a process is required. Such evolutionary sustained and systemic learning is the result of the epistemic θ-induction. It requires participatory dynamics integrating together the public and private sectors and the global economic community (Commission on Global Governance, 1995). Formation of such participatory future, which is the result of circular causation between interacting and integrating agencies that are receptive to evolutionary learning in the unification experience, is an example of systemic unification of knowledge.

Empirical Issues: Stock Market and Macroeconomic Indicators, Case of Bangladesh Stock Market Near Financial Collapse

The prevailing reasoning in economic theory relating to the financial sector as a necessary one for a modern economy has disengaged various sectors of the economy on the face of a volatile stock market that inherits the dissociated and competing nature of the economy instead of a complementary one. We take the case of Bangladesh where the stock market volatility neared financial crash. This brought agony to the shareholders, most of whom are marginal savers led away to raise capital from the stock market to become rich by easy buck. But the dream was dashed.

Stock market turmoil started in Bangladesh near to 1210 after a resilient performance in earlier years. The causes cannot be attributed to fluctuations in short-term interest rates, because the discount rate of Bangladesh Bank remained fixed at 5 per cent throughout the period 2006 t0 2009, for which data are available.

Instead of fluctuation in short-term interest rates as the cause of stock market volatility the data near to the year of capital-market turmoil in Bangladesh point out that in spite of a slight easing in the rate of inflation the rate of change in manufacturing GDP as a share of total GDP declined throughout the period. This implies that adequate diversification of the Bangladesh economy in the direction of increasing manufacturing did not occur. Hence the total productivity in Bangladesh did not show the resilience that should be expected by manufacturing diversification. Diversification here is shown by the rate of change of the percentage share of manufacturing GDP. This remained low and declining on the time-trend.

The debt syndrome was also a factor in the stock market volatility. On a trend, the growth rate of external debt outstanding remained high, around an average annual of 6.71 percentage between 2006 and 2009. Thus external flow of investments and global confidence on Dhaka stock market remained weak. The only way to resuscitate the failing stock market was external remittances. This also indicated an unproductive use of remittances in the face of a failing diversification, and thereby productivity of the manufacturing sector.

It is then questionable why the stock prices of most companies in Bangladesh nose-dived as explained later. By mutual exclusion of the above factors by virtue of the data, it is probable that the main cause of the downturn was the lack of diversification and real sector productivity, and the debt problem in Bangladesh economy. Consequently, there was weakening link between the monetary sector and the real economic sector. This fact is further indicated by the continued high percentage distribution of Quasi Money (= Total Quantity of Money – M1) compared to the low percentage of M1. The meaning here is that real money did not flow into the real economy to generate output and thereby productivity. Much of the monetary aggregates in the form of quasi-money were locked in financial savings without a productive backing -- only to increase by interest income. Stock market was a key non-banking sector that used the savings of the banking sector on the basis of financial interest returns. This is sheer speculation intensity in the monetary usage. Whereas, what ought to have been the case of stabilization by and for sustainability would be the complementary linkage between money (i.e. M1), the financial sector (thus banks and stock markets), and the real economy (productivity and economic diversification).

The result of such sectoral segmentation in the otherwise much needed money, finance, and real economy complementary linkages, caused eroding confidence in the investors. Consequently, a flight of capital took place out of Bangladesh stock market. Those who could illegally transfer money out of stock market into the foreign holdings benefited from their corrupt practices at the expense of the marginal savers in the Dhaka stock market.

True asset pricing that would depend most significantly on economic productivity and diversity that are caused by sustained linkages between the monetary sector, the financial sector, and the real economy failed to exist. Thus it is the link between these sectors that otherwise is fundamental for the stabilization and sustainability of the economy and its growing resilience. The stock market became the Achilles' heel for stock market volatility and its near dissolution close to the year 2010.

To come out of the erosion of investor confidence, and to restore confidence by the systemic signs of stabilization and sustainability, the state of the economy reflected in the kind of stock market model would be to pursue complementary linkages between the monetary sector and the real economy by means of appropriate financial instruments. The Bangladeshi foreign remittances can then be utilized in investments that would respond to the productivity gains generated by the complementary linkages causing diversification.

This paper therefore developed a generalized system and cybernetic model in the form of a complementary inter-sectoral participative model. The model while being of a system and cybernetic type is also deeply structural and strategic in nature. It invokes fundamental changes that remain embedded by the robust effect of monetary policy, central bank and commercial bank relations, and the responses of the real economy to productive spending in order to support the development of diversified productive projects. Financial instruments that systemically reduce speculation and replace it by increasing levels of financial mobilization are the appropriate ones. We refer to such a participative and inter-sectoral complementary model of money, finance, and real economy linkages as the MFRE model (Mufeedh Choudhury, 2009).

An example of Dhaka Stock Exchange trade summary for February 16, 2012 points out the following picture on stock market volatility: 82 listed firms reported positive net percentage change for the trading day. 185 listed firms reported non-positive net percentage change for the same trading day. The total net percentage change was -161.68%.

CONCLUSION

Our study of the nature and volatility of stock market prices and yields was cast against the theory and performance of some principal macroeconomic indicators. The existing theory of macroeconomic coordination to stabilize the economy has deepened the problem of instability, volatility and unsustainable development due to the failure to complement the good things (indicated by variables) that would stabilize the economy and at the same time maintain the stability and growth of wellbeing. Money and Spending regimes and their inherent policies were complemented together by the endogenous learning process between them across evolutionary knowledge flows. These knowledge flows were derived on basis of the epistemic premise of unity of knowledge idea of inter-variable complementary relations.

Economic theory between monetarism (Friedman) and fiscalism (spending as per Keynes) is fractured beyond repair to date. Instead, a theory of complementary dynamics is required that can be useful for establishing sustainability and stabilization over the long-run. A new theory emerges that designs the complementary and participative dynamics of monetary and fiscal (spending) regimes for accelerated development. This kind of thinking and implementation of the design of the new monetary, fiscal, spending and real economy interrelations was formulated in an analytical model called the MFSRE model.

Economic analysis carried out in the framework of the MFSRE model presented an altogether new perspective of economic stabilization and sustainability by the principle of pervasive complementarities in the case of interest rate being replaced by participatory financial instruments that mobilize savings into the real economy, rather than accumulate them into bank savings. The resulting real economy in such a pervasive complementary systemic framework is the social economy that produces, consumes, distributes and trades in the good things of life. This assumes the design of dynamic basic-needs regime of sustainable development.

The case study of Dhaka Stock Exchange in Bangladesh is discussed as an example. The country is found to rely on old macroeconomic theory, perspectives, indicators and policies. This has established traditional beliefs on the stock market volatility. The experience proves that Bangladesh orientation in macroeconomic theory and its effects on the stock market remains outmoded. A new design of macroeconomic arrangement needs to be formalized and practiced in the interest of economic stabilization and social wellbeing. Such a model was our prescriptive MFSRE model and its conceptual analysis explaining theory and revealing the same by empirical facts.

REFERENCES

Blaug, M. (1993). *The Methodology of Economics*. Cambridge, UK: Cambridge University Press.

Choudhury, M. (2009). *Money, Finance, and the Real Economy in Islamic Banking and Finance: Perspectives from the Maqasid as-Shari'ah* (Unpublished MSC Dissertation). Department of Economics, University of Stirling, UK.

Choudhury, M. A. (2011). *Islamic Economics and Finance: an Epistemological Inquiry*. Bingley, UK: Emerald.

Choudhury. (2012). A probabilistic model of random fields. *International Journal of Operations Research*.

Commission on Global Governance. (1995). Global Civic Ethic. In *Our Global Neighbourhood, a Report of the Commission on Global Governance*. New York, NY: Oxford University Press.

Dreyfus, H.L. & Rabinow, P. (1983). *M. Foucault: Beyond structuralism and hermeneutics, the archeology of the human sciences*. Chicago, IL: University of Chicago Press.

Farmer, R. E. A. (2010). *Will monetary and fiscal policy work?*. In *How the Economy Works*. Oxford, UK: Oxford University Press.

Friedman, M. (1960). *A Program for Monetary Stability*. New York, NY: Fordham University Press.

Friedman, M. (1989). Quantity Theory of Money. New Palgrave: Money. doi:10.1007/978-1-349-19804-7_1

Hayek, F. A. (1999). Towards a free market monetary system. In Good Money, Part II, the Standard. Chicago, IL: The University of Chicago Press.

Henderson, J. M., & Quandt, R. E. (1971). *Microeconomic Theory*. New York: McGraw-Hill.

Holton, R. L. (1992). *Economy and Society*. London: Routledge.

Kaldor, N. (1975). What is wrong with economic theory? *The Quarterly Journal of Economics*, *89*, 347–357.

Maturana, H. R., & Varela, F. J. (1987). *The Tree of Knowledge*. London: New Science Library.

Meera, A. K. M. (2004). *The Theft of Nations, Returning to Gold*. Kuala Lumpur, Malaysia: Pelanduk.

Mishkin, F. S. (2007a). What should Central Banks do? In *Monetary Policy Strategy* (pp. 37–58). Cambridge, MA: The MIT Press.

Mishkin, F. S. (2007b). The transmission mechanism and the role of asset prices in monetary policy. In *Monetary Policy Strategy* (pp. 59–74). Cambridge, MA: The MIT Press.

Myrdal, G. (1957). *An unexplained general traits of social reality. In Rich Lands and Poor, the Road to World Prosperity*. New York, NY: Harper & Row.

Myrdal, G. (1958). The principle of cumulation. In P. Streeten (Ed.), *Value in Social Theory, a Selection of Essays on Methodology by Gunnar Myrdal* (pp. 198–205). New York, NY: Harper & Brothers Publishers.

Parsons, T. (1964). *The Structure of Social Actions*. New York, NY: The Free Press of Glencoe.

Parsons, T., & Smelser, N. (1956). *Economy and Society*. London: Routledge & Kegan Paul.

Rawls, J. (1971). *A Theory of Justice*. Cambridge, MA: Harvard University Press.

Streeten, P. (1981). From Growth to Basic Needs. In *Development Perspectives*. New York: St. Martin's Press. doi:10.1007/978-1-349-05341-4_18

Toner, P. (1999). Conclusion. In *Main Currents in Cumulative Causation, the Dynamics of Growth and Development*. Houndmills, UK: Macmillan Press Ltd. doi:10.1007/978-0-333-98289-1_7

Ventelou, B. (2005). Economic thought on the eve of the General Theory. In *Millennial Keynes*. Armonk, NY: M.E. Sharpe.

Von Mises, L. (1981). The return to sound money. In *The Theory of Money and Credit* (pp. 477–500). Indianapolis, IN: Liberty Fund.

Yeager, L. B. (1997). *The Fluttering Veil, Essays on Monetary Disequilibrium*. Indianapolis, IN: The Liberty Press, reprint.

Young, A. (1928). Increasing returns and economic progress. *The Economic Journal*, *88*(152), 527–542. doi:10.2307/2224097

ENDNOTES

[1] Consider the following compound function between **M**oney, **S**pending, **G**rowth, **P**rice, and **Pro**ductivity, $F(M,S,G,P,Pr)$ = Constant. By the Implicit Function Theorem, $M = F1(S,G,P,Pr)$; $S = F2(M,G,P,Pr)$. By the Keynesian argument a full-employment target is attainable by (P,G)-stable relationship. Yet if a further monetary expansion occurs around the full-employment point of (P,G), the built-in income and money multipliers will push the economy into an inflationary phase and still maintain the neutrality of money and spending on the level of output. Thus a contradiction arises between monetary and fiscal regime in a productively expanding economy.

[2] Consider the rate of change in real money denoted by $m = M/P$: $\log(m) = \log M - \log P$, yielding $\dot{m} = \dot{M} - \dot{P} = [(a\dot{y} + b\dot{r}) - \dot{P}]$, according to the LM-curve in (y,r). Thus, increasing m-values imply $\dot{m} > 0$. That is, $(a\dot{y} + b\dot{r}) - \dot{P} > 0$; or, $\dot{y} > (\dot{P} - b\dot{r})/a > 0$. Since monetary policy is expected to contribute to market process and real sector growth according to the adage of monetarism, therefore, $\dot{P} > b\dot{r}$, even with parametric positive variations in variable 'b' according to monetarist perspective. Consequently, as r increases along the LM-curve by monetary supply, therefore $\dot{P}$ increases as well. Stability in (r,P) is lost. Y is drawn back.

[3] Foucault, M. "By *episteme* we mean … the total set of relations that unite, at a given period, the discursive practices that give rise to epistemological figures, sciences, and possibly formalized systems … The episteme is not a form of knowledge (*connaissance*) or type of rationality which, crossing the boundaries of the most varied sciences, manifests the sovereign unity of a subject, a spirit, or a period; it is the totality of relations that can be discovered, for a given period, between the sciences when one analyses them at the level of discursive regularities."

[4] Price of stock in perpetuity of \$1 yield is written as, $P = 1/i$. Thereby, as i varies randomly, so also P in the portfolio of long-term assets becomes volatile.

[5] Let Y_0 denote GDP at time $t = 0,1,2,\dots$; s_t denote saving ratio at time $t = 0,1,2,\dots$; g denote a constant growth rate of GDP at time $t = 0,1,2,\dots$
Disposable income after saving at time $t = 0$ is $Y_0(1-s)$, which increases to national income Y_1 at time $t = 1$. $Y_1 = Y_0(1-s)(1+g)$. Likewise, $Y_t = Y_0 \cdot (1+g)^t (1-s)^t$.
Now consider, $\partial Y_t/\partial s = -t Y_0 \cdot (1+g)^t (1-s)^{t-1} < 0$
$\partial Y_t/\partial g = t Y_0 \cdot (1-s)^t (1+g)^{t-1} > 0$
only due to the positive effect of g but dampened by the negative effect of s.
These results remain true irrespective of a moment of time and in the continuous sense. Besides, the argument that a higher volume of savings would grow into more resources for investment in the future contradicts the fact that at any moment of time that volume of savings is a resource withdrawal. That amount of potential resource could otherwise have been used to perpetuate economic growth and thereby development and social wellbeing.

[6] By definition, effective exchange rate (e) is
$e = P_X/P_M = [(\Sigma p_{xi}.X_i)/\Sigma X_i]/[(\Sigma p_{mj}.M_j)/\Sigma M_j] = [\Sigma M_j/\Sigma X_i].[(\Sigma p_{xi}.X_i)/ (\Sigma p_{mj}.M_j)] = \alpha.T$
where, P_X denotes average price of total exports X. p_M denotes average price of total imports M. X_i denote specific (i) export quantities. M_j denote specific (j) import quantities. p_{xi} denote specific (i) prices of imports. p_{mj} denote specific (j) import prices.
$\alpha = [\Sigma M_j/\Sigma X_i]$ is a stabilizing constant in a dynamic basic-needs of sustainability.
$T = [(\Sigma p_{xi}.X_i)/(\Sigma p_{mj}.M_j)]$ denotes stable terms-of-trade (T) in a dynamic basic-needs regime of development.

Hence, exchange rates remain stable and avoid the interest-rate and exchange rate policed mechanism. This replacement comes about by the active epistemic conduct of wellbeing by θ-ranked values that reflect the actual and the simulated levels of unity of knowledge by complementarities between the variables in economic stabilization. In the end, effective exchange rate formula in the productivity driven dynamic basic-needs regime of development is given by,

$[e = \alpha.T][\theta]$; now with the extended vector of circular causation relations between the variables, $\{y,p,M,F,f,r,u,\rho,\text{Imports, Exports, Export prices, Import prices, e, T, }\alpha)[\theta]$. Note here the endogenous nature of all the variables in circular causation relations under the induction by θ-ranked values causes the coefficient-like parameter α to be variable under the dynamic effects of learning in the sustainability of the dynamic basic-needs of development.

Section 5

Chapter 14
Comprehension of Technology in Parent–Child Activities Using Bloom's Taxonomy of the Cognitive Domain

Tzu-Hsiang Ger
National Science and Technology Museum, Taiwan

Yao-Ming Chu
National Kaohsiung Normal University, Taiwan

Mei-Chen Chang
National Science and Technology Museum, Taiwan

ABSTRACT

The objective of this study is to investigate the influence of life creativity contests held by museums for elementary school children and their parents on the participants' conceptual cognition of water conservation technologies. A survey is designed to evaluate the change in the participants' conceptual cognition of the technologies, and includes questionnaires on water consumption habits in daily lives, understanding of the water resources in the Taiwan region, and uses of and opinions on water-saving devices. A method on which the assessment of the conceptual knowledge of the participants was based was a content analysis of the interviews. The findings of this study suggested: (a) the creativity contest provided diverse opportunities to improve the participants' cognitive concepts of water conservation; (b) this activity also has positively influenced the learning of knowledge, attitudes, and behaviors of water conservation technologies.

DOI: 10.4018/978-1-5225-1779-5.ch014

INTRODUCTION

Learning from "extracurricular activities" is an important channel for learning. For example, the real items and exhibitions offered by museums provide a learning environment for students to learn by themselves, which is significantly different from the lecture-based school education. *Life Creativity Contest on Water Conservation* was one of the *Energy Saving Creativity Contests* held by the National Science and Technology Museum in Kaohsiung in 2009. The contest invited elementary school children, together with their family members, to participate and involved them in data collection, current situation analysis, meeting discussion, creativity strategic analysis, model creation, and final presentation during their participation in a series of activities. By conducting surveys on the activities of the *Life Creativity Contest on Water Conservation*, uses Bloom's taxonomy theory to conduct quantitative and qualitative data analyses. This study investigates the influence of the contest on the cognition of school children and their family members on water conservation technologies.

LITERATURE REVIEW

Creativity Contests Improve Learning Motivation

Focus concept-based exploration can prompt learners to think and integrate information (Erickson, 2002).Creativity contests provide a "do-it-yourself" learning opportunity and have become an effective way of learning, in which the participants could apply what they have memorized from the past to the contests, or even amend it to establish correct new knowledge. Hong suggested that the purpose of creativity contests is to promote innovation (Hong, 2003); and creativity design-themed activities could strengthen the creativity designs of life technologies and the core abilities of creation (Hou, 2005). It is hoped that the participants' capabilities of creativity thinking and creation can be stimulated through their participation in the contests, and that they will have memorable experiences and develop deep understanding of the basic principles of science and technology (Chou, 2005).

These types of activities can allow students to link their life experiences and technology. Through practical design activities, discussions, thinking, and the exercise of judgment, the students' higher-order thinking ability is cultivated and their values are established (Lin and Yu, 2004).

Creativity contests emphasize being ready to respond, unconfined by predetermined mindset; not only having to effectively apply past experiences to new challenges, but also needing to think and try more. In addition to knowing how to do it, one needs to learn how to think so as to develop their ability in critical thinking and creativity (Lumsdaine, 1995). Lin (2002) indicated that parents' creativity approach toward upbringing is highly correlated with the life experiences of senior elementary school children about creativity. Creativity is also one of the key ingredients of playfulness (Staempfli, 2005 & Huang, 2006).

Concept of Water Conservation Technologies

Technology has a diverse and extensive influence on human's daily lives. Williams (1985) described technology as purposefully utilizing knowledge and material resources to satisfy human's needs. Wright and Lauda (1993) suggested that technology is the embodiment of knowledge and action produced through the use of various resources in designing, manufacturing, and operating products, primarily to control and improve the natural and man-made environments, and to systematically extend human potentials. On the other hand, Lee (1993) defined technology from a problem-solving perspective as "the intention and endeavor human exerts to effectively solve practical problems and adjusting the relationship between human and the environment by using their knowledge, resources, and creativity".

Concept is a basic unit of cognition and thinking; therefore, people often use concepts to organize and categorize the things in the environment and their experiences, so as to facilitate their thinking and interpersonal communications. Concept is also a basic unit of learning (Chu, 2010).

Technology concept refers to one's fundamental cognition of technology; one needs to go through a number of concept levels, including materialization, recognition, deduction, and application, to obtain the correct ideas about the implication of the essence of the entire technology and its application. The formation of technology concept is a process of concept transformation, which is the change of concept induced by experiences based on existing knowledge (Huang, 1984).

As for the conceptual knowledge of water conservation, it is classified according to the assessment of the conceptual knowledge of water conservation proposed by Chang and Wang (2005), including the environmental knowledge, utilization, essence, method, and solution of water conservation, and these were deduced into three dimensions of technology, as shown in Table 1.

Taxonomy of Conceptual Cognition

The technology cognition of the present study is analyzed according to the factual, conceptual, procedural, and metacognitive knowledge in the knowledge dimension of Bloom's taxonomy.

By considering these two dimensions and the correlation between the dimensions, one could effectively control the range and key points of the questions and the process of cognitive change during the competition activities.

Table1. Classification of the implications of water conservation technologies

Title	Classification	Implication
Technology Development	Essence of Technology	Definition, meaning, and objective
		Classification of technology
		Factor, mode, or system of technology
	Evolution of Technology	Development and trend of technology
	Technology and Society	Influence and impact of the relationship between technology and society
Technology Application	Categories	Common water-saving devices, equipment's, and end products
	Importance	The importance of water conservation for daily lives
	Method	The principles, techniques, and methods of technology
Technology Innovation	Solution	The present study uses actual practice to provide the public with the learning of knowledge of technology and the opportunities to search for knowledge, hoping to improve the public's understanding of the process of technology innovation through the explanations.

Source: Chang et al.,[15].

Bloom's theory of cognition taxonomy is divided into two dimensions, including the knowledge dimension and cognitive process dimension:

1. The knowledge dimension classifies four types of knowledge, including factual, conceptual, procedural, and meta-cognitive knowledge. Factual and conceptual knowledge refer to the knowledge of "what"; procedural knowledge relates to the knowledge of "how", referring mostly to a series or a string of procedures; meta-cognitive knowledge refers to cognition-related knowledge, including knowledge of cognition and the control, monitoring, and regulation of cognitive processes.
2. Cognitive process dimension classifies six categories of cognitive processes, including remember, understand, apply, analyze, evaluate, and create, which are further divided into 19 subcategories. Like the old taxonomy, the revised edition appears to have levels. However, unlike the "accumulated levels" of the old taxonomy, which implies that the previous category is the basis for the next category, it has "increasing complexity levels", which means that the category levels reflect the increase in cognitive complexity (Chang & Wang, 2011).

In the cognitive science perspective, knowledge originates from the process of comprehending concepts, rather than from mechanical memorizing. Conceptual comprehension can help solve problems. Based on the cognitive processes outlined by Bloom, the term *comprehension of technology* refers to the concrete behaviors that people demonstrate after internalizing technological knowledge. These behaviors can be displayed through high and low levels of performance.

The extensive connotation of technology includes related knowledge and the evolution of technology, as well as the relationship and influence between technology and other categories.

Based on the taxonomic notion of conceptual knowledge in Bloom's knowledge dimension and the factual knowledge basis required for forming conceptual knowledge, we generalized the conceptual knowledge dimension regarding technology into three categories, namely, essence, implications, and the evolution and development of technology (Chu, 2010).

Learning Theory of Parent-Child Interaction

Learning should start from families and apply to families. What children need are not only the daily supplies from their parents, but the nourishment of life. When children and their parents learn together, they are using the time they spend together as fibers to weave the vision of their family (Krathwohl, 2002).

According to Piaget's stage theory of cognitive development, most elementary school children are at the stage of concrete operational period; thus, it is necessary to consider parents as important educational subjects when investigating students' learning activities. Unlike at schools where students spend a fixed duration of time learning, learning and sharing at home is not limited to a fixed time period, but is rather a natural sharing and learning with family members in their everyday lives.

Through parent-child interactions, children and their parents mutually influence the attitudes, emotions, and behaviors of each other, which further alter the behavioral mode of the parent-child interaction.

As a result, the purpose of a learning family is to achieve the involvement of all family members in learning activities. The growth of some family members could influence the co-learning of other family members, resulting in sharing of learning experiences or thoughts with each other, and further promoting the growth and development of individuals and the family. The real spirits of family learning is not on the amount of contents learned, but the ability to convert the obtained concepts and behaviors to continuously strengthen the life adaptability of the family.

Wang (2005) noted that parent-child co-learning is not limited to co-learning between parents and their children; rather, the definition of the co-learning participants should be extended to include the adults and children of an immediate family. Parents' involvement in their children's learning activities provides the children with a more diverse learning stimulation and helps them build a positive learning attitude to improve their learning effectiveness and motivation. Meanwhile, parents could gain an insight into how well or poor their children learn through parent-child co-learning, which contributes to the harmony of the parent-child relationship in the family and improves the interaction between the parents and the children.

RESEARCH METHODS

The research subject of this study is directed to families. The activities were joined by teams of elementary school students, designated as the leaders of their teams, and their family members. A total of 83 teams were registered, with only 24 teams submitting proposals and 16 teams entering the final competition. The competition schedule is shown in Table 2.

To assess the cognitive change on water conservation knowledge of the participants during the contests, the analyses of concept in this study adopted Bloom's taxonomy of conceptual knowledge of educational objectives (revised edition) and were conducted in the knowledge dimension and the cognitive process dimension. Besides analyzing the surveys taken before and after the contests, analysis of the conceptual knowledge of the qualitative interviews and content analysis of the documents created by the participants (including a proposal in the preliminary and 4 finished products in the final) were conducted to evaluate the knowledge of water conservation of the participants. Qualitative and quantitative methods were performed in parallel for the analyses.

Table 2. Creativity Competition Schedule

December	Online discussion platform (Energy Wizard)
January	Announcement, promotion, and notifying schools
Early March	Online registration
Mid-March	Education training courses
May	Submission of water-saving proposals
June	Announcement of the initial candidate list
July	Creating the physical model
End of August	Final-round evaluation

Table 3. Bi-directional analysis of the survey

Knowledge Dimension	Cognitive Process Dimension				
	Remember	Understand	Apply	Analysis	Total
Factual Knowledge	3	3	1	1	8
Conceptual Knowledge	2	2	3	3	10
Procedural Knowledge	1	2	2	1	6
Total	6	7	6	5	**24**

Survey

According to Anderson, Krathwohl, Airasian, Cruikshank, Mayer, and Pintrich's (2001) study, the knowledge dimension and cognition dimension in the Bloom's taxonomy of educational objectives were used as the horizontal axis and the vertical axis. Content validity of the survey was examined bi-directionally, and the survey was developed from questionnaires selected by difficulty analysis, discriminant analysis, and the point-biserial correlation coefficient. Content of the questionnaire in the survey was reviewed by experts, and was revised and edited according to the combined opinions of the experts. To increase the discrimination of the test, the survey of this study was designed in a multiple-choice (one out of four possible answers) format.

Completed survey (24 questions) was pre-tested on the participants entering the preliminary. The survey was then revised according to the results of the pre-test (146 surveys returned) and was used for post-testing (18 questions after revision). Results from the pre-test and post-test were compared to determine the conceptual change of the participants.

The comprehension of technology manifested through relevant connotations and explorations was adopted to enable people to demonstrate more concrete behaviors regarding various technological implications through different levels of learning during the learning process. In addition, we hoped to distinguish the performance differences between comprehension levels, such as lower-level illustration and interpretation and higher-level comparison and explanation methods. Therefore, this study employed a two-way detail table of technology comprehension. The analysis used four taxonomic items, namely, the knowledge classification, cognitive process comprehension of technology, and comprehension characterization (interview topic) dimensions, as shown in Tables 4 through 7.

Interview

A semi-structured interview, in which the interviewees talk about the subjective feelings of their life experiences, was conducted to evaluate the participants' cognition and thoughts of water conservation. Researcher employed the leading questions based on the interviewees' answers to allow the interviewed students and parents to talk about their thoughts in details without any psychological burden.

Each interview took approximately 10 minutes. All interviews were agreed by the interviewees and were audio-recorded in full. Contents of the interviews were typed into verbatim transcripts, followed by extraction into abstracts. Analyses were finally performed on the extracted abstracts.

Table 4. Illustrating examples of the knowledge classification dimensions

Dimension A	Dimension B	Illustrating Example
Factual knowledge	Terminology	Nouns and terms related to bottled water, groundwater, sewages, debris flow, and rivers
	Specific details	Technical terms such as gray water systems, reverse osmosis water, deep water, and alkaline water
Conceptual knowledge	Classification	Type of water-saving tools
	Principle	Application methods for technology products, such as water-saving tools
	Structure	Taiwan water resource characteristics and strategies and plans related to water saving.
Procedural knowledge	Technique and algorithms	Calculation of water costs
	Methods	Using recycled water to achieve the goal of water saving
	Procedures	Understanding the flow procedures of water recycling
Meta-cognitive knowledge	Learning strategy	Collecting knowledge related to water saving through the Internet
	Context	Will you tell your family about water-saving methods in any circumstance? Please provide the reason.
	Self-knowledge	Knowing methods to effectively save water on a personal level

Table 5. Illustrating examples of the cognitive process dimension

Dimension	Illustrating example
Remember	Dual-flush toilet and sink
Understand	Understand the reason for debris flow formation
Apply	Use known water-saving methods in daily life
Analyze	Understand the relationship between water shortages and the environment
Evaluate	Assess different water-saving methods
Create	Employ existing knowledge and experience to conceive alternative ideas regarding water-saving tool production

Table 6. Illustrating examples of the technology comprehension dimension

Dimension A	Dimension B	Illustrating Example
Technology development	Essence of technology	Inventing and developing new methods to change the environment and improve human life
	Evolution of technology	The evolving process of water-using appliances (e.g., the toilet)
	Technology and society	Influence of constructing a reservoir on the ecology and human culture
Technology applications	Categories	Types of toilets and faucets
	Importance	Pros and cons for water saving, and the effects of not saving water
	Methods	How to achieve the goal of water saving
Technology innovation	Design cognition	Understand the goals of and the required knowledge for model production
	Production cognition	Understand the characteristics of various materials and how tools are used

Table 7. Illustrating examples of the comprehension characterization dimension

Dimension	Illustrating Example
Interpretation (description)	Describe how you achieve water saving in daily life.
Illustration	Name some available water-saving devices
Classification	Water-saving methods that recycle water include rainwater, hand-washing water, and rice-rinsing water.
Summary	What do you find most interesting in the whole activity?
Inference	What will life be like if water conservation is not implemented?
Comparison	Changes in the participants before and after participating in the activity
Explanation	Principles applied in model production

Document Analysis

The document herein refers to the *Water Conservation Proposal*, whose contents are diverse, which include the analysis of family members on the current situations of family water conservation, analysis of creativity strategies, records of meeting discussions, and design and making of the models. The proposal revealed the relevant sources of technology cognition, methods of group coordination, decision-making of proposal topic, and analysis of factors of the family members during the activities. The proposal was not only the key document to be assessed for entering into the final, but also the source of data on the correlation of activity process and technology cognition; therefore, the *Water Conservation Proposal* submitted in the preliminary was photocopied and saved as the supplemental document for the research analysis.

RESEARCH RESULTS

Quantitative Analysis

The first part of the survey focuses on the life experience of the participants in water conservation, which was answered by the participants according to their actual experiences. Attitude is not inherent, but acquired through learning. After experiencing the activities, what are the changes in attitude toward water conservation of the parent-child participants?

The questionnaire developed for this study was finalized following a discussion between the research team and the advisor and a review by experts. A total of 155 questionnaires were distributed in northern, central, and southern Taiwan during the education training period from March 21, 2009, to April 5, 2009. The questionnaire recovery was completed on April 5, 2009, with 146 valid questionnaires, attaining a recovery rate of 94.2%. Subsequently, the SPSS statistical software was used to conduct a *t* test and a one-way analysis of variance (ANOVA). Participants comprised 63 parents and 83 students, most of whom were higher-grade students. The participants from southern Taiwan accounted for the majority of the sample because of convenience due to geographical proximity.

Attitude Toward Water Conservation in Daily Lives

As shown in Table 8, attitude performance of the parents and students has improved after the activity, and the difference in performance between the students and parents is lower after the activity as well. Studies found that the positive attitudes of parents toward water conservation have led students to participate in the activity, and the attitudes of students toward water conservation have positively transformed and grown after the activity.

As shown in Table 9, the average values of all the questions were higher after the activity than those before the activity, especially the difference in average values for E2 was the highest among all the questions, indicating the most attitude change; and the smallest difference was observed in E10. It is worth

Table 8. t-Tests on the attitude toward water conservation of the parent-child participants before and after the activity

	Subject	Number of Participants	Average	S.D.	Difference of Averages	Standard Error of Difference	*t*-Value
Pretest	Parents	63	4.40	0.592	0.321	0.089	3.614***
	Students	83	4.08	0.479			
Posttest	Parents	15	4.67	0.325	0.273	0.121	2.255*
	Students	30	4.40	0.407			

*p<.05 ***p<.001

Table 9. Difference in average values before and after the activity

Q.No	Question	Difference in Avg.
E1:	I often pay attention to the information on my water bills, such as the total water used and the amount due.	0.43
E2:	I feel it is a waste of resource to purchase bottled water when I go out.	0.60
E3:	I always feel it is a waste of water when taking a bath.	0.36
E4:	It is a pity to see rainwater flowing directly into the drainages without being reused.	0.33
E5:	I would pay attention to the water-saving devices at home, such as dual-flash toilets, aerators, adjustable faucet, or water-saving toilets.	0.36
E6:	When water has kept flowing from faucets not properly turned off, I would want to turn the faucet off immediately.	0.17
E7:	I would suggest my family to use water-saving devices, such as dual-flash toilets, aerators, adjustable faucet, or water-saving toilets.	0.38
E8:	The amount of rainfall in Taiwan is large, but the rainfall distribution in time and location is uneven, and the average amount of usable rainfall per person is 1/5 of the world average; so, I think Taiwan is a water shortage area.	0.44
E9:	When hearing of any effective water-saving technique, I would try to tell my family and friends about it.	0.20
E10:	I often hear about water conservation-related advocacies.	0.04
E11:	I think there is plenty of water on earth; it is not that necessary to conserve water.	0.13
E12:	Water resource has become a crucial problem threatening the human development of the 21st century.	---
Average		0.31

noting that the reason for the small change in E10 might be either "The water conservation activity did not attract the participants' attention on the water conservation advocacy" or "The water conservation advocacy of the relevant authorities was not effective".

The overall attitude of the participants of the activity toward water conservation technologies is positive and affirmative, and the performance of the participants was stronger after the activity than that before the activity. Also, the parents performed better than the students.

Water Conservation-Related Knowledge and Learning of Cognitive Concepts

The second part of the survey focuses on the 7 issues of the discussion. As shown in Table 10, analysis of the *t*-tests indicated that the scores of both the parents and the children participants were significantly improved in the posttest, and the performance of the parents was stronger than that of the children in the posttest as well.

Table 11 shows the results of the *t*-tests performed based on the conceptual cognition dimension, which revealed significant differences in the performance of the "factual knowledge", "conceptual knowledge", and "procedural knowledge" dimensions between the parent-child participants in the pretest, and that the parents' scores were significantly higher than the students'; however, no significant difference was observed in the posttest. Among the 7 issues, 4 questions in the pretest exhibited significant differences between the two groups of the participants; the parents scored higher on the "Environmental Sensitivity" issue than the students, but poorer on the "Importance of Water", "Water Usage Procedure", and "Action Strategy for Water Conservation" issues. Meanwhile, significant differences were shown in 5 questions in the posttest; the parents scored higher than the students on all 5 questions, especially on the question of the "Environmental Sensitivity" issue. Also, performance of the parents before and after the activity was both stronger than that of the students.

The positive and affirmative attitudes of the parent participants have prompted the involvement of parents and children in the water conservation activity. Through parent-child co-learning, the parents and students participated in the activity showed different degrees of growth in the understanding of water conservation-related issues or learning of cognitive concepts after the activity. This also indicated that the learning between parents and their children has influence on each other.

In the meta-cognitive dimension analysis, Table 12 shows that the participants tended to choose "family" rather than "teachers" before the activity. After the activity, the participants had an increased selection rate only for "teachers" among the nine options of learning methods. Although a parent-child activity was designed for this study, elementary school students tended to inquire their teacher when

Table 10. Statistics on the average scores, standard deviation, and t-values of the parent-child participants

	Subject	No.	Avg.	S. D.	D. A.	S. Error of Difference	t-Value
Pretest	Parents	63	16.43	1.146	-0.150	0.529	-0.283
	Students	83	16.58	4.641			
Posttest	Parents	15	16.60	0.737	2.100	0.400	5.254***
	Students	30	14.50	1.925			

***p<.001

Table 11. t-Test analysis (significant) of the scores of the parent-child participants in the questions of the surveyed issues

Time	Issue of Discussion	No.	Parents' S. R.	Students' S. R.	T
Pretest	Importance of Water	Q11	0.19	0.46	-3.60***
	Environmental Sensitivity	Q15	0.84	0.65	2.72**
	Water Usage Procedure	Q16	0.25	0.48	-2.92**
	Action Strategy for Water Conservation	Q20	0.37	0.58	-2.59*
Posttest	Environmental Sensitivity	Q2	0.93	0.60	2.96**
		Q4	1.00	0.80	2.69*
		Q18	1.00	0.80	2.69*
	Action Strategy for Water Conservation	Q6	1.00	0.87	2.11*
	Basic Knowledge of Water	Q7	1.00	0.73	3.25**

*p<.05 **p<.01 ***p<.001

Table 12. Comparison of learning about water-saving knowledge, skills, and tools

	Participating in Water-Saving Activities	Websites	Reading Books	Family	Press	Teachers	DIY	Classroom Lessons	Peer Discussion
Before activity	0.88	0.88	0.73	0.52	0.49	**0.48**	0.72	0.53	0.43
After activity	0.84	0.53	0.69	0.47	0.44	**0.60**	0.40	0.04	0.04
Difference	-0.04	-0.27	-0.04	-0.05	-0.05	**0.12**	-0.32	-0.49	-0.39

encountering problems during the activity. We infer that this phenomenon occurred because practical activities required more skills, and the information provided by the family mostly concerned daily water-saving methods, which were insufficient to meet the requirement of practical activities. Thus, the students consulted the teachers rather than the family about professional water-saving knowledge.

Table 13 shows that participants gained further understanding regarding the water cost structure and became more aware of water costs. When "high-rate water costs" and "self-pay water costs" were considered, individual water-saving behavior could be further implemented. However, whether the low water costs in Taiwan contribute to a lack of water-saving habits among the Taiwanese people is an issue worth discussing.

In the education training that occurred before the activity, many courses related to water saving were designed, including one on the water cost structure. After the activity, a number of participants expressed that the amount of water costs was a factor determining their water-saving behavior, indicating that the participants still tended to be unengaged in water-saving actions and prioritized their personal interests. The time required for cultivating environmental cognition and attitudes is shorter than the time required for demonstrating environmental behaviors. This research result showed that the participants acquired relevant water-saving information primarily through television, which, nonetheless, publicizes few environmental issues.

Table 13. Comparison of effective water-saving learning methods

	Competition Participation	High-Rate Water Cost	Online Information	Water Restriction Policies	Relatives and Friends	Environmental Demands	Self-Pay Water Cost	Others
Pretest	0.77	0.55	0.64	0.49	0.42	0.62	0.31	0.07
Posttest	0.71	0.71	0.64	0.47	0.36	0.58	0.69	0.27
Difference	-0.06	0.16	0.01	-0.02	-0.06	-0.05	0.38	0.20

Qualitative Analysis

Through interviews with the participants, water-saving concepts were used to evoke their memory, and the content of their recollection represents the participants' concepts regarding water saving. By interviewing the participants before, during, and after the activity, the participant concepts were investigated to provide a basis for the influence of interpretation activities on participants' comprehension of technology.

The interview results were organized and analyzed according to technology development, application, and innovation, as shown in Table 14.

The changes in the participants' understanding of water conservation before and after the contest activities are detailed in Table 15.

Table 14. The changes in the technology implications of the participants before and after the activity

	Before Activity:	After Activity:
Technology Development	(1) Students associate "water conservation" with water conservation-related containers; parents' association of "water conservation" is influenced by the economy and convenience. (2) The purpose of water conservation is to make our lives easier, and water conservation is correlated with the environment. (3) The participants think they could influence others by self-practicing water conservation.	(1) Association of the concept of "water conservation" is no longer limited to containers, but extended to the methods and procedures involving the related technological fields. (2) The purpose of technology development is to make our lives easier, and natural environments must be taken into account when developing technologies. (3) The participants do not exhibit strong willingness to advocate for water conservation. (4) Parents' involvement helps students' learning and promotes the parent-child relationship.
Technology Application	(1) Most participating families already have water-saving habits, and the parents' knowledge and application of water conservation influence the children's cognition and learning. (2) Implementation of water conservation in families is easier to succeed when family members influence each other. (3) Knowledge of technology is better acquired through exhibitions.	(1) Knowledge of the procedures of water conservation expands. (2) Knowledge of the process and result of technology application needs to be reinforced. (3) The convenience brought by technology makes people depend more on technology.
Technology Innovation	(1) Creativity of the water-saving models comes from life experiences, and the creativity decision is mostly made based on equal weights of creativity and practicability. (2) Learning route of technology knowledge before the activity is experience-based, and default solution strategy is used.	(1) The design of technology products comes from life habits, and public acceptance of the products needs to be considered. (2) The activity strengthens the innovative design and cognition of technology, and improves the ability of self-learning. (3) The choice of techniques and materials is the main reason for difficult production.

Table 15. Changes in the understanding of water conservation before and after the activity

Technology Understanding Dimension	Changes in Understanding After the Activity
Technology Development	1. Cognition of the essence of technology expanded from "Technology is an article" to "Technology is a method and procedure". 2. Willingness to promote water conservation decreases. 3. Involvement of parents promotes the development of parent-child relationship. 4. Specific expression: improvements in the ability to interpret, compare, and deduce.
Technology Application	1. Can compare the different practices of water conservation, and point out the pros and cons of those practices. 2. Knowledge of water conservation procedures expands. 3. Able to understand the importance of water conservation, but unable to make deeper explanations. 4. Specific expression: stronger performance in interpretation, comparison, and analysis.
Technology Innovation	1. Understand that knowledge is the basis for innovative actions, and would take the initiative to search for information and learn to improve the ability of self-learning. 2. Correct the mode of problem-solving, and learn to choose the strategy for problem-solving. 3. Specific expression: stronger performance in the ability to abstract, deduce, compare, and explain.

The results indicated larger differences in "the concept of water resource" and "the development of water conservation" of the participants. Most elementary school students do not have enough cognition about the water resources in Taiwan, and have few chances of learning about the development of water conservation in their daily lives or school classes. However, participants of the contest showed better learning growths on "water conservation actions" and better understanding about the "difficulties of practicing water conservation". These phenomena are supposed to be correlated with students' life experiences, since most of the participating families have already put water-saving actions into practice in their daily lives, and thus were more active in the learning of "water conservation actions". Overall, this activity has positively influenced the learning of knowledge, attitudes, and behaviors of water conservation.

CONCLUSIONS AND RECOMMENDATIONS

In the three dimensions of technology implications (i.e., technology development, application, and innovation) categorized in this study, the participants exhibited improved performance after the activity, indicating that the creativity competition activity of this study helped the students understand water-saving technologies during the activity, trained them to proactively engage in exploratory learning, and improved their creative thinking and problem solving skills. In addition, the activity effectively enhanced the participants' water-saving concepts.

Through this type of technology creativity competition, students could also perceive group learning as enjoyable. Therefore, replacing lectures with activities is the best learning method for developing multiple intelligences. The research findings are provided below:

1. The creativity contest provided diverse opportunities to improve the participants' cognitive concepts of water conservation; and
2. This activity also has positively influenced the learning of knowledge, attitudes, and behaviors of water conservation technologies.

Where the cognitive concept transition is summarized and described below:

Participants' Cognitive Concepts of Water Conservation before the Activity

1. There were no differences in cognitive concept between the parent-child participants, but the performance of the parents on water conservation-related issues was stronger than that of the students.
2. Participants' understanding of water conservation was mostly limited to the containers used in their daily lives. When asked to describe their thoughts, the participants mainly used "exemplary" and "comparative" methods to express themselves, without making any deeper explanations. Their learning of water conservation knowledge was influenced by their parents.

Participants' Cognitive Concepts of Water Conservation after the Activity

1. No significant difference in the cognitive concept of water conservation was observed between the parents and children after the activity, but the parents had significantly stronger "basic knowledge of water" and "environmental sensitivity" than the students.
2. Participants' understanding of water conservation has extended to the "methods" and "procedures" involving the technology-related fields. In addition to being able to "compare" and "interpret" different methods, the participants showed improvement in the ability to "analyze" and "explain" and were more active in learning about water conservation.

Transformation and Investigation of Participants' Cognitive Concepts of Water Conservation after the Activity

1. The implementation stage of this activity provides diverse opportunities, including group cooperation, information searching, strategy choosing, and hands-on operation, to improve the participants' cognitive concepts of water conservation. The activity improved the "analysis" and "deduction" abilities of the participants; and although there were improvements in the ability to "explain", it was only reflected on the model principles of their teams.

The role of parents in this activity transitioned from being a guide to a helper. Parent-child co-learning is the learning between family members, who influence each other in the co-learning process. Many family members joined their teams half way through the activity, and the educational effect spread after the activity was the most anticipated part of our study. Parents showed better "environmental sensitivity" both before and after the activity; it was their high sensitivity to the environment that prompted the involvement of their family members in this activity. Parents are anticipated to help stimulate elementary school children's attention and care for the environment.

TEACHING SUGGESTIONS

Encourage Parents to Accompany Students to Participate in Activities, which Facilitates Student Learning

We recommend teachers and parents to encourage and accompany students to involve in similar technology creativity activities. The involvement of the parents could properly provide correct assistance and encouragement to the children during the activity, which is helpful for the children's learning and makes the journey of learning happier for the children.

Designing Class Activities Related to Life Situations

The design should be more flexible and more life-integrative, in order to create a real situation, in which students could have the opportunities to reflect on themselves. We recommend schools to co-host these activities with extramural organizations, and the educational institutes may provide related information and rewards to enhance students' willingness to join the activities.

The Necessity of Educational Training

There could be differences between the required abilities for the activity and the actual personal abilities; therefore, hosting institutes should conduct a holistic investigation before the activity and provide concepts of different difficulties to students in different grades.

ACKNOWLEDGMENT

This study was supported by grants from the National Science Council of the Republic of China under Contract Number NSC 101-3113-S-017-001 and NSC 97-2514-S-359 -001 -NEP.

REFERENCES

Anderson, L. W., Krathwohl, D. R., Airasian, P. W., Cruikshank, K. A., Mayer, R. E., & Pintrich, P. R. et al. (2001). *A Taxonomy for Learning, Teaching, and Assessing*. New York: Addison Wesley Longman.

Chang, M. C., & Wang, Y. H. (2011). A study on visitors' understanding of water-saving technology through museum hands-on activities. *Technology Museum Review*, *15*(1), 10.

Chen, H. K. (2005). Technology Concept Scale Development - dissemination of scientific and technical education to the secondary level. *Living Technology Education*, *38*(4), 35–54.

Chou, C. M. (2005). *Originality thinking training*. Taipei: Chuan Hwa Publishing Ltd.

Chu, Y. M. (2010). *A study on the current situations and the development of assessment tools for technology conceptual knowledge in junior high schools*. Kaohsiung: Liwen Publishers Co., Ltd.

Chu, Y. M. (2010). *Current status and development of conceptual knowledge evaluation instrument for science and technology curricula in junior high school. Kaohsiung City*. Liwen Publishers Co., Ltd.

Erickson, H. L. (2002). *Concept Based Curriculum and Instruction*. Thousand Oaks, CA: Corwin.

Hong, J. C. (2003). *Knowledge innovation and learning organization* (2nd ed.). Taipei: Wu-Nan Book Inc.

Hou, S. K. (2005). Strengthen the core abilities for living technology by creative design activities. *Living Technology Education*, *38*(8), 1–15.

Huang, H. C. (2006). *The relationship between demographic variables, playfulness, motivation of teaching, perceived happiness and creative teaching among junior high school teachers* (Unpublished Master's Thesis). Institute of Education, National Sun Yat-sen University, Kaohsiung.

Huang, I. C. (1984). Study of the concept and its significance. *Living Technology Education, 66,* 44–56.

Krathwohl, D. R. (2002). A revision of Bloom's taxonomy: An overview. *Theory into Practice, 41*(4), 212–219. doi:10.1207/s15430421tip4104_2

Lee, L. S. (1993). Seeing different things from different perspectives – multiple views on technology education. *Technological and Vocational Education Bimonthly, 13,* 18–20.

Lin, K. Y., & Yu, K. C. (2004). The study of developing students' creativity through technological literacy curriculum in elementary and secondary school. *Journal of National University Tainan: Mathematics, Science, and Technology, 38*(2), 15–30.

Lin, S. Y. (2002). *The relationship between creative parenting, reading parenting, reading motivation and behavior, and creativity* (Unpublished Master's Thesis). Graduate School of Education, National Cheng Chi University, Taipei.

Lumsdaine, E., & Lumsdaine, M. (1995). *Creative problem solving: Thinking skills for a changing world.* New York: McGraw-Hill.

Staempfli, M. B. (2005). *Adolescent playfulness, leisure and well-being* (Unpublished Doctoral Dissertation). University of Waterloo, Ontario, Canada.

Wang, L. (2005). *An effective study of "Parent-Child English Co-Learning Project" in a social education organization: The Chin-Chin branch of Taipei Public Library experience.* (Unpublished Master's Thesis). Graduate School of Educational Policy and Management, National Taipei Teachers College, Taipei.

Williams, P. H. E. (1985). *Teaching craft, design and technology five to thirteen.* London: Croom Helm.

Wright, T., & Lauda, D. (1993). Technology education-a position statement. *Technology Teacher, 52*(6), 3–5.

Chapter 15
Teachers Conceptions and Approaches to Blended Learning:
A Literature Review

Vicki Caravias
Swinburne University of Technology, Australia

ABSTRACT

This paper presents a critical review and synthesis of research literature in higher education exploring teachers' conceptions of blended learning and their approaches to both design and teaching. Definitions of blended learning and conceptual frameworks are considered first. Attention is given to Picciano's Blending with Purpose Multimodal framework. This paper builds upon previous research on blended learning and conceptual framework by Picciano by exploring how objectives from Picciano's framework affect teachers' approaches to both design and teaching in face-to-face and online settings. Research results suggest that teachers use multiple approaches including face-to-face methods and online technologies that address the learning needs of a variety of students from different generations, personality types and learning styles.

INTRODUCTION

Over the past two decades the integration of Internet and Information and Communication Technologies (ICT) have enhanced knowledge and performance in many university courses (S. Jones, Johnson-Yale, Millermaier, & Pérez, 2008).

During this time universities have incorporated learning management systems, such as Blackboard and Moodle, into their teaching practices (R. A. Ellis, Goodyear, Prosser, & O'Hara, 2006; R. A. Ellis, Steed, & Applebee, 2006) to support teachers in delivering material to students. Learning Management Systems (LMS) provide the opportunity to deliver blended learning approaches that combine a mix

DOI: 10.4018/978-1-5225-1779-5.ch015

of ICT with various learning resources and delivery methods. Coates et al. (2005) outline several key features of LMSs:

1. Asynchronous and synchronous communication between teacher-student and student-student (discussion boards, emails, live chats);
2. Content development and delivery (lecture notes, readings, practical activities);
3. Formative and summative assessment (submission of assignments, quizzes, collaborative work feedback, grades); and
4. Class and user management (enrolling students, displaying timetable) (p. 20-21).

Early adopters of blended learning argued that there are many possibilities offered by the technologies for Australian educators in higher education (Garrison, Anderson, & Archer, 1999). There are several reasons behind the drive to incorporate ICT into the educational process. First, pressure to utilise ICT at a university level comes from changes in the student demography. According to Concannon, Flynn and Campbell (Concannon, Flynn, & Campbell, 2005) the surge in "full time part time students is a phenomenon of recent years, where school leavers take part-time jobs whilst attending university" (p.502). For students who work full time, the flexible design accommodates their busy schedules. Without this flexibility, the students may not be able to pursue their degrees. Blended learning environments suit students who prefer face-to-face interaction in addition to students who prefer online learning.

Second, blended learning has the potential to promote lifelong learning in higher education (Dzakiria, Wahab, & Rahman, 2012). In their qualitative study, Dzakiria, Wahab and Rahman investigated the learning experiences of a student's undertaking studies at University Utara Malaysia. They found that blended learning's "flexibility nature can promote lifelong learning anywhere, and anytime" (p. 299). This is supported by research carried out by Masalela (Masalcla, 2009) whose qualitative study examined factors that influenced fifteen faculty members' decision to use blended learning and found that learners become self-directed, develop critical thinking skills and become independent thinkers through blended courses. In addition, develop lifelong skills to use when they leave the university.

Third, changes in the market for delivery of education comes from innovation in new technologies. In the case of University of Central Florida (Dziuban & Moskal, 2001), a three hour classroom instruction was replaced with a two hour online instruction session. The university was able to operate multiple classes in one classroom using the technological infrastructure of the university. In addition, blended learning enables multi-university offerings (Jefferies, Grodzinsky, & Griffin, 2003) and facilitates elective courses (Verkroost, Meijerink, Lintsen, & Veen, 2008). Lastly, there is pressure from government for universities to increase participation and widen access to higher education (N. Jones & Lau, 2010).

In sum, the current environment of higher education requires a careful consideration of the role of blended learning in addressing a number issues related to teaching and learning such as generational differences, personality types and learning styles. The goal of this review is to present an investigation of the research currently available on teachers' conceptions of blended learning and their approaches to both design and teaching in higher education using Picciano's Blending with Purpose Multimodal framework. This proposes that teachers consider their objectives and understand how to apply the technologies and approaches that will work best for their students. This paper contributes to the field of blended learning by exploring how objectives from Picciano's framework affect teachers' approach to both design and teaching in face-to-face and online settings such as content, social/emotional contexts, dialectic/questioning activities, synthesis/evaluation tools, collaboration/student-generated content, and reflection opportunities.

Structurally, this paper consists of five thematic sections with relevant sub-sections. First, the author defines blended learning. Secondly, the advantages and disadvantages of blended learning approach will be discussed. The third section of this paper explores the literature available on teachers' conceptions on blended learning and their approaches to both design and teaching in higher education using Picciano's Blend with Purpose Multimodal framework. In the fourth section the author describes the method for choosing the studies in this literature review. The fifth section presents findings and provides suggestions for how this literature review could help researchers approach and study teachers' conceptions on blended learning environments in the future.

LITERATURE REVIEW

There are a few literature reviews on blended learning (Bliuc, Goodyear, & Ellis, 2007; Charles R Graham, Allen, & Ure, 2003; Shivetts, 2011; Vignare, 2007). Apart from published texts (Bonk & Graham, 2006; Littlejohn & Pegler, 2007; A. G. Picciano, Dziuban, & Graham, 2013; E. Stacey & Gerbic, 2009) there are a small number of publications focusing on teachers' conceptions using blended learning environments (Gerbic, 2011).

This section presents a critical review and synthesis of the research literature in the field being investigated by this paper: how teachers experience and perceive the blended learning approach in higher education. The literature review commences by defining blended learning. The advantages and disadvantages of the blended learning approach are then discussed. This is followed by a review of the research literature on teachers' conceptions of blended learning and their approaches to both design and teaching in higher education using Picciano's Blending with Purpose Multimodal framework.

There are many definitions for blended learning.

Defining Blended Learning

Blended learning has been defined in a number of ways and a generally accepted definition does not exist. It is used interchangeably with distance learning, online learning, eLearning, blended teaching, e-teaching, blended e-learning, hybrid learning and flexible learning. The literature defines blended learning in many different ways according to instructional methods. The three most common definitions documented by Graham, Allen and Ure (C. R. Graham, Allen, & Ure, 2005), are:

1. Combining instructional modalities (or delivery media). From a training perspective, Skill and Young (2002) view blended learning as "a combination of in-class teaching and learning modalities with robust electronically mediated experiences" (p.25). Singh (2003) sees blended learning as a combination of multiple delivery media designed to complement each other and promote meaningful learning.

2. Combining instructional methods. According to Welker and Berardino (2006) blended learning is "the use of electronic learning tools that supplement but do not replace face-to-face learning" (p.33). Blended learning is an infusion of web-based technologies into face-to-face learning to create blended learning. Alternatively the combination of instructional methods is known as hybrid

learning (De Witt & Kerres, 2003; Hermann, Popyack, Char, & Zoski, 2004; Kaleta, Skibba, & Joosten, 2007).

3. Combining online learning and face-to-face instruction (Garrison & Kanuka, 2004; Ginns & Ellis, 2007; Ginns, Prosser, & Barrie, 2007; Mortera-Gutierrez, 2006; Tang & Byrne, 2007).

Wu, Tenniyson and Hsia (Wu, Tennyson, & Hsia, 2010) state that blended learning is also noted as "blended e-learning system" that "refers to an instructional system that combines multiple delivery methods, including most often face-to-face classroom with asynchronous and/or synchronous online learning. It is characterised as maximising the best advantages of face-to-face and online education" (p. 155). This view is supported by Littlejohn and Pegler (2007).

A significant amount of blended learning research has already been done from the learning context of face-to-face activities and to which an online or web-based activity had been added. Skill and Young (2002) stated that "blended learning moves well beyond the concept of bolting a Website onto a traditional classroom-based course" (p.25). Furthermore, Graham (2006) defined blended learning as "the combination of the instruction from two historically separate models of teaching and learning: traditional face-to-face learning systems and distributed learning systems" (p.5) with an emphasis on the role of computer-based technologies. However, in a criticism of blended learning, Oliver and Trigwell (2005) argued that blended learning is really concerned with the process of blending media, teaching processes and presentation, rather than student's learning. They suggested that blended learning could be redeemed "by a closer analysis of the critical aspects of the subject matter that are in variation in the act of using blended learning" (p.24). Furthermore, Garrison and Kanuka (Garrison & Kanuka, 2004) state that blended learning should not be "just adding on to the existing dominant approach or method" (p.97) but should be transformative in higher education and increase the opportunities for critical and reflective thinking.

Advantages of the Blended Learning Approach

It has been widely argued in the literature that there are four main advantages for teachers to incorporate the blended learning approach into teaching practice:

1. Greater flexibility of time. Freedom for students to decide when each online lesson will be learned (Bouhnik & Marcus, 2006; Demetriadis & Pombortsis, 2007);
2. Lack of dependence on the time constraints of the teacher (Edginton & Holbrook, 2010; Lock, 2006);
3. Time for reflection. Freedom for students to express thoughts, and ask questions, without limitations (Chamberlin & Moon, 2005; Liaw, Huang, & Chen, 2007); and
4. Meeting different needs and learning styles (Ho, Lu, & Thurmaier, 2006).

These advantages can support students to develop more responsibility for their learning (Rodriguez & Anicete, 2010) and improve critical thinking (Saundercook & Cooper, 2003). These perceptions are consistent with the literature that suggests that the blended learning approach can transform learning experiences (Garrison & Anderson, 2003; Knight, 2009). In particular, it has been argued that the blended learning approach can improve students' written communication skills, problem solving skills, and increase the opportunities for critical and reflective thinking (Garrison et al., 1999). Lapadat (Lapadat, 2002) found that with asynchronous text-based communication students have the time to carefully compose their thoughts and ideas into a written-form communication. This attention to writing, in combination with asynchronous communication, provides students with opportunities for critical reflection which is necessary for higher-order thinking (Garrison & Anderson, 2003).

The blended learning approach can provide students access to online learning materials and engage learners interactively (Concannon et al., 2005; Sharpe, 2006). Motteram (2006) found that the blended learning approach enhanced the learning experience as the course structure enabled them to deal with topics in their own time and to organise themselves better around the tasks in their own time. In two studies, one in the UK and one in Australia, the use of blended learning environments together with access to online learning materials were found to be determining factors behind increased student engagement and motivation (Concannon et al., 2005; De Lange, Suwardy, & Mavondo, 2003). In keeping with Motteram observations, (2006) Rodriguez and Anicete (2010) found that the blended learning approach enhanced the learning experience as the course structure enabled students to deal with topics in their own time and to organise themselves better around the tasks in their own time. Rodriguez and Anicete (2010) also argue that learning management systems, such as Modular Object Oriented Dynamic Learning Environment (MOODLE), can support students to develop more responsibility for their learning. This view is supported by Masalela (Masalela, 2009). Furthermore, Garrison and Anderson (2003) argue that access to information is an important part of learning however student's learning is largely achieved through engagement and interaction with other students. This view is supported by Chen and Looi (Chen & Looi, 2007) who indicated that online discussion contains more opportunities for the practice of in depth clarification and inference skills.

The younger generations according to Prensky's (2010) "digital natives" use online technologies for their social and informational activities whilst older generations use these technologies less so. Furthermore, students engage in ways they prefer according to their preferences, interests or abilities.

The blended learning approach can meet the different needs and learning styles of students. Kupetz and Ziegenmeyer (Kupetz & Ziegenmeyer, 2005) discussed and evaluated a model of blended learning for teaching English and focussed on how different types of learners can be supported and their research covers a wide range of activities: classroom recordings, multimedia-based case stories, electronic interviews and mini-practices. Each of these activities was designed to support different aspects of student learning and to be flexible enough to respond to the needs of different types of learners. Similarly, Julian and Boone (2001) found that "the importance of a blended learning approach to learning is that it ensures the widest possible impact of a learning experience" (p. 58) and proves to be very useful in improving teachers' abilities to respond a wide range of students' needs. In addition, Ho (2006) found that blended learning courses result in lower dropout rates compared to fully online courses. This view is supported by Dzuiban and Moskal (Dziuban & Moskal, 2001) who reported that students' withdrawal rates were reduced in blended learning courses.

Research literature elsewhere indicates that the blended learning approach can bring teachers and students closer together (Aspden & Helm, 2004; Graetz & Goliber, 2002). Aspden and Helm (2004) explored student engagement and interaction with students in the context of a blended learning situation and argue that the blended learning approach can help bring teachers and students together by making appropriate use of a mix of technologies students can feel increased connectivity with both their fellow students and university staff.

To increase the likelihood of positive student learning outcomes using the blended learning approach teachers must adopt new technologies (Piccoli, Ahmad, & Ives, 2001). Teachers publish their learning resources in learning management systems and students participate through computer networks. Teachers who use a learning management system can share course materials, syllabus, opinions and online assessments as well as use e-mail, discussion boards, calendars, blogs, journals, along with traditional face-to-face activities such as lectures and tutorials. Simply placing existing material online does not serve the students. Gerbic (2011) refers to this as "juxtaposition of two pedagogical settings" (p.222). Instead, the focus should be on recognising the potential of the blended learning approach to enhance student's learning outcomes. Garrison and Vaughan (2008) state that blended courses require these elements:

1. In-class activities that link the online assignments so as to reinforce the intent of activities outside the classroom;
2. Shift from teacher-centred to learner-centred activities in class as well as online;
3. Focus on student responsibility for navigating online resources and conducting online research; and
4. Evaluation instruments that provide frequent feedback.

A positive attitude towards computers and the Internet, for example, where teaching staff are not afraid of the complexity of using computers, will result in effective learners in a blended learning environment (Piccoli ct al., 2001). Research results suggested that applying online technology in the classroom enhances students' achievement (Masalela, 2009). Evaluation instruments can provide frequent feedback such as an electronic grade book that captures students' accomplishments, reviewing course materials and communicating with teachers can be carried out more efficiently. In their quantitative study Amrein-Beardsley, Foulger and Toth (2007) investigated nine instructors perceptions of their students' and their own experiences with hybrid courses. From the questionnaires they concluded that students found the online grade book and announcements most useful. Students appreciated instructors who graded assignments and posted them in the grade book in a timely and efficient manner. Students found the course document downloads, Internet sites and links sent to them from the instructors equally useful in terms of technology tools that enhanced their learning.

Despite these advantages for teachers to incorporate the blended learning approach into teaching practice, thorough reviews of the literature have yet to show a reliable body of knowledge indicating that these benefits are an outcome for all students. Much of the research on blended learning reveals that deep learning is not easily achieved using the blended learning approach (Garrison & Vaughan, 2008; Kanuka, 2008). These findings are consistent with prior research that has shown that these benefits are not easily achieved in face-to-face teaching (Biggs, 1999; P. Ramsden, 1991).

Other authors found that blended learning courses had negative outcomes.

Disadvantages of the Blended Learning Approach

A review of the literature suggests that there are five disadvantages for teachers to incorporate the blended learning approach into teaching practice:

1. Possibility of negative effects such as innovation fatigue amongst staff and students (Oliver & Trigwell, 2005);
2. Not enough guidance for students;
3. LMS technical issues;

4.   Lack of interaction on the LMS; and
5.   Unsatisfactory use of the face-to-face teaching time (Heinze & Procter, 2004).

Research indicates students' attitudes towards computers and the Internet is an important factor in the effectiveness of the blended learning approach (J. Arbaugh et al., 2009) (J. B. Arbaugh, 2002; Garrison & Vaughan, 2008; Piccoli et al., 2001; Sharpe & Benfield, 2005). Furthermore, several researchers indicate that technology quality affects student satisfaction with blended learning environments (Piccoli et al., 2001; Webster & Hackley, 1997). Research has shown that the learning environment is an alterable educational variable that can directly influence student outcomes (Waxman, Huang, & Wang, 1997).

Furthermore, studies have suggested that, in addition to adjusting to the technology delivered instruction, students must also adapt to the "learning approach" adopted by the tertiary institution. According to Garrison and Vaughan (2008, p. ix) "those who have grown up with interactive technology are not always comfortable with the information transmission approach of large lectures. Students expect a relevant and engaging learning approach" (p.ix). The idea of the "digital native" (Prensky, 2001) suggests that students will be able to use online methods of engagement, such as blogs, social media, wikis and mobile devices effectively and efficiently having grown up with the technologies. Prensky (2006) argues "today's students are no longer the people our educational system was designed to teach" (p. 2). This suggests that students who have grown up with technology may be better suited to the blended learning approach (Laurillard, 2002; Palloff & Pratt, 1999).

Elsewhere in the literature, Chen and Looi (Chen & Looi, 2007) found that in-class online discussion lacked interaction, because most of the online postings were task oriented, independent postings without replies and comments on postings by others. Secondly, too much online discussion in-class may slow the progress of the class. Thirdly, in-class online discussion does not assure that every learner will read the online postings, because reading online discussion was not a compulsory practice. Chen and Looi (Chen & Looi, 2007) research examined how to incorporate online discussion in a face-to-face classroom learning study comprising of sixteen Heads of Departments of Information Technology from Singapore schools who attended a professional development course. These findings are consistent with Collis et al's (Collis, Bruijstens, & van Veen, 2003) statement that online learning often requires a large amount of self-discipline on the part of the learners and Salmon (Gilly Salmon, 2002) who states that one of the main disadvantages of blended learning is the lack of interaction between students. In addition, Ellis and Calco (R. Ellis & Calvo, 2004) found that undergraduate students could not connect the discussions in face-to-face teaching time and online to the goals of the course. These finding are consistent with Molesworth (Molesworth*, 2004) who found a lack of participation in computer-mediated classes with students wanting more integration into the overall course.

It has been suggested in the literature that teachers require better skills to incorporate the blended learning approach in their teaching (Coates et al., 2005). Salmon (2005) states that uploading PowerPoint slides into the learning management system is not enough to create good quality online learning materials. This view is supported by Heinze and Proctor's action research study that examined staff opinions regarding the delivery of a program at the University of Salford using blended learning. Heinze and Proctor (2004) found that simply using a learning management system instead of web pages to deliver handouts and presentations and combining it with discussion boards resulted in staff stating that they were not really doing any e-learning on the course.

Picciano's Blending with Purpose Multimodal model was derived from discussions above on blending learning environments, generations, personality types and learning styles.

Blending with Purpose: The Multimodal Model

The structure of this paper is based on Picciano's Blending with Purpose Multimodal framework (see Figure 1 below). Picciano (2009) Blending with Purpose Multimodal framework recognises that because students represent different generations, different personality types, and different learning styles, teachers should seek use multiple approaches including face-to-face methods and online technologies to meet the needs of a wide scope of students.

A significant component of this model is that teachers need to carefully consider their objectives and understand how to apply the technologies and approaches that will work best for their students. There are six pedagogical objectives used in the model above: content, social/emotional contexts, dialectic/ questioning activities, synthesis/evaluation tools, collaboration/student-generated content, and reflection opportunities. Learning management systems and other online tools provide a number of mechanisms for assisting teachers meet these objectives.

Figure 1. Blending with Purpose: The Multimodal Model
Source: Picciano (A. Picciano, 2009) (p.11)

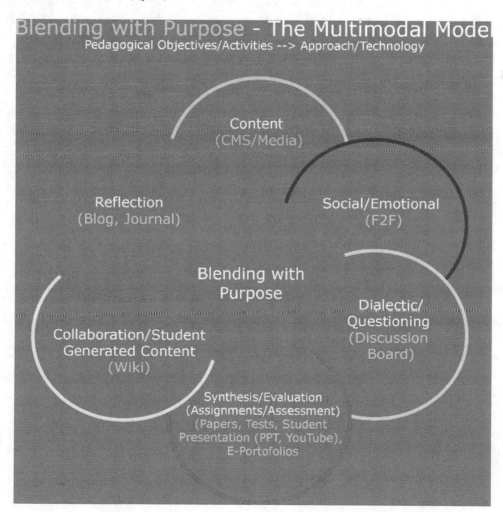

Teachers' Conceptions of Blended Learning

Considerable research has been carried out into teachers' conceptions of face-to-face teaching (Paul Ramsden, 2003; Saljo, 1979; Trigwell, Prosser, & Taylor, 1994) and what impact this may have on the way university teachers carry out their teaching. Entwistle (2005) suggests that there are relationships between teachers' conceptions of teaching (including their beliefs about teaching) and their approaches to teaching. An understanding of teachers' conceptions is therefore likely to help in the process of understanding and improving teaching (Prosser, Trigwell, & Taylor, 1994). Kember and Kwan (2000) identified two main approaches to teaching: 'content centred', in which teachers focus on the content to be taught; and 'learner centred' where teachers focus on the learning process.

As this literature review shows, there are thirteen studies focussed on teachers' conceptions, beliefs and experiences of blended learning and their approaches to both design and teaching in face-to-face and online settings. Teachers' conceptions of blended learning have been investigated with five studies reported research into teaching with e-learning (R. A. Ellis, Steed, et al., 2006; Gonzalez, 2009; Lameras, Paraskakis, & Levy, 2008; McConnell & Zhao, 2006; Roberts, 2003). From these five studies, one had been conducted in a 'distance education' setting (Gonzalez, 2009) and one reported conceptions of blended teaching (R. A. Ellis, Steed, et al., 2006). A couple of studies have investigated teachers' "beliefs", which are considered different from "conceptions" according to the literature (Elizabeth Stacey & Wiesenberg, 2007; Steel, 2009). The six remaining studies focussed on teachers' conceptions and experiences of working with learning management systems (Gedik, Kiraz, & Ozden, 2013; Jokinen & Mikkonen, 2013; King & Arnold, 2012; McShane, 2004; Napier, Dekhane, & Smith, 2011; Ocak, 2011).

Picciano's (2009) Blended with Purpose Multimodal framework comprises of six objectives: content; socially and emotionally; dialectic/questioning; collaboration; synthesis/evaluation and reflection. These six objectives affect teachers' approaches to both design and teaching in face-to-face and online settings. Much of the research in one objective impacts the other objectives.

First, the Blending with Purpose Multimodal framework suggests that delivering content is one of the main objectives of teaching and there are many ways in which content can be delivered and presented to students. Blended learning allows teachers an ongoing opportunity to experiment with new approaches to learning and introduce new types of educational technology into their teaching such as the Web and learning management systems. Learning management systems enable the delivery of a variety of media including text, video and audio. In providing and presenting content, the Blending with Purpose Multimodal framework suggests that multiple technologies and media be utilised. Research results suggest the teachers' conceptions of blended learning as a way to provide information to students by way of lecture notes, online learning resources and links to external websites (McConnell & Zhao, 2006; Oh & Park, 2009; Roberts, 2003).

McConnell and Zhao (2006) research examined the ways in which Chinese higher education teachers think about e-learning and e-teaching, and the ways in which they implement e-learning in a qualitative study. From twenty-four interviews they found a set of categories of conceptions:

1. The centrality of the learner (p.516);
2. Online co-operative learning (p.517);
3. Network learning (p.518);
4. Student learning (p.518); and
5. Infrastructure and access (p.519).

Their research findings suggest that face-to-face instruction using lectures were the preferred method of teaching with each teacher acknowledging the "sheer power of the lecture in the Chinese higher education system" (p.519). These results are supported by another study that examined faculty involvement in blended instruction and their attitudes towards the instructional method. Oh's (2009) quantitative study involved one hundred and fifty-one universities classified by the Carnegie Foundation. One hundred and thirty-three faculty members completed a survey and reported that the most commonly selected instructional delivery format used by faculty was "face-to-face instruction with supplementary online instructional components" (p.333). These results suggest that e-learning is conceived by teachers as not a good way to deliver course content to students with teachers preferring face-to-face methods.

In addition, Robert's (2003) phenomenographic study investigated the use of e-learning for teaching and the extent and nature of Web use for teaching and learning in a Scottish university. From a Web-based survey and interviews with seventeen teachers three conceptions of teaching using the Web were discovered, as well as a set of strategies to describe the approaches taken by lecturers. Conceptions of teaching using the web that were discovered are:

1. The web as a source of subject information (p.145): in this conception the Web is used the medium used to distribute information to students. Teachers upload learning materials such as lecture notes and direct students to websites to retrieve information.
2. The web is used for individual and independent self-paced learning (p.146): students use the Web to complete subject activities.
3. The web is used for group analysis, decision making and dialogue (p.147): the Web is used for students to interact with one another and create communities of inquiry (Garrison & Arbaugh, 2007).

These conceptions are consistent with McConnell and Zhao (McConnell & Zhao, 2006) definition of networked learning and Picciano's definition of content (A. Picciano, 2009) where teachers place material online and students are expected to learn at their own pace. At the University of Central Florida, learning to use technology to modify their teaching methods was cited as one of the outcomes that faculty liked most about teaching on the Web (Dziuban & Moskal, 2001). The fundamental principles underlying networked learning are learner-centred where the learning is outcome-focused and requires engagement, group collaboration and the creation of communities of inquiry (Garrison & Arbaugh, 2007).

Research results from this study are consistent with previous research outcomes from Kember and Khan (2000) who suggested that teachers rely on 'content-centred' approaches to transmit information to students. Like Roberts and McConnell and Zhao, Gonzalez also found teachers' conceptions focused on access to learning materials and information transfer. Gonzalez's (2009) phenomenographic study investigated what university teachers think eLearning is good for in their teaching. From interviews with seven teachers from the Faculty of Health Sciences three conceptions using eLearning were identified:

1. For individual access to learning materials and information, and for individual assessment (p.312);
2. For learning-related communication (p.312); and
3. For networked learning (p.312).

Gonzalez (2009) found that university teachers "having a 'content-centred' approach to teaching can be defined as 'informative-individual learning focused'; while those university teachers having a 'transitional or learner-centred' approach can be defined as 'communicative-networked learning focused'" (2009, p. 311).

Similar to the 'content-centred' conceptions found in the above studies, outcomes from Lameras, Paraskakis and Levy (2012) showed that teachers conceived eLearning as a way to transfer information to students where learning resources were uploaded for students to use on their own. This enables students to learn at their own pace. Lameras, Paraskasis and Levy (2012) qualitative study investigated Greek university teachers' conceptions of and approaches to teaching using digital technology in blended settings. Their interviews with twenty-five Computer Science teachers identified four categories that describe the use of virtual learning environments as a means of supporting:

1. Information transfer (p.145);
2. Application and clarification of concepts (p.145);
3. Exchange and development of ideas, and resource exploration and sharing (p.145); and
4. Collaborative knowledge-creation, and development of process awareness and skills (p.145).

The first and second category of conceptions support the content-centred approaches of the virtual management system and are supported by research carried out by McConnell and Zhao as well as Roberts (McConnell & Zhao, 2006; Roberts, 2003).The third and fourth category of conceptions support the learner-centred of the virtual management system and are supported by research carried out by Ellis, Steed and Applebee as well as McConnell and Zhao (R. A. Ellis, Steed, et al., 2006; McConnell & Zhao, 2006).

Second, the Blended with Purpose Multimodal framework suggests that email and electronic communications enable collaboration between students. Research results indicate teachers' conceptions of 'eLearning as a way to engage in communication-collaboration-knowledge building' (Gonzalez, 2010) and seen to engage students in discussion, developing understanding and building knowledge (R. A. Ellis, Steed, et al., 2006). In addition, blended learning is conceived as a way of engaging students in learning activities that may lead to higher-level learning experiences (Garrison & Kanuka, 2004).

In their qualitative study, Ellis, Steed and Applebee (2006) investigated the conceptions of blended learning and teaching by teachers in two campus-based Australian universities, and the relationships between these conceptions to their approaches to integrating online and face-to-face environments. From their interviews with twenty-two teachers they identified four conceptions of blended teaching:

1. Blended teaching as helping students develop and apply new concepts (p.324);
2. Blended teaching as developing student understanding through aligning media to intended learning outcomes (p.324);
3. Blended teaching as providing students with information (p.325); and
4. Blended teaching as replacing part of the responsibility of being a teacher (p.326).

The researchers found that teachers recognised a connection between students achieving their learning outcomes and the role of technology in blended settings helping students develop higher order thinking. Garrison and Kanuka (2004) argued that blended environments can support and transform universities by building a Community of Inquiry (Garrison & Arbaugh, 2007) and develop higher order thinking.

Third, the Blending with Purpose Multimodal framework suggests that the social and emotional needs of students should be considered by teachers when designing blended learning courses (McShane, 2004; Elizabeth Stacey & Wiesenberg, 2007). Stacey and Weisenberg (2007) study investigated teachers' beliefs about teaching face-to-face and online in two case studies of ten Australian and twelve Canadian university teachers. From an online open-ended questionnaire about teaching philosophies and approaches together with the Teaching Perspective Inventory which measures teachers beliefs. They found that twenty-two teachers regarded themselves as more teacher-centred in face-to-face settings and more learner-centred in online settings. The Australian teachers had a preference for teaching face-to-face because they believed that it enabled them to build better relationships with their students. In contrast, the Canadian teachers had a stronger preference for teaching online because they believed the mode could support multiple perspectives.

These conceptions are supported by research carried out by McShane's (2004) case study that investigated the personal experiences of five Australian lecturers who teach using an online learning management system (Web CT or Top Class) to organise the online components of their subjects. Five themes emerged across the individual case studies:

1. Enhanced relationships with students (p.8);
2. Planning and teaching becomes very conscious tasks (p.9);
3. Expansion, extension, augmentation (time and space) (p.10);
4. Scrutiny and reflexivity (p.11); and
5. The centrality of learning (p.12).

McShane (2004) found that university teachers perceived their teaching approaches where no different when they were teaching face-to-face to when they were teaching online. These findings were inconsistent with studies identified in this literature that show that teachers' approaches can differ considerably when changing modes of teaching.

The fourth objective from the Blending with Purpose Multimodal framework suggests that dialectic/questioning is an important activity that allows faculty to explore what students know and to refine their knowledge. For dialectic and questioning activities, a well- organised discussion board activity generally seeks to present a topic or issue and have students respond to questions, provide their own perspectives while also evaluating and responding to the opinions of others (Steel, 2009). Research results indicate that teachers are advised to take deliberate action once courses begin towards creating a community of inquiry (Garrison & Arbaugh, 2007) such as monitoring and responding to online discussion board postings (Conrad, 2005).

Steel (2009) investigated the relationship between teacher beliefs and their learning designs for learning management systems in large undergraduate classes in her qualitative study. Three award winning university teachers from an Australian university were interviewed. The research identified "strong affective components" (p.414) of the teachers' belief systems that demonstrate a commitment to engage with their students, build learning communities and use technologies to support social justice and equity. Faculty who have taught blended learning courses have observed that students do a better job of writing, learning course material, mastering concepts, and applying what they have learned compared to traditional face-to-face courses (Aycock, Garnham, & Kaleta, 2002). This viewpoint is captured in a comment from a faculty member at the University of Wisconsin who teaches blended courses, "My students have done better that I have ever seen; they are motivated, enthused and doing their best work" (p.3).

The fifth objective from the Blending with Purpose Multimodal framework suggests that students receive feedback from teachers regarding their academic progress. Learning management systems provide a number of mechanisms for assisting teachers to assess their student's learning and provide feedback.

Major methods include electronic tests, assignments and portfolios (Gedik et al., 2013; Jokinen & Mikkonen, 2013; King & Arnold, 2012). In sum, learning management systems provides an on-going record that can be referred to over and over again by both students and teachers. Gedik, Kiraz and Ozden (2013) qualitative study investigated instructor experiences relating to the design, development and implementation processes of a blended course. They found several themes emerged: arousal of student's interest and participation, flexibility, time conservation, improvement of interaction, collaboration and communication opportunities and the ability to track student's progress.

In another qualitative study, King and Arnold (2012) explored five professors who teach in blended learning environments and examined whether course preparation and design, communication and motivation are taken into consideration when designing their courses. All the professors used a learning management system for the online component. From a survey and interviews with five professors from the college of education at a Mid-western research university, four factors were found to contribute to the success of blended learning courses:

1. Course preparation (p.51): The professors prepared their blended courses in various ways and used technology, such as Skype, wikis and blogs in addition to the learning management system.
2. Course design (p.52): The professors used the content feature of the learning management system to post course documents and assignments which support the content-centred approach of teaching (Kember & Kwan, 2000).
3. Communication (p.53): The importance of communicating with students in a timely manner is consistent with research findings in blended learning Ho, Lu and Thurmaier (Ho et al., 2006). The professors used the discussion board in various ways. One professor required the students to complete weekly journals that were viewed by student and professor only enabling a confidential dialogue and the student's time to reflect on what they had learnt.
4. Motivation (p.53). These results are supported by research carried out by Aycock, Garnham and Kaleta (Aycock et al., 2002).

According to King and Arnold (King & Arnold, 2012) "preparing for a blended learning course requires more discipline and preparation time than a traditional face-to-face course" (p.51). The literature records challenges to the use of blended learning environments in other studies. The commonly found issues were increased time commitment and workload (Edginton & Holbrook, 2010; Gedik et al., 2013; King & Arnold, 2012; Napier et al., 2011). The increased time commitment involved in designing a blended course is regarded as the number one challenge by faculty (Dziuban & Moskal, 2001). This view is echoed in Napier (2011) research (discussed below) where several success factors for teaching and designing blended learning courses were identified:

1. Play to your strengths;
2. Utilize technology;
3. Build a classroom without walls;
4. Provide tutoring and on-line support; and
5. Creatively manage out-of-class time.

Napier (2011) examined the perceptions of instructors teaching blended learning courses at a small public liberal arts college and found that instructors invest more time becoming familiar with available technology, creating in-class activities and reflecting on course structure. These results are also supported by research carried out by Edginton and Holbrook (2010) who found that teachers teaching blended learning courses can expect to invest more time becoming familiar with available technology and creating in-class activities. These research results contradict Garrison and Vaughan's (2008) argument. They argued that, blended learning environments can ease the workload. Similarly, all faculty members involved in a blended learning program at the University of Wisconsin, Milwaukee stated that they will continue to teach blended learning courses as they believe that their time was wisely invested in improving the learning environment for both students and faculty members (Aycock et al., 2002).

Jokinen and Mikkonen (2013) qualitative study described teachers' experiences of planning and implementing teaching and learning in a blended learning based nursing programme. Nine themes emerged from the data including: collaborative planning; integration; student group; face-to-face teaching; online learning; learning activities; teaching and learning methods; learning in and about work; and confirming competences (2013, p. 526).

These researchers found that teachers experienced the blended learning approach positively despite challenges from the viewpoint of planning and design. According to the study careful planning is required by teachers to ensure the combination of face-to-face learning and learning in practice with technology-mediated learning activities. These findings are supported by previous studies of Salmon (2005) as well as Heinze and Proctor (2004). Moreover, while planning for blended learning, teachers should include a variety of learning activities to meet the needs of different learners (A. Picciano, 2009).

Lastly, the Blending with Purpose Multimodal framework suggests that the ability to share one's reflection with others can be most beneficial however this objective is the least researched objective. Pedagogical activities that require students to reflect on what they are learning and to share their reflection with their teachers and fellow students are viewed very positively. Blogs and blogging, whether as group activities or for individual journaling activities, are appropriate tools for students reflecting on what is being learned. Ocak (2011) qualitative study examined problems and challenges faculty members encountered in blended learning environments and found class discussions that take place on discussion boards or blogs and provide teachers with an electronic record that can be reviewed over and over again to examine how students have participated and progressed over time.

These predominantly qualitatively studies draw attention to the importance of teachers' conceptions and beliefs of teaching in face-to-face and online settings.

METHOD

A comprehensive literature review was conducted to locate papers on teachers' perceptions on blended learning using search engines and educational databases such as Academic Search Elite, ProQuest, ERIC (Education Resources Information Centre), and Google Scholar. The keywords used were blended learning, blended learning environments, blended teaching, online teaching, eLearning, teacher perceptions, teachers conceptions (as well as combinations of these). Literature related to teachers working across face-to-face and online environments were included in this review.

Selecting only those papers, which specifically focussed on blended learning in higher education, and reported the results of empirical research, further refined this search. Conference papers and dissertations were not included. References from the articles included in the review were examined in order to identify other relevant studies. Following this literature search a database including approximately ninety-seven titles was created using EndNote.

There are four published texts (Bonk & Graham, 2006; Littlejohn & Pegler, 2007; A. G. Picciano et al., 2013; E. Stacey & Gerbic, 2009); there were few publications, which directly discussed teacher's perspectives on blended teaching.

DISCUSSION

Blended learning research on teachers' conceptions, beliefs and experiences of teaching in face-to-face and online settings reflects all six objectives of the Blending with Purpose Multimodal framework but student-generated content and reflection were not used to their fullest capacity. Teachers focused mainly on content, social/emotional aspects of blended learning courses for their students, and synthesis/evaluation tools. The studies in this literature review contained faculty-driven rather than student-generated content, as was suggested by Picciano (2009) as part of the design of the multimodal model. This literature review shows the importance of teachers' conceptions, beliefs and experiences and their approaches to both designing and teaching in face-to-face and online settings including learning management systems. In addition, relationships between conceptions and approaches found in previous research have been confirmed. Research results indicate that teachers use multiple approaches including face-to-face methods and online technologies that address the learning needs of a variety of students from different generations, personality types and learning styles.

Even though these studies have been conducted in different settings and by different researchers, many similarities in research results can be seen. Research results indicate that teachers merge several objectives of the Blending with Purpose Multimodal framework together to create learning experiences. Teachers utilise multiple approaches and technologies as a way to transfer information to students. Learning resources are uploaded for students to use on their own and teachers provide information to students in the form of lecture notes, online resources and websites. This enables students to learn at their own pace. Teachers can engage in communications and learning activities with students including email, blogs and discussion boards. Electronic communications enable collaboration between students. Teachers develop pedagogical activities that require students to reflect on what they are learning and to share their reflection with their teachers and fellow students are viewed very positively. Teachers use discussion to present a topic or issue and have students respond to questions, provide their own perspectives while also evaluating and responding to the opinions of others.

The research in blended learning so far has focused more on what teachers need to know in order to integrate technology into their teaching (Mishra & Koehler, 2006) rather than on personal support tools to enable students to use blended learning environments effectively and to learn efficiently. Most studies have been conducted as case studies. Yin (2009) argued that "a case study investigates a contemporary phenomenon within its real-life context" (p.13). Even though the case study has this advantage, this research area needs other research methods. The Blending with Purpose Multimodal framework used in this paper can be used as a conceptual framework to examine the effectiveness of blended learning courses. The Blending with Purpose Multimodal framework shows what objectives teachers should consider when designing blended learning courses.

As this literature review shows, teachers' conceptions and approaches to both design and teaching using blended learning environments is still a developing issue. More research is also needed to gain a more comprehensive understanding of teachers' perceptions and problems that these teachers face when integrating pedagogy and content knowledge into blended learning environments, the strategies they employ to address these problems, and how they use the blended learning tools (e.g., learning management systems) to overcome these challenges. Discovering what type of pedagogical and technology changes are being made to blended learning courses, being able to identify design problems, and finding solutions to design and development issues are extremely important to blended learning. The Blending with Purpose Multimodal framework (A. Picciano, 2009) should also be compared to other frameworks to discover to what extent pedagogical frameworks are helping teachers to integrate pedagogy and content knowledge into blended learning environments.

REFERENCES

Amrein-Beardsley, A., Foulger, T. S., & Toth, M. (2007). Examining the Development of a Hybrid Degree Program: Using Student and Instructor Data to Inform Decision-Making. *Journal of Research on Technology in Education*, *39*(4), 27. doi:10.1080/15391523.2007.10782486

Arbaugh, J., Godfrey, M. R., Johnson, M., Pollack, B. L., Niendorf, B., & Wresch, W. (2009). Research in online and blended learning in the business disciplines: Key findings and possible future directions. *The Internet and Higher Education*, *12*(2), 71–87. doi:10.1016/j.iheduc.2009.06.006

Arbaugh, J. B. (2002). Managing the on-line classroom. *The Journal of High Technology Management Research*, *13*(2), 203–223. doi:10.1016/S1047-8310(02)00049-4

Aspden, L., & Helm, P. (2004). Making the Connection in a Blended Learning Environment. *Educational Media International*, *41*(3), 245–252. doi:10.1080/09523980410001680851

Aycock, A., Garnham, C., & Kaleta, R. (2002). Lessons learned from the hybrid course project. *Teaching with Technology Today, 8*(6), 9-21.

Biggs, J. (1999). *Teaching for quality learning at university: what the student does*. Buckingham, UK: Society for Research into Higher Education.

Bliuc, A.-M., Goodyear, P., & Ellis, R. A. (2007). Research focus and methodological choices in studies into students experiences of blended learning in higher education. *The Internet and Higher Education*, *10*(4), 231–244. doi:10.1016/j.iheduc.2007.08.001

Bonk, C., & Graham, C. (2006). *The Handbook of Blended Learning: Global Perspectives, Local Designs*. San Francisco, CA: Pfeiffer.

Bouhnik, D., & Marcus, T. (2006). Interaction in distance,Äêlearning courses. *Journal of the American Society for Information Science and Technology*, *57*(3), 299–305. doi:10.1002/asi.20277

Brabazon, T. (2002). *Digital hemlock: Internet education and the poisoning of teaching*. Sydney: UNSW Press.

Chamberlin, S., & Moon, S. (2005). Model-eliciting activities: An introduction to gifted education. *Journal of Secondary Gifted Education*, *17*(1), 37–47.

Chen, W., & Looi, C. (2007). Incorporating online discussion in face to face classroom learning: A new blended learning approach. *Australasian Journal of Educational Technology, 23*(3), 307. doi:10.14742/ajet.1255

Coates, H., James, R., & Baldwin, G. (2005). A critical examination of the effects of learning management systems on university teaching and learning. *Tertiary Education and Management, 11*, 19-36.

Collis, B., Bruijstens, H., & van Veen, J. K. (2003). Course redesign for blended learning: Modern optics for technical professionals. *International Journal of Continuing Engineering Education and Lifelong Learning, 13*(1), 22–38. doi:10.1504/IJCEELL.2003.002151

Concannon, F., Flynn, A., & Campbell, M. (2005). What campus-based students think about the quality and benefits of e-learning. *British Journal of Educational Technology, 36*(3), 501–512. doi:10.1111/j.1467-8535.2005.00482.x

Conrad, D. (2005). Building and maintaining community in cohort-based online learning. *Journal of Distance Education, 20*(1), 1.

De Lange, P., Suwardy, T., & Mavondo, F. (2003). Integrating a virtual learning environment into an introductory accounting course: Determinants of student motivation. *Accounting Education, 12*(1), 1–14. doi:10.1080/0963928032000064567

De Witt, C., & Kerres, M. (2003). A didactical framework for the design of blended learning arrangements. *Journal of Educational Media, 28*(2/3), 101–114. doi:10.1080/1358165032000165653

Delialioglu, O., & Yildirim, Z. (2008). Design and development of a technology enhanced hybrid instruction based on MOLTA model: Its effectiveness in comparison to traditional instruction. *Computers & Education, 51*(1), 474–483. doi:10.1016/j.compedu.2007.06.006

Demetriadis, S., & Pombortsis, A. (2007). E-lectures for flexible learning: A study on their learning efficiency. *Journal of Educational Technology and Society, 10*(2), 147.

Dzakiria, H., Wahab, M. S. D. A., & Rahman, H. D. A. (2012). Blended Learning (BL) as Pedagogical Alternative to Teach Business Communication Course: Case Study of UUM Executive Diploma Program. *Turkish Online Journal of Distance Education, 13*(3).

Dziuban, C., & Moskal, P. (2001). Evaluating distributed learning at metropolitan universities. *EDUCAUSE Quarterly, 24*(4), 60–61.

Edginton, A., & Holbrook, J. (2010). A blended learning approach to teaching basic pharmacokinetics and the significance of face-to-face interaction. *American Journal of Pharmaceutical Education, 74*(5), 88. doi:10.5688/aj740588 PMID:20798797

Ellis, R., & Calvo, R. (2004). Learning through discussions in blended environments. *Educational Media International, 41*(3), 263–274. doi:10.1080/09523980410001680879

Ellis, R. A., Goodyear, P., Prosser, M., & OHara, A. (2006). How and what university students learn through online and face-to-face discussion: Conceptions, intentions and approaches. *Journal of Computer Assisted Learning, 22*(4), 244–256. doi:10.1111/j.1365-2729.2006.00173.x

Ellis, R. A., Steed, A. F., & Applebee, A. C. (2006). Teacher conceptions of blended learning, blended teaching and associations with approaches to design. *Australasian Journal of Educational Technology*, *22*(3), 312. doi:10.14742/ajet.1289

Entwistle, N. (2005). Learning outcomes and ways of thinking across contrasting disciplines and settings in higher education. *Curriculum Journal*, *16*(1), 67–82. doi:10.1080/09585170042000336818

Garrison, D. R., & Anderson, T. (2003). *E-learning in the 21st century: A framework for research and practice*. Routledge.

Garrison, D. R., Anderson, T., & Archer, W. (1999). Critical inquiry in a text-based environment: Computer conferencing in higher education. *The Internet and Higher Education*, *2*(2), 87–105. doi:10.1016/S1096-7516(00)00016-6

Garrison, D. R., & Arbaugh, J. B. (2007). Researching the community of inquiry framework: Review, issues, and future directions. *The Internet and Higher Education*, *10*(3), 157–172. doi:10.1016/j.iheduc.2007.04.001

Garrison, D. R., & Kanuka, H. (2004). Blended learning: Uncovering its transformative potential in higher education. *The Internet and Higher Education*, *7*(2), 95–105. doi:10.1016/j.iheduc.2004.02.001

Garrison, D. R., & Vaughan, N. (2008). *Blended learning in higher education; framework, principles, and guidelines* (Vol. 23). Academic Press.

Gedik, N., Kiraz, E., & Ozden, M. Y. (2013). Design of a blended learning environment: Considerations and implementation issues. *Australasian Journal of Educational Technology*, *29*(1). doi:10.14742/ajet.6

Gerbic, P. (2011). Teaching using a blended approach - what does the literature tell us? *Educational Media International*, *48*(3), 221–234. doi:10.1080/09523987.2011.615159

Ginns, P., & Ellis, R. (2007). Quality in blended learning: Exploring the relationships between on-line and face-to-face teaching and learning. *The Internet and Higher Education*, *10*(1), 53–64. doi:10.1016/j.iheduc.2006.10.003

Ginns, P., Prosser, M., & Barrie, S. (2007). Students perceptions of teaching quality in higher education: The perspective of currently enrolled students. *Studies in Higher Education*, *32*(5), 603–615. doi:10.1080/03075070701573773

Gonzalez, C. (2009). Conceptions of, and approaches to, teaching online: A study of lecturers teaching postgraduate distance courses. *Higher Education*, *57*(3), 299–314. doi:10.1007/s10734-008-9145-1

Gonzalez, C. (2010). What do university teachers think eLearning is good for in their teaching? *Studies in Higher Education*, *35*(1), 61–78. doi:10.1080/03075070902874632

Graetz, K. A., & Goliber, M. J. (2002). Designing collaborative learning places: Psychological foundations and new frontiers. *New Directions for Teaching and Learning*, *2002*(92), 13–22. doi:10.1002/tl.75

Graham, C. R. (2006). Blended Learning Systems. Definitions, current trends and future directions. In C. J. Bonk & C. R. Graham (Eds.), The Handbook of Blended Learning: Global Perspectives, Local Designs (pp. 3-21). San Francisco: Pfeiffer.

Graham, C. R., Allen, S., & Ure, D. (2003). *Blended learning environments: A review of the research literature.* Unpublished manuscript, Provo, UT.

Graham, C. R., Allen, S., & Ure, D. (2005). Benefits and challenges of blended learning environments. In M. Khosrow-Pour (Ed.), *Encyclopedia of information science and technology* (pp. 53–259). Hershey, PA: Idea Group. doi:10.4018/978-1-59140-553-5.ch047

Heinze, A., & Procter, C. (2004). *Reflections on the use of blended learning.* Academic Press.

Hermann, N., Popyack, J. L., Char, B., & Zoski, P. (2004). *Assessment of a course redesign: introductory computer programming using online modules.* Academic Press.

Ho, A., Lu, L., & Thurmaier, K. (2006). Testing the reluctant professor's hypothesis: evaluating a blended-learning approach to distance education. *Journal of Public Affairs Education*, 81-102.

Jefferies, P., Grodzinsky, F., & Griffin, J. (2003). Advantages and problems in using information communication technologies to support the teaching of a multi-institutional computer ethics course. *Journal of Educational Media*, 28(2-3), 191–202. doi:10.1080/1358165032000165644

Jokinen, P., & Mikkonen, I. (2013). Teachers experiences of teaching in a blended learning environment. *Nurse Education in Practice*, 13(6), 524–528. doi:10.1016/j.nepr.2013.03.014 PMID:23608218

Jones, N., & Lau, A. M. S. (2010). Blending learning: Widening participation in higher education. *Innovations in Education and Teaching International*, 47(4), 405–416. doi:10.1080/14703297.2010.518424

Jones, S., Johnson-Yale, C., Millermaier, S., & Pérez, F. S. (2008). Academic work, the Internet and US college students. *The Internet and Higher Education*, 11(3-4), 165–177. doi:10.1016/j.iheduc.2008.07.001

Julian, E., & Boone, C. (2001). *Blended learning solutions: Improving the way companies manage intellectual capital: An IDC whitepaper.* IDC.

Kaleta, R., Skibba, K., & Joosten, T. (2007). *Discovering, designing, and delivering hybrid courses. Blended Learning: Research Perspectives.* Needham, MA: The Sloan Consortium.

Kanuka, H. (2008). Understanding e-learning technologies-in-practice through philosophies-in-practice. *The theory and practice of online learning*, 91-118.

Kanuka, H., & Kelland, J. (2008). Has e-learning delivered on its promises? Expert opinion on the impact of e-learning in higher education. *Canadian Journal of Higher Education*, 38(1), 45–65.

Kember, D., & Kwan, K.-P. (2000). Lecturers approaches to teaching and their relationship to conceptions of good teaching. *Instructional Science*, 28(5), 469–490. doi:10.1023/A:1026569608656

King, S. E., & Arnold, K. C. (2012). Blended Learning Environments in Higher Education: A Case Study of How Professors Make It Happen. *Mid-Western Educational Researcher*, 25(1), 44–59.

Knight, S. (2009). *Effective practice in a digital age.* Bristol, UK: JISC Innovation Group, University of Bristol.

Kupetz, R., & Ziegenmeyer, B. (2005). Blended Learning in a Teacher Training Course: Integrated Interactive E-Learning and Contact Learning. *ReCALL*, 17(2), 179–196. doi:10.1017/S0958344005000327

Lameras, P., Levy, P., Paraskakis, I., & Webber, S. (2012). Blended university teaching using virtual learning environments: Conceptions and approaches. *Instructional Science, 40*(1), 141–157. doi:10.1007/s11251-011-9170-9

Lameras, P., Paraskakis, I., & Levy, P. (2008). *Conceptions of teaching using virtual learning environments: preliminary findings from a phenomenographic inquiry.* Paper presented at the 6th International Conference on Networked Learning.

Lapadat, J. C. (2002). Written interaction: A key component in online learning. *Journal of Computer-Mediated Communication, 7*(4).

Laurillard, D. (2002). *Rethinking university teaching: a conversational framework for the effective use of learning technologies.* London: RoutledgeFalmer. doi:10.4324/9780203304846

Liaw, S.-S., Huang, H.-M., & Chen, G.-D. (2007). An activity-theoretical approach to investigate learners‚Äô factors toward e-learning systems. *Computers in Human Behavior, 23*(4), 1906–1920. doi:10.1016/j.chb.2006.02.002

Littlejohn, A., & Pegler, C. (2007). *Preparing for Blended Learning. Milton Park.* Abingdon, UK: Routledge.

Lock, J. V. (2006). A new image: Online communities to facilitate teacher professional development. *Journal of Technology and Teacher Education, 14*(4), 663–678.

Masalela, R. K. (2009). Potential benefits and complexities of blended learning in higher education: The case of the University of Botswana. *Turkish Online Journal of Distance Education, 10*(1), 66–82.

McConnell, D., & Zhao, J. (2006). Chinese higher education teachers' conceptions of e-Learning: Preliminary outcomes. Paper presented at the 23rd Annual Ascilite Conference: Who's Learning? Whose technology?

McShane, K. (2004). Integrating face-to-face and online teaching: Academics' role concept and teaching choices. *Teaching in Higher Education, 9*(1), 3–16.

Mishra, P., & Koehler, M. J. (2006). Technological Pedagogical Content Knowledge: A Framework for Teacher Knowledge. *Teachers College Record, 108*(6), 1017–1054. doi:10.1111/j.1467-9620.2006.00684.x

Molesworth, M. (2004). Collaboration, reflection and selective neglect: campus-based marketing students' experiences of using a virtual learning environment. *Innovations in Education and Teaching International, 41*(1), 79-92.

Mortera-Gutierrez, F. (2006). Faculty Best Practices Using Blended Learning in E-Learning and Face-to-Face Instruction. *International Journal on E-Learning, 5*(3), 313–337.

Motteram, G. (2006). Blended education and the transformation of teachers: A long term case study in postgraduate UK Higher Education. *British Journal of Educational Technology, 37*(1), 17–30. doi:10.1111/j.1467-8535.2005.00511.x

Napier, N. P., Dekhane, S., & Smith, S. (2011). Transitioning to Blended Learning: Understanding Student and Faculty Perceptions. *Journal of Asynchronous Learning Networks, 15*(1), 20–32.

Ocak, M. A. (2011). Why are faculty members not teaching blended courses? Insights from faculty members. *Computers & Education, 56*(3), 689–699. doi:10.1016/j.compedu.2010.10.011

Oh, E., & Park, S. (2009). How are universities involved in blended instruction? *Journal of Educational Technology & Society, 12*(3), 327–342.

Oliver, M., & Trigwell, K. (2005). Can'Blended Learning'Be Redeemed? *E-Learning and Digital Media, 2*(1), 17–26.

Palloff, R. M., & Pratt, K. (1999). *Building learning communities in cyberspace: effective strategies for the online classroom.* San Francisco: Jossey-Bass Publishers.

Picciano, A. (2009). Blending with purpose: The multimodal model. *Journal of the Research Center for Educational Technology, 5*(1), 4–14.

Picciano, A. G., Dziuban, C. D., & Graham, C. R. (2013). *Blended learning: Research perspectives* (Vol. 2). United States of America: The Sloan Consortium.

Piccoli, G., Ahmad, R., & Ives, B. (2001). Web-Based Virtual Learning Environments: A Research Framework and a Preliminary Assessment of Effectiveness in Basic IT Skills Training. *Management Information Systems Quarterly, 25*(4), 401–426. doi:10.2307/3250989

Prendergast, G. (2004). *Blended collaborative learning: online teaching of online educators.* Global Educator.

Prensky, M. (2001). Digital natives, digital immigrants Part 1. *On the horizon, 9*(5), 1–6. doi:10.1108/10748120110424816

Prensky, M. (2006). Adopt and adapt. *Edutopia, 1*(9), 42–45.

Prensky, M. (2010). *Teaching Digital Natives.* London: SAGE Ltd.

Prosser, M., Trigwell, K., & Taylor, P. (1994). A phenomenographic study of academics conceptions of science learning and teaching. *Learning and Instruction, 4*(3), 217–231. doi:10.1016/0959-4752(94)90024-8

Ramsden, P. (1991). A performance indicator of teaching quality in higher education: The Course Experience Questionnaire. *Studies in Higher Education, 16*(2), 129–150. doi:10.1080/03075079112331382944

Ramsden, P. (2003). *Learning to teach in higher education.* New York: RoutledgeFalmer.

Roberts, G. (2003). Teaching using the web: Conceptions and approaches from a phenomenographic perspective. *Instructional Science, 31*(1-2), 127–150. doi:10.1023/A:1022547619474

Rodriguez, M. A., & Anicete, R. C. R. (2010). Students' Views of a Mixed Hybrid Ecology Course. *MERLOT Journal of Online Learning and Teaching, 6*, 791–798.

Saljo, R. (1979). *Learning in the learner's perspective. I. Some common-sense conceptions.* ERIC Clearinghouse.

Salmon, G. (2002). *E-tivities: the key to active online learning.* Falmer Press, Limited.

Salmon, G. (2005). Flying not flapping: A strategic framework for e-learning and pedagogical innovation in higher education institutions. *ALT-J, 13*(3), 201–218. doi:10.1080/09687760500376439

Saundercook, J., & Cooper, P. (2003). *4th annual technology and student success in higher education. A research study on faculty perceptions of technology and student success.* Toronto: McGraw-Hill Ryerson.

Sharpe, R. (2006). *The undergraduate experience of blended e-learning: a review of UK literature and practice.* The Higher Education Academy York.

Sharpe, R., & Benfield, G. (2005). The Student Experience of E-learning in Higher Education. *Brookes eJournal of Learning and Teaching, 1*(3).

Shivetts, C. (2011). *E-Learning and Blended Learning: The Importance of the Learner--A Research Literature Review* (Vol. 10, pp. 331–337). Association for the Advancement of Computing in Education.

Singh, H. (2003). Building effective blended learning programs. *Educational Technology, 43*(6), 51–54.

Skill, T. D., & Young, B. A. (2002). Embracing the hybrid model: Working at the intersections of virtual and physical learning spaces. *New Directions for Teaching and Learning, 2002*(92), 23–32. doi:10.1002/tl.76

Stacey, E., & Gerbic, P. (2009). Introduction to blended learning practices. *Effective blended learning practices: Evidence-based perspectives in ICT-facilitated education*, 1-20.

Stacey, E., & Wiesenberg, F. (2007). A study of face-to-face and online teaching philosophies in Canada and Australia. *The Journal of Distance Education/Revue de l'Éducation à Distance, 22*(1), 19-40.

Steel, C. (2009). Reconciling university teacher beliefs to create learning designs for LMS environments. *Australasian Journal of Educational Technology, 25*(3), 399–420. doi:10.14742/ajet.1142

Tang, M., & Byrne, R. (2007). Regular versus Online versus Blended: A Qualitative Description of the Advantages of the Electronic Modes and a Quantitative Evaluation. *International Journal on E-Learning, 6*(2), 257–266.

Trigwell, K., Prosser, M., & Taylor, P. (1994). Qualitative differences in approaches to teaching first year university science. *Higher Education, 27*(1), 75–84. doi:10.1007/BF01383761

Verkroost, M. J., Meijerink, L., Lintsen, H., & Veen, W. (2008). Finding a balance in dimensions of blended learning. *International Journal on E-Learning, 7*(3), 499–522.

Vignare, K. (2007). Review of literature, blended learning: Using ALN to change the classroom–will it work. *Blended learning: Research perspectives*, 37-63.

Waxman, H. C., Huang, S. Y. L., & Wang, M. C. (1997). Investigating the classroom learning environment of resilient and non-resilient students from inner-city elementary schools. *International Journal of Educational Research, 27*(4), 343–353. doi:10.1016/S0883-0355(97)90016-1

Webster, J., & Hackley, P. (1997). Teaching Effectiveness in Technology-Mediated Distance Learning. *Academy of Management Journal, 40*(6), 1282–1309. doi:10.2307/257034

Welker, J., & Berardino, L. (2006). Blended Learning: Understanding the Middle Ground between Traditional Classroom and Fully Online Instruction. *Journal of Educational Technology Systems*, *34*(1), 33–55. doi:10.2190/67FX-B7P8-PYUX-TDUP

Wu, J.-H., Tennyson, R. D., & Hsia, T.-L. (2010). A study of student satisfaction in a blended e-learning system environment. *Computers & Education*, *55*(1), 155–164. doi:10.1016/j.compedu.2009.12.012

Yin, R. K. (2009). *Case study research: Design and methods* (Vol. 5). Sage Publications, Inc.

Chapter 16
A Techno–Economic Perspective of Constrained Application Protocol

Tapio Levä
Aalto University, Finland

Miika Komu
Ericsson Research, Finland

Mahya Ilaghi
Aalto University, Finland

Nicklas Beijar
Ericsson Research, Finland

Vilen Looga
Aalto University, Finland

Oleksiy Mazhelis
University of Jyväskylä, Finland

ABSTRACT

Among billions of Internet enabled devices that are expected to surround us in the near future, many will be resource constrained, i.e., will have limited power supply, processing power and memory. To cope with these limitations, the Constrained Application Protocol (CoAP) has been recently introduced as a lightweight alternative to HTTP for connecting the resource limited devices to the Web. Although the new protocol offers solid technical advantages, it remains uncertain whether a successful uptake will follow, as it depends also on its economic feasibility for the involved stakeholders. Therefore, this paper studies the techno-economic feasibility of CoAP using a systematic methodological framework. Based on eleven expert interviews complemented with a literature survey, the paper identifies potential deployment challenges for CoAP, both technical and business-related, and suggests approaches to overcome them. The findings should facilitate the uptake of CoAP by supporting the potential adopters of the protocol in their decision-making.

DOI: 10.4018/978-1-5225-1779-5.ch016

INTRODUCTION

INTERNET of Things (IoT) envisions to connect billions of devices to the Internet. However, many of these devices, known as smart objects, have limited power supply, processing power and memory (Lerche, Hartke, & Kovatsch, 2012). The market is currently dominated by the in-house solutions and proprietary protocols, which are now being challenged by sector specific protocols, such as ZigBee and Z-wave, as well as by stardard protocols, such as Bluetooth Low Energy (Gallen, 2014). On the other hand, the widely deployed HyperText Transfer Protocol (HTTP) is believed to be a poor match for resource-constrained devices because of its chatty communication model and reliance on the stateful transmission control protocol (TCP) (Bormann, Castellani & Shelby, 2012).

To overcome the limitations of HTTP and to provide a standardized alternative to the sector specific protocols, the Internet Engineering Task Force (IETF) has introduced the Constrained Application Protocol (CoAP) (Shelby, Hartke, Bormann and Frank, 2013), which is designed specifically for constrained nodes and networks. CoAP is a simplified and optimized alternative to HTTP, which allows easy mapping between the two protocols (Bormann et al., 2012). The advantage of CoAP is that it supports efficient communication between resource-limited devices (Villaverde, Pesch, Alberola, Fedor & Boubekeur, 2012) by providing a generic HTTP-like protocol with small communications overhead (Shelby, Hartke, et al., 2013). As a generic application-layer protocol, CoAP can potentially be used to connect arbitrary things to the Web without the business sector specific limitations of other protocols. Therefore, CoAP is suitable for a wide range of application scenarios, including home automation, smart energy, street lightning, and asset tracking.

The performance gains attainable through the use of CoAP have been the focus of recent research efforts. Colitti et al. (Colitti, Steenhaut & Caro, 2011) studied the energy consumption of CoAP and HTTP data transfers and found that for frequent request-response sessions, CoAP allows the energy footprint to be cut roughly by 50% compared to HTTP. Levä et al. (Tapio Levä, Mazhelis and Suomi, 2013) found that the use of the CoAP's "observe" option in push-like applications enables a factor of six reduction in the energy footprint. Furthermore, the CoAP's energy impact and smaller communication overhead, when combined with a large number of frequently communicating devices, provides significant cost savings for CoAP-based solutions compared to the HTTP-based ones. Finally, Bandyopadhyay et al. (Bandyopadhyay & Bhattacharyya, 2013) compared the energy footprint of CoAP and MQTT for the push-like applications, and found CoAP to systematically outperform MQTT, due to data overhead of latter caused by its reliance on TCP and the inclusion of the topic definitions in the payload.

Nevertheless, the performance improvements alone cannot guarantee the success of CoAP, since a protocol needs also be economically feasible for the potential adopters and other stakeholders participating in protocol deployment. Analyzing the feasibility of CoAP is crucial in order to target it to the most suitable use cases, to identify its potential deployment challenges and to suggest strategies to foster its deployment. Therefore, this paper applies the framework of Levä and Suomi (Tapio Levä & Suomi, 2013) to analyze the feasibility of CoAP from the techno-economic perspective. The data are collected by reviewing the literature and interviewing eleven IoT experts with both technical and business expertise.

The remainder of the paper is organized as follows: Section II introduces the research methods, including the feasibility analysis framework and the interview process. Then Section III presents the necessary background on the technical architecture, deployment actions, stakeholder roles and deployment environment of CoAP. Section IV analyzes the interview results concerning the techno-economic feasibility of CoAP. Finally, Section V discusses the role of CoAP in the evolving IoT ecosystem, before Section VI concludes the paper.

RESEARCH METHODS

This paper applies a single case study approach, where the focus is on analyzing the CoAP case in depth. The qualitative case study is especially suitable for evaluating the feasibility of an emerging technology, such as CoAP, as it allows studying a specific phenomenon in detail (Yin, 2003) without the need for quantitative data that would be challenging to get due to the limited deployment. The case study follows the feasibility analysis framework of Levä and Suomi (T Levä & Suomi, 2013) that provides a systematic process description for identifying the potential deployment challenges of the investigated protocol and strategies to solve them. The framework is suitable for this study since it has been developed for analyzing the feasibility of Internet protocols still under development. The framework and its development version have been applied earlier to analyze the feasibility of Multipath TCP (MPTCP) (T Levä and Suomi, 2013), Host Identity Protocol (HIP) (T Levä, Komu, Keränen & Luukkainen, 2013) and web real-time communications (WebRTC) (Tabakov, 2014).

The framework consists of six analysis steps. Each step answers a set of questions and these answers are used as input in the following steps. The first four steps defining the 1) use cases, 2) technical architecture, 3) value network and 4) deployment environment scope the analysis so that the feasibility of the protocol for the relevant stakeholders can be analyzed in step 5. The output of the feasibility analysis is a list of deployment challenges. Finally, solutions to these challenges are identified in step 6.

The data to answer the questions of the framework were collected both by reviewing existing literature and interviewing a set of 11 technical experts and business managers working in the field of IoT. An interview study was selected as the data collection method, because the potential deployment challenges and related strategies to improve the feasibility of CoAP were not available in written sources, and because the feasibility of a protocol is heavily based on subjective evaluation of different stakeholders participating in protocol deployment.

The interviews were conducted in two phases. The first nine interviews in Spring 2013 involved mostly technical experts and provided information regarding all the steps of the framework. In order to avoid unnecessary bias, the interviewees covered both CoAP experts and people involved with substitute technologies. The initial results of these interviews were reported in a conference paper (Ilaghi, Levä & Komu, 2014). The interview study was extended in Spring 2014 by interviewing two business experts that presented different stakeholders of CoAP. In these additional interviews the focus was on the feasibility of CoAP for its stakeholders. The interviewees are listed in Table 1.

Each interview took 30-60 minutes. Eight interviews were carried out face to face, the rest over Skype. The semi-structured interviews followed the questions posed by the feasibility analysis framework, but the emphasis varied depending on each interviewee's area of expertise. The recorded interviews were transcribed and appropriate tabulations were used to increase the validity of the results.

Despite all the steps of the framework were covered in the interviews, the interview results are reported directly only for the feasibility and solution analysis steps covered in Section IV. However, the results were also used to scope the literature study of Section III that features the other steps of the framework.

BACKGROUND

This section analyzes the technical architecture, deployment actions, stakeholder roles and deployment environment of CoAP by reviewing the existing literature.

Table 1. List of interviewees

	Title	Expertise	Stakeholder group
1	PhD student	CoAP	Academia
2	CTO	Smart Energy Solutions	Service provider
3	Professor	Energy Efficient Computing	Academia
4	PhD student	Wireless Sensor Networks	Academia
5	PhD student	CoAP	Academia
6	Post-doc	Technology Adoption	Academia
7	Researcher	IoT	Service provider
8	Researcher	Web Services	Service provider
9	CTO	CoAP standardization	Software provider
10	CEO	Cleantech sensor solutions	Service provider
11	Research manager	Next generation networking	Research institution

Technical Architecture of CoAP

CoAP (Shelby, Hartke, et al., 2013) is an application layer protocol designed to scale down to small battery-powered devices with limited memory and processing capabilities. To be more exact, CoAP is suitable to be implemented on so-called Class 1 devices (100 KB ROM and 10 KB of RAM) that can support IP connectivity, but are unable to provide a full protocol stack with TCP and HTTPS support. In addition to the devices, also the network may be constrained. Therefore, all CoAP messages are in binary format to minimize the packet sizes.

CoAP follows the design principles of RESTful architectures: messaging follows the request-response pattern, and each request from a client must provide a complete information to process the request at the server. In general, this improves service-side scalability, because the server does not have to maintain the state. Additionally, the "observe" extension (Hartke, 2014) to CoAP allows a service to register and receive events automatically from a constrained device without constantly pulling information over the wireless network. This saves battery life, because wireless communications consume a considerable amount of overall energy. However, this extension does not conform to RESTful design, since it introduces a state at the server.

Resources in CoAP are identified via their uniform resource locators (URLs) indicating the logical path of the resource together with the corresponding device address. For example, readings from a temperature sensors could be accessed as a resource at the URL "coap://[fe80::ff:3d:6c14]/sensors/temp". To ease automatic configuration, devices provide a discovery mechanism (Shelby, 2012) allowing other nodes to detect their local resources and obtain the corresponding URLs and attributes. The mechanism uses CoAP for accessing the local resource directory itself as a resource at a fixed URL "/.well-known/core". A limited search functionality is supported, allowing queries on attributes with simple wildcards for prefix matching.

Besides the CoAP protocol itself, the protocol stack typically involves other protocol layers which all contribute to making CoAP feasible in constrained environments. Unlike HTTP, CoAP generally runs over User Datagram Protocol (UDP) and the optional reliability is provided by a layer in CoAP with less overhead and complexity than in TCP. However, UDP is not mandatory and TCP-based alternative has been specified (Bormann, 2013).

Datagram Transport Layer Security (DTLS) provides optional security for CoAP when UDP is used (Shelby, Hartke, et al., 2013). The security of DTLS is based either on pre-shared symmetric keys or asymmetric keys (with or without a certificate). In all cases, some security credentials (symmetric keys, public keys or certificates) are assumed to be distributed to the constrained devices before deployment. In other words, automated bootstrapping procedures for security are not defined in the specification.

Because of the high number of addresses required for IoT devices, IPv6 is typically used instead of IPv4. The low bandwidth version of IPv6, called IPv6 over Low-Power Wireless Personal Area Networks (6LoWPAN), usually replaces the ordinary IPv6 protocol. In the physical and data link layers, various technologies including IEEE 802.15.4, Bluetooth Low-Energy, and IEEE 802.11ah can be used. These standards are designed for low power consumption and low data transfer rate in constrained devices. The protocol stack as a whole affects the deployment, since all involved layers must be supported by the nodes, either locally between neighboring nodes (6LoWPAN and the physical/link layer) or end-to-end (UDP, DTLS and IPv6).

Figure 1 illustrates the technical architecture of CoAP with two architectural alternatives. Firstly, the constrained nodes can connect to the server directly with CoAP. Being a new protocol, CoAP may meet problems with middleboxes on the path, such as firewalls and NATs. This is further complicated due to the use of UDP and DTLS as transport instead of TCP. Secondly, the RESTful web architecture allows HTTP and CoAP to interoperate (Shelby, Hartke, et al., 2013). An intermediary (proxy) converts between the two protocols by operating as a server on one side and as a client on the other side of communication (Bormann et al., 2012). In this mode, the lightweight CoAP is utilized in the constrained network, while HTTP offers compatibility with devices in the normal Internet and provides better traversal of middleboxes. Mapping between HTTP and CoAP is rather straightforward because CoAP has direct mappings to the GET, PUT, POST and DELETE methods (Castellani, Loreto, Rahman, Fossati and Dijk, 2014).

Intermediaries can also provide additional services. For example, caching is important in a scenario, where devices conserve energy by periodically entering a sleep mode. Energy conservation can be sup-

Figure 1.

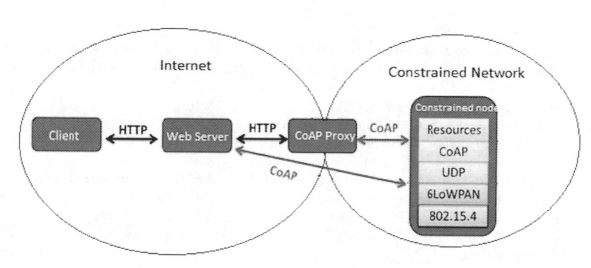

ported by employing a resource directory, which maintains descriptions of all the resources available in the network (Shelby, Bormann and Krco, 2013). Instead of querying each device separately, the centralized directory is queried. This allows the resources hosted by a device to be discovered and looked up also when the device is asleep or when multicast to all devices is not feasible.

CoAP can also be used for automated device management including bootstrapping, registration and configuration of devices as well as status and error reporting. This is possible through OMA LWM2M - a lightweight adaptation of the widely used OMA Device Management protocol defined by the Open Mobile Alliance (OMA) - that uses CoAP as one of its underlying protocols. OMA LWM2M defines manageable resources trough an extensible objects and resource model.

Deployment of CoAP

In order to advance the protocol from the specifications into actual use on the Internet, the one deploying the protocol needs to proceed through the following actions:

1. Implement and install CoAP libraries in the smart objects;
2. Implement and install CoAP libraries in the web server *or* deploy a CoAP-HTTP proxy;
3. Enable IPv6 support (if needed);
4. Allow CoAP to pass middleboxes;
5. Provide and adopt IoT services based on CoAP.

These deployment actions are helpful in defining the related value network and the ecosystem including the involved stakeholders and their roles (Tapio Levä and Suomi, 2013). Previous studies (Eurich et al., 2010; Kaleelazhicathu, 2004; Schlautmann, Levy, Keeping and Pankert, 2011; Stanoevska-Slabeva, 2010) have identified multiple organizational roles that an IoT value network and ecosystem includes. The number of roles varies depending on the application scenario. In some scenarios, most of the deployment actions are taken by a single company that implements, installs, operates and uses the service based on CoAP. However, to cover all potentially relevant stakeholders, the list below includes all the stakeholder roles that relate to the deployment of CoAP.

- **Original Equipment Manufacturers (OEMs):** Typically install CoAP libraries into the smart objects. Due to the tight integration of hardware and software, the software is typically installed already by the manufacturer. Consequently, the manufacturers also decide the configuration methods available to the end users.
- **Service Providers:** Offer (web) services to the end users. The providers own, rent or otherwise manage the web servers and install CoAP to them. In case of complex applications, the implementation and/or operation of the service may be outsourced to *System integrators*.
- **Software (Platform) Vendors:** Implement CoAP libraries and back-end software. They license the software to the service providers and OEMs.
- **End Users:** Use the IoT services provided by the service providers. They include both individual end users (consumers) and businesses. The end users either own the smart objects (e.g., heart rate meters) or then they use their web clients to access the data provided by the service provider

owned objects (e.g., weather sensors). When middleboxes are involved, the end users must ensure that they allow CoAP traffic.

- **Infrastructure Providers:** Such as communications service providers (CSPs), and cloud providers offer connectivity, computational and other resources for the smart objects, proxies and web servers. The deployment of CoAP may require the participation from these providers in order to enable IPv6, to allow the CoAP traffic through their networks or to provide a CoAP-HTTP proxy.

Deployment Environment of CoAP

The current deployment state of CoAP can be characterized as embryonic. The protocol is just leaving the research labs making its way into the industrial products and solutions, while the protocol standardization is being finalized, approaching the Internet Standard phase. The proponents of CoAP, such as Ericsson, INRIA, Lulea, NXP, Sensinode, SICS, STMicroelectronics, Watteco and Wisenet, are testing their CoAP implementations and their interoperability (Lerche et al., 2012). At the time of writing, only few reported examples of using the protocol in commercial products, such as Sensinode's NanoService, could be found. Gartner estimates the current CoAP adoption to amount for only 1-5% of its target market (Ramamoorthy, 2013).

According to (Tushman and Murmann, 2003), the introduction of a new major product or process breakthrough initiates a new technological cycle that starts with the period of variation, selection and retention. This period, referred to as the era of ferment, is characterized by the intense competition among alternative technologies. It usually results in the emergence of a new dominant design, i.e. the set of design decisions adopted by the majority of the products.

The emergence of Internet-enabled constrained smart objects represents the technological discontinuity that initiates the era of ferment. In this situation, CoAP is to compete both with available generic protocols, such as XMPP, MQTT and HTTP, as well as with sector-specific alternatives, such as Z-wave, KNX and X10 used in the building and home automation solutions, WirelessHART used for process automation, and Bluetooth low energy, WiFi low energy, Dash7 and Mbath. Therefore, the competition is still upcoming between the HTTP-, MQTT-, and XMPP-based and sector-specific solutions, on the one hand, and the CoAP-based solutions, on the other hand, for the position of the new dominant design in future IoT applications. According to (Tushman and Murmann, 2003), the economic forces, along with social and political, will determine whether the CoAP will emerge as the element of the new dominant design.

CoAP standardisation and adoption can also be seen in the context of the IoT business ecosystem which both shapes the protocol development and is affected by its uptake. The IoT business ecosystem represents the community of interacting companies and individuals along with their socio-economic environment, where the companies are competing and cooperating by utilizing a common set of core assets in a form of hardware and software products, platforms or standards (Mazhelis, Luoma and Warma, 2012) . As such, the CoAP, if widely deployed, can be seen as one of the core assets in this ecosystem.

At the moment, the IoT ecosystem is in a formation phase, with no clear keystone leading the ecosystem development (Sundmaeker, Guillemin, Friess and Woelfflé, 2010). It is expected, however, that the platform providers - i.e., the vendors of service platform handling device specific tasks, including fault detection, management of SIM cards, etc. - will take the central role, and thus be able to create and appropriate the greatest portion of the value in the ecosystem (Schlautmann et al., 2011). This is no surprise that dozens of IoT platforms have recently emerged (Mazhelis and Tyurväinen, 2014), and that many of the large ICT players, such as NSN, Alcatel-Lucent, Vodafone, and Telefonica are pushing their platforms to the market (Schlautmann et al., 2011). For the success of the CoAP, it is crucial to have the support for the protocol provided by these platforms, e.g., in a form of CoAP libraries included in their software packages.

TECHNO-ECONOMIC FEASIBILITY OF COAP

This section analyzes the techno-economic feasibility of CoAP based on the results of the expert interviews. Where possible, the interview results are validated with literature.

Evaluation of Potential Use Cases for CoAP

We asked our interviewees about potential use cases for CoAP. All of the interviewees, including the ones who were initially not familiar with CoAP, could see several potential use cases. Almost all of interviewees saw getting data from sensors (including humidity, temperature, light, etc.) as the main functionality of CoAP. Second most often mentioned functionality was using CoAP to control actuators, such as light switches, and turning on and off electronics. Thus, most of our interviewees saw CoAP as the "last mile" connection to edge nodes for data retrieving and control systems. In the following we describe the use cases that were seen most potential by the interviewees.

- **Home Automation:** By far the most popular use case mentioned by the interviewees. They saw a significant advantage of CoAP to allow devices and sensors at home that connect seamlessly to the Internet and provide a slew of new services to the customers.
- **Smart Cities:** An extension to the previous use case, where monitoring of various infrastructure (e.g. streetlights, sewers) and environmental measures (e.g. temperature, road conditions) is needed. Interviewees thought that CoAP can provide a simple API between various data sources and multiple users (city management, utility companies) having interest to access their data.
- **Asset Management and Logistics:** Also mentioned by a few experts as a case where it's necessary to save energy and cellular bandwidth, thus being a good target for CoAP. For cases like tracking wireless devices and shipping containers CoAP would provide substantial monetary savings in roaming charges sue to its small communication overhead.

The use cases above are in line with the IoT applications listed in (Atzori, Iera and Morabito, 2010). However, one interviewee mentioned a different use case where a CSP is planning to use CoAP end-to-end as the control plane for *network equipment management and configuration*. Here, CoAP would allow the CSP to monitor and control their infrastructure without overloading their network with management traffic.

Comparison to Substitute Technologies

In order to be an attractive alternative to its potential adopters, CoAP needs to provide relative advantage over the existing solutions and other new proposals entering the market. Therefore, the interviewees

Table 2. Comparison of selected technologies

	CoAP	HTTP	MQTT	ZigBee
Scope[1]	E2E, E2G	E2E	E2E	E2G
Radio	Any	Any	Any	IEEE 802.15.4
Transport	UDP, (TCP)	TCP	TCP, UDP	ZigBee
Communication[2]	C-S, Pub-Sub	C-S	Pub-Sub	C-S
Overhead	Low	High	Low (MQTT-S)	Low
Standardization	IETF	IETF	IBM, OASIS	ZigBee Alliance
Adoption	Low	High	Medium	Medium
Maturity	Low	High	Medium	High

were asked to name the key substitutes of CoAP and evaluate their pros and cons. Due to the fragmentation of the market, the interviewees mentioned a large number of alternatives to CoAP. The evaluation here focuses on the substitutes mentioned most often, which include HTPP, MQTT, ZigBee, and sector specific, proprietary protocols grouped together. The evaluation is summarized in Table 2 that compares the properties of the selected protocols by focusing on the factors affecting the attractiveness of the protocols to the potential adopters.

In many application domains, sector specific standards and proprietary protocols have been designed to meet the domain-specific requirements and the limitations of constrained devices. These typically cover the whole stack from radio to application. Examples include the BACnet, LonWorks, and KNX and DALI in industrial and building automation, as well as Z-Wave and Insteon for home automation (Mazhelis et al., 2013). Further alternatives include WirelessHART, Bluetooth low energy, Dash7 and Mbath. Common to these solutions is the dependency on a gateway to enable Internet access. For example, Z-Wave only works on top of Z-Wave proprietary radio and the standard does not specify the interoperability with the Internet protocols, thus requiring a gateway to convert the Z-Wave application protocols into another presentation format (Gomez and Paradells, 2010). Likewise, the KNX protocols specify the layers from link up to application layer, with a dedicated gateway device needed for conversion to TCP/IP. Despite this, one interviewee told that simple custom protocols are often sufficient due to their simplicity and energy efficiency. This is particularly relevant for the most restricted devices - a category CoAP is actually not targeting. Moreover, the sector-specific and proprietary protocols are typically more mature and optimized for solving a specific problem.

More recently, the standardization groups have devoted significant efforts to make the communication standards more domain independent and interoperable. For instance, the ZigBee Alliance promoting the ZigBee protocol stack running on top of IEEE 802.15.4 radio complements the network (originally non-IP) and application level protocols by defining the so-called public application profiles that enable cross-vendor interoperability within specific application domains. While ZigBee has gained trust, interviews also reveal concerns about the multitude of variants and the compatibility problems between them.

The horizontal domain-independent approach is also followed by MQTT (Locke, 2010) that is a lightweight, non-RESTful, publish/subscribe messaging protocol developed at IBM. It can use both TCP and UDP for transport, even though the UDP-based variant MQTT-S (Stanford-Clark and Truong, 2013) was considered as a more relevant competitor to CoAP by the interviewees. The architecture of MQTT is based on a broker, which relays messages between publishers and subscribers based on the message topic. MQTT is agnostic to the payload content; the application developer has to define a suitable information representation format on top of the protocol. Interviewees noted that MQTT has been existing longer than CoAP and therefore has more supporters. Technically MQTT-S was not seen to be superior to CoAP. An interesting example of the current fragmentation in the market is that one interviewee considers providing gateways using both CoAP and MQTT.

In the interviews, HTTP 1.1 was generally considered as the main competitor to CoAP. In many cases HTTP is sufficient, especially if the solution is not battery-constrained. According to one interviewee, companies do not care about energy consumption as it will be marginal compared to the other costs. It was also mentioned that many devices have enough processing power and have HTTP already implemented. Developing on top of HTTP is easy and it has no problems with middleboxes. On the other hand, some expected a tipping point not to be far away, where CoAP becomes the de-facto standard for IoT. The updated version 2.0 of HTTP currently being specified (Belshe, Peon, & Thomson, 2014) may further improve the attractiveness of HTTP since it implements many of CoAP's technical advantages. However, HTTP 2.0 runs over TCP with security based on SSL/TLS, which reduces its suitability for constrained environments.

Deployment Challenges of CoAP

The interviews were also asked about the potential deployment challenges of CoAP, i.e., the issues that may hinder its adoption. The findings are clustered around seven generalized deployment challenges.

Several interviewees mentioned the general lack of technological ecosystem around CoAP as a problem, which is mostly caused by the immaturity of CoAP. This refers to the supporting elements for the deployment and use of CoAP-based services, including for example native support for CoAP in web browsers, availability of CoAP in software platforms and solutions for managing sensors. The issue that CoAP does not specify the semantics was also seen as a problem for the stakeholders who would like to get the whole system at once. The CoAP experts actually mentioned multiple ongoing efforts on building the systems standards (e.g., OMA LWM2M) around CoAP, but the non-experts were not yet familiar with these, likely due to their immaturity.

CoAP is vulnerable to the common Internet attacks, including the denial of service attack that could drain the battery of constrained nodes. The problem is not the lack of available security solutions, but the fact that implementations often do not support those to avoid overhead (Sethi, Arkko and Keränen, 2012). Additionally, some interviewees did not trust the Internet security mechanisms, thus favoring not to connect sensitive sensors to the Web at all.

Several interviewees anticipated middlebox-related problems. Currently, middleboxes pass HTTP traffic over TCP very well, but CoAP uses UDP and has its own port number. Therefore, middleboxes may drop CoAP-based datagrams. Moreover, CoAP proxies complicate the implementations by breaking end-to-end connectivity. They may also become potential security hazards and their protocol translation may include unpredictable bugs.

Many existing solutions used in wireless sensor networks do not include any application or transport-layer protocols, but rather function at the network layer or even at lower layers. According to a couple of interviewees with sensor network background, the additional transport and application layers make CoAP inefficient and cause reliability problems compared to the non-IP solutions running directly on top of link layer. Additionally, since the lower layers already compress the data, the benefit of compression at the higher layers is small. This line of arguments conflicts with the CoAP experts' statements of

CoAP being very lightweight. This is understandable, because the comparison points differ from each other (low-layer WSN solutions vs. IP stack with TCP+HTTP).

Only few commercial products are available in the market even though several manufacturers are implementing and experimenting with the protocol (Probe-IT, 2012). According to the interviewees, service providers are reluctant to provide CoAP-based services due to the missing demand for the service and poor availability of CoAP devices and software, whereas the end users cannot adopt due to lack of services. Since very few companies are willing to carry the cost of trying out new technology, this will remain a"chicken and egg" problem of CoAP for some time.

Existing solutions, such as HTTP and Zigbee, decrease demand for CoAP. Related to that is a long-term concern that at some point the hardware might become capable and cheap enough, so it would be possible to run HTTP on it, thus making CoAP irrelevant. For the stakeholders that already implement and use other solutions, changing to CoAP requires effort and causes costs. Additionally, some stakeholders favor their proprietary solutions in order to restrict competition. Consequently, CoAP needs to provide significant benefits over the existing solutions in order to convince the stakeholders to incorporate it into their products.

CoAP smart objects might be more expensive than the very constrained, non-IP devices on the one hand, and the less resource-constrained but more widely available HTTP smart objects, on the other hand. This holds true especially in the early phases of CoAP deployment when the economies of scale are not yet available. Even though the difference in unit cost would be minor, it may translate into major difference in total cost because many practical application scenarios require the deployment of a huge number of smart objects. Also, since CoAP requires a full IP stack, it might consume more energy, which in turn would raise running costs of large installations. On the other hand, CoAP has been found to provide cost-savings compared to HTTP, especially when the smart objects are large in number, deployed in the field, and communicate frequently over a communications channel charged based on the traffic volume (Tapio Levä et al., 2013).

Strategies to Foster the Deployment of CoAP

After identifying potential deployment challenges, the interviewees were asked to suggest potential solutions to solve these challenges and strategies to facilitate the adoption of CoAP. The five solutions presented below can improve the feasibility of CoAP, thus making it more attractive to potential adopters.

One practical strategy for facilitating the deployment of CoAP is trying to convince the IoT service providers to use CoAP by showing the actual benefits of the CoAP compared to its substitutes. Businesses are namely reluctant to adopt a new protocol, if they already have the knowledge and have invested into their own proprietary technology. Convincing businesses to switch to CoAP requires the demonstration of long-term flexibility and cost-savings compared to proprietary solutions. According to an interviewee, the CoAP developers have taken this path by evaluating a telematics device manufacturer's proprietary protocol against CoAP (Becker, Kuladinithi, Pötsch and Görg, 2013). The result was acceptable, but did not lead to an immediate transition to CoAP. However, the manufacturer became interested in the standardized protocols that would reduce their lock-in to CSPs and cloud operators providing their current, proprietary solution. Even a better way to demonstrate the feasibility and increase the credibility of CoAP would be to get the industry giants, such as a prominent service provider (e.g., Google) or sensor manufacturer (e.g., Texas Instruments) to adopt CoAP in their products.

Many interviewees were not familiar with all the developments around CoAP. Additionally, one interviewee mentioned that although their company is starting to deploy CoAP based on a recommendation from a research institute, it was not clear to them, why is it necessary. This shows a clear need for educating potential adopters. Thus, more means to promote CoAP are needed, such as blog posts, conference and industry presentations, tutorials, etc. This would allow potential adopters to find out on their own what CoAP is, whether it is suitable for them, and how can they adopt it for their particular use. Since CoAP standard is soon finalized, the time is ripe for promotion and commercialization efforts.

In order to demonstrate the benefits of using CoAP, developers should target use cases which would be easy and beneficial to implement with CoAP, but hard to implement with alternative technologies. Discovery of these kinds of use cases could motivate vendors to provide CoAP devices and service providers to introduce CoAP-based services. Based on our analysis, it would be beneficial to focus on the following use cases:

- A suit of vertical products that would take advantage of unified CoAP layer (e.g several systems both internal and web-based needing access to various sensors in different geographic locations)
- CSPs could benefit from the small communications overhead of CoAP through the decreased load in their networks. Reaping the benefits requires that the operators would move from a volume-based pricing model into a transaction-based model.
- Sensors that need to be connected seamlessly to the Internet (e.g home automation, network equipment monitoring and configuration)

Availability of open source implementations for different operating systems, such as Android, Linux and Windows, would allow easy experimentation with CoAP. Implementations that can be taken into production use can provide immediate cost savings compared to developing own protocol or buying proprietary solutions. Also, the open nature of CoAP allows it to be easily incorporated into various development and management tools.

For solving CoAP security issues, IETF mailing lists ("solace" and "ace") have already been established. The security experts need to come up with a reliable end-to-end security solution to increase the trustworthiness of the protocol. A number of security-related drafts has emerged, but the IETF consensus is still missing.

DISCUSSION

The analysis of the conducted interviewes suggests that CoAP bears a great potential to multiple stakeholders, is technically sound for a set of use cases, and hence has good chances of becoming widely used, if not dominant IoT protocol. There are, however, factors that may intervene in the process; some of them are discussed below.

According to (Tyrväinen & Mazhelis, 2009), the *vertical software* industry — including the IoT solutions in different vertical application domains—is evolving from vertically integrated solutions developed in-house by the vertical industry firms, towards vertically disintegrated standardized software products utilizing a dominant design with standard interfaces and protocols, possibly including CoAP as its element. However, a small market size, high degree of market regulation, degree of required customer-specific tailoring, the need to coordinate innovation efforts, internal complexity of the business processes being automated by the software, and the need to maintain compatibility with older systems, among other issues (Tushman and Murmann, 2003; Tyrväinen & Mazhelis, 2009), may negatively affect the evolution and adoption of a new technology in general and CoAP in particular.

The fact that the IoT is composed of different application *sub-domains with distinct use cases* and hence different requirements (McCourt et al., 2014) may thus have a negative effect on the widespread adoption of the new protocol. Indeed, even though CoAP tries to be a jack-of-all-trades of the IoT world, it may still not be suitable for all the possible use cases. The technology selection in the IoT world seems to be still based on the use case in hand. CoAP is a midway solution between the solutions targeted to the very constrained (Class 0) devices and fairly resourceful (Class 2) devices. Being pressured by the solutions from both sides, the question remains, if there is a sufficient room in between to warrant a dedicated protocol. Likewise, some of the IoT use cases, such as infrequent delivery of video streams from security cameras, poorly match the design objectives of CoAP, and thus are unlikely to benefit from using the protocol.

Further, while *Web-compliance* has been promoted as one of the key benefits of the CoAP, in many use cases the Web connectivity is not needed and thus does not bring any additional value when selecting the technology. In addition to the lack of interest, also the security reasons may prohibit connecting the smart objects directly, or through a gateway, to the Web. This is the case for example in factories and hospitals, where exposing smart objects to the Web could risk the production or peoples' lives.

The *co-evolution of the alternative protocols* makes it even more difficult to predict the chances of CoAP becoming the dominant IoT protocol. For instance, some of the interviewed experts believe that in long-term, the development of HTTP 2.0 combined with lower costs of constrained devices will make CoAP obsolete. Thus, in their view, investing into CoAP to replace the current solutions is a waste of resources, especially if CoAP does not provide significant benefits in the use cases they have in mind. It shall be noted that, although HTTP will likely become suitable for constrained devices in future, it is difficult to tell when this might happen. Therefore, since moving from CoAP to HTTP is claimed relatively straightforward, there is little reason for adopters to stall moving to CoAP for the sake of waiting for HTTP to become suitable for their needs.

Finally, according to the technology acceptance models, the adoption depends on the expected performance and the perceived ease of use (Venkatesh, Morris, Davis and Davis, 2003). So far, CoAP is being developed by the IETF with relatively modest industry support. Although academic members behind the IETF CoAP effort might see it as a logical extension of Web to the constrained devices, it is not necessarily a view shared by the industry. This is evident form the fact that although several of our industry experts mentioned that they understand the motivations behind CoAP, it is not clear to them why should they be replacing their existing technologies. When promoting CoAP it is necessary to understand that existing (proprietary) solutions were adopted for strong business reasons - off-the-shelf solutions, practical knowledge etc. This should not be ignored, otherwise the CoAP effort might seem an academic exercise, with no regards to the realities of business. In case the CoAP protocol provides only minor benefits as compared with alternative protocols such as HTTP or MQTT, requires significant investments that are unlikely to pay off, or is complex to implement, its adoption and therefore the emergence of new dominant design is likely to be hindered, similarly to the failure of WAP protocol in the past (Sigurdson, 2001).

CONCLUSION

The widespread adoption of CoAP, the newly introduced application protocol for constrained devices, depends on its feasibility for the involved stakeholders. In this paper, the techno-economic feasibility of CoAP has been analyzed using a systematic methodological framework. Based on the available literature and conducted expert interviews, the paper identified key technological and business challenges for CoAP deployment, including limited market penetration, the lack of technological ecosystem around it, and strong competition from substitute technologies, among others. The paper further outlines approaches to address these challenges, e.g., by using focused promotion among industrial adopters and providing multi-platform production grade implementations. These findings are deemed beneficial for the potential adopters of CoAP when deciding on which protocol to use, as well as for the protocol developers when striving to understand the inhibitors and facilitators of the protocol adoption. In future work, the relative importance of the identified challenges shall be evaluated by using a survey over a large sample of stakeholders, possibly complemented by the stakeholder-specific studies on the costs and benefits of using the protocol in different application scenarios.

REFERENCES

Atzori, L., Iera, A., & Morabito, G. (2010). The Internet of Things: A survey. *Computer Networks*, *54*(15), 2787–2805. doi:10.1016/j.comnet.2010.05.010

Bandyopadhyay, S., & Bhattacharyya, A. (2013). Lightweight Internet protocols for web enablement of sensors using constrained gateway devices. In *Computing, Networking and Communications (ICNC), 2013 International Conference on* (pp. 334–340). doi:10.1109/ICCNC.2013.6504105

Becker, M., Kuladinithi, K., Pötsch, T., & Görg, C. (2013). *Wireless Freight Supervision Using Open Standards. Communication Networks, TZI*. University of Bremen.

Belshe, M., Peon, R., & Thomson, M. (2014). *Hypertext Transfer Protocol version 2*. Retrieved from http://www.rfc-editor.org/info/rfc7540

Bormann, C. (2013). *A TCP transport for CoAP*. Retrieved from https://tools.ietf.org/html/draft-bormann-core-coap-tcp-00

Bormann, C., Castellani, A. P., & Shelby, Z. (2012). CoAP: An Application Protocol for Billions of Tiny Internet Nodes. *IEEE Internet Computing*, *16*(2), 62–67. doi:10.1109/MIC.2012.29

Castellani, A., Loreto, S., Rahman, A., Fossati, T., & Dijk, E. (2014). *Guidelines for HTTP-CoAP Mapping Implementations*. Retrieved from http://www.w3.org/TR/json-ld/(Jan. 2014)

Colitti, W., Steenhaut, K., & De Caro, N. (2011). De Integrating Wireless Sensor Networks with the Web. In *Proceedings of Workshop on Extending the Internet to Low power and Lossy Networks*.

Eurich, M., Lavoisy, O., Forest, F., Ytterstad, P., Akselsen, S., Tierno, A., … Villalonga, C. (2010). *Business models and Value Creation*. SENSEI project. Deliverable 1.4.

Gallen, C. (2014, March). *More than Half-a-billion Wireless Smart Home Monitoring Devices to be Installed Worldwide by 2018, Finds ABI Research.* Academic Press.

Gomez, C., & Paradells, J. (2010). Wireless home automation networks: A survey of architectures and technologies. *Communications Magazine, IEEE, 48*(6), 92–101. doi:10.1109/MCOM.2010.5473869

Hartke, K. (2014, April). *Observing Resources in CoAP.* Retrieved from https://tools.ietf.org/html/draft-ietf-core-observe-13

Ilaghi, M., Levä, T., & Komu, M. (2014). Techno-economic feasibility analysis of constrained application protocol. In *2014 IEEE World Forum on Internet of Things* (WF-IoT) (pp. 153–158). doi:10.1109/WF-IoT.2014.6803138

Kaleelazhicathu, R. K. (2004). *Business models in telecommunications.* Retrieved from http://ecosys.optcomm.di.uoa.gr

Lerche, C., Hartke, K., & Kovatsch, M. (2012). Industry Adoption of the Internet of Things: A Constrained Application Protocol Survey. In *Proceedings of the 7th International Workshop on Service Oriented Architectures in Converging Networked Environments* (SOCNE 2012). doi:10.1109/ETFA.2012.6489787

Levä, T., Komu, M., Keränen, A., & Luukkainen, S. (2013). Adoption barriers of network layer protocols: The case of host identity protocol. *Computer Networks, 57*(10), 2218–2232. doi:10.1016/j.comnet.2012.11.024

Levä, T., Mazhelis, O., & Suomi, H. (2013). *Comparing the cost-efficiency of CoAP and {HTTP} in Web of Things applications.* Decision Support Systems. Retrieved from; doi:10.1016/j.dss.2013.09.009

Levä, T., & Suomi, H. (2013). Techno-economic feasibility analysis of Internet protocols: Framework and tools. *Computer Standards and Interfaces, 36*(1), 76–88. Retrieved from10.1016/j.csi.2013.07.011

Levä, T., & Suomi, H. (2013). Techno-economic feasibility analysis of Internet protocols: Framework and tools. *Computer Standards & Interfaces, 36*(1), 76–88. doi:10.1016/j.csi.2013.07.011

Locke, D. (2010). *MQ Telemetry Transport MQTT V3.1 Protocol Specification.* International Business Machines Corporation Technical Report.

Mazhelis, O., Luoma, E., & Warma, H. (2012). Defining an Internet-of-Things Ecosystem. In S. Andreev, S. Balandin, & Y. Koucheryavy (Eds.), *Internet of Things, Smart Spaces, and Next Generation Networking* (Vol. 7469, pp. 1–14). Springer Berlin Heidelberg; doi:10.1007/978-3-642-32686-8_1

Mazhelis, O., & Tyurväinen, P. (2014). A Framework for Evaluating Internet-of-Things Platforms: Application Provider Viewpoint. In *Proc. of the IEEE World Forum on Internet of Things (WF-IoT).* doi:10.1109/WF-IoT.2014.6803137

Mazhelis, O., Warma, H., Leminen, S., Ahokangas, P., Pussinen, P., Rajahonka, M., & Myllykoski, J. (2013). *Internet-of-Things Market, Value Networks, and Business Models: State of the Art Report.* Academic Press.

McCourt, T. C., Leopold, S., Louthan, F. G., Mosesmann, H., Smigie, J. S., Tillman, T., … Sklar, A. (2014). *The Internet of Things: A Study in Hype, Reality, Disruption, and Growth.* Academic Press.

Probe-IT. (2012). *CoAP white paper*. Retrieved from http://www.probe-it.eu/?p=522

Ramamoorthy, G. (2013). *Hype cycle for embedded software and systems*. Gartner, Research Note. Retrieved from http://www.gartner.com/newsroom/id/2575515

Schlautmann, A., Levy, D., Keeping, S., & Pankert, G. (2011). Wanted: Smart market-makers for the "Internet of Things". *Prism, 2*, 35–47.

Sethi, M., Arkko, J., & Keränen, A. (2012). End-to-end security for sleepy smart object networks. In *37th Annual IEEE Conference on Local Computer Networks* (LCN Workshops) (pp. 964–972). doi:10.1109/LCNW.2012.6424089

Shelby, Z. (2012). *Constrained RESTful Environments (CoRE)*. Link Format; doi:10.1109/MIC.2012.29

Shelby, Z., Bormann, C., & Krco, S. (2013). *CoRE Resource Directory*. Retrieved from https://tools.ietf.org/html/draft-ietf-core-resource-directory-02

Shelby, Z., Hartke, K., Bormann, C., & Frank, B. (2013, June). *Constrained Application Protocol (CoAP)*. Retrieved from https://datatracker.ietf.org/doc/draft-ietf-core-coap/

Sigurdson, J. (2001). WAP OFF---Origin, Failure, and Future, Prepared for the Japanese. Retrieved from http://www2.hhs.se/eijswp/135.PDF

Stanford-Clark, A., & Truong, H. L. (2013). *MQTT for Sensor Networks MQTT-SN Protocol Specification Version 1.2*. International Business Machines Corporation IBM, Technical Report.

Stanoevska-Slabeva, K. (2010). *Business Models - Opportunities and Barriers*. Retrieved from http://www.ict-ccast.eu

Sundmaeker, H., Guillemin, P., Friess, P., & Woelfflé, S. (2010). Vision and Challenges for Realizing the Internet of Things. Brussels, Belgium: Academic Press.

Tabakov, B. (2014). *Techno-Economic Feasibility of Web Real-Time Communications*. Aalto University.

Tushman, M. L., & Murmann, J. P. (2003). *Managing in the modular age: architectures, networks, and organizations* (R. Garud, A. Kumaraswamy, & R. N. Langlois, Eds.). Oxford, UK: Blackwell Publishers.

Tyrväinen, P., & Mazhelis, O. (2009). *Vertical Software Industry Evolution: Analysis of Telecom Operator Software*. Physica Verlag. doi:10.1007/978-3-7908-2352-3

Venkatesh, V., Morris, M. G., Davis, G. B., & Davis, F. D. (2003). User acceptance of information technology: Toward a unified view. *Management Information Systems Quarterly, 27*(3), 425–478.

Villaverde, B. C., Pesch, D., Alberola, R. D. P., Fedor, S., & Boubekeur, M. (2012). Constrained Application Protocol for Low Power Embedded Networks: A Survey. In *Innovative Mobile and Internet Services in Ubiquitous Computing (IMIS), 2012 Sixth International Conference on* (pp. 702–707). doi:10.1109/IMIS.2012.93

Yin, R. K. (2003). *Case Study Research: design and methods*. Sage Publications Inc.

ENDNOTES

[1]   E2E = end-to-end, E2G = end-to-gateway
[2]   C-S = client-server model, pub-sub = publish-subscribe model

Compilation of References

Abdillah, A., & Husin, N. M. (2016). A longitudinal examination corporate social responsibility reporting practice among top bank in Malaysia. *Procedia Economics and Finance*, *35*, 10–16. doi:10.1016/S2212-5671(16)00004-6

Acs, Z., Szerb, L., & Autio, E. (2015). *Global Entrepreneurship Index 2015, Global Entrepreneurship and Development Institute*. CreateSpace Independent Publishing Platform.

Adler, P. A., & Adler, P. (1987). *Membership roles in field research*. Newbury Park, CA: SAGE. doi:10.4135/9781412984973

Adolfsson, E. T., Smide, B., Gregeby, E., Fernstro"m, L., & Wikblad, K. (2004). Implementing empowerment group education in diabetes. *Patient Education and Counseling*, *53*(3), 319–324. doi:10.1016/j.pec.2003.07.009 PMID:15186870

Afuah, A., & Tucci, C. L. (2012). Crowdsourcing as a solution to distant search. *Academy of Management Review*, *37*(3), 355–375. doi:10.5465/amr.2010.0146

Aiman-Smith, L., & Green, S. G. (2002). Implementing New Manufacturing Technology: "The Related Effects of Technology Characteristics and User Learning Activities. *Academy of Management Journal*, *45*(2), 421–430. doi:10.2307/3069356

Akçomak, İ. S., & ter Weel, B. (2009). Social capital, innovation and growth: Evidence from Europe. *European Economic Review*, *53*(5), 544–567. doi:10.1016/j.euroecorev.2008.10.001

Akhtar, S. (2010). 2G-4G Networks: Evolution of technologies, standards, and deployment. In *Encyclopedia of Multimedia Technology and Networking*. Ideas Group Publisher. Retrieved from http://faculty.uaeu.ac.ae/s.akhtar/EncyPaper04.pdf

Alaimo, S., & Heckman, S. (2008). Introduction: Emerging modes of materiality in feminist theory. In Material Feminisms (pp. 1–19). Bloomington, IN: Indiana University Press.

Alani. J. (2012). Effects of Technological Progress and Productivity on Economic Growth In Uganda. *Revue Procedia Economics and Finance*, (1), 14 – 23.

Alan, S. (2004). *News Culture* (3rd ed.). Maidenhead, UK: Open University Press.

Albers-Miller, N. D., & Gelb, D. B. (1996). Business advertising appeals as a mirror of cultural dimensions: A study of *eleven* countries. *Journal of Advertising*, *25*(4), 57–70. doi:10.1080/00913367.1996.10673512

Al-Hawari, M. A. A. (2014). Does customer sociability matter? Differences in e-quality, e-satisfaction, and e-loyalty between introvert and extravert online banking users. *Journal of Services Marketing*, *28*(7), 538–546. doi:10.1108/JSM-02-2013-0036

Allen, T. J. (1977). Managing the Flow of Technology: Technology Transfer and the Dissemination of Technological Information Within the R&D Organization. Cambridge, MA: Academic Press.

Ambler, T., & Styles, C. (1997). Brand development versus new product development: Toward a process model of extension decisions. *Journal of Product and Brand Management, 6*(4), 222–234. doi:10.1108/10610429710186752

Ambroise, A., Barnaud, M., Manchon, O., & Vedel, G. (1998). Bilan de l'expérience des plans de développement durable du point de vue de la relation agriculture-environnement. *Courrier de l'environnement de l'INRA, 34*.

Amrein-Beardsley, A., Foulger, T. S., & Toth, M. (2007). Examining the Development of a Hybrid Degree Program: Using Student and Instructor Data to Inform Decision-Making. *Journal of Research on Technology in Education, 39*(4), 27. doi:10.1080/15391523.2007.10782486

Anderson, L. W., Krathwohl, D. R., Airasian, P. W., Cruikshank, K. A., Mayer, R. E., & Pintrich, P. R. et al. (2001). *A Taxonomy for Learning, Teaching, and Assessing*. New York: Addison Wesley Longman.

Anderson, R. E., & Srinivasan, S. (2003). E-satisfaction and E-Loyalty: A Contingency Framework. *Psychology and Marketing, 20*(2), 123–138. doi:10.1002/mar.10063

Andreu, L., Aldas, J., Bigne, E., & Mattila, A. (2010). An analysis of e-business adoption and its impact on relational quality in travel agency-supplier relationships. *Tourism Management, 31*(6), 777–787. doi:10.1016/j.tourman.2009.08.004

Anisimova, T. A. (2007). The Effect of Corporate Brand attributes on Attitudinal And Behavioral Consumer Loyalty. *Journal of Consumer Marketing, 24*(7), 395–405. doi:10.1108/07363760710834816

Arbaugh, J. B. (2002). Managing the on-line classroom. *The Journal of High Technology Management Research, 13*(2), 203–223. doi:10.1016/S1047-8310(02)00049-4

Arbaugh, J., Godfrey, M. R., Johnson, M., Pollack, B. L., Niendorf, B., & Wresch, W. (2009). Research in online and blended learning in the business disciplines: Key findings and possible future directions. *The Internet and Higher Education, 12*(2), 71–87. doi:10.1016/j.iheduc.2009.06.006

Arctice. (2014). *Arctice is on Facebook*. Reviewed 29 March from https://www.facebook.com/pages/Arctice/586348848092936

Arikunto, S. (2010). *Prosedur penelitian: Suatu Pendekatan Praktik*. Jakarta: Rineja Cipta.

Arvidsson, A. (2005). Brands: A critical perspective. *Journal of Consumer Culture, 5*(2), 235–258. doi:10.1177/1469540505053093

Asim, M., & Hashmi, Y. (2005). *E-Loyalty: Companies Secret Weapon On the Web*. Lulea University of Technology.

Aspden, L., & Helm, P. (2004). Making the Connection in a Blended Learning Environment. *Educational Media International, 41*(3), 245–252. doi:10.1080/09523980410001680851

Atakan-Duman, S., & Ozdora-Aksak, E. (2014). The role of corporate social responsibility in online identity construction: An analysis of Turkey's banking sector. *Public Relations Review, 40*(5), 862–864. doi:10.1016/j.pubrev.2014.07.004

Attaran, H. J., Divandari, A., & Adinov, H. (2012). Identifying effective factors in market integration (realization of sustainable co mpetitive advantage) the banking services in Mellat Bank based on source -centered approach. *Journal of Public Administration, 12*(4), 91–112.

Atzori, L., Iera, A., & Morabito, G. (2010). The Internet of Things: A survey. *Computer Networks, 54*(15), 2787–2805. doi:10.1016/j.comnet.2010.05.010

Audretsch, O. B. (2002). *Entrepreneurship: A survey of literature*. London: CEPR.

Austin, A. C., Heffernan, M., & David, N. (2008). *Academic Authorship, Publishing Agreements and Open Access (Research Report)*. Brisbane, Australia: Queensland University of Technology.

Australian Law Reform Commission. (2012). *Copyright and the Digital Economy (IP 42)* (Government Report, Canberra). Retrieved June 18, 2013, from http://www.alrc.gov.au/publications/copyright-ip42

Australian Law Reform Commission. (2013). *Copyright and the Digital Economy (DP 79)* (Government Report, Canberra). Retrieved on June 18, 2013, from http://www.alrc.gov.au/publications/copyright-ip42

Aycock, A., Garnham, C., & Kaleta, R. (2002). Lessons learned from the hybrid course project. *Teaching with Technology Today, 8*(6), 9-21.

Baack, D. W., & Singh, N. (2007). Culture and web communications. *Journal of Business Research, 60*(3), 181–188. doi:10.1016/j.jbusres.2006.11.002

Baer, M., & Frese, M. (2003). Innovation is not enough: Climates for initiative and psychological safety, process innovations, and firm performance. *Journal of Organizational Behavior, 24*(1), 45–68. doi:10.1002/job.179

Baldwin, C., & von Hippel, E. (2011). Modeling a paradigm shift: From producer innovation to user and open collaborative innovation. *Organization Science, 22*(6), 1399–1417. doi:10.1287/orsc.1100.0618

Balogun, J., Best, K., & Lê, J. (2015). Selling the object of strategy: How frontline workers realize strategy through their daily work. *Organization Studies, 36*(10), 1285–1313. doi:10.1177/0170840615590282

Balston, D. M. (1993). *Cellular Radio Systems*. Artech House.

Bandyopadhyay, S., & Bhattacharyya, A. (2013). Lightweight Internet protocols for web enablement of sensors using constrained gateway devices. In *Computing, Networking and Communications (ICNC), 2013 International Conference on* (pp. 334–340). doi:10.1109/ICCNC.2013.6504105

Baporikar, N. (2015). Drivers of Innovation. In P. Ordoñez de Pablos, L. Turró, R. Tennyson, & J. Zhao (Eds.), *Knowledge Management for Competitive Advantage During Economic Crisis* (pp. 250–270). Hershey, PA: Business Science Reference; doi:10.4018/978-1-4666-6457-9.ch014

Baporikar, N. (2015a). *Innovation Knowledge Management Nexus. In Innovation Management* (pp. 85–110). Berlin: De Gruyter.

Baporikar, N. (2016a). Organizational Barriers and Facilitators in Embedding Knowledge Strategy. In *Business Intelligence: Concepts, Methodologies, Tools, and Applications* (pp. 1585–1610). Hershey, PA: Business Science Reference.

Baporikar, N. (2016b). Strategies for Enhancing the Competitiveness of MNEs. In M. Khan (Ed.), *Multinational Enterprise Management Strategies in Developing Countries* (pp. 50–71). Hershey, PA: Business Science Reference.

Baporikar, N. (2016c). Lifelong Learning in Knowledge Society. In P. Ordóñez de Pablos & R. Tennyson (Eds.), *Impact of Economic Crisis on Education and the Next-Generation Workforce* (pp. 263–284). Hershey, PA: Information Science Reference.

Baporikar, N. (2016d). Talent Management Integrated Approach for Organizational Development. In A. Casademunt (Ed.), *Strategic Labor Relations Management in Modern Organizations* (pp. 22–48). Hershey, PA: Business Science Reference.

Baporikar, N. (2016e). Stakeholder Approach for Quality Higher Education. In W. Nuninger & J. Châtelet (Eds.), *Handbook of Research on Quality Assurance and Value Management in Higher Education* (pp. 1–26). Hershey, PA: Information Science Reference.

Baporikar, N. (2017a). Knowledge Transfer Issues in Teaching: Learning Management. In N. Baporikar (Ed.), *Innovation and Shifting Perspectives in Management Education* (pp. 58–78). Hershey, PA: Business Science Reference.

Baporikar, N. (2017b). *Innovation and Shifting Perspectives in Management Education* (pp. 1–352). Hershey, PA: IGI Global.

Barad, K. (2003). Posthumanist performativity: Toward an understanding of how matter comes to matter. *Signs (Chicago, Ill.), 28*(3), 801–831. doi:10.1086/345321

Barad, K. (2007). *Meeting the universe halfway: Quantum physics and the entanglement of matter and meaning*. Durham, NC: Duke University Press. doi:10.1215/9780822388128

Barley, S. R. (1990). The alignment of technology and structure through roles and networks. *Administrative Science Quarterly, 31*(1), 61–103. doi:10.2307/2393551

Barnard, C. I. (1938). *The Functions of the Executive*. Cambridge, MA: Harvard University Press.

Bart, Y., Shankar, V., Sultan, F., & Urban, G. L. (2005). Are the drivers and role of online trust the same for all web sites and consumers? A large scale e xploratory empirical study. *Journal of Marketing, 69*(4), 133–152. doi:10.1509/jmkg.2005.69.4.133

Ba, S., Whinston, A. B., & Zhang, H. (2003). Building trust in online auction markets through an economic incentive mechanism. *Decision Support Systems, 35*(3), 273–286. doi:10.1016/S0167-9236(02)00074-X

Battarbee, K., & Koskinen, I. (2005). Co-experience: User experience as interaction. *CoDesign, 1*(1), 5–18. doi:10.1080/15710880412331289917

Baum, J. R., & Locke, E. A. (2004). The relationship of entrepreneurial traits, skill, and motivation to subsequent venture growth. *Journal of Applied Phycology, 89*(4), 589–598.

Bech, M., & Kristensen, B. (2009). Differential Response Rates in Postal and Web-based Surveys among Older Respondents. *Survey Research Methods, 3*(1), 1–6.

Becker, M., Kuladinithi, K., Pötsch, T., & Görg, C. (2013). *Wireless Freight Supervision Using Open Standards. Communication Networks, TZI*. University of Bremen.

Behlendorf, B. (1999). Open Source as a Business Strategy. In C. DiBona, S. Ockman, & M. Stone (Eds.), *Open Sources: Voices from the Open Source Revolution* (pp. 149–170). O'Reilly.

Belanger, B., Hiller, S. B., & Smith, W. J. (2002). Trustworthiness in electronic commerce: The role of privacy, security, and site attributes. *The Journal of Strategic Information Systems, 11*(3-4), 245–270. doi:10.1016/S0963-8687(02)00018-5

Belch, G.E. (1982). The effect of television commercial repetition on cognitive response and message acceptance. *Journal of Consumer Research, 9*(1), 56–65.

Bell, H., Nelson, K., & Tang, N. K. (1998). The effective of commercial Internet websites: A user's perspective. *Electronic Networking Applications and Policy, 8*(3), 219–228. doi:10.1108/10662249810217768

Belshe, M., Peon, R., & Thomson, M. (2014). *Hypertext Transfer Protocol version 2*. Retrieved from http://www.rfc-editor.org/info/rfc7540

Bendapudi, N., & Leone, R. P. (2003). Psychological implications of customer participation in co-production. *Journal of Marketing, 67*(1), 14–28. doi:10.1509/jmkg.67.1.14.18592

Bendix, R. (1956). *Work and authority in industry: Managerial Ideologies in the Case of Industrialization.* New York: John Wiley.

Benedicktus, R. L. (2011). The Effects of 3rd Party Consensus Information on Service Expectations and Online Trust. *Journal of Business Research, 64*(8), 846–853. doi:10.1016/j.jbusres.2010.09.014

Benkler, Y. (2001). Coase's Penguin, or: Linux and the Nature of the Firm. *The Yale Law Journal, 112*(3), 369–446. doi:10.2307/1562247

Benkler, Y. (2005). Coase's penguin, or, linux and the nature of the firm. In R. A. Ghosh (Ed.), *CODE: Collaborative Ownership and the Digital Economy* (pp. 169–206). Cambridge, MA: The MIT Press.

Bergquist, M., & Ljungberg, J. Bertil Rolandsson. "A Historical Account of the Value of Free and Open Source Software: From Software Commune to Commercial Commons. In S. Hissam, B. Russo, M. de Mendonça Neto, & F. Kon (Eds.), *Open Source Systems: Grounding Research* (pp. 196–207). Boston: Springer.

Berlo, D. K., Lemert, J. B., & Mertz, R. J. (1969). Dimensions for evaluating the acceptability of message sources. *Public Opinion Quarterly, 33*(4), 563–576. doi:10.1086/267745

Berne Convention for the Protection of Literary and Artistic Works, July 24, 1971.

Berry, L. L., Wall, A. E., & Carbon, L. P. (2006). Service clues and customer assessment of the service experience: Lesson from marketing. *The Academy of Management Perspectives, 20*(2), 43–57. doi:10.5465/AMP.2006.20591004

Bertalanffy, L. (1956). General System theory. In *General Systems. In Yearbook of the Society for the Advancement of General System Theory* (10th ed.). Ann Arbor, MI: Academic Press.

Bertalanffy, L. (1968). *General System Theory: Foundations, Development, Applications.* New York: George Braziller.

Bhattacherjee, A. (2002). Individual Trust in Online Firms: Scale Development and Initial Test. *Journal of Management Information Systems, 19*(1), 211–241.

Biggs, J. (1999). *Teaching for quality learning at university: what the student does.* Buckingham, UK: Society for Research into Higher Education.

Birkstedt, R. (2012). *Between the deliberate and the emergent - Constructing corporate brand meaning in MNCs* (Doctoral dissertation). University of Turku.

Blank, S. (2013, May). Why the lean start-up changes everything. *Harvard Business Review, 91*(5), 63–72.

Blaug, M. (1993). *The Methodology of Economics.* Cambridge, UK: Cambridge University Press.

Blau, P. M., & Scott, W. R. (1962). *Formal organizations: A comparative approach.* San Francisco, CA: Chandler Publishing.

Blazy, J.-M., Carpentier, A., & Thomas, A. (2011). The willingness to adopt agro-ecological innovations: Application of choice modelling to Caribbean banana planters. *Revue Ecological Economics, 72*, 140–150. doi:10.1016/j.ecolecon.2011.09.021

Bliuc, A.-M., Goodyear, P., & Ellis, R. A. (2007). Research focus and methodological choices in studies into students experiences of blended learning in higher education. *The Internet and Higher Education, 10*(4), 231–244. doi:10.1016/j.iheduc.2007.08.001

Bogoviyeva, E. (2009). *Brand development: The effects of customer brand co-creation on self-brand connection* (Doctoral Dissertation). University of Mississippi. ProQuest LLC.

Bonk, C., & Graham, C. (2006). *The Handbook of Blended Learning: Global Perspectives, Local Designs*. San Francisco, CA: Pfeiffer.

Bormann, C. (2013). *A TCP transport for CoAP*. Retrieved from https://tools.ietf.org/html/draft-bormann-core-coap-tcp-00

Bormann, C., Castellani, A. P., & Shelby, Z. (2012). CoAP: An Application Protocol for Billions of Tiny Internet Nodes. *IEEE Internet Computing, 16*(2), 62–67. doi:10.1109/MIC.2012.29

Bosma, N., & Van Praag, M., & de Wit, G. (2000). Determinants of successful entrepreneurship. Scientific analysis of Entrepreneurship and SMEs (SCALES) Research Report 0002/E The Concept of an Integrated Idea Management. *Int. J. Technology, Policy, and Management, 7*(3).

Boudreau, M. C., & Robey, D. (2005). Enacting integrated information technology: A human agency perspective. *Organization Science, 16*(1), 3–18. doi:10.1287/orsc.1040.0103

Boughanmi. H. (1995). *Les principaux volets des politiques agricoles en Tunisie: évolution, analyse et performances agricoles*. CIHEAM-options méditerranéennes, ser.B/n 14, les agricultures maghrébines à l'aube de l'an 2000.

Bouhnik, D., & Marcus, T. (2006). Interaction in distance‚Äêlearning courses. *Journal of the American Society for Information Science and Technology, 57*(3), 299–305. doi:10.1002/asi.20277

Boulding, K. E. (1956). General systems theory the skeleton of science. *Management Science, 2*(3), 197–208. doi:10.1287/mnsc.2.3.197

Bourdieu, P. (1990). *The Logic of Practice*. Cambridge, MA: Polity Press.

Bowden, J. L. H. (2009). The process of customer engagement: A conceptual framework. *Journal of Marketing Theory and Practice, 17*(1), 63–74. doi:10.2753/MTP1069-6679170105

Bowman, C., & Ambrosini, V. (2003). How the resource-based and the dynamic capability views of the firm inform corporate -level strategy. *British Journal of Management, 14*(1), 289–303. doi:10.1111/j.1467-8551.2003.00380.x

Boyd, D. E., Clarke, T., & Spekman, R. (2014). The emergence and impact of consumer brand empowerment in online social networks: A proposed ontology. *Journal of Brand Management, 21*(6), 516–531. doi:10.1057/bm.2014.20

Brabazon, T. (2002). *Digital hemlock: Internet education and the poisoning of teaching*. Sydney: UNSW Press.

Brabham, D. C. (2008). Crowdsourcing as a model for problem solving an introduction and cases. *Convergence (London), 14*(1), 75–90. doi:10.1177/1354856507084420

Brakus, J. J., Schmitt, B. H., & Zarantonello, L. (2009). Brand Experience: What is It? How Is It Measured? Does It Affect Loyalty? *Journal of Marketing, 73*(3), 52–68. doi:10.1509/jmkg.73.3.52

Brannen, J. (2004). Working Qualitatively and Quantitatively. In C. Seale, D. Silverman, J. F. Gubrium, & G. Gobo (Eds.), *Qualitative Research Practice* (pp. 312–315). London: Sage Publications. doi:10.4135/9781848608191.d25

Brazeal, D. V., & Herbert, T. T. (1999). The genesis of entrepreneurship. *Entrepreneurship Theory and Practice, 23*, 29–25.

Brem, A., & Voigt, K. (2007). Innovation management in emerging technology ventures –The concept of an integrated idea management. *Int. J. Technology, Policy, and Management, 7*(3).

Brown, S. L., & Eisenhardt, K. M. (1995). Product development: Past research, present findings, and future directions. *Academy of Management Review, 20*, 343–378.

Buchanan, E. A. (2004). *Readings in Virtual Research Ethics: Issues and Controversies*. Hershey, PA: Idea Group Publishing. doi:10.4018/978-1-59140-152-0

Bucy, E. P., Lang, A., Potter, R. F., & Grabe, M. E. (1998). *Structural features of cyberspace: A content analysis of the World Wide Web*. Paper presented at the 1998 Conference of the Association for Education in Journalism and Mass Communication, Theory and Methodology Division, Baltimore, MD.

Budeanu, A. (2013). Sustainability and Tourism Social Media. *Tourism Social Science Series*, *18*, 87–103.

Bunge, M. (1977). Treatise on basic philosophy: Vol. 3. *Ontology I: The furniture of the World*. Boston: Reidel.

Bunge, M. (1979). Treatise on basic philosophy: Vol. 4. *Ontology II: A World of systems*. Boston: Reidel.

Burgelman, R. A. (1991). Intraorganizational ecology of strategy making and organizational adaptation: Theory and field research. *Organization Science*, *2*(3), 239–262. doi:10.1287/orsc.2.3.239

Burger-Helmchen, T., & Pénin, J. (2010). The limits of crowdsourcing inventive activities: What do transaction cost theory and the evolutionary theories of the firm teach us. In *Workshop on Open Source Innovation*, Strasbourg, France.

Burris, V., Smith, E., & Strahm, A. (2000). White supremacist network on the Internet. *Sociological Focus*, *33*(2), 215–234. doi:10.1080/00380237.2000.10571166

Büscher, B., & Igoe, J. (2013). 'Prosuming' conservation? Web 2.0, nature and the intensification of value-producing labour in the late capitalism. *Journal of Consumer Culture*, *13*(3), 283–305. doi:10.1177/1469540513482691

Butler, J. (2006). *Hankala sukupuoli* [Gender trouble: Feminism, and the subversion of identity]. Helsinki: Gaudeamus.

Bygrave, W. D., & Hofer, C. W. (1991). Theorizing about entrepreneurship. *Entrepreneurship Theory and Practice*, *16*, 13–22.

Cabiddu, F., De Carlo, M., & Piccoli, G. (2014). Social media affordances: Enabling customer engagement. *Annals of Tourism Research*, *48*, 75–192. doi:10.1016/j.annals.2014.06.003

Cadilhon, J.-J., Fearne, A. P., Giac Tam, P. T., Moustier, P., & Poole, N. D. (2006). Quality incentives and dependence in vegetable supply chains to Ho Chi Minh City. *Acta Horticulturae*, (699), 111–117. doi:10.17660/ActaHortic.2006.699.11

Cantatore, F. (2011). *Authors, Copyright and the Digital Evolution*. Retrieved on November 20, 2011, from http://www.surveymonkey.com

Cantatore, F. (2012). *Negotiating a changing landscape: Authors, Copyright and the Digital Evolution* (Unpublished doctoral dissertation). Bond University, Queensland, Australia.

Capaldo, G., Iandoli, L., & Ponsiglione, C. (2004). *Entrepreneurial competencies and training needs of small firms*. Paper presented at the 14th Annual International Entrepreneurial Conference, Napoli.

Carbon, L. P., & Haeckel, S. H. (1994). Engineering Customer Experiences. *Marketing Management*, *3*(3), 9–19.

Carduff, K. (2010). *Corporate Reporting: From Stewardship to Contract*. The Annual Reports of the United States Steel Corporation (1902-2006).

Carlile, P. R. (2002). A pragmatic view of knowledge and boundaries: Boundary objects in new product development. *Organization Science*, *13*(4), 442–455. doi:10.1287/orsc.13.4.442.2953

Carrol, A. B. (1991). The pyramid of corporate social responsibility: Toward the moral management of organisasional stakeholders. *Business Horizons*, *34*(4), 39–48. doi:10.1016/0007-6813(91)90005-G

Carter, C., Clegg, S. R., & Kornberger, M. (2008). So!apbox: editorial essays: Strategy as practice? *Strategic Organization*, *6*(1), 83–99. doi:10.1177/1476127007087154

Castellani, A., Loreto, S., Rahman, A., Fossati, T., & Dijk, E. (2014). *Guidelines for HTTP-CoAP Mapping Implementations*. Retrieved from http://www.w3.org/TR/json-ld/(Jan. 2014)

CEMA. (2014). *Promouvoir le développement rural et agricole en Afrique grâce à la mécanisation agricole (MA) avancée*. Comité Européen des groupements de constructeurs du machinisme agrico.

Chamberlin, S., & Moon, S. (2005). Model-eliciting activities: An introduction to gifted education. *Journal of Secondary Gifted Education, 17*(1), 37–47.

Chandler, A. (1962). *Strategy and structure*. Cambridge, MA: MIT Press.

Chandler, G., Keller, C., & Lyon, D. (2000). Unravelling the determinants and consequences of an innovation-supportive organizational culture. *Entrepreneurship Theory and Practice, 25*, 59–76.

Chang, M. C., & Wang, Y. H. (2011). A study on visitors' understanding of water-saving technology through museum hands-on activities. *Technology Museum Review, 15*(1), 10.

Chan, H. C., Tan, C. H., & Teo, H. H. (2014). Data Modeling: An Ontological Perspective of Pointers. *Database Management, 25*(4), 17–37. doi:10.4018/JDM.2014100102

Chaston, I., Badger, B., & Sadler-Smith, E. (1999). Organisational learning: Research issues and application in SME sector firms. *International Journal of Entrepreneurial Behavior & Research, 5*(4), 191–203. doi:10.1108/13552559910293146

Chaudhuri, A., & Holbrook, M. B. (2001). The Chain of Effects From Brand Trust and Brand Affect to Brand Performance: The Role of Brand Loyalty. *Journal of Marketing, 65*(2), 81–94. doi:10.1509/jmkg.65.2.81.18255

Cheema, A., & Papatla, P. (2010). Relative importance of online versus offline information for Internet purchases: Product category and Internet experience effects. *Journal of Business Research, 63*(9-10), 979–985. doi:10.1016/j.jbusres.2009.01.021

Chellappa, R. K., & Paol, A. P. (2002). Perceived information security, financial liability and consumer trust in electronic commerce transactions. *Logistic Information Management, 15*(5-6), 358–368. doi:10.1108/09576050210447046

Cheng, M. I., Dainty, A. R. J., & Moore, D. R. (2003). The differing faces of managerial competency in Britain and America. *Journal of Management Development, 22*(6), 526–537. doi:10.1108/02621710310478495

Chen, H. K. (2005). Technology Concept Scale Development - dissemination of scientific and technical education to the secondary level. *Living Technology Education, 38*(4), 35–54.

Chen, S. C., & Dhillon, G. S. (2003). Interpreting dimensions of consumer trust in e-commerce. *Information Technology Management, 4*(2-3), 303–318. doi:10.1023/A:1022962631249

Chen, W., & Looi, C. (2007). Incorporating online discussion in face to face classroom learning: A new blended learning approach. *Australasian Journal of Educational Technology, 23*(3), 307. doi:10.14742/ajet.1255

Chesbrough, H. (2006). Open innovation: A new paradigm for understanding industrial innovation. In H. Chesbrough, W. Vanhaverbeke, & J. West (Eds.), Open innovation: Researching a new paradigm (pp. 1–14). Oxford, UK: Oxford University Press.

Cheung, R., & Lam, P. (2009). How travel agency survive in e-business world? *Communications of the IMIBA, 10*, 85–92.

Chia, R., & MacKay, B. (2007). Post-processual challenges for the emerging strategy-as-practice perspective: Discovering strategy in the logic of practice. *Human Relations, 60*(1), 217–242. doi:10.1177/0018726707075291

Choi, . (1997). *The Economics of Electronic Commerce*. Macmillan Technical Publications.

Choi, J. N., & Chan, J. Y. (2009). Innovation Implementation in the Public Sector: An Integration of Institutional Collective Dynamics. *The Journal of Applied Psychology*, *94*(1), 245–253. doi:10.1037/a0012994 PMID:19186909

Choi, M. S., & Rifon, N. J. (2010). Antecedents and consequences of Web advertising credibility: A study of consumer response to banner ads. *Journal of Interactive Advertising*, *3*(1), 12–24. doi:10.1080/15252019.2002.10722064

Chong, H. G. (2008). Measuring performance of small and medium sized enterprises: The grounded theory approach. *Journal of Business and Public Affairs*, *2*, 1.

Chou, C. M. (2005). *Originality thinking training*. Taipei: Chuan Hwa Publishing Ltd.

Choudhury, M. (2009). *Money, Finance, and the Real Economy in Islamic Banking and Finance: Perspectives from the Maqasid as-Shari'ah* (Unpublished MSC Dissertation). Department of Economics, University of Stirling, UK.

Choudhury. (2012). A probabilistic model of random fields. *International Journal of Operations Research*.

Choudhury, M. A. (2011). *Islamic Economics and Finance: an Epistemological Inquiry*. Bingley, UK: Emerald.

Christodoulides, G., & de Chernatony, L. (2004). Dimensionalising on- and offline brands' composite equity. *Journal of Product and Brand Management*, *13*(3), 168–179. doi:10.1108/10610420410538069

Chroneer, D. (2005). The impact of supply chain information and networking on product development in Swedish process industry. *International Journal of Logistics Systems and Management*, *1*(2), 127–148. doi:10.1504/IJLSM.2005.005968

Chung, C. J., Kim, H., & Kim, J. H. (2010). An anatomy of the credibility of online newspapers. *Online Information Review*, *34*(5), 669–685. doi:10.1108/14684521011084564

Chu, Y. M. (2010). *A study on the current situations and the development of assessment tools for technology conceptual knowledge in junior high schools*. Kaohsiung: Liwen Publishers Co., Ltd.

Chu, Y. M. (2010). *Current status and development of conceptual knowledge evaluation instrument for science and technology curricula in junior high school. Kaohsiung City*. Liwen Publishers Co., Ltd.

Clark, J. S., & Youngblood, C. E. (1992). Estimating Duality Models with Biased Technical Change: A Time Series Approach. *American Journal of Agricultural Economics*, *74*(2), 353–360. doi:10.2307/1242489

Clay, E.J. (1982). Technical innovation and public polic: agricultural development in the Kosi Region, Bihar, India. *Agricultural Administration, 9*, 189-210.

Coates, H., James, R., & Baldwin, G. (2005). A critical examination of the effects of learning management systems on university teaching and learning. *Tertiary Education and Management, 11*, 19-36.

Colitti, W., Steenhaut, K., & De Caro, N. (2011). De Integrating Wireless Sensor Networks with the Web. In *Proceedings of Workshop on Extending the Internet to Low power and Lossy Networks*.

Collins, R. (1975). *Conflict Sociology: Toward an Exploratory Science*. New York: Academic Press.

Collis, B., Bruijstens, H., & van Veen, J. K. (2003). Course redesign for blended learning: Modern optics for technical professionals. *International Journal of Continuing Engineering Education and Lifelong Learning*, *13*(1), 22–38. doi:10.1504/IJCEELL.2003.002151

Commission on Global Governance. (1995). Global Civic Ethic. In *Our Global Neighbourhood, a Report of the Commission on Global Governance*. New York, NY: Oxford University Press.

Concannon, F., Flynn, A., & Campbell, M. (2005). What campus-based students think about the quality and benefits of e-learning. *British Journal of Educational Technology*, *36*(3), 501–512. doi:10.1111/j.1467-8535.2005.00482.x

Conrad, D. (2005). Building and maintaining community in cohort-based online learning. *Journal of Distance Education, 20*(1), 1.

Constantinides, E. (2004). Influencing The Online Consumer's Behavior: The Web Experience. *Internet Research, 14*(2), 111–126. doi:10.1108/10662240410530835

Copyright Act 1968 (Cth) (Australia).

Copyright Act 1976 (USA).

Copyright, Designs and Patents Act 1988 (UK).

Costco Wholesale Corp. v Omega, SA 131 S.C. 565 US (2010).

Creyer, E. H. (1997). The Influence of Firm Behavior on Purchase Intention: Do Consumers Really Care About Business Ethics? *Journal of Consumer Marketing, 14*(6), 421–432. doi:10.1108/07363769710185999

Cross, S. E., Kippelen, B., & Berthelot, Y. H. (2014). Reaching Across the Pond: Extending a Regional Innovation Ecosystem Strategy, In B. Galbraith (Ed.), *European Conference on Innovation and Entrepreneurship* (p. 128). Academic Conferences International Limited.

Culnan, M. J., & Milne, R. G. (2001). *The Culnan-Milne survey on consumers and online privacy notices: summary of responses.* Federal Trade Commission. Available at: http://www.ftc.gov/bcp/workshops/glb/supporting/culnan-milne.pdf

Cunliffe, A. L. (2010). Retelling tales of the field. In search of organizational ethnography 20 years on. *Organizational Research Methods, 13*(2), 224–239. doi:10.1177/1094428109340041

Czarniawska, B. (2004). *Narratives in Social Science Research.* London: Sage. doi:10.4135/9781849209502

Daft, R. L. (1995). *Organization theory and design.* New York: West Publishing.

Dahlander, L., & Magnusson, M. (2008). How do firms make use of open source communities? *Long Range Planning, 41*(6), 629–649. doi:10.1016/j.lrp.2008.09.003

Dahlander, L., & Magnusson, M. G. (2005). Relationships between open source software companies and communities: Observations from Nordic firms. *Research Policy, 34*(4), 481–493. doi:10.1016/j.respol.2005.02.003

Dahlén, M. (2002). Thinking and feeling on the World Wide Web:the impact of product type and time on World Wide Web advertising effectiveness. *Journal of Marketing Communications, Vol, 8*(2), 115–125. doi:10.1080/13527260210142347

Dahlén, M., & Bergendahl, J. (2001). Informing and transforming on the web: An empirical study of response to banner ads for functional and expressive products. *International Journal of Advertising, 20*(2), 189–205.

Dahlén, M., Murray, M., & Nordenstam, S. (2004). An empirical study of perceptions of implicit meanings in World Wide Web advertisements versus print advertisements. *Journal of Marketing Communications, 10*(1), 35–47. doi:10.1080/1352726042000177391

Dahlman, E., Skold, J., & Beming, P. (2008). *3G Evolution: HSPA and LTE for Mobile Broadband.* Academic Press.

Dalsgaard, S. (2008). Facework on Facebook: The presentation of self in virtual life and its role in the US elections. *Anthropology Today, 24*(6), 8–12. doi:10.1111/j.1467-8322.2008.00626.x

Dameron, S., Lê, J. K., & LeBaron, C. (2015). Materializing strategy and strategizing material: Why matter matters. *British Journal of Management, 26*, 1–12. doi:10.1111/1467-8551.12084

Davidaviciene, V., Gatautis, R., Paliulis, N., & Petrauskas, R. (2009). Electronic Business. Vilnius: VGTU.

Davis, F. D. (1989). Perceived usefulness, perceived ease of use and user acceptance of information technology. *Management Information Systems Quarterly*, *13*(3), 319–340. doi:10.2307/249008

Day, G. (1999). *The market-driven organization: understanding, attracting and keeping valuable customers*. New York: The Free Press.

De Certeau, M. (1984). *The practice of everyday life*. Berkeley, CA: University of California Press.

de Chernatony, L., & Christodoulides, G. (2004). Taking the brand promise online: Challenges and opportunities. *Interactive Marketing*, *5*(3), 238–251. doi:10.1057/palgrave.im.4340241

de Laat, P. B. (2005). Copyright or copyleft?: An analysis of property regimes for software development. *Research Policy*, *34*(10), 1511–1532. doi:10.1016/j.respol.2005.07.003

De Lange, P., Suwardy, T., & Mavondo, F. (2003). Integrating a virtual learning environment into an introductory accounting course: Determinants of student motivation. *Accounting Education*, *12*(1), 1–14. doi:10.1080/0963928032000064567

De Witt, C., & Kerres, M. (2003). A didactical framework for the design of blended learning arrangements. *Journal of Educational Media*, *28*(2/3), 101–114. doi:10.1080/1358165032000165653

Dean, J. W. Jr, & Bowen, D. E. (1994). Management Theory and Total Quality: Improving Research and Practice Through Theory Development. *Academy of Management Review*, *19*(3), 392–418.

Delchet, K. (2004). *Qu'est-ce que le développement durable?*. Academic Press.

Delgado-Ballester, E. (2001). *Development and validation of a brand trust scale*. Twin Cities, MN: University of Minnesota.

Delgado-Ballester, E., & Munuera-Aleman, J. L. (2001). Brand trust in the context of consumer loyalty. *European Journal of Marketing*, *11*(12), 1238–1258. doi:10.1108/EUM0000000006475

Delialioglu, O., & Yildirim, Z. (2008). Design and development of a technology enhanced hybrid instruction based on MOLTA model: Its effectiveness in comparison to traditional instruction. *Computers & Education*, *51*(1), 474–483. doi:10.1016/j.compedu.2007.06.006

Demetriadis, S., & Pombortsis, A. (2007). E-lectures for flexible learning: A study on their learning efficiency. *Journal of Educational Technology and Society*, *10*(2), 147.

Demir, R. (2015). Strategic activity as bundled affordances. *British Journal of Management*, *26*, S125–S141. doi:10.1111/1467-8551.12083

Denzin, N. K., & Lincoln, Y. S. (Eds.). (2005). *Handbook of Qualitative Research* (2nd ed.). London: Sage Publications.

Dewar, R. D., & Dutton, J. E. (1986). The adoption of radical and incremental innovations: An empirical analysis. *Management Science*, *32*(11), 1422–1433. doi:10.1287/mnsc.32.11.1422

Dinev, T., & Hart, P. (2006, January1). Internet privacy concerns and social awareness as determinants of intention to transact. *International Journal of Electronic Commerce*, *10*(2), 7–29. doi:10.2753/JEC1086-4415100201

Ding, X. D., Huang, Y., & Verma, R. (2011). Customer experience in online financial services: A study of behavioral intentions for techno-ready market segments. *Journal of Service Management*, *22*(3), 344–366. doi:10.1108/09564231111136863

Dou, R., Wu, J., Zhang, S., & Liang, W. (2010). A Web-based advertising content analysis platform. *Future Information Technology and Management Engineering (FITME),International Conference*.

Dreyfus, H.L. & Rabinow, P. (1983). *M. Foucault: Beyond structuralism and hermeneutics, the archeology of the human sciences*. Chicago, IL: University of Chicago Press.

Drucker, P. F. (1993). The Ecological Vision: Reflections on the American Condition. Transaction Publishers.

Drucker, P. F. (1961). The Technological Revolution--Notes on the Relationship of Technology, Science and Culture. *Technology and Culture, 2*(4), 342–351. doi:10.2307/3100889

Drucker, P. F. (1976). *The Unseen Revolution: How Pension Fund Socialism Came to America.* New York: Harper and Row.

Dubouloz, J. (2006). Acception et défense des loca publica dans les Variae de Cassiodore, Un point de vue juridique sur la cité. dans M. Ghilardi, Ch. J. Goddard et P. Porena dir., Les cités de l'Italie tardo-antique (IVe –VIe siècle), Institutions, économie, société, culture et religion. *Actes du colloque de l'Ecole française de Rome, 369,* 53-74.

Dunning, J. H. (2000). The eclectic paradigm as an envelope for economic and business theories of MNE activity. *International Business Review, 9*(2), 163–190.

Durvasula, S., & Lysonski, S. (2001). Are there global dimensions of beliefs toward advertising in general: A multicultural investigation. In C. P. Rao (Ed.), Globalization and its managerial implications (pp. 184–202). Westport, CT: Quorum Books.

Dzakiria, H., Wahab, M. S. D. A., & Rahman, H. D. A. (2012). Blended Learning (BL) as Pedagogical Alternative to Teach Business Communication Course: Case Study of UUM Executive Diploma Program. *Turkish Online Journal of Distance Education, 13*(3).

Dziuban, C., & Moskal, P. (2001). Evaluating distributed learning at metropolitan universities. *EDUCAUSE Quarterly, 24*(4), 60–61.

Earls, N. (2008). *Submission to Productivity Commission, Canberra.* Retrieved on November 20, 2011, from http://www.pc.gov.au/projects/study/books/submissions#initial

Eastlick, M. A., Lotz, S. L., & Warrington, P. (2006). Understanding Online B-toC Relationships: An Integrated Model of Privacy Concern, Trust and Commitment. *Journal of Business Research, 59*(8), 2006. doi:10.1016/j.jbusres.2006.02.006

Edginton, A., & Holbrook, J. (2010). A blended learning approach to teaching basic pharmacokinetics and the significance of face-to-face interaction. *American Journal of Pharmaceutical Education, 74*(5), 88. doi:10.5688/aj740588 PMID:20798797

Edmondson, A. C. (1999). Psychological safety and learning behaviour in work teams. *Administrative Science Quarterly, 44*(2), 350–383. doi:10.2307/2666999

Edmondson, A. C., Bohmer, R., & Pisano, G. P. (2001). Disrupted routines: Team learning and new technology adaptation. *Administrative Science Quarterly, 46,* 685–716. doi:10.2307/3094828

Edward, M., & Sahadev, S. (2012). Modeling The Consequences of Customer Confusion in A Service Marketing Context: An Empirical Study. *Journal of Service Research, 12*(2), 127–146.

Eisenhardt, K. M., & Martin, J. A. (2000). Dynamic capabilities: What are they? *Strategic Management Journal, 21*(10-11), 1105–1121. doi:10.1002/1097-0266(200010/11)21:10/11<1105::AID-SMJ133>3.0.CO;2-E

Ellis, R. A., Goodyear, P., Prosser, M., & OHara, A. (2006). How and what university students learn through online and face-to-face discussion: Conceptions, intentions and approaches. *Journal of Computer Assisted Learning, 22*(4), 244–256. doi:10.1111/j.1365-2729.2006.00173.x

Ellis, R. A., Steed, A. F., & Applebee, A. C. (2006). Teacher conceptions of blended learning, blended teaching and associations with approaches to design. *Australasian Journal of Educational Technology, 22*(3), 312. doi:10.14742/ajet.1289

Ellis, R., & Calvo, R. (2004). Learning through discussions in blended environments. *Educational Media International, 41*(3), 263–274. doi:10.1080/09523980410001680879

Ellis, S. T., & Griffith, D. (2001). The Evaluation of IT Ethical Scenarios Using a Multidimensional Scale. *The Data Base for Advances in Information Systems, 32*(1), 75–85. doi:10.1145/506740.506750

Emirbayer, M., & Mische, A. (1998). What is agency? *American Journal of Sociology, 103*(4), 962–1023. doi:10.1086/231294

Entwistle, N. (2005). Learning outcomes and ways of thinking across contrasting disciplines and settings in higher education. *Curriculum Journal, 16*(1), 67–82. doi:10.1080/09585170420000336818

Erickson, H. L. (2002). *Concept Based Curriculum and Instruction.* Thousand Oaks, CA: Corwin.

Eriksson, P., & Kovalainen, A. (2008). *Qualitative methods in business research.* New York, NY: Simon & Schuster. doi:10.4135/9780857028044

Eriksson, P., & Kovalainen, A. (2008). *Qualitative Methods in Business Research.* Sage Publications Ltd.

Eriksson, P., & Kovalainen, A. (2015). *Qualitative Methods in Business Research. 2nd extended edition.* London: SAGE.

Esposti, R. (2002). Public agricultural R&D design and technological spill-ins a dynamic model. *Revue Research Policy, 31*, 693–717.

Estevez, B., & Domon, G. (1999). Les enjeux sociaux de l'agriculture durable un débat de société nécessaire? Une perspective nord-américaine. *Courrière de l'environnement, 36.*

Ettlie, J. E. (1983). Organizational policy and innovation among suppliers to the food processing sector. *Academy of Management Journal, 26*(1), 27–44. doi:10.2307/256133

Ettlie, J. E. (2006). *Managing Innovation, New Technology, New Products, and New Services in a Global Economy.* Burlington, MA: Elsevier Butterworth-Heinemann Publications.

Etzioni, A. (1964). *Modern Organizations.* Upper Saddle River, NJ: Prentice Hall.

Eurich, M., Lavoisy, O., Forest, F., Ytterstad, P., Akselsen, S., Tierno, A., ... Villalonga, C. (2010). *Business models and Value Creation.* SENSEI project. Deliverable 1.4.

Faber, R. J., Lee, M., & Nan, X. (2004). Advertising and the consumer information environment online. *The American Behavioral Scientist, 48*(4), 447–466. doi:10.1177/0002764204270281

Fadavi, R., Keyhani, A., & Mohtasebi, S. S. (2010, December). Estimation of a Mechanization Index in Apple Orchard in Iran. *The Journal of Agricultural Science, 2*(4).

Fagerberg, J., Mowery, D. C., & Nelson, R. R. (Eds.). (2006). *The Oxford handbook of innovation.* Oxford, UK: Oxford University Press. doi:10.1093/oxfordhb/9780199286805.001.0001

Farmer, R. E. A. (2010). *Will monetary and fiscal policy work?. In How the Economy Works.* Oxford, UK: Oxford University Press.

Feder. G & Umali. D. L. (1993). The Adoption of Agricultural Innovations. *Technological Forecasting and Social Change, 43*, 215-239.

Feijoo, C., Maghiros, I., Abadie, F., & Gomer-Barroso, J. L. (2009). Exploring a Heterogeneous and Fragmented Digital Ecosystem: Mobile Content. *Telematics and Informatics, 26*(3), 173–292. doi:10.1016/j.tele.2008.11.009

Fernandez, M. T. F., Jimenez, F. J. B., & Roura, J. R. C. (2015). Business incubation: Innovative services in an entrepreneurship ecosystem. *Service Industries Journal, 35*(14), 783–800. doi:10.1080/02642069.2015.1080243

Fersino, V., & Petruzzella, D. (2002). Organic agriculture in the Mediterranean area: state of the art.Options Méditerranéennes: Série B. Etudes et Recherches, 40, 9- 51.

Fetterman, D. M. (2010). *Ethnography: Step-by-step*. Thousand Oaks, CA: SAGE Publications.

Fitzgerald, B. (2006). The transformation of open source software. *Management Information Systems Quarterly, 30*(3), 587–598.

Flanagin, A. J., & Metzger, M. J. (2007). The role of site features, user attributes, and information verification behaviors on the perceived credibility of web-based information. *New Media and Society, 9*.

Fligstein, N., & Mara-Drita, I. (1996). How to make a market: Reflections on the European Union's Single Market Program. *American Journal of Sociology, 102*, 1–33. doi:10.1086/230907

Floyd, S. W., & Wooldridge, B. (2000). *Building strategy from the middle: Reconceptualizing strategy process*. Thousand Oaks, CA: Sage.

Fontana, A., & Frey, J. H. (2005). The Interview: From Neutral Stance to Political Involvement. In N. K. Denzin & Y. S. Lincoln (Eds.), *Handbook of Qualitative Research* (3rd ed.; pp. 695–728). London: Sage Publications.

Foster, C., & Heeks, R. (2013). Conceptualising Inclusive Innovation: Modifying systems of innovation frameworks to understand diffusion of new technology to low-income consumers. *European Journal of Development Research, 25*(3), 333–355. doi:10.1057/ejdr.2013.7

Foster, R. J. (2009). The Work of the New Economy: Consumers, Brands, and Value Creation. *Cultural Anthropology, 22*(4), 707–731. doi:10.1525/can.2007.22.4.707

Foucault, M. (1977). *Discipline and Punish: The Birth of the Prison*. New York: Random House.

Foxman, E. R., Muehling, D. D., & Berger, P. W. (1990). An investigation of factors contributing to consumer brand confusion. *The Journal of Consumer Affairs, 24*(1), 170–189. doi:10.1111/j.1745-6606.1990.tb00264.x

Frey, K., Lüthje, C., & Haag, S. (2011). Whom should firms attract to open innovation platforms? The role of knowledge diversity and motivation. *Long Range Planning, 44*(5), 397–420. doi:10.1016/j.lrp.2011.09.006

Friedman, M. (1989). Quantity Theory of Money. New Palgrave: Money. doi:10.1007/978-1-349-19804-7_1

Friedman, M. (1960). *A Program for Monetary Stability*. New York, NY: Fordham University Press.

Frosch, D. L., Krueger, P. M., Honrik, R. C., Cronholm, P. F., & Barg, F. K. (2007). "Creating Demand for Prescription Drugs: A Content Analysis of Television Direct-to-Consumer Advertising", 1 (January). *Annals of Family Medicine*, 16–13.

Frosch, R. A., & Gallopoulos, N. E. (1989). Strategies for manufacturing. *Scientific American, 261*(3), 144–152. doi:10.1038/scientificamerican0989-144

Frutiger, M., Narasimhan, S., & Slaughter, S. (2014). A Business Ecosystem Perspective on Open Platforms and Outsourcing Relationships: A Software Industry Case Study. In R. Hirschheim, A. Heinzl, & J. Dibbern (Eds.), *Information Systems Outsourcing* (pp. 501–515). Mannheim, Germany: Springer. doi:10.1007/978-3-662-43820-6_20

Gächter, S., von Krogh, G., & Haefliger, S. (2010). Initiating private-collective innovation: The fragility of knowledge sharing. *Research Policy, 39*(7), 893–906. doi:10.1016/j.respol.2010.04.010

Gallen, C. (2014, March). *More than Half-a-billion Wireless Smart Home Monitoring Devices to be Installed Worldwide by 2018, Finds ABI Research*. Academic Press.

Gamble, J., Thompson, A., & Peteraf, M. (2014). *Essentials of Strategic Management: The Quest for Competitive Advantage*. McGraw-Hill/Irwin.

Ganalassi, S. (2008). The Influence of the Design of Web Survey Questionnaires on the Quality of Responses. *Survey Research Methods*, *2*(1), 21–32.

Garener, M. P., Mitchell, A. A., & Russo, E. J. (1985). Low involvement strategies for processing advertisements. *Journal of Advertising*, *14*(2), 4–56. doi:10.1080/00913367.1985.10672941

Garrison, D. R., & Anderson, T. (2003). *E-learning in the 21st century: A framework for research and practice*. Routledge.

Garrison, D. R., & Vaughan, N. (2008). *Blended learning in higher education; framework, principles, and guidelines* (Vol. 23). Academic Press.

Garrison, D. R., Anderson, T., & Archer, W. (1999). Critical inquiry in a text-based environment: Computer conferencing in higher education. *The Internet and Higher Education*, *2*(2), 87–105. doi:10.1016/S1096-7516(00)00016-6

Garrison, D. R., & Arbaugh, J. B. (2007). Researching the community of inquiry framework: Review, issues, and future directions. *The Internet and Higher Education*, *10*(3), 157–172. doi:10.1016/j.iheduc.2007.04.001

Garrison, D. R., & Kanuka, H. (2004). Blended learning: Uncovering its transformative potential in higher education. *The Internet and Higher Education*, *7*(2), 95–105. doi:10.1016/j.iheduc.2004.02.001

Gary, M. S. (2005). Implementation Strategy and Performance Outcomes in Related Diversification. *Strategic Management Journal*, *26*(7), 643–664. doi:10.1002/smj.468

Gaskill, L. A. R., & Van Auken, H. E. (1993). A factor analytic study of the perceived causes of small business failure. *Journal of Small Business Management*, *31*(4), 18–31.

Gaziano, C., & McGrath, K. (1986). Measuring the concept of credibility. *The Journalism Quarterly*, *63*(3), 451–462. doi:10.1177/107769908606300301

Gedik, N., Kiraz, E., & Ozden, M. Y. (2013). Design of a blended learning environment: Considerations and implementation issues. *Australasian Journal of Educational Technology*, *29*(1). doi:10.14742/ajet.6

Gençer, M., Oba, B., Özel, B., & Tunalıoğlu, V. S. (2006). Forking: The GPL coherent technology for flexible organizing in foss development. European Group of Organizational Studies 2006 Colloqium, Bergen, Norway.

Gençer, M., & Oba, B. (2011). Organising the digital commons: A case study on engagement strategies in open source. *Technology Analysis and Strategic Management*, *23*(9), 969–982. doi:10.1080/09537325.2011.616698

George, G., McGahan, A. M., & Prabhu, J. (2012). Innovation for inclusive growth: Towards a theoretical framework and a research agenda. *Journal of Management Studies*, *49*(4), 661–683. doi:10.1111/j.1467-6486.2012.01048.x

Gerbic, P. (2011). Teaching using a blended approach - what does the literature tell us? *Educational Media International*, *48*(3), 221–234. doi:10.1080/09523987.2011.615159

Gerschenfeld, N., & Vasseur, J. P. (2014). As objects go online. *Foreign Affairs*, *93*(2), 60–67.

Gerstenfeld, P. B., Grant, D. R., & Chiang, C. (2003). Hate Online: A Content Analysis of Extremist Internet Sites. *Analyses of Social Issues and Public Policy (ASAP)*, *3*(1), 29–44. doi:10.1111/j.1530-2415.2003.00013.x

Giddens, A. (1984). *The Constitution of Society. Outline of the Theory of Structuration.* Berkeley, CA: University of California Press.

Giddens, A. (2001). *Sociology* (4th ed.). Cambridge, UK: Polity Press.

Gimpel, G., & Westerman, G. (2012). *Shaping the Future: Seven Enduring Principles for Fast Changing Industries.* Working Paper-MIT Center for Digital Business.

Ginns, P., & Ellis, R. (2007). Quality in blended learning: Exploring the relationships between on-line and face-to-face teaching and learning. *The Internet and Higher Education, 10*(1), 53–64. doi:10.1016/j.iheduc.2006.10.003

Ginns, P., Prosser, M., & Barrie, S. (2007). Students perceptions of teaching quality in higher education: The perspective of currently enrolled students. *Studies in Higher Education, 32*(5), 603–615. doi:10.1080/03075070701573773

Goldstein, P. (2003). *Copyright's highway: From Gutenberg to the Celestial Jukebox.* Stanford, CA: Stanford University Press.

Gomez, C., & Paradells, J. (2010). Wireless home automation networks: A survey of architectures and technologies. *Communications Magazine, IEEE, 48*(6), 92–101. doi:10.1109/MCOM.2010.5473869

Gommans, M., Krishnan, K. S., & Scheffold, K. B. (2001). From Brand Loyalty to e-Loyalty: A Conceptual Framework. *Journal of Economic and Social Research, 3*(1), 43-58.

Gonzalez, C. (2009). Conceptions of, and approaches to, teaching online: A study of lecturers teaching postgraduate distance courses. *Higher Education, 57*(3), 299–314. doi:10.1007/s10734-008-9145-1

Gonzalez, C. (2010). What do university teachers think eLearning is good for in their teaching? *Studies in Higher Education, 35*(1), 61–78. doi:10.1080/03075070902874632

Gouldner, A. W. (1959). Organizational analysis. Sociology Today, 400-428.

Graetz, K. A., & Goliber, M. J. (2002). Designing collaborative learning places: Psychological foundations and new frontiers. *New Directions for Teaching and Learning, 2002*(92), 13–22. doi:10.1002/tl.75

Graham, C. R. (2006). Blended Learning Systems. Definitions, current trends and future directions. In C. J. Bonk & C. R. Graham (Eds.), The Handbook of Blended Learning: Global Perspectives, Local Designs (pp. 3-21). San Francisco: Pfeiffer.

Graham, C. R., Allen, S., & Ure, D. (2003). *Blended learning environments: A review of the research literature.* Unpublished manuscript, Provo, UT.

Graham, C. R., Allen, S., & Ure, D. (2005). Benefits and challenges of blended learning environments. In M. Khosrow-Pour (Ed.), *Encyclopedia of information science and technology* (pp. 53–259). Hershey, PA: Idea Group. doi:10.4018/978-1-59140-553-5.ch047

Gretzel, U., Kyung, H. Y., & Purifoy, M. (2007). *Online travel review study. Role & impact of online travel reviews.* Laboratory for intelligent systems in tourism. Retrieved from http://www.tripadvisor.com/pdfs/OnlineTravelReviewReport.pdf

Gunasekaran, A., Lai, K. H., & Cheng, T. C. E. (2008). Responsive supply chain: A competitive strategy in a networked economy. *The International Journal of Management Science, Omega, 36*(4), 549-564.

Gunasekaran, A., Marri, H. B., McGaughey, R. E., & Nebhwani, M. D. (2002). E-commerce and its impact on operations management. *International Journal of Production Economics, 75*(1-2), 185–197. doi:10.1016/S0925-5273(01)00191-8

Haeckel, S. (1999). *Adaptive enterprise: Creating and leading sense-and-respond organizations*. Boston: Harvard School of Business.

Hage, J. T. (1999). Organizational innovation and organizational change. *Annual Review of Sociology, 25*(1), 597–622. doi:10.1146/annurev.soc.25.1.597

Ha, H.-Y., & Perks, H. (2005). Effect of Consumer Perceptions of Brand Experience on The Web: Brand Familiarity, Satisfaction, and Brand Trust. *Journal of Consumer Behaviour, 4*(6), 438–452. doi:10.1002/cb.29

Ha, L. (2008). Online Advertising Research Advertising Journals: A Review. *Journal of Current Issues and Research in Advertising, 30*(1), 31–48. doi:10.1080/10641734.2008.10505236

Hall, E. T. (1976). Beyond Culture. Doubleday.

Hall, M. (2008). Santa Claus, place branding and competition. *Fennia, 186*(1), 59–67.

Halonen, T., Romero, J., & Melero, J. (2003). *GSM, GPRS and edge performance: evolution towards 3G/UMTS*. John Wiley & sons Ltd. doi:10.1002/0470866969

Hanafizadeh, P., & Behboudi, M. (2012). *Online advertising and Promotion, New Technologies for Marketing*. IGI-Global. doi:10.4018/978-1-4666-0885-6

Hanafizadeh, P., Behboudi, M., Ahadi, F., & Ghaderi Varkani, F. (2012). Internet Advertising Adoption; a Structural Equation Model for Iranian SMEs. *Internet Research, 22*(4), 499–526. doi:10.1108/10662241211251015

Hanif, A., & Marnavi, I. A. (2009). Influence of quality, innovation and new product/services design on small and medium enterprises.*Proceedings of the World Congress on Engineering*.

Harden, L., & Heyman, B. (2009). *Digital engagement: internet marketing that captures customers and builds intense brand loyalty*. New York: AMAKOM.

Hargreaves, I. (2011). Digital opportunity: A review of intellectual property and growth. London: Government Research Report.

Harper, I. (2015). *Competition Policy Review*. Australian Government. Retrieved on 13 April at http://competitionpolicyreview.gov.au/

Harris, L. C., & Goode, M. M. H. (2004). The Four of Loyalty and The Pivitol Role of Trust: A Study of Online Service Dynamics. *Journal of Retailing, 80*(2), 139–158. doi:10.1016/j.jretai.2004.04.002

Hartke, K. (2014, April). *Observing Resources in CoAP*. Retrieved from https://tools.ietf.org/html/draft-ietf-core-observe-13

Hauge, O., Sorensen, C. F., & Conradi, R. (2008). Adoption of open source in the software industry. In B. Russo, E. Damiani, S. Hissam, B. Lundell, & G. Succi (Eds.), Open Source Development, Communities and Quality. Springer.

Hauschildt, J. (2004). *Innovation management*. Munchen: Vahlen.

Haveman, H. A. (1993). Follow the leader: Mimetic isomorphism and entry into new markets. *Administrative Science Quarterly*, 593–627.

Hawryszkiewycz, I. (2010). *Knowledge Management: Organizing Knowledge Based Enterprises*. Hampshire, UK: Palgrave MacMillan.

Hayek, F. A. (1999). Towards a free market monetary system. In Good Money, Part II, the Standard. Chicago, IL: The University of Chicago Press.

Haythornthwaite, C. (2009, January). Crowds and communities: Light and heavyweight models of peer production. In *System Sciences, 2009. HICSS'09. 42nd Hawaii International Conference* on (pp. 1-10). IEEE.

Heeks, R., Amalia, M., Kintu, R., & Shah, N. (2013). Inclusive Innovation: Definition, Conceptualisation and Future Research Priorities.*Annual Conference of the Academy of Innovation and Entrepreneurship.*

Heidarzadeh Hanzaee, K., Behboudi, M., & Sadr, F. (2011). Emerging New Concept of Electronic Police and its Impact on the Websites' Sales. *Interdisciplinary Journal of Research in Business, 1*(3), 8–14.

Heinonen, K., Strandvik, T., Mickelsson, K., Edvardsson, B., Sundström, E., & Andersson, P. (2010). A customer-dominant logic of service. *Journal of Service Management, 21*(4), 531–548. doi:10.1108/09564231011066088

Heinonen, K., Strandvik, T., & Voima, P. (2013). Customer-dominant value formation in service. *European Business Review, 25*(2), 104–123. doi:10.1108/09555341311302639

Heinze, A., & Procter, C. (2004). *Reflections on the use of blended learning.* Academic Press.

Henderson, J. M., & Quandt, R. E. (1971). *Microeconomic Theory.* New York: McGraw-Hill.

Henrik, B. (2007). Risk conception and risk management in corporate innovation: Lessons from two Swedish cases. *International Journal of Innovation Management, 11*(4), 497–513. doi:10.1142/S1363919607001849

Heracleous, L., & Jacobs, C. D. (2011). *Crafting strategy: Embodied metaphors in practice.* Cambridge, UK: Cambridge University Press. doi:10.1017/CBO9780511975516

Hermann, N., Popyack, J. L., Char, B., & Zoski, P. (2004). *Assessment of a course redesign: introductory computer programming using online modules.* Academic Press.

Heunks, F. J. (1998). Innovation, creativity and success. *Small Business Economics, 10*(3), 263–272. doi:10.1023/A:1007968217565

Himmelman, A. T. (2001). On coalitions and the transformation of power relations: Collaborative betterment and collaborative empowerment. *American Journal of Community Psychology, 29*(2), 277–284. doi:10.1023/A:1010334831330

Ho, A., Lu, L., & Thurmaier, K. (2006). Testing the reluctant professor's hypothesis: evaluating a blended-learning approach to distance education. *Journal of Public Affairs Education*, 81-102.

Hoffman, D. L., Novak, T. P., & Peralta, M. (1999). Building consumer trust online. *Communications of the ACM, 42*(4), 80–85. doi:10.1145/299157.299175

Hofmeister-Toth, A., & Nagy, P. (2011). The content analysis of adver-games in Hungary. *Qualitative Market Research: An International Journal, 14*(3), 289–303. doi:10.1108/13522751111137514

Holahan, P. J., Aronson, Z. H., Jurkat, M. P., & Schoorman, F. D. (2004). Implementing computer technology: A multiorganizational test of Klein and Sorra's model. *Journal of Engineering and Technology Management, 21*(1-2), 31–50. doi:10.1016/j.jengtecman.2003.12.003

Holbrook, M. B., & Hirschman, E. C. (1982). The experiential aspects of consumption: Consumer fantasies, feelings, and fun. *The Journal of Consumer Research, 9*(2), 132–140. doi:10.1086/208906

Holidayworld. (2014a). Retrieved from http://www.holidayworld.com/holiblog/2014/03/05/deep-fried-question-fabulous-flop/

Holidayworld. (2014b). Retrieved from http://www.holidayworld.com/holiblog/2014/03/13/sweet-question/

Holidayworld. (2014c). Retrieved from https://www.facebook.com/HolidayWorld?sid=b660a4148829021a9b66f8005 420e3c1&ref=search

Holidayworld. (2014d). Retrieved from https://plus.google.com/+holidayworld/posts

Holton, R. L. (1992). *Economy and Society*. London: Routledge.

Hong, J. C. (2003). *Knowledge innovation and learning organization* (2nd ed.). Taipei: Wu-Nan Book Inc.

Hooper, R. (2012). *The Hooper Report*. London: Government Research Report. Retrieved on June 6, 2013 at http://www.ipo.gov.uk/types/hargreaves.htm

Hornby, A. S. (2015). *The Oxford advanced learner's dictionary of current English*. Oxford, UK: Oxford University Press.

Hou, S. K. (2005). Strengthen the core abilities for living technology by creative design activities. *Living Technology Education, 38*(8), 1–15.

Howe, J. (2006). The rise of crowdsourcing. *Wired Magazine, 14*(6), 1-4.

Hoyer, W. D., Chandry, R., Dorotic, M., Krafft, M., & Singh, S. S. (2010). Consumer co-creation in new product development. *Journal of Service Research, 13*(3), 283–296. doi:10.1177/1094670510375604

Huang, H. C. (2006). *The relationship between demographic variables, playfulness, motivation of teaching, perceived happiness and creative teaching among junior high school teachers* (Unpublished Master's Thesis). Institute of Education, National Sun Yat-sen University, Kaohsiung.

Huang, I. C. (1984). Study of the concept and its significance. *Living Technology Education, 66*, 44–56.

Huffman, C., & Kahn, B. E. (1998). Variety for sale: Mass customization or mass confusion? *Journal of Retailing, 74*(4), 491–513. doi:10.1016/S0022-4359(99)80105-5

Huffman, D. L., Kalsbeek, W. D., & Novak, T. P. (1996). Internet and web use in the United States: Baselines for commercial development. *Communications of the ACM, 39*, 36–46.

Humphreys, A., & Grayson, K. (2008). The intersecting roles of consumer and producer: A critical perspective on co-production, co-creation and prosumprion. *Social Compass, 2*(3), 963–980. doi:10.1111/j.1751-9020.2008.00112.x

Hung, H., & Mondejar, R. (2005). Corporate directors and entrepreneurial innovation: An empirical study. *Journal of Entrepreneurship, 14*(2), 117–129. doi:10.1177/097135570501400203

IAB.net. (2011). *Internet Advertising Revenues Hit $7.3 Billion in Q1 '11 Highest First-Quarter Revenue Level on Record According to IAB and PwC*. Retrieved from www.iab.net

Ilaghi, M., Levä, T., & Komu, M. (2014). Techno-economic feasibility analysis of constrained application protocol. In *2014 IEEE World Forum on Internet of Things* (WF-IoT) (pp. 153–158). doi:10.1109/WF-IoT.2014.6803138

Ind, N. (2015). How participation is changing the practice of managing brands. *Journal of Brand Management, 21*(S9), 734–742. doi:10.1057/bm.2014.35

Infante, D. A., Parker, K. R., Clarke, C. H., Wilson, L., & Nathu, I. A. (1983). A comparison of factor and functional approaches to source credibility. *Communication Quarterly, 31*(1), 43–48. doi:10.1080/01463378309369484

Insch, A. (2011). Conceptualization and anatomy of green destination brands, *International Journal of Culture. Tourism and Hospitality Research, 5*(3), 282–290.

Internetworldstats.com. (2012). *Internet Users and Population Statistics for 35 countries and regions in Asia.* Retrieved from: http://www.internetworldstats.com/stats3.htm

Isenberg, D. (2011). *The entrepreneurship ecosystem strategy as a new paradigm for economic policy: principles for cultivating entrepreneurship.* The Babson entrepreneurship ecosystem project. Retrieved December 20, 2015. from http://www.wheda.com/root/uploadedFiles/Website/About_Wheda/Babson%20Entrepreneurship%20Ecosystem%20Project.pdf

Isherwood, D. & Coetzee, M. (2011). Enhancing digital business ecosystem trust and reputation with centrality measures. *Information Security South Africa (ISSA),* 1-8.

Itproportal.com. (2011). *Number Of Domain Names Registered Approaching 200 Million.* Retrieved from: http://www.itproportal.com/2010/02/23/number-domain-names-registered-approaching-200-million/

Jaipuriar, V. (2012, Jan 6). *Aadhaar ATMs on doorstep.* Retrieved June 15, 2013, from The Telegraph: http://www.telegraphindia.com/1120106/jsp/jharkhand/story_14969269.jsp#.Ucd_fhYtsII

Janevski, T. (2009). 5G mobile phone concept. In *Consumer Communications and Networking Conference,* (pp. 1-2). IEEE.

Jarzabkowski, P. & Kaplan, S. (2015). Strategy tools-in-use: A framework for understanding "technologies of rationality" in practice. *Strategic Management Journal, 36,* 537–558.

Jarzabkowski, P. & Pinch, T. (2013). Sociomateriality is 'the New Black': Accomplishing repurposing, reinscripting and repairing in context. *M@n@gement, 16*(5), 579–592.

Jarzabkowski, P. (2005). Strategy as practice: An activity-based approach. *Sage.*

Jarzabkowski, P., Balogun, J., & Seidl, D. (2007). Strategizing: The challenges of a practice perspective. *Human Relations, 60*(1), 5–27. doi:10.1177/0018726707075703

Jarzabkowski, P., Burke, G., & Spee, P. (2015). Constructing spaces for strategic work: A multimodal perspective. *British Journal of Management, 26,* S26–S47. doi:10.1111/1467-8551.12082

Jarzabkowski, P., & Spee, A. P. (2009). Strategy as practice: A review and future directions for the field. *International Journal of Management Reviews, 11*(1), 69–95. doi:10.1111/j.1468-2370.2008.00250.x

Jarzabkowski, P., Spee, A. P., & Smets, M. (2013). Material artifacts: Practices for doing strategy with 'stuff'. *European Management Journal, 31*(1), 41–54. doi:10.1016/j.emj.2012.09.001

Jarzabkowski, P., & Spee, P. (2009). Strategy-as-practice: A review and future directions for the field. *International Journal of Management Reviews, 11*(1), 69–95.

Jauch, L. R., & Osborn, R. N. (1981). Toward an integrated theory of strategy. *Academy of Management Review, 6*(3), 491–498.

Jeannerat, H., & Crevoisier, O. (2011). Non-techonolgical innovation and multi-local territorial knowledge dynamics in the Swiss watch industry. *International Journal of Innovation and Regional Development, 3*(1), 26–44. doi:10.1504/IJIRD.2011.038061

Jefferies, P., Grodzinsky, F., & Griffin, J. (2003). Advantages and problems in using information communication technologies to support the teaching of a multi-institutional computer ethics course. *Journal of Educational Media, 28*(2-3), 191–202. doi:10.1080/1358165032000165644

Jelinek, M. (2004). Managing Design, Designing Management. In R. Boland & F. Callopy (Eds.), *Managing as Designing.* Stanford.

Jenkins, H. (2006). *Convergence Culture: Where Old and New Media Collide*. New York University Press.

Jia, S., Lansdall-Welfare, T., Sudhahar, S., Carter, C., & Cristianini, N. (2016). Women are seen more than heard in online newspapers. *PLoS ONE, 11*(2), 1–11. doi:10.1371/journal.pone.0148434

Johannisson, B. (1993). Designing supportive contexts for emerging enterprises. In C. Karlsson, B. Johannisson, & D. Storey (Eds.), *Small business dynamics: International, national and regional perspectives*. London: Routledge.

John Wiley & Sons, Inc. v Kirtsaeng 54F. 3d 210 (2d Cir. 2011).

Johnson, G., Melin, L., & Whittington, R. (2003). Micro strategy and strategizing: Towards an activity-based view. *Journal of Management Studies, 40*(1), 3–22. doi:10.1111/1467-6486.t01-2-00002

Jokinen, P., & Mikkonen, I. (2013). Teachers experiences of teaching in a blended learning environment. *Nurse Education in Practice, 13*(6), 524–528. doi:10.1016/j.nepr.2013.03.014 PMID:23608218

Jones, B. (2011). Book Industry Strategy Group Report. Canberra, Australia: Government Research Report.

Jones, N., & Lau, A. M. S. (2010). Blending learning: Widening participation in higher education. *Innovations in Education and Teaching International, 47*(4), 405–416. doi:10.1080/14703297.2010.518424

Jones, S., Johnson-Yale, C., Millermaier, S., & Pérez, F. S. (2008). Academic work, the Internet and US college students. *The Internet and Higher Education, 11*(3-4), 165–177. doi:10.1016/j.iheduc.2008.07.001

Jorde, T. M., & Teece, D. J. (1989). Competition and cooperation: Striking the right balance. *California Management Review, 31*(3), 25–37. doi:10.2307/41166568

Julian, E., & Boone, C. (2001). *Blended learning solutions: Improving the way companies manage intellectual capital: An IDC whitepaper*. IDC.

Kaldor, N. (1975). What is wrong with economic theory? *The Quarterly Journal of Economics, 89*, 347–357.

Kaleelazhicathu, R. K. (2004). *Business models in telecommunications*. Retrieved from http://ecosys.optcomm.di.uoa.gr

Kaleta, R., Skibba, K., & Joosten, T. (2007). *Discovering, designing, and delivering hybrid courses. Blended Learning: Research Perspectives*. Needham, MA: The Sloan Consortium.

Kallivroussis. L, A. Natsis. N & Papadakis. G. (2002). The Energy Balance of Sunflower Production for Biodiesel in Greece. *Biosystems Engineering Revue, 81*(3), 347–354.

Kamuzora, F. (2005). The Internet as an Empowering Agent for Small, Medium and Micro Tourism Enterprises in Poor Countries. *e-Review of Tourism Research, 3*(4), 82-89.

Kanuka, H. (2008). Understanding e-learning technologies-in-practice through philosophies-in-practice. *The theory and practice of online learning*, 91-118.

Kanuka, H., & Kelland, J. (2008). Has e-learning delivered on its promises? Expert opinion on the impact of e-learning in higher education. *Canadian Journal of Higher Education, 38*(1), 45–65.

Kapferer, J.-N. (2008). *The New Strategic Brand Management: Creating and Sustaining Brand Equity Long Term*. London: Kogan Page.

Kaplan, S. (2011). Strategy and PowerPoint: An inquiry into the epistemic culture and machinery of strategy making. *Organization Science, 22*(2), 320–346. doi:10.1287/orsc.1100.0531

Karakas, F. (2009). Welcome to World 2.0: The new digital ecosystem. *The Journal of Business Strategy, 30*(4), 23–30. doi:10.1108/02756660910972622

Karimi, J., Somers, T. M., & Bhattacherjee, A. (2007). The Impact of ERP Implementation on Business Process Outcomes: A Factor-Based Study. *Journal of Management Information Systems, 24*(1), 101–134. doi:10.2753/MIS0742-1222240103

Kariyawasam, R. (2010). Next Generation Networks: A New Digital Divide? *International Journal of Innovation in the Digital Economy, 1*(3), 1–21. doi:10.4018/jide.2010070101

Keat, T. K., & Mahon, A. (2004). Integration of TAM based electronic commerce models for trust. *Journal of American Academy of Business, 5*(1/2), 404–410.

Keevers, L., Treleaven, L., Sykes, C., & Darcy, M. (2012). Made to measure: Taming practices with results-based accountability. *Organization Studies, 33*(1), 97–120. doi:10.1177/0170840611430597

Keller, K. L. (1993). Conceptualizing, Measuring, and Managing Customer Based Brand Equity. *Journal of Marketing, 57*(1), 1–22. doi:10.2307/1252054

Kelly, J. (2009). *Publish and be damned.* Retrieved on May 19, 2011 from http://www.abc.net.au

Kelly, L., Gayle, K., & Drennan, J. (2010). Avoidance of Advertising in Social Networking Sites: The Teenager Perspective. *Journal of Interactive Advertising, 10*(2), 16–27. doi:10.1080/15252019.2010.10722167

Kember, D., & Kwan, K.-P. (2000). Lecturers approaches to teaching and their relationship to conceptions of good teaching. *Instructional Science, 28*(5), 469–490. doi:10.1023/A:1026569608656

Kemp, R., Loorbach, D., & Rotmans, J. (2007). Transition management as a model for managing processes of co-evolution towards sustainable development. *International Journal of Sustainable Development and World Ecology, 14*(1), 78–91.

Keneally, T. (2008). *Submission to Productivity Commission, Canberra.* Retrieved on November 20, 2011, from http://www.pc.gov.au/projects/study/books/submissions#initial

Kenney, M., & Pon, B. (2011). Structuring the Smartphone Industry: Is the Mobile Internet OS Platform the Key? *Journal of Industry, Competition and Trade, 11*(3), 239–261. doi:10.1007/s10842-011-0105-6

Khaled, R., & Hammas, L. (2014). Macroeconomic and institutional determinants of the irrigation system and their impact on development and economic sustainability of the agricultural sector in MSEC: A new result by using panel data. *International Journal of Sustainable Economies Management, 3*(3), 54–66. doi:10.4018/ijsem.2014070104

Khaled, R., & Hammas, L. (2016). Technological innovation and the agricultural sustainability: What compatibility for the mechanization? *International Journal of Innovation in the Digital Economy, 7*(4).

Khanna, T., & Palepu, K. G. (2005). *Spotting Institutional Voids in Emerging Markets.* Harvard Business School Publishing Note 106-014.

Khanna, T., & Raina, A. (2012). *Aadhaar: India's' Unique Identification' System.* Harvard Business School Strategy Unit Case, 712-412.

Khanna, T., & Palepu, K. G. (2010). *Winning in emerging markets: A road map for strategy and execution.* Harvard Business School Press.

Kim, D., & Tohnson, T. J. (2005). *Media credibility: comparing internet and traditional news sources in South Korea.* Paper presented at the International Communication Association Conference, New York, NY.

Kim, D., & Benbasat, I. (2003). Trust-related arguments in internet stores: A framework for evaluation. *Journal of Electronic Commerce Research*, *4*(2), 49–64.

Kim, W. C., & Mauborgne, R. (2005). Blue ocean strategy: From theory to practice. *California Management Review*, *47*(3), 105–121. doi:10.2307/41166308

Kim, W., Jeong, O., Kim, C., & So, J. (2011). The dark side of the internet: Attacks, cost and responses. *Information Systems*, *36*, 675–705. doi:10.1016/j.is.2010.11.003

King, S. E., & Arnold, K. C. (2012). Blended Learning Environments in Higher Education: A Case Study of How Professors Make It Happen. *Mid-Western Educational Researcher*, *25*(1), 44–59.

Kirtsaeng v John Wiley & Sons 568 U.S. WL 1104736 (U.S. Mar. 19, 2013).

Klag, M., & Langley, A. (2013). Approaching the conceptual leap in qualitative research. *International Journal of Management Reviews*, *15*(2), 149–166. doi:10.1111/j.1468-2370.2012.00349.x

Klein, K. J., Conn, A. B., & Sorra, J. S. (2001). Implementing Computerized Technology: An Organizational Analysis. *The Journal of Applied Psychology*, *86*(5), 811–824. doi:10.1037/0021-9010.86.5.811 PMID:11596799

Klein, K. J., & Ralls, R. S. (1995). The organizational dynamics of computerized technology implementation: A review of the empirical literature. In L. R. Gomez-Mejia & M. W. Lawless (Eds.), *Implementation management of high technology* (pp. 31–79). Greenwich, CT: JAI Press.

Klein, K. J., & Sorra, J. S. (1996). The Challenge of Innovation Implementation. *Academy of Management Review*, *21*(4), 1055–1080.

Klein, K. J., & Sorra, J. S. (1996). The challenge of innovation implementation. *Academy of Management Review*, *21*, 1055–1080.

Knight, S. (2009). *Effective practice in a digital age*. Bristol, UK: JISC Innovation Group, University of Bristol.

Koch, J. (2008). *Strategic Paths and Media Management-A Path Dependency Analysis of the German Newspaper Branch of High Quality Journalism*. Available at SSRN 1101643

Korgaonkar, P. K., & Wolin, L. D. (1999). A multivariate analysis of web usage. *Journal of Advertising Research*, *39*(2), 53–68.

Korhonen, J. (2001). Four ecosystem principles for an industrial ecosystem. *Journal of Cleaner Production*, *9*(3), 253–259. doi:10.1016/S0959-6526(00)00058-5

Kotler, P. (2001). Marketing Management. Prentice Hall.

Kotler, P. (1986). The prosumer movement: A new challenge for marketers. *Advances in Consumer Research. Association for Consumer Research (U. S.)*, *13*(1), 510–513.

Kotler, P., & Keller, K. L. (2012). *Marketing Management*. Pearson Education, Inc.

Kotler, P., & Lee, N. (2005). *Corporate Social Responsibility Doing the Must Good for Your Company and Your Couse*. John Wiley and Son Inc.

Koufaris, M., & Hampton-Sosa, W. (2004). The development of initial trust in an online company by new customers. *Information & Management*, *41*(3), 377–397. doi:10.1016/j.im.2003.08.004

Kozinets, R. V., Hemetsberger, A., & Jensen Schau, H. (2008). The Wisdom of Consumer Crowds: Collective Innovation in the Age of Networked Marketing. *Journal of Macromarketing*, *28*(4), 339–354. doi:10.1177/0276146708325382

Krathwohl, D. R. (2002). A revision of Bloom's taxonomy: An overview. *Theory into Practice, 41*(4), 212–219. doi:10.1207/s15430421tip4104_2

Krogstie, J. (2012). Modeling of Digital Ecosystems: Challenges and Opportunities. In L. M. Camarinha-Matos, L. Xu, & H. Afsarmanesh (Eds.), International Federation for Information Processing, (pp. 137-145). Springer.

Krowne. (2012, Dec 13). *Visa launches new payment service in India – links Indian UID with Visa accounts.* Retrieved June 18, 2013, from C-ITV: http://security-news-tv.com/2012/12/13/visa-launches-new-payment-service-in-india-links-indian-uid-with-visa-accounts/

Kuo, T., & Wu, A. (2008). *The determinants of organizational innovation and performance: An examination of Taiwanese electronics industry.* Unpublished Paper. National Chengchi University, Taiwan.

Kupetz, R., & Ziegenmeyer, B. (2005). Blended Learning in a Teacher Training Course: Integrated Interactive E-Learning and Contact Learning. *ReCALL, 17*(2), 179–196. doi:10.1017/S0958344005000327

Kylänen, M., & Rusko, R. (2011). Unintentional coopetition in the service industries: The case of Pyhä-Luosto tourism destination in the Finnish Lapland. *European Management Journal, 29*(3), 193–205. doi:10.1016/j.emj.2010.10.006

La Ferle, C., Edwards, S. M., & Lee, W. (2008). Culture, attitudes, and media patterns in China, Taiwan, and the U.S. balancing standardization and localization decisions. *Journal of Global Marketing, 21*(3), 191–205. doi:10.1080/08911760802152017

La Ferle, C., & Kim, H. (2006). Cultural influences on internet motivations and communication styles: A comparison of Korean and US consumers. *International Journal of Internet Marketing and Advertising, 3*(2), 142–157. doi:10.1504/IJIMA.2006.010296

Laine, M., Bamberg, J., & Jokinen, P. (2007). Tapaustutkimuksen käytäntö ja teoria. In Tapaustutkimuksen taito, (pp. 9-38). Gaudeamus.

Laine, P.-M., & Vaara, E. (2015). Participation in Strategy Work. In Cambridge Handbook of Strategy as Practice. Cambridge University Press. doi:10.1017/CBO9781139681032.036

Laine, P.-M. (2010). *Toimijuus strategiakäytännöissä: Diskurssi- ja käytäntöteoreettisia avauksia.* Turku School of Economics.

Lamberg, J.-A., Näsi, J., Ojala, J., & Sajasalo, P. (Eds.). (n.d.). *The Evolution of Competitive Strategies in Global Forestry Industries.* Dordrecht, The Netherlands: Springer.

Lameras, P., Paraskakis, I., & Levy, P. (2008). *Conceptions of teaching using virtual learning environments: preliminary findings from a phenomenographic inquiry.* Paper presented at the 6th International Conference on Networked Learning.

Lameras, P., Levy, P., Paraskakis, I., & Webber, S. (2012). Blended university teaching using virtual learning environments: Conceptions and approaches. *Instructional Science, 40*(1), 141–157. doi:10.1007/s11251-011-9170-9

Langley, A. (1999). Strategies for theorizing from process data. *Academy of Management Journal, 24*, 691–710.

Langlois, R. N. (1990). Creating external capabilities: Innovation and vertical disintegration in the microcomputer industry. *Business and Economic History, 19*, 93–102.

Lapadat, J. C. (2002). Written interaction: A key component in online learning. *Journal of Computer-Mediated Communication, 7*(4).

Lappi, T., Haapasalo, H., & Aaltonen, K. (2015). Business Ecosystem Definition in Built Environment Using a Stakeholder Assessment Process. *Management, 10*(2), 110–129.

LaTour, M. S., & Hawthorne, T. (1994). Ethical judgments of Sexual appeals in print advertising. *Journal of Advertising, 23*(3), 81–90. doi:10.1080/00913367.1994.10673453

Laurillard, D. (2002). *Rethinking university teaching: a conversational framework for the effective use of learning technologies*. London: RoutledgeFalmer. doi:10.4324/9780203304846

Laurtent, G., & Kaoferer, J. (1985). Measuring consumer involvement profiles. *JMR, Journal of Marketing Research, 22*(1), 41–53. doi:10.2307/3151549

Lavassani, K., Movahedi, B., & Kumar, V. (2010). Electronic collaboration ontology: The case of readiness analysis of electronic marketplace adoption. *Journal of Management & Organization, 16*(3), 454–466. doi:10.1017/S183336720000208X

Law, R., Qi, S., & Buhalis, D. (2010). Progress in tourism management: A review of website evaluation in tourism research. *Tourism Management, 31*(3), 297–313. doi:10.1016/j.tourman.2009.11.007

Lê, J. K., & Spee, A. (2015). The role of materiality in the practice of strategy. In Cambridge Handbook of Strategy as Practice. Cambridge, UK: Cambridge University Press.

Leavitt, H. J. (1965). Applied organizational change in industry: structural, technical and humanistic approaches. In Handbook of Organizations, (pp. 1144-1170). John Wiley & Sons.

Leek, S., & Kun, D. (2006). Consumer Confusion in the Chinese Personal Computer Market. *Journal of Product and Brand Management, 15*(3), 184–193. doi:10.1108/10610420610668621

Lee, L. S. (1993). Seeing different things from different perspectives – multiple views on technology education. *Technological and Vocational Education Bimonthly, 13*, 18–20.

Lehdonvirta, V. (2013). Helsinki Spring: An essay on entrepreneurship and cultural change. *Research on Finnish Society, 6*, 25–28.

Leonard-Barton, D. (1992). Core capabilities and core rigidities: A paradox in managing new product development. *Strategic Management Journal, 13*(S1), 111–125. doi:10.1002/smj.4250131009

Lerche, C., Hartke, K., & Kovatsch, M. (2012). Industry Adoption of the Internet of Things: A Constrained Application Protocol Survey. In *Proceedings of the 7th International Workshop on Service Oriented Architectures in Converging Networked Environments* (SOCNE 2012). doi:10.1109/ETFA.2012.6489787

Levä, T., & Suomi, H. (2013). Techno-economic feasibility analysis of Internet protocols: Framework and tools. *Computer Standards and Interfaces, 36*(1), 76–88. Retrieved from 10.1016/j.csi.2013.07.011

Levä, T., Komu, M., Keränen, A., & Luukkainen, S. (2013). Adoption barriers of network layer protocols: The case of host identity protocol. *Computer Networks, 57*(10), 2218–2232. doi:10.1016/j.comnet.2012.11.024

Levä, T., Mazhelis, O., & Suomi, H. (2013). *Comparing the cost-efficiency of CoAP and {HTTP} in Web of Things applications*. Decision Support Systems. Retrieved from; doi:10.1016/j.dss.2013.09.009

Liao, H., Proctor, R. W., & Salvendy, G. (2008). Content preparation for cross-cultural e-commerce: A review and a model. *Behaviour & Information Technology, 27*(1), 43–61. doi:10.1080/01449290601088424

Liaw, S.-S., Huang, H.-M., & Chen, G.-D. (2007). An activity-theoretical approach to investigate learners,Äô factors toward e-learning systems. *Computers in Human Behavior, 23*(4), 1906–1920. doi:10.1016/j.chb.2006.02.002

Li, D., Browne, G., & Wetherbe, J. (2006). Why do internet users stick with a specific website? a relationship perspective. *International Journal of Electronic Commerce, 10*(4), 105–141. doi:10.2753/JEC1086-4415100404

Li, J., Merenda, M., & Venkatachalam, A. R. (2009). Business process digitalization and new product development: An empirical study of small and medium-sized manufacturers. *International Journal of E-Business Research, 5*(1), 49–64. doi:10.4018/jebr.2009010103

Lilien, G., Morrison, P. D., Searls, K., Sonnack, M., & von Hippel, E. (2002). Performance assessment of the lead user idea-generation process for the new product development. *Management Science, 48*(8), 1042–1059. doi:10.1287/mnsc.48.8.1042.171

Lin, S. Y. (2002). *The relationship between creative parenting, reading parenting, reading motivation and behavior, and creativity* (Unpublished Master's Thesis). Graduate School of Education, National Cheng Chi University, Taipei.

Line, N. D., & Runyan, R. C. (2014). Destination marketing and the service-dominant logic: A resource-based operationalization of strategic marketing assets. *Tourism Management, 43*, 91–102. doi:10.1016/j.tourman.2014.01.024

Lin, K. Y., & Yu, K. C. (2004). The study of developing students' creativity through technological literacy curriculum in elementary and secondary school. *Journal of National University Tainan: Mathematics, Science, and Technology, 38*(2), 15–30.

Linsey, R., Jackson, T. W., & Cooke, L. (2011). Adapted technology acceptance model for mobile policing. *Journal of Systems and Information Technology, 13*(4), 389–407. doi:10.1108/13287261111183988

Lippke, R. L. (1989). Advertising and the social conditions of autonomy. *Business & Professional Ethics Journal, 8*(4), 35–58. doi:10.5840/bpej19898417

Littlejohn, A., & Pegler, C. (2007). *Preparing for Blended Learning. Milton Park*. Abingdon, UK: Routledge.

Litz, R. A., & Kleysen, R. F. (2001). Your old men shall dream dreams, your young men shall see visions: Toward a theory of family firm innovation with help from the Brubeck family. *Family Business Review, 14*(4), 335–352. doi:10.1111/j.1741-6248.2001.00335.x

Liu, C., Arnett, K. P., Capella, L. M., & Beatty, R. C. (1997). websites of the Fortune 500 companies: Facing customers through home pages. *Information & Management, 31*(6), 335–345. doi:10.1016/S0378-7206(97)00001-3

Locke, D. (2010). *MQ Telemetry Transport MQTT V3.1 Protocol Specification*. International Business Machines Corporation Technical Report.

Lock, J. V. (2006). A new image: Online communities to facilitate teacher professional development. *Journal of Technology and Teacher Education, 14*(4), 663–678.

Loukakis, A. (2010) *Warning: More ebook loopholes*. Retrieved on December 10, 2010, http://www.asauthors.org

Lu, C., Rong, K., You, J., & Shi, Y. (2014). Business ecosystem and stakeholders' role transformation: Evidence from Chinese emerging electric vehicle industry. *Expert Systems with Applications, 41*(10), 4579–4595. doi:10.1016/j.eswa.2014.01.026

Luecke, R & Katz, R. (2003). *Managing Creativity and Innovation*. Boston, MA: Harvard Quarterly.

Lumsdaine, E., & Lumsdaine, M. (1995). *Creative problem solving: Thinking skills for a changing world*. New York: McGraw-Hill.

Lundell, B., Lings, B., & Lindqvist, E. (2010). Open source in Swedish companies: Where are we? *Information Systems Journal, 20*(6), 519–535. doi:10.1111/j.1365-2575.2010.00348.x

Luo, Y. (2004a). *Coopetition in International Business*. Copenhagen Business School Press.

Lusch, R. F., & Vargo, S. L. (2006). Service-dominant logic: Reactions, reflections and refinements. *Marketing Theory*, *6*(3), 281–288. doi:10.1177/1470593106066781

Lusch, R. F., Vargo, S. L., & O'Brien, M. (2007). Competing through service: Insights from service-dominant logic. *Journal of Retailing*, *83*(1), 5–18. doi:10.1016/j.jretai.2006.10.002

Lusch, R. F., Vargo, S. L., & Wessels, G. (2008). Toward a conceptual foundation for service science: Contributions from service-dominant logic. *IBM Systems Journal*, *47*(1), 5–14. doi:10.1147/sj.471.0005

Lusch, R. F., & Webster, F. E. (2011). A stakeholder-Unifying, co-creation philosophy for marketing. *Journal of Macromarketing*, *31*(2), 129–134. doi:10.1177/0276146710397369

Lyytinen, K., & Newman, M. (2014). A tale of two coalitions – marginalising the users while successfully implementing an enterprise resource planning system. *Information Systems Journal*, *25*(2), 71–101. doi:10.1111/isj.12044

Mahadeoa, J. D., Oogarah-Hanumana, V., & Soobaroyen, T. (2011). Changes in social and environemntal reporting practices in an emerginh economy (2004-2007): Exploring the relevance of staeholder and legitimacy theory. *Accounting Forum*, *35*(3), 158–175. doi:10.1016/j.accfor.2011.06.005

Mair, J., Marti, I., & Ventresca, M. J. (2012). Building inclusive markets in rural Bangladesh: How intermediaries work institutional voids. *Academy of Management Journal*, *55*(4), 819–850. doi:10.5465/amj.2010.0627

Mantere, S. (2005). Strategic practices as enablers and disablers of championing activity. *Strategic Organization*, *3*(2), 157–284. doi:10.1177/1476127005052208

Mantere, S. (2008). Role expectations and middle manager strategic agency. *Journal of Management Studies*, *45*(2), 294–316.

Mantere, S., & Vaara, E. (2008). On the problem of participation in strategy: A critical discursive perspective. *Organization Science*, *19*(2), 341–358. doi:10.1287/orsc.1070.0296

March, J. G., & Simon, H. A. (1958). *Organizations*. New York: Wiley.

Mariani, M. M. (2007). Coopetition as an emergent Strategy. *International Studies of Management & Organization*, *37*(2), 97–126. doi:10.2753/IMO0020-8825370205

Marshall, C., & Rossman, G. B. (2010). *Designing Qualitative Research* (5th ed.). London: Sage Publications.

Masalela, R. K. (2009). Potential benefits and complexities of blended learning in higher education: The case of the University of Botswana. *Turkish Online Journal of Distance Education*, *10*(1), 66–82.

Mascarenhas, O. A., Kesavan, R., & Bernacchi, M. (2006). Lasting Customer Loyalty: A Total Customer Experience Approach. *Journal of Consumer Marketing*, *23*(7), 397–405. doi:10.1108/07363760610712939

Mashelkar, R. A. (2012). *Global Research Alliance Working Paper*. Retrieved on 16 July 2014 from http://www.theglobalresearchalliance.org/en/What-we-do/~/media/Files/Resources/What%20is%20Inclusive%20Innovation_Global%20Research%20Alliance.ashx

Maturana, H. R., & Varela, F. J. (1987). *The Tree of Knowledge*. London: New Science Library.

Mazhelis, O., Warma, H., Leminen, S., Ahokangas, P., Pussinen, P., Rajahonka, M., & Myllykoski, J. (2013). *Internet-of-Things Market, Value Networks, and Business Models: State of the Art Report*. Academic Press.

Mazhelis, O., Luoma, E., & Warma, H. (2012). Defining an Internet-of-Things Ecosystem. In S. Andreev, S. Balandin, & Y. Koucheryavy (Eds.), *Internet of Things, Smart Spaces, and Next Generation Networking* (Vol. 7469, pp. 1–14). Springer Berlin Heidelberg; doi:10.1007/978-3-642-32686-8_1

Mazhelis, O., & Tyurväinen, P. (2014). A Framework for Evaluating Internet-of-Things Platforms: Application Provider Viewpoint. In *Proc. of the IEEE World Forum on Internet of Things (WF-IoT)*. doi:10.1109/WF-IoT.2014.6803137

McCole, P., Ramsey, E., & Williams, J. (2010). Trust Considerations on Attitudes Toward Online Purchasing: The Moderating Effect on Privacy and Security Concerns. *Journal of Business Research*, *63*(9-10), 1018–1024. doi:10.1016/j.jbusres.2009.02.025

McConnell, D., & Zhao, J. (2006). Chinese higher education teachers' conceptions of e-Learning: Preliminary outcomes. Paper presented at the 23rd Annual Ascilite Conference: Who's Learning? Whose technology?

McCourt, T. C., Leopold, S., Louthan, F. G., Mosesmann, H., Smigie, J. S., Tillman, T., … Sklar, A. (2014). *The Internet of Things: A Study in Hype, Reality, Disruption, and Growth*. Academic Press.

McDermott, G. A. (2002). *Embedded politics: Industrial networks and institutional change in Postcommunism*. Ann Arbor, MI: University of Michigan Press. doi:10.3998/mpub.12137

McDonald, H., & Adam, S. (2003). A Comparison of Online and Postal Data Collection Methods in Marketing Research. *Marketing Intelligence & Planning*, *21*(2), 85–95. doi:10.1108/02634500310465399

McKnight, D. H., Choudhury, V., & Kacmar, C. (2002a). Developing and validating trust measures for e-commerce: An integrative typology. *Information Systems Research*, *13*(3), 334–359. doi:10.1287/isre.13.3.334.81

McKnight, D. H., Choundhury, V., & Kacmar, C. (2002b). The Impact of Initial Consumer Trust on Intentions to Transact With a Website: A Trust Building Model. *The Journal of Strategic Information Systems*, *11*(3-4), 297–323. doi:10.1016/S0963-8687(02)00020-3

McLuhan, M., & Nevitt, B. (1972). *Take today: The executive as dropout*. New York: Harcourt Brace Jovanovich.

McShane, K. (2004). Integrating face-to-face and online teaching: Academics' role concept and teaching choices. *Teaching in Higher Education*, *9*(1), 3–16.

Meadows. D, Randers. J & William. W. (1972). *The limits to growth. A report for the club of Rome's project on the predicament of mankind*. Academic Press.

Meera, A. K. M. (2004). *The Theft of Nations, Returning to Gold*. Kuala Lumpur, Malaysia: Pelanduk.

Metzger, M. J., Flanagin, A. J., Eyal, K., Lemus, D. R., & McCann, R. M. (2003). Credibility for the 21st century: integrating perspectives on source, message, and media credibility in the contemporary media environment. In P. J. Kalbfleisch (Ed.), *Communications Yearbook* (Vol. 27, pp. 293–335). Mahwah, NJ: Lawrence Erlbaum Associates. doi:10.1080/23808985.2003.11679029

Mickelsson, K. J. (2013). Customer activity in service. *Journal of Service Management*, *24*(5), 534–552. doi:10.1108/JOSM-04-2013-0095

Miller, M. M., & Henthorne, T. L. (2007). In Search of Competitive Advantage in Caribbean Tourism Websites: Revisiting the Unique Selling Proposition. *Journal of Travel & Tourism Marketing*, *21*(2), 49–62. doi:10.1300/J073v21n02_04

Milling, P. M., & Maier, F. H. (1996). Invention, Innovation and Diffusion: A Simulation Analysis of the management of new products. Berlin: Academic Press.

Mintzberg, H., Ahlstrand, B., & Lampel, J. (1998). *The Complete Guide through the Wilds of Strategic Management.* FT Prentice Hall.

Mishkin, F. S. (2007a). What should Central Banks do? In *Monetary Policy Strategy* (pp. 37–58). Cambridge, MA: The MIT Press.

Mishkin, F. S. (2007b). The transmission mechanism and the role of asset prices in monetary policy. In *Monetary Policy Strategy* (pp. 59–74). Cambridge, MA: The MIT Press.

Mishra, P., & Koehler, M. J. (2006). Technological Pedagogical Content Knowledge: A Framework for Teacher Knowledge. *Teachers College Record, 108*(6), 1017–1054. doi:10.1111/j.1467-9620.2006.00684.x

Mitchell, V. W., & Papavassiliou, V. (1999). Marketing causes and implications of consumer confusion. *Journal of Product and Brand Management, 8*(4), 319–339. doi:10.1108/10610429910284300

Mitchell, V.-W., Walsh, G., & Yamin, M. (2005). Towards a Conceptual Model of Consumer Confusion. *Advances in Consumer Research. Association for Consumer Research (U. S.), 32*, 143–150.

MITSloan Management Review. (2014, January 7). Retrieved from http://sloanreview.mit.edu/article/the-nine-elements-of-digital-transformation/

Mladenow, A., Bauer, C., & Strauss, C. (2014). Social Crowd Integration in New Product Development: Crowdsourcing Communities Nourish the Open Innovation Paradigm. *Global Journal of Flexible Systems Management,* 1-10.

Moisander, J., & Stenfors, S. (2009). Exploring the edges of theory-practice gap: Epistemic cultures in strategy-tool development and use. *Organization, 16*(2), 227–247. doi:10.1177/1350508408100476

Moisander, J., & Valtonen, A. (2006). *Qualitative Marketing Research: A Cultural Approach.* London: Sage Publications. doi:10.4135/9781849209632

Moisio, L., & Rökman, M. (2011). Musician's, fans' and record company's value creation in internet. In *Proceedings of the Naples Forum on Services: Service- Dominant-Logic, Service Science, and Network Theory.* Available at: http://www.naplesforumonservice.it/uploads//files/Moisio,%20Rokman%20Musici an.pdf

Molesworth, M. (2004). Collaboration, reflection and selective neglect: campus-based marketing students' experiences of using a virtual learning environment. *Innovations in Education and Teaching International, 41*(1), 79-92.

Moon, J., & Kim, Y. (2001). Extending the TAM for a World-Wide-Wen Context. *Information & Management, 38*(4), 217–230. doi:10.1016/S0378-7206(00)00061-6

Moore, C. M., & Birtwistle, G. (2004). The Burberry business model: Creating an international luxury fashion brand. *International Journal of Retail & Distribution Management, 32*(8), 412–422. doi:10.1108/09590550410546232

Moore, J. (1993). Predators and Prey: A New Ecology of Competition. *Harvard Business Review, 71*(3), 75–86.

Morgan, R. M., & Hunt, S. D. (1994). The Commitment-Trust Theory of Relationship Marketing. *Journal of Marketing, 58*(3), 20–38. doi:10.2307/1252308

Morgan-Thomas, A., & Veloutsou, C. (2013). Beyond technology acceptance: Brand relationships and online brand experience. *Journal of Business Research, 66*(21-27), 21-27.

Mortera-Gutierrez, F. (2006). Faculty Best Practices Using Blended Learning in E-Learning and Face-to-Face Instruction. *International Journal on E-Learning, 5*(3), 313–337.

Moskowitz, H. R., & Saguy, I. S. (2013). Reinventing the role of consumer research in today's open innovation ecosystem. *Critical Reviews in Food Science and Nutrition, 53*(7), 682–693. doi:10.1080/10408398.2010.538093

Motteram, G. (2006). Blended education and the transformation of teachers: A long term case study in postgraduate UK Higher Education. *British Journal of Educational Technology, 37*(1), 17–30. doi:10.1111/j.1467-8535.2005.00511.x

Murphy, P. E. (1998). Ethics in advertising, review, analysis, and suggestions. *Journal of Public Policy & Marketing, 17*(2), 316–319.

Musson, G., & Duberley, J. (2007). Change, change or be exchanged: The discourse of participation and the manufacture of identity. *Journal of Management Studies, 44*(1), 143–164. doi:10.1111/j.1467-6486.2006.00640.x

Muzellec, L., Ronteau, S., & Lambkin, M. (2015). Two-sided Internet platform: A business model lifecycle perspective. *Industrial Marketing Management, 45*(2), 139–150. doi:10.1016/j.indmarman.2015.02.012

Myrdal, G. (1957). *An unexplained general traits of social reality. In Rich Lands and Poor, the Road to World Prosperity.* New York, NY: Harper & Row.

Myrdal, G. (1958). The principle of cumulation. In P. Streeten (Ed.), *Value in Social Theory, a Selection of Essays on Methodology by Gunnar Myrdal* (pp. 198–205). New York, NY: Harper & Brothers Publishers.

Nacar, R., & Burnaz, S. (2011). A cultural content analysis of multinational companies' web sites. *Qualitative Market Research, An International Journal, 14*(3), 274–288. doi:10.1108/13522751111137505

Nafiou. M.M. (2009). Impact de l'aide publique au développement sur la croissance économique du Niger. *Revue africaine de l'Intégration, 3*(2).

Nairn, A., & Dew, A. (2007). Pop-ups, pop-under, banners and buttons: The ethics of online advertising to primary school children. *Journal of Direct, Data and Digital Marketing Practice,* (May), 30–46. Available at http://www.palgrave-journals.com/dddmp/journal/v9/n1/full/4350076a.html

Napier, N. P., Dekhane, S., & Smith, S. (2011). Transitioning to Blended Learning: Understanding Student and Faculty Perceptions. *Journal of Asynchronous Learning Networks, 15*(1), 20–32.

Narayan, D. (2009). *Moving Out of Poverty: The Promise of Empowerment and Democracy in India* (Vol. 3). Washington, DC: World Bank. doi:10.1596/978-0-8213-7215-9

Närvänen, E. (2013). *Extending the Collective Consumption of Brands* (Doctoral dissertation). University of Tampere.

Nebenzahl, I. D., & Jaffe, E. D. (1998). Ethics dimensions of advertising executions. *Journal of Business Ethics, 17*(7), 805–815. doi:10.1023/A:1005850812845

Newton, K. (2001). *Management Skills for Small Business.* Small Business Policy Brand.

Nielsen. (2009). *Global Consumer Confidence Survey.* Nielsen Company.

Nikula, U. (2005, July). Quantifying the Interest in Open Source Systems: Case South-East Finland Sami Jantunen. *Source,* 192-195.

Nilssen, J., Bertheussen, B. A., & Dreyer, B. (2015). Sustained competitive advantage based on high quality input. *Marine Policy, 52,* 145–154. doi:10.1016/j.marpol.2014.10.011

Nix, G. (2008). *Submission to Productivity Commission, Canberra.* Retrieved on November 20, 2011, from http://www.pc.gov.au/projects/study/books/submissions#initial

Nograsek, J., & Vintar, M. (2014). E-government and organisational transformation of government: Black box revisited? *Government Information Quarterly, 31*(1), 108–118. doi:10.1016/j.giq.2013.07.006

Nokia. (2011a). *Story of Nokia (Nokia's first century to Nokia Now)*. Retrieved from http://blog.a4add.com/story-of-nokianokias-first-century-to-nokia-now/special-news/create-free-Website-a4add.com

Nokia. (2011b). *Form 20-F 2010 (Annual Report of Nokia 2010)*. Nokia.

Nokia. (2011c). *Historia lyhyesti*. Retrieved from http://www.nokia.fi/nokia/tietoa-yhtiosta/historia/historia-lyhyesti

Nokia. (2012). *Annual report 2011*. Nokia.

Nokia. (2013). *The Nokia Story*. Retrieved from http://www.nokia.com/global/about-nokia/about-us/the-nokia-story/

Nokia. (2016a). *Nokia ja Alcatel-Lucent juhlistavat tänään toimintansa aloittamista yhdistyneenä yhtiönä*. Retrieved from http://company.nokia.com/fi/uutiset/lehdistotiedotteet/2016/01/14/nokia-ja-alcatel-lucent-juhlistavat-tanaan-toimintansa-aloittamista-yhdistyneena-yhtiona

Nokia. (2016b). *Our businesses*. http://company.nokia.com/en/our-businesses

Nord, W. R., & Tucker, S. (1987). *Implementing routine and radical innovations*. San Francisco: New Lexington Press.

Norman, D. A., & Verganti, R. (2014). Incremental and Radical Innovation: Design Research vs. Technology and Meaning Change. *Design Issues, 30*(1), 78–96. doi:10.1162/DESI_a_00250

Normann, R., & Ramirez, R. (1993). From value chain to value constellation: Designing interactive strategy. *Harvard Business Review, 71*(4), 65–77.

North, D. C. (1990). *Institutions, institutional change and economic performance*. New York: Cambridge University Press. doi:10.1017/CBO9780511808678

Novak, T. P., Huffman, D. L., & Yung, Y. (2000). Measuring the customer experience in online environments: A structural modeling approach. *Marketing Science, 19*(1), 22–42. doi:10.1287/mksc.19.1.22.15184

Nurvitadhi, E. (2003). *Trends in Mobile Computing: A Study of Mobile Phone Usage in the United States and Japan*. Oregon State University.

Nutt, P. C. (1986). Tactics of implementation. *Academy of Management Journal, 29*(2), 230–261. doi:10.2307/256187

Oakes, L. (2001). *Language and national identity: Comparing France and Sweden*. Philadelphia: John Benjamins Publishing Company. doi:10.1075/impact.13

Oba, B., & Semercioz, F. (2005). Antecedents of trust in industrial districts: An empirical analysis of inter-firm relations in a turkish industrial district. *Entrepreneurship and Regional Development, 17*(3), 163–182. doi:10.1080/08985620500102964

Ocak, M. A. (2011). Why are faculty members not teaching blended courses? Insights from faculty members. *Computers & Education, 56*(3), 689–699. doi:10.1016/j.compedu.2010.10.011

OCDE. (1999). *Développement durable les grands questions?*. Author.

OECD Communication Outlook. (2011). OECD.

OECD. (2015). Retrieved from: http://www.oecd.org/internet/broadband/oecdkeyictindicators.htm

Oh, E., & Park, S. (2009). How are universities involved in blended instruction? *Journal of Educational Technology & Society, 12*(3), 327–342.

Ojo, O. (2003). *Fundamentals of research methods*. Lagos: Standard Publications.

Okazaki, S. (2004). Do multinationals standardize or localize? The cross-cultural dimensionality of product-based web sites. *Internet Research: Electronic Networking Applications and Policy, 14*(1), 81–94. doi:10.1108/10662240410516336

Oliver, C. (1997). Sustainable Competitive Advantage: Combining Institutional and Resource-based View. *Strategic Management Journal, 18*(9), 697–713. doi:10.1002/(SICI)1097-0266(199710)18:9<697::AID-SMJ909>3.0.CO;2-C

Oliver, M., & Trigwell, K. (2005). Can'Blended Learning'Be Redeemed? *E-Learning and Digital Media, 2*(1), 17–26.

O'Mahony, S., & Ferraro, F. (2007). The emergence of governance in an open source community. *Academy of Management Journal, 50*(5), 1079–1106. doi:10.5465/AMJ.2007.27169153

Oman, M. (2008). *Measuring innovation in developing countries*. Regional Workshop on Science and Technology Statistics by Institute of Statistics. Retrieved from: www.uis.unesco.org

Ong, J. (2011). *Google overtakes Nokia as top smartphone platform maker.* Retrieved from: http://www.appleinsider.com/articles/11/01/31/google_overtakes_nokia_as_maker_of_top_smartphone_platform.html

Orlikowski, W. J. (2000). Using technology and constituting structures. *Organization Science, 11*(4), 404–428. doi:10.1287/orsc.11.4.404.14600

Orlikowski, W. J. (2007). Sociomaterial practices: Exploring technology at work. *Organization Studies, 28*(9), 1435–1448. doi:10.1177/0170840607081138

Orlikowski, W. J. (2015). Engaging practice in research: Phenomenon, perspective, and philosophy. In D. Golsorkhi, L. Rouleau, D. Seidl, & E. Vaara (Eds.), *Cambridge handbook of strategy as practice* (2nd ed.; pp. 33–43). Cambridge, UK: Cambridge University Press. doi:10.1017/CBO9781139681032.002

Orlikowski, W. J., & Scott, S. (2008). Sociomateriality: Challenging the separation of technology, work and organization. *The Academy of Management Annals, 2*(1), 433–474. doi:10.1080/19416520802211644

Palloff, R. M., & Pratt, K. (1999). *Building learning communities in cyberspace: effective strategies for the online classroom.* San Francisco: Jossey-Bass Publishers.

Palmer, A. (2004). The internet challenge for destination marketing organizations. *Destination Branding, 128*.

Panetto, H., Jardim-Goncalves, R., & Molina, A. (2012). Enterprise Integration and Networking: Theory and practice. *Annual Reviews in Control, 36*(2), 284–290. doi:10.1016/j.arcontrol.2012.09.009

Papacharissi, Z., & Alan, R. M. (2000). Predictors of internet use. *Journal of Broadcasting & Electronic Media, 44*(2), 175–196. doi:10.1207/s15506878jobem4402_2

Parker, I. (2011, Oct 3). *The ID Man: Can a software mogul's epic project help India's poor?* Retrieved Oct 5, 2012, from The New Yorker: http://www.newyorker.com/reporting/2011/10/03/111003fa_fact_parker

Parsons, T. (1964). *The Structure of Social Actions.* New York, NY: The Free Press of Glencoe.

Paschke, A., Athan, T., Sottara, D., Kendall, E., & Bell, R. (2015). A Representational Analysis of the API4KP Metamodel. In R. Cuel & R. Yound (Eds.), *Formal Ontologies Meet Industry, Proceedings of the 7th International Workshop 2015.* doi:10.1007/978-3-319-21545-7_1

Patton, M. Q. (2002). *Qualitative Research and Evaluation Methods* (3rd ed.). London: Sage Publications.

Paunov, C. (2013). *Innovation and Inclusive Development: A Discussion of the Main Policy Issues (No. 2013/1).* OECD Publishing. doi:10.1787/18151965

Pek-Hooi, S., Mahmood, I. P., & Mitchell, W. (2004). Dynamic inducements in R&D investment: Market signals and network locations. *Academy of Management Journal, 47*(6), 907–917. doi:10.2307/20159630

Pelkonen, K., & Yliniemi, A. (2005). *The history of the Arctic Circle in Rovaniemi.* Rovaniemi: Osviitta.

Perry, M., & Bodkin, C. (2000). Content analysis of Fortune 100 company Web sites. *Corporate Communications An International Journal, 5*(2), 87–96. doi:10.1108/13563280010338331

Peslak, A. R. (2006). PAPA revisited: A current empirical study of the Mason framework. *Journal of Computer Information Systems, 46*(3), 117–123.

Peteraf, M., & Barney, J. (2003). Unraveling The Resource-Based Tangle. *Managerial and Decision Economics, 24*(4), 309–323. doi:10.1002/mde.1126

Pettigrew, A. (1990). Longitudinal field research on change: Theory and practice. *Organization Science, 1*(3), 267–292. doi:10.1287/orsc.1.3.267

Petty, R. E., & John, C. T. (1984). The Effects of Involvement on Responses to Argument Quantity and Quality: Central and Peripheral Routes to Persuasion. *Journal of Personality and Social Psychology, 46*(1), 69–81. doi:10.1037/0022-3514.46.1.69

Petty, R. E., John, C. T., & Schumann, D. (1983). Central and Peripheral Routes to Advertising Effectiveness: The Moderating of Involvement. *The Journal of Consumer Research, 10*(2), 135–146. doi:10.1086/208954

Pfeffer, J., & Salancik, G. R. (1978). *The external control of organization: A resource dependence perspective.* New York: Harper and Row.

Pfeffer, J., & Sutton, R. I. (2000). *The knowing–doing gap: How smart companies turn knowledge into action.* Boston: Harvard Business School Press.

Phelps, J. D., D'Souza, G., & Nowak, G. J. (2000b). Antecedents and consequences of consumer Privacy concerns: An empirical investigation. *Journal of Interactive Marketing, 15*(4), 2–17. doi:10.1002/dir.1019

Phelps, J., Nowak, G., & Ferrell, E. (2000a). Privacy concerns and consumer willingness to provide personal information. *Journal of Public Policy & Marketing, 19*(1), 27–41. doi:10.1509/jppm.19.1.27.16941

Phillips, D. (2001). Managing reputation in cyberspace. *Journal of Communication Management, 5*(3), 300–304.

Picciano, A. (2009). Blending with purpose: The multimodal model. *Journal of the Research Center for Educational Technology, 5*(1), 4–14.

Picciano, A. G., Dziuban, C. D., & Graham, C. R. (2013). *Blended learning: Research perspectives* (Vol. 2). United States of America: The Sloan Consortium.

Piccoli, G., Ahmad, R., & Ives, B. (2001). Web-Based Virtual Learning Environments: A Research Framework and a Preliminary Assessment of Effectiveness in Basic IT Skills Training. *Management Information Systems Quarterly, 25*(4), 401–426. doi:10.2307/3250989

Pilinkiene, V., & Maciulis, P. (2014). Comparison of different ecosystem analogies: The main economic determinants and levels of impact. *Procedia: Social and Behavioral Sciences, 156*, 365–370. doi:10.1016/j.sbspro.2014.11.204

Piller, F., Vossen, A., & Ihl, C. (2012). From Social Media to Social Product Development: The Impact of Social Media on Co-Creation of Innovation. Die Unternehmung, *65*(1).

Pinho, J. C. M. R., & Soares, A. M. (2011). Examining the technology acceptance model in the adoption of social networks. *Journal of Research in Interactive Marketing*, *5*(2/3), 116–129. doi:10.1108/17505931111187767

Pitelis, C. (2002). *The Growth of the Firm. The Legacy of Edith Penrose*. Oxford University Press.

Pittaway, L., Rodriguez-Falcon, E., Aiyegbayo, O., & King, A. (2011). The Role of entrepreneurship clubs and societies in entrepreneurial learning. *International Small Business Journal*, *29*(1), 37–57. doi:10.1177/0266242610369876

Planning Commission (2011). *Faster, Sustainable and More Inclusive Growth: An Approach to the Twelfth Five-Year Plan (2012-17)*. Government of India, Planning Commission Document.

Polgreen, L. (2011, Sept 2). *Scanning 2.4 Billion Eyes, India Tries to Connect Poor to Growth*. Retrieved Oct 10, 2012, from New York Times: http://www.nytimes.com/2011/09/02/world/asia/02india.html?pagewanted=all

Poole. N. (2006). *L'innovation: enjeux, contraintes et opportunités pour les ruraux pauvres*. Document de synthèse, Janvier.

Posner, B. Z., & Kouzes, J. M. (1988). Relating leadership and credibility. *Psychological Reports*, *63*(2), 527–530. doi:10.2466/pr0.1988.63.2.527

Poster, M. (2004). Consumption and digital commodities in the everyday. *Cultural Studies*, *18*(2-3), 409–423.

Prahalad, C. K. (2004). *The fortune at the bottom of the pyramid: Eradicating poverty through profits*. Philadelphia: Wharton School Publishing.

Prahalad, C. K., & Ramaswamy, V. (2000). Co-opting customer competence. *Harvard Business Review*, *78*(1), 79–90.

Prahalad, C. K., & Ramaswamy, V. (2004). Co-creation experiences: The next practice in value creation. *Journal of Interactive Marketing*, *18*(3), 5–14. doi:10.1002/dir.20015

Prendergast, G. (2004). *Blended collaborative learning: online teaching of online educators*. Global Educator.

Prensky, M. (2001). Digital natives, digital immigrants Part 1. *On the horizon*, *9*(5), 1–6. doi:10.1108/10748120110424816

Prensky, M. (2006). Adopt and adapt. *Edutopia*, *1*(9), 42–45.

Prensky, M. (2010). *Teaching Digital Natives*. London: SAGE Ltd.

Probe-IT. (2012). *CoAP white paper*. Retrieved from http://www.probe-it.eu/?p=522

Productivity Commission. (2009). *Restrictions on the Parallel Importation of Books*. Retrieved on November 20, 2011, from http://www.pc.gov.au/projects/study/books/report

Prosser, M., Trigwell, K., & Taylor, P. (1994). A phenomenographic study of academics conceptions of science learning and teaching. *Learning and Instruction*, *4*(3), 217–231. doi:10.1016/0959-4752(94)90024-8

PTI. (2012, Oct 18). *Micro-ATM using Aadhaar data delivers cash to villagers*. Retrieved June 20, 2013 from The Hindu: http://www.thehindubusinessline.com/news/microatm-using-aadhaar-data-delivers-cash-to-villagers/article4009641.ece

Public Law, 111–5, American Recovery and Reinvestment Act of 2009. (n.d.). Retrieved December 1, 2015. from https://www.gpo.gov/fdsys/pkg/PLAW-111publ5/pdf/PLAW-111publ5.pdf

Pullen, A., & Rhodes, C. (2014). Corporeal ethics and the politics of resistance in organizations. *Organization*, *21*(6), 782–796. doi:10.1177/1350508413484819

Pullman, M. E., & Gross, M. A. (2004). Ability of Experience Design Element to Elicit Emotin and Loyalty Behaviors. *Decision Sciences*, *35*(3), 551–578. doi:10.1111/j.0011-7315.2004.02611.x

Quality King Distributors, Inc. v. L'anza Research Int'l, Inc. - 523 U.S. 135 (1998).

Radin, T. J., Calkins, M., & Predmore, C. (2007). New Challenges to Old Problems: Building Trust In E-marketing. *Business and Society Review, 112*(1), 73–98. doi:10.1111/j.1467-8594.2007.00287.x

Rajala, R., Westerlund, M., & Möller, K. (2012). Strategic flexibility in open innovation–designing business models for open source software. *European Journal of Marketing, 46*(10), 1368–1388. doi:10.1108/03090561211248071

Ramamoorthy, G. (2013). *Hype cycle for embedded software and systems.* Gartner, Research Note. Retrieved from http://www.gartner.com/newsroom/id/2575515

Ramaswamy, V. & Ozcan, K. (2016). Brand value co-creation in a digitalized world: An integrative framework and research implications. *International Journal of Research and Marketing.* 10.1016/j.ijresmar.2015.07.001

Ramaswamy, V., & Gouillart, F. (2010). *The power of co-creation.* New York, NY: Simon & Schuster.

Ramsden, P. (1991). A performance indicator of teaching quality in higher education: The Course Experience Questionnaire. *Studies in Higher Education, 16*(2), 129–150. doi:10.1080/03075079112331382944

Ramsden, P. (2003). *Learning to teach in higher education.* New York: RoutledgeFalmer.

Ranaweera, C., & Prabhu, J. (2003). The influence of satisfaction, trust and switching barriers on customer retention in a continuous purchasing setting. *International Journal of Service Industry Management, 14*(4), 374–395. doi:10.1108/09564230310489231

Rashidi, R., Yousefpour, S., Sani, Y., & Rezaei, S. (2013). Presenting a butterfly ecosystem for digital entrepreneurship development in knowledge age. *Proceedings of 7th conference on Application of Information and Communication Technologies (AICT).* doi:10.1109/ICAICT.2013.6722798

Rawlins, G. J. E. (1993). Publishing over the next decade. *Journal of the American Society for Information Science, 44*(8), 474–479. doi:10.1002/(SICI)1097-4571(199309)44:8<474::AID-ASI6>3.0.CO;2-3

Rawls, J. (1971). *A Theory of Justice.* Cambridge, MA: Harvard University Press.

Razzouk, N. Y., Setiz, V., Lamuda, K., & Kepekci, A. C. (2005). A Content Analysis of Value-Based Advertising on the Internet. *Journal of Website Promotion, 1*(3), 61–73. doi:10.1300/J238v01n03_05

Reckwitz, A. (2002). Toward a Theory of Social Practices. A Development in Culturalist Theorizing. *European Journal of Social Theory, 5*(2), 243–263. doi:10.1177/13684310222225432

Repenning, N. P. (2002). A Simulation-Based Approach to Understanding the Dynamics of Innovation Implementation. *Organization Science, 13*(2), 109–127. doi:10.1287/orsc.13.2.109.535

Repenning, N. P., & Sterman, J. D. (2002). Capability traps and self-confirming attribution errors in the dynamics of process improvement. *Administrative Science Quarterly, 47*(2), 265–295. doi:10.2307/3094806

Richards, J. I., & Curran, C. M. (2002). Oracles on Advertising: Searching for a Definition. *Journal of Advertising, 31*(2), 63–77. doi:10.1080/00913367.2002.10673667

Riederer, J. P., Baier, M., & Graefe, G. (2005). Innovation management – An overview and some best practices. *C-LAB Report, 4*, 3.

Ries, E. (2011). *The lean startup. How today's entrepreneurs use continuous innovation to create radically successful businesses.* New York: Crown Publishing Group.

Ring, P. S., & van de Ven, A. H. (1994). Developmental processes of cooperative interorganizational relationships. *Academy of Management Review, 19*(1), 90–118.

Ritala, P. (2001). Coopetition Strategy - When is it Successful? Empirical Evidence on Innovation and market performance. *British Journal of Management.*

Ritzer, G. (2013). Prosumption: Evolution, revolution or eternal return of the same? *Journal of Consumer Culture,* 1–22.

Ritzer, G., & Jurgenson, N. (2010). Production, Consumption, Prosumption The nature of capitalism in the age of the digital 'prosumer'. *Journal of Consumer Culture, 10*(1), 13–36. doi:10.1177/1469540509354673

Roberts, G. (2003). Teaching using the web: Conceptions and approaches from a phenomenographic perspective. *Instructional Science, 31*(1-2), 127–150. doi:10.1023/A:1022547619474

Rodgers, S., & Thorson, E. (2000). The Interactive Advertising Model: How Users Perceive and Process Online Ads. *Journal of Interactive Advertising, 1*(1), 42–61. doi:10.1080/15252019.2000.10722043

Rodgers, S., Wang, Y., Rettie, R., & Alpert, F. (2007). The Web Motivation Inventory Replication, extension and application to internet advertising. *International Journal of Advertising, 26*(4), 447–476.

Rodriguez, M. A., & Anicete, R. C. R. (2010). Students' Views of a Mixed Hybrid Ecology Course. *MERLOT Journal of Online Learning and Teaching, 6,* 791–798.

Roger, E. M. (2003). Diffusion of Innovations. New York: Academic Press.

Romero, D., Galeano, N., & Molina, A. (2008). Innovation in manufacturing networks. In A. Azevedo (Ed.), *International Federation for Information Processing, 266* (pp. 47–56). Boston: Springer.

Rong, K., Hu, G., Lin, Y., Shi, Y., & Guo, L. (2015). Understanding business ecosystem using a 6C framework in Internet-of-Things-based sectors, *International Journal of Production Economics, 159,* 41-55.

Rong, K., Wu, J., Shi, Y., & Guo, L. (2015). Nurturing business ecosystems for growth in a foreign market: Incubating, identifying and integrating stakeholders. *Journal of International Management, 21*(4), 293–308. doi:10.1016/j.intman.2015.07.004

Rosario Perello-Marin, M., Marin-Garcia, J. A., & Marcos-Cuevas, J. (2013). Towards a path dependence approach to study management innovation. *Management Decision, 51*(5), 1037–1046. doi:10.1108/MD-08-2012-0605

Rossiter, J. R., & Percy, L. (1991). Emotions and motivations in advertising. *Advances in Consumer Research. Association for Consumer Research (U. S.), 18,* 100–110.

Rossiter, J. R., & Percy, L. (1992). A model of brand awareness and brand attitude advertising strategies. *Psychology and Marketing, 9*(4), 263–274. doi:10.1002/mar.4220090402

Rossiter, J. R., & Percy, L. (1997). *Advertising Communications and Promotion Management.* McGraw-Hill.

Rotfeld, H.J. (1988). Fear appeals and persuasion: Assumption and errors in advertising research. *Current Issues and Research in Advertising, 11*(1), 221-40.

Rothschild, M. (1990). *Bionomics: Economy as Business Ecosystem.* New York: Beard.

Rouleau, L. (2005). Micro-Practices of Strategic Sensemaking and Sensegiving: How Middle Managers Interpret and Sell Change Every Day. *Journal of Management Studies, 42*(7), 1413–1441. doi:10.1111/j.1467-6486.2005.00549.x

Rouleau, L., & Balogun, J. (2011). Middle managers, strategic sensemaking, and discursive competence. *Journal of Management Studies, 48*(5), 953–983. doi:10.1111/j.1467-6486.2010.00941.x

Rubens, N., Still, K., Huhtamaki, J., & Russell, M.G. (2011). A network analysis of investment firms as resource routers in Chinese innovation ecosystem. *Journal of Software*, *6*(9), 1737-1745.

Rusko, R. (2013). The Redefined Role of Consumer as a Prosumer: Value Co-Creation, Coopetition, and Crowdsourcing of Information Goods. In Production and Manufacturing System Management: Coordination Approaches and Multi-Site Planning (pp. 162- 174). Academic Press.

Rusko, R. (2012). Strategic Processes and Turning Points in ICT Business: Case Nokia. *International Journal of Innovation in the Digital Economy*, *3*(3), 25–34.

Rusko, R. T., Kylänen, M., & Saari, R. (2009). Supply chain in tourism destinations: The case of Levi Resort in Finnish Lapland. *International Journal of Tourism Research*, *11*(1), 71–87. doi:10.1002/jtr.677

Rusko, R., Merenheimo, P., & Haanpää, M. (2013). Coopetition, Resource-Based View and Legend: Cases of Christmas Tourism and City of Rovaniemi. *International Journal of Marketing Studies*, *5*(6).

Ruttan, V.-W. (1974). Induced innovation and agricultural development. *RE:view*, *64*(May), I-14.

Ruttan, V.-W. (1989). Institutional-Innovation and Agricultural Development. *Review World Development*, *17*(9), 1375–138. doi:10.1016/0305-750X(89)90079-X

Ryker, R., LaFleur, E., McManis, B., & Cox, C. K. (2002). Online privacy policies:An assessment of the fortuneE-50. *Journal of Computer Information Systems*, *42*(4), 15–20.

Sahin, A., Zehir, C., & Kitapci, H. (2011). The Effects of Brand Experiences, Trust and Satisfaction on Building Brand Loyalty; An Empirical Research On Global Brands. *Procedia: Social and Behavioral Sciences*, *24*, 1288–1301. doi:10.1016/j.sbspro.2011.09.143

Saljo, R. (1979). *Learning in the learner's perspective. I. Some common-sense conceptions*. ERIC Clearinghouse.

Salmon, G. (2002). *E-tivities: the key to active online learning*. Falmer Press, Limited.

Salmon, G. (2005). Flying not flapping: A strategic framework for e-learning and pedagogical innovation in higher education institutions. *ALT-J*, *13*(3), 201–218. doi:10.1080/09687760500376439

Salo, J., & Karjaluoto, H. (2007). A Conceptual Model of Trust in the Online Environment. *Online Information Review*, *31*(5), 604–621. doi:10.1108/14684520710832324

Sanchez, R. A., Hueros, A. D., & Ordaz, M. G. (2013). E-learning and the University of Huelva: A study of WebCT and the technological acceptance model. *Campus-Wide Information Systems*, *30*(2), 135–160. doi:10.1108/10650741311306318

Saundercook, J., & Cooper, P. (2003). *4th annual technology and student success in higher education. A research study on faculty perceptions of technology and student success*. Toronto: McGraw-Hill Ryerson.

Saur, C., & Willcocks, L. P. (2002). The evolution of organizational architect. *MIT Sloan Management Review*, *43*(3), 41–49.

Savikas, A. (2013). *The future of publishing*. Podcast, January 15, 2013. Retrieved on June 18, 2013 from http://nextmarket.co/blogs/conversations/7178184-andrew-savikas-ceo-of-safari-books-on-book-publishing-models-social-reading-and-more

Sawhney, M., Verona, G., & Prandelli, E. (2005). Collaborating to create: The Internet as a platform for customer engagement in product innovation. *Journal of Interactive Marketing*, *19*(4), 4–17. doi:10.1002/dir.20046

Sawyer, A. (1981). Repetition, cognitive responses and persuasion. In R. E. Petty, T. M. Ostrom, & T. C. Brock (Eds.), *Cognitive Responses in Persuasion* (pp. 237–262). Lawrence Erlbaum Associates.

Schafer, J. A. (2002). Spinning the web of hate: Web-based hate propagation by extremist organizations. *Journal of Criminal Justice and Popular Culture, 69–88*. Available at http://www.albany.edu/scj/jcjpc/vol9is2/schafer.pdf

Schatzki, T. R. (2001). Practice theory. In T. R. Schatzki, K. Knorr-Cetina, & E. von Savigny (Eds.), *The practice turn in contemporary theory* (pp. 1–14). London: Routledge.

Schindehutte, M., Morris, M. H., & Kocak, A. (2008). Understanding Market-Driving Behavior: The Role of Entrepreneurship. *Journal of Small Business Management, 46*(1), 4–26. doi:10.1111/j.1540-627X.2007.00228.x

Schlautmann, A., Levy, D., Keeping, S., & Pankert, G. (2011). Wanted: Smart market-makers for the "Internet of Things". *Prism, 2*, 35–47.

Schlosser, E. A., Shavitt, S., & Kanfer, A. (1999). Survey of internet users' attitudes toward internet advertising. *Journal of Interactive Marketing*, 34–54.

Schmitt, B. H. (1999a). Experiential Marketing. *Journal of Marketing Management, 15*(1-3), 53–67. doi:10.1362/026725799784870496

Schmitt, B. H. (1999b). *Experiential Marketing: How to Get Customers to Sense, Feel, Think, Act, and Relate to Your Company and Brand*. New York: The Free Press.

Schmitt, B. H. (2009). The Concept of Brand Experience. *Journal of Brand Management, 16*(7), 417–419. doi:10.1057/bm.2009.5

Schuh, G., Kuhlmann, K., Pitsch, M., & Komorek, N. (2013, July). Digitalization as a key enabler for efficient value creation networks in the tool and die making industry. In *Technology Management in the IT-Driven Services (PICMET), 2013 Proceedings of PICMET'13* (pp. 1976-1984). IEEE.

Schumpeter, J. A. (1934). *The theory of economic development*. Cambridge, MA: Harvard University Press.

Schumpeter, J. A. (1939). *Business Cycles: A Theoretical*. New York: Historical, and Statistical Analysis of the Capitalist Process.

Schumpeter, J. A. (1996). *Capitalism*. London: Socialism and Democracy.

Scott, S., & Orlikowski, W. J. (2012). Reconfiguring relations of accountability: Materialization of social media in the travel sector. *Accounting, Organizations and Society, 37*(1), 26–40. doi:10.1016/j.aos.2011.11.005

Scott, W. R. (2003). *Organizational: Rational, Natural, and Open Systems*. Upper Saddle River, NJ: Prentice-Hall.

Sethi, M., Arkko, J., & Keränen, A. (2012). End-to-end security for sleepy smart object networks. In *37th Annual IEEE Conference on Local Computer Networks* (LCN Workshops) (pp. 964–972). doi:10.1109/LCNW.2012.6424089

Sharma, R., & Yetton, P. (2003). The contingent effects of management support and task interdependence on successful information systems implementation. *Management Information Systems Quarterly, 27*, 533–555.

Sharpe, R., & Benfield, G. (2005). The Student Experience of E-learning in Higher Education. *Brookes eJournal of Learning and Teaching, 1*(3).

Sharpe, R. (2006). *The undergraduate experience of blended e-learning: a review of UK literature and practice*. The Higher Education Academy York.

Shavitt, S., Lowrey, P., & Haefner, J. (1998). Public Attitudes Toward Advertising: More Favorable Than You Might Think. *Journal of Advertising Research, 38*(4), 7–22.

Sheehan, K. B. (2002). Of surfing, searching, and newshounds: A typology of Internet users online sessions. *Journal of Advertising Research*, *42*(5), 62–71. doi:10.2501/JAR-42-5-62-71

Shelby, Z., Bormann, C., & Krco, S. (2013). *CoRE Resource Directory*. Retrieved from https://tools.ietf.org/html/draft-ietf-core-resource-directory-02

Shelby, Z., Hartke, K., Bormann, C., & Frank, B. (2013, June). *Constrained Application Protocol (CoAP)*. Retrieved from https://datatracker.ietf.org/doc/draft-ietf-core-coap/

Shen, C.-H., Wu, M.-W., Chen, T.-H., & Fang, H. (2016). To engage or not to engage in corporate social responsibility: Empirical evidence from global banking sector. *Economic Modelling*, *55*(June), 207–225. doi:10.1016/j.econmod.2016.02.007

Sheng, M. L., & Teo, T. S. H. (2012). Product attributes and brand equity in the mobile domain: The mediating role of customer experience. *International Journal of Information Management*, *32*(2), 139–146. doi:10.1016/j.ijinfomgt.2011.11.017

Sheth, J., Sisodia, R., & Sharma, A. (2000). The Antecedents and Consequences of Customer-Centric Marketing. *Journal of the Academy of Marketing Science*, *28*(Winter), 55–66. doi:10.1177/0092070300281006

Shivetts, C. (2011). *E-Learning and Blended Learning: The Importance of the Learner--A Research Literature Review* (Vol. 10, pp. 331–337). Association for the Advancement of Computing in Education.

Shnayder, L., van Rijnsoeve, F. J., & Hekkert, M. P. (2016). Motivations for Corporate Social Responsibility in the packaged food industry: An institutional and stakeholder management perspective. *Journal of Cleaner Production*, *122*(May), 212–227. doi:10.1016/j.jclepro.2016.02.030

Sigurdson, J. (2001). WAP OFF---Origin, Failure, and Future, Prepared for the Japanese. Retrieved from http://www2.hhs.se/eijswp/135.PDF

Simonin, B. L. (1999). Transfer of Marketing Know-How in International Strategic Alliances: An Empirical Investigation of the Role and Antecedents of Knowledge Ambiguity. *Journal of International Business Studies*, *30*(3), 463–491. doi:10.1057/palgrave.jibs.8490079

Singh, H. (2003). Building effective blended learning programs. *Educational Technology*, *43*(6), 51–54.

Singh, J., & Sirdeshmukh, D. (2000). Agency and trust mechanisms in consumer satisfaction and loyalty judgments. *Journal of the Academy of Marketing Science*, *28*(1), 150–167. doi:10.1177/0092070300281014

Singh, S. (2010). Digital divide in India: Measurement, determinants and policy for addressing the challenges in bridging the digital divide. *International Journal of Innovation in the Digital Economy*, *1*(2), 1–24. doi:10.4018/jide.2010040101

Sipola, S. (2015). *Understanding growth and non-growth in entrepreneurial economies. Analysis of startup industries and experimental winner generation in Finland, Israel and Silicon Valley* (Doctoral dissertation). Acta Universitatis Ouluensis, G Oeconomica 73.

Skill, T. D., & Young, B. A. (2002). Embracing the hybrid model: Working at the intersections of virtual and physical learning spaces. *New Directions for Teaching and Learning*, *2002*(92), 23–32. doi:10.1002/tl.76

So, K. K. F., King, C., Sparks, B. A., & Wang, Y. (2016). Enhancing customer relationships with retail service brands: The role of customer engagement. *Journal of Service Management*, *27*(2).

Soni, P., Taewichit, C., & Salokhe, V. M. (2013). Energy consumption and CO2 emissions in rainfed agricultural production systems of Northeast Thailand. *Agricultural Systems*, *116*, 25–36. doi:10.1016/j.agsy.2012.12.006

Spee, A. P., & Jarzabkowski, P. (2011). Strategic planning as a communicative process. *Organization Studies*, *32*(9), 1217–1245. doi:10.1177/0170840611411387

Spottke, B., Wulf, J., & Brenner, W. (2015). Consumer-Centric Information Systems: A Literature Review and Avenues for Further Research. *Proceedings of Thirty Sixth InternationalConference on Information Systems.*

Stacey, E., & Gerbic, P. (2009). Introduction to blended learning practices. *Effective blended learning practices: Evidence-based perspectives in ICT-facilitated education,* 1-20.

Stacey, E., & Wiesenberg, F. (2007). A study of face-to-face and online teaching philosophies in Canada and Australia. *The Journal of Distance Education/Revue de l'Éducation à Distance, 22*(1), 19-40.

Staempfli, M. B. (2005). *Adolescent playfulness, leisure and well-being* (Unpublished Doctoral Dissertation). University of Waterloo, Ontario, Canada.

Stake, R. E. (2005). Qualitative Case Studies. In N. K. Denzin & Y. S. Lincoln (Eds.), *Handbook of Qualitative Research* (3rd ed.; pp. 443–466). London: Sage Publications.

Stam, E., Gibcus, P., Telussa, J., & Garnsey, E. (2008). *Employment growth of new firms.* JENA Economic Research Papers, 08-005.

Stanford-Clark, A., & Truong, H. L. (2013). *MQTT for Sensor Networks MQTT-SN Protocol Specification Version 1.2.* International Business Machines Corporation IBM, Technical Report.

Stanoevska-Slabeva, K. (2010). *Business Models - Opportunities and Barriers.* Retrieved from http://www.ict-ccast.eu

Steel, C. (2009). Reconciling university teacher beliefs to create learning designs for LMS environments. *Australasian Journal of Educational Technology, 25*(3), 399–420. doi:10.14742/ajet.1142

Stieger, D., Matzler, K., Chatterjee, S., & Ladstaetter-Fussenegger, F. (2012). Democratizing strategy: How crowdsourcing can be used for strategy dialogues. *California Management Review, 54*(4), 44–68. doi:10.1525/cmr.2012.54.4.44

Strebler, M., Robinson, D., & Heron, P. (1997). *Getting the Best Out of Your Competencies.* Brighton, UK: Institute of Employment Studies, University of Sussex.

Streeten, P. (1981). From Growth to Basic Needs. In *Development Perspectives.* New York: St. Martin's Press. doi:10.1007/978-1-349-05341-4_18

Suchman, L. A. (2007). *Human–machine reconfigurations: Plans and situated actions.* Cambridge, UK: Cambridge University Press.

Sundar, S. S., & Nass, C. (2001). Conceptualizing sources in online news. *Journal of Communication, 51*(1), 52–72. doi:10.1111/j.1460-2466.2001.tb02872.x

Sundmaeker, H., Guillemin, P., Friess, P., & Woelfflé, S. (2010). Vision and Challenges for Realizing the Internet of Things. Brussels, Belgium: Academic Press.

Survey Monkey. (2013). Retrieved on June 17, 2013 from http://www.surveymonkey.com

Sydow, J., Schreyögg, G., & Koch, J. (2005). *Organizational paths: Path dependency and beyond.* Free University of Berlin.

Sylvander, B., Schieb-Bienfait, N., Le Floch-Wadel, A., & Couallier, C. (2004). The strategic turn of Organic Farming in Europe: a resource based approach of Organic Marketing Initiatives.*XI World Congress of Rural Sociology Special session II: Peasant between Social Movements and the markets.*

Tabakov, B. (2014). *Techno-Economic Feasibility of Web Real-Time Communications.* Aalto University.

Talouselämä. (2013). *Gartner: The market share of Nokia declined extremely low.* Author. (in Finnish)

Tang, M., & Byrne, R. (2007). Regular versus Online versus Blended: A Qualitative Description of the Advantages of the Electronic Modes and a Quantitative Evaluation. *International Journal on E-Learning*, *6*(2), 257–266.

Tanrikulu, Z., & Celilbatur, N. (2013). Trust Factor Affectng E-Ticket Purchasing. *Procedia: Social and Behavioral Sciences*, *73*, 115–119. doi:10.1016/j.sbspro.2013.02.030

Taylor, C. (1985). *Philosophy and the human sciences*. Cambridge, UK: Cambridge University Press. doi:10.1017/CBO9781139173490

Teece, D. J., Pisano, G., & Shuen, A. (1997). Dynamic capabilities and strategic management. *Strategic Management Journal*, *18*(7), 509–533. doi:10.1002/(SICI)1097-0266(199708)18:7<509::AID-SMJ882>3.0.CO;2-Z

Tellis, G. J. (1997). Effective frequency: one exposure or three factors?. *Journal of Advertising Research*, 75–80. Available at http://papers.ssrn.com/sol3/papers.cfm?abstract_id=906019

The Authors Guild et al v Google, Inc , (2009) US District Court, Southern District of New York, No. 05-08136 1.

The Economist . (2012a, Jan 14). *India's identity scheme- The magic number: A huge identity scheme promises to help India's poor—and to serve as a model for other countries*. Retrieved April 5, 2012, from The Economist: http://www.economist.com/node/21542763/print

The History of Ericsson. (2016). Retrieved From: http://www.ericssonhistory.com/

Thirtle, C., Townsend, R., & Van Zyl, J. (1998). Testing the Induced Innovation Hypothesis in South African Agriculture (An Error Correction Approach). *Agricultural Economics*, (19), 145–157. doi:10.1016/S0169-5150(98)00030-9

Thomas, R. (2009). Critical management studies on identity: Mapping the terrain. In The Oxford Handbook of Critical Management Studies (pp. 166-185). Oxford University Press.

Thomas, L., & Ambrosini, V. (2015). Materializing strategy: The role of comprehensiveness and management controls in strategy formation in volatile environments. *British Journal of Management*, *26*, S105–S124. doi:10.1111/1467-8551.12075

Thorson, E. (1996). Advertising. In An integrated Approach to Communication Theory and Research (pp. 211-230). Mahwah, NJ: Lawrence Erlbaum.

Tietokone. (2006). *Matkapuhelintekniikka täyttää 50 vuotta*. Tero Lehto.

Timmer, C.P. (1992). agricultural and economic development revisited. *Agricultural Systems, 40*, 21-58.

Tischer, S., Meyer, M., Wodak, R., & Vetter, E. (2000). *Methods of Text and Discourse Analysis*. London: SAGE.

Tjiptono, F., Arli, D., & Bucic, T. (2014). Consumer confusion proneness: Insights from a developing economy. *Marketing Intelligence & Planning*, *32*(6), 722–734. doi:10.1108/MIP-05-2013-0082

TNN. (2012, Oct 22). *UID helps detect 4k fake beneficiaries*. Retrieved 29 Oct, 2012, from The Times of India: http://timesofindia.indiatimes.com/city/mumbai/UID-helps-detect-4k-fake-beneficiaries/articleshow/16907738.cms

Toffler, A. (1980). *The third wave*. New York: Bantam books.

Toffler, A., & Toffler, H. (2006). *Revolutionary Wealth*. New York: Doubleday.

Toner, P. (1999). Conclusion. In *Main Currents in Cumulative Causation, the Dynamics of Growth and Development*. Houndmills, UK: Macmillan Press Ltd. doi:10.1007/978-0-333-98289-1_7

Tong, M. C., & Robertson, K. (2008). Political and cultural representation in Malaysian websites. *International Journal of Design*, *2*(2), 67–79.

Trigwell, K., Prosser, M., & Taylor, P. (1994). Qualitative differences in approaches to teaching first year university science. *Higher Education, 27*(1), 75–84. doi:10.1007/BF01383761

Tripadvisor. (2014a). Retrieved from http://www.tripadvisor.com/ShowUserReviews-g189922-d591471-r172227191-Santa_Claus_Village-Rovaniemi_Lapland.html

Tripadvisor. (2014b). *TripAdvisor.com, Community, Destination Experts.* Author.

Trott, P. (2005). Innovation management and new product development (3rd ed.). Essex, UK: Pearson Education Limited.

Turban, E., King, D., McKay, J., Marshall, P., & Lee, L. K. (2008). *Electronic Commerce 2008: A Managerial Perspective.* Pearson Prentice Hall. Available at: www.pearsonhighered.com

Turnbull, P. W., Leek, S., & Ying, G. (2000). Customer confusion: The mobile phone market. *Journal of Marketing Management, 16*(January-April), 143–163. doi:10.1362/026725700785100523

Tushman, M. L., & Murmann, J. P. (2003). *Managing in the modular age: architectures, networks, and organizations* (R. Garud, A. Kumaraswamy, & R. N. Langlois, Eds.). Oxford, UK: Blackwell Publishers.

Tyrväinen, P., & Mazhelis, O. (2009). *Vertical Software Industry Evolution: Analysis of Telecom Operator Software.* Physica Verlag. doi:10.1007/978-3-7908-2352-3

U.S Census Bureau News. (2011). *Monthly and Annual Retail Trade.* Retrieved from http://www.censuse.gov/www/ecomm.htm/

UIDAI. (2010). *UIDAI Strategy Overview: Creating a Unique Identity Number for every resident in India.* Planning Commission, Government of India Document.

UIDAI. (2012). *Aadhaar Enabled Service Delivery.* Planning Commission, Government of India Document.

United Nations (2014). *Millennium Development Goals report.* Author.

Vaara, E. & Whittington, R. (2012). Strategy-as-practice. Taking social practices seriously. *The Academy of Management Annals,* 1–52.

Vaara, E., Sorsa, V., & Palli, P. (2010). On the force potential of strategy texts, a critical discourse analysis of a strategic plan and its power effects in a city organization. *Organization, 17*(6), 685–702. doi:10.1177/1350508410367326

van der Linden, F., Lundell, B., & Marttiin, P. (2009). Commodification of industrial software: A case for open source. *Software, IEEE., 26*(4), 77–83. doi:10.1109/MS.2009.88

Van Doorn, J., Lemon, K. N., Mittal, V., Nass, S. D. P., Pirner, P., & Verhoef, P. C. (2010). Customer engagement behaviour: Theoretical foundations and research directions. *Journal of Service Research, 13*(3), 253–266. doi:10.1177/1094670510375599

Van Rijn, F., Bulte, E., & Adekunle, A. (2012). Social capital and agricultural innovation in Sub-Saharan Africa. *Revue Agricultural Systems, 108,* 112–122.

Vargo, S. L., & Lusch, R. F. (2004). Evolving to a new dominant logic for marketing. *Journal of Marketing, 68*(1), 1–17. doi:10.1509/jmkg.68.1.1.24036

Vargo, S. L., & Lusch, R. F. (2006). *Service-dominant logic. The service-dominant logic of marketing: Dialog, debate, and directions.* Armonk, NY: ME Sharpe.

Vattyam, S., & Lubbers, C. A. (1999). *A content analysis of the web pages of large U.S corporations: What is the role of public relations and marketing?*. Paper submitted to the Public Relations Division of the AEJMC for review for the 1999 Conference.

Vaughan, R. (1986). How advertising works: A planning model. *Journal of Advertising Research, 1*(1), 57–66.

Venkatesh, V., Morris, M. G., Davis, G. B., & Davis, F. D. (2003). User acceptance of information technology: Toward a unified view. *Management Information Systems Quarterly, 27*(3), 425–478.

Ventelou, B. (2005). Economic thought on the eve of the General Theory. In *Millennial Keynes*. Armonk, NY: M.E. Sharpe.

Vergne, J.-P., & Durand, R. (2010). The missing link between the theory and empirics of path dependence: Conceptual clarification, testability issue, and methodological implications. *Journal of Management Studies, 47*(4), 736–759.

Verkroost, M. J., Meijerink, L., Lintsen, H., & Veen, W. (2008). Finding a balance in dimensions of blended learning. *International Journal on E-Learning, 7*(3), 499–522.

Verona, G. (1999). A resource-based view of product development. *Academy of Management Review, 24*(1), 132–142.

Vignare, K. (2007). Review of literature, blended learning: Using ALN to change the classroom–will it work. *Blended learning: Research perspectives*, 37-63.

Vigneron, F., & Johnson, L. W. (1999). A Review and a Conceptual Framework of Prestige-Seeking Consumer Behavior. *Academy of Marketing Science Review, 99*(1), 1–15.

Villaverde, B. C., Pesch, D., Alberola, R. D. P., Fedor, S., & Boubekeur, M. (2012). Constrained Application Protocol for Low Power Embedded Networks: A Survey. In *Innovative Mobile and Internet Services in Ubiquitous Computing (IMIS), 2012 Sixth International Conference on* (pp. 702–707). doi:10.1109/IMIS.2012.93

von Hippel, E. (2006). *Democratizing Innovation*. MIT Press.

von Hippel, E., & von Krogh, G. (2003). Open source software and the "private-collective" innovation model: Issues for organization science. *Organization Science, 14*(2), 209–223. doi:10.1287/orsc.14.2.209.14992

von Krogh, G., Rossi-Lamastra, C., & Haefliger, S. (2012). Phenomenon-based research in management and organisation science: When is it rigorous and does it matter? *Long Range Planning, 45*(4), 277–298. doi:10.1016/j.lrp.2012.05.001

Von Mises, L. (1981). The return to sound money. In *The Theory of Money and Credit* (pp. 477–500). Indianapolis, IN: Liberty Fund.

Voorveld, H. A. M., Neijens, P. C., & Smit, E. G. (2011). The Relation Between Actual and Perceived Interactivity, What Makes the Web Sites of Top Global Brands Truly Interactive. *Journal of Advertising, 40*(2), 77–92. doi:10.2753/JOA0091-3367400206

Walker, E., Loughton, K., & Brown, A. (1999). The relevance of non-financial measures of success for micro business owners.*International Council for Small Business, NaplesConference Proceedings*.

Walsh, G., Hennig-Thurau, T., & Mitchel, V.-W. (2007). Consumer confusion proneness: Scale development, validation, and application. *Journal of Marketing Management, 23*(7/8), 697–721. doi:10.1362/026725707X230009

Walsh, G., & Mitchel, V.-W. (2010). The Effect of Consumer Confusion Proneness on Word of Mouth, Trust, and Customer Satisfaction. *European Journal of Marketing, 44*(6), 838–859. doi:10.1108/03090561011032739

Wand, Y., & Weber, R. (1990). An ontological model of an information system. *IEEE Transactions on Software Engineering, 16*(11), 1281–1291. doi:10.1109/32.60316

Wand, Y., & Weber, R. (1993). On the ontological expressiveness of information systems analysis and design grammars. *Journals of Information Systems, 3*(4), 217–237. doi:10.1111/j.1365-2575.1993.tb00127.x

Wang, L. (2005). *An effective study of "Parent-Child English Co-Learning Project" in a social education organization: The Chin-Chin branch of Taipei Public Library experience.* (Unpublished Master's Thesis). Graduate School of Educational Policy and Management, National Taipei Teachers College, Taipei.

Wang, A., & Marquardt, W. (2009). An Ontological Conceptualization of multiscale models. *Computers & Chemical Engineering, 33*(4), 822–837. doi:10.1016/j.compchemeng.2008.11.015

Watson, R. T., Boudreau, M. C., York, P. T., Greiner, M. E., & Wynn, D. Jr. (2008). The business of open source. *Communications of the ACM, 51*(4), 41–46. doi:10.1145/1330311.1330321

Waxman, H. C., Huang, S. Y. L., & Wang, M. C. (1997). Investigating the classroom learning environment of resilient and non-resilient students from inner-city elementary schools. *International Journal of Educational Research, 27*(4), 343–353. doi:10.1016/S0883-0355(97)90016-1

Weare, C., & Lin, W. Y. (2000). Content Analysis of the World Wide Web Opportunities and Challenges. *Social Science Computer Review, 18*(3), 272-292.

Webster, J., & Hackley, P. (1997). Teaching Effectiveness in Technology-Mediated Distance Learning. *Academy of Management Journal, 40*(6), 1282–1309. doi:10.2307/257034

Weill, P., & Woerner, S. (2015). Thriving in an Increasingly Digital Ecosystem, *MIT. Sloan Management Review, 56*(4), 27–34.

Weiss, D. (2005). Internetnutzung im studium – Erklarung and vorhersage der internetnutzung von studierenden in Deutschland und Osterreich. *Psychologie–Medienpsychologie, 135*(1-3), 135.

Welker, J., & Berardino, L. (2006). Blended Learning: Understanding the Middle Ground between Traditional Classroom and Fully Online Instruction. *Journal of Educational Technology Systems, 34*(1), 33–55. doi:10.2190/67FX-B7P8-PYUX-TDUP

Werle, F., & Seidl, D. (2015). The layered materiality of strate- gizing: Epistemic objects and the interplay between material artefacts in the exploration of strategic topics. *British Journal of Management, 26*, S67–S89. doi:10.1111/1467-8551.12080

Westerman, G., Bonnet, D., & McAfee, A. (2014). *The Nine Elements of Digital Transformation.* Academic Press.

West, J. (2003). How open is open enough?melding proprietary and open source platform strategies. *Research Policy, 32*(7), 1259–1285. doi:10.1016/S0048-7333(03)00052-0

West, J., & O'Mahony, S. (2008). The role of participation architecture in growing sponsored open source communities. *Industry and Innovation, 15*(2), 145–168. doi:10.1080/13662710801970142

Whittington, R. (2015). The massification of strategy. *British Journal of Management, 26*, S13–S16. doi:10.1111/1467-8551.12078

Whittington, R., Cailluet, L., & Yakis-Douglas, B. (2011). Opening Strategy: Evolution of a Precarious Profession. *British Journal of Management, 22*(3), 531–544. doi:10.1111/j.1467-8551.2011.00762.x

Whittington, R., Molloy, E., Mayer, M., & Smith, A. (2006). Practices of strategizing/organising. Broadening strategy work and skills. *Long Range Planning, 39*, 615–629. doi:10.1016/j.lrp.2006.10.004

Wiedmann, K.-P. (2015). The future of brand and brand management – Some provocative propositions from a more methodological perspective. *Journal of Brand Management, 21*(9), 743–757.

Wijen, F., & Ansari, S. (2007). Overcoming inaction through collective institutional entrepreneurship: Insights from regime theory. *Organization Studies, 28*(7), 1079–1100. doi:10.1177/0170840607078115

Williams, O. W., Stewart, K., & Larsen, D. (2011). Toward an agenda of high-priority tourism research. *Journal of Travel Research, 51*(1), 3–11. doi:10.1177/0047287511427824

Williams, P. H. E. (1985). *Teaching craft, design and technology five to thirteen*. London: Croom Helm.

Wills, J., Samli, C. A., & Jacobs, L. (1991). Developing global products and construct and a research agenda. *Journal of the Marketing Strategies: Academy of Marketing Science, 19*(1), 1–10.

Wind, Y. J., & Rangaswamy, A. (2000). *Customerization: The Next Revolution in Mass Customization*. Marketing Science Institute Working Paper No. 00-108. Cambridge, MA: Marketing Science Institute.

Wood, J. C., & Wood, M. C. (Eds.). (2005). *Peter F. Drucker: Critical evaluations in business and management*. New York, NY: Routledge.

Wright, T., & Lauda, D. (1993). Technology education-a position statement. *Technology Teacher, 52*(6), 3–5.

Wu, J.-H., Tennyson, R. D., & Hsia, T.-L. (2010). A study of student satisfaction in a blended e-learning system environment. *Computers & Education, 55*(1), 155–164. doi:10.1016/j.compedu.2009.12.012

Yadav, V. (2014). Unique Identification Project for 1.2 billion People in India:Can it fill Institutional Voids and enable 'Inclusive' Innovation? *Contemporary Readings in Law and Social Justice, 6*(1), 38–48.

Yang, C. (1997). An exploratory study of the effectiveness of interactive advertisements on the Internet. *Journal of Marketing Communications, 3*(2), 61–85. doi:10.1080/135272697345970

Yang, M. H., Natalyn, C., Lin, B., & Cho, H. Y. (2009). The effect of perceived ethical performance of websites on consumer trust. *Journal of Computer Information Systems, 50*(1), 15.

Yeager, L. B. (1997). *The Fluttering Veil, Essays on Monetary Disequilibrium*. Indianapolis, IN: The Liberty Press, reprint.

Yin, R. K. (2002). *Case study research: Design and methods*. Newbury Park, CA: Sage.

Yin, R. K. (2003). *Case Study Research: design and methods*. Sage Publications Inc.

Yin, R. K. (2014). *Case Study Research: Design and Methods*. New York: Sage.

Young, A. (1928). Increasing returns and economic progress. *The Economic Journal, 88*(152), 527–542. doi:10.2307/2224097

Young, S. (2007). *The book is dead, long live the book*. Sydney: The University of New South Wales Press Ltd.

Yuchtman, E., & Seashore, S. (1967). A system approach to organizational effectiveness. *American Sociological Review, 32*(6), 891–903. doi:10.2307/2092843

Yusuf, A. (1995). Critical success factors for small business: Perceptions of South Pacific entrepreneurs. *Journal of Small Business Management, 33*(2), 68–73.

Zaltman, G., Duncan, R., & Holbeck, J. (1973). *Innovations and Organizations*. New York.

Zaltman, G., Duncan, R., & Holbek, J. (1973). *Innovations and organizations*. New York: Wiley.

Zeng, D., Chen, H., Lusch, R., & Li, S. H. (2010). Social media analytics and intelligence. *IEEE Intelligent Systems*, *25*(6), 13–16. doi:10.1109/MIS.2010.151

Zhang, C., Xue, L., & Dhaliwal, J. (2016). Alignments between the depth and breadth of inter-organizational systems deployment and their impact on firm performance. *Information & Management*, *53*(1), 79–90. doi:10.1016/j.im.2015.08.004

Zhao, L., & Elbaum, S. (2003). Quality assurance under the open source development model. *Journal of Systems and Software*, *66*(1), 65–75. doi:10.1016/S0164-1212(02)00064-X

About the Contributors

Ionica Oncioiu holds a Ph.D. in economy and accounting. Her research interests include the development of SMEs innovation, Project Management, Accounting Information Systems, Asset Management and E-Commerce Marketing. She has had more than 10 years of experience in this area and has published 10 text books and more than 70 papers in scholarly peer reviewed international journals, also authoring eight books.

* * *

Elia Ardyan earned his Bachelor of economics in Managemement from Satya Wacana Christiany University in 2005. He Received his Master of Business Administration from Gadjah Mada University, Indonesia in 2010. Now, he is a doctoral candidate in the marketing program at Diponegoro University, Indonesia. He begin the doctoral program in 2012. He is a lecturer and researcher at STIE Surakarta, Indonesia. He begin to be lecturer dan researcher from 2011 until now. He taught courses in marketing management. His area research in online marketing, customer behavior and Hospitality. His Studies have published in local journal in Indonesia (jurnal.stiesurakarta.ac.id).

Vincent Didiek Wiet Aryanto obtained his Ph.D (Commerce) in International Business Management from The Catholic University of the Philippines Santo Tomas in 1998. He was a recipient of a Fulbright Scholarship in 2002 allowing him to complete his post-doctoral studies at Marquette University, Milwaukee Wisconsin USA. He is currently a full-time professor at Universitas Dian Nuswantoro in the Faculty of Economics and Business Management, at both a graduate and undergraduate level, specializing in e-commerce marketing, international marketing and international management. He is also a professor of marketing at Ph.D (doctoral) program of Business Management Universitas Diponegoro in Semarang Indonesia. Professor Aryanto's research interests concern digital economy, e-marketing and international marketing management and he is a published author of the International Journal of Innovation in the Digital Economy, Journal of Business Administration Online, International Journal of Internet, e-Commerce and Management, The International Journal of Accountancy and Management Research, Journal of Business and Economics Studies and International Journal of Applied Behavioral Economics, International Journal of Technoethics, International Journal of Social Ecology and Sustainable Development, Contaduria Y Administracion, International Journal of Online Marketing etc. Professor Aryanto is an experienced research fellow and has presented at many international seminars including in The Netherlands, ISS The Hague, The University of New Castle Upon Tyne United Kingdom, The

Chinese University of Hong Kong, Providence University Taiwan, Assumption University Thailand. Australian Catholic University in Brisbane Australia. Currently, he is an active reviewer in the Asia Pacific Management Review Elsevier.

Neeta Baporikar is currently Director/Professor (Business Management) at Harold Pupkewitz Graduate School of Business (HP-GSB), Namibia University of Science and Technology, Namibia. Prior to this she was Head-Scientific Research, with Ministry of Higher Education CAS-Salalah, Sultanate of Oman, Professor (Strategy & Entrepreneurship) at IIIT Pune and BITS India. With more than a decade of experience in industry, consultancy and training, she made a lateral switch to research and academics in 1995. Dr. Baporikar holds D.Sc. (Management Studies) USA, PhD in Management, University of Pune INDIA with MBA (Distinction) and Law (Hons.) degrees. Apart from this she is an External Reviewer, Oman Academic Accreditation Authority (OAAA), Accredited Management Teacher from All India Management Association (AIMA), Qualified Trainer from Indian Society for Training & Development (ISTD), International PhD Examiner, Doctoral Guide and Board Member of Academics and Advisory Committee in accredited B-Schools. Reviewer for international journals, she has to her credit 5 conferred doctorates, several refereed research papers, and authored books in the area of Entrepreneurship, Strategy, Management and Higher Education.

Mehdi Behboudi is a Lecturer of Online Advertising and Interactive Marketing at Department of Business Management, School of Management and Accountancy, Islamic Azad University, Qazvin Branch, Qazvin, Iran. Mehdi Behboudi is also serving as a guest Lecturer and Head of Business Administration Department as well as Manager of Research Affairs at Ghazali Higher Education Institute. He also is Director of the Online Advertising and Internet Marketing Department at Management and Productivity Research Center, MPRC. Moreover, Mehdi Behboudi has authored four highly successful books in Iran namely: "Internet Advertising", "International Marketing" "Successful Entrepreneurs" and "How launch an e-Bay based business" as well as many papers in Persian in various Iranian academic journals and conference proceedings. He is known as an online advertising and Internet marketing Author, Speaker, and Consultant. He has delivered many speeches for different companies in marketing and advertising context. He has knowledgeable experience in online branding, online advertising strategies, inverse advertising, and search engine advertising and viral advertising strategies.

Nicklas Beijar received his D.Sc. in networking technology from Aalto University, Finland in 2010 and his M.Sc. from Helsinki University of Technology, Finland in 2002. He joined Ericsson Research as a guest researcher in 2013 to work with Internet of Things. His current field is cloud technology, with a focus on distributed cloud for IoT. His interests also include gateway selection and management of IoT devices. Prior to this, he has been working at Aalto University as a research scientist and postdoc with topics related to IP telephony, routing protocols for ad hoc network, peer-to-peer systems and distributed search algorithms.

Francina Cantatore holds a Doctorate in Copyright Law with the following qualifications: BA, LLB (Hons), MA, Grad Diploma in Legal Practice (Hons), PhD. After practising in South Africa as a barrister for many years, she relocated to Australia where she continued her law practice and academic studies. She currently lectures in Property Law and Media and Communications Law at the Faculty of

Law, Bond University, Australia and is the Director of the Bond Law Clinic Program. She also practices as a Special Counsel with a law firm. Her PhD research was conducted in Copyright Law to provide insight into authors' relationships with copyright and challenges faced by authors in the digital era. Her broader research interests lie in the areas of Intellectual Property Law, Consumer and Competition Law and Legal Education. She has published internationally in these areas and has presented papers at international conferences on consumer law issues and copyright.

Vicki Caravias has been teaching at Swinburne University of Technology for 14 years. Before commencing at Swinburne, Vicki spent 10 years managing IT projects for the retail sector. Vicki also has experience in developing training programs for corporate clients. In addition, Vicki has taken part in programme and curriculum development and implementation for onshore and offshore programs. Vicki has successfully completed the following qualifications: Bachelor of Computing (Victoria University of Technology); Master of Business (Information Systems) (Victoria University of Technology); Master of Training and Development (University of Melbourne); Diploma of Business (Frontline Management) (Swinburne University of Technology); Certificate IV in Workplace Assessment and Training (Swinburne University of Technology). Vicki Caravias is a PhD candidate in the Faculty of Arts, Education and Human Development at Victoria University. Vicki Caravias has devoted herself to researching the area of blended learning. My research problem is focussed around teachers' conceptions and approaches to integrating pedagogy and content knowledge using blended learning environments at Swinburne University.

Mei-Chen Chang is an associate researcher in the Division of Technology Education at National Science & Technology Museum, Taiwan (R.O.C.). She got her Ph.D. in Industrial Technology Education from National Kaohsiung Normal University and Master of Industrial Technology from University of North Dakota in USA. Her current research interests include creative design, technology education, energy education, and museum education. She also hosted several projects, such as the "Innovative Design Competition and Promotion Activities on Energy Education", and "Design, Implementation, and evaluation of A multiple Learning Scenario for Energy-Saving and Reducing Carbon Dioxide Emission in Senior High School".

Masudul Alam Choudhury earned his Masters and Doctorate Degrees from the University of Toronto. He then specialized in the area of Economics of Human Capital Theory and Economic Growth. Presently Professor Choudhury specializes in epistemological problems of economic theory, political economy, world-systems and socio-scientific issues. In these fields he has original contributions in a vast number of journal papers and scholarly books published by reputed publishers. Professor Choudhury is also a founder member of the Postgraduate Program in Islamic Economics and Finance, Trisakti University, Jakarta, Indonesia where he lectures and supervises Ph.D. theses.

Yao-Ming Chu is a professor in the department of Industrial Technology Education and a director of library at the National Kaohsiung Normal University (NKNU), Taiwan. His current research interests are: blended learning, informal technology education, technology development and philosophy, creative competition activities, and international education. Yao-Ming Chu received his B.S in the industrial education in 1983 form the NKNU, Taiwan, and his M.S. in technology education in 1989 from the University of North Dakota, USA. He received his Ph.D. in workforce education and development in 1996 from the Pennsylvania State University, USA.

Mehmet Gençer is Associate Professor of Organization Studies at Istanbul Bilgi University, Faculty of Engineering. His research areas include empirical studies on collaboration in virtual communities, innovation dynamics, and computational socio-economic system models. He has published several journal articles and book chapters nationally and internationally, in the areas of strategic management, innovation ecosystems, and software innovation. His articles appeared in Technology Analysis & Strategic Management Journal, International Journal of IT Standards and Standardization Research, IEEE Computers and Communications, among others.

Tzu-Hsiang Ger is an assistant researcher in the Secretariat Division at National Science & Technology Museum, Taiwan (R.O.C.). He current research interests include the extending and planning of Sustainable architecture, environmental improving, resources recycling, energy conservation and cooperation with other affiliations to hold the environmental protection activities. Now he entered Industrial Technology Education, National Kaohsiung Normal University to pursue his Ph. D degree.

Mahya Ilaghi finished a double master's degree in distributed system in Aalto University, Finland and Technical University of Berlin in 2014. During her studies she was involved in IoT research projects. Mahya is working as software engineer with interest in big data and cloud computing research and development challenges.

Rachida Khaled is PhD student in economics at the Faculty of Economic Science and Management of Sousse Tunisia.

Miika Komu finished his doctoral studies in Aalto University in 2012. Besides Aalto, he has been working for Helsinki Institute for Information technology and is now working for Ericsson research in Finland. Miika has been involved with IETF standardization for many years, and is currently working on IoT and cloud related topics.

Pikka-Maaria Laine works as an Associate Professor of Management at the University of Lapland, Finland. She also holds a position of an Adjunct Professor of Strategic Management at the University of Eastern Finland. Her research interests revolve around strategy making, subjectivities, power and resistance, and she has published in academic journals. In addition to her university position she also works as a facilitator in dialogical strategy work. She has acted as a leading member of strategy-as-practice standing working group at EGOS, and a board member of Finnish Strategic Management Society.

Tapio Levä received his M.Sc. from Helsinki University of Technology, Finland in 2009 and his D.Sc. in network economics from Aalto University, Finland, in 2014. The topic of his dissertation was feasibility analysis of new Internet protocols. Tapio is currently working at TeliaSonera. His research interests include techno-economics of Internet architecture evolution, Internet standards adoption, information-centric networking and Internet of things.

Vilen Looga started his doctoral studies at DCS Lab under the supervision of Prof. Antti Ylä-Jääski after graduating with a double Master's degree (NordSecMob – an English language Master's Programme) from Aalto and Tartu universities in 2010. At first he was focusing on energy efficient traffic transmission on single devices, but soon realized that there is a huge opportunity for achieving energy savings with network-level traffic control, especially in different Internet of Things (IoT) scenarios. After that insight, his research work crystallized into a bottom-up approach of gaining energy savings by traffic control, starting from device level and all the way up to large-scale network level.

Oleksiy Mazhelis is a post-doc researcher at the Department of Computer Science and Information Systems, University of Jyväskylä, Finland. He received a degree of M.Sc. (Specialist) from Kharkov National University of Radio-Electronics, Ukraine in 1997, and received his licentiate and doctoral degrees from the University of Jyväskylä in 2004 and 2007, respectively, on the subject of masquerader detection in mobile phone environment. Starting from 2004, he has been working in various research projects conducted in collaboration with industrial partners. His current research interests encompass techno-economics, systems analysis, machine learning, and pattern recognition, applied to the domains of software industry evolution, internet-of-things, telecommunications and cloud software, as well as intelligent transportation systems.

Petra Merenheimo, Diplom-Kauffrau, graduated from the Johann Wolfgang von Goethe University, Frankfurt am Main. She is now doctoral student at the University of Lapland. Her research topic is entrepreneurship and the role of power, in the caring sector. Her other research interests are competition and gender.

Bahar Movahedi, Ph.D., has served as reviewer, associate editor, program chair, and coordinator of several international conferences and journals. She has published over 60 papers in journals, books and proceedings. She has received several awards honoring the quality of her scholarly works from prestigious academic organizations in Canada, the U.S. and the U.K.

Beyza Oba is Professor of Organization Studies at İstanbul Bilgi University, Department of Business Administration. Her research interests include empirical studies on trust, governance, hegemony and innovation in different contexts. She has published in journals like Business History, Entrepreneurship and Regional Development, Journal of Technology Analysis and Strategic Management and Corporate Governance. She also has several journal articles in Turkish. Additionally, she has presented research papers in EIASM European Institute in Advanced Studies in Management), EGOS (European Group of Organization Studies) and British Academy of Management conferences.

Olu Ojo is a Lecturer in the Department of Business Administration at Osun State University, Okuku, Nigeria. He received his B. Sc. and MBA degrees in Management from Usmanu Danfodiyo University, Sokoto. Prior to joining the faculty at Osun State University, he had taught at The Polytechnic, Ile-Ife and Covenant University, Ota. His research interests include general management, strategic management, production and operations management, quantitative techniques, and entrepreneurship. His research work has appeared in Journal of Business Administration and Management, Lex ET Scientia International Journal, Manager Journal, Business Intelligence Journal, Petroleum-Gas University of Ploiesti Bulletin: Economic Sciences Series among others. He is the author of Fundamentals of Research Methods (2003) and co-author of Operations Research in Decision Analysis and Production Management (2006). He is on the editorial board of Annals of University of Bucharest: Economic and Administrative Sciences and Lex ET Scientia International Journal. Mr. Ojo is respected for excellence in both research and teaching.

Piritta Parkkari is a PhD candidate in management and organization at the University of Lapland. She develops the research streams of Entrepreneurship-as-Practice and Critical Entrepreneurship Studies. She has done extensive ethnographic work in a student- and other volunteer-led Entrepreneurship Society -organization and its network in Finland. She is interested in the role of entrepreneurship in contemporary societies and the dynamics of social inclusion and exclusion.

Rauno Rusko, PhD, Lic. Soc. Sc., graduated from the University of Lapland and from the University of Oulu. He is Lecturer of management and entrepreneurship at the University of Lapland. He has been also lecturer of Economics in the University of Vaasa and in the University of Lapland. His research activities focus on cooperation, coopetition, strategic management, supply chain management and entrepreneurship mainly in the branches of information communication technology, forest industry and tourism. His articles appeared in the European Management Journal, Forest Policy and Economics, Industrial Marketing Management, Managing Leisure, International Journal of Innovation in the Digital Economy and International Journal of Tourism Research among others.

Vanita Yadav is an Assistant Professor in the area of Strategy, Innovation and Entrepreneurship at IRMA, a premier Business School in India. She is a Fulbright Fellow and a Postdoc from MIT, USA. Vanita was also a Research Affiliate at the South Asia Institute, Harvard University for 2012-13. She has a Doctorate in Management from MDI Gurgaon, India. Vanita has published and presented more than 30 research papers in refereed International Journals like JGIM and JITTA, Conferences like AoM, PACIS and SMS, and book chapters. She has published two best-selling case studies at the Harvard Business School publications online. Vanita is also the Associate Editor of the International Journal of Rural Management, Sage. She has worked on research projects funded by the Government of India, European Union and other institutional funded projects. Before joining academia, she worked in the Indian IT Industry with NIIT Ltd.

Index

Recommended Reference Books

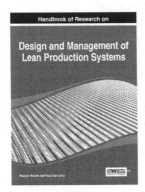

ISBN: 978-1-4666-5039-8
© 2014; 487 pp.
List Price: $260

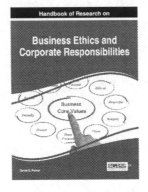

ISBN: 978-1-4666-7476-9
© 2015; 508 pp.
List Price: $212

ISBN: 978-1-4666-6182-0
© 2014; 325 pp.
List Price: $180

ISBN: 978-1-4666-4474-8
© 2014; 735 pp.
List Price: $276

ISBN: 978-1-4666-5950-6
© 2014; 290 pp.
List Price: $156

ISBN: 978-1-4666-6595-8
© 2015; 406 pp.
List Price: $156

Publishing Information Science and Technology Research Since 1988

www.igi-global.com   Sign up at www.igi-global.com/newsletters   facebook.com/igiglobal   twitter.com/igiglobal

Support Your Colleagues and Stay Current on the Latest Research Developments

Become a Reviewer

In this competitive age of scholarly publishing, constructive and timely feedback significantly decreases the turn-around time of manuscripts from submission to acceptance, allowing the publication and discovery of progressive research at a much more expeditious rate.

The overall success of a refereed journal is dependent on quality and timely reviews.

Several IGI Global journals are currently seeking highly qualified experts in the field to fill vacancies on their respective editorial review boards. Reviewing manuscripts allows you to stay current on the latest developments in your field of research, while at the same time providing constructive feedback to your peers.

Reviewers are expected to write reviews in a timely, collegial, and constructive manner. All reviewers will begin their role on an ad-hoc basis for a period of one year, and upon successful completion of this term can be considered for full editorial review board status, with the potential for a subsequent promotion to Associate Editor.

Join this elite group by visiting the IGI Global journal webpage, and clicking on "**Become a Reviewer**".

Applications may also be submitted online at:
www.igi-global.com/journals/become-a-reviewer/.

Applicants must have a doctorate (or an equivalent degree) as well as publishing and reviewing experience.

If you have a colleague that may be interested in this opportunity, we encourage you to share this information with them.

Any questions regarding this opportunity can be sent to:
journaleditor@igi-global.com.

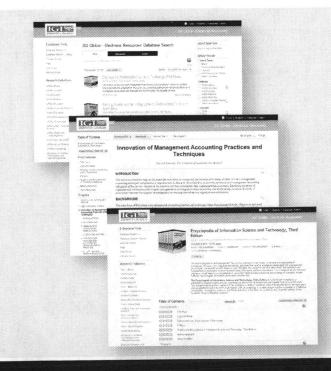

Printed in the United States
By Bookmasters

T·H·E
ENCYCLOPAEDIA
O·F ILLUSTRATION

T·H·E
ENCYCLOPAEDIA
O·F ILLUSTRATION

· A COMPILATION OF MORE THAN ·
5,000 ILLUSTRATIONS AND DESIGNS

Research and Introduction by Gerard Quinn

STUDIO EDITIONS
LONDON

The Clip Art Book

first published in 1990 by Studio Editions
an imprint of Studios Editions Ltd
Princess House, 50 Eastcastle Street
London W1N 7AP, England

Design by David Wire

ISBN 0 85170 360 8

Printed and bound in Czechoslovakia

Publishers' Note

The Clip Art Book is a new compilation of illustrations
that are in the public domain. The individual illustrations
are copyright free and may be reproduced without
permission or payment. However the selection of illustrations
and their layout is the copyright of the publishers, so that
one page or more may not be photocopied or reproduced without
first contacting the publishers.

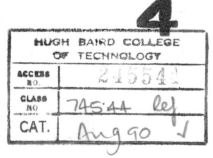

C·O·N·T·E·N·T·S

INTRODUCTION

In the late eighteenth century in England the woodcut was alive and well and enjoying something of a revival at the hands of Thomas Bewick who had pulled it from obscurity. We are fortunate that he adapted it to the needs of mass production at exactly the right time to match developments in printing during the Industrial Revolution. The instigator of an English school of illustration and a forerunner of the Romantic movement, of Blake *(Centre L.214)*, Palmer and Calvert, Bewick's influence however was technical rather than artistic. He innovated a technique of woodcut properly called wood-engraving. Woodcuts were gouged out of the plank side of a piece of wood, Bewick used the harder end-grain. His images were worked out of a black ground in half-tone and white, giving his figures a painterly three dimensional quality and a solidity that was quite new.

Bewick has been criticised for failing to pay attention to the composition of the page as a whole. But whatever he may have lacked in design he made up for in fresh unclouded intimacy of his observations from the natural world.

In contrast to Bewick's deeply poetic approach to nature stands the work of the French caricaturist J.J. Grandville. There is a European tradition of expressing fantasy through the graphic media which "The Public and Private Life of Animals", 1842, exemplifies. Grandville is at his disturbing best when drawing the menacing forms of beetles and other insects engaged in specifically human activities. His greater relevance to art historians lies beyond the artistic merit of his work and his influence on contemporaries Tenniel and Lear, *(266)*. He is acknowledged to be precursor to the Symbolist and Surrealist movements.

The nineteenth century if inconsistent in standards of craftsmanship was one of the richest, most formative periods for illustration. A growth in literacy and a surge in the size of the population generated an increasing demand for illustrated books of all kinds which the new mechanical presses were able to supply. Because a wide readership was assured editions no longer had to be limited, and the result was more and more popular editions aimed at the new book buying public.

The new social order stimulated the minds of artists and writers, but not always to generosity. George Cruickshank, a committed fighter for social reform, attacked with a fierce humour the injustices and cruelty of the industrial age. In the same satirical tradition as Hogarth and Rowlandson, Cruickshank elected to use etching as his medium. It was ideally suited to his fluid descriptive line and the distortions and exaggerations of caricature. His most successful work and the best known, are the illustrations for Dickens' novels. The medium and the subject matter of the dark spaces in gloomy gas-lit Victorian London are in complete harmony.

Contemporary with Cruickshank were John Leech and Charles Keene, both humorists who worked in gentler, less spleenful vein. Drawing for the satirical journal "Punch" they burlesqued the manners and customs of the new middle classes, laughing at their attempts to cope with an accident fraught modern age, *(Bottom R. 164, bottom L. 102.).*

The mood of nineteenth century "fin de siècle" will always be associated with the decadent and grotesque designs of Aubrey Beardsley. His eclectic mix of Japanic style and mediaeval decoration combine in illustrations of exceptional beauty. The intricacy of his drawing was impossible for wood engraving, but his mastery of the line block method brought the sparkling greys of his ornately patterned costumes to perfection, *(Top R. 161).*

The closing years of the century saw a growing distrust of the machine in the eyes of at least one artist. William Morris was prompted to revive the craft of the illustrated book at the Kelmscott Press. Although Morris published some notable editions he was fighting against the tide, *(Top R. 235)*. The challenges of the new century had to be met, the increasing pre-eminence of photography, the growing absorbtion of design and illustration by advertising which would inspire the art movements of the 1960s, and possibilities in even greater mass production. Whatever doubts Morris had about the new age, however, we can still concur which his statement that the illustrated book is not perhaps absolutely necessary to man's life, but it gives us such endless pleasure . . . that it must remain one of the very worthiest things towards the production of which reasonable man should strive."

No. 100.—Dr. Gall.

No. 101.—Hewlett, Actor.

13

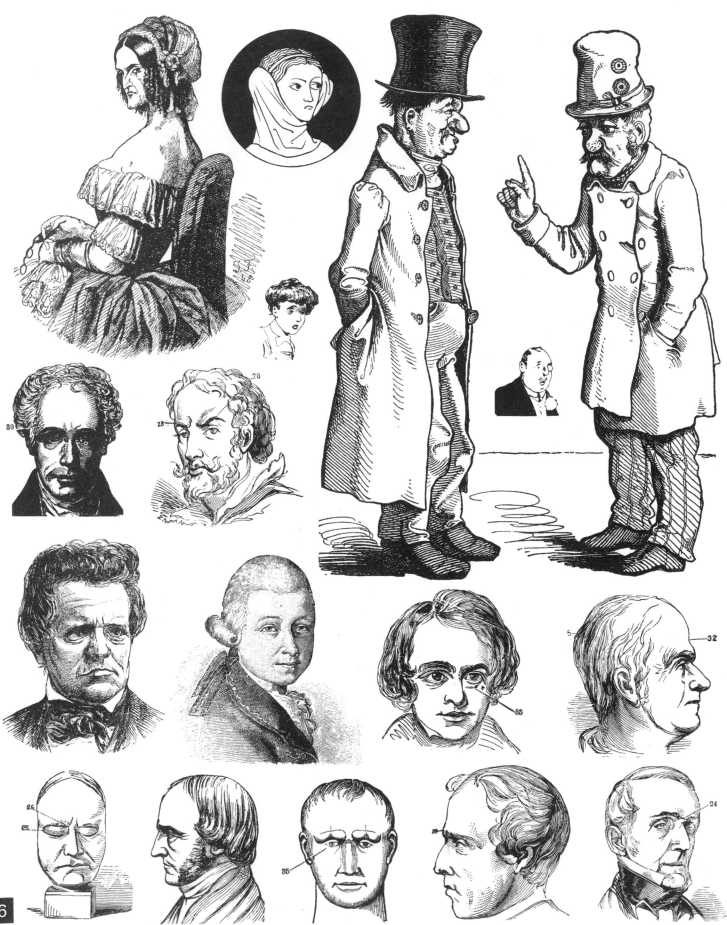

PEOPLE

22

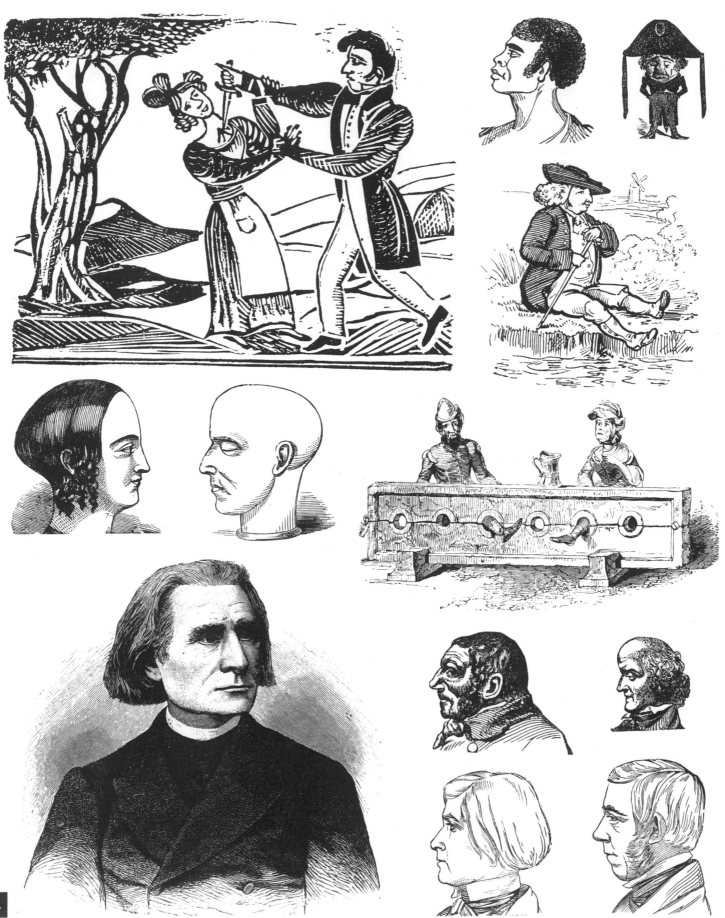

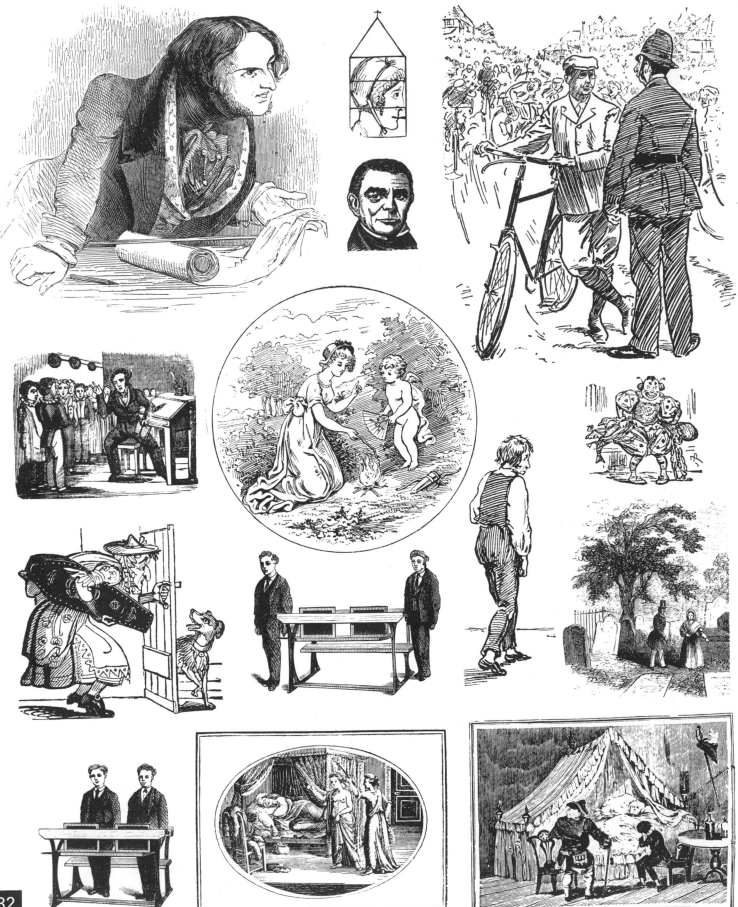

IRON AND SON,
SHOES FOR MEN
AND BEASTS.

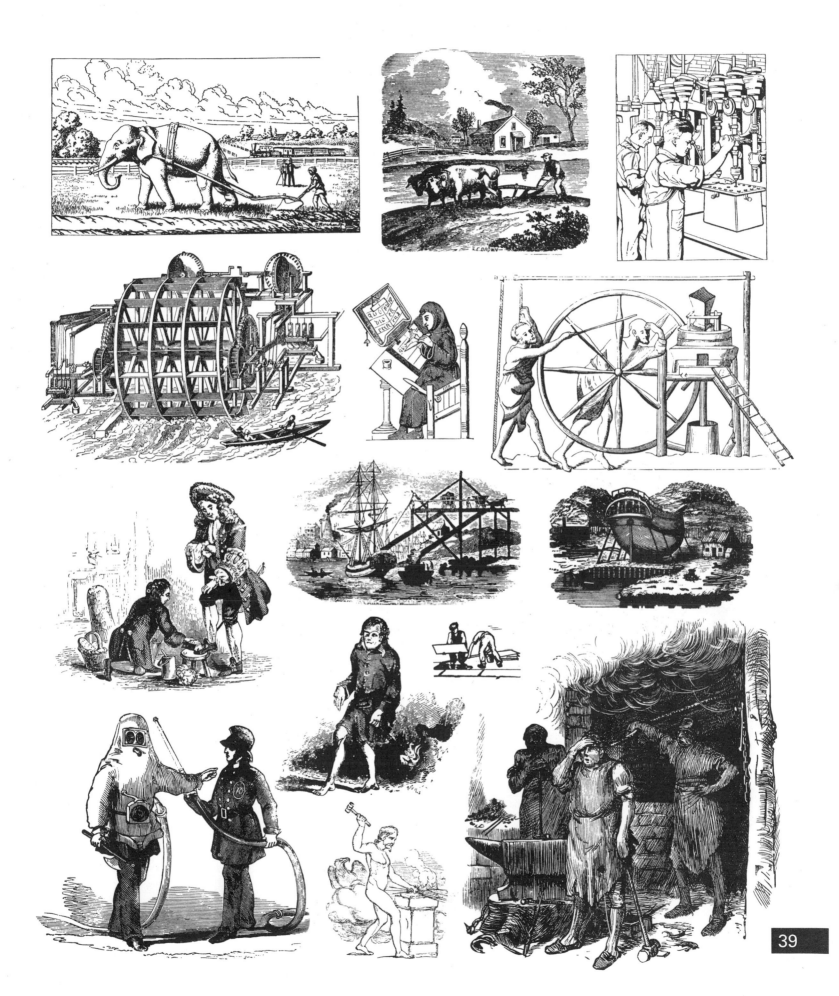

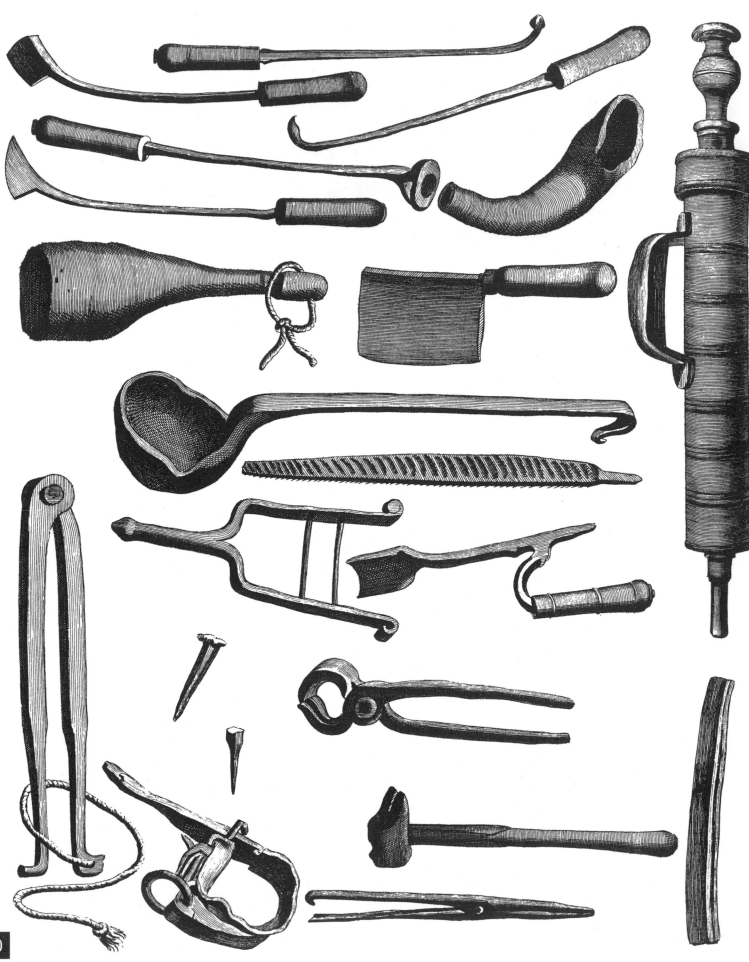

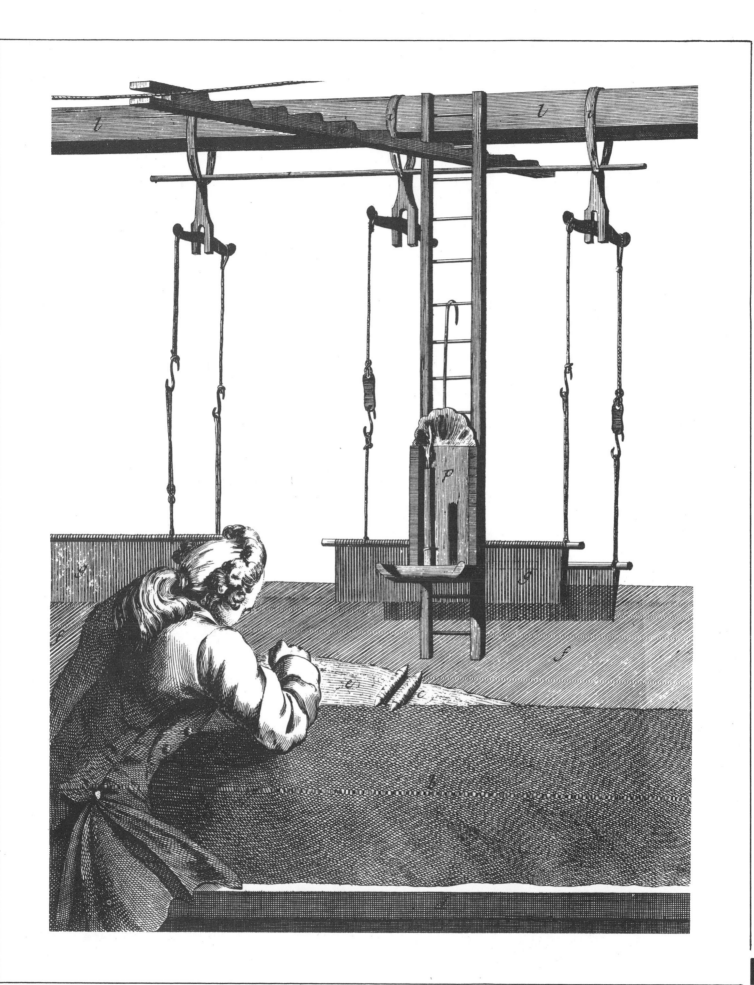

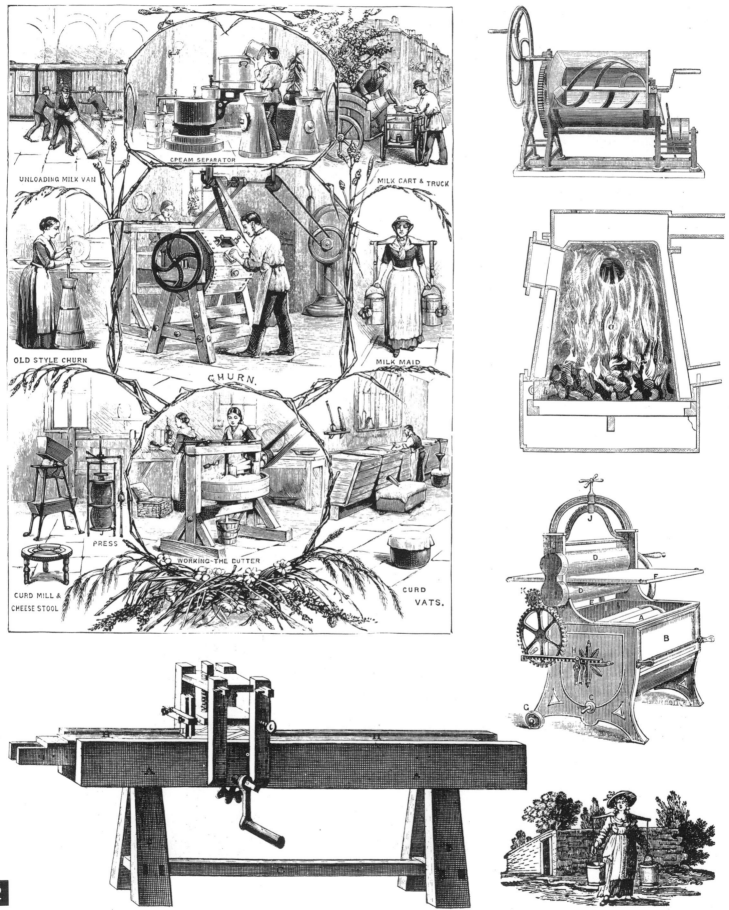

UNLOADING MILK VAN

CREAM SEPARATOR

MILK CART & TRUCK

OLD STYLE CHURN

MILK MAID

CHURN.

PRESS

WORKING THE BUTTER

CURD MILL & CHEESE STOOL

CURD VATS.

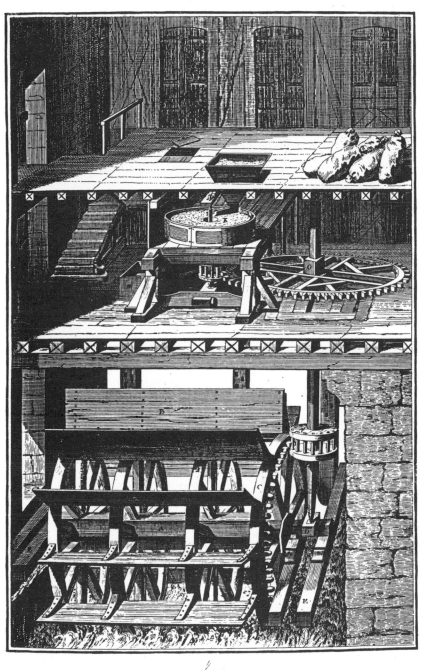

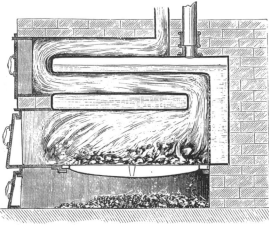

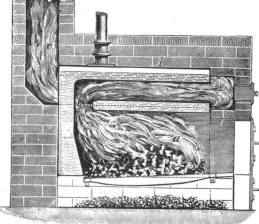

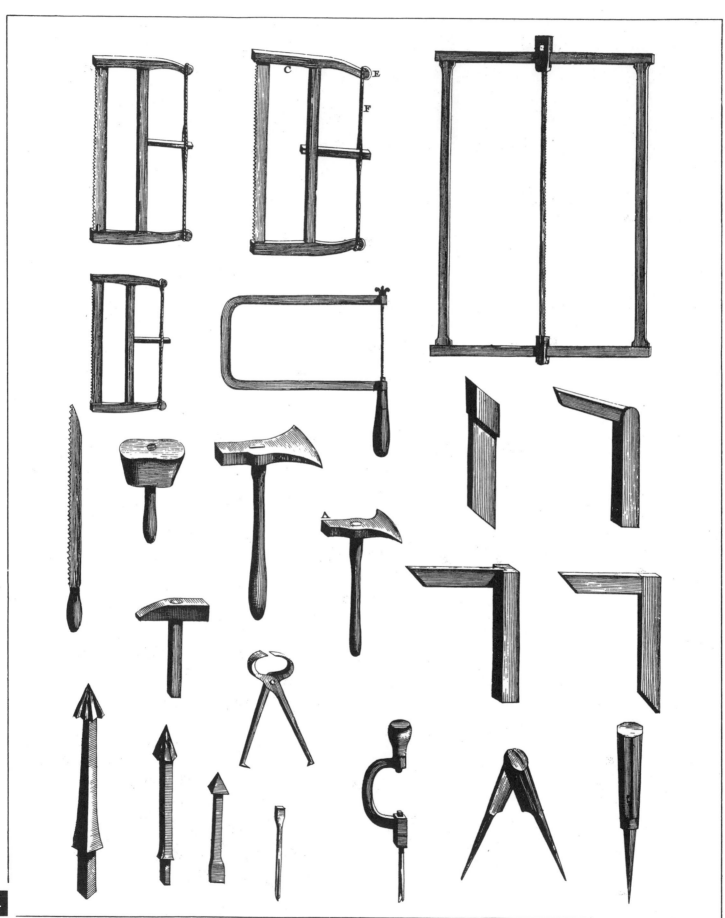

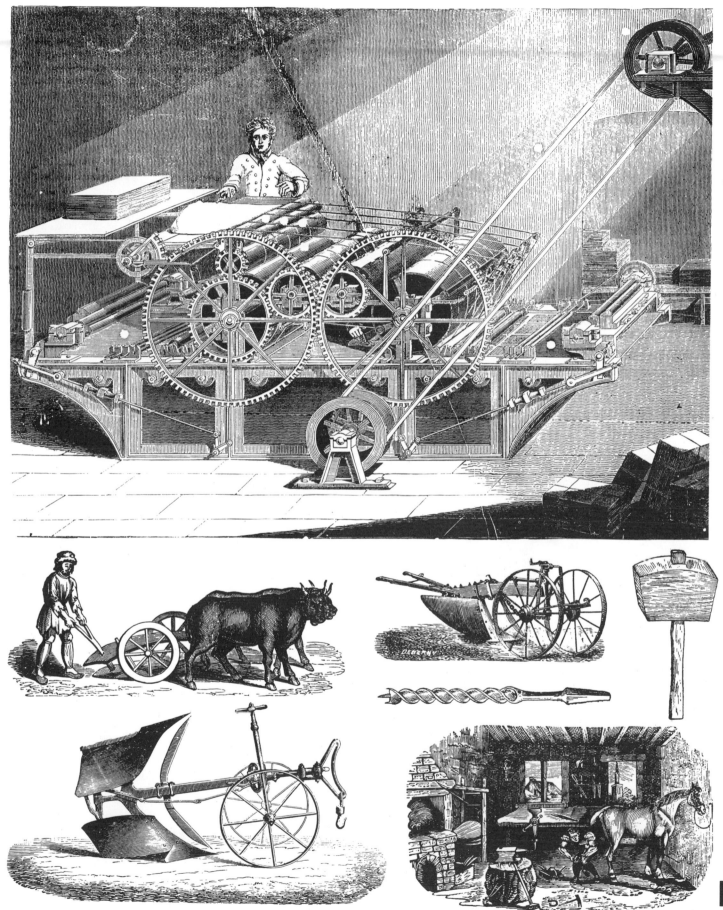

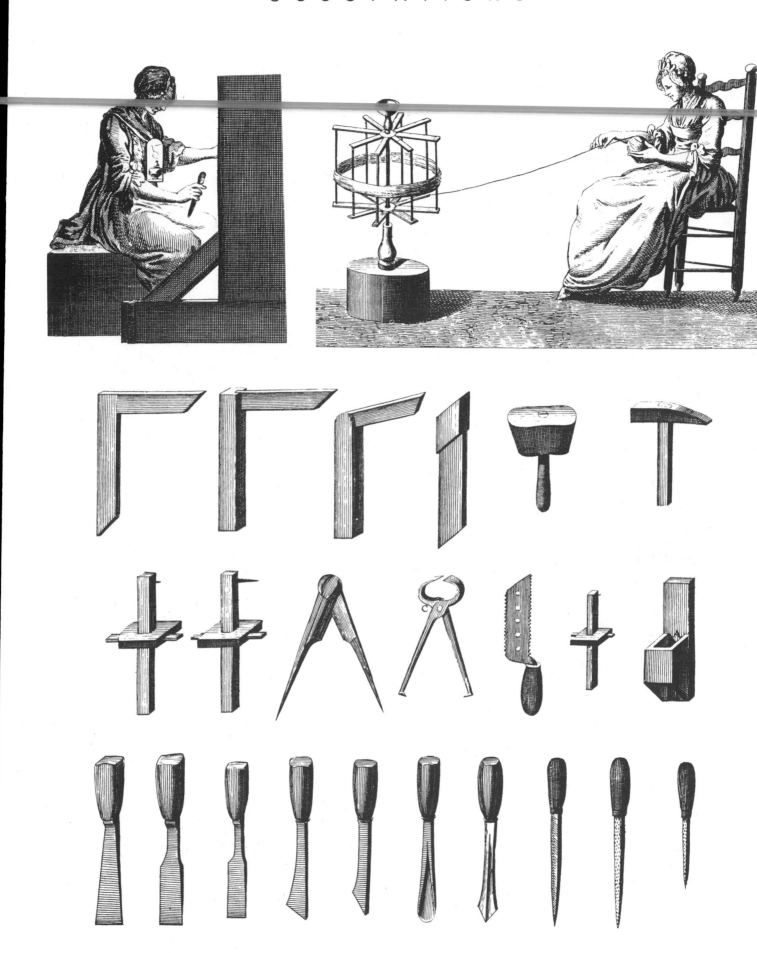

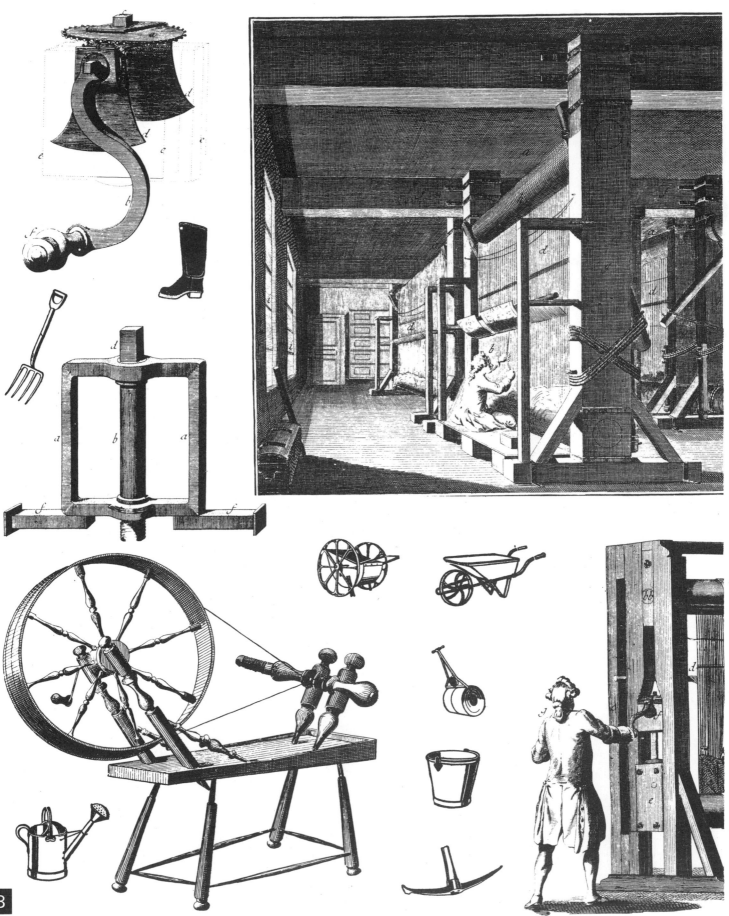

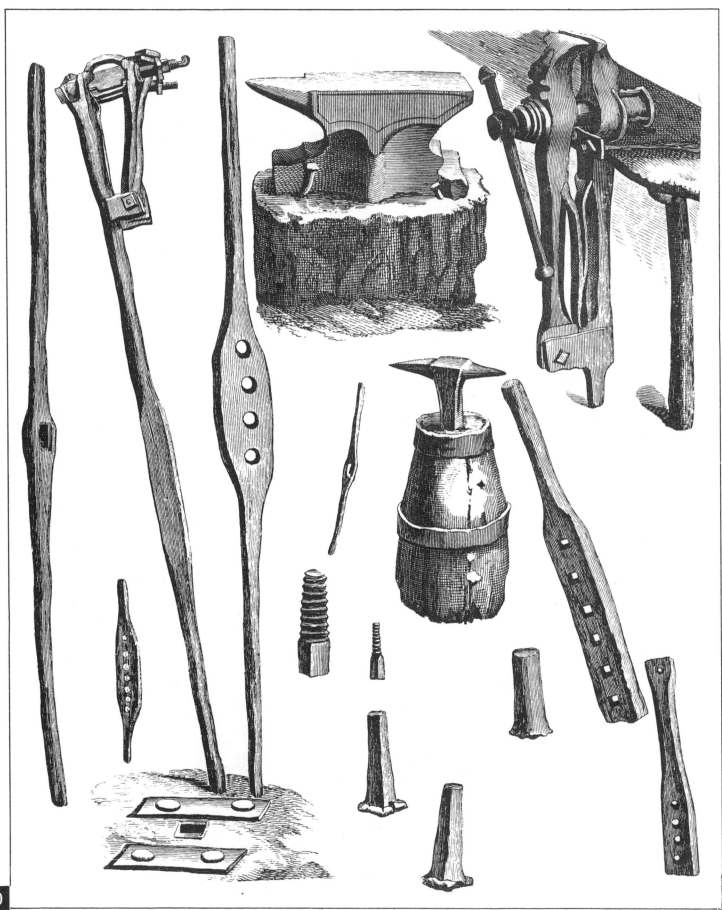

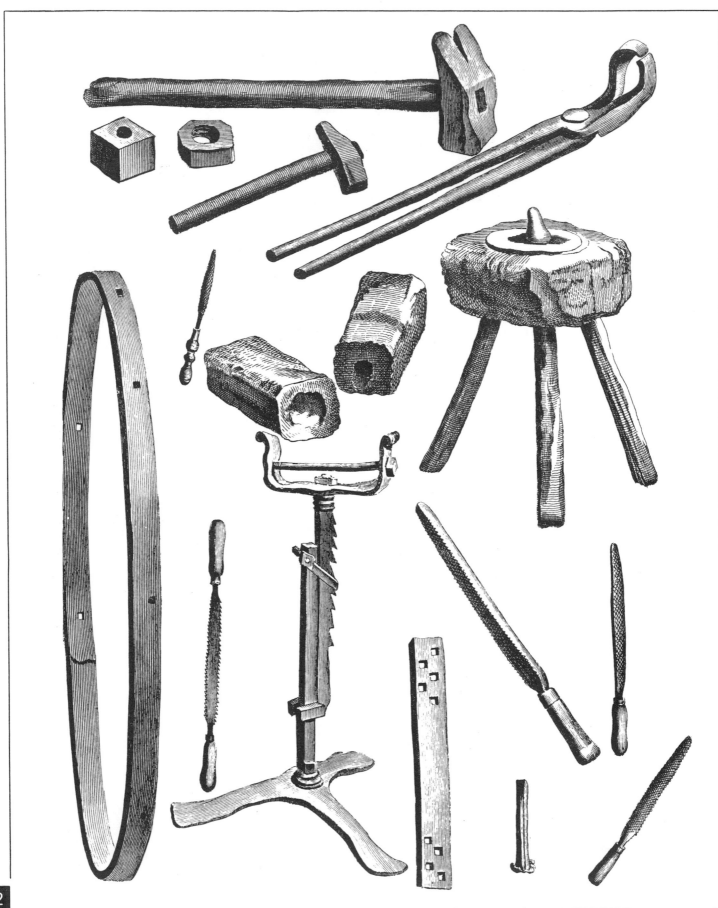

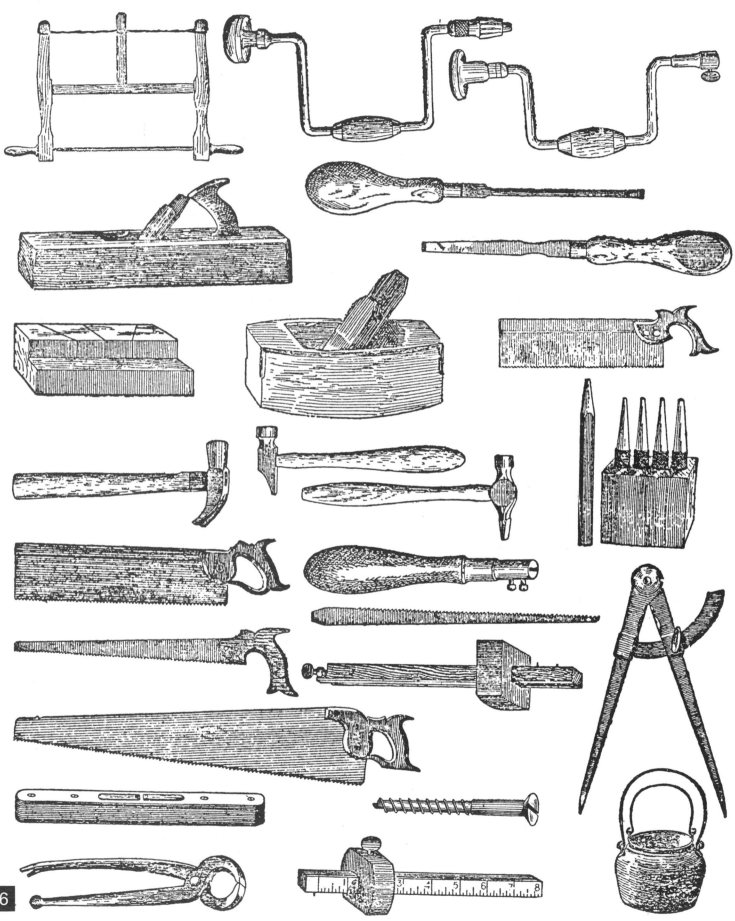

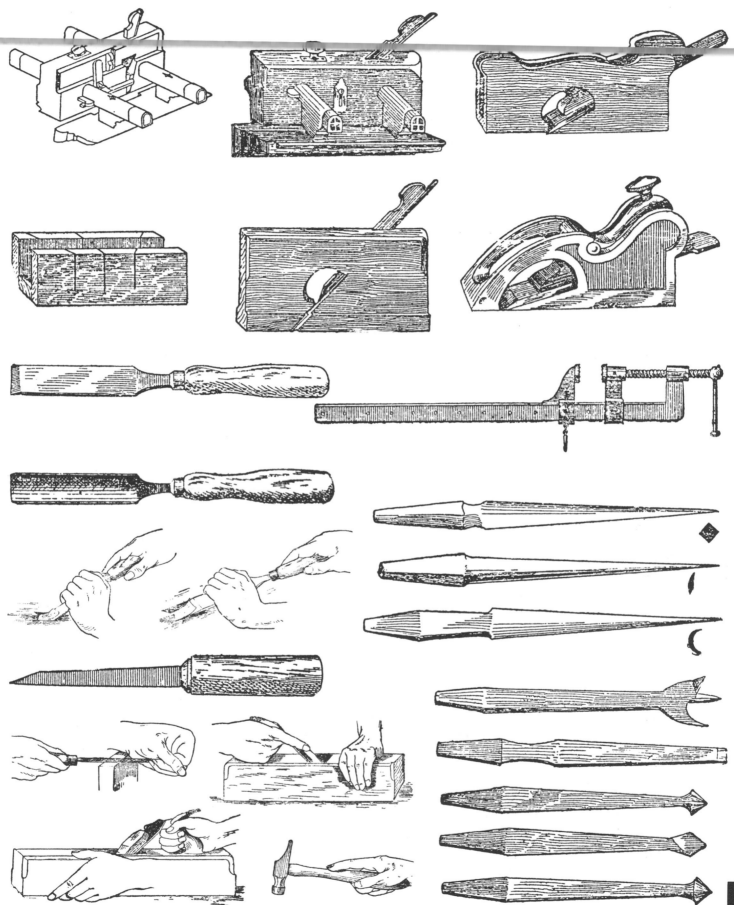

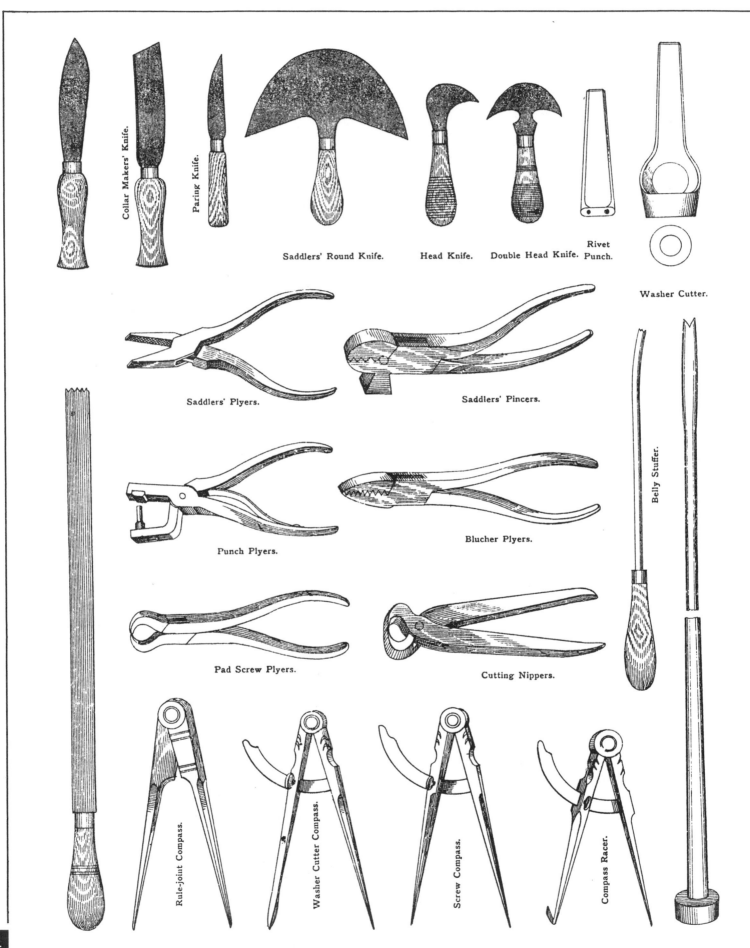

Collar Makers' Knife.

Paring Knife.

Saddlers' Round Knife.

Head Knife.

Double Head Knife.

Rivet Punch.

Washer Cutter.

Saddlers' Plyers.

Saddlers' Pincers.

Punch Plyers.

Blucher Plyers.

Belly Stuffer.

Pad Screw Plyers.

Cutting Nippers.

Rule-joint Compass.

Washer Cutter Compass.

Screw Compass.

Compass Racer.

64

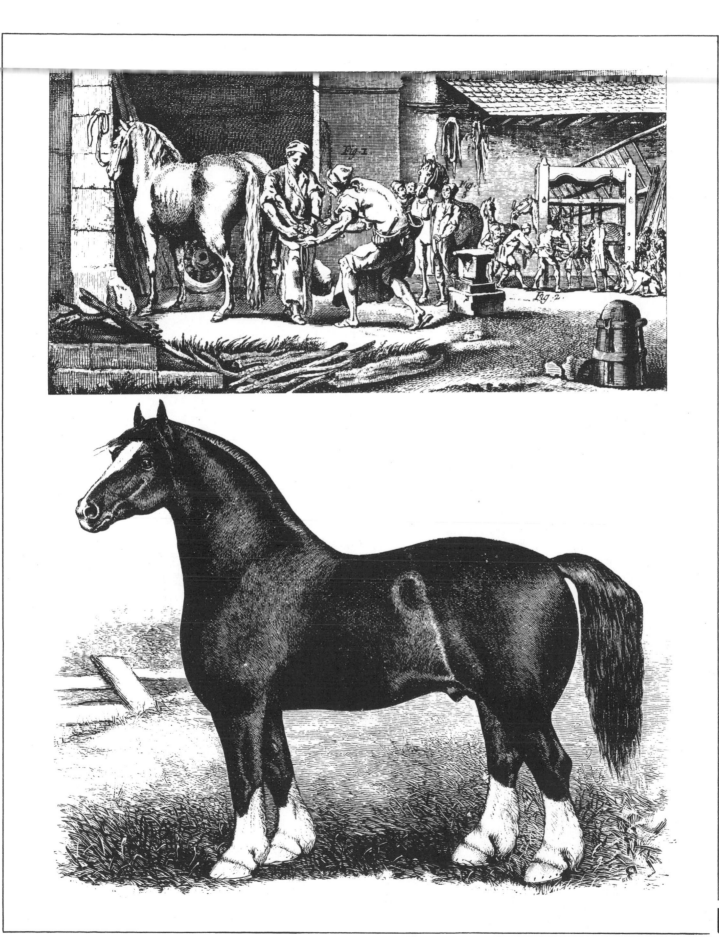

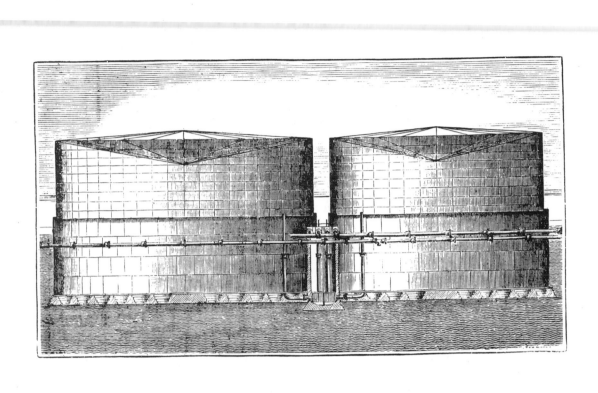

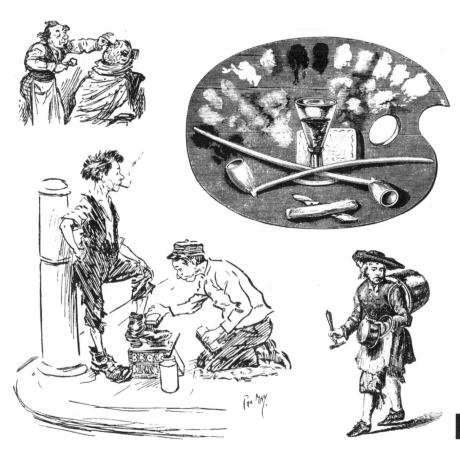

Poop.

Talar

Wale.

Prow.

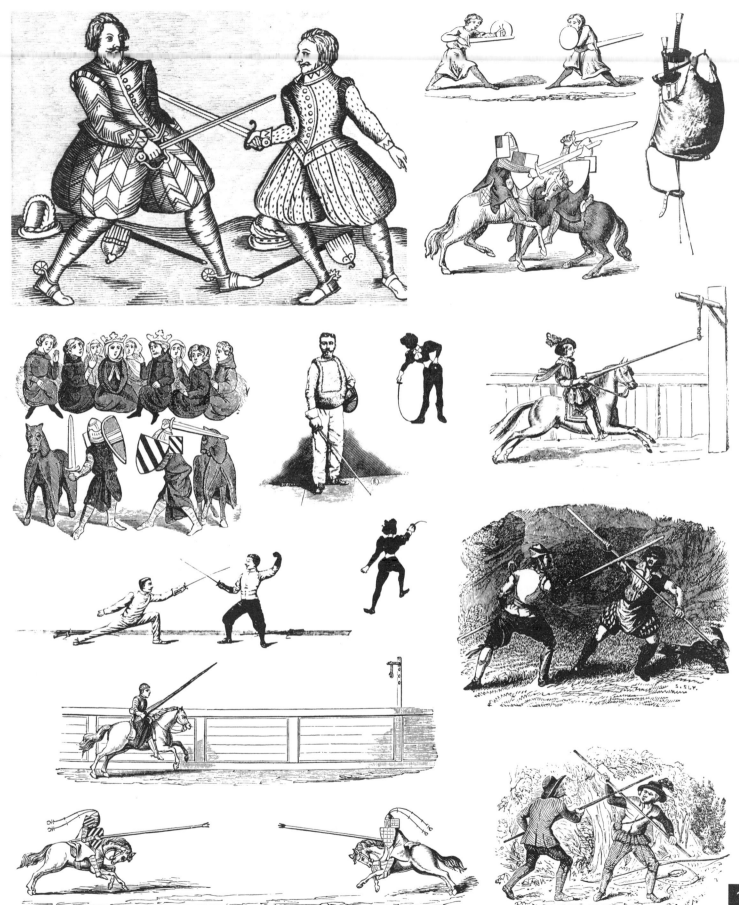

Fig. 2.

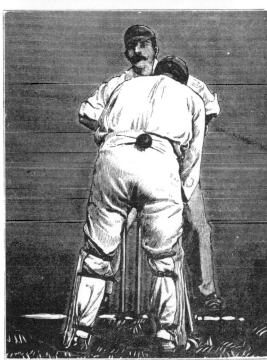

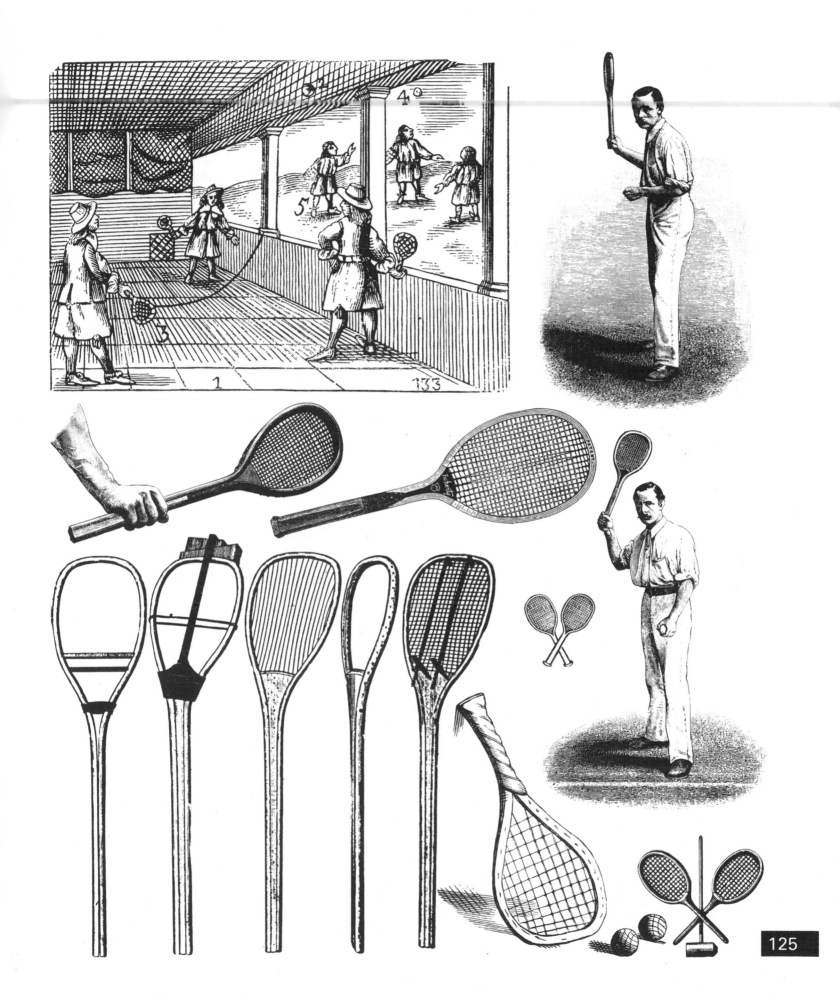

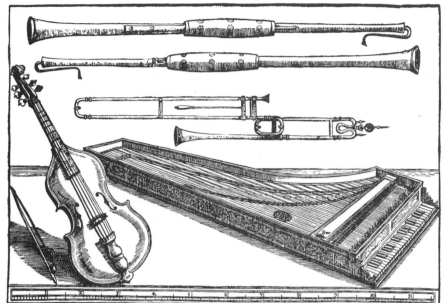

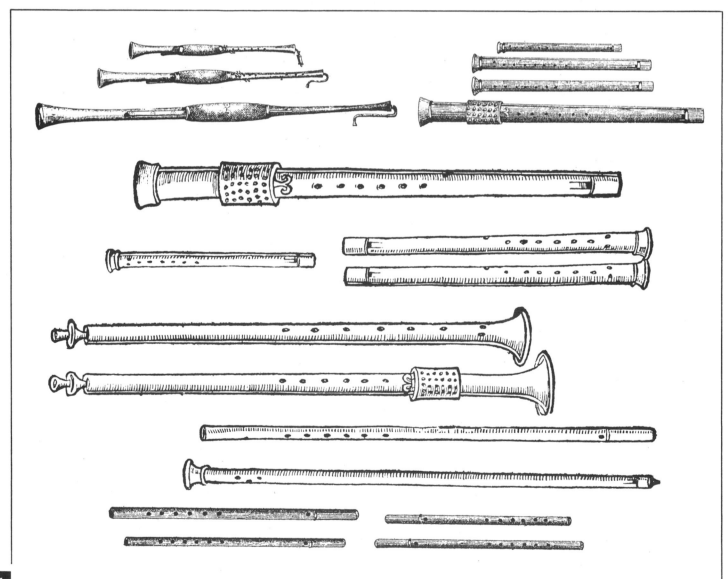

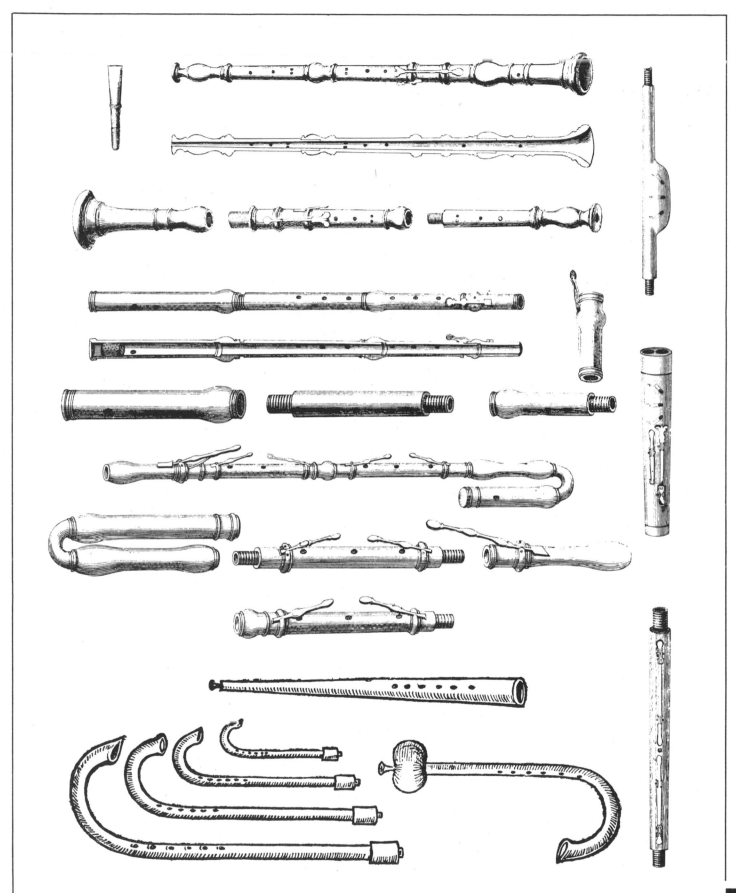

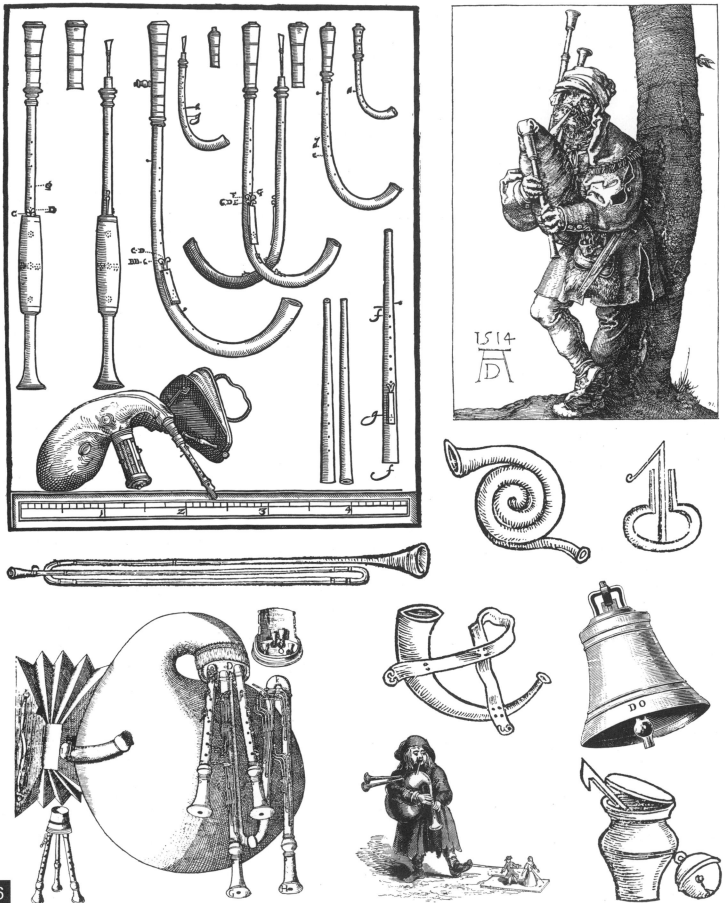

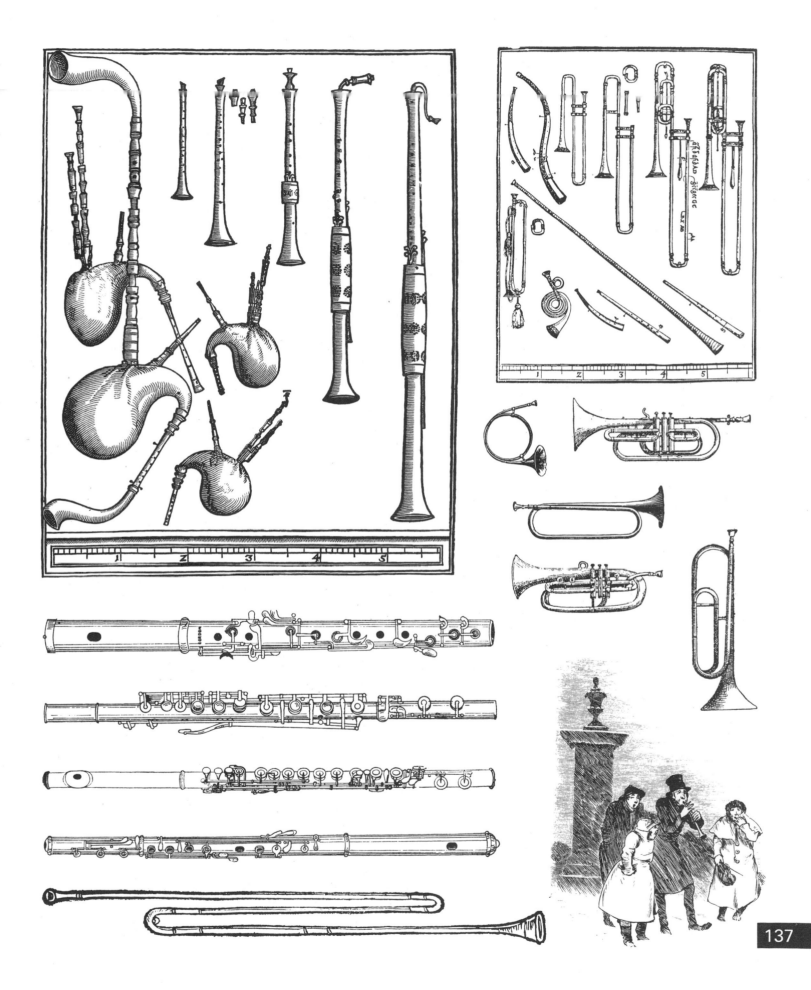

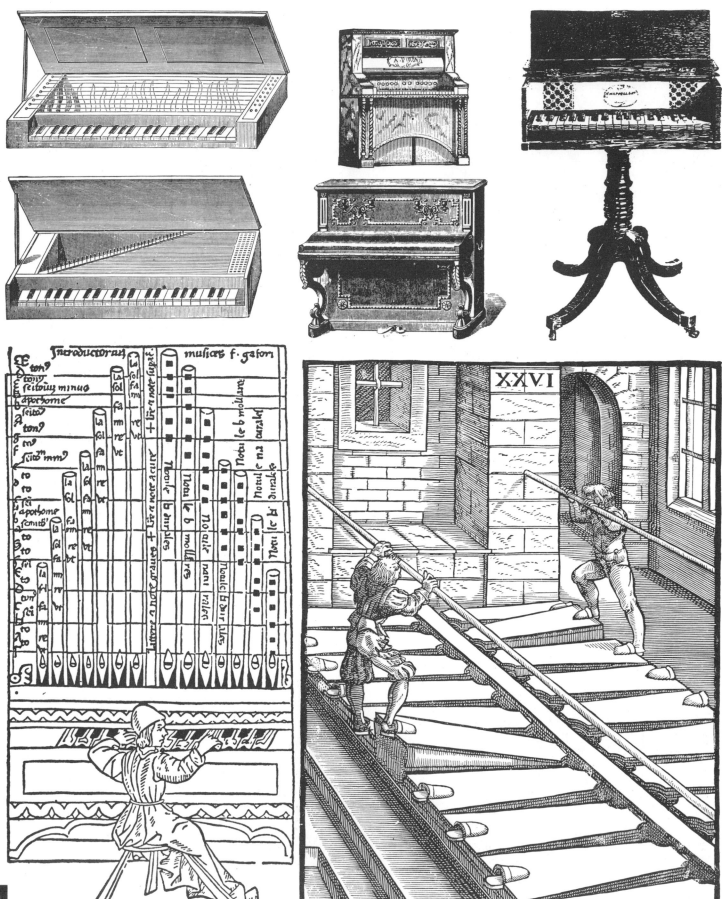

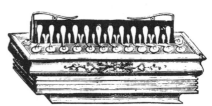

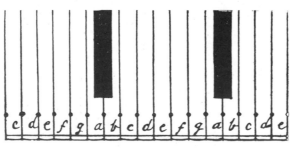

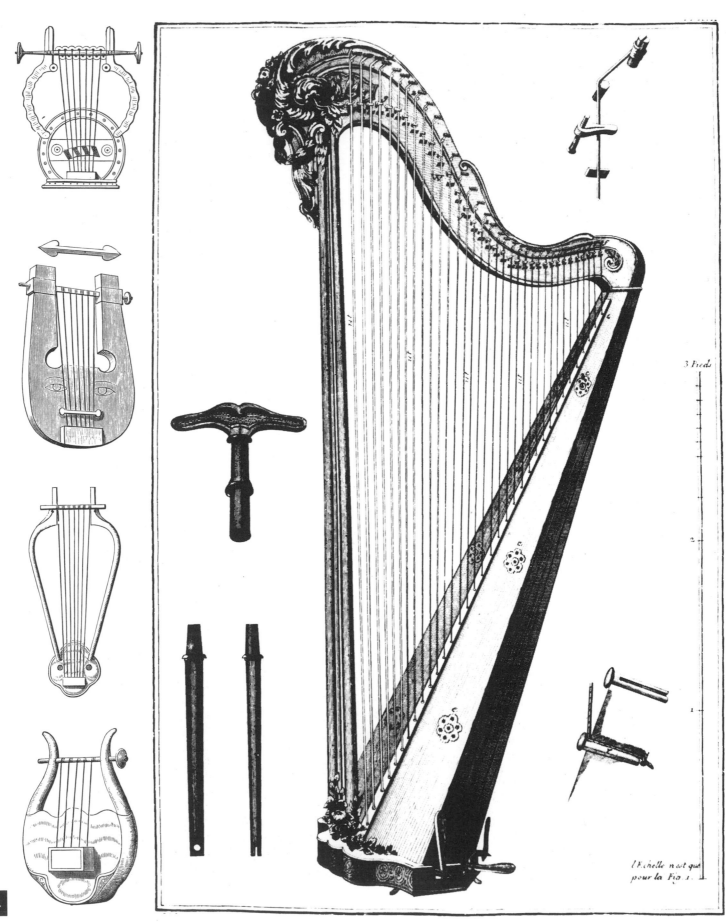

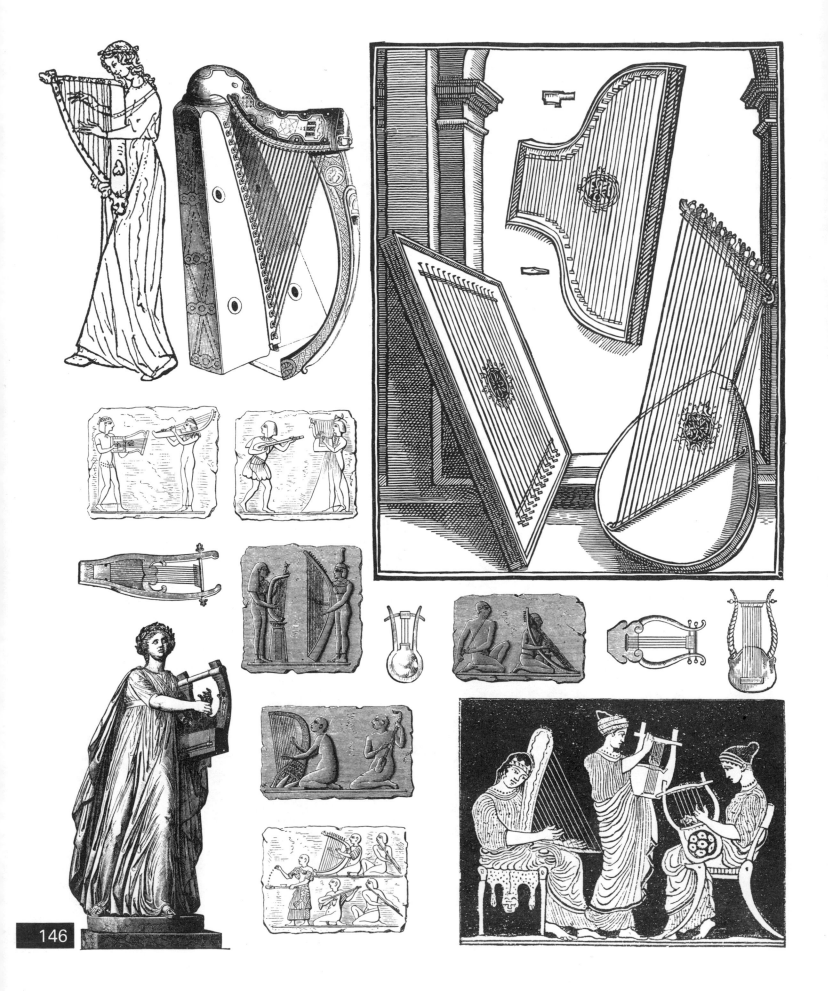

146

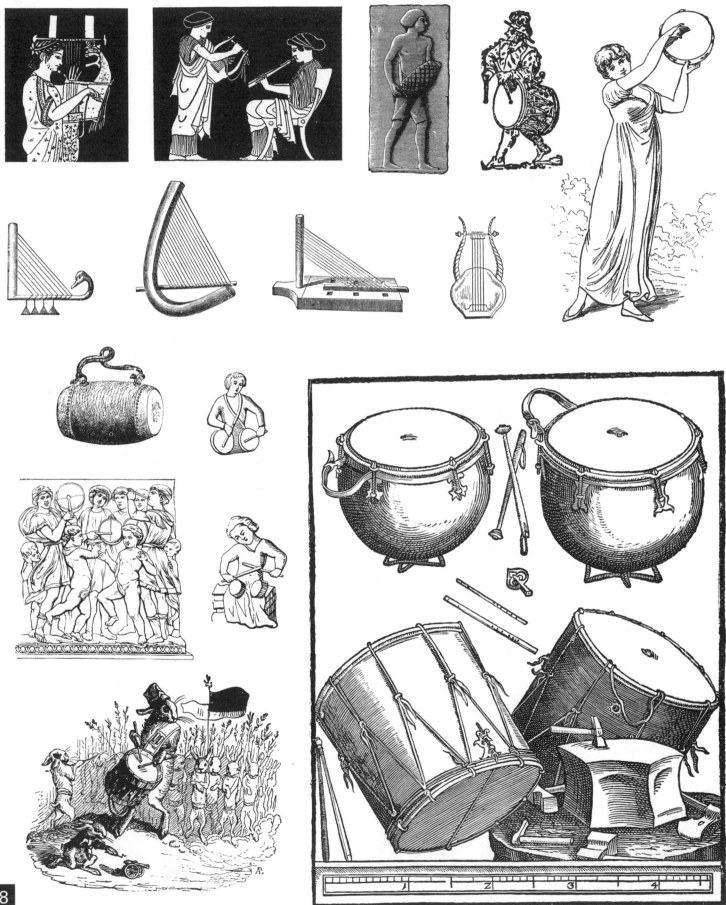

161

JOSEPHVS ROMANOR. IMPERATOR

COSTUME

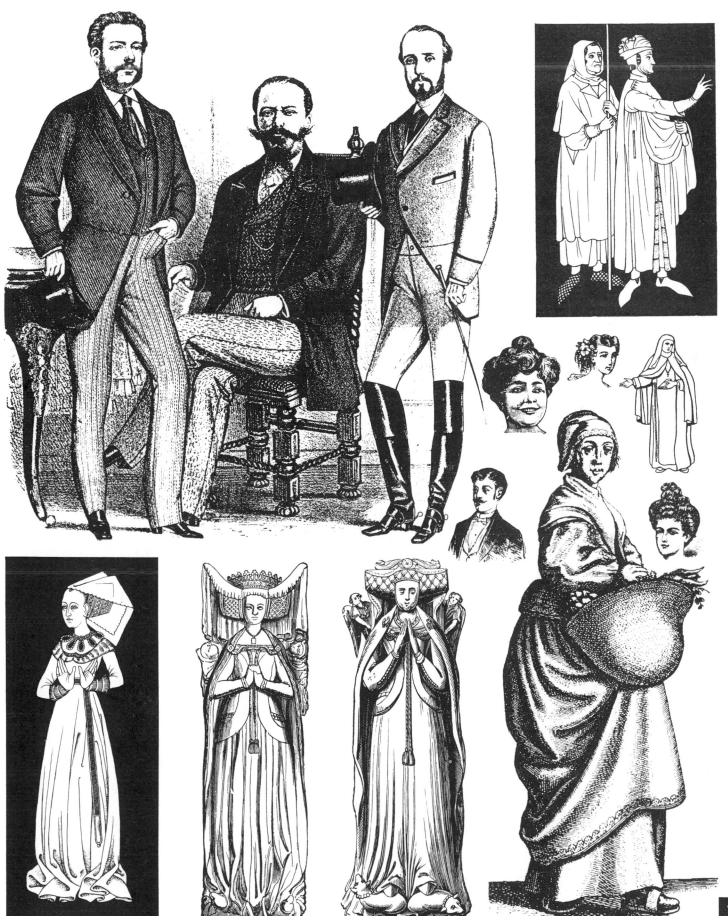

173

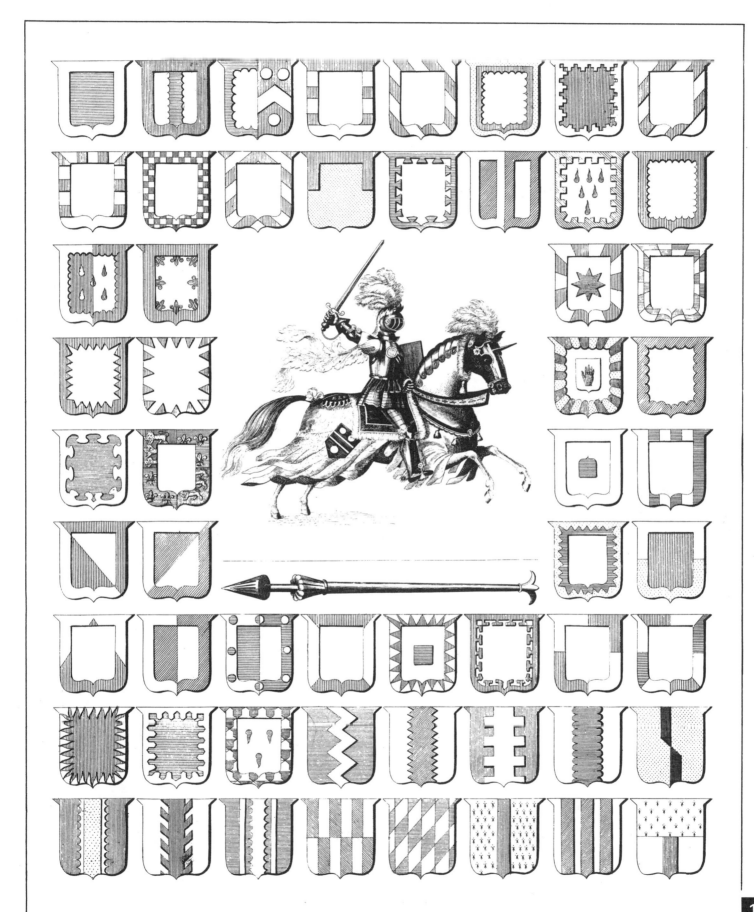

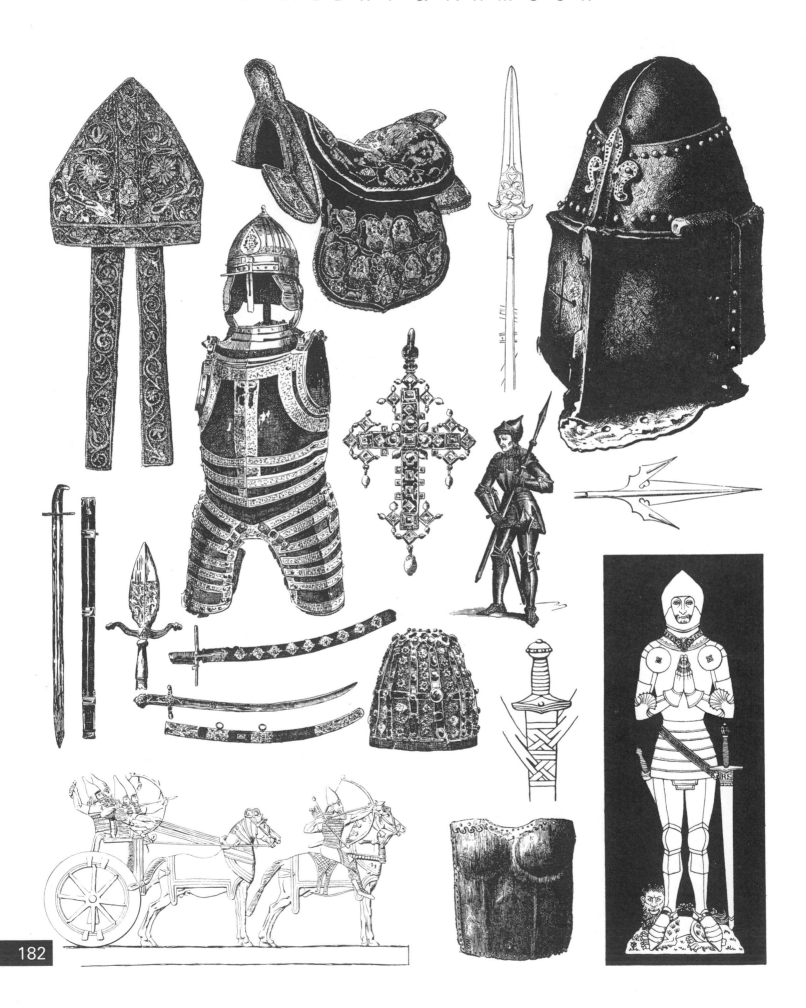

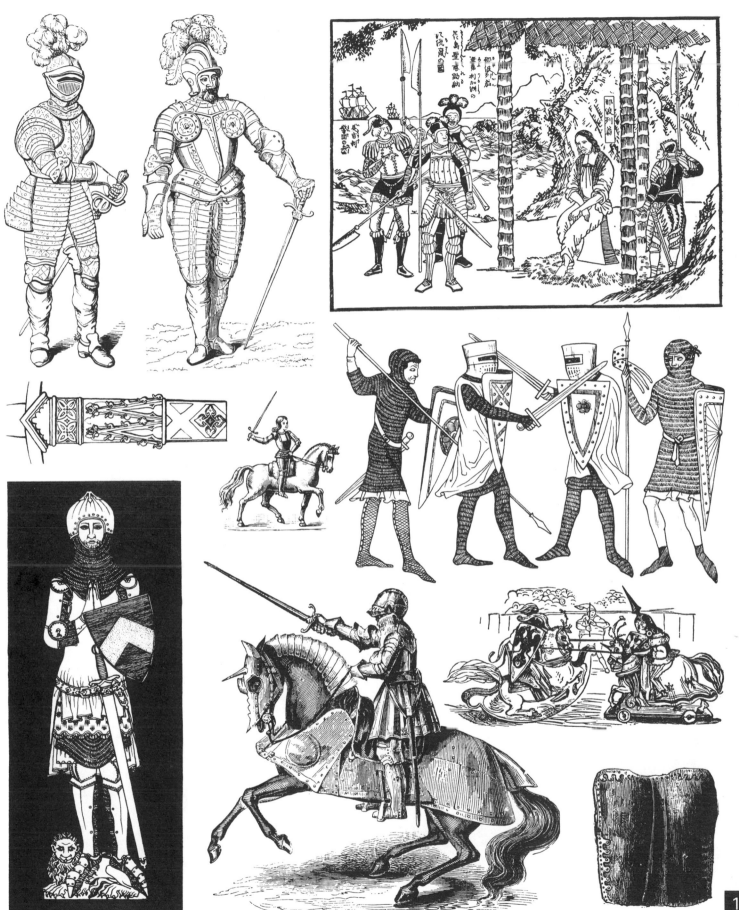

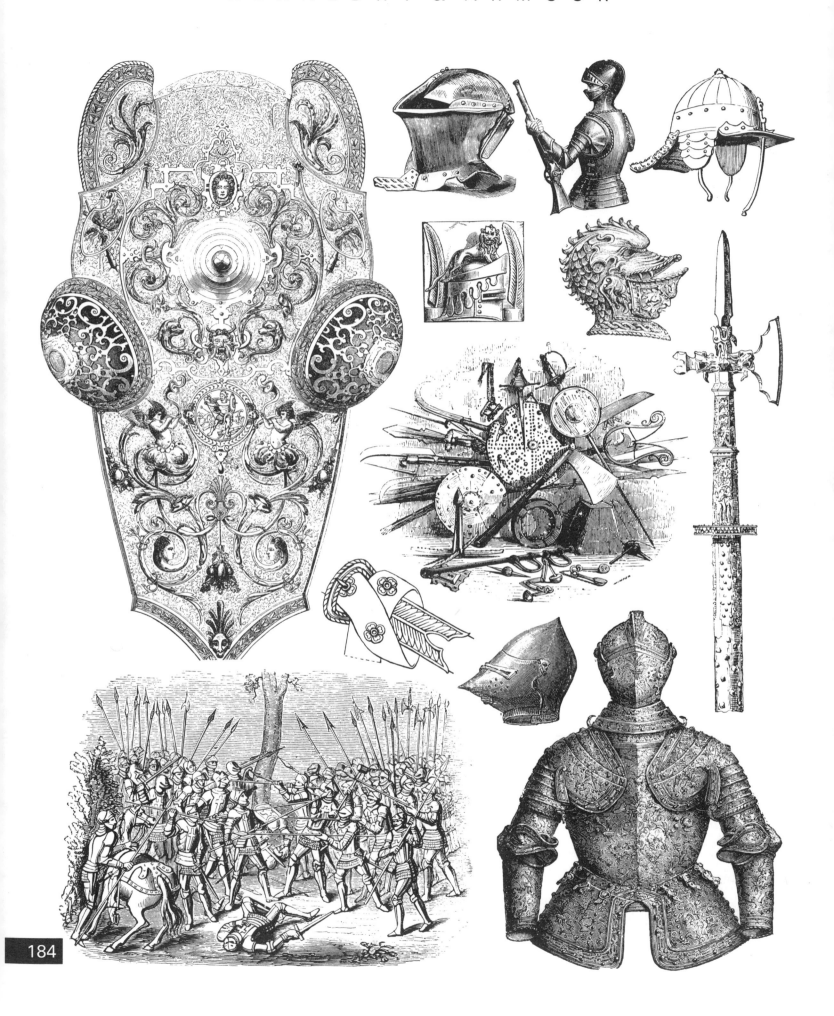

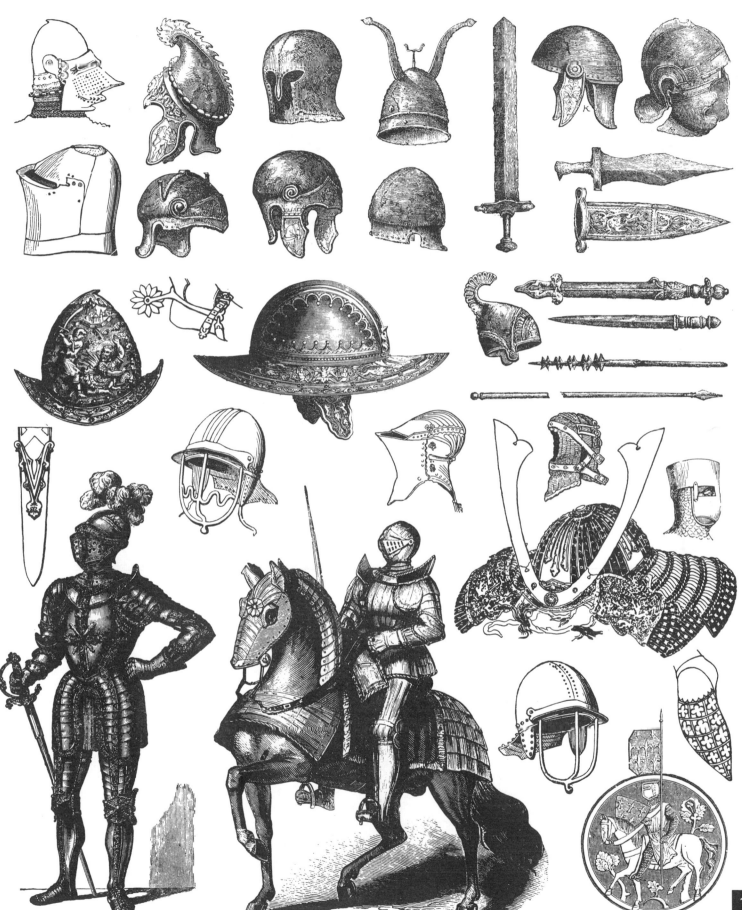

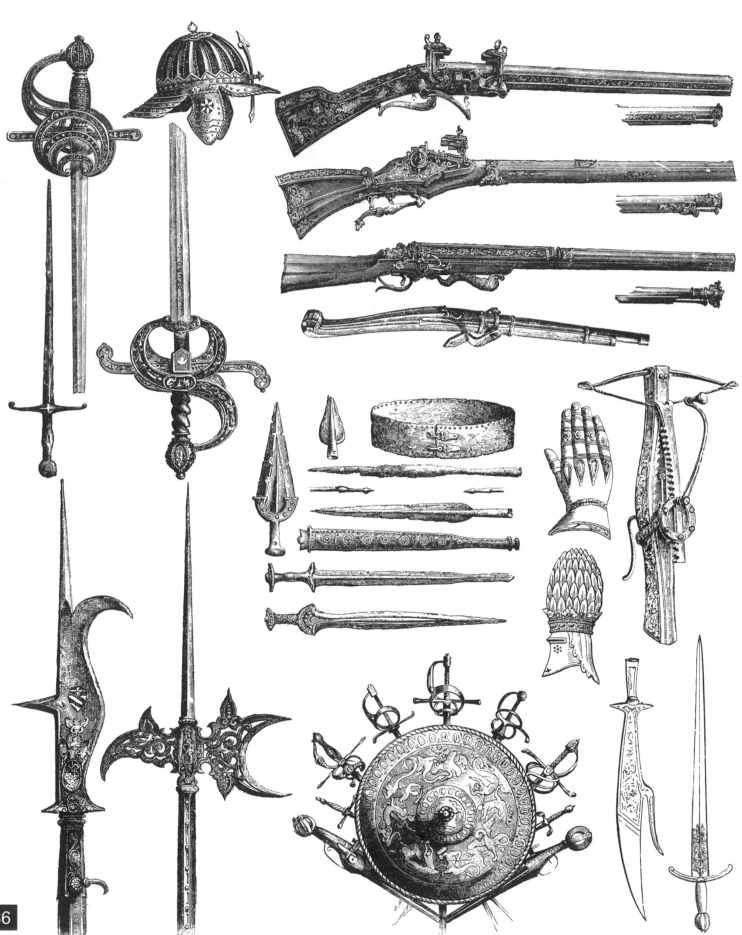

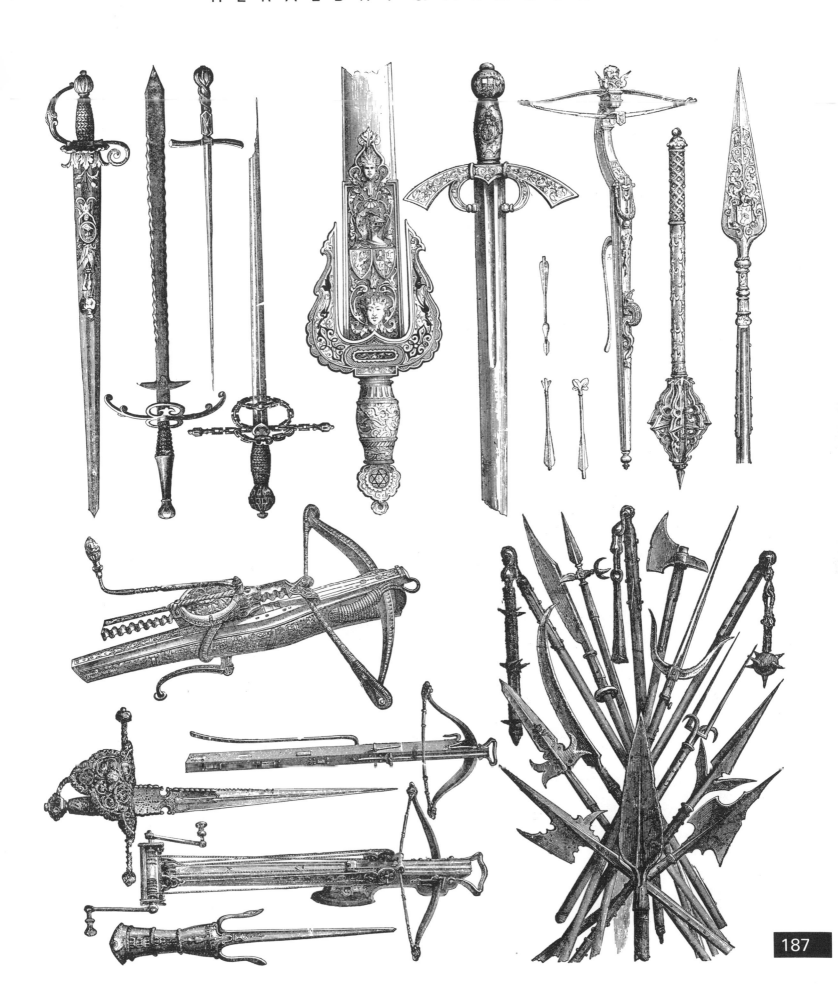

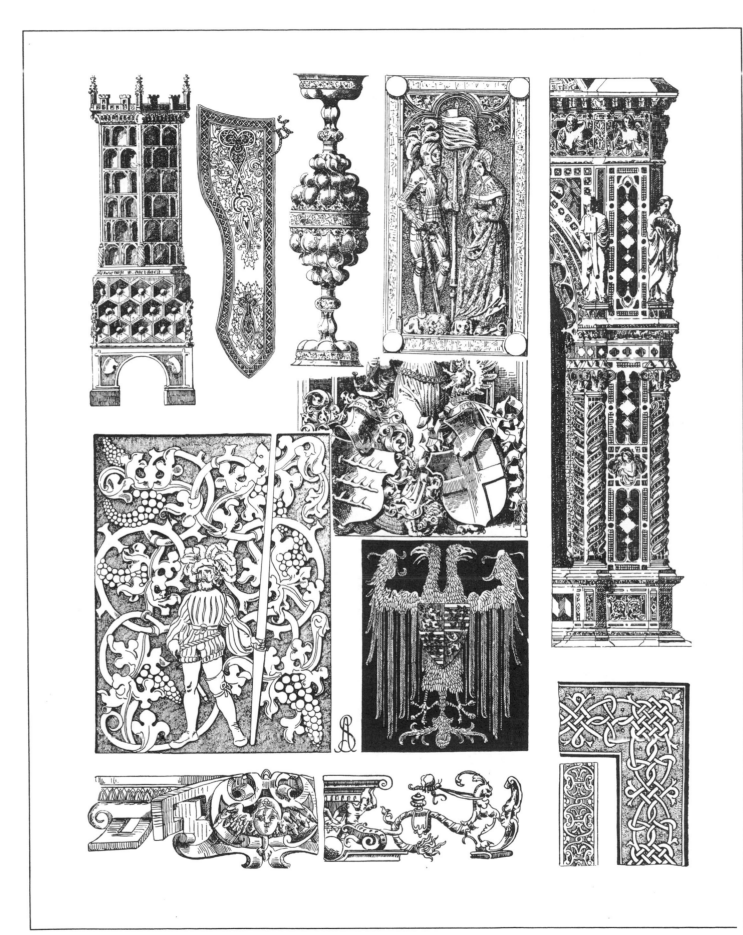

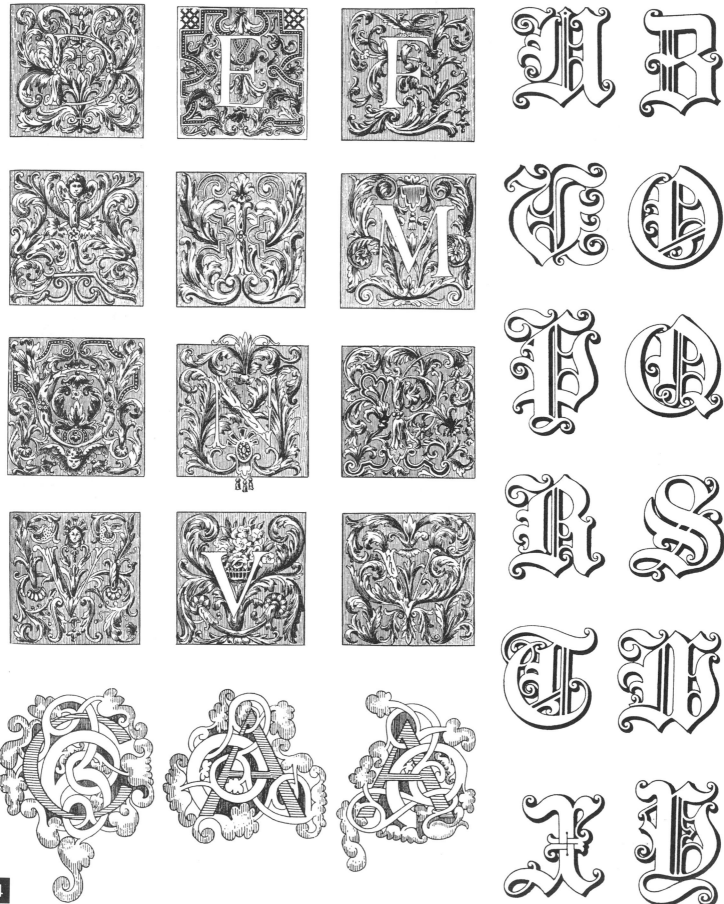

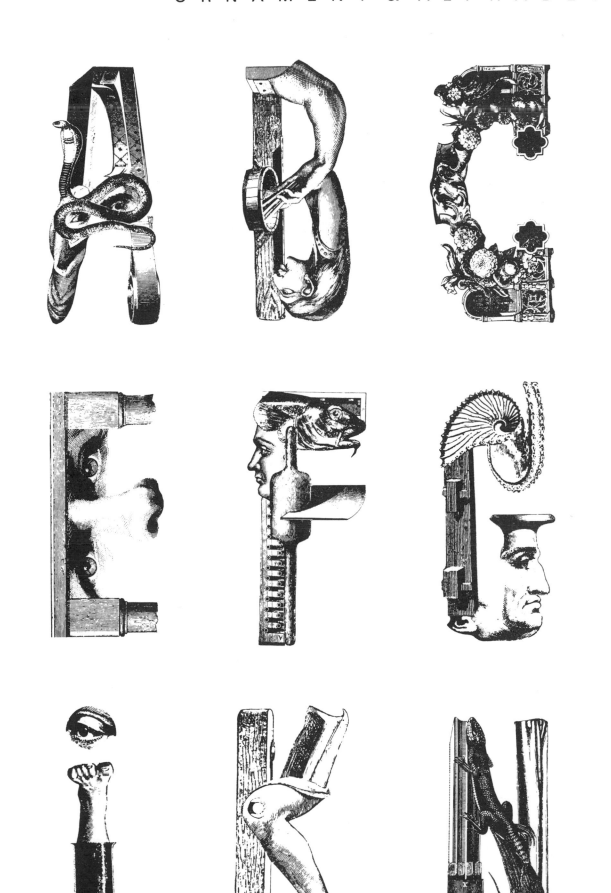
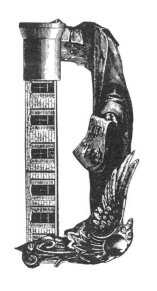

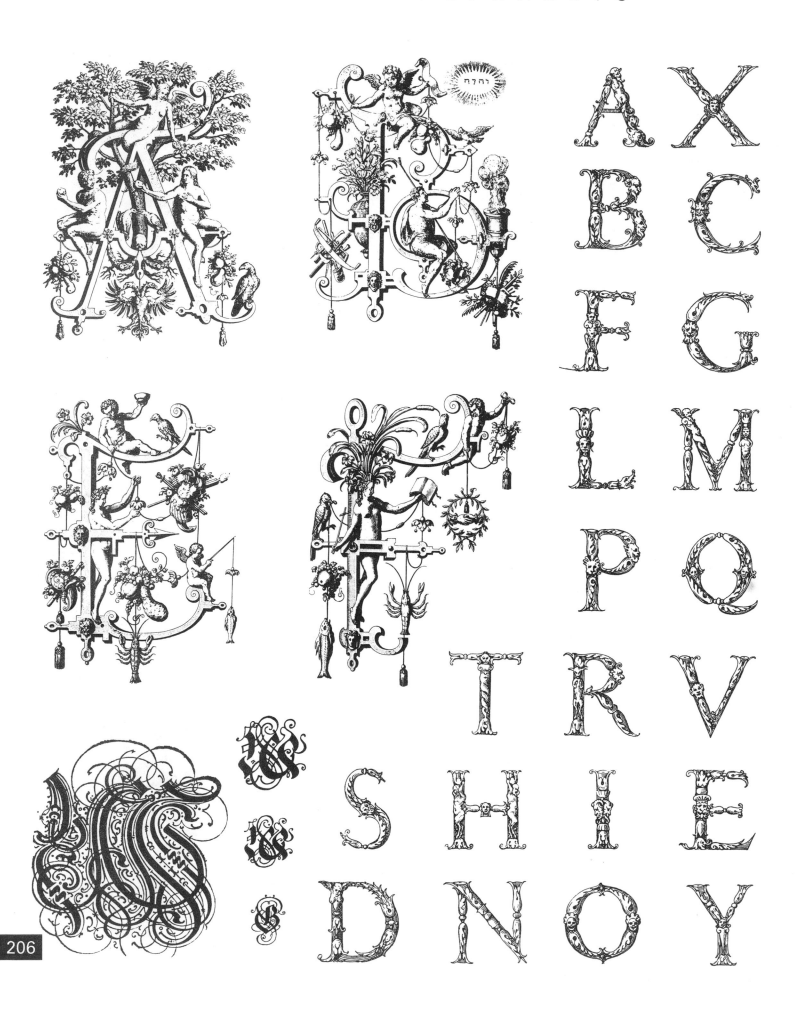

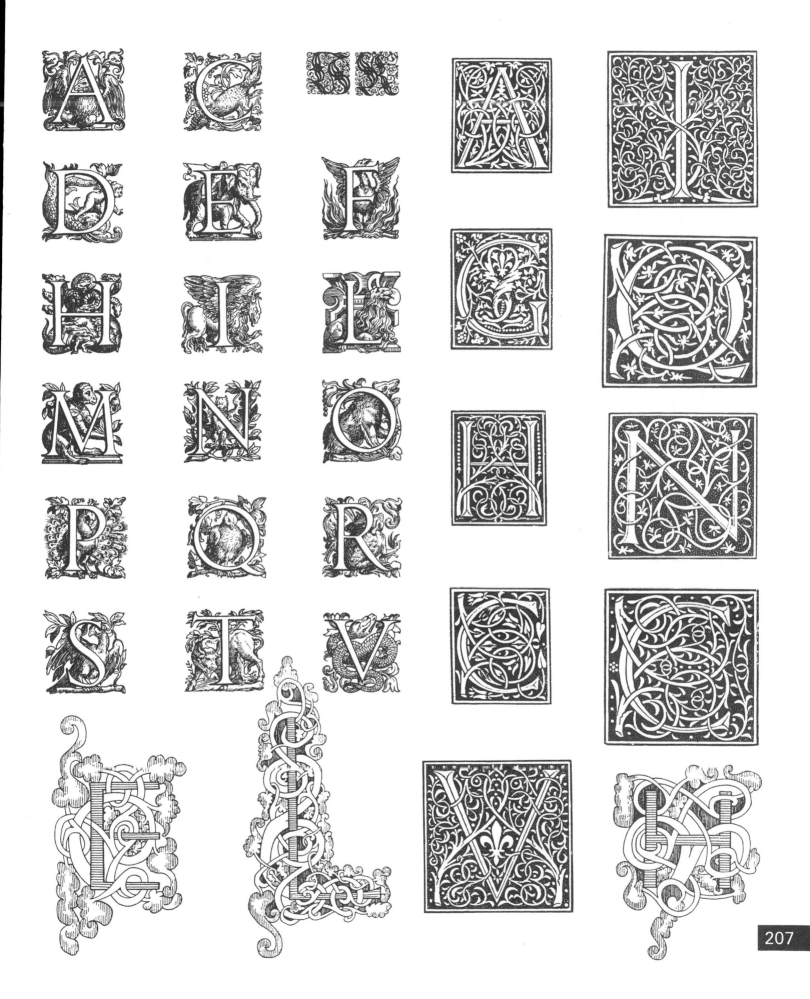

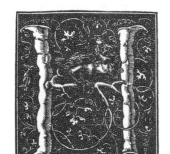

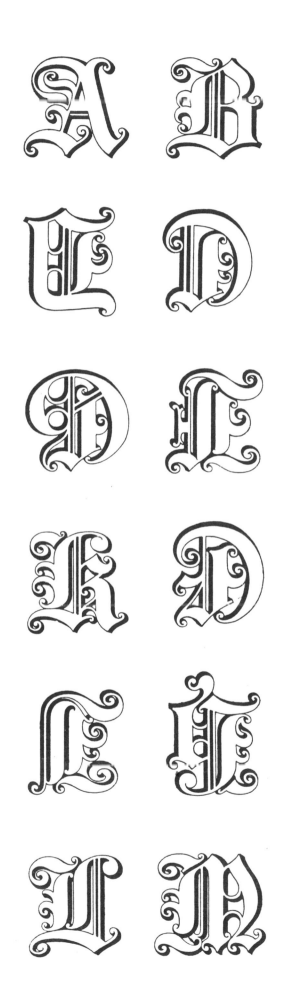

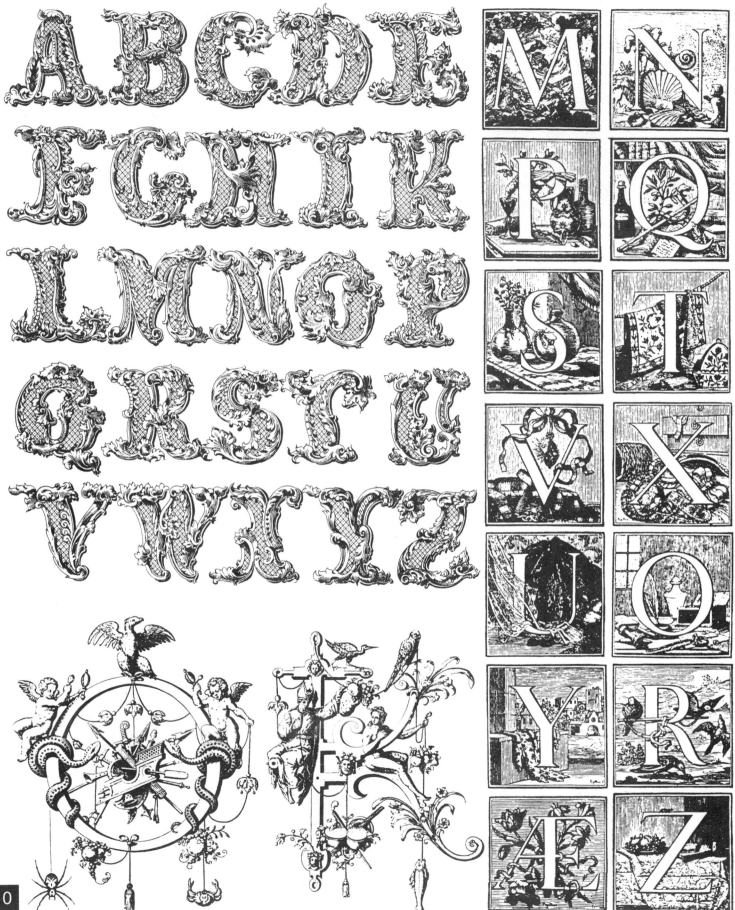

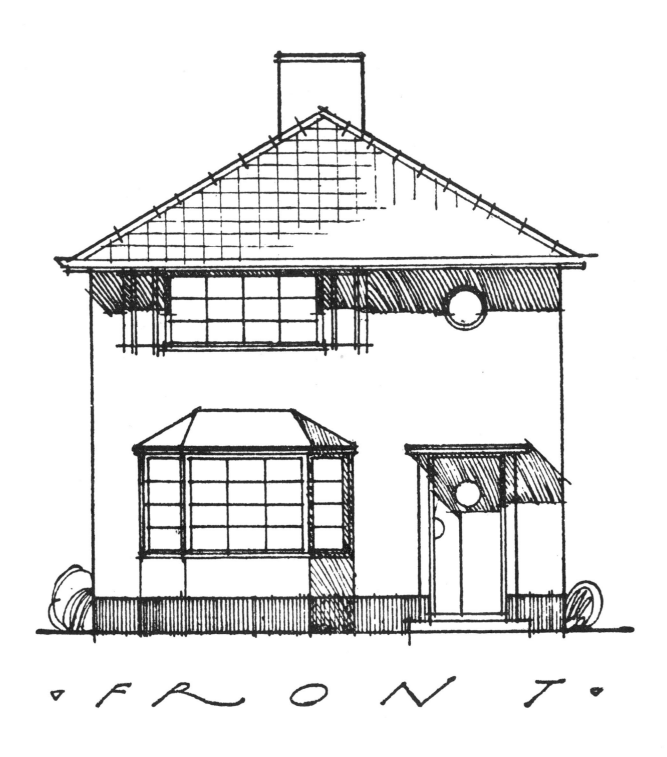

·F R O N T·

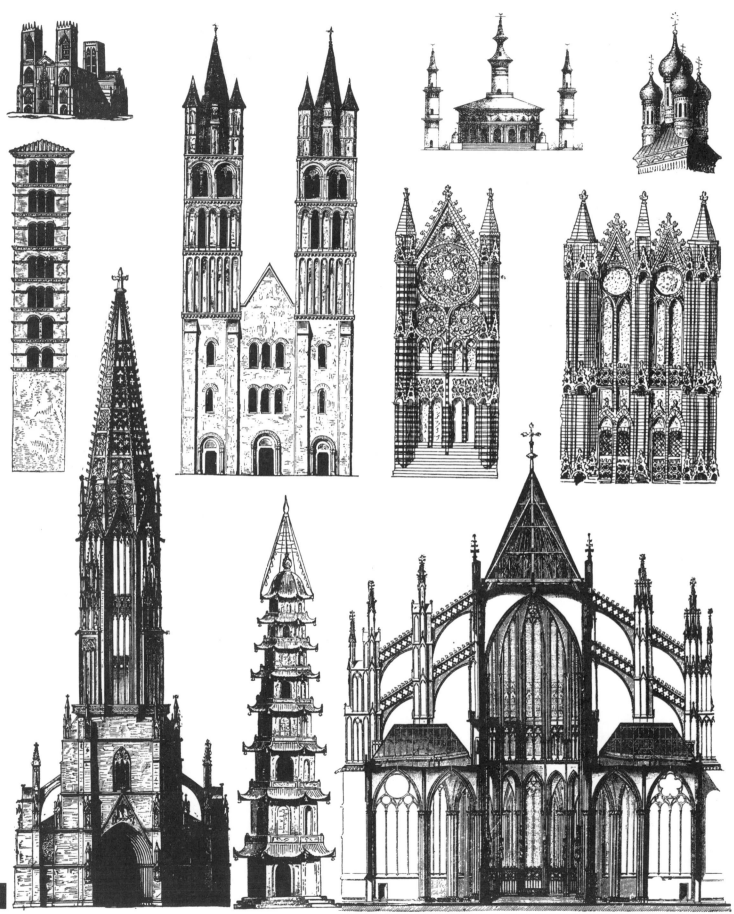

ARCHITECTURE

223

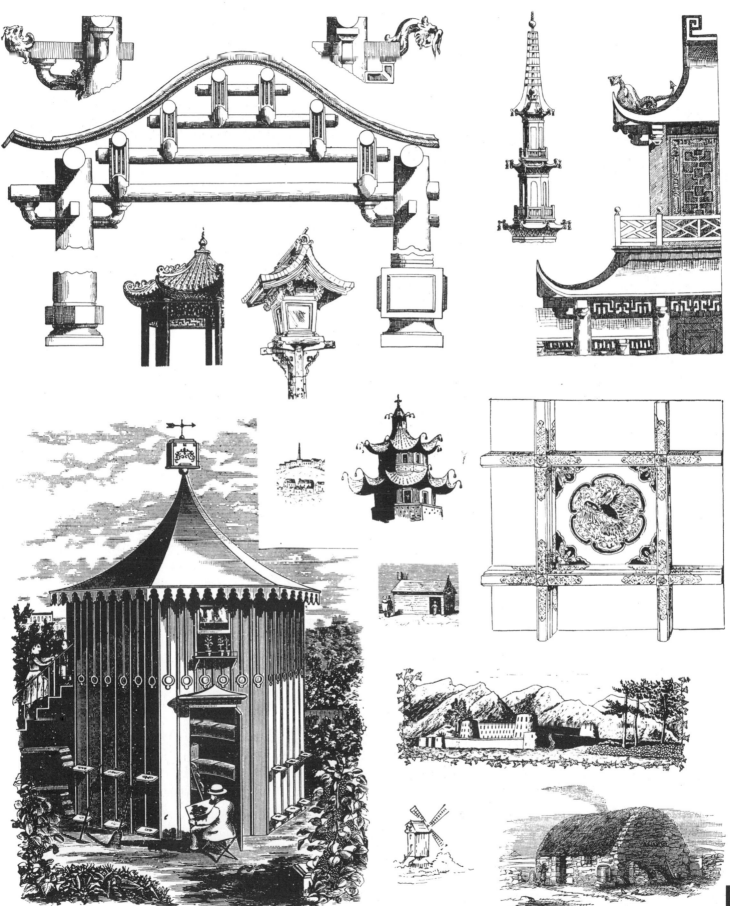

THIS IS THE PICTURE OF THE OLD HOUSE BY THE THAMES TO WHICH THE PEOPLE OF THIS STORY WENT. HEREAFTER FOLLOWS THE BOOK IT. SELF WHICH IS CALLED NEWS FROM NOWHERE OR AN EPOCH OF REST & IS WRITTEN BY WILLIAM MORRIS.

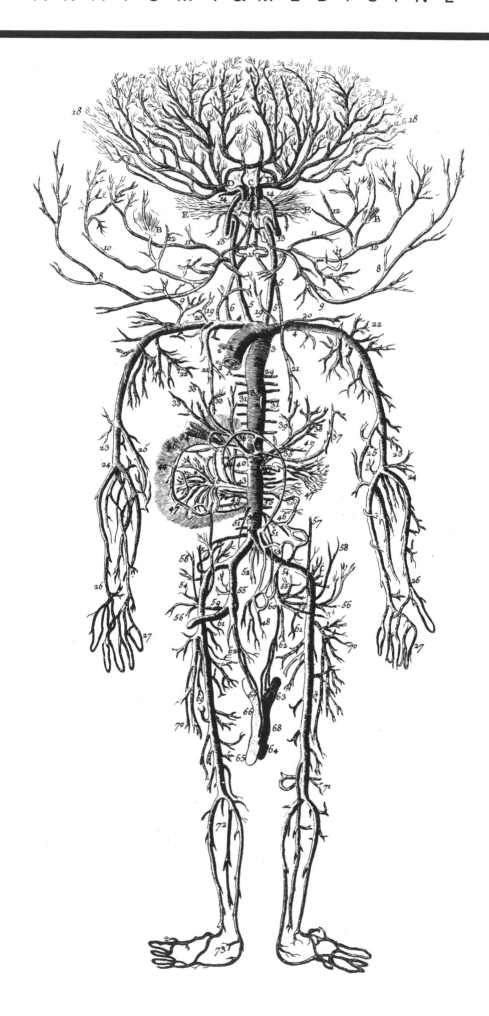

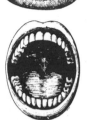

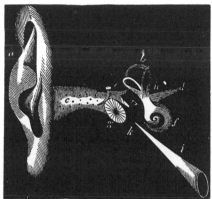

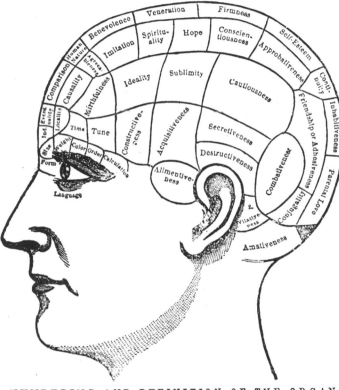

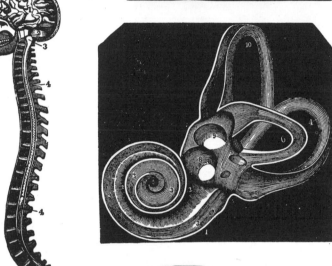

NUMBERING AND DEFINITION OF THE ORGANS.

1. **AMATIVENESS**, Love between the sexes.
A. **CONJUGALITY**, Matrimony—love of one. [etc.
2. **PARENTAL LOVE** Regard for offspring, pets,
3. **FRIENDSHIP**, Adhesiveness—sociability.
4. **INHABITIVENESS**, Love of home.
5. **CONTINUITY**, One thing at a time.
E. **VITATIVENESS**, Love of life.
6. **COMBATIVENESS**, Resistance—defence.
7. **DESTRUCTIVENESS**, Executiveness—force.
8. **ALIMENTIVENESS**, Appetite—hunger.
9. **ACQUISITIVENESS**, Accumulation.
10. **SECRETIVENESS**, Policy—management.
11. **CAUTIOUSNESS** Prudence—provision.
12. **APPROBATIVENESS**, Ambition—display.
13. **SELF-ESTEEM**, Self-respect—dignity.
14. **FIRMNESS**, Decision—perseverance.
15. **CONSCIENTIOUSNESS**, Justice, equity.
16. **HOPE**, Expectation—enterprise.
17. **SPIRITUALITY**, Intuition—faith—credulity.
18. **VENERATION**, Devotion—respect.
19. **BENEVOLENCE**, Kindness—goodness.

20. **CONSTRUCTIVENESS**, Mechanical ingenuity.
21. **IDEALITY**, Refinement—taste—purity.
B. **SUBLIMITY**, Love of grandeur—infinitude.
22. **IMITATION**, Copying—patterning.
23. **MIRTHFULNESS**, Jocoseness—wit—fun.
24. **INDIVIDUALITY**, Observation.
25. **FORM**, Recollection of shape.
26. **SIZE**, Measuring by the eye.
27. **WEIGHT**, Balancing—climbing.
28. **COLOR**, Judgment of colors.
29. **ORDER**, Method—system—arrangement.
30. **CALCULATION**, Mental Arithmetic.
31. **LOCALITY**, Recollection of places.
32. **EVENTUALITY**, Memory of facts.
34. **TIME**, Cognizance of duration.
34. **TUNE**, Sense of harmony and melody.
35. **LANGUAGE**, Expression of ideas.
36. **CAUSALITY**, Applying causes to effect.
37. **COMPARISON**, Inductive reasoning.
C. **HUMAN NATURE**, Perception of motives.
D. **AGREEABLENESS**—Pleasantness—suavity.

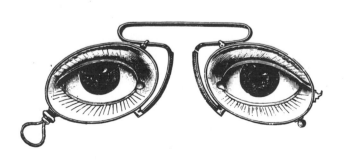

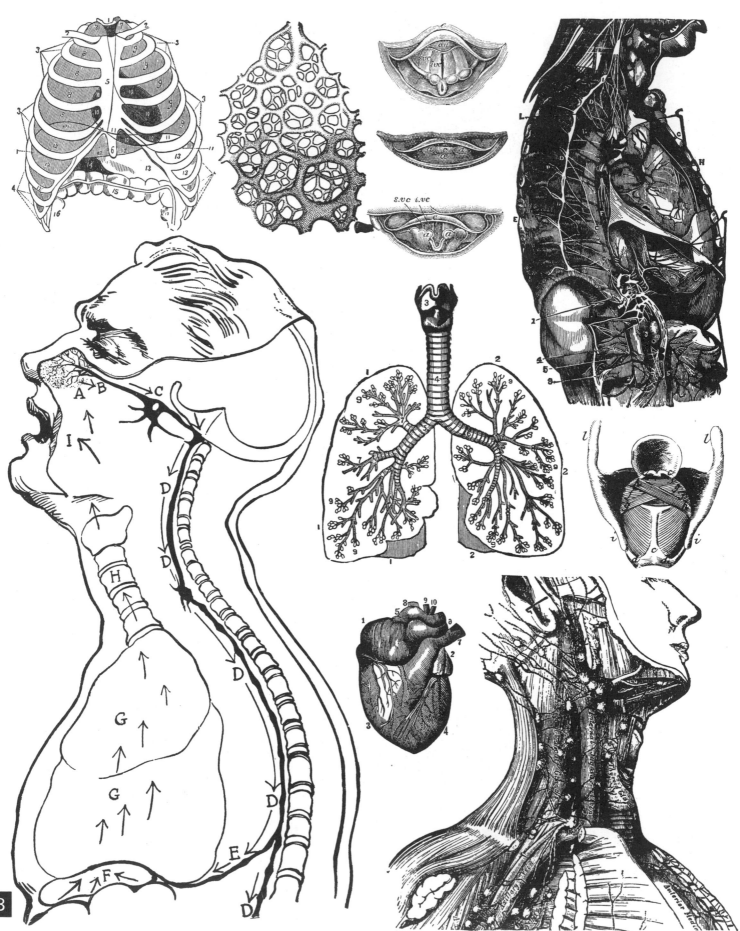

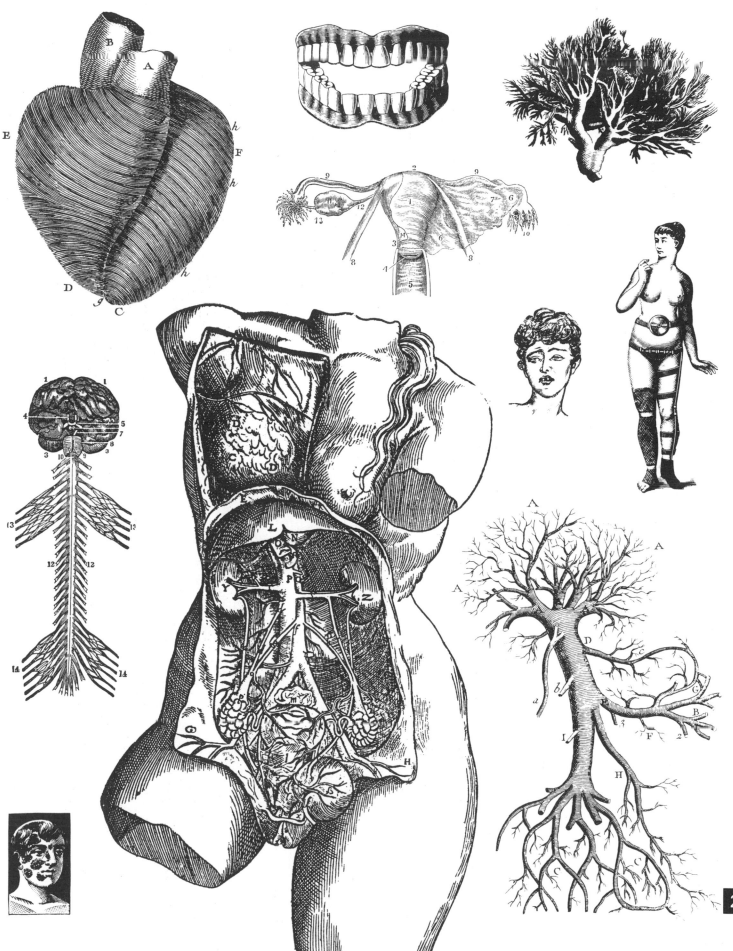

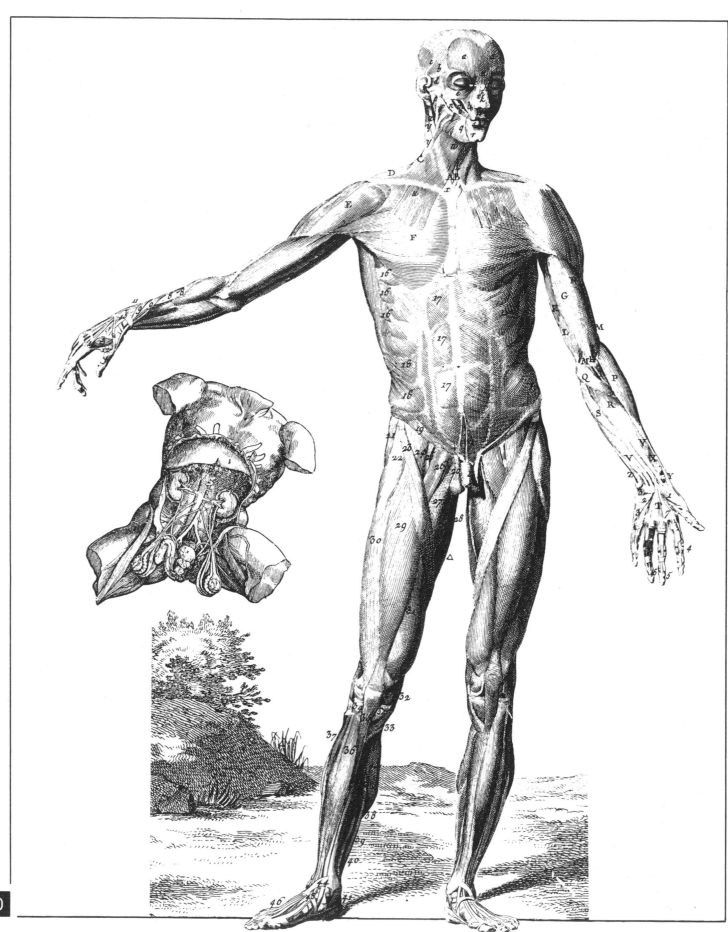

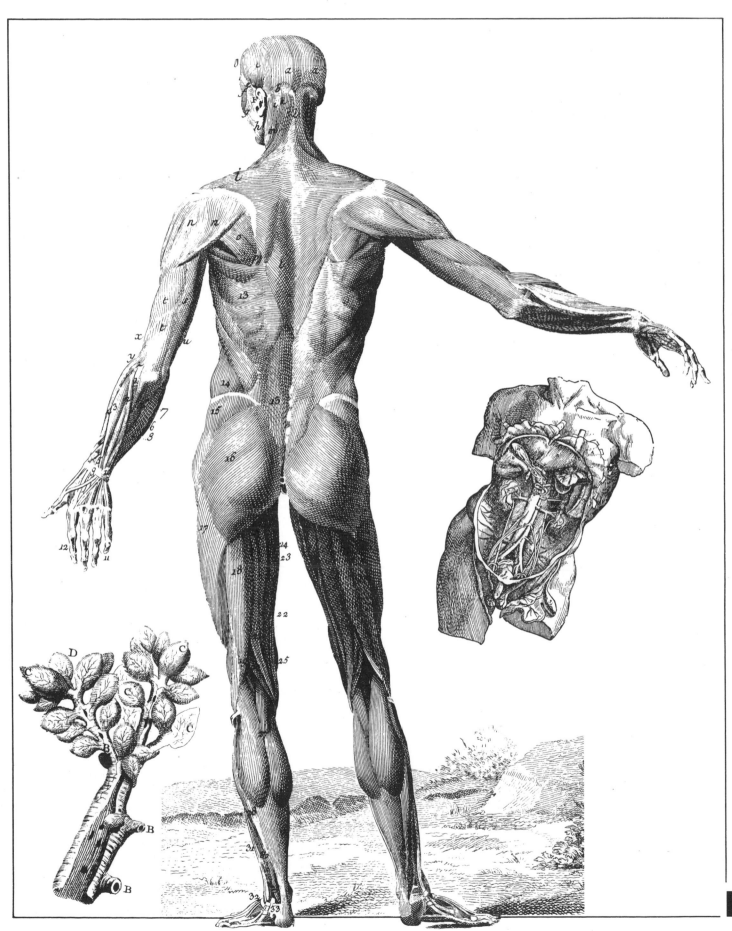

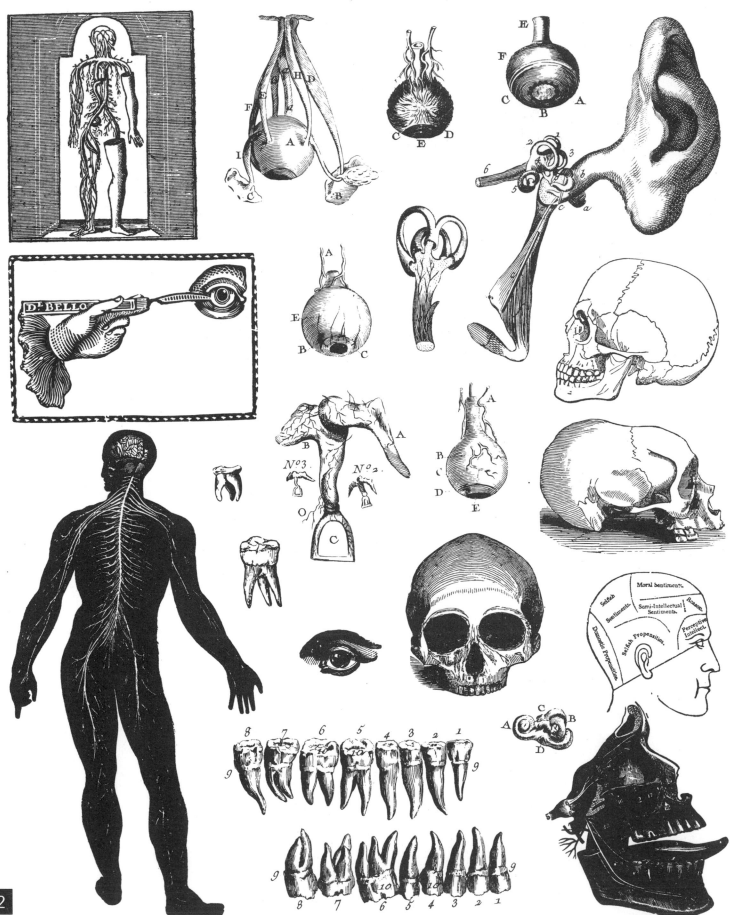

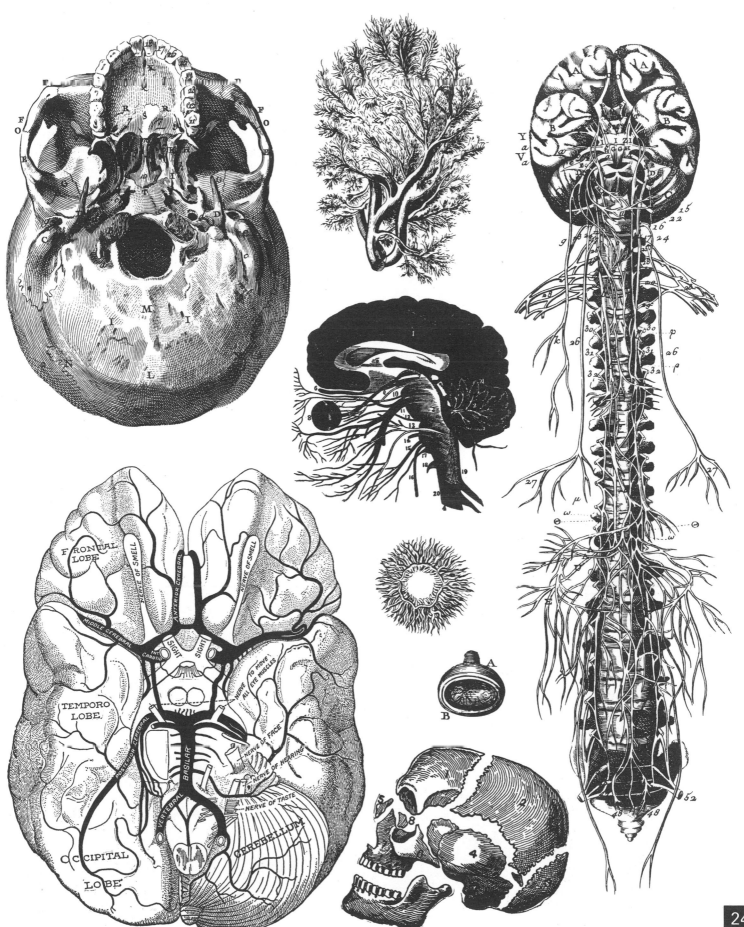

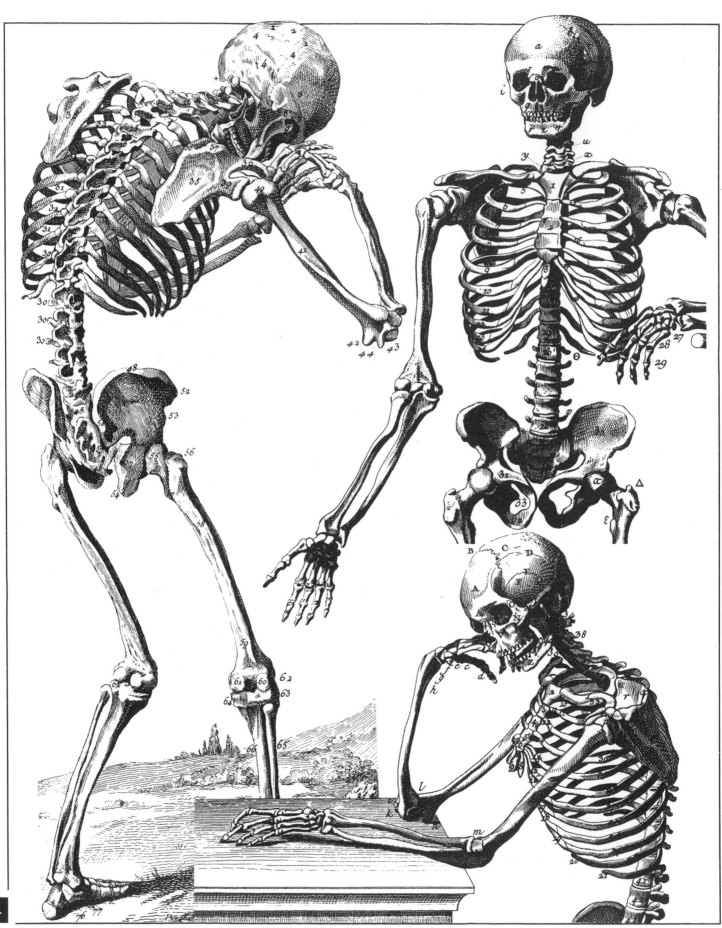

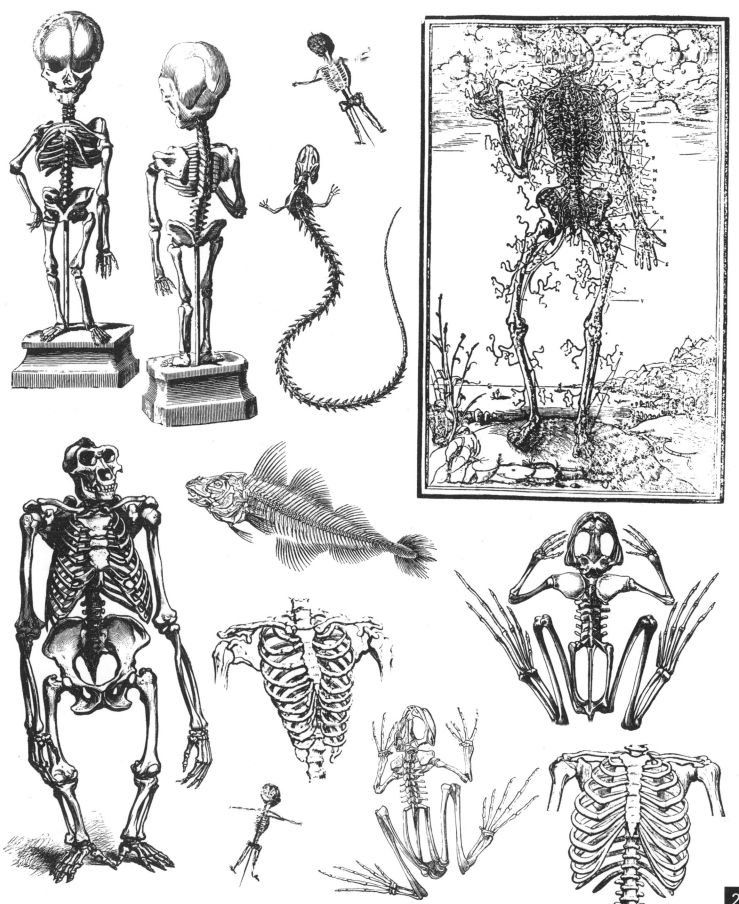

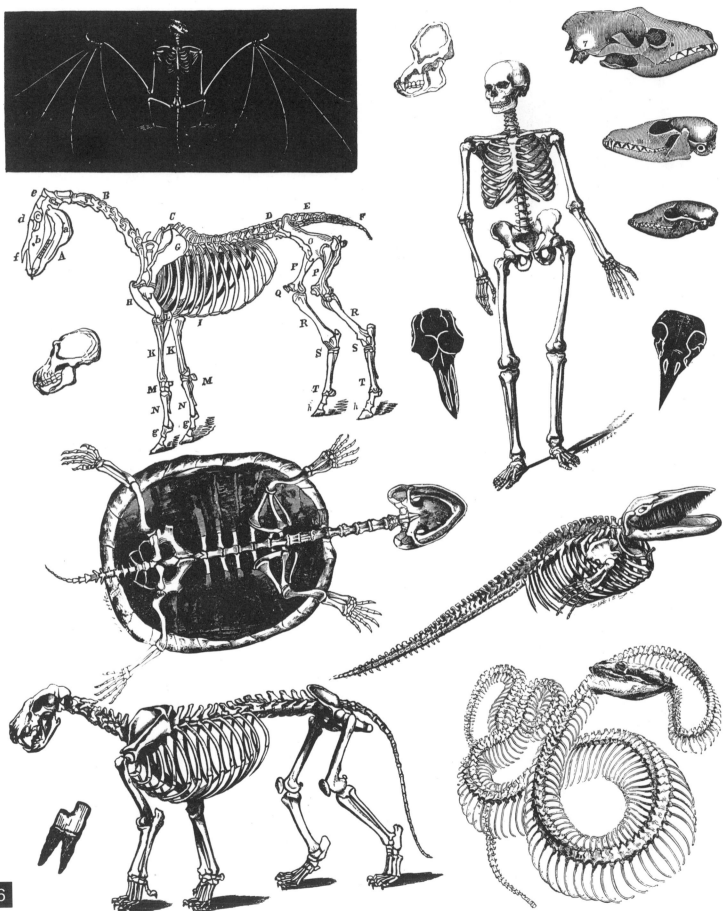

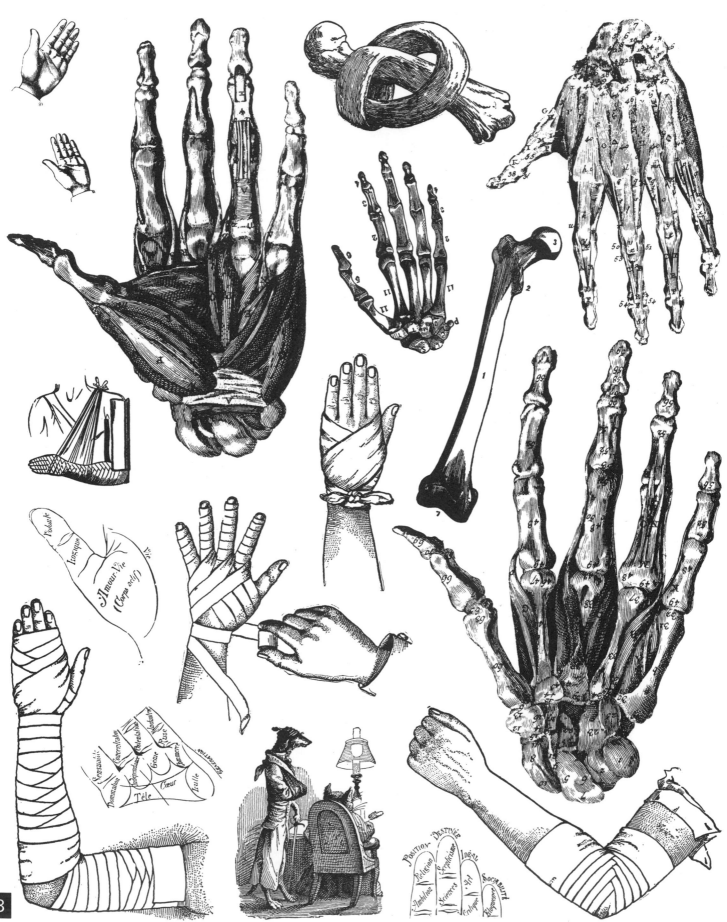

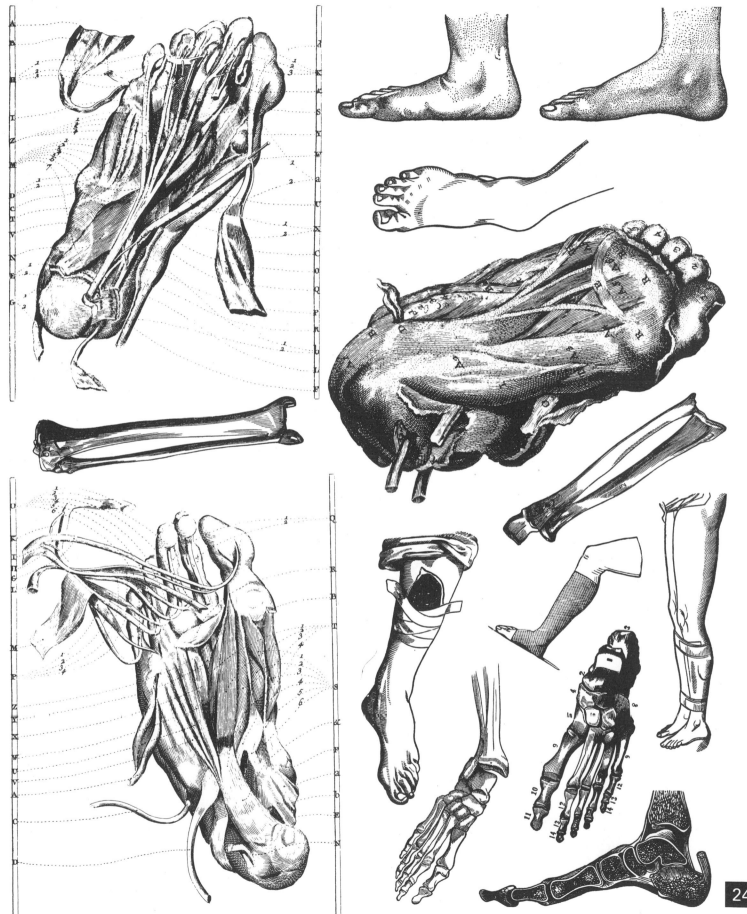

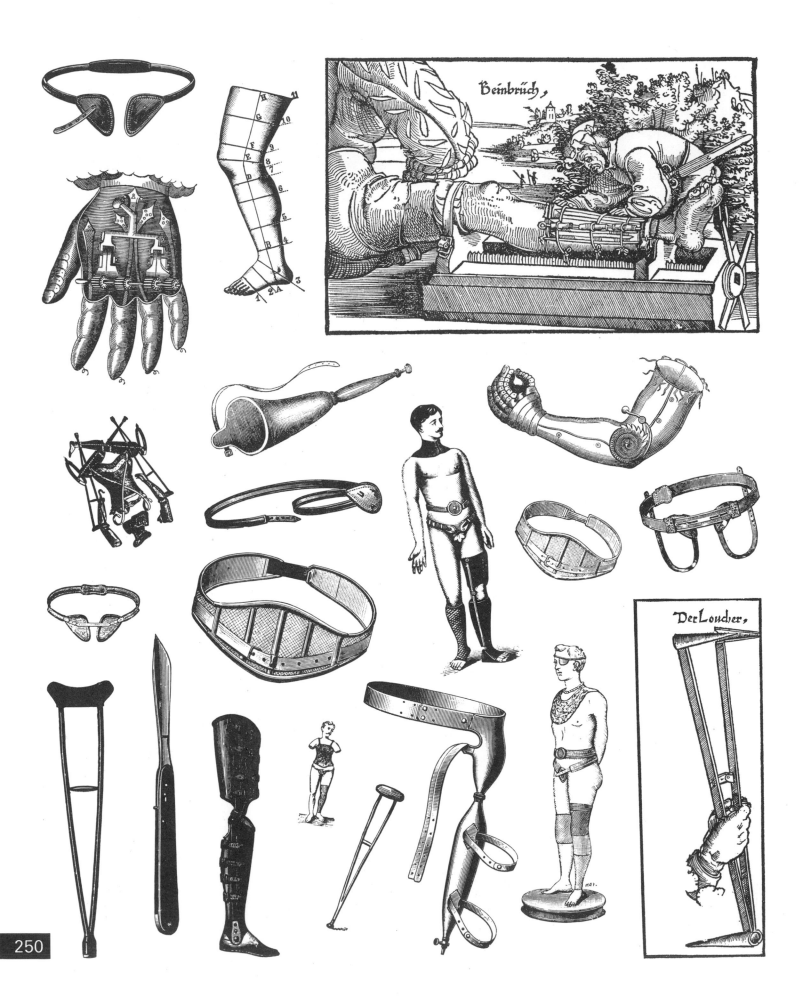

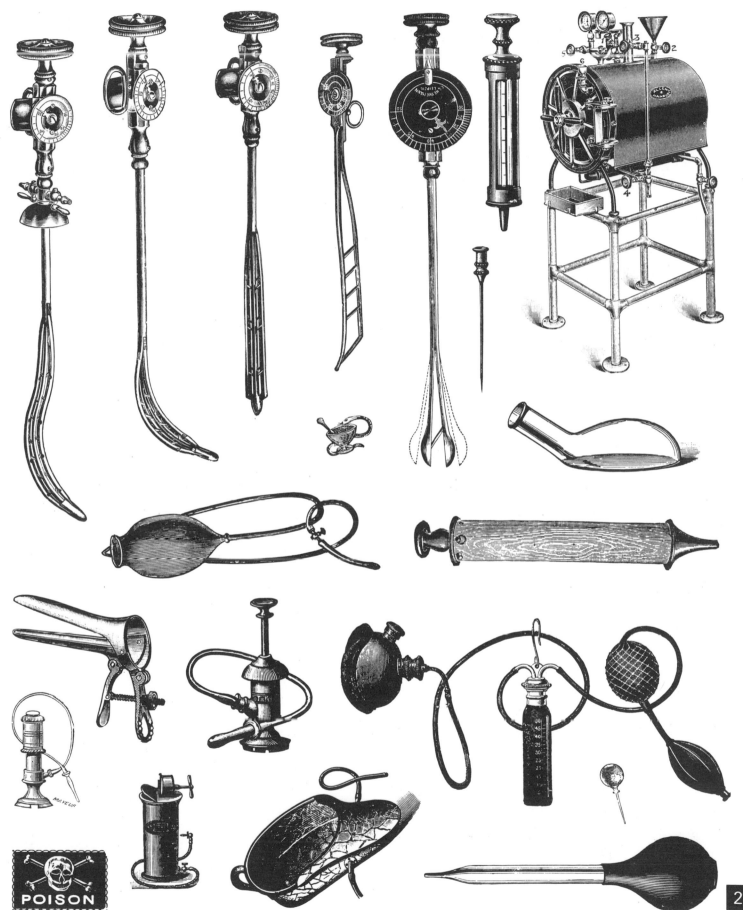

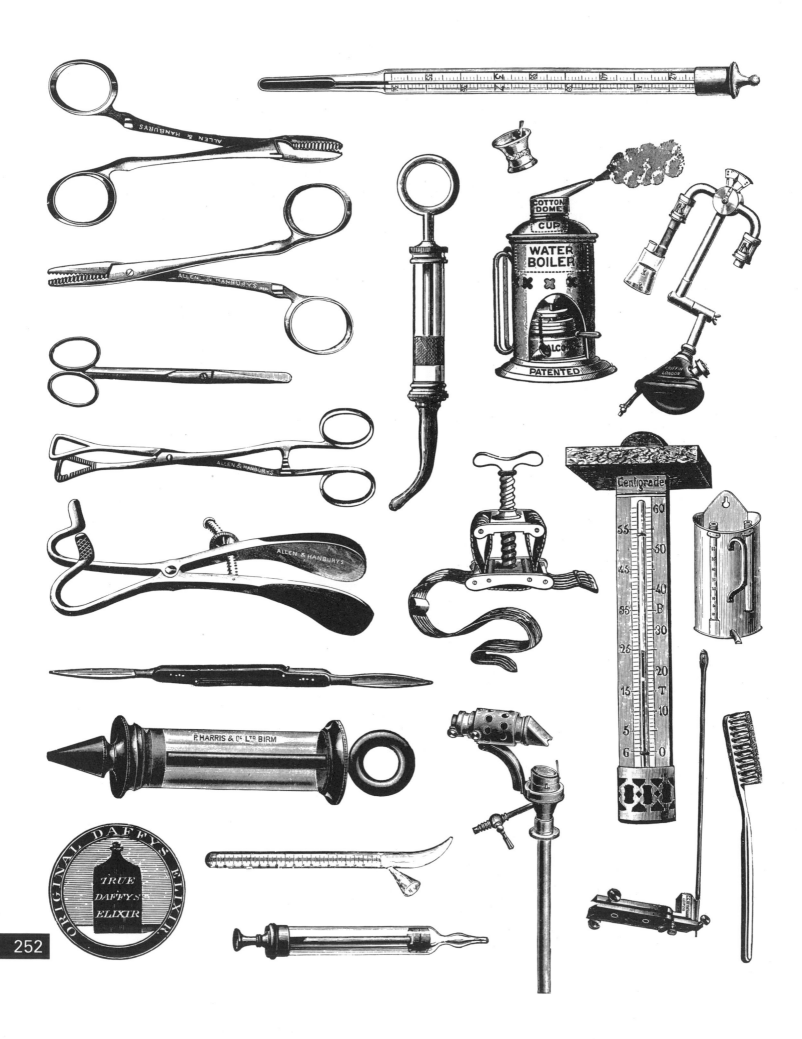

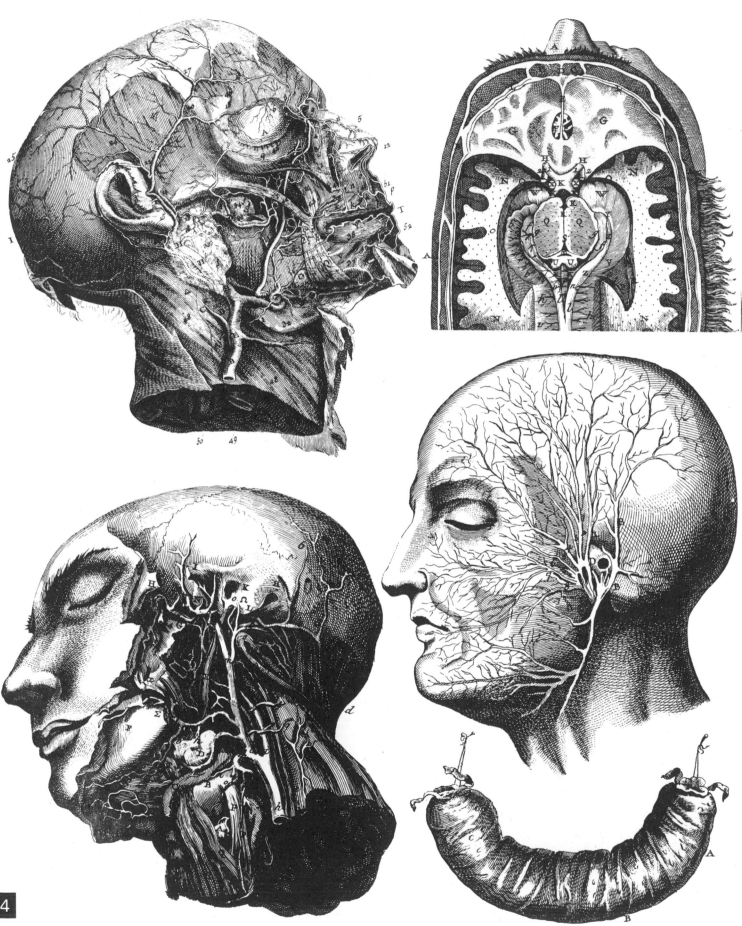

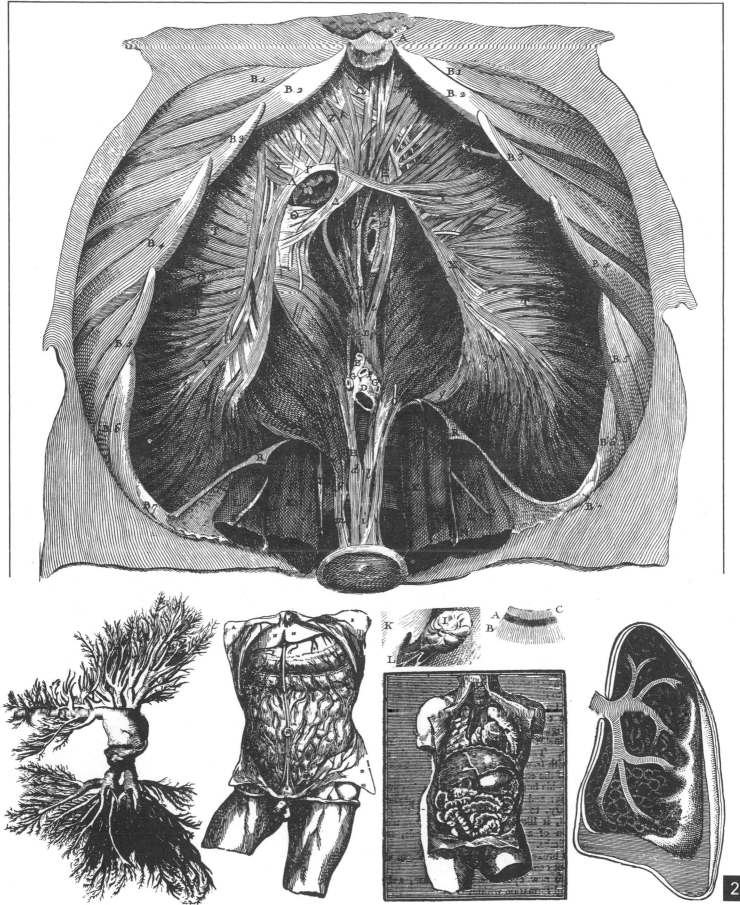

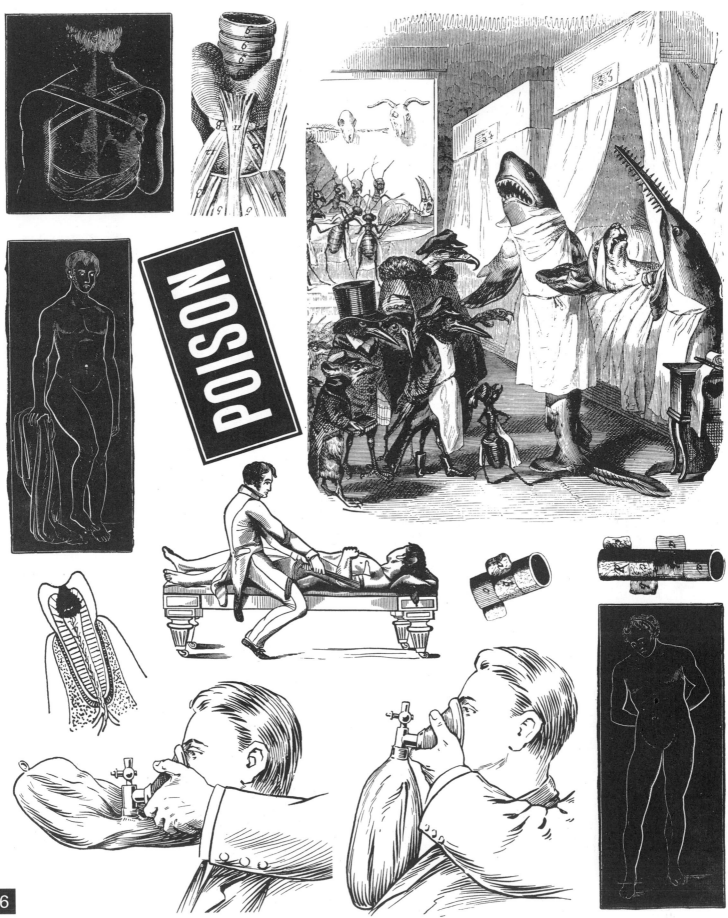

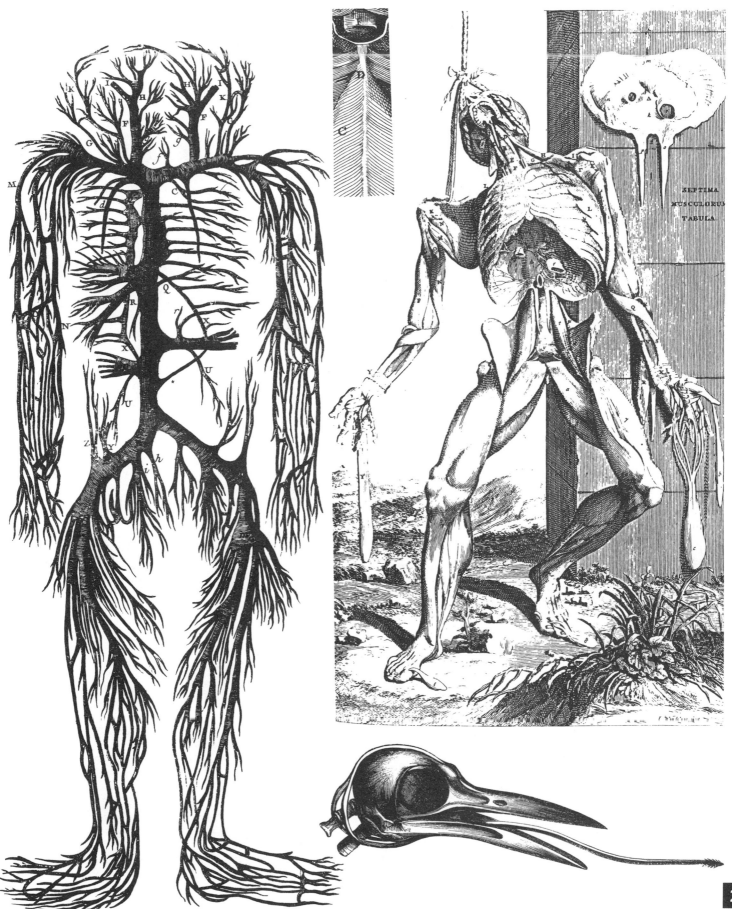

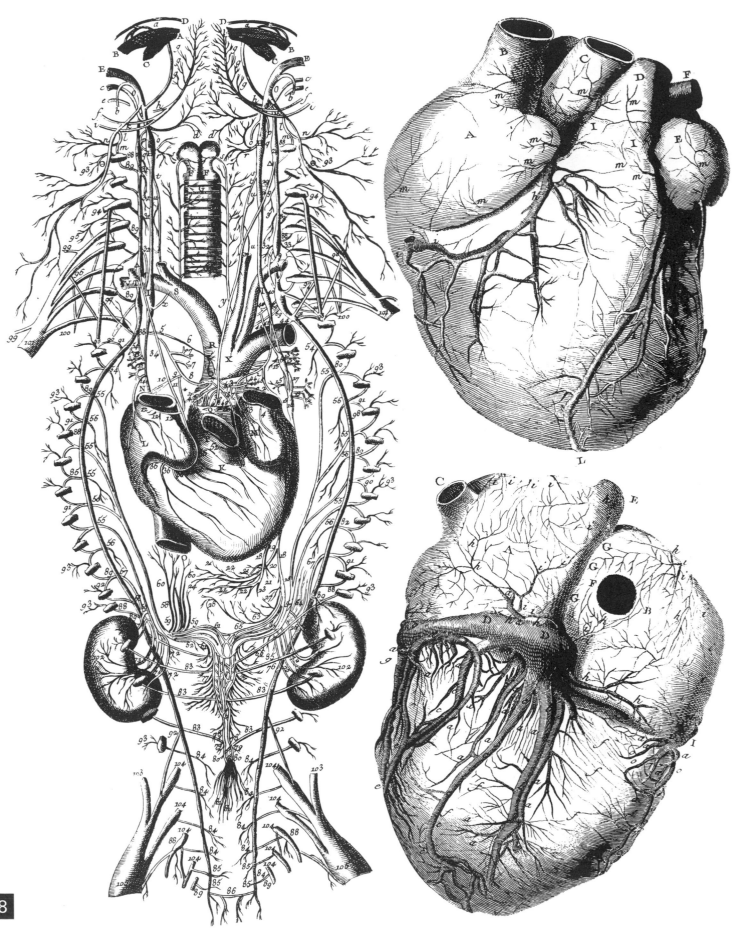

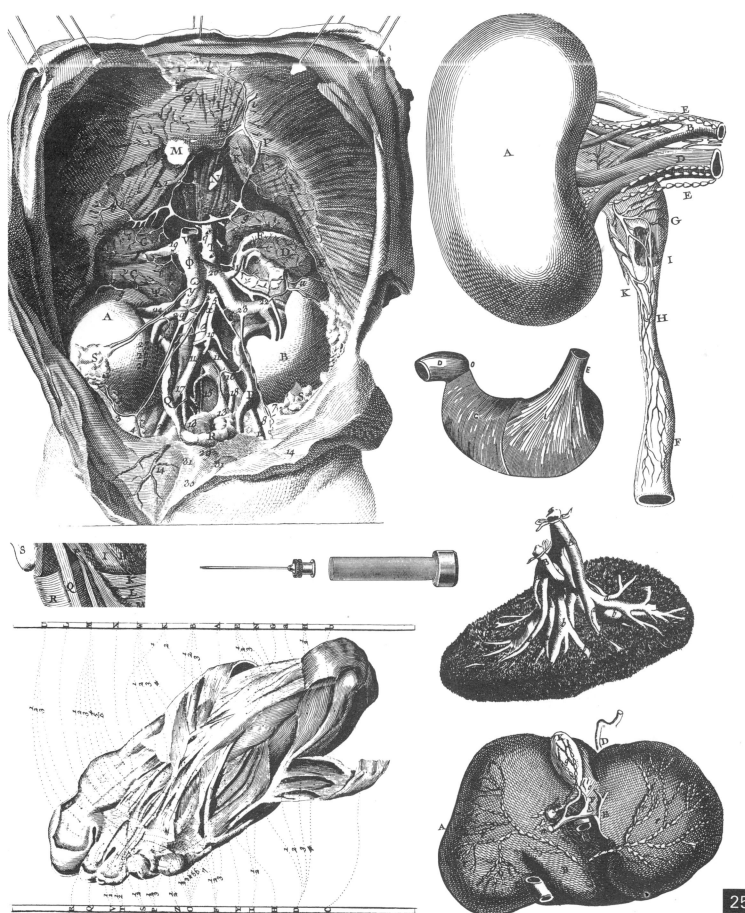

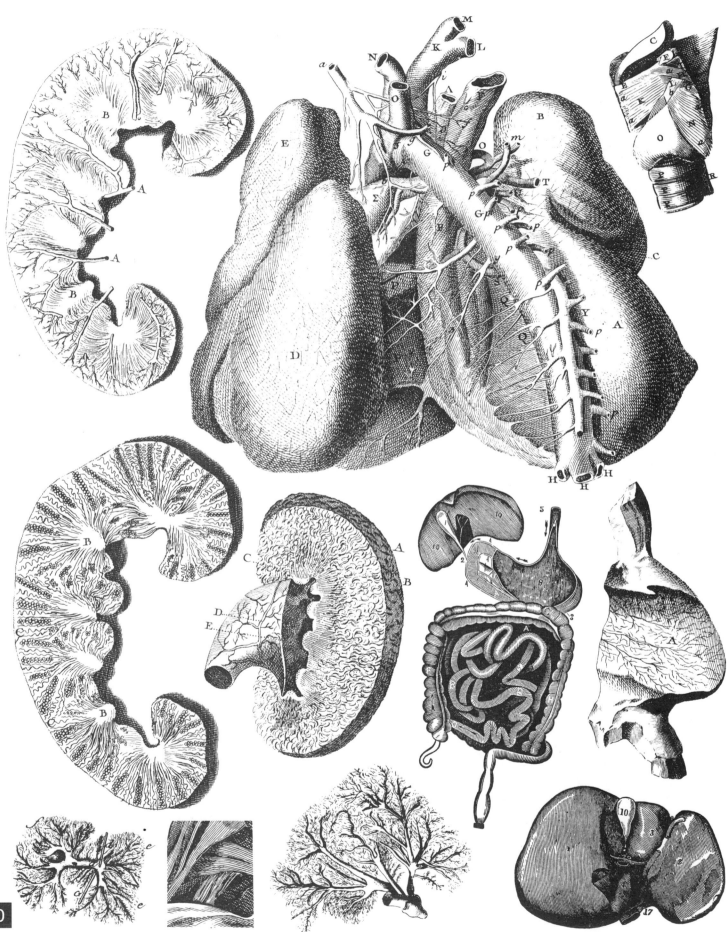

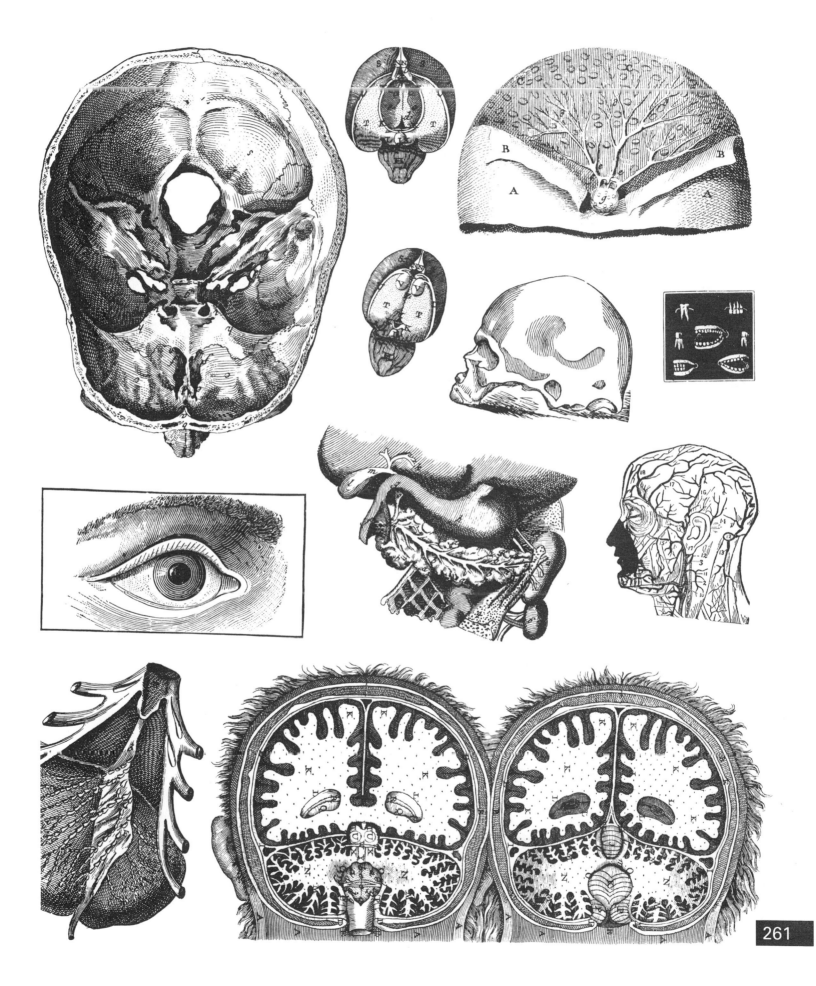

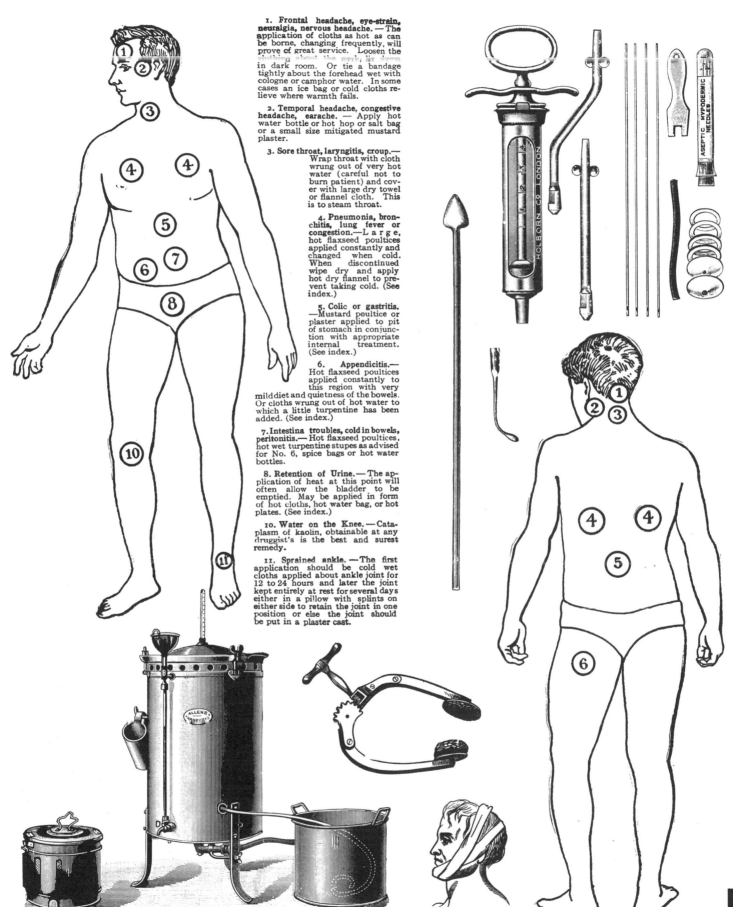

1. **Frontal headache, eye-strain, neuralgia, nervous headache.** — The application of cloths as hot as can be borne, changing frequently, will prove of great service. Loosen the clothing about the neck, if sitting in dark room. Or tie a bandage tightly about the forehead wet with cologne or camphor water. In some cases an ice bag or cold cloths relieve where warmth fails.

2. **Temporal headache, congestive headache, earache.** — Apply hot water bottle or hot hop or salt bag or a small size mitigated mustard plaster.

3. **Sore throat, laryngitis, croup.** — Wrap throat with cloth wrung out of very hot water (careful not to burn patient) and cover with large dry towel or flannel cloth. This is to steam throat.

4. **Pneumonia, bronchitis, lung fever or congestion.** — L a r g e, hot flaxseed poultices applied constantly and changed when cold. When discontinued wipe dry and apply hot dry flannel to prevent taking cold. (See index.)

5. **Colic or gastritis.** — Mustard poultice or plaster applied to pit of stomach in conjunction with appropriate internal treatment. (See index.)

6. **Appendicitis.** — Hot flaxseed poultices applied constantly to this region with very mild diet and quietness of the bowels. Or cloths wrung out of hot water to which a little turpentine has been added. (See index.)

7. **Intestinal troubles, cold in bowels, peritonitis.** — Hot flaxseed poultices, hot wet turpentine stupes as advised for No. 6, spice bags or hot water bottles.

8. **Retention of Urine.** — The application of heat at this point will often allow the bladder to be emptied. May be applied in form of hot cloths, hot water bag, or hot plates. (See index.)

10. **Water on the Knee.** — Cataplasm of kaolin, obtainable at any druggist's is the best and surest remedy.

11. **Sprained ankle.** — The first application should be cold wet cloths applied about ankle joint for 12 to 24 hours and later the joint kept entirely at rest for several days either in a pillow with splints on either side to retain the joint in one position or else the joint should be put in a plaster cast.

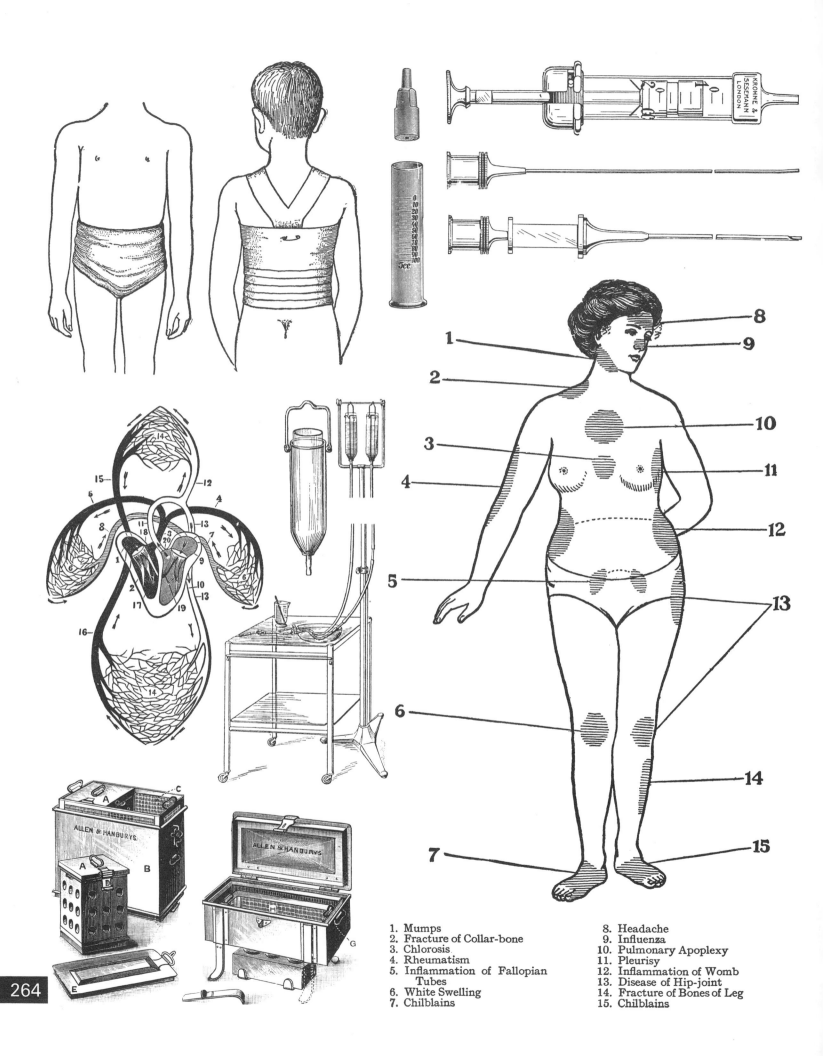

1. Mumps
2. Fracture of Collar-bone
3. Chlorosis
4. Rheumatism
5. Inflammation of Fallopian Tubes
6. White Swelling
7. Chilblains
8. Headache
9. Influenza
10. Pulmonary Apoplexy
11. Pleurisy
12. Inflammation of Womb
13. Disease of Hip-joint
14. Fracture of Bones of Leg
15. Chilblains

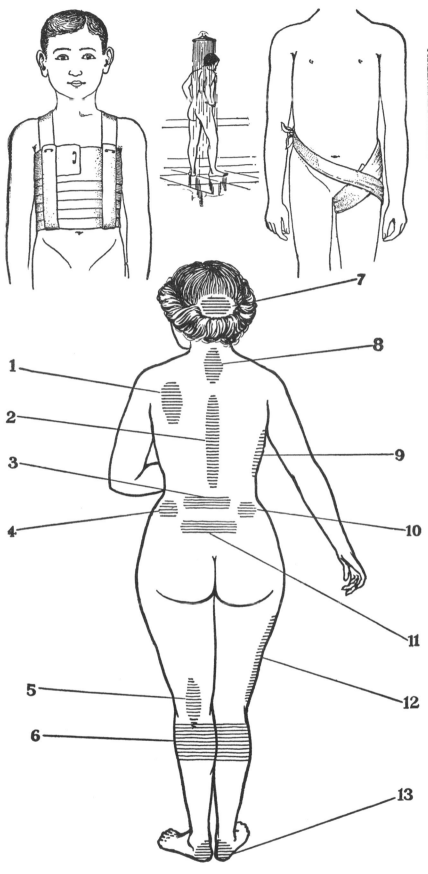

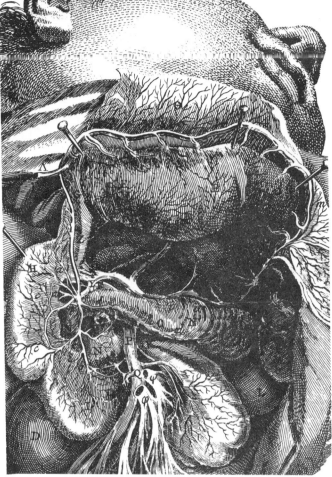

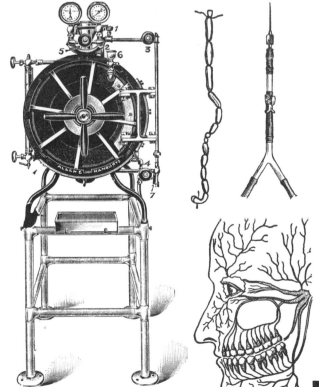

1. **Fracture of Shoulder-blade**
2. **Inflammation of Spinal Cord**
3. **Lumbago**
4. **Inflammation of Kidneys**
5. **Varicose Veins**
6. **Milk Leg**
7. **Brain Disease**
8. **Cerebro-Spinal Fever**
9. **Fracture of Ribs**
10. **Inflammation of Kidneys**
11. **Falling of Womb**
12. **Sciatica**
13. **Neurasthenia**

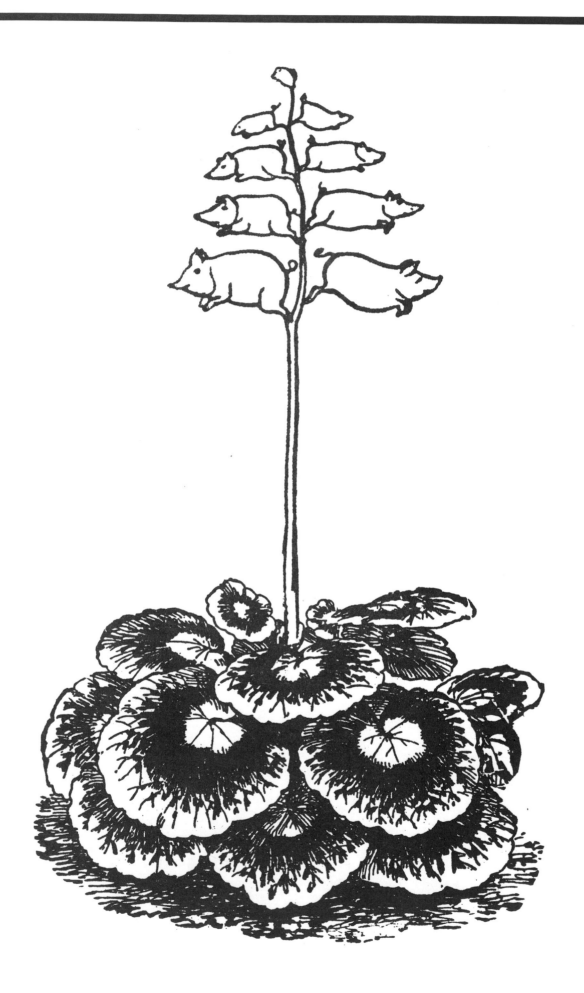

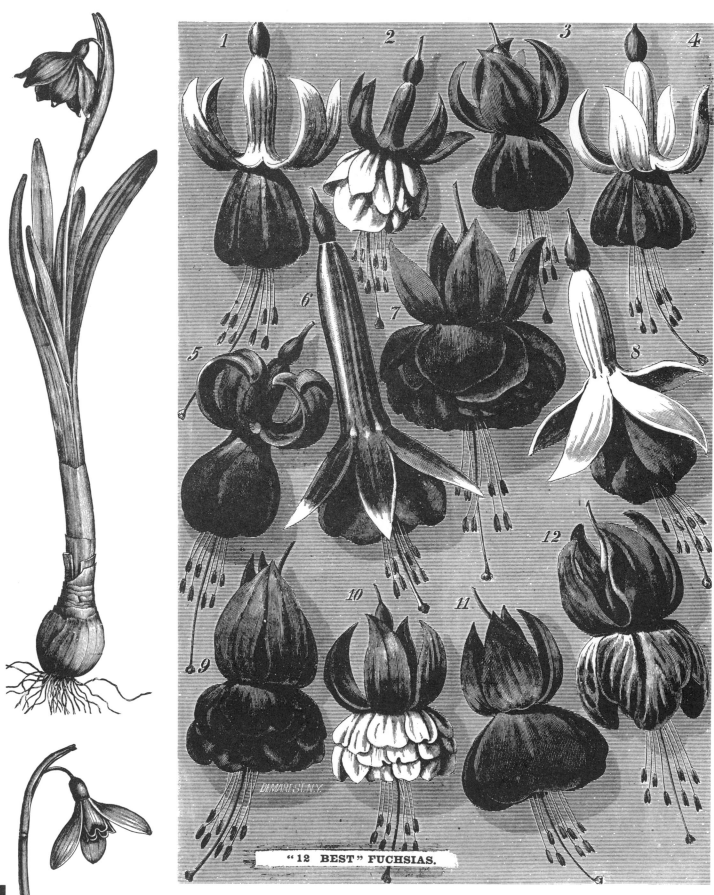

"12 BEST" FUCHSIAS.

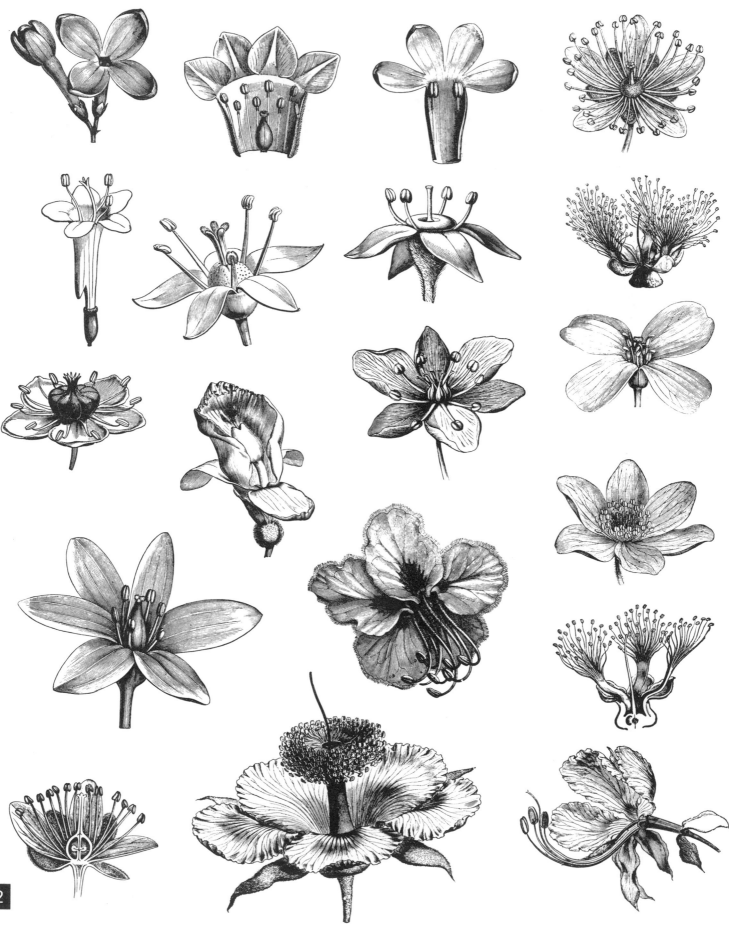

273

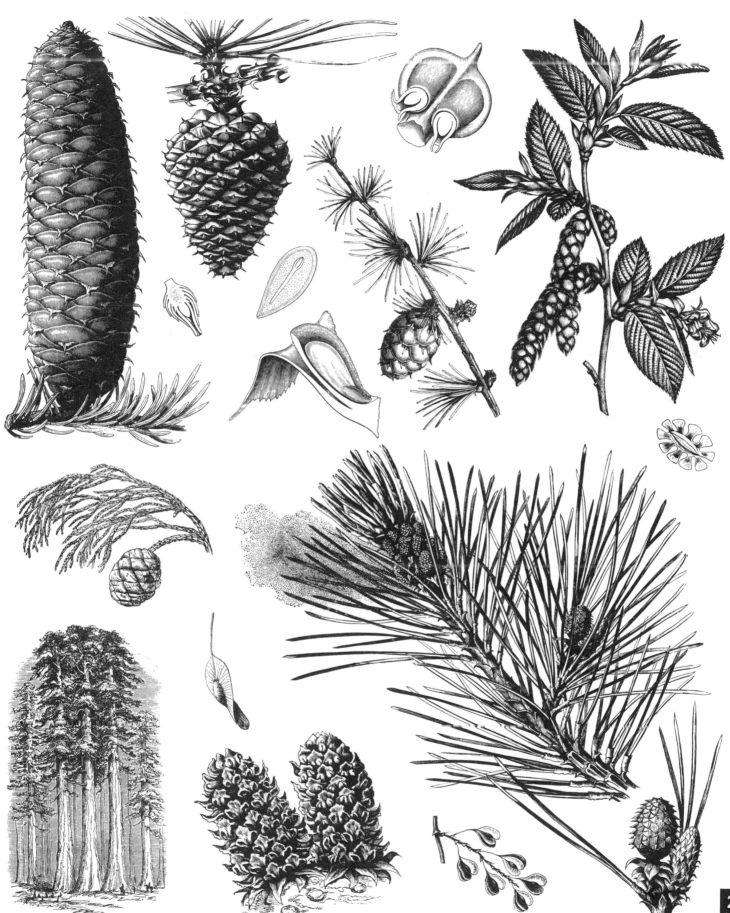

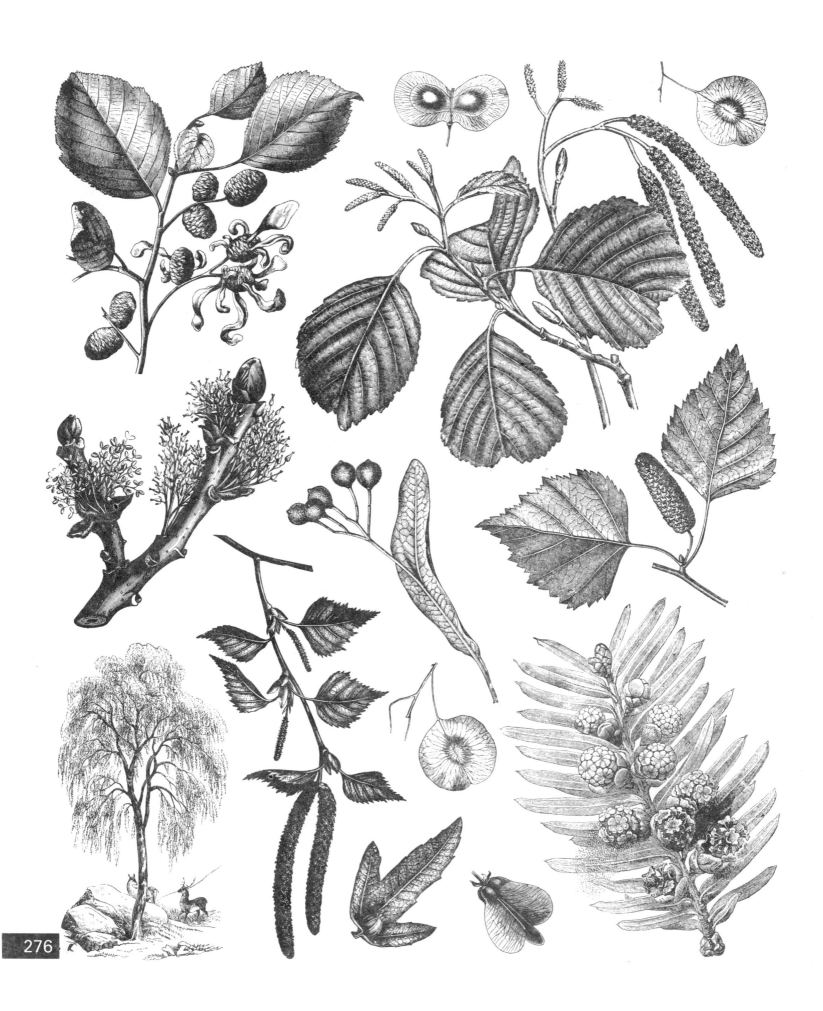

277

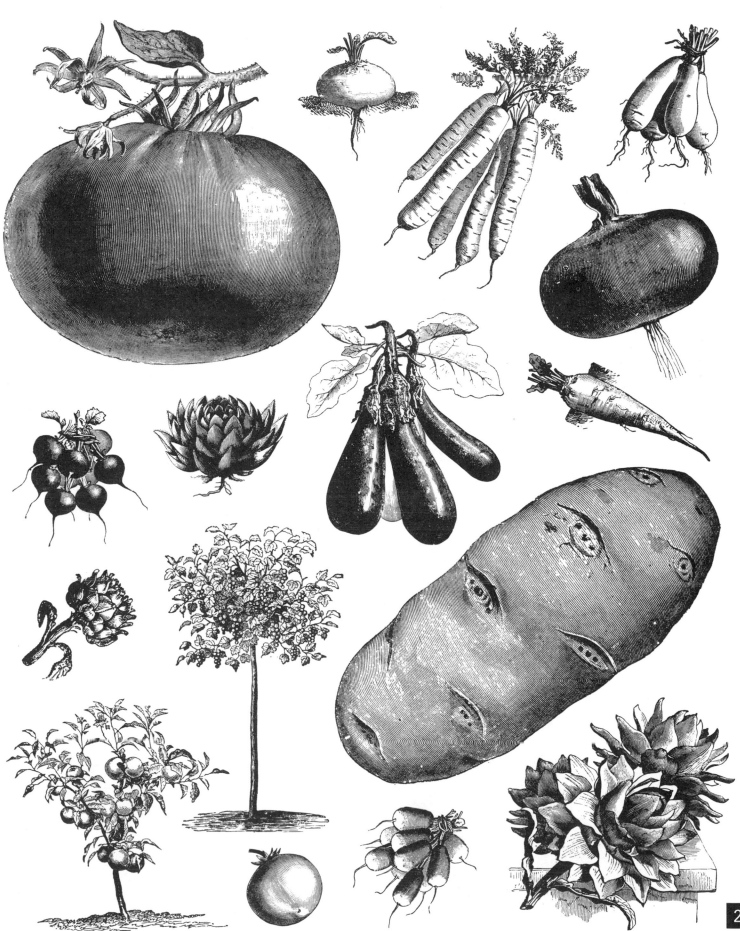

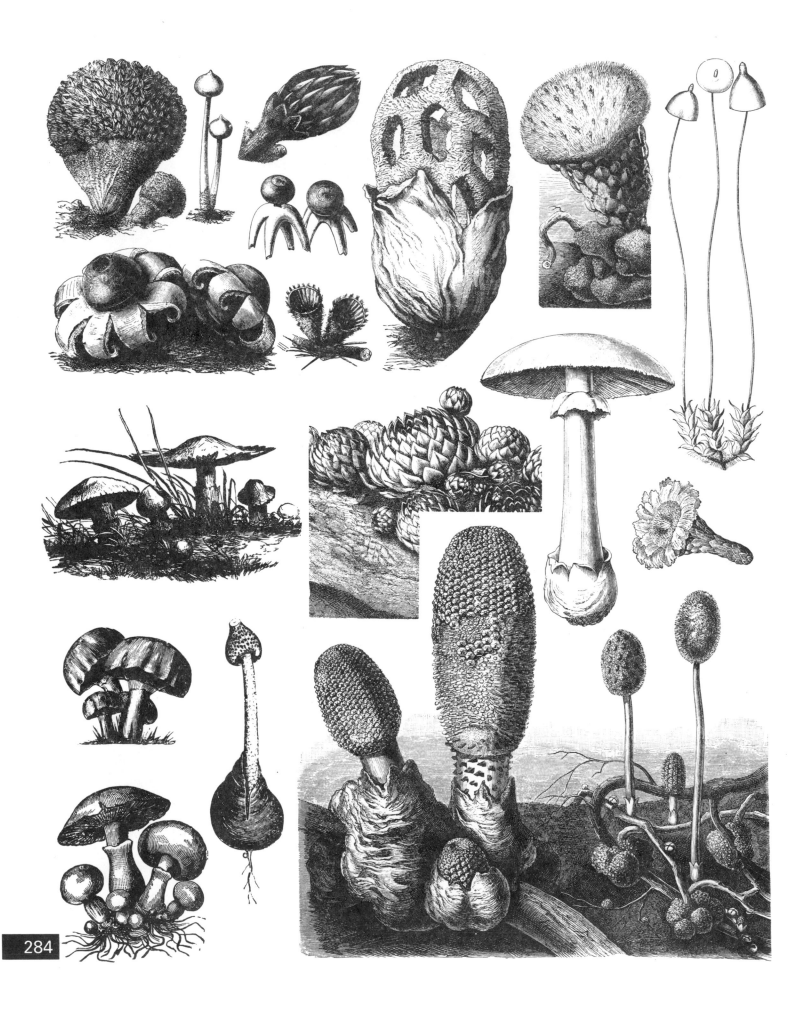

285

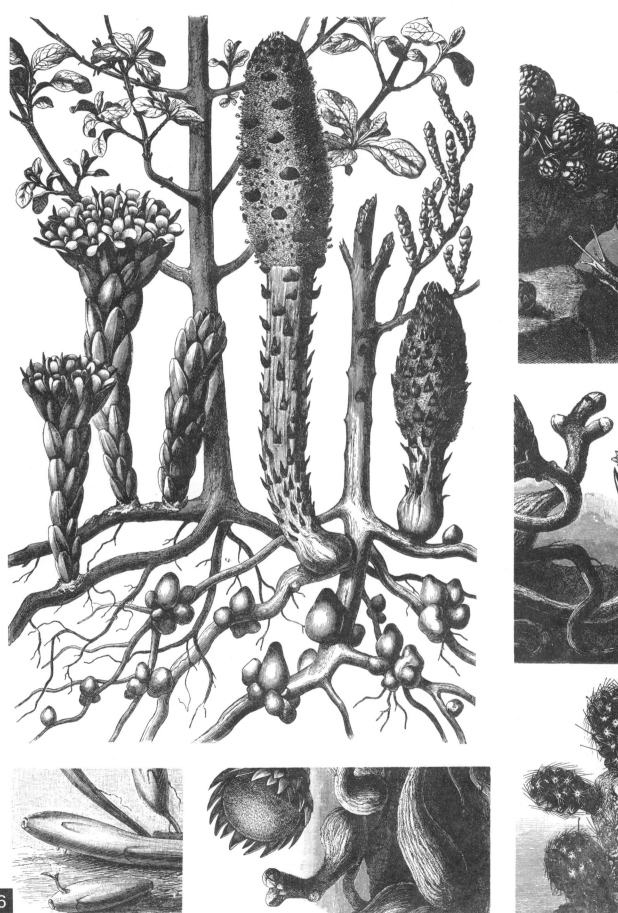

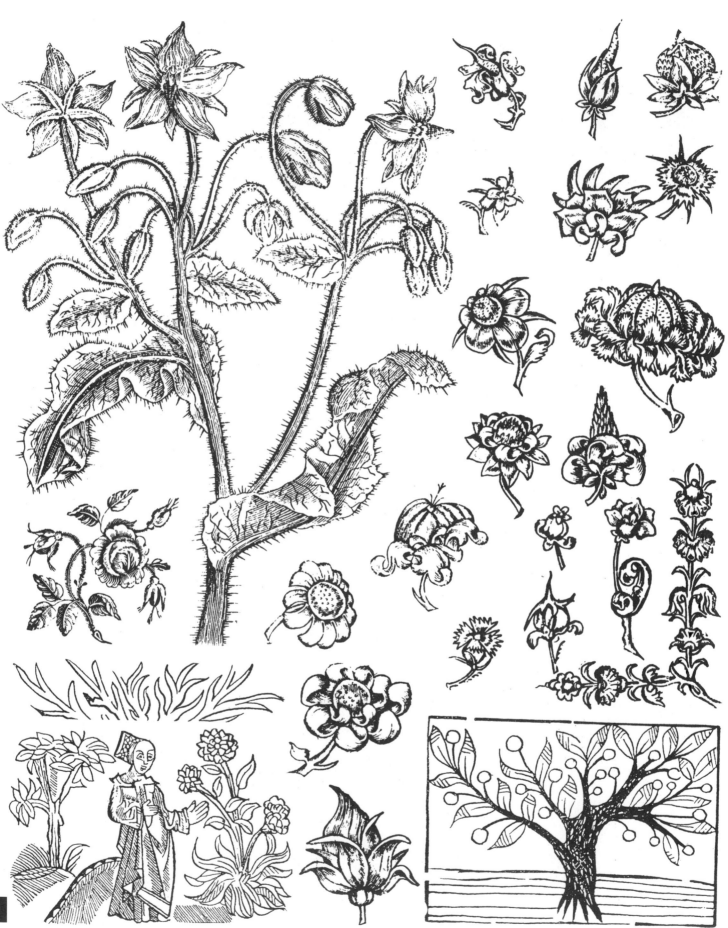

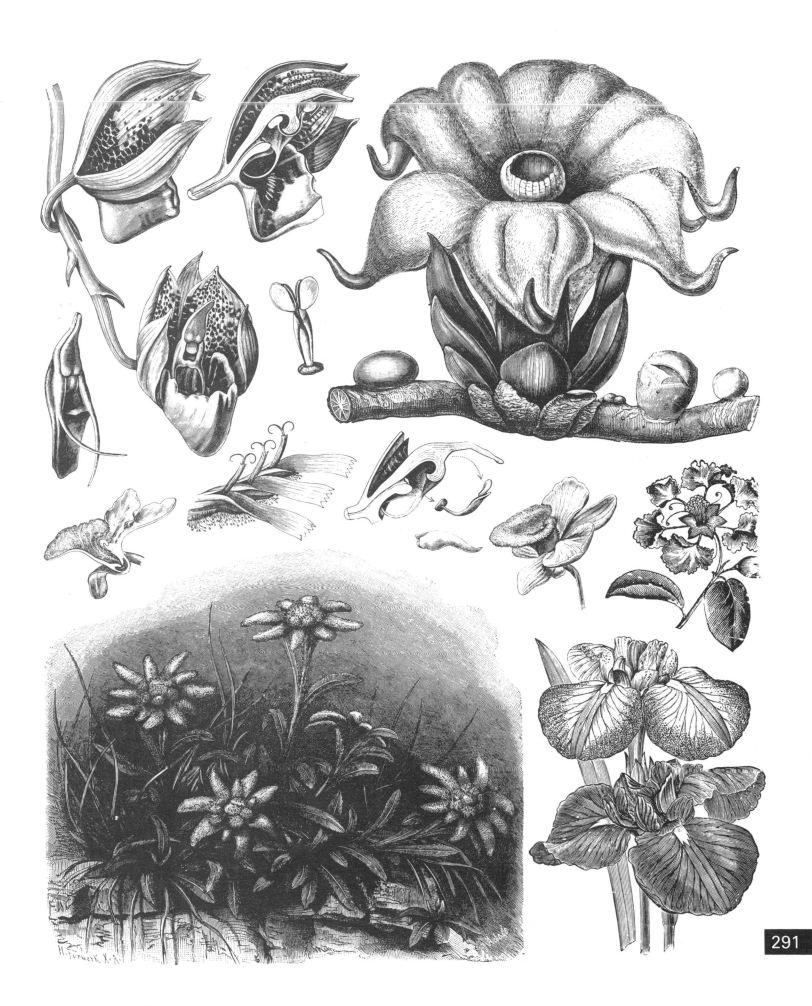

·MAISCH·NURNBERG·

313

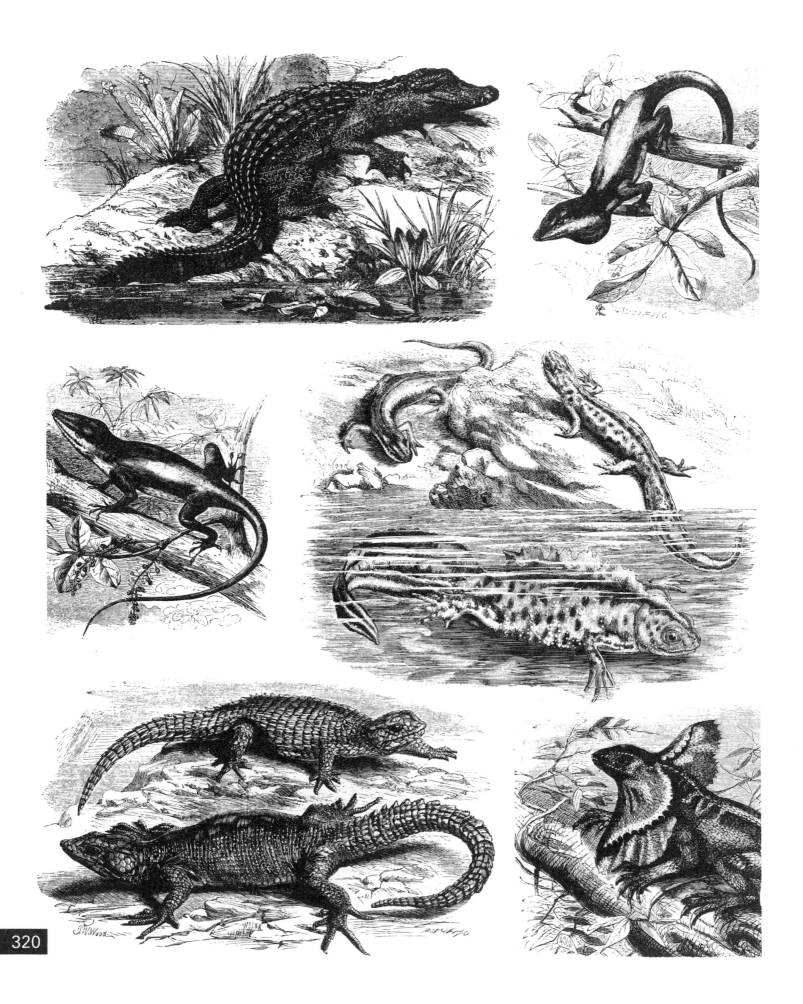

337

Teal Quail Snipe Plover Ruff

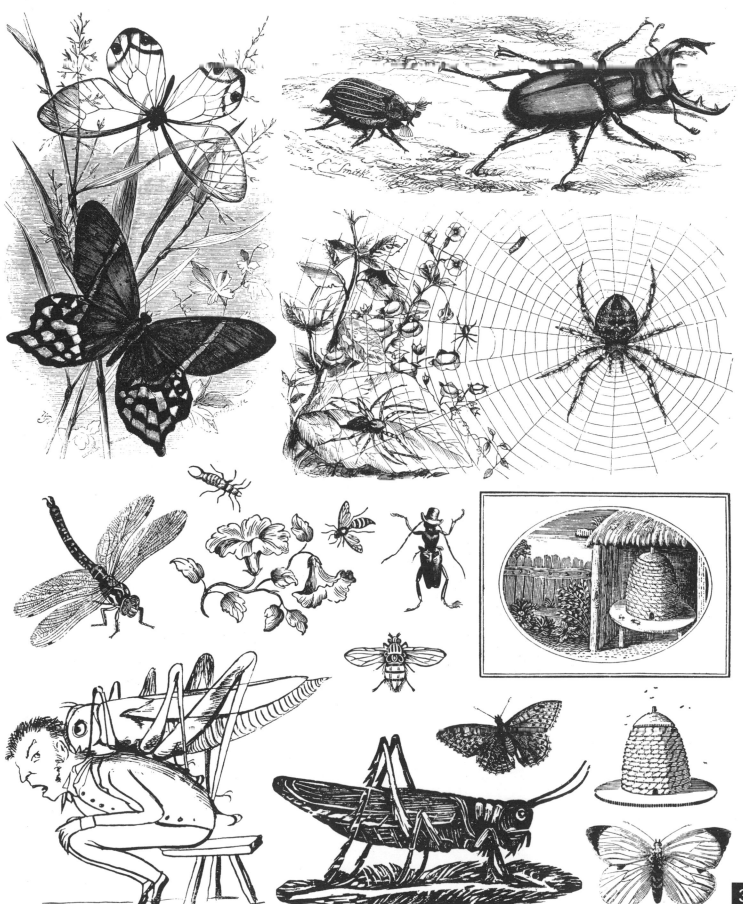

343

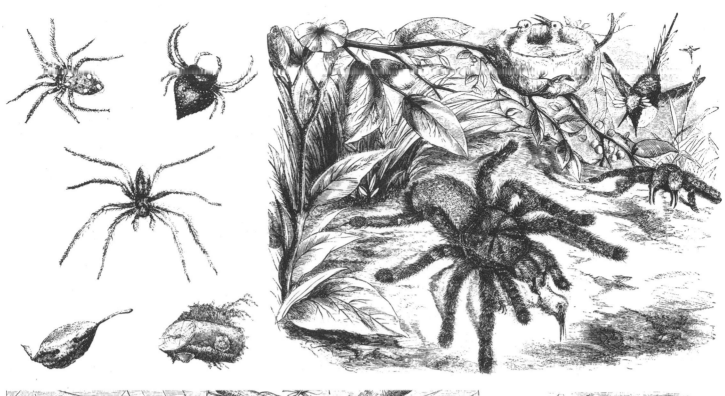

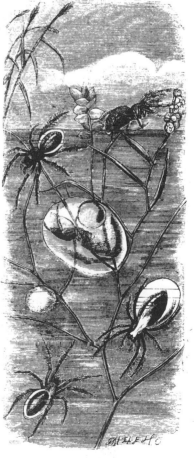

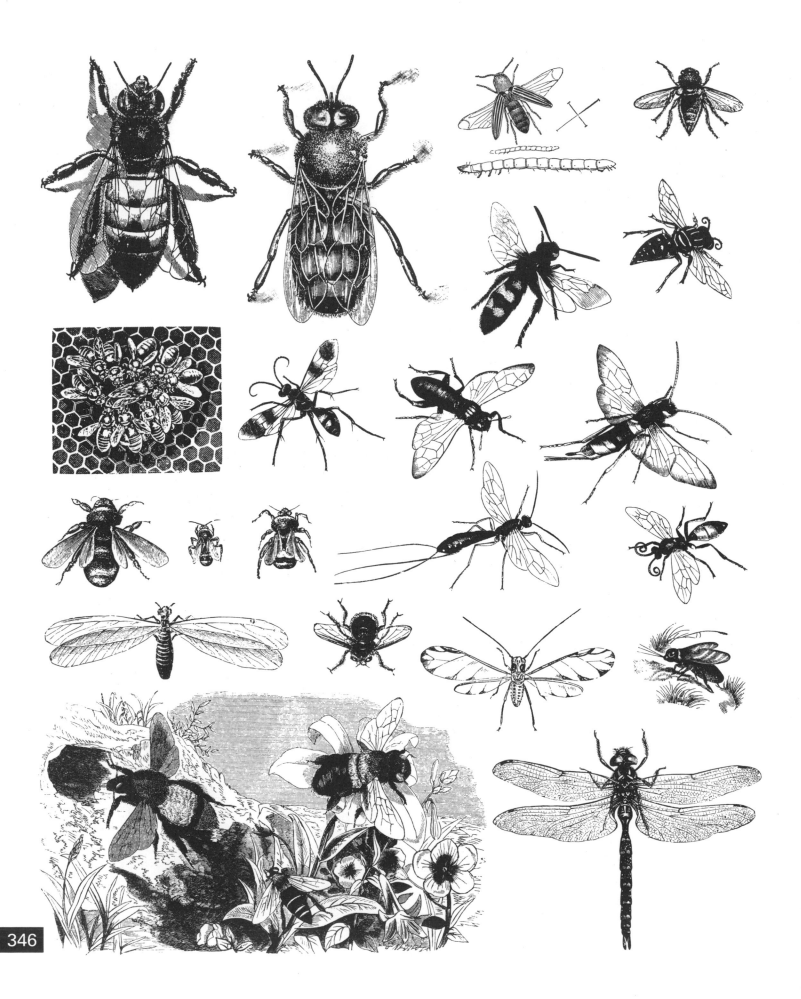

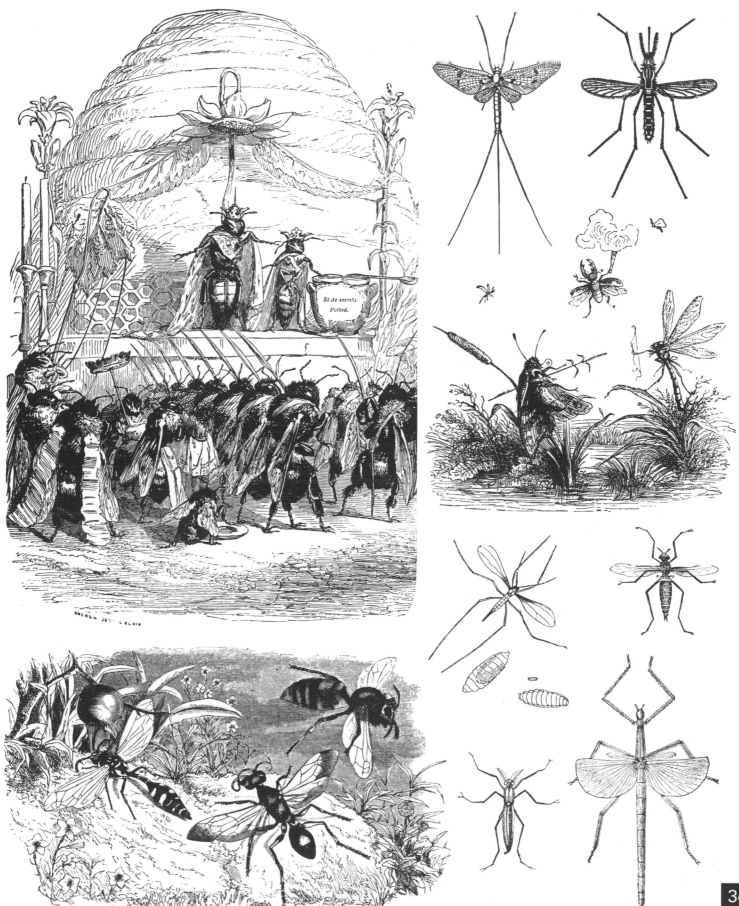

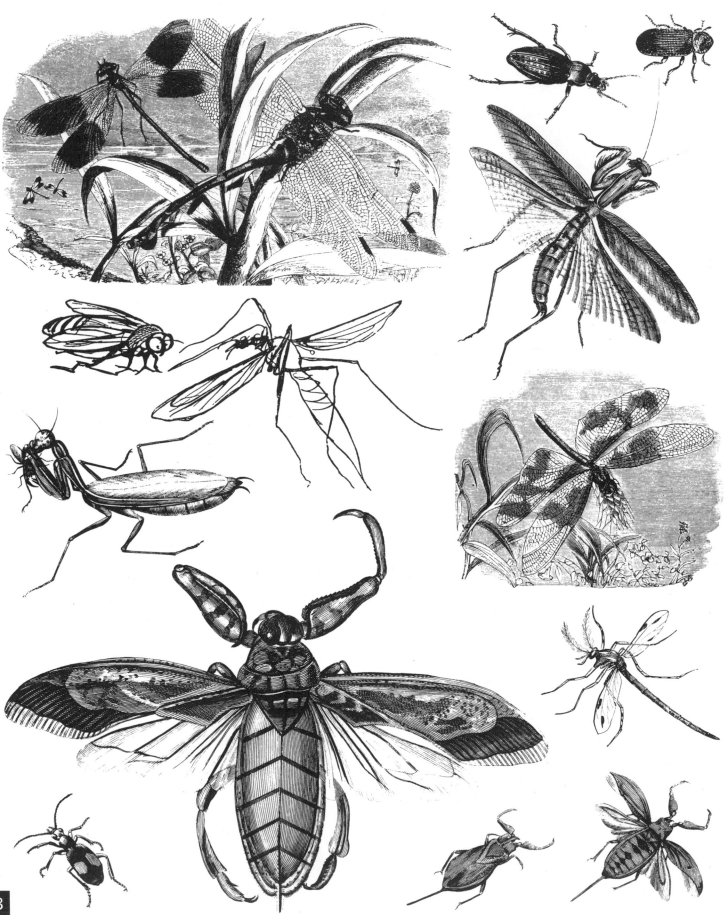

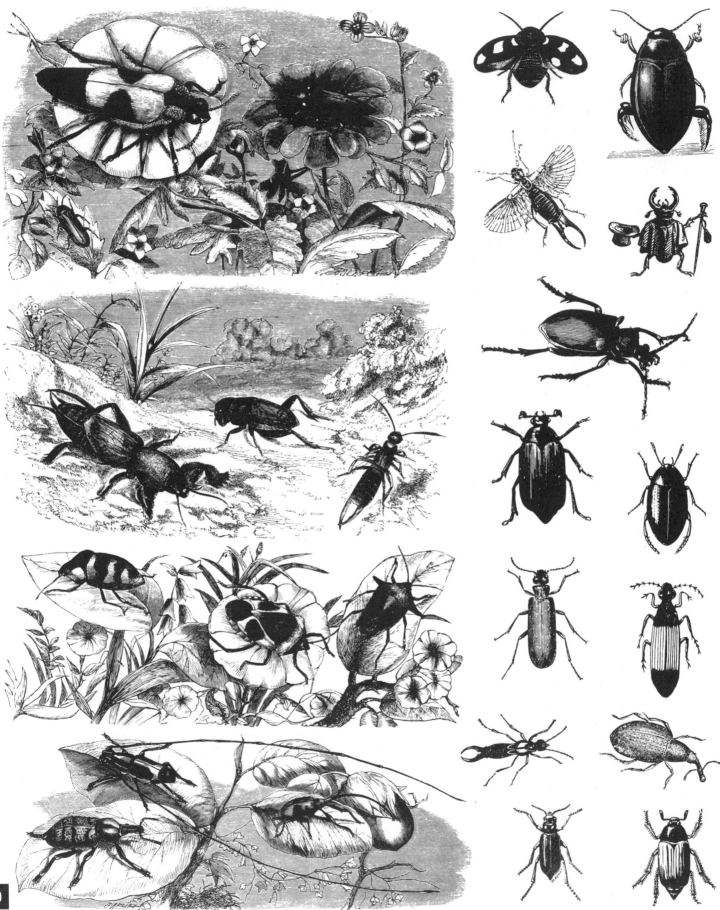

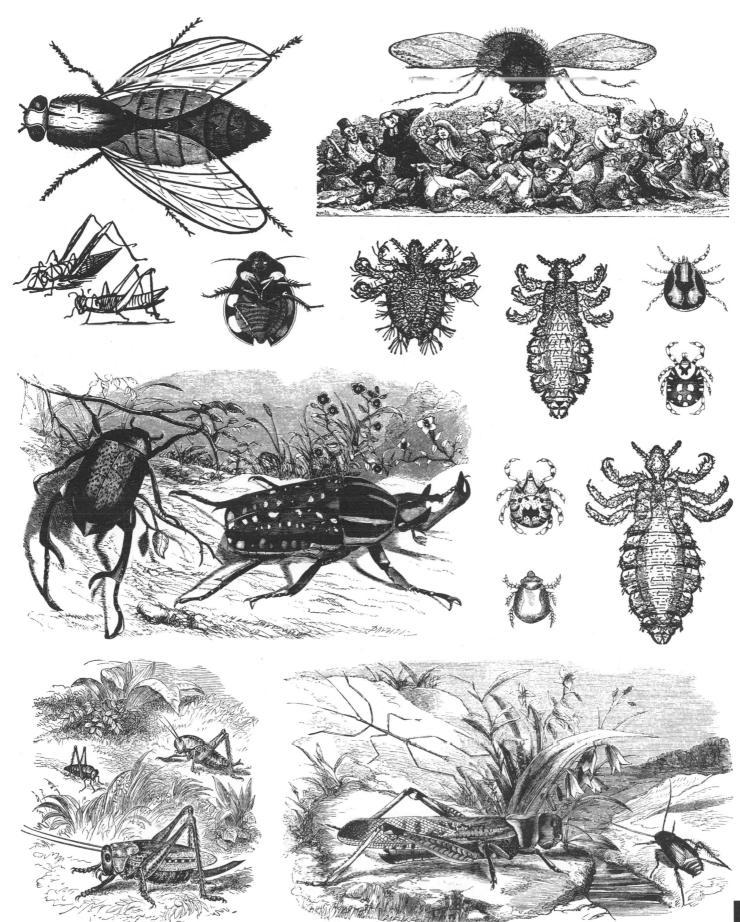

351

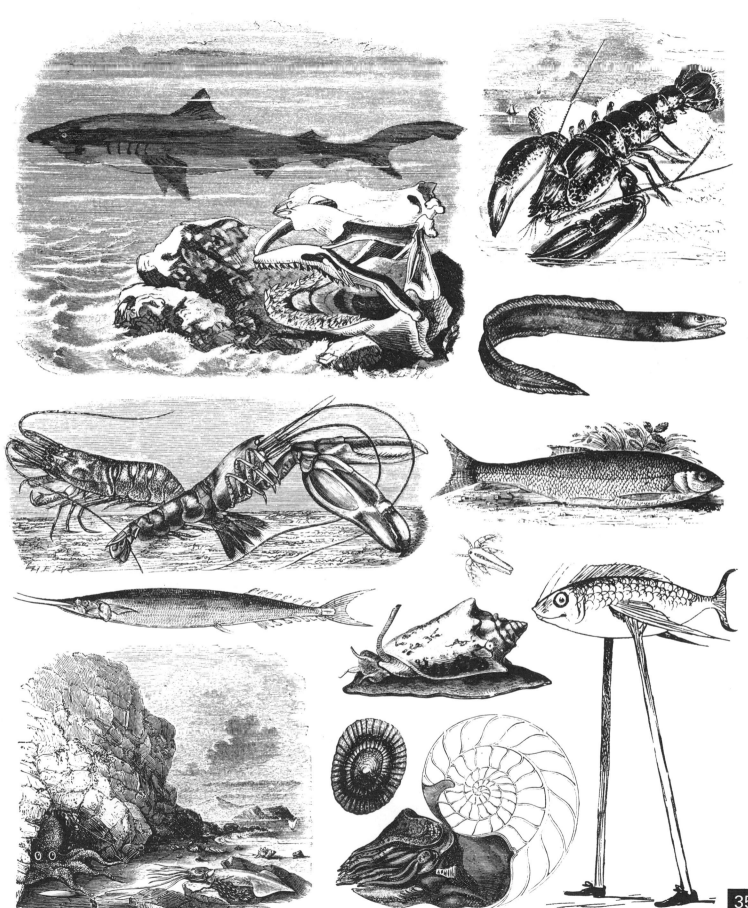

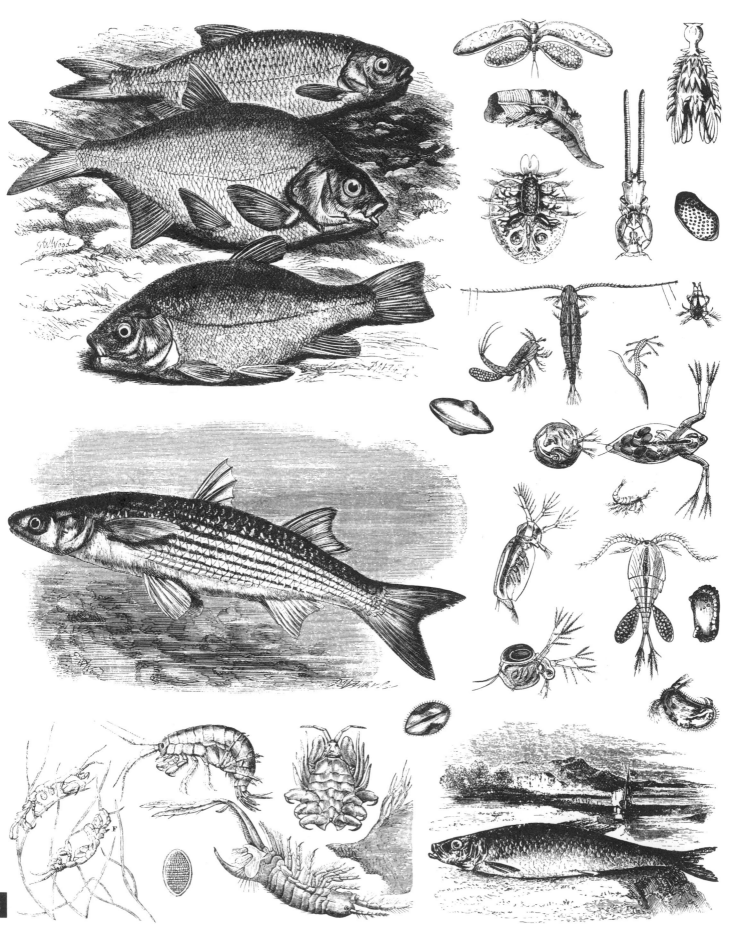

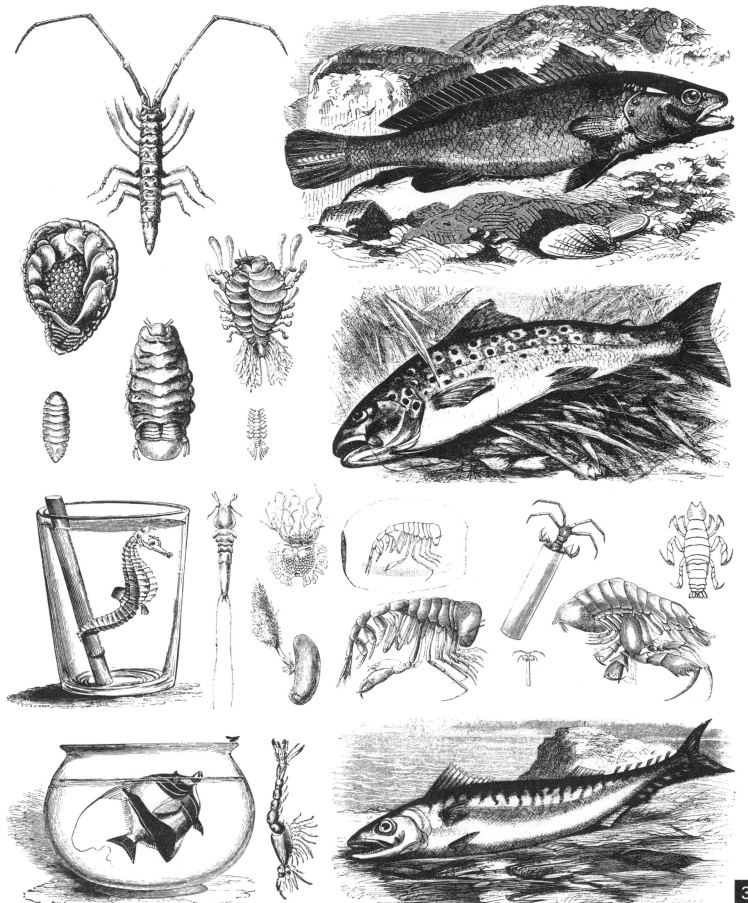

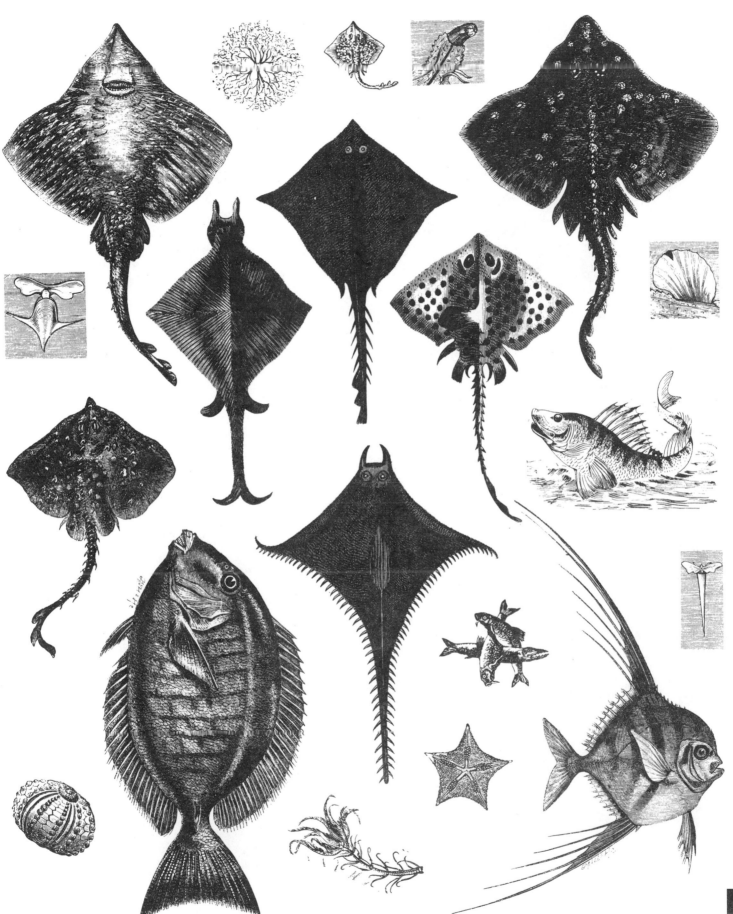

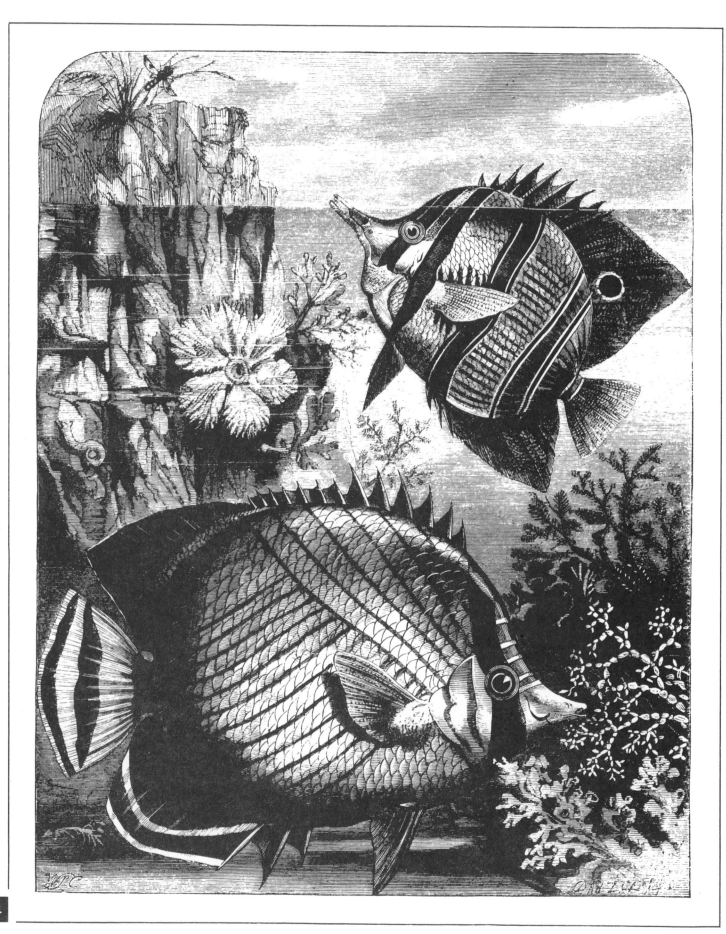

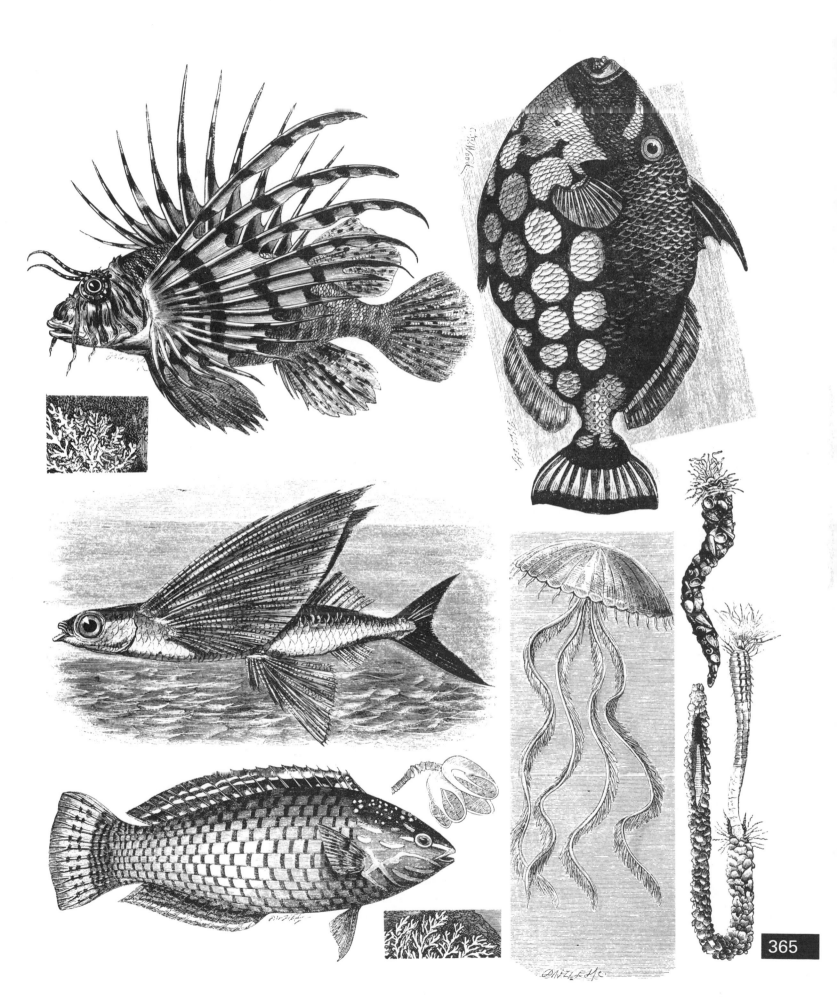

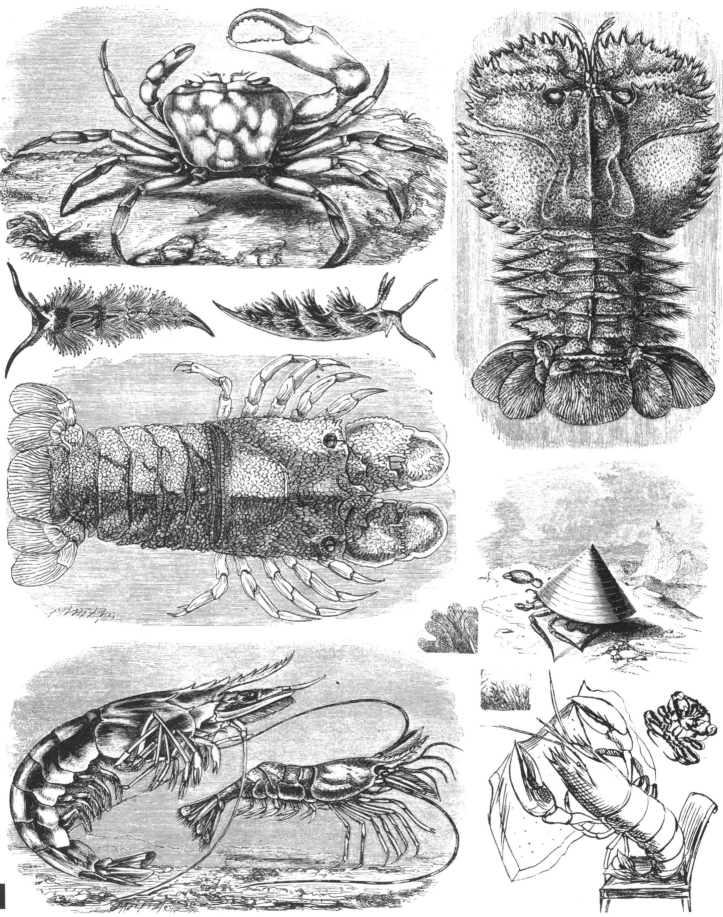

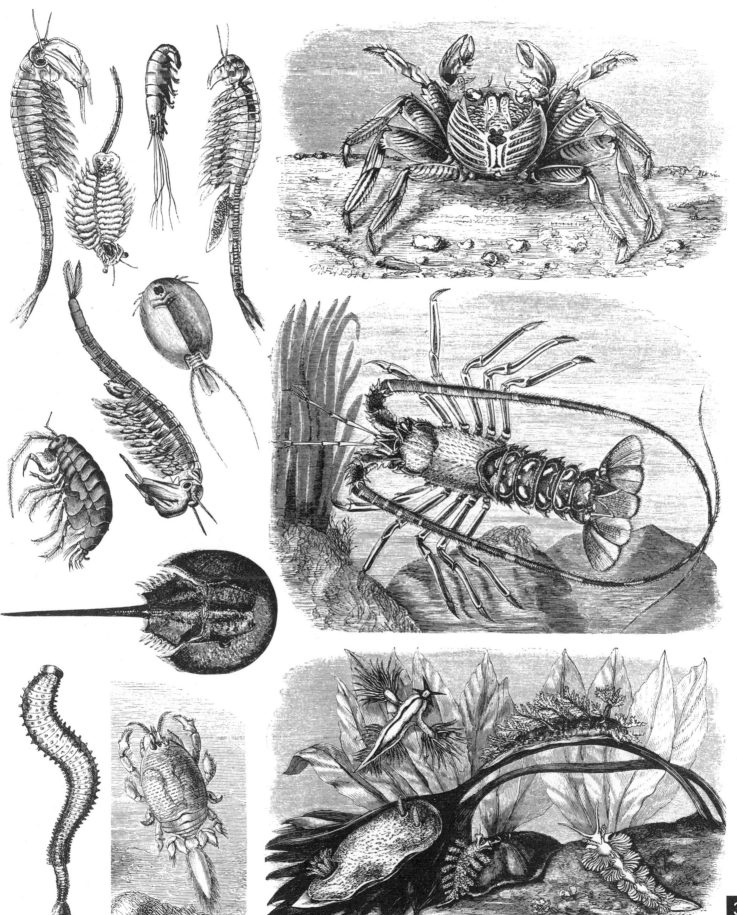

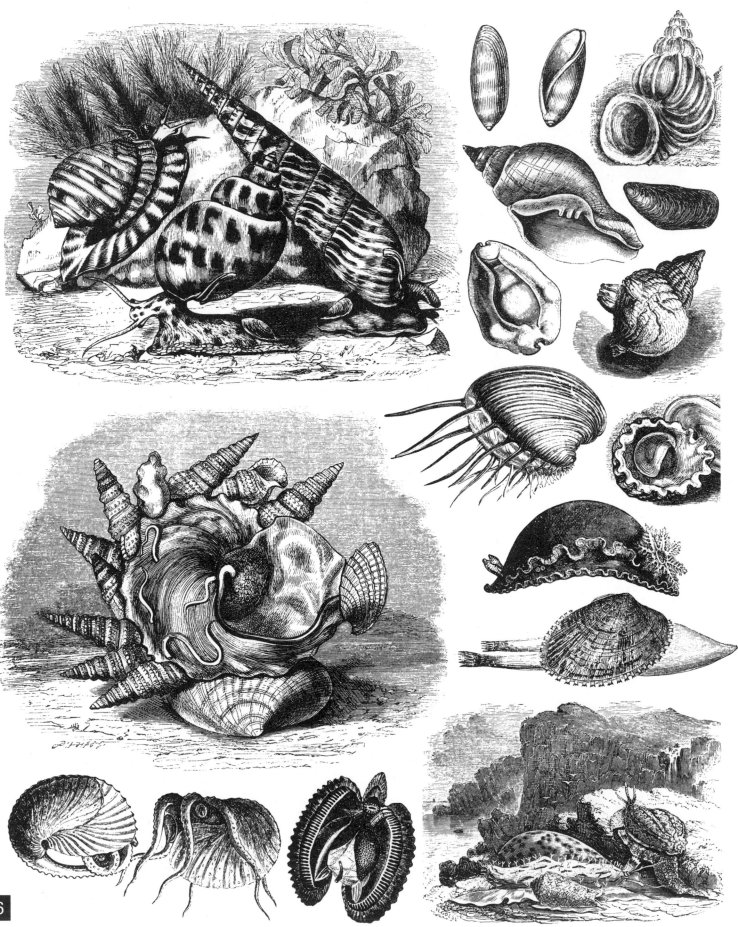

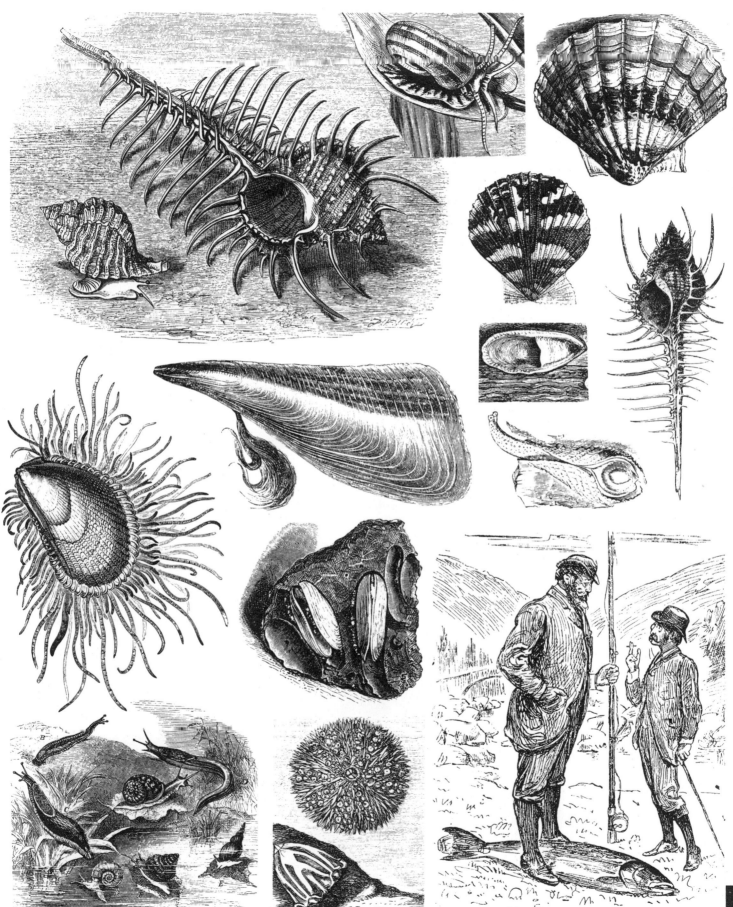

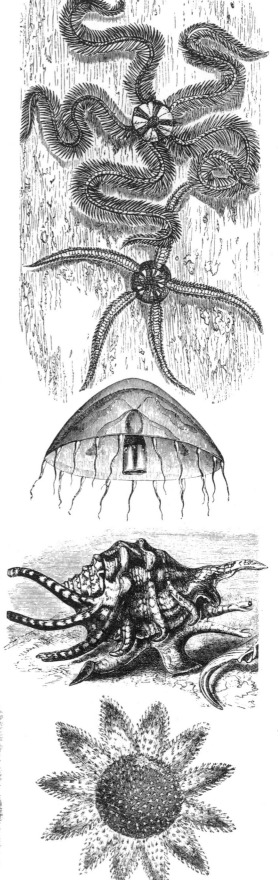

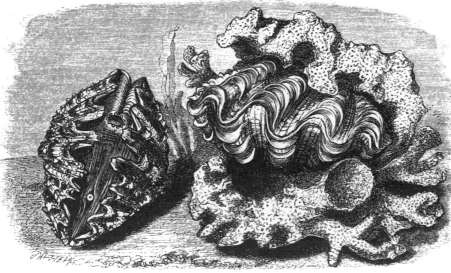

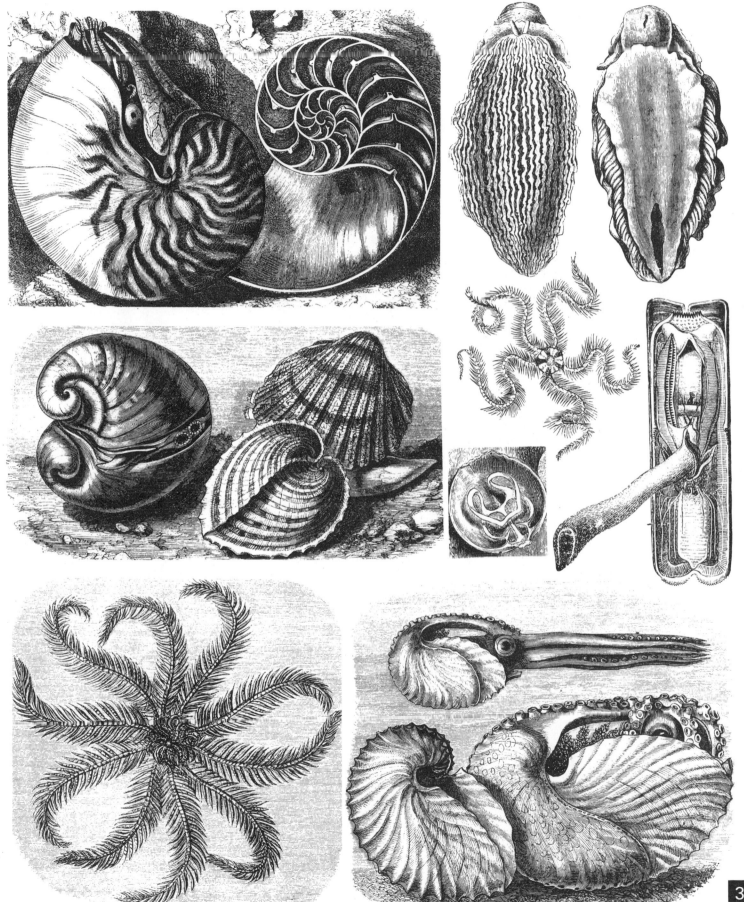

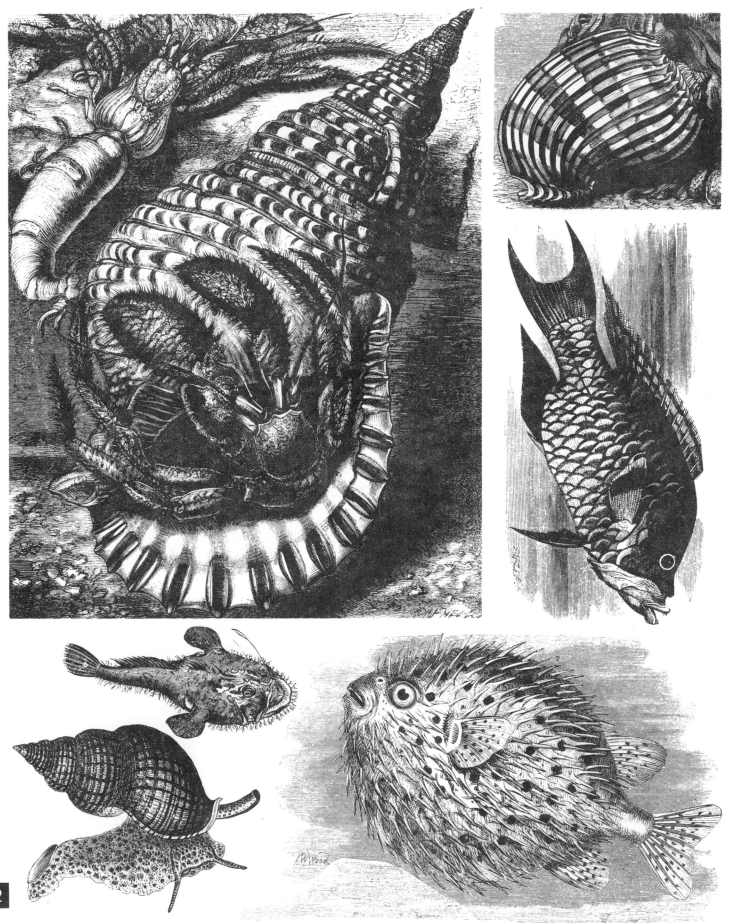